Book 2

Literature & Comprehension

Writing Skills

Language Arts

Lesson Guide

Book Staff and Contributors

Beth Zemble   *Director, Alternative Learning Strategies; Director, English Language Arts*
Marianne Murphy   *Senior Content Specialist*
Amy Rauen   *Senior Instructional Designer*
Mariana Holliday, Lenna King, David Shireman   *Instructional Designers*
Mary Beck Desmond   *Senior Text Editor*
Suzanne Montazer   *Creative Director, Print and ePublishing*
Sasha Blanton   *Art Director, Print and ePublishing*
Carol Leigh   *Print Visual Designer*
Stephanie Shaw Williams   *Cover Designer*
Anna Day   *Director, Instructional Design for Language Arts and Humanities*
Tim Mansfield, Lisa Moran   *Writers*
Amy Eward   *Senior Manager, Writers*
Susan Raley   *Senior Manager, Editors*
Alden Davidson   *Senior Project Manager*
David Johnson   *Director, Program Management Grades K–8*

Maria Szalay   *Executive Vice President, Product Development*
John Holdren   *Senior Vice President, Content and Curriculum*
David Pelizzari   *Vice President, K12 Content*
Kim Barcas   *Vice President, Creative*
Laura Seuschek   *Vice President, Assessment and Research*
Christopher Frescholtz   *Senior Director, Program Management*

Lisa Dimaio Iekel   *Director, Print Production and Manufacturing*
Ray Traugott   *Production Manager*

Credits

About K12 Inc.

K12 Inc., a technology-based education company, is the nation's leading provider of proprietary curriculum and online education programs to students in grades K–12. K12 provides its curriculum and academic services to online schools, traditional classrooms, blended school programs, and directly to families. K12 Inc. also operates the K12 International Academy, an accredited, diploma-granting online private school serving students worldwide. K12's mission is to provide any child the curriculum and tools to maximize success in life, regardless of geographic, financial, or demographic circumstances. K12 Inc. is accredited by CITA. More information can be found at www.K12.com.

978-1-60153-302-9
Printed by LSC Communications, Roanoke, VA, USA, April, 2017

Contents

Literature & Comprehension

Writing Skills

K¹² Language Arts Purple

General Overview

K¹² Language Arts Purple lays a strong foundation for readers and writers. A well-balanced Language Arts program provides instruction on understanding the meaning of the words on the page (comprehension) as well as putting words on the page (writing). According to the National Reading Panel, a comprehensive reading program includes fluency, text comprehension, spelling, vocabulary, and writing skills. K¹² Language Arts Purple provides this instruction through five separate-yet-related programs.

You will spend about two hours a day working with Language Arts Purple. The tables describe the programs, the time you can expect to spend on them, and the overarching big ideas that are covered.

Program	Daily Lesson Time (approximate)	Online/Offline
K¹² Language Arts Purple Literature & Comprehension	50 minutes	Lessons may be all online, all offline, or a combination, moving from online to offline.

Big Ideas

- *Fluency*   The ability to decode text quickly, smoothly, and automatically allows readers to focus on comprehension.
- *Comprehension*   Comprehension is the reason why we read. Reading strategies are conscious plans that readers apply and adapt to make sense of text. Comprehension requires readers to actively think, ask themselves questions, and synthesize information to make meaning from their reading. There are a variety of strategies that proficient readers employ to make sense of text, and these strategies should be actively practiced, self-evaluated, and reinforced.
- *Analysis and Interpretation*   Comprehension is a prerequisite to analysis. Following comprehension of literal meaning, readers must read "between the lines" to understand how an author creates meaning. Readers must pay careful attention to organizational structure, language, and literary elements to appreciate the underlying meaning or message of an author's work.
- *Application and Evaluation*   The ability to apply and evaluate what one has read demonstrates not only comprehension, but also the ability to think critically about ideas. Readers need to synthesize, draw conclusions about, evaluate, and interpret what they have read. Readers must be able to make connections between and among the texts that they have read and relate what they read to the world around them.
- *Enjoyment*   To develop a lifelong love of reading, readers should independently read for their own enjoyment.

Program	Daily Lesson Time (approximate)	Online/Offline
K[12] Language Arts Purple Spelling	15 minutes	Each unit: 4 offline lessons, 1 online review
Big Ideas		

- Spelling represents sounds, syllables, and meaningful parts called *morphemes*.
- The spelling of all English words can be explained by rules or patterns related to word origins.

Program	Daily Lesson Time (approximate)	Online/Offline
K[12] Language Arts Purple Vocabulary	10 minutes	All online
Big Ideas		

- Vocabulary words are words we need to know to communicate and understand.
- A *speaking vocabulary* includes the words we know and can use when speaking.
- A *reading vocabulary* includes the words we know and can read with understanding.
- A *listening vocabulary* includes the words we know and understand when we hear them.
- A *writing vocabulary* includes the words we know and understand when we write.
- The more we read, the more our vocabulary grows.
- Early learners acquire vocabulary through active exposure (by talking and listening, being read to, and receiving explicit instruction).

Program	Daily Lesson Time (approximate)	Online/Offline
K¹² Language Arts Purple Writing Skills	35 minutes (Days 1–90) 45 minutes (Days 91–180)	Lessons may be all online, all offline, or a combination, moving from online to offline.

Big Ideas

Composition

- Developing writers should study models of good writing.
- The study of writing models provides students with opportunities to read, analyze, and emulate good models.
- Writing can be broken out into a series of steps, or a process, that will help developing writers become more proficient.
- Teaching the writing process encourages students to organize their ideas before they write and to revise their work after they write.
- Writing varies by purpose and audience. The specific reason for writing and the writer's intended readers (audience) determine the correct form and language to use.
- Following a specific organizational structure is a useful tool for novice writers; however, writers require the freedom and flexibility to follow their ideas to completion.
- Writing requires thought and planning.
- Writers must be able to articulate a main idea and support it with appropriate details.
- All writers revise, and revision is best performed in discrete tasks.
- Good writers carefully check their work for errors.
- To improve, writers require frequent practice.

Grammar, Usage, and Mechanics (GUM)

- To be effective communicators, writers and speakers should recognize and use complete sentences.
- Sentence combining—teaching students to construct complex, sophisticated sentences—is an effective instructional strategy and an important element in learning to write well.
- Using different kinds of sentences helps writers and speakers express their ideas accurately.
- A noun is a basic part of speech. Understanding nouns gives students a basic vocabulary for building sentences and understanding how language works.
- Recognizing and using action verbs helps writers make their work specific and interesting to readers.
- Using pronouns to take the place of some nouns helps writers avoid repetition.
- The use of descriptive adjectives can turn an ordinary piece of writing into one that enables the audience to form clear mental pictures of a scene.
- Using a wide range of adverbs allows a writer to convey specific information about how, when, where, or why an action occurs.

Program	Daily Lesson Time (approximate)	Online/Offline
K¹² Language Arts Purple Cursive Handwriting	10 minutes	All offline

Big Ideas
• Instruction in posture, pencil grip, and letter formation improves students' handwriting skills.
• Proper modeling of letter formation is imperative for developing handwriting skills.
• Students who have formal instruction in handwriting are more engaged in composition writing.

Structure

Literature & Comprehension, Spelling, Vocabulary, Writing Skills, and Cursive Handwriting are independent programs that work together to give students a complete, well-balanced education in Language Arts.

1. **Literature & Comprehension**   Students read independently in a variety of genres—fiction, poetry, drama, and nonfiction—to suit diverse tastes. Students are expected to apply comprehension strategies before and during their reading. Activities emphasize literal and inferential comprehension, analysis, evaluation, and application. There is a balance among oral, written, and project work. Students work on literal and inferential comprehension lessons, as well as those lessons that are designed to emulate standardized test-taking formats.

2. **Spelling**   Students learn to focus on spelling patterns that are necessary to be fluent, proficient readers, writers, and spellers.

3. **Vocabulary**   Students increase their vocabulary by learning the meanings of groups of conceptually related words. Vocabulary skills help students read and compose written material.

4. **Writing Skills**   Students study writing models and then use the writing process to write a variety of compositions. They learn about grammar, usage, and mechanics skills and apply those skills as they revise and proofread their work. In addition, students work on language, vocabulary, spelling, and writing-strategy skills in lessons that are designed to emulate standardized test-taking formats.

5. **Cursive Handwriting**   For the first half of the year, students practice cursive handwriting at a pace that meets their needs. For the second part of the year, students may continue to practice handwriting skills as they complete written work in other programs.

Flexible Lesson Planning

A key aspect of K[12] is the flexibility we offer students. Doing things that work best for them is vital to students' mastery. The structure of K[12] Language Arts Purple, with the separate programs, allows you to work on one skill at a time, which gives you flexibility. You will be able to

- **Find content more easily.** The descriptive titles, both in the lesson lists online and in the Lesson Guide, allow you to find lessons and activities quickly.
- **Manage progress more easily.** You can track progress, mastery, and attendance by program so you can see at a glance how a student is progressing in each. This tracking will allow you to better customize your schedule to meet students' needs.
- **Pace work appropriately for students.** The focused lessons enable you to identify skills that students need to spend more or less time on and make adjustments. You can decide the pace that works best for students in each program. For example, a student may work through two Vocabulary lessons at a time but need to spend some extra time on Writing Skills.
- **Control your own schedule.** You can arrange lessons to meet your needs.

TIP Get to know the different lesson types and then set up your lesson schedule in the best way for you and your students.

How to Work Through a Lesson

Preview and Prepare

1. **Prepare in advance** by scheduling time to plan at the beginning of each week and before each school day. You may want to look ahead at any assessments or writing assignments so you know what students are working toward in each unit.

2. **Check the Lesson Guide or the online lesson** to see the lesson plan and read any instructions for completing the lesson.

3. **Complete Advance Preparation** before you begin a lesson. Look for Advance Preparation in the Lesson Guide or the online lesson.

4. **Preview the Lesson Guide** so that you are prepared to provide support during the offline activities. You may also want to preview the online lesson and the word lists for Vocabulary.

5. **Gather the materials** listed in the Lesson Guide or the online lesson before you begin. You should always have paper and pencil available in addition to any other materials that are listed.

6. **Set up the workspace** for offline activities or move students to the computer to complete online activities.

TIP You might want to check the materials and Advance Preparation for the week in addition to reviewing them before each lesson so you know of any materials or tasks that may require some extra time or planning. For example, you may need to plan a trip to the library to get a book or go to the craft store for special materials.

Where to Begin?

For programs with both online and offline components, there is more than one way to begin a lesson. Either way will get you where you need to go.

Beginning Online   If you begin from the online lesson, the lesson screens will walk you through what you need to do, including gathering materials and moving offline if necessary.

- ► If the lesson begins with online activities, students will need to come to the computer to complete them.
- ► If the lesson begins with offline activities, gather the materials listed and begin the activities described in the lesson plan with students when you're ready.

Beginning Offline   You may choose to begin a lesson by first checking the lesson plan for the day in the Lesson Guide. The table on the first page of the lesson plan will indicate whether the lesson begins with online or offline activities.

- ► If the lesson begins with online activities, students will need to move to the computer to complete them.
- ► If the lesson begins with offline activities, gather the materials listed and begin the activities described in the lesson plan with students when you're ready.

Complete Activities with Students

Offline Activities   During offline activities, you will work closely with students away from the computer. Follow the instructions in the Lesson Guide for completing these activities.

Online Activities   Online activities take place at the computer. At first, you may need to help students learn how to navigate and use the online activities. You may also need to provide support when activities cover new or challenging content. Eventually, students will complete online activities with minimal support from you.

Work with Students to Complete Assessments

Offline Assessments   Students will complete offline assessments in Literature & Comprehension, Writing Skills, and Spelling. After students complete the assessments offline, you will need to enter assessment scores in the Online School.

Online Assessments   Students will complete online assessments in Literature & Comprehension, Writing Skills, and Vocabulary. Because these assessments are online, the computer will score them for you. You do not need to enter these assessment scores in the Online School.

Track Progress in Portfolios

K[12] recommends keeping students' work samples in a portfolio as a record of their progress. A simple folder, large envelope, or three-ring binder would work. Place offline assessments, unit project pages, compositions, Activity Book pages, and handwriting samples in the portfolio. Look back through the portfolio monthly and at the end of the year with students. Celebrate their progress and achievements.

How to Use This Book

K[12] *Language Arts Lesson Guide* contains information that will be helpful to you as you begin K[12] Language Arts Purple and on a daily basis as you work through the programs. Here is what the Lesson Guide contains and how to use it:

Lesson Guide Contents	What to Do with It
Overviews of each of the programs included in K[12] Language Arts Purple, including instructional philosophies, materials, and unit and lesson structure for the programs	• **Read the overviews** of the programs as you begin K[12] Language Arts Purple. • **Refer to the overview** information if you have questions as you work through the programs.
Glossary of key terms used in Literature & Comprehension and Writing Skills	• **Use the keywords list** in the back of the book any time you need to look up a keyword used in Literature & Comprehension or Writing Skills.
Lesson plans for teaching • Literature & Comprehension lessons • Writing Skills lessons	• **Scan the unit and lesson overviews** for the lessons you will be working on each day. • **Follow the instructions** in the lesson plans to complete the activities with students. • **Use the answer keys** to check students' work on Activity Book pages and offline assessments.

Following are examples of the unit overview, lesson overview, and activity instructions that you will see in the lesson plans for teaching a Literature & Comprehension or Writing Skills lesson.

Unit Overview

There is one unit overview page per unit.

Unit Title
Each unit has a unique title that reflects the purpose or content of the unit.

Unit Focus
This section presents an overview of unit content and purpose, written to the Learning Coach.

Unit Plan
This table lists all the lessons in the unit, their duration, and online/offline icons and identification.

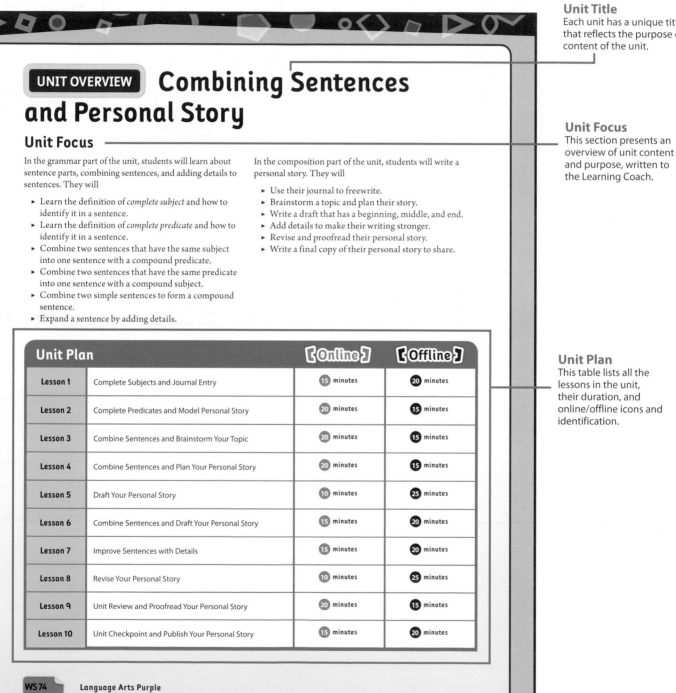

UNIT OVERVIEW Combining Sentences and Personal Story

Unit Focus

In the grammar part of the unit, students will learn about sentence parts, combining sentences, and adding details to sentences. They will

- Learn the definition of *complete subject* and how to identify it in a sentence.
- Learn the definition of *complete predicate* and how to identify it in a sentence.
- Combine two sentences that have the same subject into one sentence with a compound predicate.
- Combine two sentences that have the same predicate into one sentence with a compound subject.
- Combine two simple sentences to form a compound sentence.
- Expand a sentence by adding details.

In the composition part of the unit, students will write a personal story. They will

- Use their journal to freewrite.
- Brainstorm a topic and plan their story.
- Write a draft that has a beginning, middle, and end.
- Add details to make their writing stronger.
- Revise and proofread their personal story.
- Write a final copy of their personal story to share.

Unit Plan		〖Online〗	〖Offline〗
Lesson 1	Complete Subjects and Journal Entry	15 minutes	20 minutes
Lesson 2	Complete Predicates and Model Personal Story	20 minutes	15 minutes
Lesson 3	Combine Sentences and Brainstorm Your Topic	20 minutes	15 minutes
Lesson 4	Combine Sentences and Plan Your Personal Story	20 minutes	15 minutes
Lesson 5	Draft Your Personal Story	10 minutes	25 minutes
Lesson 6	Combine Sentences and Draft Your Personal Story	15 minutes	20 minutes
Lesson 7	Improve Sentences with Details	15 minutes	20 minutes
Lesson 8	Revise Your Personal Story	10 minutes	25 minutes
Lesson 9	Unit Review and Proofread Your Personal Story	20 minutes	15 minutes
Lesson 10	Unit Checkpoint and Publish Your Personal Story	15 minutes	20 minutes

WS 74   Language Arts Purple

Lesson Overview

Each Literature & Comprehension and Writing Skills lesson has a lesson overview page.

Lesson Title
The title indicates the lesson topic.

Lesson Overview Table
This table has an overview of the lesson's activities, their approximate times, and whether they take place offline or online.

This section of the lesson overview page includes Advance Preparation, Big Ideas, and Content Background, if any, that you need to know.

Advance Preparation
This information is what you need to prepare before beginning the lesson.

Big Ideas
Students will work toward these major organizing ideas in Language Arts.

Content Background
You might need this information to help you better understand the content you will be teaching.

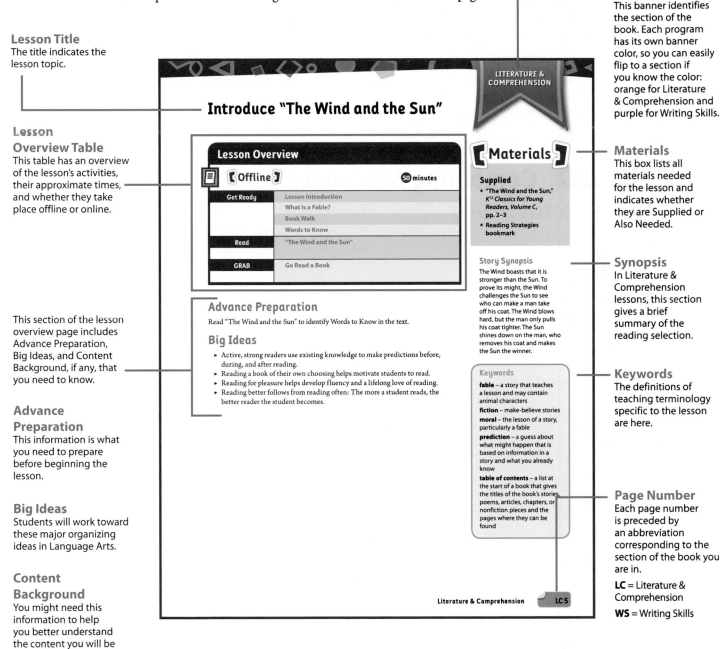

Introduce "The Wind and the Sun"

LITERATURE & COMPREHENSION

Lesson Overview

Offline — **50 minutes**

Get Ready	Lesson Introduction
	What Is a Fable?
	Book Walk
	Words to Know
Read	"The Wind and the Sun"
GRAB	Go Read a Book

Advance Preparation
Read "The Wind and the Sun" to identify Words to Know in the text.

Big Ideas
▸ Active, strong readers use existing knowledge to make predictions before, during, and after reading.
▸ Reading a book of their own choosing helps motivate students to read.
▸ Reading for pleasure helps develop fluency and a lifelong love of reading.
▸ Reading better follows from reading often: The more a student reads, the better reader the student becomes.

Materials

Supplied
- "The Wind and the Sun," *K¹² Classics for Young Readers, Volume C,* pp. 2–3
- Reading Strategies bookmark

Story Synopsis
The Wind boasts that it is stronger than the Sun. To prove its might, the Wind challenges the Sun to see who can make a man take off his coat. The Wind blows hard, but the man only pulls his coat tighter. The Sun shines down on the man, who removes his coat and makes the Sun the winner.

Keywords
fable – a story that teaches a lesson and may contain animal characters
fiction – make-believe stories
moral – the lesson of a story, particularly a fable
prediction – a guess about what might happen that is based on information in a story and what you already know
table of contents – a list at the start of a book that gives the titles of the book's stories, poems, articles, chapters, or nonfiction pieces and the pages where they can be found

Literature & Comprehension — **LC 5**

Program Name
This banner identifies the section of the book. Each program has its own banner color, so you can easily flip to a section if you know the color: orange for Literature & Comprehension and purple for Writing Skills.

Materials
This box lists all materials needed for the lesson and indicates whether they are Supplied or Also Needed.

Synopsis
In Literature & Comprehension lessons, this section gives a brief summary of the reading selection.

Keywords
The definitions of teaching terminology specific to the lesson are here.

Page Number
Each page number is preceded by an abbreviation corresponding to the section of the book you are in.

LC = Literature & Comprehension

WS = Writing Skills

Activity Instructions

Lesson plans in the Literature & Comprehension and Writing Skills sections of the Lesson Guide include detailed instructions for each activity.

Program Name
This banner identifies the section of the book. Literature & Comprehension has an orange banner and Writing Skills has a purple banner.

Activity Type
This label tells you what kind of activity you are working on.

Activity Description
This text describes what will happen in the activity. For offline activities, it provides step-by-step instructions. Answers are in magenta text.

Objectives
These learning goals indicate what students should be able to do as a result of the lesson.

Activity Book Page Answer Key
A miniature version of the Activity Book page is included in the Lesson Guide, with answers to help you check students' work.

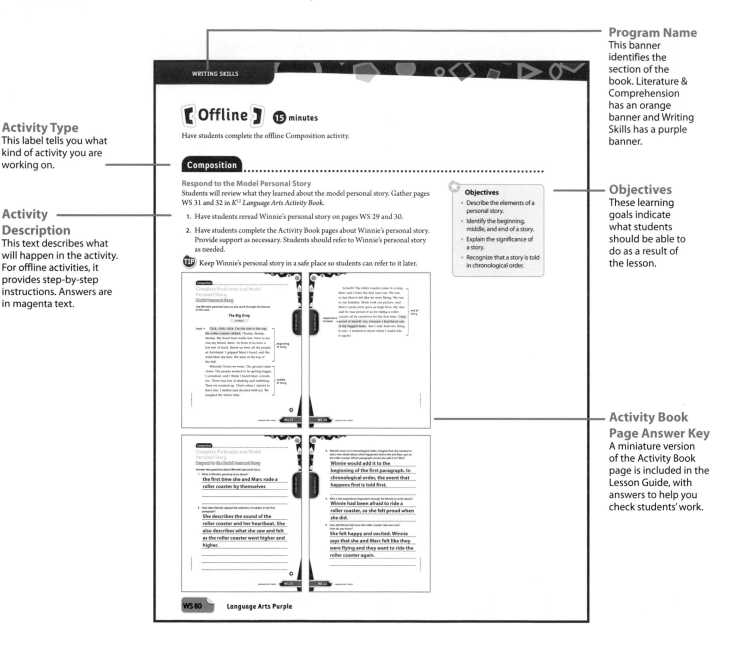

Look for Icons

The lesson plans contain icons to help you quickly see key elements as you work through the lesson. Look for these icons as you use the lesson plans.

Icon	Description
🖥 【Online】	Shows that an activity is online.
📄 【Offline】	Shows that an activity is offline.
TIP	Offers additional advice to help you explain the content.
✏	Appears next to activities that provide students with the opportunity to practice their handwriting.
🎖	Indicates that students have reached a milestone that should be rewarded, usually by adding a sticker to the My Accomplishments chart.
⊕ OPTIONAL:	Indicates that an activity is optional.
➲ Learning Coach Check-In	Indicates an opportunity for you to check in on students' work or progress before they continue.

TIP Use a bookmark or a sticky note to mark the lesson that you are working on in Literature & Comprehension and in Writing Skills. These markers will help you quickly find the page you need each day.

My Accomplishments Chart

Research shows that rewarding students for quality work can increase their motivation. To help you reward students, you will receive a My Accomplishments chart and sticker sheet for use throughout K[12] Language Arts Purple. This chart gives students a tangible record of their progress and accomplishments throughout Literature & Comprehension, Spelling, Vocabulary, and Writing Skills. There is also extra space that you can use to track progress for other accomplishments, such as reading additional books, if you wish.

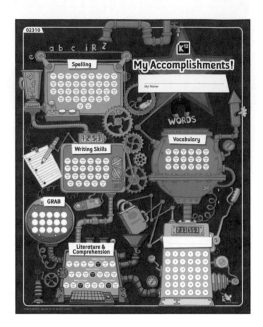

Help students proudly display and share their accomplishments with others by placing the chart somewhere visible, such as on the refrigerator or wall. Throughout the lessons, look for the reward icon 🏅, which indicates when and where students should place a sticker on the chart. Encourage students to set goals and watch their stickers accumulate. Praise students to help them understand the connection between their own growing skill set and the My Accomplishments chart. (For specific information about how to use the chart in each program, see the My Accomplishments Chart section in the individual program overviews.)

K[12] My Journal

Research demonstrates that emerging writers are more motivated and become more confident when writing about self-selected topics. Journal writing allows young writers to explore and express themselves in a nonthreatening environment and make connections to their present knowledge. You will receive *K[12] My Journal* for use throughout K[12] Language Arts Purple. Students will use the journal as they complete some lessons in Writing Skills, but they can also use the journal to write on their own. The journal has three sections that students will use as they work through lessons or on their own.

▸ **Writing Skills** has prompts that students will use to freewrite and make connections to the things that they learn as they complete the lessons in Writing Skills. When appropriate, students may use their freewriting as the basis for their assigned composition.

▸ **Thoughts and Experiences** has prompts to help students start writing. Students can use the pages in this section at any time.

▸ **Ideas** has blank pages, without prompts, on which students can write freely on topics of their choice. Students can use the pages in this section at any time.

K¹² Language Arts Purple Literature & Comprehension Overview

Program	Daily Lesson Time (approximate)	Online/Offline
K¹² Language Arts Purple Literature & Comprehension	50 minutes	Lessons may be all online, all offline, or a combination, moving from online to offline.

Structure and Materials	
22 units that vary in length and structure, depending on the number and length of literary selections • 11 units of fiction, nonfiction, and poetry • 4 Reader's Choice units • 5 Critical Skills Practice units • 2 Semester Review and Checkpoint units	**Materials** • *K¹² Language Arts Lesson Guide* • *K¹² Language Arts Activity Book* • *K¹² Language Arts Assessments* • *K¹² Classics for Young Readers, Volume C* • *K¹² World: Weather or Not* • *George Washington: Soldier, Hero, President* • *The Glory of Greece* • Reading Strategies bookmark

Philosophy

K¹² Language Arts Purple Literature & Comprehension engages students in classic works of literature from various genres. Works are grouped thematically to help students see the connections among texts or genres. The program requires students to read often, think critically about what they have read, and evaluate the ideas and apply the skills they have learned.

The scaffolded approach to each reading selection requires students to prepare for reading by activating prior knowledge, read independently, comprehend what they have read, analyze the language or structure of the text to find its meaning, evaluate the ideas in selections and form substantiated analyses about them, and apply the ideas or skills they have learned to other texts or to the broader world. This consistent pattern—from inward knowledge to outward application—is developed through the lesson activity structure, which is designed to help students model the habits of mind to make them proficient and critical readers, writers, and communicators. The pyramid represents the skills—from lower- to higher-order thinking skills—that students encounter in each lesson and unit in Literature & Comprehension. With each lesson and reading experience, students begin at the foundation of the pyramid and work their way through the lessons and unit, tackling increasingly complex questions and assignments that require them to use higher-order thinking skills.

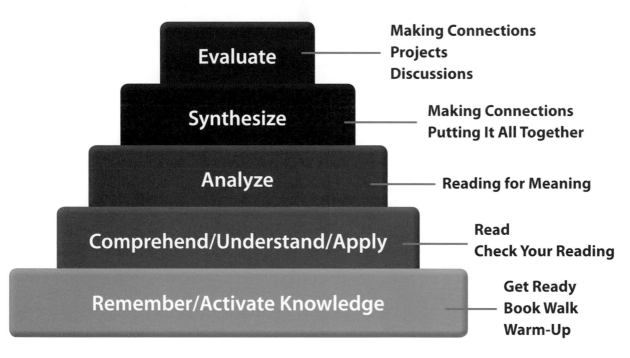

Evaluate — **Making Connections**
Projects
Discussions

Synthesize — **Making Connections**
Putting It All Together

Analyze — **Reading for Meaning**

Comprehend/Understand/Apply — **Read**
Check Your Reading

Remember/Activate Knowledge — **Get Ready**
Book Walk
Warm-Up

TIP Look in the first lesson of the first unit of this program for more information about the different approaches to reading in K¹² Language Arts Purple.

Overview of Literature & Comprehension Lessons

Materials

The following materials are supplied for Literature & Comprehension:

K¹² Language Arts Lesson Guide

K¹² Language Arts Activity Book

K¹² Language Arts Assessments

K¹² Classics for Young Readers, Volume C

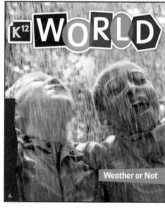

K¹² World: Weather or Not

The following trade books are also supplied:

- *George Washington: Soldier, Hero, President* by Justine and Ron Fontes
- *The Glory of Greece* by Beth Zemble and John Holdren

Also included in your materials is a GRAB (Go Read a Book) bag where students can store their reading materials. Encourage them to keep a list of all the works they complete and praise their efforts.

You should always have paper and pencils available. You will also need the following general materials to complete Activity Book pages:

- ▶ crayons or coloring pencils
- ▶ glue
- ▶ scissors (Safety note: When students are working with scissors, please supervise them to make sure they use their scissors safely and stay seated.)

Additional materials, ranging from index cards to library books, may be needed for certain lessons.

Using the Activity Book

Keep in mind that students will write in and tear out pages from the Activity Book; you may want to store loose Activity Book pages in a three-ring binder. Remember to build students' portfolios with completed Activity Book pages.

TIP Look for instructions in Advance Preparation and tips within activities for saving and gathering materials that get used in more than one lesson.

Unit Structure

Literature & Comprehension consists of 22 units: 17 Literature & Comprehension units and 5 Critical Skills Practice units. Each lesson within each unit should take about 50 minutes to complete.

- ▶ **Literature & Comprehension units**   In these units, students focus on reading selections from *K¹² Classics for Young Readers, Volume C*, an anthology; *K¹² World: Weather or Not*, a nonfiction magazine; the trade books *George Washington: Soldier, Hero, President* and *The Glory of Greece*; and the Reader's Choice book list. The number of lessons in a unit varies and the lessons themselves have different combinations of activities, but the activities include prereading, reading, and postreading instruction.

- ▶ **Critical Skills Practice units**   In these units, students read a variety of passages and practice answering questions similar to those found on standardized assessments, including multiple choice and extended response (writing to a prompt) items. Students read and answer questions about fiction, nonfiction, forms, instructions, poetry, and paired passages. Each unit contains five lessons, with four instructional lessons and one Unit Checkpoint lesson.

Lesson Activities

Lesson plans in the Literature & Comprehension section of this Lesson Guide include detailed instructions for each activity. Literature & Comprehension activity types include the following:

- **Get Ready (Offline or Online)**   The Get Ready activities prepare students for that day's reading selection and lesson. They include a brief overview of the lesson, instructions to help students build background knowledge, and strategies needed for comprehension or to activate their own prior knowledge or experience. Prereading activities include discussions and becoming familiar with the text through the Book Walk and review of Words to Know, words from the selection with which students should become familiar.

- **Warm-Up (Online)**   Students listen to a model of a text being read aloud and then record themselves reading that same text aloud. The text usually is one they have read in the previous lesson. The purpose of this activity is for students to demonstrate their reading fluency—their pace and ability to read text fluidly and with proper expression. Fluency is a prerequisite to comprehension. This activity is a regular feature of the first semester. By the end of the first semester, proficient readers will not require a model of fluent reading.

- **Read (Offline)**   Students read the selection using the comprehension strategies they have reviewed in the Get Ready. **Note:** Watch for **Learning Coach Check-In** opportunities in these activities. You check in with students after they read and ask a few basic questions (which are provided) to ensure that students comprehend the reading selection.

- **Read (Online)**   A second type of **Read** activity appears in Days 91–180. In this activity, students record themselves reading aloud a text they have not seen previously. The purpose of this activity is for students to demonstrate their reading fluency. Unlike the Warm-Up activity in the first semester, this activity does not include a model of fluent reading.

- **GRAB (Offline)**   GRAB stands for Go Read a Book. Research indicates that dedicated, daily reading (of works of one's own choosing) helps develop reading fluency skills and a lifelong habit of reading.

- **Check Your Reading (Online)**   Students answer online multiple choice questions to demonstrate literal and inferential comprehension of the reading selection. In most cases, these questions require students to know what happened in the selection or to identify elements of the selection. These questions become more difficult as the year progresses, requiring students to apply terms and ideas learned in earlier units to later selections.

- **Reading for Meaning (Online)**   Students develop a deeper understanding of the reading selection through application of comprehension strategies and analysis of the selection. These activities have both instruction and practice components. Students may be asked to refer to the reading selection as they go through these activities.

- **Making Connections (Offline)**   Students apply the reading selection information and strategies learned from lessons. They also evaluate the selection and communicate their ideas using textual evidence in support of statements. This activity often involves students' making a connection between and among texts or between the text and themselves or the larger world. This activity may or may not have an Activity Book page.

- **OPTIONAL Beyond the Lesson (Offline)**   This activity is for students who have extra time and interest in exploring the reading selection further. Beyond the Lesson activities are not required and can be skipped.

- **OPTIONAL Peer Interaction (Offline)**   You lead a discussion with students about the reading selection. Ideally, students should discuss their reading with their peers. Peer Interaction activities are not required.

- **Putting It All Together (Offline)**   Students apply information, skills, and strategies learned during the unit. This activity often involves students making a connection among the texts read in the unit. This activity may or may not have an Activity Book page. You score students' work using a checklist and enter the results online.

- **Performance Review (Online)**   You listen to the recordings that students have made during the Warm-Up or Read activities and score students' reading fluency using a checklist. This activity is optional in the first semester but is required in the second semester.

- **Semester Review (Online and Offline)**   Students review skills to prepare for the Semester Checkpoint.

- **Unit and Semester Checkpoints (Online and Offline)**   Students apply the skills learned in the program as they read fiction, nonfiction, and poetry selections. Critical Skills Practice units include a Unit Checkpoint, which tests the skills students have learned in the unit. A Semester Checkpoint covers the concepts learned in the entire semester.

- **More Practice (Online)**   After each Checkpoint, activities are provided to aid review and to practice areas where students may need extra work.

- **Learn (Online)**   In Critical Skills Practice units, students learn strategies for analyzing and responding to various types of questions similar to those found on standardized tests, including answering objective multiple choice questions and responding to a writing prompt. Though students learn the strategies as they particularly relate to the testing formats, the reading, writing, and comprehension skills are taught elsewhere in the course.

- **Try It (Online)**   In Critical Skills Practice units, students practice using skills by completing online exercises. These questions give students experience answering the kinds of items found on common standardized assessments.

My Accomplishments Chart

Rewards in Literature & Comprehension are tied to completing units. When students complete a unit, have them add a sticker for that unit to the My Accomplishments chart.

Reader's Choice Units

Throughout K[12] Language Arts Purple Literature & Comprehension, Planning and Progress in the Online School will alert you to an approaching Reader's Choice unit. These units are designed to give students an opportunity to choose books to read while fine-tuning their comprehension skills. Research indicates that providing opportunities for choice enhances performance and motivates early readers.

In each of the Reader's Choice units, you and your students will select a work from a bank of possible texts. K[12] suggests that you discuss the possible texts with students to guarantee that they will read the texts that interest them. Reader's Choice units are 11 lessons each. There are three important differences from other units in the program.

1. **You will need to acquire these texts on your own, through a library or bookstore.** To help you choose a text for a Reader's Choice unit, K[12] includes a brief synopsis of the story and information about grade and interest level. If you have difficulty locating a work, try your local library. The older works are time-honored classics. Newer works should be readily available online.

2. When you have selected the text, you will be prompted to *print* the accompanying lesson guide and activity pages. **You must print these pages because they are not provided in this Lesson Guide or the Activity Book.**

3. To keep students engaged, deepen comprehension, and develop public speaking capabilities, they are required to complete a unit project as part of each Reader's Choice unit. There are eight possible unit projects that students can choose to complete. Detailed instructions for creating, grading, and presenting each unit project can be found in the online support materials for each Reader's Choice unit. **Once students have chosen which project they will complete, you must print the applicable unit project pages because they are not provided in this Lesson Guide or the Activity Book.**

K¹² Language Arts Purple Spelling Overview

Program	Daily Lesson Time (approximate)	Online/Offline
K¹² Language Arts Purple Spelling	15 minutes	Each unit: 4 offline lessons, 1 online review
Structure and Materials		
36 units with 5 lessons each	**Materials** • *K¹² Spelling Handbook*	

The Spelling materials are separate from the K¹² Language Arts Purple materials, so you will not find Spelling lesson plans in *K¹² Language Arts Lesson Guide* or activity pages in *K¹² Language Arts Activity Book*. Please refer to *K¹² Spelling Handbook* for all materials related to the program.

K¹² Language Arts Purple Vocabulary Overview

Program	Daily Lesson Time (approximate)	Online/Offline
K¹² Language Arts Purple Vocabulary	10 minutes	All online
Structure and Materials		
18 units with 10 lessons each	**Materials** • *K¹² Language Arts Vocabulary Word Lists* Online Book	

Vocabulary is entirely online. Students will work through the online lessons with your supervision. You can access the word lists for all the units from the online lessons.

K¹² Language Arts Purple Writing Skills Overview

Program	Daily Lesson Time (approximate)	Online/Offline
K¹² Language Arts Purple Writing Skills	35 minutes (Days 1–90) 45 minutes (Days 91–180)	Lessons may be all online, all offline, or a combination, moving from online to offline.

Structure and Materials	
23 units that vary in length and structure • 17 Writing Skills units • 4 Critical Skills Practice units • 2 Semester Review and Checkpoint units	**Materials** • *K¹² Language Arts Lesson Guide* • *K¹² Language Arts Activity Book* • *K¹² Language Arts Assessments* • *K¹² My Journal*

Philosophy

Learning to express one's ideas in writing is a fundamental requirement of an educated person. K¹² Language Arts Purple Writing Skills prepares students to express themselves as educated people in the twenty-first century. Grammar, Usage, and Mechanics (GUM) lessons teach students the nuts and bolts of communicating in standard written English. Knowing how to form strong sentences, use verbs and subjects that work together correctly, and capitalize and punctuate their writing without distracting errors helps students communicate their ideas in an understandable way. Composition lessons teach students how to put their ideas together in a form that is appropriate for their purpose and audience. Students will learn how to plan, write, revise, and proofread their writing so that their ideas are presented effectively for their readers. Most Writing Skills units encompass both GUM and Composition.

Grammar, Usage, and Mechanics (GUM)

What Is It?   The grammar, usage, and mechanics lessons give students practice as they learn about sentences and the parts of sentences, including the subject and predicate. They learn about using the eight parts of speech—nouns, verbs, pronouns, adjectives, adverbs, conjunctions, prepositions, and interjections— in sentences. They learn how to use verb tense so that they can express their thoughts in a logical manner, and they discover how capitalization and punctuation marks aid in conveying the message of sentences.

Why We Do It   While it is true that knowing grammar does not make someone a good writer, understanding how grammar works makes writing easier. When students understand basic grammar skills such as how to write a complete sentence, what kind of punctuation is used within a sentence and at the end of a sentence, and which words need capital letters, they can spend their time focusing on ideas. When the focus is on ideas, not on mechanics, writing becomes more fluent and expressive.

Composition

What Is It?   In composition lessons, students do a great deal of writing to practice presenting their ideas fluently and expressively. To help students' writing become more fluent and expressive, each Writing Skills unit begins with a lesson that includes journal writing. Journal writing allows students to freewrite—to write what they want and as much as they want with the knowledge that journal writing is ungraded. Journal writing also helps students warm up for the rest of the composition unit, where they will explore a model that presents the form of writing they will be doing. It might be a narrative, an informational piece, an opinion, a letter, or a research report. During the rest of the unit, students see how one student brainstorms ideas, chooses a topic, makes a plan for writing, drafts, revises, proofreads, and finally publishes the writing as they then do the same with their own writing. In addition, some units end with an oral presentation, where students can hone their speaking skills and choose media to enhance their presentation.

Why We Do It   Research shows that daily writing practice is essential for the developing writer. The lessons are based on a process-writing model of instruction. Research demonstrates that engaging in a variety of prewriting techniques (such as freewriting in a journal or brainstorming) and planning activities (using graphic organizers or outlines) helps novice writers learn to transform their ideas into organized writing. Throughout each unit, students practice skills in discrete stages, and they ultimately write a polished piece of writing that is ready to be "published" or shared. Students learn that the writing process is not a straight line forward and that writing always means rewriting for improvement. As you help students through these lessons, encourage them to express their thoughts and ideas. Student writing is not adult writing. Expect errors in sentence structure and mechanics, but encourage students to express their thoughts in written form.

Overview of Writing Skills Lessons

Materials

The following materials are supplied for Writing Skills:

K¹² *Language Arts Lesson Guide*   K¹² *Language Arts Activity Book*   K¹² *Language Arts Assessments*

K¹² *My Journal*

You should always have paper and pencils available for students. You will also need the following general materials to complete some assignments:

- craft materials (crayons or coloring pencils, glue, scissors, and so forth) (Safety note: When students are working with scissors, please supervise them to make sure they use their scissors safely and stay seated.)
- 3½ x 5-inch index cards

Using the Activity Book

Students write in and tear out pages of the Activity Book, so periodically place the Activity Book pages in a student writing portfolio. In addition, save students' graphic organizers, drafts, and published compositions in the portfolio to keep track of their growth as writers. Consult the portfolio regularly and keep it as a record to share with teachers. Also, share the work with students so that they can see the progress they have made and celebrate it. Remember that student writing is not adult writing. Do not expect perfection, but rather look for progress over time and clarity of thought and intent.

The Activity Book contains pages with examples of different types of writing or other kinds of materials that students refer to over the course of a unit. Look for tips in the Lesson Guide alerting you to store these materials for further use. Be sure to keep these pages in a safe place so you can easily find and refer to them.

TIP Look for instructions in Advance Preparation and tips within activities for saving and gathering materials that get used in more than one lesson.

Using the Journal

As students complete Writing Skills lessons, they freewrite about topics and ideas in
K¹² My Journal. Specific instructions in the Lesson Guide help students get started
and encourage their writing. Students may use the Thoughts and Experiences and
Ideas sections of the journal to write on their own.

(TIP) You can print additional copies of the journal pages used in the Writing Skills
lessons from the online lessons.

Unit Structure

Writing Skills consists of 23 units: 19 Writing Skills units and 4 Critical Skills
Practice units. For Days 1–90, lessons should take about 35 minutes to complete. For
Days 91–180, lessons should take about 45 minutes to complete.

▸ **Writing Skills units**   In these units, students learn grammar, usage, and
   mechanics (GUM) skills; write compositions; and complete related projects
   or presentations. The number of lessons in a unit varies and the lessons
   themselves have different combinations of activities, but the activities
   generally include both GUM and composition instruction.

▸ **Critical Skills Practice units**   In these units, students review a variety of
   writing strategies and language, vocabulary, and spelling skills. They practice
   answering questions similar to those found on standardized assessments,
   including multiple choice and extended response (writing to a prompt) items.
   Students read and answer questions about such topics as main idea and
   supporting details, purpose and audience for writing, sentences and parts of
   sentences, subject and verb agreement, prefixes and suffixes, synonyms and
   antonyms, homophones, and spelling vowel suffixes. Each unit contains five
   lessons, with four instructional lessons and one Unit Checkpoint lesson.

Lesson Activities

Lesson plans in the Writing Skills section of this Lesson Guide include detailed descriptions or instructions for each activity. Writing Skills activity types include the following:

▸ **GUM (Online/Offline)**   Online GUM activities provide instruction and practice in grammar, usage, and mechanics concepts. Offline GUM activities, found on Activity Book pages, provide additional practice.

▸ **Composition (Online/Offline)**   Online composition activities introduce the composition assignments and model the steps needed to complete them. Offline Composition activities allow students to apply what they've learned by taking writing assignments through the entire writing process, from prewriting to publishing. Students also complete freewriting activities by responding to prompts in their journal during some offline Composition activities. **Note:** Watch for **Learning Coach Check-In** opportunities in some of the Composition activities. After students have finished a first draft of their composition, you have the opportunity to print a feedback sheet from the online lesson and use it offline to share with students the strengths and weaknesses of their writing. Each feedback sheet is customized for the particular type of composition students are writing. By sharing your responses to students' writing, you not only provide ways that students can improve their writing, you also give students confidence through the positive feedback you include.

▸ **OPTIONAL Beyond the Lesson (Offline)**   Students with extra time have an opportunity to complete additional entries in *K¹² My Journal*. Beyond the Lesson activities are not required and can be skipped.

▸ **Skills Update (Online)**   Students complete a few short exercises to check the GUM skills covered in the previous lesson. If students struggle with the exercises, suggestions for review activities are provided. Completion of these activities is strongly encouraged before continuing with new concepts.

▸ **OPTIONAL Peer Interaction (Offline)**   Most composition assignments include a Peer Interaction activity, in which students share their writing with a peer or anyone else willing to give feedback. Students can benefit from this interaction by using the feedback to revise their work, as appropriate. Peer Interaction activities are not required.

▸ **Unit and Semester Review (Online)**   Units with GUM content include an online activity as an opportunity to review and practice the GUM skills students have learned in preparation for the Unit Checkpoint. A Semester Review covers the GUM and Critical Skills Practice concepts learned in preparation for the Semester Checkpoint.

▸ **Unit and Semester Checkpoints (Online)**   Units with GUM content and Critical Skills Practice units include a Unit Checkpoint, which tests the skills that students have learned in the unit. A Semester Checkpoint covers the GUM and Critical Skills Practice concepts learned in the entire semester.

- ▸ **Write Now (Offline)**   Composition assignments end with students completing the assignment that they have been planning, drafting, and revising throughout the unit or over multiple units. You evaluate students' writing on a three-point scale for purpose and content, structure and organization, and grammar and mechanics. Sample papers (available online) help evaluate the strength of the writing and areas in which students can improve.

- ▸ **More Practice (Online/Offline)**   After Unit Review, Semester Review, Unit Checkpoint, Semester Checkpoint, and Write Now, activities are usually provided to aid review and to practice areas where students may need extra work, along with links to access these materials.

- ▸ **Get Ready (Online)**   In Critical Skills Practice units, the Get Ready is a short activity to prepare students for the skills that they will learn in the lesson. Often the Get Ready draws on students' previous knowledge or builds background knowledge in preparation for the skill.

- ▸ **Learn (Online)**   In Critical Skills Practice units, students learn strategies for analyzing and responding to various types of test questions, including answering multiple choice questions and responding to a writing prompt.

- ▸ **Try It (Online)**   Students practice using the skills that they have learned by completing online exercises.

My Accomplishments Chart

Rewards in Writing Skills are tied to completing both Unit Checkpoints and Write Now assignments satisfactorily. When students score 80 percent or higher on a Unit Checkpoint and/or when students' writing achieves "meets objectives" in all three categories on the grading rubric, have them add a sticker for that unit to the My Accomplishments chart.

If students score lower than 80 percent on a Unit Checkpoint, review each Checkpoint exercise with them and work with them to correct any exercises they missed. If students' composition work scores "does not meet objectives" in any category, help them review and revise their work to achieve "meets objectives."

K¹² Language Arts Purple Cursive Handwriting Overview

Program	Daily Lesson Time (approximate)	Online/Offline
K¹² Language Arts Purple Cursive Handwriting	10 minutes	All offline

Structure and Materials	
18 units with 5 lessons each	**Materials** • *Cursive Handwriting* • *3rd Grade Cursive Teacher's Guide* • lined paper

Philosophy

K¹² supplies the proven Handwriting Without Tears® program for students in kindergarten through grade 3. This gentle, multisensory approach focuses on careful practice at a pace that suits students' fine motor skills development.

The Handwriting Without Tears website (www.hwtears.com) is full of helpful tips, demonstration videos, and other resources. **Use the passcode found on the cover of the *3rd Grade Cursive Teacher's Guide*** to create an account and gain access to A Click Away. There you will be able to use the Digital Teaching Tools, A+Worksheet Maker, and Screener of Handwriting Proficiency. In addition, visit www.hwtears.com/k12 for information on ordering supplemental materials and teaching aids.

Overview of Cursive Handwriting Lessons

Materials

The following books and materials are supplied for Cursive Handwriting:

- *Cursive Handwriting*
- *3rd Grade Cursive Teacher's Guide*
- one package of specially lined writing paper for Handwriting Without Tears If you need more of this paper, the following options are available:
  - Online lesson openers provide a handwriting sheet that you can print and photocopy.
  - You can order more wide double-lined notebook paper directly from Handwriting Without Tears at http://www.hwtears.com/.

These materials are separate from *K¹² Language Arts Lesson Guide* and *K¹² Language Arts Activity Book*.

Lesson Structure

K[12] Cursive Handwriting is entirely offline and uses the supplied Handwriting Without Tears materials. Before beginning the program, become familiar with *3rd Grade Cursive Teacher's Guide*. The guide includes a Teaching Guidelines chart to help you plan students' handwriting lessons.

In each lesson, you work with students for 10 minutes. (You may want to set a timer for 10 minutes; most students enjoy the Cursive Handwriting program, so it's easy to lose track of time and do too much in one day.)

Students should complete as many workbook pages as they can, picking up where they left off during the previous Cursive Handwriting lesson and continuing from there. They are not expected to complete a set number of pages during the 10-minute lessons. Be sure to monitor students' writing time so you can help them develop good letter formation habits.

Depending on students' pace, the workbook should provide about eight weeks of instruction. Move as quickly or as slowly as students need. When students have completed the workbook, have them use the packaged lined writing paper from Handwriting Without Tears to practice their handwriting. Also look for the Handwriting icon throughout the Lesson Guide. This icon indicates that the associated activity provides a perfect opportunity to practice proper handwriting, and if students pay careful attention to their handwriting, this time can also count as Cursive Handwriting time.

Literature & Comprehension

Stories That Teach

Unit Focus

In this unit, students will read three stories and a play. They will identify the basic story elements of each work, and they will explore the moral, lesson, or theme of each selection. Students will explore these works in *K¹² Classics for Young Readers, Volume C*:

- ▸ "The Necklace of Truth"
- ▸ "The Stone in the Road"
- ▸ "Bruce and the Spider"
- ▸ "The Calabash Kids" (a play)

Unit Plan		Online	Offline
Lesson 1	Introduce "The Necklace of Truth"		50 minutes
Lesson 2	Explore "The Necklace of Truth"	40 minutes	10 minutes
Lesson 3	Introduce "The Stone in the Road"		50 minutes
Lesson 4	Explore "The Stone in the Road"	40 minutes	10 minutes
Lesson 5	Introduce "Bruce and the Spider"		50 minutes
Lesson 6	Explore "Bruce and the Spider"	40 minutes	10 minutes
Lesson 7	Introduce "The Calabash Kids"		50 minutes
Lesson 8	Explore "The Calabash Kids"	40 minutes	10 minutes
Lesson 9	Reflections on Stories That Teach		40 minutes
Lesson 10	Your Choice	varies	50 minutes

Introduce "The Necklace of Truth"

Lesson Overview

[Offline]   50 minutes

Get Ready	Lesson Introduction
	Review Lessons, Morals, and Themes
	Book Walk
	Words to Know
Read	"The Necklace of Truth"
GRAB	Go Read a Book

Content Background

Students may be familiar with stories of King Arthur and his magician friend Merlin. This story is a tale about Merlin. As necessary, explain to students that Merlin was a very wise man and trusted adviser to the legendary King Arthur of England. There are other Welsh and Scottish tales that feature Merlin as a prophet or sage.

Big Ideas

▸ Active, strong readers employ reading strategies such as making connections between text and self.
▸ Reading better follows from reading often: The more a student reads, the better reader the student becomes.

[Materials]

Supplied

● "The Necklace of Truth," *K¹² Classics for Young Readers, Volume C,* pp. 78–85
● Reading Strategies bookmark

Story Synopsis

In a story set long ago, a young girl named Pearl has a problem: She likes to tell lies. Her parents take her to the magician Merlin for help. Merlin gives Pearl a special necklace that changes whenever the girl lies. Pearl is embarrassed by the changes and soon learns to tell the truth.

Keywords

moral – the lesson of a story, particularly a fable
theme – the author's message or big idea

[Offline] 50 minutes

Work **together** with students to complete offline Get Ready, Read, and GRAB activities.

Get Ready

Lesson Introduction

Prepare students to read "The Necklace of Truth."

1. Explain to students that before they read "The Necklace of Truth," they will discuss with you

   ▸ What a moral and a theme are
   ▸ Their predictions about the text
   ▸ Important words to know in the text

2. Tell students that while they read, you will check in to make sure they understand what they are reading.

3. Tell students that after they read, they will answer questions about the story.

> **Objectives**
> - Define *moral* or *lesson learned.*
> - Define *theme.*
> - Connect text with prior knowledge.
> - Use text organizational features to locate and comprehend information (table of contents).
> - Use before-reading strategies.
> - Increase concept and content vocabulary.

Review Lessons, Morals, and Themes

Help students recall what morals and themes are and have them give examples.

1. Remind students that some stories have lessons, or **morals**. Have students tell what a moral is. the lesson of a story, particularly a fable

2. Have students briefly retell a story they have read and tell the moral of the story. For example, students may recall "The Bundle of Sticks" and its moral that people are stronger when they stick together than when they fight or work separately.

3. Remind students that some stories do not have a moral, but they may have a **theme**. Have students tell what a theme is or review it for them. the author's message or big idea

4. Review the differences between lessons and morals, and themes. Tell students that morals are often stated at the end of a story. Themes are not usually stated. Explain that lessons and morals are usually easier to figure out. Themes, on the other hand, must be determined by looking carefully at what happens in a story and the choices that the characters make and the consequences of those choices.

5. Tell students that "The Necklace of Truth" is a story with a lesson.

Book Walk

Have students lead you through a Book Walk of "The Necklace of Truth." Remind them to use the **title** and **illustrations** to make predictions about what will happen in the story.

Words to Know

Remind students that they will find the Words to Know at the bottoms of the pages in the selection.

Read

"The Necklace of Truth"

Have students read "The Necklace of Truth." Remind them to use the strategies on their Reading Strategies bookmark.

 Learning Coach Check-In This reading assignment should take about 15 minutes. After students finish reading, ask the following questions to assess their comprehension of the selection:

▸ Why do Pearl's parents take her to see Merlin? to see if he can help her stop lying

▸ What does Merlin give Pearl, and what does it do? a necklace that changes when the person wearing it tells a lie

If students have trouble answering these questions, ask them what reading strategies they used and suggest they reread the selection.

Objectives
- Read literature independently and proficiently.
- Apply information read to answer questions.
- Evaluate reading strategies.

GRAB

Go Read a Book

Have students read a book or magazine of their own choosing for at least 20 minutes. Remind students to use the strategies on their Reading Strategies bookmark before and during reading to help them understand the text.

TIP Remember: The more students read, the better readers they become.

Objectives
- Read literature independently and proficiently.
- Read a variety of texts for information and pleasure.

Explore "The Necklace of Truth"

Lesson Overview

🖥 【Online】 ⏱40 minutes

Check Your Reading	Comprehend "The Necklace of Truth"
Reading for Meaning	Identify Problem and Solution
	Identify Choices and Consequences

📄 【Offline】 ⏱10 minutes

Making Connections	Map the Story

【Materials】

Supplied

- "The Necklace of Truth," *K¹² Classics for Young Readers, Volume C*, pp. 78–85
- *K¹² Language Arts Activity Book*, pp. LC 75–77

Keywords

consequence – what happens because of an action or event

problem – an issue a character must solve in a story

solution – how a character solves a problem in a story

Content Background

Just as languages have a grammar, stories have a grammar—meaning that stories are put together in a way that helps readers understand them. When we ask students to recall the elements of a story, we are asking them to identify the story grammar. These elements are characters, setting, plot, and problem and solution. To understand the deeper meaning of stories, students must first be able to identify the story grammar. We ask students to think about the story grammar and the way stories are put together because it helps them improve their reading and writing skills. If students are having difficulty identifying and explaining these basic story elements at this point in the year, it would be wise to seek outside assistance from a teaching professional or reading specialist.

Big Ideas

- ▶ To understand and interpret a story, readers need to understand and describe characters and what they do.
- ▶ Readers need to understand literary conflicts and their resolutions in order to analyze characters and themes.
- ▶ Identifying choices and consequences helps readers understand characters and the central message in a story.
- ▶ Understanding story grammar helps students comprehend text and strengthen their self-monitoring skills.

[Online] ④⓪ minutes

Students will work **independently** to complete online Check Your Reading and Reading for Meaning activities.

Check Your Reading ....

Comprehend "The Necklace of Truth"

Students will answer questions about "The Necklace of Truth" to demonstrate their literal and inferential comprehension of the story.

Objectives
- Identify concrete answers to questions.
- Infer answers to questions.
- Apply information read to answer questions.

Reading for Meaning ....

Identify Problem and Solution

Students will identify story elements, focusing on the problem and the solution, to help them understand the main character.

Objectives
- Identify the problem a character faces.
- Identify the solution to a problem a character faces.
- Identify choices that a character makes and their consequences.

Identify Choices and Consequences

Students will look at the choices the main character makes in "The Necklace of Truth" and think about how she changes as a result of the consequences of her actions.

⟦ Offline ⟧ 🔟 minutes

Work **together** with students to complete the offline Making Connections activity.

Making Connections ···

Map the Story

Students will review the who, what, where, when, why, and how of the story, as well as the story's lesson. Turn to pages LC 75–77 in *K¹² Language Arts Activity Book*.

1. Have students read the directions.

2. Have them complete the Activity Book pages.

3. If students have difficulty recalling a story to which they can compare this one, remind them of "The Boy Who Cried Wolf" or "Pinocchio."

(TIP) Keep the Activity Book pages in a safe place so students can refer to them later.

> **Objectives**
> - Identify story grammar.
> - Determine the theme, moral, or lesson of a work of literature.
> - Make connections between text and self, text and world, and text to text.
> - Compare and contrast literary elements in two or more literary selections.

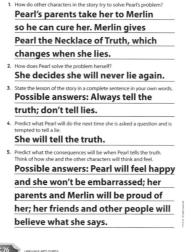

Making Connections

Explore "The Necklace of Truth"

Map the Story

Fill in the boxes. Then answer the questions.

| Title | "The Necklace of Truth" |

Setting: Possible answer: long, long ago in a place with a castle

Characters:
Main character: Pearl
Other characters: Pearl's parents; Merlin; Pearl's friends

Problem and Solution: Pearl tells lies and then learns to stop lying.

LANGUAGE ARTS PURPLE — LC 75

1. How do other characters in the story try to solve Pearl's problem?
Pearl's parents take her to Merlin so he can cure her. Merlin gives Pearl the Necklace of Truth, which changes when she lies.

2. How does Pearl solve the problem herself?
She decides she will never lie again.

3. State the lesson of the story in a complete sentence in your own words.
Possible answers: Always tell the truth; don't tell lies.

4. Predict what Pearl will do the next time she is asked a question and is tempted to tell a lie.
She will tell the truth.

5. Predict what the consequences will be when Pearl tells the truth. Think of how she and the other characters will think and feel.
Possible answers: Pearl will feel happy and she won't be embarrassed; her parents and Merlin will be proud of her; her friends and other people will believe what she says.

LC 76 — LANGUAGE ARTS PURPLE

6. Write at least five sentences comparing and contrasting this story with another story about a character who lies.
Students should compare and contrast this story with a similar one, such as "The Boy Who Cried Wolf" or "Pinocchio." They should tell how the setting, characters, problems and solutions, choices, consequences, and lessons are similar and different.

LANGUAGE ARTS PURPLE — LC 77

Introduce "The Stone in the Road"

Lesson Overview

[Offline]   50 minutes

Get Ready	Lesson Introduction
	Discuss Responsibility
	Book Walk
	Words to Know
Read	"The Stone in the Road"
GRAB	Go Read a Book

Big Ideas

▶ Active, strong readers employ reading strategies such as making connections between text and self.

▶ Active, strong readers use existing knowledge to make predictions before, during, and after reading.

▶ Reading for pleasure helps develop fluency and a lifelong love of reading.

[Materials]

Supplied

● "The Stone in the Road," *K¹² Classics for Young Readers, Volume C,* pp. 86–89

● Reading Strategies bookmark

Story Synopsis

This folktale illustrates the importance of taking responsibility for doing the right thing. A stone lies in a road, and everyone who passes complains about it but does not move it. Finally, the king reveals that he put the stone in the road and hid treasures underneath for the one who moved the stone.

Keywords

folktale – a story, which usually teaches a lesson important to a culture, that is passed down through many generations

[Offline] **50** minutes

Work **together** with students to complete offline Get Ready, Read, and GRAB activities.

Get Ready

Lesson Introduction

Prepare students to read "The Stone in the Road."

1. Explain to students that before they read "The Stone in the Road," they will discuss with you

   ▸ What *responsibility* means
   ▸ Their predictions about the text
   ▸ Important words to know in the text

2. Tell students that while they read, you will check in to make sure they understand what they are reading.

3. Tell students that after they read, they will answer questions about the story.

> **Objectives**
> - Connect text with prior knowledge.
> - Use text organizational features to locate and comprehend information (table of contents).
> - Use before-reading strategies.
> - Increase concept and content vocabulary.

Discuss Responsibility

Discuss the topic of responsibility with students to prepare them for the theme of the folktale "The Stone in the Road."

1. Ask students what they think of when they hear the word *responsibility*.

2. Tell them responsibility is doing your part or your duty. Have students tell how they show that they are responsible, or do what they are supposed to do.

3. Remind students that some responsibilities are understood—no one tells you to do them, but you know they are the right thing to do because they help other people, your family, your neighbors, or your community.

4. Tell students that "The Stone in the Road" is a story about responsibility.

Book Walk

Have students lead you through a Book Walk of "The Stone in the Road." Remind them to use the **title** and **illustrations** to make predictions about what will happen in the story.

Words to Know

Remind students that they will find the Words to Know at the bottoms of the pages in the selection.

Read

"The Stone in the Road"

Have students read "The Stone in the Road." Remind them to use the strategies on their Reading Strategies bookmark.

➲ **Learning Coach Check-In** This reading assignment should take about 15 minutes. After students finish reading, ask the following questions to assess their comprehension of the selection:

► What do most people do when they come to the stone in the road? go around it and complain that no one has moved it

► How did the stone get there? The king put it there.

If students have trouble answering these questions, ask them what reading strategies they used and suggest they reread the selection.

Objectives
- Read literature independently and proficiently.
- Apply information read to answer questions.
- Evaluate reading strategies.

GRAB

Go Read a Book

Have students read a book or magazine of their own choosing for at least 20 minutes. Remind students to use the strategies on their Reading Strategies bookmark before and during reading to help them understand the text.

Objectives
- Read literature independently and proficiently.
- Read a variety of texts for information and pleasure.

Explore "The Stone in the Road"

Lesson Overview

🖥 [Online]   **40** minutes

Check Your Reading	Comprehend "The Stone in the Road"
Reading for Meaning	Identify Problems, Solutions, and Theme

📄 [Offline]   **10** minutes

Making Connections	Map the Story

Big Ideas

▸ To understand and interpret a story, readers need to understand and describe characters and what they do.
▸ Readers need to understand literary conflicts and their resolutions in order to analyze characters and themes.
▸ Understanding story grammar helps students comprehend text and strengthen their self-monitoring skills.

[Materials]

Supplied

● "The Stone in the Road,"
  *K¹² Classics for Young
  Readers, Volume C,*
  pp. 86–89
● *K¹² Language Arts Activity
  Book,* pp. LC 79–80

Keywords

problem – an issue a
character must solve in a
story
solution – how a character
solves a problem in a story
theme – the author's
message or big idea

 **40 minutes**

Students will work **independently** to complete online Check Your Reading and Reading for Meaning activities.

Check Your Reading

Comprehend "The Stone in the Road"
Students will answer questions about "The Stone in the Road" to demonstrate their literal and inferential comprehension of the story.

Objectives
- Identify concrete answers to questions.
- Infer answers to questions.
- Apply information read to answer questions.

Reading for Meaning

Identify Problems, Solutions, and Theme
Students will explore the plot of "The Stone in the Road" and focus on the problem to determine the theme of the story.

Objectives
- Identify the problem a character faces.
- Identify the solution to a problem a character faces.
- Define *theme*.
- Identify theme.

[Offline] ⏱ 10 minutes

Work **together** with students to complete the offline Making Connections activity.

Making Connections •

Map the Story

Students will review the who, what, where, when, why, and how of the story, as well as its theme. Turn to pages LC 79 and 80 in *K¹² Language Arts Activity Book*.

1. Have students read the directions.

2. Have them complete the Activity Book pages.

TIP Keep the Activity Book pages in a safe place so students can refer to them later.

> ⭐ **Objectives**
> - Identify story grammar.
> - Identify theme.
> - Make connections between text and self, text and world, and text to text.

Making Connections

Explore "The Stone in the Road"

Map the Story

Complete the story web. Then answer the questions.

Characters
people on the road; the king

Problem
There is a stone in the road.

Theme
Possible answer: Be responsible and fix a problem when you see it, even if the problem is not your fault.

Characters' Solution to the Problem
Leave the stone and complain about it.

Better Solution to the Problem
Move the stone out of the way.

LANGUAGE ARTS PURPLE · **LC 79**

---

1. Write about a time when the theme of this story was important in your own life.

   Answers will vary, but students should describe a time when it was important for them or someone they know to take responsibility and fix a problem.

2. Describe a problem in your neighborhood and tell how you could take responsibility to help fix it.

   Example: Students might describe litter in a public place that they could put in the trash.

LC 80 · LANGUAGE ARTS PURPLE

Introduce "Bruce and the Spider"

Lesson Overview

[Offline]   **50** minutes

Get Ready	Lesson Introduction
	What Is a Legend?
	Book Walk
	Words to Know
Read	"Bruce and the Spider"
GRAB	Go Read a Book

Content Background

This legend is about Robert the Bruce, a medieval king of Scotland who led his army in a fight against England to free Scotland from English rule. After many battles in which the Scottish army was outnumbered, Robert the Bruce eventually triumphed and was made king of Scotland. As king, he was called Robert I of Scotland.

Big Ideas

▸ Active, strong readers employ reading strategies such as making connections between text and self.
▸ Reading a book of their own choosing helps motivate students to read.

[Materials]

Supplied

● "Bruce and the Spider," *K¹² Classics for Young Readers, Volume C,* pp. 90–93
● Reading Strategies bookmark

Also Needed

● map, world

Story Synopsis

In this legend, Robert the Bruce, a king of Scotland from long ago, is ready to give up the fight against his enemies. In his hideout, Bruce sees a spider repeatedly try to build a web. Bruce is inspired by the spider's persistence and decides to fight on.

Keywords

legend – a story that is passed down for many years to teach the values of a culture; a legend may or may not contain some true events or people
setting – when and where a story takes place

[Offline] 50 minutes

Work **together** with students to complete offline Get Ready, Read, and GRAB activities.

Get Ready

Lesson Introduction

Prepare students to read "Bruce and the Spider."

1. Explain to students that before they read "Bruce and the Spider," they will discuss with you

   ▶ What a legend is
   ▶ Their predictions about the text
   ▶ Important words to know in the text

2. Tell students that while they read, you will check in to make sure they understand what they are reading.

3. Tell students that after they read, they will answer questions about the story.

> ### Objectives
> - Define *legend*.
> - Define *setting*.
> - Identify setting(s).
> - Use text organizational features to locate and comprehend information (table of contents).
> - Use before-reading strategies.
> - Increase concept and content vocabulary.

What Is a Legend?

Discuss what a legend is and the setting of the story "Bruce and the Spider." Gather a world map.

1. Tell students that the story they are about to read is a **legend**. Explain what a legend is: a story that is passed down for many years to teach the values of a culture. A legend may or may not contain some true events or people.

2. Have students tell about any legends they might have read, such as stories about King Arthur who was believed to be a real king of England.

3. Have students tell what a **setting** is: when and where a story takes place. Explain that the setting of this legend is a country called Scotland. Help students find Scotland on the world map.

4. On the map, show students England and point out that it shares the same large island with Scotland. Tell students that "Bruce and the Spider" is about a real king of Scotland from long ago who led his people in a fight to free Scotland from being ruled by England.

Book Walk

Have students lead you through a Book Walk of "Bruce and the Spider." Remind them to use the **title** and **illustrations** to make predictions about what will happen in the story.

Words to Know
Remind students that they will find the Words to Know at the bottoms of the pages in the selection.

Read

"Bruce and the Spider"
Have students read "Bruce and the Spider." Remind them to use the strategies on their Reading Strategies bookmark.

➲ **Learning Coach Check-In** This reading assignment should take about 15 minutes. After students finish reading, ask the following questions to assess their comprehension of the selection:

► What does Robert Bruce decide at the beginning of the story, when he is hiding out in the hut? He is going to give up the fight against his enemies.
► What does Bruce watch the spider do? try seven times to make a web in the rafters

If students have trouble answering these questions, ask them what reading strategies they used and suggest they reread the selection.

Objectives
- Read literature independently and proficiently.
- Apply information read to answer questions.
- Evaluate reading strategies.

GRAB

Go Read a Book
Have students read a book or magazine of their own choosing for at least 20 minutes. Remind students to use the strategies on their Reading Strategies bookmark before and during reading to help them understand the text.

Objectives
- Read literature independently and proficiently.
- Read a variety of texts for information and pleasure.

Explore "Bruce and the Spider"

Lesson Overview

🖥 〖Online〗   40 minutes

Check Your Reading	Comprehend "Bruce and the Spider"
Reading for Meaning	Analyze How the Main Character Changes
	Learn What the Legend Teaches

📄 〖Offline〗   10 minutes

Making Connections	Map the Story

Big Ideas

▶ To understand and interpret a story, readers need to understand and describe characters and what they do.

▶ Readers need to understand literary conflicts and their resolutions in order to analyze characters and themes.

▶ Understanding story grammar helps students comprehend text and strengthen their self-monitoring skills.

▶ Readers need to synthesize, draw conclusions about, and interpret what they have read.

〖Materials〗

Supplied

● "Bruce and the Spider,"
  *K¹² Classics for Young
  Readers, Volume C,*
  pp. 90–93

● *K¹² Language Arts Activity
  Book,* pp. LC 81–83

Keywords

legend – a story that is passed down for many years to teach the values of a culture; a legend may or may not contain some true events or people

main character – an important person, animal, or other being who is central to the plot

problem – an issue a character must solve in a story

solution – how a character solves a problem in a story

theme – the author's message or big idea

[Online] 40 minutes

Students will work **independently** to complete online Check Your Reading and Reading for Meaning activities.

Check Your Reading •••

Comprehend "Bruce and the Spider"
Students will answer questions about "Bruce and the Spider" to demonstrate their literal and inferential comprehension of the story.

Objectives
- Identify concrete answers to questions.
- Infer answers to questions.
- Apply information read to answer questions.

Reading for Meaning •••

Analyze How the Main Character Changes
Students will look at how the main character changes in "Bruce and the Spider" to begin to identify the theme of the legend.

Learn What the Legend Teaches
Students will think about how the legend "Bruce and the Spider" teaches readers about the values of the people of Scotland, and they will identify the theme of the story.

Objectives
- Identify the problem a character faces.
- Identify the solution to a problem a character faces.
- Describe characters by what they say, what they do, or what others say about them.
- Describe how a character changes.
- Define *theme*.
- Determine the theme, moral, or lesson of a work of literature.
- Understand a variety of literature representing different cultures and traditions.

 **10** minutes

Work **together** with students to complete the offline Making Connections activity.

Making Connections •••

Map the Story
Students will review the who, what, where, when, why, and how of the story, as well as its theme. Turn to pages LC 81–83 in *K¹² Language Arts Activity Book*.

1. Have students read the directions.

2. Have them complete the Activity Book pages.

TIP Keep the Activity Book pages in a safe place so students can refer to them later.

Making Connections
Explore "Bruce and the Spider"
Map the Story

Fill in the boxes. Then answer the questions.

| Title | "Bruce and the Spider" |

Setting — long ago in Scotland

Main Character — Robert Bruce, King of Scotland

Problem — Bruce and his army have lost many battles, and he and his soldiers are in hiding.

LANGUAGE ARTS PURPLE — **LC 81**

LC 82 — LANGUAGE ARTS PURPLE

1. How does Robert Bruce solve his problem?
He goes back into battle and fights harder than he ever has. He wins and frees his country.

2. What happens that makes Robert Bruce decide to go back into battle?
He sees a spider try again and again to build a web. The spider gives Bruce courage. He decides to try again because the spider continues to try and eventually succeeds.

3. How does Robert Bruce change in the story?
At the beginning, he is feeling defeated and like he wants to quit. At the end, he feels brave and decides to fight hard and not give up.

---

4. Tell the theme of the story in your own words.
Possible answer: You should keep trying if something is important to you, even if it's hard.

5. Describe a time when this theme was important in your own life.
Answers will vary, but students should describe a time when they had to keep trying to do something difficult and eventually succeeded.

LANGUAGE ARTS PURPLE — **LC 83**

Introduce "The Calabash Kids"

Lesson Overview

[Offline]   50 minutes

Get Ready	Lesson Introduction
	What Is Drama?
	Book Walk
	Words to Know
Read	"The Calabash Kids"
GRAB	Go Read a Book

Big Ideas

► Active, strong readers employ reading strategies such as making connections between text and self.
► Reading better follows from reading often: The more a student reads, the better reader the student becomes.

[Materials]

Supplied

- "The Calabash Kids," *K¹² Classics for Young Readers, Volume C,* pp. 94–113
- Reading Strategies bookmark

Also Needed

- map, world

Play Synopsis

This play from Tanzania tells the story of a widow who lives alone and yearns for children. The woman receives magic gourd seeds, and the gourds turn into children. One day the woman gets angry at her favorite child, and he turns back into a gourd. The woman regrets her behavior, and the child returns.

Keywords

drama – another word for *play*

folktale – a story, which usually teaches a lesson important to a culture, that is passed down through many generations

narrator – the teller of a story

[Offline] 🔟 minutes

Work **together** with students to complete offline Get Ready, Read, and GRAB activities.

Get Ready

Lesson Introduction

Prepare students to read "The Calabash Kids."

1. Explain to students that before they read "The Calabash Kids," they will discuss with you

   ▸ What drama is
   ▸ Their predictions about the text
   ▸ Important words to know in the text

2. Tell students that while they read, you will check in to make sure they understand what they are reading.

3. Tell students that after they read, they will answer questions about the story.

What Is Drama?

Discuss what drama is and the elements of drama in "The Calabash Kids." Gather a world map.

1. Tell students that the story they are about to read is a play, and another word for *play* is **drama**.

2. Have students use the table of contents in *K¹² Classics for Young Readers, Volume C,* to find the play "The Calabash Kids."

3. Using the book, point to and explain the elements of a drama.

   ▸ Show the cast of characters and setting at the beginning. Have students tell what a **narrator** is: the teller of a story.
   ▸ Show the first line of the play. Explain that the name in boldface type before the colon is the name of the person speaking. The sentences after that are the words that the character would say on a stage. The actors don't speak the name of the character.
   ▸ Show students the words in parentheses on page 97 (the fourth page of the play). Explain that these are stage directions—words that tell the actor how to say the lines or that describe something else happening on the stage. They are not read aloud but will help students as they read the play.

4. Go back to the first page of the play and have students identify the setting.

5. Tell students that Tanzania is a country in Africa. Have students find it on the world map.

6. Explain that this play is also a **folktale** from Tanzania. Have students tell what a folktale is: a story that usually teaches a lesson important to a culture and is passed down through many generations. Remind them to think about the lessons in the tale as they read.

Objectives

- Define *drama*.
- Identify parts of a drama.
- Define *folktale*.
- Identify setting(s).
- Use text organizational features to locate and comprehend information (table of contents).
- Use before-reading strategies.
- Increase concept and content vocabulary.

Book Walk

Have students lead you through a Book Walk of "The Calabash Kids." Remind them to use the **title** and **illustrations** to make predictions about what will happen in the story.

Words to Know

Remind students that they will find the Words to Know at the bottoms of the pages in the selection.

 Read •••

"The Calabash Kids"

Have students read "The Calabash Kids." Remind students to use the strategies on their Reading Strategies bookmark.

> ⮑ **Learning Coach Check-In** This reading assignment should take about 15 minutes. After students finish reading, ask the following questions to assess their comprehension of the selection:
>
> > ► What does Shindo [pronounced SHEE-an-doh] want? children
> > ► Where do the children come from? gourds grown from magic seeds

If students have trouble answering these questions, ask them what reading strategies they used and suggest they reread the selection.

Objectives
- Read literature independently and proficiently.
- Apply information read to answer questions.
- Evaluate reading strategies.

GRAB •••

Go Read a Book

Have students read a book or magazine of their own choosing for at least 20 minutes. Remind students to use the strategies on their Reading Strategies bookmark before and during reading to help them understand the text.

Objectives
- Read literature independently and proficiently.
- Read a variety of texts for information and pleasure.

Explore "The Calabash Kids"

Lesson Overview

🖥 【Online】   ⑩ minutes

Check Your Reading	Comprehend "The Calabash Kids"
Reading for Meaning	Stage the Play

📄 【Offline】   ⑩ minutes

Making Connections	Map the Story

Big Ideas

▸ To understand and interpret a story, readers need to understand and describe characters and what they do.

▸ Readers need to understand literary conflicts and their resolutions in order to analyze characters and themes.

▸ Understanding story grammar helps students comprehend text and strengthen their self-monitoring skills.

【Materials】

Supplied

- "The Calabash Kids," *K¹² Classics for Young Readers, Volume C,* pp. 94–113
- *K¹² Language Arts Activity Book,* pp. LC 85–87

Keywords

drama – another word for *play*

folktale – a story, which usually teaches a lesson important to a culture, that is passed down through many generations

[Online] **40** minutes

Students will work **independently** to complete online Check Your Reading and Reading for Meaning activities.

Check Your Reading ......

Comprehend "The Calabash Kids"
Students will answer questions about "The Calabash Kids" to demonstrate their literal and inferential comprehension of the story.

Objectives
- Identify concrete answers to questions.
- Infer answers to questions.
- Apply information read to answer questions.

Reading for Meaning ......

Stage the Play
Students will think about how the play might be acted out onstage as a way to help them understand the main character, Shindo, and how she feels and behaves.

Objectives
- Make inferences and draw conclusions about the structure and elements of drama.
- Explain the elements of plot, character, and dialogue.
- Describe characters by what they say, what they do, and what others say about them.
- Use information gained from illustrations to demonstrate understanding of, for example, mood, character, or setting.

[Offline] **10** minutes

Work **together** with students to complete the offline Making Connections activity.

Making Connections

Map the Story

Students will review the who, what, where, when, why, and how of the story, as well as its lessons. Turn to pages LC 85–87 in *K¹² Language Arts Activity Book*.

1. Have students read the directions.

2. Have them complete the Activity Book pages.

TIP Keep the Activity Book pages in a safe place so students can refer to them later.

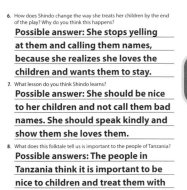

Objectives

- Identify story grammar.
- Define important questions that need to be answered: *who, what, when, where, why,* and *how.*
- Describe how a character changes.
- Understand a variety of literature representing different cultures and traditions.
- Make connections between text and self, text and world, and text to text.

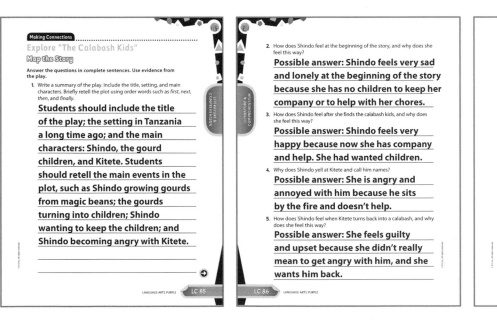

Making Connections

Explore "The Calabash Kids"

Map the Story

Answer the questions in complete sentences. Use evidence from the play.

1. Write a summary of the play. Include the title, setting, and main characters. Briefly retell the plot using order words such as *first, next, then,* and *finally.*

Students should include the title of the play; the setting in Tanzania a long time ago; and the main characters: Shindo, the gourd children, and Kitete. Students should retell the main events in the plot, such as Shindo growing gourds from magic beans; the gourds turning into children; Shindo wanting to keep the children; and Shindo becoming angry with Kitete.

2. How does Shindo feel at the beginning of the story, and why does she feel this way?

Possible answer: Shindo feels very sad and lonely at the beginning of the story because she has no children to keep her company or to help with her chores.

3. How does Shindo feel after she finds the calabash kids, and why does she feel this way?

Possible answer: Shindo feels very happy because now she has company and help. She had wanted children.

4. Why does Shindo yell at Kitete and call him names?

Possible answer: She is angry and annoyed with him because he sits by the fire and doesn't help.

5. How does Shindo feel when Kitete turns back into a calabash, and why does she feel this way?

Possible answer: She feels guilty and upset because she didn't really mean to get angry with him, and she wants him back.

6. How does Shindo change the way she treats her children by the end of the play? Why do you think this happens?

Possible answer: She stops yelling at them and calling them names, because she realizes she loves the children and wants them to stay.

7. What lesson do you think Shindo learns?

Possible answer: She should be nice to her children and not call them bad names. She should speak kindly and show them she loves them.

8. What does this folktale tell us is important to the people of Tanzania?

Possible answers: The people in Tanzania think it is important to be nice to children and treat them with kindness. It is important to be patient with children.

LANGUAGE ARTS PURPLE **LC 85**

LC 86 LANGUAGE ARTS PURPLE

LANGUAGE ARTS PURPLE **LC 87**

Reflections on Stories That Teach

Lesson Overview

📄 [Offline] 40 minutes

Get Ready	Lesson Introduction
	Review Compare and Contrast
Putting It All Together	Compare and Contrast Stories

🖥 [Online] varies

More Practice	Review the Skills
Read	Read Fluently "The Crab and the Monkey"
Performance Review	Fluency Check

[Materials]

Supplied

- "The Necklace of Truth," "The Stone in the Road," "Bruce and the Spider," "The Calabash Kids," *K¹² Classics for Young Readers, Volume C,* pp. 78–113
- *K¹² Language Arts Activity Book,* pp. LC 75–77, 79–83, 85–87, 89
- Putting It All Together Assessment Checklist (printout)
- "Tit for Tat" (printout)
- "The Crab and the Monkey" (printout)
- Fluency Performance Checklist (printout)

Also Needed

- stopwatch

Advance Preparation

For Putting It All Together, print "Tit for Tat" from the online lesson and read it before beginning the lesson. If possible, find peers to discuss the story. Also have students gather completed pages LC 75–77, 79–83, and 85–87 (Map the Story) in *K¹² Language Arts Activity Book*. For the Performance Review, print "The Crab and the Monkey."

Big Ideas

- ▸ Fluent readers expend less energy on decoding and therefore have more energy for comprehension.
- ▸ Active, strong readers employ reading strategies such as making connections between and among texts.
- ▸ Understanding story grammar helps students comprehend text and strengthen their self-monitoring skills.
- ▸ Comprehension requires an understanding of story structure.

Keywords

adage – a saying that contains a lot of ideas in very few words, or embodies an idea using a metaphor *Example:* The early bird catches the worm.

compare – to explain how two or more things are alike

contrast – to explain how two or more things are different

folktale – a story, which usually teaches a lesson important to a culture, that is passed down through many generations

〔Offline〕 50 minutes

Work **together** with students to complete the offline Get Ready and Putting It All Together activities.

Get Ready ....

Lesson Introduction

Prepare students to compare and contrast a new story, "Tit for Tat," with the stories they have read in this unit.

1. Tell students that you are going to read aloud a new story. Before you read the story, they will discuss with you
   - ► How to compare and contrast different works of literature
   - ► What a folktale is

2. Tell students that as they listen to the story, they will complete a story map about it.

3. Tell students that after you finish reading the story, they will have a discussion about this story and the other stories they've read in the unit.

> **Objectives**
> - Define *compare* and *contrast*.
> - Use before-reading strategies.

Review Compare and Contrast

Review how to compare and contrast various works of literature from the same or similar genres.

1. Have students tell what they do when they **compare** and **contrast** two stories. tell how the stories are similar and how they are different

2. Have students tell the names of the stories in this unit. "The Necklace of Truth," "The Stone in the Road," "Bruce and the Spider," "The Calabash Kids"

3. Have students compare and contrast the stories in the unit by telling their similarities and their differences. Possible answers: They are similar because they take place long ago and in other countries; they all teach a lesson; they all have main characters that change and learn lessons. The stories are different in their genres, main characters settings, and lessons.

4. Tell students that they are going to compare and contrast a new story with the ones they have read in this unit.

Putting It All Together

Compare and Contrast Stories

Students will demonstrate their understanding of the story "Tit for Tat" and participate in a discussion comparing and contrasting the story to others in the unit. Ideally students should discuss the story with their peers, but if necessary you can have the discussion with them. Gather the completed Map the Story pages and turn to page LC 89 in *K¹² Language Arts Activity Book*. Also gather the printout of "Tit for Tat."

1. Tell students you are going to read to them "Tit for Tat." Do not provide the passage to students to read independently. This exercise is intended to assess their listening skills as well as their comprehension ability.

2. Tell them that as you read, they are to complete the Activity Book page. Read the story and have students complete the page.

3. Review students' completed page with them. Then lead a discussion about the story.

   ▸ How do you think the camel feels when the villagers chase him and beat him? Possible answers: afraid; angry; worried

   ▸ How does the camel feel about the way his friend the jackal behaved after he ate? Possible answers: He's angry that his friend made so much noise and got the villagers' attention; he doesn't think it's fair that the jackal got to eat his dinner but caused the camel to miss his.

   ▸ Why do you think the camel chooses to roll in the river and throw off the jackal? Possible answers: He wants to get back at the jackal for ruining his dinner; he wants to give the jackal a taste of his own medicine and have him feel what it's like to have your friend do something that hurts you.

   ▸ What are the consequences of the jackal's choice to make noise after dinner? Possible answer: The villagers come and beat the camel. His friend the camel is angry at him and seeks revenge by dumping him in the river.

   ▸ What lesson do you think the jackal learns from having the camel dump him in the river? Possible answers: You should think about the consequences of your actions before you do anything; you should think about how your behavior might affect others; if you do something that hurts someone else, you can expect them to be mad at you or even try to get back at you; you should treat people the way you want them to treat you.

   ▸ *Tit for tat* is a common expression or *adage*. An adage is a saying that contains a lot of ideas in very few words, or embodies an idea using a metaphor. What do you think the title "Tit for Tat" means? Possible answers: You get what you deserve; treat people the way you want to be treated; if you do something that hurts someone else, you might get hurt in return.

   ▸ There is an adage that is known as the Golden Rule. It says, "Do unto others as you would have them do unto you." How do you think this adage relates to this story? Possible answer: The jackal should have thought about how his actions would affect the camel before he began howling. Then he might not have made so much noise, and the camel wouldn't have been mad at him.

Objectives

- Compare texts from different cultures and time periods.
- Compare and contrast literary elements in two or more literary selections.
- Demonstrate understanding of common features of legends, myths, folktales, fairy tales, and classic stories.
- Read and discuss texts from different cultures, traditions, and time periods.
- Ask for clarification and further explanation as needed about the topics and texts under discussion.
- Follow agreed-upon rules for discussions (for example, gaining the floor in respectful ways, listening to others with care, speaking one at a time about the topics and texts under discussion).
- Identify the main ideas and supporting details of a text read aloud, or information presented in a variety of media and formats.
- Ask and answer questions about information from a speaker, offering appropriate elaboration and detail.
- Understand the meaning of common adages, proverbs, and idioms.
- Explain one's own ideas and understanding in light of discussion with peers.
- Ask and answer questions about information from a speaker with enough detail to demonstrate understanding.
- Contribute meaningfully to group discussions by being prepared, explaining one's own ideas, building upon others' comments, and asking questions.

▶ Look at the Activity Book pages you completed on the other stories in this unit. Compare and contrast this story with the others in this unit. How are they similar, and how are they different? Possible answers: The stories are similar because they teach lessons. They are different because the settings are different; this story has animals as main characters; the lesson is different from the others.

▶ How is the lesson in this story similar to the other stories in this unit, and how is it different? Possible answer: The lessons are similar because they teach you how to behave in a good way: don't lie, take responsibility, keep trying, and treat others with kindness. The lesson is different because it teaches you to treat others nicely so they will treat you nicely, which is similar to "The Calabash Kids" but different from the other stories in the unit.

4. When students have completed the discussion, use the materials and instructions in the online lesson to evaluate students' work.

5. Enter the answers (Yes or No) for each line of the assessment checklist online.

Making Connections

Explore "The Necklace of Truth"

Map the Story

Fill in the boxes. Then answer the questions.

Title **"The Necklace of Truth"**

Setting: **Possible answer: long, long ago in a place with a castle**

Characters —
Main character **Pearl**
Other characters **Pearl's parents; Merlin; Pearl's friends**

Problem and Solution: **Pearl tells lies and then learns to stop lying.**

---

1. How do other characters in the story try to solve Pearl's problem?
   Pearl's parents take her to Merlin so he can cure her. Merlin gives Pearl the Necklace of Truth, which changes when she lies.

2. How does Pearl solve the problem herself?
   She decides she will never lie again.

3. State the lesson of the story in a complete sentence in your own words.
   Possible answers: Always tell the truth; don't tell lies.

4. Predict what Pearl will do the next time she is asked a question and is tempted to tell a lie.
   She will tell the truth.

5. Predict what the consequences will be when Pearl tells the truth. Think of how she and the other characters will think and feel.
   Possible answers: Pearl will feel happy and she won't be embarrassed; her parents and Merlin will be proud of her; her friends and other people will believe what she says.

---

6. Write at least five sentences comparing and contrasting this story with another story about a character who lies.
   Students should compare and contrast this story with a similar one, such as "The Boy Who Cried Wolf" or "Pinocchio." They should tell how the setting, characters, problems and solutions, choices, consequences, and lessons are similar and different.

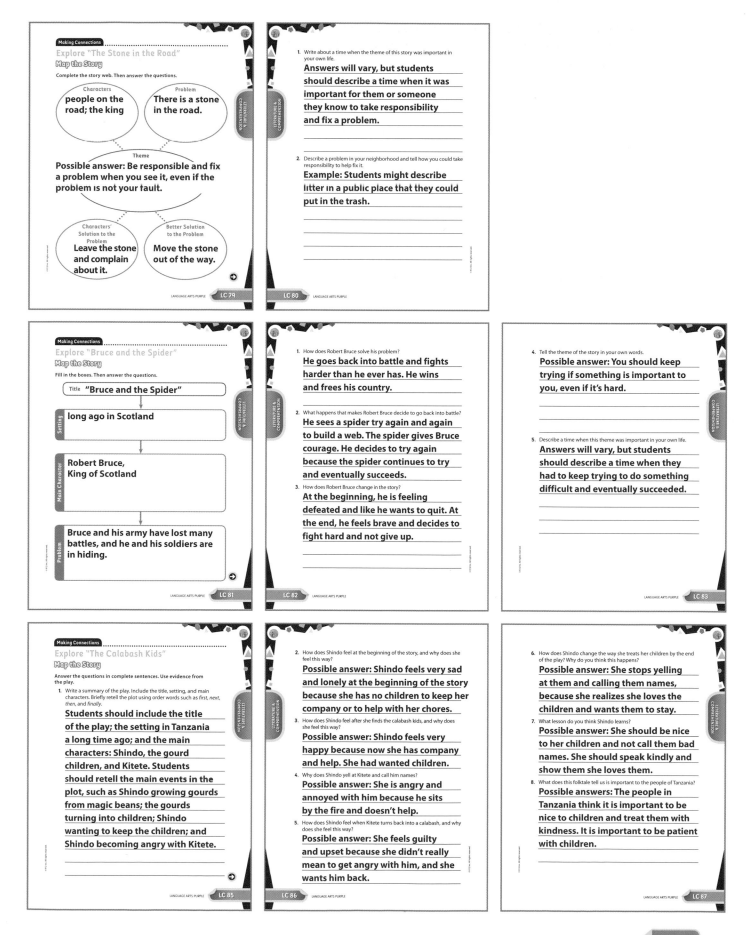

Making Connections

Explore "The Stone in the Road"

Map the Story

Complete the story web. Then answer the questions.

Characters
people on the road; the king

Problem
There is a stone in the road.

Theme
Possible answer: Be responsible and fix a problem when you see it, even if the problem is not your fault.

Characters' Solution to the Problem
Leave the stone and complain about it.

Better Solution to the Problem
Move the stone out of the way.

LANGUAGE ARTS PURPLE   LC 79

LC 80   LANGUAGE ARTS PURPLE

1. Write about a time when the theme of this story was important in your own life.

Answers will vary, but students should describe a time when it was important for them or someone they know to take responsibility and fix a problem.

2. Describe a problem in your neighborhood and tell how you could take responsibility to help fix it.

Example: Students might describe litter in a public place that they could put in the trash.

Making Connections

Explore "Bruce and the Spider"

Map the Story

Fill in the boxes. Then answer the questions.

Title **"Bruce and the Spider"**

Setting **long ago in Scotland**

Main Character **Robert Bruce, King of Scotland**

Problem **Bruce and his army have lost many battles, and he and his soldiers are in hiding.**

LANGUAGE ARTS PURPLE   LC 81

LC 82   LANGUAGE ARTS PURPLE

1. How does Robert Bruce solve his problem?

He goes back into battle and fights harder than he ever has. He wins and frees his country.

2. What happens that makes Robert Bruce decide to go back into battle?

He sees a spider try again and again to build a web. The spider gives Bruce courage. He decides to try again because the spider continues to try and eventually succeeds.

3. How does Robert Bruce change in the story?

At the beginning, he is feeling defeated and like he wants to quit. At the end, he feels brave and decides to fight hard and not give up.

---

4. Tell the theme of the story in your own words.

Possible answer: You should keep trying if something is important to you, even if it's hard.

5. Describe a time when this theme was important in your own life.

Answers will vary, but students should describe a time when they had to keep trying to do something difficult and eventually succeeded.

LANGUAGE ARTS PURPLE   LC 83

Making Connections

Explore "The Calabash Kids"

Map the Story

Answer the questions in complete sentences. Use evidence from the play.

1. Write a summary of the play. Include the title, setting, and main characters. Briefly retell the plot using order words such as first, next, then, and finally.

Students should include the title of the play; the setting in Tanzania a long time ago; and the main characters: Shindo, the gourd children, and Kitete. Students should retell the main events in the plot, such as Shindo growing gourds from magic beans; the gourds turning into children; Shindo wanting to keep the children; and Shindo becoming angry with Kitete.

LANGUAGE ARTS PURPLE   LC 85

LC 86   LANGUAGE ARTS PURPLE

2. How does Shindo feel at the beginning of the story, and why does she feel this way?

Possible answer: Shindo feels very sad and lonely at the beginning of the story because she has no children to keep her company or to help with her chores.

3. How does Shindo feel after she finds the calabash kids, and why does she feel this way?

Possible answer: Shindo feels very happy because now she has company and help. She had wanted children.

4. Why does Shindo yell at Kitete and call him names?

Possible answer: She is angry and annoyed with him because he sits by the fire and doesn't help.

5. How does Shindo feel when Kitete turns back into a calabash, and why does she feel this way?

Possible answer: She feels guilty and upset because she didn't really mean to get angry with him, and she wants him back.

---

6. How does Shindo change the way she treats her children by the end of the play? Why do you think this happens?

Possible answer: She stops yelling at them and calling them names, because she realizes she loves the children and wants them to stay.

7. What lesson do you think Shindo learns?

Possible answer: She should be nice to her children and not call them bad names. She should speak kindly and show them she loves them.

8. What does this folktale tell us is important to the people of Tanzania?

Possible answers: The people in Tanzania think it is important to be nice to children and treat them with kindness. It is important to be patient with children.

LANGUAGE ARTS PURPLE   LC 87

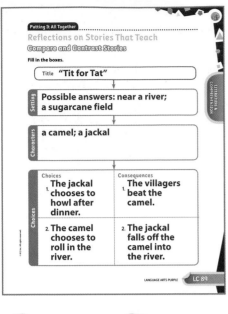

Putting It All Together
Reflections on Stories That Teach
Compare and Contrast Stories
Fill in the boxes.

Title "Tit for Tat"

Setting Possible answers: near a river; a sugarcane field

Characters a camel; a jackal

Choices
1. The jackal chooses to howl after dinner.
2. The camel chooses to roll in the river.

Consequences
1. The villagers beat the camel.
2. The jackal falls off the camel into the river.

LANGUAGE ARTS PURPLE LC 89

Online varies

Students will work **independently** to complete the online More Practice and Read activities.

More Practice

Review the Skills

If students scored less than 80 percent or had difficulty meeting the objectives of the Putting It All Together activity, have them go online for more practice.

Objectives

- Compare and contrast literary elements in two or more literary selections.
- Identify plot elements: problem and solution.
- Identify choices that a character makes and their consequences.
- Describe how a character changes.
- Determine the theme, moral, or lesson of a work of literature.
- Identify theme.

Read

Read Fluently "The Crab and the Monkey"

Students will read aloud and record a passage. The purpose of this activity is to assess students' oral reading and fluency. Have students read the passage aloud and record their reading. Note that this is a new passage to them, and there is no audio for them to hear a model reading. This will allow the recording to accurately reflect students' fluency ability.

> **Objectives**
> - Read poetry and prose aloud.
> - Read aloud grade-level text with appropriate automaticity, prosody, accuracy, and rate.

Performance Review

Fluency Check

Evaluate students' performance on the fluency reading. Gather the stopwatch and printout of "The Crab and the Monkey."

1. Listen to students' recordings and use the Fluency Performance Checklist to review fluency and the story printout to track performance.

2. Keep the completed checklist so you can review students' progress over time.

3. Follow the advice on the checklist regarding appropriate interventions for students who do not receive high scores on the Fluency Performance Checklist. If students aren't able to score above 12 points on the checklist, it is advisable to seek outside help from a teaching professional or reading specialist to improve students' reading fluency.

> **Objectives**
> - Read poetry and prose aloud.
> - Read aloud grade-level text with appropriate automaticity, prosody, accuracy, and rate.

Reward: If students score 80 percent or more on the Putting It All Together activity and 18 or more on the Fluency Check, add a sticker for this unit on the My Accomplishments chart. If students did not score 80 percent or more on the Putting It All Together activity and 18 or more on the Fluency Check, work with them to revise their writing and practice their fluency until they earn those scores and then add a sticker to the My Accomplishments chart.

Nature's Way

Unit Focus

In this unit, students will read six poems about nature. They will review the basic elements of poetry, such as stanza, speaker, and rhyme, as well as identify two new forms of figurative language: personification and metaphor. Students will explore these poems in *K¹² Classics for Young Readers, Volume C*:

- ► "April Rain Song"
- ► "The Secret"
- ► "The Building of the Nest"
- ► "The Raindrop's Ride"
- ► "Winter Jewels"
- ► "Pussy Willows"

Unit Plan		〖Online〗	〖Offline〗
Lesson 1	Introduce Songs and Secrets		**50** minutes
Lesson 2	Explore Songs and Secrets	**40** minutes	**10** minutes
Lesson 3	Introduce Castles in the Air		**50** minutes
Lesson 4	Explore Castles in the Air	**40** minutes	**10** minutes
Lesson 5	Introduce Nature's Metaphors		**50** minutes
Lesson 6	Explore Nature's Metaphors	**40** minutes	**10** minutes
Lesson 7	Reflections on Nature's Way	varies	**40** minutes
Lesson 8	Your Choice		**50** minutes

Introduce Songs and Secrets

Lesson Overview

[Offline]   50 minutes

Get Ready	Lesson Introduction
	Review the Basic Elements of Poetry
	Book Walk
	Words to Know
Read	Songs and Secrets
GRAB	Go Read a Book

Big Ideas

► Active, strong readers employ reading strategies such as making connections between text and self, between and among texts, and between text and the real world.
► Poems are different from prose in structure and content. They are generally organized in lines and often contain rhymes.
► Reading for pleasure helps develop fluency and a lifelong love of reading.

[Materials]

Supplied

- "April Rain Song," "The Secret," *K¹² Classics for Young Readers, Volume C,* pp. 114–117
- Poetry Reading Strategies bookmark
- Reading Strategies bookmark

Poetry Synopses

In "April Rain Song," using personification to express a love of rain, the speaker describes the rain as having human qualities. In "The Secret," the speaker hints at a secret told by a mother robin to a tree in order to create a sense of wonder about the discovery of a bird's nest.

Keywords

poet – one who writes poetry
poetry – writing that uses language, sound, and rhythm to make readers feel, experience, or imagine something
rhyme – the use of words that end with the same sounds; for example, *cat* and *hat* rhyme
rhyme scheme – the pattern of rhymes made by the last sounds in the lines of a poem, shown by a different letter of the alphabet to represent each rhyme
speaker – the narrator of a poem
stanza – a group of lines in a poem

〔 Offline 〕 50 minutes

Work **together** with students to complete offline Get Ready, Read, and GRAB activities.

Get Ready ....

Lesson Introduction
Prepare students to read the poems "April Rain Song" and "The Secret."

1. Explain to students that before they read "April Rain Song" and "The Secret" they will discuss with you

   ▸ The basic elements of poetry
   ▸ Their predictions about the text
   ▸ Important words to know in the text

2. Tell students that while they read, you will check in to make sure they understand what they are reading.

3. Tell students that after they read, they will answer questions about the poems.

Review the Basic Elements of Poetry
Review the basic structure of poetry, including lines and stanzas, as well as speaker and rhyme.

1. Tell students they are going to read poems. Have them tell what a poem is and describe some of the characteristics of **poetry**. Give them some of the characteristics if they have trouble recalling. Ask them how poetry differs from prose or drama. Students should recall that poetry is writing that uses special language and sounds to express feelings, ideas, or images. They may also remember that poetry is usually written in lines, and it often has rhymes. The structure of poetry is different from prose or drama.

2. Have students use the table of contents in *K¹² Classics for Young Readers, Volume C*, to find the poem "The Secret." Ask them to point out the name of the poet and tell how the **poet** is different from the **speaker** in the poem. The poet is the person who wrote the poem. The speaker is like a narrator and is the person talking or describing things in the poem.

3. Have students tell what a **stanza** is. Then have them point to a stanza in the poem and tell how many stanzas the poem has. A stanza is a group of lines in a poem. There are three stanzas in "The Secret."

4. Ask students to read the words at the end of the last four lines of the poem. Have them tell which lines **rhyme**. The first two lines rhyme, and the last two rhyme.

5. Remind students that a **rhyme scheme** is the pattern of rhymes in a poem, with a different letter given to each rhyme.

Objectives
- Define *stanza*.
- Identify stanzas in a poem.
- Define *rhyme*.
- Define *speaker*.
- Distinguish between speaker and author.
- Differentiate among literary genres.
- Use before-reading strategies.
- Differentiate among genres and identify their salient characteristics, including those of poetry, prose, and drama.
- Recognize the characteristics of poetry.
- Identify rhyme in a literary selection.

Book Walk

Have students lead you through a Book Walk of "April Rain Song" and "The Secret." Remind them to discuss the features of the poems, such as lines and stanzas, and to use the **titles** and **illustrations** to make predictions about the poems.

Words to Know

Remind students that they will find the Words to Know at the bottoms of the pages in the selections.

Read

Songs and Secrets

Have students read "April Rain Song" and "The Secret." Remind them to use the strategies on their Poetry Reading Strategies bookmark. For example, they may want to read each poem once silently to themselves and then a second time aloud. Tell students that reading poetry aloud will help them appreciate rhyme, meter, and other poetic elements.

➲ **Learning Coach Check-In** This reading assignment should take 5–10 minutes. After students finish reading, ask the following questions to assess their comprehension of the selections:

> ▶ How does the speaker in "April Rain Song" feel about the rain?
> The speaker loves it.
> ▶ In the poem "The Secret," who are the three keeping a secret? the robin, the cherry tree, and the speaker

If students have trouble answering these questions, ask them what reading strategies they used and suggest they reread the selections.

Objectives
- Read literature independently and proficiently.
- Apply information read to answer questions.
- Evaluate reading strategies.
- Read poetry and prose aloud.

GRAB

Go Read a Book

Have students read a book or magazine of their own choosing for at least 20 minutes. Remind students to use the strategies on their Reading Strategies bookmark before and during reading to help them understand the text.

TIP Remember: The more students read, the better readers they become.

Objectives
- Read literature independently and proficiently.
- Read a variety of texts for information and pleasure.

Explore Songs and Secrets

Lesson Overview

[Online]　　　　　　　　　　**40** minutes

Check Your Reading	Comprehend Songs and Secrets
Reading for Meaning	Use Language to Create Images
	Identify Personification

[Offline]　　　　　　　　　　**10** minutes

Making Connections	Compare and Contrast Poems and Feelings

Big Ideas

▶ The use of imagery and sensory language creates detailed pictures in the reader's mind, so the reader can understand and appreciate the ideas and feelings the writer conveys.

▶ Personification is a common device in poetry and similar to imagery. The poet creates an image of an object by giving it human traits, so the reader can better understand what the poet is trying to describe.

▶ Writing helps build reading skills, and reading more helps improve writing skills.

[Materials]

Supplied

● "April Rain Song," "The Secret," *K¹² Classics for Young Readers, Volume C*, pp. 114–117

● *K¹² Language Arts Activity Book*, pp. LC 91–93

Keywords

compare – to explain how two or more things are alike

contrast – to explain how two or more things are different

figurative language – words that describe something by comparing it to something completely different
Example: Rain fell in buckets and the streets looked like rivers.

personification – giving human qualities to something that is not human
Example: The thunder shouted from the clouds.

rhyme – the use of words that end with the same sounds; for example, *cat* and *hat* rhyme

rhyme scheme – the pattern of rhymes made by the last sounds in the lines of a poem, shown by a different letter of the alphabet to represent each rhyme

speaker – the narrator of a poem

stanza – a group of lines in a poem

[Online] 40 minutes

Students will work **independently** to complete online Check Your Reading and Reading for Meaning activities.

Check Your Reading

Comprehend Songs and Secrets

Students will answer questions about "April Rain Song" and "The Secret" to demonstrate their literal and inferential comprehension of these poems. They will be asked about the poetic structure. Review poetic terms such as *stanza* and *rhyme scheme* if students have difficulty with these questions.

Objectives

- Identify concrete answers to questions.
- Infer answers to questions.
- Apply information read to answer questions.
- Identify stanzas in a poem.
- Identify rhyme scheme in a poem.

Reading for Meaning

Use Language to Create Images

Students will look at how the poet uses language in "The Secret" to create images that help the reader visualize what is being described and imagine the speaker's feelings of excitement at discovering a nest with eggs. In this poem, to emphasize the speaker's wonder and difficulty keeping the secret, the poet omits certain words that the reader anticipates.

Identify Personification

Students will learn what personification is and identify examples of this type of figurative language in the poem "April Rain Song." They will explore how the use of this device helps the poet show the speaker's positive feelings and love for the rain.

Objectives

- Identify sensory language.
- Identify rhyme in a literary selection.
- Distinguish between literal and nonliteral, or figurative, language in poetry.
- Define *personification*.
- Identify personification.
- Identify how sensory details and figurative language enhance poetry.

Offline 10 minutes

Work **together** with students to complete the offline Making Connections activity.

Making Connections

Compare and Contrast Poems and Feelings

Students will compare their own feelings to those expressed in the poems and practice creating their own figurative language to describe an element of nature. Turn to pages LC 91–93 in *K¹² Language Arts Activity Book*.

1. Have students read the directions.

2. Have them complete the Activity Book pages.

TIP Keep the Activity Book pages in a safe place for students to use later.

Objectives

- Compare and contrast using evidence from the text.
- Make connections between text and self, text and world, and text to text.
- Distinguish between literal and nonliteral, or figurative, language in poetry.
- Write examples of figurative language.
- Identify how sensory details and figurative language enhance poetry.

Making Connections

Explore Songs and Secrets
Compare and Contrast Poems and Feelings

Answer the questions in complete sentences.

1. How do you feel about the rain? What words would you use to describe it?
Answers will vary.

2. How are your feelings about the rain similar to the speaker's feelings in "April Rain Song"? How are your feelings different?
Students should compare and contrast their feelings about the rain with the speaker's feelings of love for the rain expressed in "April Rain Song."

LANGUAGE ARTS PURPLE LC 91

---

3. Describe a time when you had a secret. Did you keep it? How did it make you feel to have a secret?
Answers will vary. Students may or may not describe the actual secret.

4. How are your feelings about having a secret similar to the speaker's feelings in "The Secret"? How are your feelings different?
Answers will vary.

5. The poems "April Rain Song" and "The Secret" are both about things in nature. How do the speakers feel about nature? Why do you think this?
Students may say that the speakers seem to enjoy and love nature and think it is something other people should enjoy, too. The poets use words that tell the reader about the speakers' love for nature. In "April Rain Song," the speaker says he loves the rain. In "The Secret," the speaker is very excited about finding a bird's nest.

LC 92 LANGUAGE ARTS PURPLE

---

6. Choose something in nature—for example, a tree, a flower, the sun, the moon, the ocean, or a kind of weather. Write a literal sentence describing it and a sentence using personification to describe it.

Literal sentence: **Example: "The ocean waves are powerful."**

Sentence using personification: **Example: "The ocean waves swallowed my shovel."**

LANGUAGE ARTS PURPLE LC 93

Introduce Castles in the Air

Lesson Overview

[Offline]   **50** minutes

Get Ready	Lesson Introduction
	Make Comparisons
	Book Walk
	Words to Know
Read	Castles in the Air
GRAB	Go Read a Book

Content Background

The poem "The Raindrop's Ride" is about the water cycle. If students need a refresher on the water cycle, refer them to the article "Let It Rain" in the nonfiction magazine *K¹² World: Weather or Not*.

Big Ideas

- ▸ Active, strong readers employ reading strategies such as making connections between text and self, between and among texts, and between text and the real world.
- ▸ Poems are different from prose in structure and content. They are generally organized in lines and often contain rhymes.
- ▸ Reading better follows from reading often: The more a student reads, the better reader the student becomes.

Materials

Supplied

- "The Building of the Nest," "The Raindrop's Ride," *K¹² Classics for Young Readers, Volume C*, pp. 118–123
- "Let It Rain," *K¹² World: Weather or Not*, pp. 14–25 (optional)
- Poetry Reading Strategies bookmark
- Reading Strategies bookmark

Poetry Synopses

In "The Building of the Nest," the poet uses metaphors to describe a robin's nest. In "The Raindrop's Ride," the poet uses an extended metaphor to describe the water cycle.

Keywords

figurative language – words that describe something by comparing it to something completely different *Example:* Rain fell in buckets and the streets looked like rivers.

poetry – writing that uses language, sound, and rhythm to make readers feel, experience, or imagine something

rhyme – the use of words that end with the same sounds; for example, *cat* and *hat* rhyme

speaker – the narrator of a poem

stanza – a group of lines in a poem

[Offline] 50 minutes

Work **together** with students to complete offline Get Ready, Read, and GRAB activities.

Get Ready

Lesson Introduction

Prepare students to read the poems "The Building of the Nest" and "The Raindrop's Ride."

1. Explain to students that before they read "The Building of the Nest" and "The Raindrop's Ride" they will discuss with you

   ▶ How to make comparisons between two unlike things
   ▶ Their predictions about the text
   ▶ Important words to know in the text

2. Tell students that while they read, you will check in to make sure they understand what they are reading.

3. Tell students that after they read, they will answer questions about the poems.

> **Objectives**
> - Connect text to prior knowledge.
> - Use before-reading strategies.
> - Distinguish between literal and figurative language.
> - Use figurative language.

Make Comparisons

Review figurative language and have students make their own comparisons between two unlike things.

1. Review that poets often use **figurative language** to help readers visualize what they are trying to describe. Have students tell what figurative language is, or give them the definition. Figurative language is the use of words to describe something by comparing it to something completely different. For example, this sentence uses figurative language: "Rain fell in buckets and the streets looked like rivers."

2. Have students look out the window at the sky and use words to describe what it looks like to them. Answers will vary, but students may describe the color or things they see in the sky, such as clouds or birds.

3. Have students think about what other things the sky looks like and make a comparison. For example, the sky might be as blue as a crayon or the clouds might look like cotton balls. Answers will vary, but students should think of at least one other object they can compare the sky to, such as a marble, the ocean, a sea, or a river.

4. Tell students they are going to read two poems—one about birds and one about rain. In both, the poets use special kinds of comparisons to help readers visualize, or see in their mind, what is being described.

Book Walk

Have students lead you through a Book Walk of "The Building of the Nest" and "The Raindrop's Ride." Remind them to use the **titles** and **illustrations** to make predictions about the poems.

Words to Know

Remind students that they will find the Words to Know at the bottoms of the pages in the selections.

 Read ●●

Castles in the Air

Have students read "The Building of the Nest" and "The Raindrop's Ride." Remind students to use the strategies on their Poetry Reading Strategies bookmark. For example, they should pause in their reading at punctuation, not at the ends of the lines.

> ⊃ **Learning Coach Check-In**   This reading assignment should take 5–10 minutes. After students finish reading, ask the following questions to assess their comprehension of the selections:

> ► Where do the robins build their nests in "The Building of the Nest"?
> in apple trees
> ► In the poem "The Raindrop's Ride," what do the raindrops actually ride in? a cloud

If students have trouble answering these questions, ask them what reading strategies they used and suggest they reread the selections.

Objectives
- Read literature independently and proficiently.
- Apply information read to answer questions.
- Evaluate reading strategies.

GRAB ●●

Go Read a Book

Have students read a book or magazine of their own choosing for at least 20 minutes. Remind students to use the strategies on their Reading Strategies bookmark before and during reading to help them understand the text.

Objectives
- Read literature independently and proficiently.
- Read a variety of texts for information and pleasure.

Explore Castles in the Air

Lesson Overview

[Online]   40 minutes

Check Your Reading	Comprehend Castles in the Air
Reading for Meaning	Understand Simile and Metaphor
	Identify Metaphors in Poems

[Offline]   10 minutes

Making Connections	Compare and Contrast Poems About Rain and Birds

Big Ideas

► The use of imagery and sensory language creates detailed pictures in the reader's mind, so the reader can understand and appreciate the ideas and feelings the writer conveys.

► Readers must focus on the specific language of a text to aid in interpretation.

► Readers need to synthesize, draw conclusions about, and interpret what they have read.

► Personification is a common device in poetry: The poet creates an image of an object by giving it human traits, so the reader can better understand what the poet is trying to describe.

[Materials]

Supplied

• "April Rain Song," "The Secret," "The Building of the Nest," "The Raindrop's Ride," *K¹² Classics for Young Readers, Volume C,* pp. 114–123

• *K¹² Language Arts Activity Book,* pp. LC 95–96

Keywords

compare – to explain how two or more things are alike

contrast – to explain how two or more things are different

figurative language – words that describe something by comparing it to something completely different
Example: Rain fell in buckets and the streets looked like rivers.

metaphor – a figure of speech that compares two unlike things, without using the word *like* or *as*
Example: The cat's eyes were emeralds shining in the night.

personification – giving human qualities to something that is not human
Example: The thunder shouted from the clouds.

simile – a comparison between two things using the word *like* or *as*
Example: I didn't hear him come in because he was as quiet as a mouse.

 **Online** ⁴⁰ **minutes**

Students will work **independently** to complete online Check Your Reading and Reading for Meaning activities.

Check Your Reading •

Comprehend Castles in the Air

Students will answer questions about "The Building of the Nest" and "The Raindrop's Ride" to demonstrate their literal and inferential comprehension of the poems. They will be required to understand that "The Building of the Nest" takes place in spring and the various phases of the water cycle (starting in the sea and then returning back to the sea by way of a brook) as described in "The Raindrop's Ride."

Objectives
- Identify concrete answers to questions.
- Infer answers to questions.
- Apply information read to answer questions.
- Identify personification.

Reading for Meaning •

Understand Simile and Metaphor

Students will review similes, a kind of figurative language, and learn about metaphors, another type of figurative language used to make comparisons. They will learn how to tell the difference between metaphors and similes.

Identify Metaphors in Poems

Students will learn to identify examples of metaphors in the poems "The Building of the Nest" and "The Raindrop's Ride." They will explore how the particular metaphors the poets use help the reader appreciate the feelings conveyed in the poetry.

Objectives
- Define *simile*.
- Identify similes.
- Define *metaphor*.
- Identify the metaphor.
- Explore and explain the meaning of figurative language in poetry.

[Offline] 🔟 minutes

Work **together** with students to complete the offline Making Connections activity.

Making Connections ••

Compare and Contrast Poems About Rain and Birds

Students will compare and contrast two poems from the unit. Turn to pages LC 95 and 96 in *K¹² Language Arts Activity Book*.

1. Have students read the directions.

2. Tell students that they are to choose two poems from the unit to compare and contrast: either the bird poems "The Secret" and "The Building of the Nest," or the rain poems "April Rain Song" and "The Raindrop's Ride."

3. Have them complete the Activity Book pages. Similarities belong in the intersection of the ovals. Unique characteristics of the poems belong in each poem's own oval. Characteristics of the four poems that students might include in their Venn diagram include the following:

   ▶ "The Secret": has three stanzas; uses special punctuation to create the secret; has AABB rhyme scheme; uses personification to describe the cherry tree

   ▶ "The Building of the Nest": has four stanzas; has ABABAB rhyme scheme; uses metaphors to describe the nests

   ▶ "April Rain Song": has two stanzas; has no rhyme scheme; uses personification to describe the rain; uses language that compares the rain to a song

   ▶ "The Raindrop's Ride": has four stanzas; has ABCB rhymes scheme; uses personification to describe the raindrops; uses metaphors to describe the cloud and breeze

TIP Keep the Activity Book pages in a safe place for students to use later.

> ### Objectives
> - Compare and contrast literary elements in poetry.
> - Makes connections between text and self, text and world, and text to text.
> - Explore and explain the meaning of figurative language in poetry.

Making Connections

Explore Castles in the Air

Compare and Contrast Poems About Rain and Birds

Of the poems you've read so far in this unit, choose either the two poems about birds ("The Secret" and "The Building of the Nest") or the two poems about rain ("April Rain Song" and "The Raindrop's Ride"). Using the Venn diagram, compare and contrast the language and poetic elements of the two poems.

Poem Title A   Poem Title B

_____   _____

Characteristics of Poem A / Shared / Characteristics of Poem B

Students should compare and contrast either the two poems about birds—"The Secret" and "The Building of the Nest"—or the two poems about rain—"April Rain Song" and "The Raindrop's Ride."

LANGUAGE ARTS PURPLE **LC 95**

LC 96 LANGUAGE ARTS PURPLE

Students should refer to their Venn diagram and explain their answers using examples from the poems.

Answer the questions in complete sentences.

1. Which poem do you like best? Why?

_____
_____
_____

2. Which poet do you think does a better job of describing the topic? Why?

_____
_____
_____

3. One poet uses personification to describe the topic. The other uses metaphors. Which one works better to describe the topic? Why?

_____
_____
_____

4. Compare and contrast the feelings the poets describe. How are the feelings of their speakers similar, and how are they different?

_____
_____
_____

Introduce Nature's Metaphors

Lesson Overview

[Offline] 50 minutes

Get Ready	Lesson Introduction
	Review Metaphor
	Book Walk
	Words to Know
Read	Nature's Metaphors
GRAB	Go Read a Book

Big Ideas

► Poems are different from prose in structure and content. They are generally organized in lines and often contain rhymes.
► The use of imagery and sensory language creates detailed pictures in the reader's mind, so the reader can understand and appreciate the ideas and feelings the writer conveys.
► Reading a book of their own choosing helps motivate students to read.

[Materials]

Supplied

- "Winter Jewels," "Pussy Willows," *K¹² Classics for Young Readers, Volume C,* pp. 124–125
- Poetry Reading Strategies bookmark
- Reading Strategies bookmark

Poetry Synopses

In "Winter Jewels," the poet uses an extended metaphor to describe ice crystals in the trees as diamonds. In "Pussy Willows," the poet uses an extended metaphor to describe the buds on pussy willow plants.

Keywords

metaphor – a figure of speech that compares two unlike things, without using the word *like* or *as*
Example: The cat's eyes were emeralds shining in the night.

[Offline] **50** minutes

Work **together** with students to complete offline Get Ready, Read, and GRAB activities.

Get Ready

Lesson Introduction

Prepare students to read the poems "Winter Jewels" and "Pussy Willows."

1. Explain to students that before they read "Winter Jewels" and "Pussy Willows" they will discuss with you

   ► What a metaphor is
   ► Their predictions about the text
   ► Important words to know in the text

2. Tell students that while they read, you will check in to make sure they understand what they are reading.

3. Tell students that after they read, they will answer questions about the poems.

> ### Objectives
> - Define *metaphor*.
> - Identify the metaphor.
> - Use text organizational features to locate and comprehend information (table of contents).
> - Use before-reading strategies.
> - Increase concept and content vocabulary.

Review Metaphor

Review what a metaphor is.

1. Have students tell what a **metaphor** is, or give them the definition. A metaphor is a figure of speech that compares two unlike things without using the word *like* or *as*.

2. Have students tell how a metaphor is different from a simile. A simile makes a comparison between two unlike things using the word *like* or *as*. A metaphor doesn't use *like* or *as*.

3. Have students give an example of a metaphor, or provide one. Possible answers: The cat's eyes were emeralds shining in the night; the stars were jewels sparkling in the night sky.

4. Tell students they are going to read two poems that use metaphors to describe things in nature.

5. Ask students if they know what a pussy willow plant is or looks like. If they don't, find an example in a book or by searching for images of pussy willows on the Internet.

Book Walk

Have students lead you through a Book Walk of "Winter Jewels" and "Pussy Willows." Remind them to use the **titles** and **illustrations** to make predictions about the poems.

Words to Know

Remind students that they will find the Words to Know at the bottoms of the pages in the selections.

Read

Nature's Metaphors

Have students read "Winter Jewels" and "Pussy Willows." Remind students to use the strategies on their Poetry Reading Strategies bookmark. For example, they should try to imagine what the poets are describing.

➲ **Learning Coach Check-In** This reading assignment should take 5–10 minutes. After students finish reading, ask the following questions to assess their comprehension of the selections:

  ► What do the maidens ask for in "Winter Jewels"? jewels in the trees
  ► What time of the year is it in "Pussy Willows"? March; spring

If students have trouble answering these questions, ask them what reading strategies they used and suggest they reread the selections.

Objectives
- Read literature independently and proficiently.
- Apply information read to answer questions.
- Evaluate reading strategies.

GRAB

Go Read a Book

Have students read a book or magazine of their own choosing for at least 20 minutes. Remind students to use the strategies on their Reading Strategies bookmark before and during reading to help them understand the text.

Objectives
- Read literature independently and proficiently.
- Read a variety of texts for information and pleasure.

Explore Nature's Metaphors

Lesson Overview

🖥 [Online] 40 minutes

Check Your Reading	Comprehend Nature's Metaphors
Reading for Meaning	Identify the Metaphor in "Winter Jewels"
	Identify the Metaphors in "Pussy Willows"

📄 [Offline] 10 minutes

Making Connections	Compare and Contrast the Poems

Big Ideas

► The use of imagery and sensory language creates detailed pictures in the reader's mind, so the reader can understand and appreciate the ideas and feelings the writer conveys.
► Readers must focus on the specific language of a text to aid in interpretation.
► Readers need to synthesize, draw conclusions about, and interpret what they have read.

[Materials]

Supplied

- "Winter Jewels," "Pussy Willows," *K¹² Classics for Young Readers, Volume C,* pp. 124–125
- *K¹² Language Arts Activity Book,* pp. LC 97–99

Keywords

metaphor – a figure of speech that compares two unlike things, without using the word *like* or *as*
Example: The cat's eyes were emeralds shining in the night.

[Online] 40 minutes

Students will work **independently** to complete online Check Your Reading and Reading for Meaning activities.

Check Your Reading ....

Comprehend Nature's Metaphors
Students will answer questions about "Winter Jewels" and "Pussy Willows" to demonstrate their literal and inferential comprehension of the poems.

Objectives
- Identify concrete answers to questions.
- Infer answers to questions.
- Apply information read to answer questions.

Reading for Meaning ....

Identify the Metaphor in "Winter Jewels"
Students will identify the extended metaphor in the poem "Winter Jewels" and explore how the use of the metaphor makes the reader view the ice on the trees as something precious to be admired.

Objectives
- Define *metaphor*.
- Identify the metaphor.
- Explore and explain the meaning of figurative language used in poetry.

Identify the Metaphors in "Pussy Willows"
Students will identify examples of metaphors in the poem "Pussy Willows" and explore how the metaphors evoke a protective feeling about the new buds.

[Offline] 🔟 minutes

Work **together** with students to complete the offline Making Connections activity.

Making Connections ●●●

Compare and Contrast the Poems

Students will compare and contrast "Winter Jewels" and "Pussy Willows," as well as evaluate one of the poems. Turn to pages LC 97–99 in *K¹² Language Arts Activity Book*.

1. Have students read the directions.

2. Have them complete the Activity Book pages.

TIP Keep the Activity Book pages in a safe place for students to use later.

Objectives

- Compare and contrast literary elements in poetry.
- Make connections between text and self, text and world, and text to text.
- Explore and explain the meaning of figurative language used in poetry.
- Write a metaphor.
- Evaluate text.

Explore Nature's Metaphors
Compare and Contrast the Poems

Compare and contrast "Winter Jewels" and "Pussy Willows." In the first two columns, write the characteristics of each poem. In the third column, write characteristics that both poems share. Then answer the questions.

"Winter Jewels"	"Pussy Willows"	Both
Students should list characteristics of each poem and then list characteristics that the poems have in common. For example, they might say that one describes ice crystals, while the other describes pussy willow buds. They might say both poems use a metaphor to describe something in nature.		

LANGUAGE ARTS PURPLE LC 97

Students should use examples from the poems to explain their answers.

Answer the questions in complete sentences.

1. Which poem do you like best? Why?

2. Which poem has the best use of a metaphor? Why?

Choose one of the poems—either "Winter Jewels" or "Pussy Willows"—and answer the questions in complete sentences.

3. Explain how the metaphor helps you form a mental image of what is being described.
Students should explain how the language that describes either ice crystals as jewels or pussy willow buds as kittens helps them imagine the look and feel of the poem's subject.

LC 98 LANGUAGE ARTS PURPLE

---

4. What other words could the poet use as part of this metaphor?
Students should list words that fit the metaphor. For example, students might say that other words to describe ice crystals as diamonds could include *bright*, *shiny*, or *sparkling*. They might say that words like *soft*, *furry*, or *fuzzy* could be used to describe pussy willow buds as kittens.

5. Write your own metaphor for what the poet is describing. What would you compare the topic of the poem to?
Students should compare ice crystals or pussy willow buds to something completely different—for example, glass ornaments or slippers, respectively. Students' metaphor should not use the words *like* or *as* in the comparison.

LANGUAGE ARTS PURPLE LC 99

Reflections on Nature's Way

Lesson Overview

📄 [Offline] ⏱ 40 minutes

Get Ready	Review Elements of Poetry
Putting It All Together	Analyze a New Poem

🖥 [Online] varies

More Practice	Review the Skills
Read	Read Fluently "Color"
Performance Review	Fluency Check

Advance Preparation

For Putting It All Together, have students gather completed pages LC 91–93 (Compare and Contrast Poems and Feelings), 95–96 (Compare and Contrast Poems About Rain and Birds), and 97–99 (Compare and Contrast the Poems) in *K¹² Language Arts Activity Book*. For the Performance Review, print the poem "Color."

Big Ideas

▶ Fluent readers expend less energy on decoding and therefore have more energy for comprehension.
▶ Active, strong readers employ reading strategies such as make connections between and among texts.

[Materials]

Supplied

- "April Rain Song," "The Secret," "The Building of the Nest," "The Raindrop's Ride," "Winter Jewels," "Pussy Willows," *K¹² Classics for Young Readers, Volume C*, pp. 114–125
- *K¹² Language Arts Activity Book*, pp. LC 91–93, 95–99, 101–104
- Putting It All Together Assessment Checklist (printout)
- "Color" (printout)
- Fluency Performance Checklist (printout)

Also Needed

- crayons (optional)
- stopwatch

Keywords

compare – to explain how two or more things are alike
contrast – to explain how two or more things are different
figurative language – words that describe something by comparing it to something completely different
metaphor – a figure of speech that compares two unlike things, without using the word *like* or *as*
personification – giving human qualities to something that is not human
simile – a comparison between two things using the word *like* or *as*
speaker – the narrator of a poem

[Offline] 40 minutes

Work **together** with students to complete the offline Get Ready and Putting It All Together activities.

Get Ready

Review Elements of Poetry

Prepare students for reading and analyzing a new poem.

1. Have students tell what makes a poem different from other kinds of writing. Possible answers: Poems have lines, stanzas, and sometimes rhymes; they express ideas and feelings in a short space; they usually use imagery and figurative language.

2. Have students tell the definitions of some of the elements of poetry and give examples.

   ▸ speaker The speaker is the narrator of a poem. An example of a speaker is the girl in "The Secret" who finds a robin's nest in a cherry tree.

   ▸ rhyme and rhyme scheme Rhyme is the use of words that end with the same sounds; rhyme scheme is the pattern of rhymes made by the last sounds in the lines of a poem, shown by a different letter of the alphabet to represent each rhyme. A rhyme is *cat* and *bat*. A rhyme scheme might be ABAB.

   ▸ figurative language Figurative language is the use of words that describe something by comparing it to something completely different. An example is "Rain fell in buckets and the streets looked like rivers."

   ▸ personification Personification is giving human qualities to something that is not human. An example is "The thunder shouted from the clouds."

   ▸ simile A simile is a comparison between two things using the word *like* or *as*. An example is "I didn't hear him come in because he was as quiet as a mouse."

   ▸ metaphor A metaphor is a figure of speech that compares two unlike things without using the word *like* or *as*. An example is "The cat's eyes were emeralds shining in the night."

3. Tell students that they are going to read a new poem, and they should look for some of these elements as they read.

Objectives

- Define *speaker*.
- Define *rhyme*.
- Define *rhyme scheme*.
- Define *figurative language*.
- Define *simile*.
- Define *metaphor*.
- Define *personification*.

Putting It All Together

Analyze a New Poem

Students will demonstrate their understanding of how to analyze the use of language and the meaning of a poem, as well as how to compare and contrast poems and evaluate them. Gather the completed poetry comparisons pages and turn to pages LC 101–104 in *K¹² Language Arts Activity Book*.

1. Tell students that they are going to explore a new poem using the skills they have learned and that they will also compare and contrast the new poem with one of the other poems in this unit.

2. Have students complete the Activity Book pages. Check in with students after about 20 minutes to see if they have completed the first part of the assignment

3. Have students choose their favorite poem from the unit, and then have them practice and read it aloud in front of an audience.

4. When students have completed the Activity Book pages and read aloud presentation, use the materials and instructions in the online lesson to evaluate students' work.

5. Enter the answers (Yes or No) for each line of the assessment checklist online.

TIP If students like drawing, have them illustrate their favorite poem and explain it when they read the poem aloud.

Objectives

- Recognize the characteristics of poetry.
- Identify rhyme scheme in a poem.
- Identify stanzas in a poem.
- Distinguish between speaker and author.
- Recognize figurative language.
- Identify the metaphor.
- Compare and contrast literary elements in poetry.
- Make connections between text and self, text and world, and text to text.
- Explore and explain the meaning of figurative language used in poetry.
- Read prose and poetry aloud.
- Read aloud grade-level text with appropriate expression, accuracy, and rate.

Making Connections

Explore Songs and Secrets
Compare and Contrast Poems and Feelings

Answer the questions in complete sentences.

1. How do you feel about the rain? What words would you use to describe it?

Answers will vary.

2. How are your feelings about the rain similar to the speaker's feelings in "April Rain Song"? How are your feelings different?

Students should compare and contrast their feelings about the rain with the speaker's feelings of love for the rain expressed in "April Rain Song."

---

3. Describe a time when you had a secret. Did you keep it? How did it make you feel to have a secret?

Answers will vary. Students may or may not describe the actual secret.

4. How are your feelings about having a secret similar to the speaker's feelings in "The Secret"? How are your feelings different?

Answers will vary.

5. The poems "April Rain Song" and "The Secret" are both about things in nature. How do the speakers feel about nature? Why do you think this?

Students may say that the speakers seem to enjoy and love nature and think it is something other people should enjoy, too. The poets use words that tell the reader about the speakers' love for nature. In "April Rain Song," the speaker says he loves the rain. In "The Secret," the speaker is very excited about finding a bird's nest.

---

6. Choose something in nature—for example, a tree, a flower, the sun, the moon, the ocean, or a kind of weather. Write a literal sentence describing it and a sentence using personification to describe it.

Literal sentence: **Example: "The ocean waves are powerful."**

Sentence using personification: **Example: "The ocean waves swallowed my shovel."**

Making Connections

Explore Castles in the Air
Compare and Contrast Poems About Rain and Birds

Of the poems you've read so far in this unit, choose either the two poems about birds ("The Secret" and "The Building of the Nest") or the two poems about rain ("April Rain Song" and "The Raindrop's Ride"). Using the Venn diagram, compare and contrast the language and poetic elements of the two poems.

Poem Title A _____   Poem Title B _____

Characteristics of Poem A | Shared | Characteristics of Poem B

Students should compare and contrast either the two poems about birds—"The Secret" and "The Building of the Nest"—or the two poems about rain—"April Rain Song" and "The Raindrop's Ride."

Students should refer to their Venn diagram and explain their answers using examples from the poems.

Answer the questions in complete sentences.

1. Which poem do you like best? Why?

2. Which poet do you think does a better job of describing the topic? Why?

3. One poet uses personification to describe the topic. The other uses metaphors. Which one works better to describe the topic? Why?

4. Compare and contrast the feelings the poets describe. How are the feelings of their speakers similar, and how are they different?

Making Connections

Explore Nature's Metaphors
Compare and Contrast the Poems

Compare and contrast "Winter Jewels" and "Pussy Willows." In the first two columns, write the characteristics of each poem. In the third column, write characteristics that both poems share. Then answer the questions.

"Winter Jewels"	"Pussy Willows"	Both
Students should list characteristics of each poem and then list characteristics that the poems have in common. For example, they might say that one describes ice crystals, while the other describes pussy willow buds. They might say both poems use a metaphor to describe something in nature.		

Students should use examples from the poems to explain their answers.

Answer the questions in complete sentences.

1. Which poem do you like best? Why?

2. Which poem has the best use of a metaphor? Why?

Choose one of the poems—either "Winter Jewels" or "Pussy Willows"—and answer the questions in complete sentences.

3. Explain how the metaphor helps you form a mental image of what is being described.

Students should explain how the language that describes either ice crystals as jewels or pussy willow buds as kittens helps them imagine the look and feel of the poem's subject.

---

4. What other words could the poet use as part of this metaphor?

Students should list words that fit the metaphor. For example, students might say that other words to describe ice crystals as diamonds could include *bright*, *shiny*, or *sparkling*. They might say that words like *soft*, *furry*, or *fuzzy* could be used to describe pussy willow buds as kittens.

5. Write your own metaphor for what the poet is describing. What would you compare the topic of the poem to?

Students should compare ice crystals or pussy willow buds to something completely different—for example, glass ornaments or slippers, respectively. Students' metaphor should not use the words *like* or *as* in the comparison.

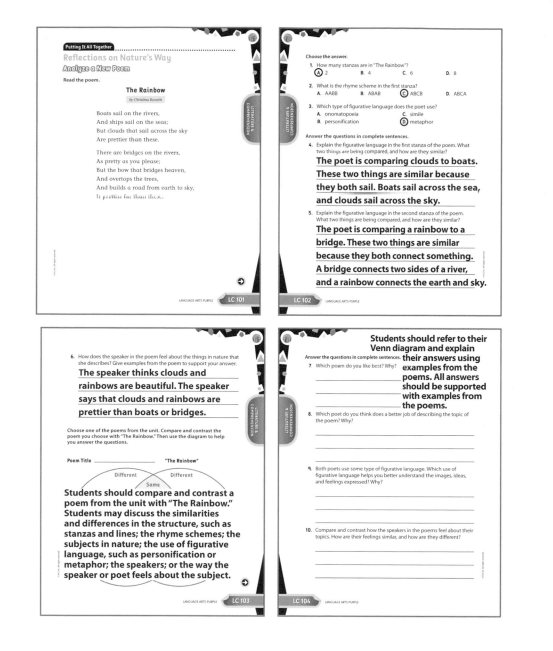

Putting It All Together

Reflections on Nature's Way
Analyze a New Poem

Read the poem.

The Rainbow
by Christina Rossetti

Boats sail on the rivers,
And ships sail on the seas;
But clouds that sail across the sky
Are prettier than these.

There are bridges on the rivers,
As pretty as you please;
But the bow that bridges heaven,
And overtops the trees,
And builds a road from earth to sky,
Is prettier far than these.

Choose the answer.

1. How many stanzas are in "The Rainbow"?
   A 2   B. 4   C. 6   D. 8

2. What is the rhyme scheme in the first stanza?
   A. AABB   B. ABAB   **C** ABCB   D. ABCA

3. Which type of figurative language does the poet use?
   A. onomatopoeia   C. simile
   B. personification   **D** metaphor

Answer the questions in complete sentences.

4. Explain the figurative language in the first stanza of the poem. What two things are being compared, and how are they similar?

   The poet is comparing clouds to boats. These two things are similar because they both sail. Boats sail across the sea, and clouds sail across the sky.

5. Explain the figurative language in the second stanza of the poem. What two things are being compared, and how are they similar?

   The poet is comparing a rainbow to a bridge. These two things are similar because they both connect something. A bridge connects two sides of a river, and a rainbow connects the earth and sky.

---

6. How does the speaker in the poem feel about the things in nature that she describes? Give examples from the poem to support your answer.

   The speaker thinks clouds and rainbows are beautiful. The speaker says that clouds and rainbows are prettier than boats or bridges.

Choose one of the poems from the unit. Compare and contrast the poem you choose with "The Rainbow." Then use the diagram to help you answer the questions.

Poem Title _____   "The Rainbow"

Different   Same   Different

Students should compare and contrast a poem from the unit with "The Rainbow." Students may discuss the similarities and differences in the structure, such as stanzas and lines; the rhyme schemes; the subjects in nature; the use of figurative language, such as personification or metaphor; the speakers; or the way the speaker or poet feels about the subject.

Answer the questions in complete sentences.

7. Which poem do you like best? Why?

   Students should refer to their Venn diagram and explain their answers using examples from the poems. All answers should be supported with examples from the poems.

8. Which poet do you think does a better job of describing the topic of the poem? Why?

9. Both poets use some type of figurative language. Which use of figurative language helps you better understand the images, ideas, and feelings expressed? Why?

10. Compare and contrast how the speakers in the poems feel about their topics. How are their feelings similar, and how are they different?

[Online] varies

Students will work **independently** to complete the online More Practice activity.

More Practice •

Review the Skills

If students scored less than 80 percent or had difficulty meeting the objectives of the Putting It All Together activity, have them go online for more practice.

Objectives

- Recognize the characteristics of poetry.
- Identify rhyme scheme in a poem.
- Identify stanzas in a poem.
- Recognize figurative language.
- Identify metaphor.

Read •

Read Fluently "Color"

Students will read aloud and record the poem "Color" by Christina Rossetti. The purpose of this activity is to improve students' oral reading and fluency. Have students read the passage aloud and record their reading. Note that this is a new passage to students, and there is no audio for them to hear a model reading. This will allow the recording to accurately reflect their fluency ability.

Objectives

- Read poetry and prose aloud.
- Read aloud grade-level text with appropriate automaticity, prosody, accuracy, and rate.

Performance Review

Fluency Check

Evaluate students' performance on the fluency reading. Gather the stopwatch and printout of "Color."

1. Listen to students' recordings and use the Fluency Performance Checklist to review fluency and the story printout to track performance.

2. Keep the completed checklist so you can review students' progress over time.

3. Follow the advice on the checklist regarding appropriate interventions for students who do not receive high scores on their Fluency Performance Checklist. If students aren't able to score above 12 points on the Fluency Performance Checklist, it is advisable to seek outside help from a teaching professional or reading specialist to improve students' reading fluency.

Reward: If students score 80 percent or more on the Putting It All Together activity and 18 or more on the Fluency Check, add a sticker for this unit on the My Accomplishments chart. If students did not score 80 percent or more on the Putting It All Together activity and 18 or more on the Fluency Check, work with them to revise their writing and practice their fluency until they attain those scores and then add a sticker to the My Accomplishments chart.

Objectives

- Read poetry and prose aloud.
- Read aloud grade-level text with appropriate automaticity, prosody, accuracy, and rate.

Critical Skills Practice 4

Unit Focus

In this unit, students will focus on reading directions, fictional passages, and nonfiction passages, and on answering multiple choice questions about those readings in a standardized test format. They will also practice responding to a writing prompt, which is a common type of question on standardized tests.

Unit Plan		〔Offline〕	〔Online〕
Lesson 1	Directions (B)		50 minutes
Lesson 2	Fiction Passages (E)		50 minutes
Lesson 3	Nonfiction Passages (D)		50 minutes
Lesson 4	Fiction Passages (F)		50 minutes
Lesson 5	Write About a Fiction Passage	20 minutes	30 minutes
Lesson 6	Unit Checkpoint	50 minutes	varies

Directions (B)

Lesson Overview

💻 **[Online]**　　　　　　　　　　　　　　**50** minutes

Get Ready	Reading Directions
Learn	Types of Questions
Try It	Practice Passage and Questions

Big Ideas

- ► Comprehension is facilitated by an understanding of physical presentation (headings, subheads, graphics, and other features).
- ► Comprehension entails an understanding of the organizational patterns of text.
- ► A set of written steps is also known as a how-to piece of writing. Think of a process of steps as a recipe or set of instructions for learning how to do something.

[Materials]

Supplied

- Types of Questions (optional printout)
- Practice Passage and Questions (optional printout)

Keywords

diagram – a drawing or design that shows how pieces of information are related

sequence – the order in which things happen

 **50 minutes**

Students will work online to complete Get Ready, Learn, and Try It activities.

Get Ready

Reading Directions

Students will review the common features of a recipe and recognize the importance of following the steps of the directions in order.

Objectives
- Identify recipes as a type of directions.
- Identify sequencing as critical to a recipe.

Learn

Types of Questions

Students will learn how to answer questions related to a set of directions by reading a recipe and working through several items.

TIP If students are not comfortable reading the passage for this activity online, print Types of Questions and have students read the printout.

Objectives
- Use graphics to answer a question about a reading.
- Follow third grade-level multistep instructions.
- Identify directions as a way to organize ideas through sequencing.
- Read instructional-level text with 90 percent accuracy.
- Identify sequencing as critical to a recipe.

Try It

Practice Passage and Questions

Students will demonstrate their comprehension by reading a recipe and then answering questions about it.

TIP If students are not comfortable reading the passage for this activity online, print Practice Passage and Questions and have students read the printout.

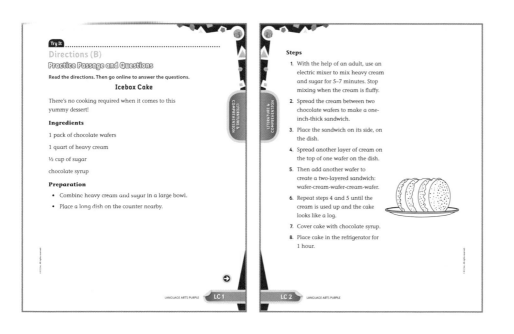
Objectives

- Use graphics to answer a question about a reading.
- Follow third grade-level multistep instructions.
- Identify directions as a way to organize ideas through sequencing.
- Read instructional-level text with 90 percent accuracy.
- Identify sequencing as critical to a recipe.

Fiction Passages (E)

Lesson Overview

Online — 50 minutes

Get Ready	Point of View, Narrators, Drawing Conclusions, Different Endings, and Dialogue
Learn	Types of Questions
Try It	Practice Passage and Questions

Big Ideas

The point of view that a story is told from determines how much information readers have about plot events and characters' feelings.

Materials

Supplied

- Types of Questions (optional printout)
- Practice Passage and Questions (optional printout)

Keywords

conclusion – a decision made about something not stated, using information provided and what is already known

dialogue – the words that characters say in a written work

narrator – the teller of a story

third-person point of view – the telling of a story by someone outside of the action, using the third-person pronouns *he*, *she*, and *they*

[Online] ⏱ 50 minutes

Students will work online to complete Get Ready, Learn, and Try It activities.

Get Ready ....

Point of View, Narrators, Drawing Conclusions, Different Endings, and Dialogue

In preparation for reading and answering questions about fictional passages, students will review the following terms:

- ► dialogue
- ► different endings
- ► drawing conclusions
- ► narrator
- ► point of view
- ► third-person narrator

Objectives
- Define *third-person point of view*.
- Define *third-person narrator*.
- Define *conclusion*.
- Identify dialogue.
- Recognize that stories include dialogue, which starts and ends with quotation marks.

Learn ....

Types of Questions

Students will learn how to answer questions about a fiction passage by reading a story and working through several items.

TIP If students are not comfortable reading the passage for this activity online, print Types of Questions and have students read the printout.

Objectives
- Identify third-person narrator.
- Describe the effect point of view has on a story.
- Draw conclusions about characters using evidence from the text.
- Identify the impact of alternative endings to a plot.
- Identify dialogue.

Learn
Fiction Passages (E)
Types of Questions

Read the passage. Then go online to answer the questions.

Waiting

Bella sat on her front step. Her eyes were fixed on the mailbox. It was almost four o'clock, but the mail had not yet been delivered. Inside, Mom swept the floor.

"Why don't you read a book, Bella?" she called out.

"I won't be able to pay attention to a book now, Mom," Bella said. "Can you call the post office and find out if the mailman got lost or something today?"

Mom laughed at that, but Bella frowned. The mailman was not lost, of course. He was just late. It was bad luck that he was late on the day Bella was to learn if she was accepted to theater camp this summer. She bit her fingernails and felt her heart beat fast.

Bella loved to act, and the camp at Otterlin College was the best in the state. She would learn so much there. She would have so much fun. But only 10 percent of kids who wanted to go to the camp actually got in. Bella stood and paced.

LANGUAGE ARTS PURPLE   **LC 1**

Then she heard it: the hum of the mail van's engine. The letter from Otterlin would arrive soon. She'd find out if she got into the camp. Suddenly, she was afraid.

Mom heard the mail van, too. She walked to the mailbox before Bella, so she met the mailman first. He was smiling as Bella walked up behind her mom.

"Just one envelope today," the mailman said. "It's thick, too. Here you go, Bella."

Bella took the envelope, took a deep breath, and then tore it open. She read for a moment. Then she smiled and started to dance.

She got in!

LC 2   LANGUAGE ARTS PURPLE

Try It

Practice Passage and Questions

Students will demonstrate their comprehension and ability to respond to questions based on a fiction passage by reading a story and then answering questions about it.

TIP If students are not comfortable reading the passage for this activity online, print Practice Passage and Questions and have students read the printout.

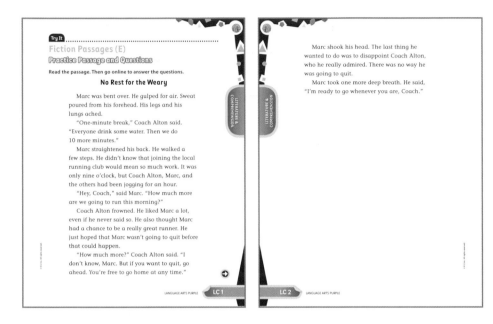

Nonfiction Passages (D)

Lesson Overview

[Online]   **50** minutes

Get Ready	How Authors Influence Readers
Learn	Types of Questions
Try It	Practice Passage and Questions

Big Ideas

▶ Nonfiction texts differ from fiction texts in that they describe real or true things in life, rather than things made up by the author.

▶ Readers must understand the relationship between main idea and supporting details.

▶ Readers need to be able to sequence, summarize, and articulate the main idea.

[Materials]

Supplied
- Types of Questions (optional printout)
- Practice Passage and Questions (optional printout)

Keywords

context clue – a word or phrase in a text that helps you figure out the meaning of an unknown word

fact – something that can be proven true

main idea – the most important point the author makes; it may be stated or unstated

opinion – something that a person thinks or believes, but which cannot be proven to be true

text feature – part of a text that helps a reader locate information and determine what is most important; some examples are the title, table of contents, headings, pictures, and glossary

50 minutes

Students will work online to complete Get Ready, Learn, and Try It activities.

Get Ready

How Authors Influence Readers
Students will learn how authors use language to influence readers and sway their opinion.

Objectives
- Describe methods authors use to influence readers' feelings.

Learn

Types of Questions
Students will learn how to answer questions about a nonfiction opinion passage.

TIP If students are not comfortable reading the passage for this activity online, print Types of Questions and have students read the printout.

Objectives
- Identify author's perspective/opinion.
- Use context clues to determine word meanings.
- Describe methods authors use to influence readers' feelings.
- Use text organizational features to locate and comprehend information (table of contents, glossary, chapter, index, title, author, illustrator, caption).
- Restate main idea.

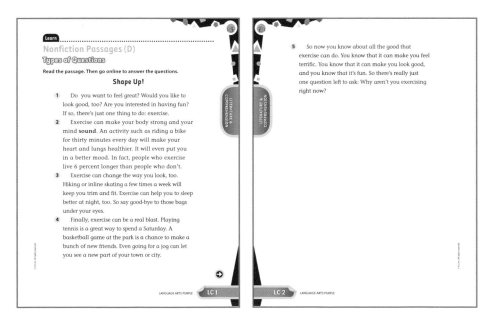

Try It ●●

Practice Passage and Questions

Students will demonstrate their comprehension of how to analyze and respond to questions about an opinion passage.

TIP If students are not comfortable reading the passage for this activity online, print Practice Passage and Questions and have students read the printout.

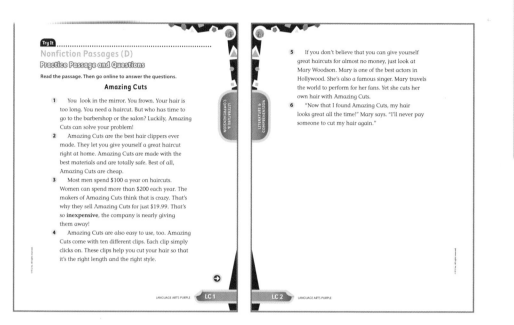

Try It

Nonfiction Passages (D)

Practice Passage and Questions

Read the passage. Then go online to answer the questions.

Amazing Cuts

1   You look in the mirror. You frown. Your hair is too long. You need a haircut. But who has time to go to the barbershop or the salon? Luckily, Amazing Cuts can solve your problem!

2   Amazing Cuts are the best hair clippers ever made. They let you give yourself a great haircut right at home. Amazing Cuts are made with the best materials and are totally safe. Best of all, Amazing Cuts are cheap.

3   Most men spend $100 a year on haircuts. Women can spend more than $200 each year. The makers of Amazing Cuts think that is crazy. That's why they sell Amazing Cuts for just $19.99. That's so **inexpensive**, the company is nearly giving them away!

4   Amazing Cuts are also easy to use, too. Amazing Cuts come with ten different clips. Each clip simply clicks on. These clips help you cut your hair so that it's the right length and the right style.

5   If you don't believe that you can give yourself great haircuts for almost no money, just look at Mary Woodson. Mary is one of the best actors in Hollywood. She's also a famous singer. Mary travels the world to perform for her fans. Yet she cuts her own hair with Amazing Cuts.

6   "Now that I found Amazing Cuts, my hair looks great all the time!" Mary says. "I'll never pay someone to cut my hair again."

LANGUAGE ARTS PURPLE   LC 1   LC 2   LANGUAGE ARTS PURPLE

Objectives

- Identify author's perspective/opinion.
- Use context clues to determine word meanings.
- Describe the methods authors use to influence readers' feelings.
- Use text organizational features to locate and comprehend information (table of contents, glossary, chapter, index, title, author, illustrator, caption).
- Restate the main idea.

Fiction Passages (F)

Lesson Overview

🖥 [Online]   50 minutes

Get Ready	Setting, Characters, Cause and Effect, and Theme
Learn	Types of Questions
Try It	Practice Passage and Questions

[Materials]

Supplied
- Types of Questions (optional printout)
- Practice Passage and Questions (optional printout)

Keywords

cause – the reason something happens

compare – to explain how two or more things are alike

contrast – to explain how two or more things are different

effect – the result of a cause

setting – when and where a story takes place

theme – the author's message or big idea

trait – a quality of a person or character

Big Ideas

To understand and interpret a story, readers need to understand and describe characters and what they do.

[Online] 🕐 50 minutes

Students will work online to complete Get Ready, Learn, and Try It activities.

Get Ready ●

Setting, Characters, Cause and Effect, and Theme

Students will review how to identify setting, theme, character traits, and cause and effect, as well as how to compare and contrast characters in a work of fiction.

> ### Objectives
> - Define *setting*.
> - Define *character traits*.
> - Define *cause* and *effect*.
> - Define *theme*.
> - Define *compare* and *contrast*.

Learn ●

Types of Questions

Students will learn how to answer questions about a fiction passage by reading a story and working through several items.

TIP If students are not comfortable reading the passage for this activity online, print Types of Questions and have students read the printout.

> ### Objectives
> - Identify setting(s).
> - Identify character traits.
> - Compare and contrast characters in a literary selection.
> - Identify a cause and its effect on events and/or relationships.
> - Identify the theme of a third-grade passage.

Learn
Fiction Passages (F)
Types of Questions

Read the passage. Then go online to answer the questions.

Far from Home

Smoke rose from the spaceship that afternoon. Murray and Wilson looked at each other. Then they looked at the green sky and the odd plants that floated in the air. If they could not fix their ship, the two astronauts would both be stuck on this planet millions of miles from earth.

"This is bad," Murray said as he paced. There was worry in his voice. "I do not like this one bit. We are in real trouble."

"Just relax," said Wilson. She was standing still and she sounded much less upset. "We can fix the ship if we work together."

"But what if we can't?" shouted Murray. "What if we never get home? We never should've gone on this mission!"

Yet Wilson was not listening to Murray. She was too busy examining their spaceship. She realized that the engine had stalled. It looked like a hose was ripped. She and Murray would have to fix the problem.

"Listen," Wilson said to Murray, "I know you're scared. I'm scared, too. But we have to get over our fear. We have to fix this engine. Now go look for another hose."

Having a chore helped Murray calm down. He found a new hose in the ship's cargo bay. Within moments, he and Wilson installed the new hose. The engine stopped smoking. The ship started to hum. It was ready for takeoff. The two astronauts looked at one another.

"Nice work," said Wilson.

"Let's get out of here," said Murray.

LANGUAGE ARTS PURPLE LC 1

LC 2 LANGUAGE ARTS PURPLE

Try It

Practice Passage and Questions

Students will demonstrate their comprehension and ability to respond to questions based on a fiction passage by reading a story and then answering questions about it.

TIP If students are not comfortable reading the passage for this activity online, print Practice Passage and Questions and have students read the printout.

Objectives
- Identify setting(s).
- Identify character traits.
- Compare and contrast characters in a literary selection.
- Identify a cause and its effect on events and/or relationships.
- Identify the theme of a third-grade passage.

Write About a Fiction Passage

Lesson Overview

💻 [Online]   **30** minutes

| Get Ready | Questions That Require a Written Answer |
| Learn | Answer with a Summary |

📃 [Offline]   **20** minutes

| Try It | Read and Write a Response |

Materials

Supplied

- *K¹² Language Arts Activity Book*, pp. LC 105–107
- Answer with a Summary (optional printout)
- Read and Write a Response: Rubric and Sample Responses (printout)

Keywords

order words – words that connect ideas or a series of steps, or create a sequence, such as *first, next, later, finally*

summarize – to tell in order the most important ideas or events of a text

summary – a short retelling that includes only the most important ideas or events of a text

Advance Preparation

This lesson includes an offline Try It in which students will write a response to an open-ended question, or writing prompt. You will evaluate this response using the tools provided in the online lesson or your own state's rubric. Print Read and Write a Response: Rubric and Sample Responses, which you will use to evaluate the open-ended response. You may wish to familiarize yourself with this tool in advance.

Big Ideas

Explicit instruction in how to summarize a text is an important element in learning how to write well.

[Online] 30 minutes

Students will work online to complete Get Ready and Learn activities.

Get Ready

Questions That Require a Written Answer

Students will learn how to identify and respond to questions similar to those found on standardized tests that require written responses. They will also review what a **summary** is and why they must be able to write one.

> **Objectives**
> • Define *summary*.

Learn

Answer with a Summary

Students will learn how to summarize a fiction passage. They will learn to use **order words** and include the most important events from the beginning, middle, and end of the story. They will learn how to analyze and respond to a writing prompt that requires a summary.

TIP If students are not comfortable reading the passage for this activity online, print Answer with a Summary and have students read the printout.

Learn
Write About a Fiction Passage
Answer with a Summary

Read the passage. Then go online to answer the questions.

Locked Out

Nina reached into her front pockets. Then she checked her back pockets.

She opened her bag. She picked up the doormat on the step. A frown spread across her face.

She was locked out of her house.

Across the street, Mr. Ackley was mowing his lawn. He wore bright green shorts and black socks with sandals. His long nose made it look as though he was always leaning his head forward. Mr. Ackley was a good friend of Nina's parents, and Nina knew him well. He was always nice to Nina. Once when she was selling cookies, he bought five boxes. He and Mrs. Ackley had dinner at Nina's house every Friday. She walked across the street now and waved her hand.

Mr. Ackley saw Nina and turned off his lawn mower. He wiped sweat from his forehead and off his long nose. Nina told him about her problem.

"Locked out, huh?" Mr. Ackley said. "That's too bad. And Mom and Dad are out?"

"Yeah. Dad's at a football game and Mom's picking up my aunt at the airport."

"What about the spare key they keep under the doormat?"

"It's not there now, Mr. Ackley," Nina told him.

"Are you sure? Let's check again," said Mr. Ackley.

So Nina walked back across the street with Mr. Ackley following. They went back up to the front door, and she again lifted the doormat. The key, of course, still wasn't there.

"Hmm," Mr. Ackley began. "This is quite a pickle. Can't open a locked door without a key. You're sure the door is locked, right?"

Nina raised her eyebrows. She never actually tried to open the door. Mr. Ackley reached out and turned the knob. Just like that, the door opened. On the other side of the door, inside the house, stood Nina's mother and her sister, Aunt Diane.

"Oh, hi, Nina. Hello, Mr. Ackley," Nina's mom said with a smile on her face and the spare key in her hand. "Aunt Diane's flight arrived early. When we got home I realized I forgot my key and had to use the spare."

LANGUAGE ARTS PURPLE   LC 1

LC 2   LANGUAGE ARTS PURPLE

[Offline] ⓴ minutes

Work **together** with students to complete the Try It activity.

Try It

Read and Write a Response

Students will write a summary of a short fiction passage. Turn to pages LC 105–107 in *K¹² Language Arts Activity Book*.

1. Direct students' attention to the Activity Book pages. Have them carefully read the passage, directions, and prompt that requires a written response.

2. Tell students they are to write a summary.

   ▸ Their summary should describe events in the same order as they occur in the passage.
   ▸ Their summary should describe only the passage's most important events and details, written in their own words. Students should not merely repeat the words of the story's author.
   ▸ Their summary should be mostly free of errors in grammar, usage, and mechanics.

3. Remind students that they should write in complete sentences, use good handwriting, and leave spaces between words so that others can read what they wrote.

4. Have students complete the Activity Book pages.

5. Use the Read and Write a Response: Rubric and Sample Responses to evaluate students' finished writing. You will be looking at students' writing to evaluate the following:

   ▸ **Purpose and Content:** The summary describes most of the important events from the story with only one or two unnecessary or minor details. It contains at least four sentences. It is mostly original and rarely repeats the words of the story's author.
   ▸ **Structure and Organization:** The summary is written in mostly the same order as the story with only one exception, and it includes events from the beginning, middle, and end of the story.
   ▸ **Grammar and Mechanics:** Most sentences are complete, and there are a few errors in grammar, punctuation, or spelling.

Objectives

- Write a summary.
- Summarize text and maintain accurate sequence.

6. If students' writing scored a 1 in any category, work with students to proofread and revise their work.

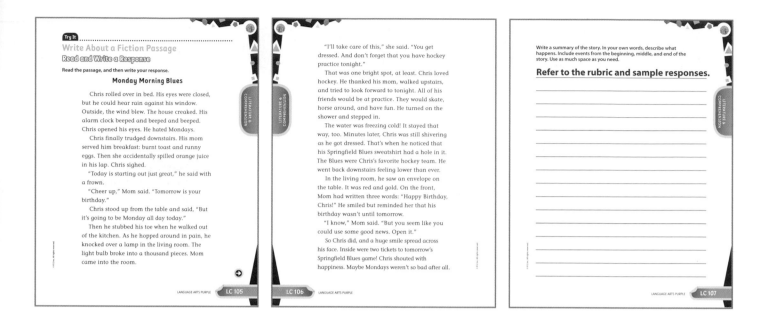

Try It

Write About a Fiction Passage

Read and Write a Response

Read the passage, and then write your response.

Monday Morning Blues

Chris rolled over in bed. His eyes were closed, but he could hear rain against his window. Outside, the wind blew. The house creaked. His alarm clock beeped and beeped and beeped. Chris opened his eyes. He hated Mondays.

Chris finally trudged downstairs. His mom served him breakfast: burnt toast and runny eggs. Then she accidentally spilled orange juice in his lap. Chris sighed.

"Today is starting out just great," he said with a frown.

"Cheer up," Mom said. "Tomorrow is your birthday."

Chris stood up from the table and said, "But it's going to be Monday all day today."

Then he stubbed his toe when he walked out of the kitchen. As he hopped around in pain, he knocked over a lamp in the living room. The light bulb broke into a thousand pieces. Mom came into the room.

LANGUAGE ARTS PURPLE **LC 105**

LC 106 LANGUAGE ARTS PURPLE

"I'll take care of this," she said. "You get dressed. And don't forget that you have hockey practice tonight."

That was one bright spot, at least. Chris loved hockey. He thanked his mom, walked upstairs, and tried to look forward to tonight. All of his friends would be at practice. They would skate, horse around, and have fun. He turned on the shower and stepped in.

The water was freezing cold! It stayed that way, too. Minutes later, Chris was still shivering as he got dressed. That's when he noticed that his Springfield Blues sweatshirt had a hole in it. The Blues were Chris's favorite hockey team. He went back downstairs feeling lower than ever.

In the living room, he saw an envelope on the table. It was red and gold. On the front, Mom had written three words: "Happy Birthday, Chris!" He smiled but reminded her that his birthday wasn't until tomorrow.

"I know," Mom said. "But you seem like you could use some good news. Open it."

So Chris did, and a huge smile spread across his face. Inside were two tickets to tomorrow's Springfield Blues game! Chris shouted with happiness. Maybe Mondays weren't so bad after all.

Write a summary of the story. In your own words, describe what happens. Include events from the beginning, middle, and end of the story. Use as much space as you need.

Refer to the rubric and sample responses.

_____
_____
_____
_____
_____
_____
_____
_____
_____
_____
_____
_____
_____
_____
_____

LANGUAGE ARTS PURPLE **LC 107**

Unit Checkpoint

Lesson Overview

Offline   50 minutes

Unit Checkpoint	Part 1: Nonfiction Passage
	Part 2: Directions
	Part 3: Fiction Passage
	Part 4: Summarize a Fiction Passage

Online   varies

More Practice	Review the Skills

Materials

Supplied
- *K¹³ Language Arts Assessments* pp. LC 47–59
- **Summarize a Fiction Passage: Rubric and Sample Responses (printout)**

Objectives

- Use graphics to answer a question about a reading.
- Follow third grade-level multistep instructions.
- Identify directions as a way to organize ideas through sequencing.
- Read instructional-level text with 90 percent accuracy.
- Identify sequencing as critical to a recipe.
- Identify third-person narrator.
- Describe the effect point of view has on a story.
- Draw conclusions about characters using evidence from the text.
- Identify the impact of alternative endings to a plot.
- Identify dialogue.
- Use context clues to determine word meanings.

- Identify author's perspective/opinion.
- Describe methods authors use to influence readers' feelings.
- Use text organizational features to locate and comprehend information (table of contents, glossary, chapter, index, title, author, illustrator, caption).
- Restate main idea.
- Identify setting(s).
- Identify character traits.
- Compare and contrast characters in a literary selection.
- Identify a cause and its effect on events and/or relationships.
- Identify the theme of a third-grade passage.
- Write a summary.
- Summarize text and maintain accurate sequence.

 **50 minutes**

Explain to students that they are going to show what they have learned about reading and answering questions about nonfiction passages, directions, and fiction passages, and about summarizing a fiction passage.

1. Give students the Unit Checkpoint pages.

2. Read the directions together.

3. Use the Answer Key to score the Checkpoint, and then enter the results online.

4. Review each exercise with students. Work with students to correct any exercise that they missed.

Part 1: Nonfiction Passage
Have students read "A Town Like No Other" and answer the questions.

Part 2: Directions
Have students read the recipe and answer the questions.

Part 3: Fiction Passage
Have students read "Sandy's Share" and answer the questions.

Part 4: Summarize a Fiction Passage
Have students write a summary of "Sandy's Share."

1. Direct students' attention to Part 4 of the Checkpoint and read the directions together, ensuring that students understand they are to write a summary of the story they read in Part 3, "Sandy's Share."

2. Have students write their summary.

3. Use the Summarize a Fiction Passage: Rubric and Sample Responses to evaluate students' finished writing. You will be looking at students' writing to evaluate the following:

- ▶ **Purpose and Content:** The summary describes most of the important events from the story with only one or two unnecessary or minor details. It contains at least four sentences. It is mostly original and rarely repeats the words of the story's author.
- ▶ **Structure and Organization:** The summary is written in mostly the same order as the story with only one exception, and it includes events from the beginning, middle, and end of the story.
- ▶ **Grammar and Mechanics:** Most sentences are complete, and there are a few errors in grammar, punctuation, or spelling.

4. If students' writing scored a 1 in any category, work with students to proofread and revise their work.

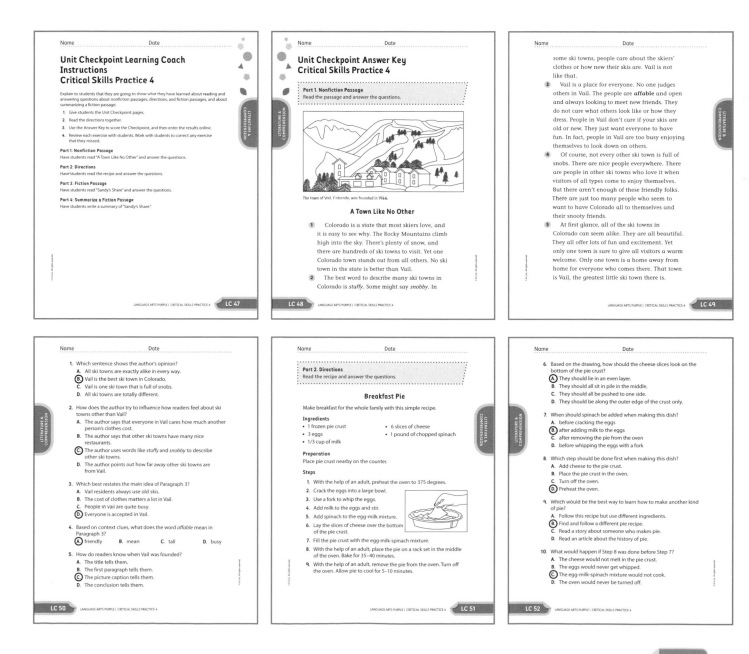

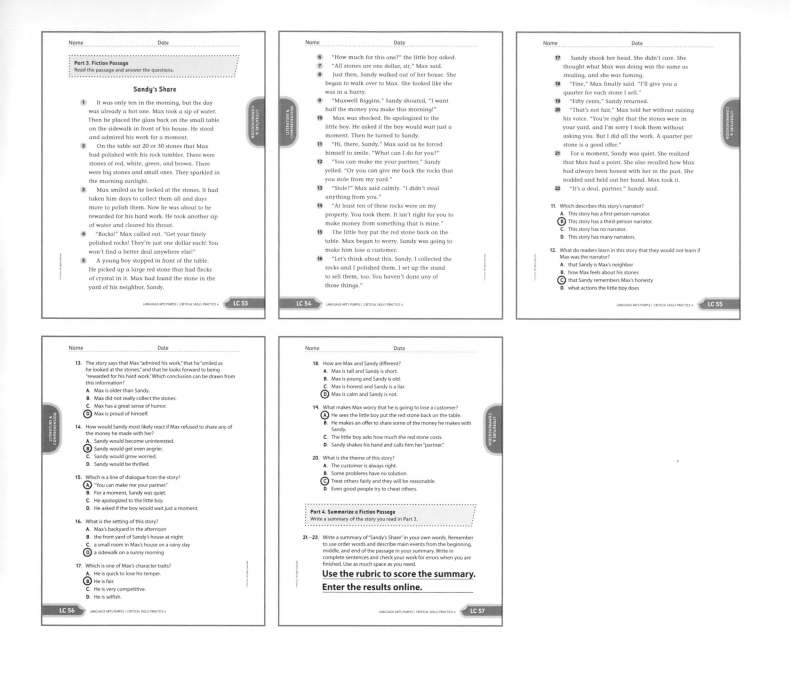

Part 3. Fiction Passage
Read the passage and answer the questions.

Sandy's Share

1 It was only ten in the morning, but the day was already a hot one. Max took a sip of water. Then he placed the glass back on the small table on the sidewalk in front of his house. He stood and admired his work for a moment.

2 On the table sat 20 or 30 stones that Max had polished with his rock tumbler. There were stones of red, white, green, and brown. There were big stones and small ones. They sparkled in the morning sunlight.

3 Max smiled as he looked at the stones. It had taken him days to collect them all and days more to polish them. Now he was about to be rewarded for his hard work. He took another sip of water and cleared his throat.

4 "Rocks!" Max called out. "Get your finely polished rocks! They're just one dollar each! You won't find a better deal anywhere else!"

5 A young boy stopped in front of the table. He picked up a large red stone that had flecks of crystal in it. Max had found the stone in the yard of his neighbor, Sandy.

6 "How much for this one?" the little boy asked.

7 "All stones are one dollar, sir," Max said.

8 Just then, Sandy walked out of her house. She began to walk over to Max. She looked like she was in a hurry.

9 "Maxwell Riggins," Sandy shouted, "I want half the money you make this morning!"

10 Max was shocked. He apologized to the little boy. He asked if the boy would wait just a moment. Then he turned to Sandy.

11 "Hi, there, Sandy," Max said as he forced himself to smile. "What can I do for you?"

12 "You can make me your partner," Sandy yelled. "Or you can give me back the rocks that you stole from my yard."

13 "Stole?" Max said calmly. "I didn't steal anything from you."

14 "At least ten of these rocks were on my property. You took them. It isn't right for you to make money from something that is mine."

15 The little boy put the red stone back on the table. Max began to worry. Sandy was going to make him lose a customer.

16 "Let's think about this, Sandy. I collected the rocks and I polished them. I set up the stand to sell them, too. You haven't done any of those things."

17 Sandy shook her head. She didn't care. She thought what Max was doing was the same as stealing, and she was fuming.

18 "Fine," Max finally said. "I'll give you a quarter for each stone I sell."

19 "Fifty cents," Sandy returned.

20 "That's not fair," Max told her without raising his voice. "You're right that the stones were in your yard, and I'm sorry I took them without asking you. But I did all the work. A quarter per stone is a good offer."

21 For a moment, Sandy was quiet. She realized that Max had a point. She also recalled how Max had always been honest with her in the past. She nodded and held out her hand. Max took it.

22 "It's a deal, partner," Sandy said.

---

11. Which describes this story's narrator?
   A. This story has a first-person narrator.
   Ⓑ This story has a third-person narrator.
   C. This story has no narrator.
   D. This story has many narrators.

12. What do readers learn in this story that they would not learn if Max was the narrator?
   A. that Sandy is Max's neighbor
   B. how Max feels about his stones
   Ⓒ that Sandy remembers Max's honesty
   D. what actions the little boy does

13. The story says that Max "admired his work," that he "smiled as he looked at the stones," and that he looks forward to being "rewarded for his hard work." Which conclusion can be drawn from this information?
   A. Max is older than Sandy.
   B. Max did not really collect the stones.
   C. Max has a great sense of humor.
   Ⓓ Max is proud of himself.

14. How would Sandy most likely react if Max refused to share any of the money he made with her?
   A. Sandy would become uninterested.
   Ⓑ Sandy would get even angrier.
   C. Sandy would grow worried.
   D. Sandy would be thrilled.

15. Which is a line of dialogue from the story?
   Ⓐ "You can make me your partner."
   B. For a moment, Sandy was quiet.
   C. He apologized to the little boy.
   D. He asked if the boy would wait just a moment.

16. What is the setting of this story?
   A. Max's backyard in the afternoon
   B. the front yard of Sandy's house at night
   C. a small room in Max's house on a rainy day
   Ⓓ a sidewalk on a sunny morning

17. Which is one of Max's character traits?
   A. He is quick to lose his temper.
   Ⓑ He is fair.
   C. He is very competitive.
   D. He is selfish.

18. How are Max and Sandy different?
   A. Max is tall and Sandy is short.
   B. Max is young and Sandy is old.
   C. Max is honest and Sandy is a liar.
   Ⓓ Max is calm and Sandy is not.

19. What makes Max worry that he is going to lose a customer?
   Ⓐ He sees the little boy put the red stone back on the table.
   B. He makes an offer to share some of the money he makes with Sandy.
   C. The little boy asks how much the red stone costs.
   D. Sandy shakes his hand and calls him "partner."

20. What is the theme of this story?
   A. The customer is always right.
   B. Some problems have no solution.
   Ⓒ Treat others fairly and they will be reasonable.
   D. Even good people try to cheat others.

Part 4. Summarize a Fiction Passage
Write a summary of the story you read in Part 3.

21.–23. Write a summary of "Sandy's Share" in your own words. Remember to use order words and describe main events from the beginning, middle, and end of the passage in your summary. Write in complete sentences and check your work for errors when you are finished. Use as much space as you need.

Use the rubric to score the summary.
Enter the results online.

LC 53 LANGUAGE ARTS PURPLE | CRITICAL SKILLS PRACTICE 4
LC 54 LANGUAGE ARTS PURPLE | CRITICAL SKILLS PRACTICE 4
LANGUAGE ARTS PURPLE | CRITICAL SKILLS PRACTICE 4 LC 55
LC 56 LANGUAGE ARTS PURPLE | CRITICAL SKILLS PRACTICE 4
LANGUAGE ARTS PURPLE | CRITICAL SKILLS PRACTICE 4 LC 57
LC 308 Language Arts Purple

 **varies**

Students will work **independently** to complete the online More Practice activity.

More Practice

Review the Skills

If students scored less than 80 percent or had difficulty meeting the objectives of the Unit Checkpoint, have them go online for more practice.

 Reward: If students score 80 percent or more on the Unit Checkpoint, add a sticker for this unit on the My Accomplishments chart. If students did not score 80 percent or more, work with them to revise their work until they do score 80 percent, and then add a sticker to the My Accomplishments chart.

Objectives
- Evaluate Unit Checkpoint results and choose activities for more practice.

Folktales from Many Lands

Unit Focus

In this unit, students will read folktales from a variety of cultures. They will focus on the differences between heroes and villains, heroic character traits, the heroes' problems and their solutions, and themes of the stories. Students will read these selections from *K¹² Classics for Young Readers, Volume C*:

▶ "The Leak in the Dike"
▶ "William Tell"
▶ "The Stone-Cutter"
▶ "Aladdin and the Wonderful Lamp"

Students will also prepare and give a speech in the role of one of the heroes from the stories to reflect their understanding of that character and his traits.

Unit Plan		Online	Offline
Lesson 1	Introduce "The Leak in the Dike"		50 minutes
Lesson 2	Explore "The Leak in the Dike"	40 minutes	10 minutes
Lesson 3	Introduce "William Tell"		50 minutes
Lesson 4	Explore "William Tell"	40 minutes	10 minutes
Lesson 5	Introduce "The Stone-Cutter"		50 minutes
Lesson 6	Explore "The Stone-Cutter"	40 minutes	10 minutes
Lesson 7	Introduce "Aladdin and the Wonderful Lamp"		50 minutes
Lesson 8	Explore "Aladdin and the Wonderful Lamp"	40 minutes	10 minutes
Lesson 9	Reflections on Folktales from Many Lands (A)		50 minutes
Lesson 10	Reflections on Folktales from Many Lands (B)	varies	40 minutes
Lesson 11	Your Choice		50 minutes

Introduce "The Leak in the Dike"

Lesson Overview

[Offline] **50** minutes

Get Ready	Lesson Introduction
	Review Folktales and Settings
	Book Walk
	Words to Know
Read	"The Leak in the Dike"
GRAB	Go Read a Book

[Materials]

Supplied

- "The Leak in the Dike,"
  *K¹² Classics for Young
  Readers, Volume C,*
  pp. 126–133
- Reading Strategies
  bookmark

Also Needed

- globe

Content Background

This story takes place in a country in western Europe called the Netherlands, or
Holland. Holland borders the North Sea. A large part of the land is lower than the
level of the sea. The people have built great walls, called dikes, to keep the sea from
flooding their cities and homes. These dikes are high and wide, and are sometimes
covered with buildings and trees.

Big Ideas

- ▶ Folktales are stories that are passed down from older people to younger people
  in order to teach important lessons or values.
- ▶ Active, strong readers employ reading strategies such as making connections
  between text and self, between and among texts, and between text and the
  real world.
- ▶ Folktales help readers understand a culture's values, hopes, and fears.

Story Synopsis

This story is set in Holland
long ago. A young boy named
Peter is returning from an
errand across one of Holland's
dikes. On his way home, he
notices a small leak in the
dike. Peter climbs down the
side of the dike and puts his
finger in the hole to hold back
the water. He remains there
for an entire night until he is
discovered.

Keywords

folktale – a story, which
usually teaches a lesson
important to a culture, that is
passed down through many
generations

setting – when and where a
story takes place

[Offline] 50 minutes

Work **together** with students to complete offline Get Ready, Read, and GRAB activities.

Get Ready ....

Lesson Introduction

Prepare students to read "The Leak in the Dike."

1. Explain to students that before they read "The Leak in the Dike," they will discuss with you

   ▸ What a folktale is
   ▸ The setting for the story
   ▸ Their predictions about the text
   ▸ Important words to know in the text

2. Tell students that while they read, you will check in to make sure they understand what they are reading.

3. Tell students that after they read, they will answer questions about the story.

Objectives

- Define *folktale*.
- Identify setting(s).
- Use text organizational features to locate and comprehend information (table of contents).
- Use before-reading strategies.
- Increase concept and content vocabulary.

Review Folktales and Settings

Review what a folktale is and discuss the setting of "The Leak in the Dike." Gather the globe.

1. Tell students they are going to read a **folktale** and have them tell what a folktale is. a story, which usually teachers a lesson important to a culture, that is passed down through many generations

2. Tell students the story takes place in a country in western Europe called the Netherlands, also known as Holland. Help students find Holland on the globe.

3. Explain the system of dikes in Holland.
   Say: Holland borders the North Sea. There is something very unusual about the land of Holland. A large part of the land is lower than the level of the sea. The people have built great walls, called dikes, to keep the sea from flooding their cities and homes. These dikes are high and wide, and are sometimes covered with buildings and trees. You are going to read an old story from Holland.

Book Walk

Have students lead you through a Book Walk of "The Leak in the Dike." Remind them to use the **title** and **illustrations** to make predictions about what will happen in the story.

Words to Know

Remind students that they will find the Words to Know at the bottoms of the pages in the selection.

Read

"The Leak in the Dike"

Have students read "The Leak in the Dike." Remind students to use the strategies on their Reading Strategies bookmark. For example, they may want to stop at the end of each page of the story and ask themselves questions about what they just read.

➲ **Learning Coach Check-In** This reading assignment should take about 20 minutes. After students finish reading, ask the following questions to assess their comprehension of the selection:

- ▸ What does the boy Peter see? a hole in a dike
- ▸ What does he do about what he sees? Peter puts his finger in the hole to stop the leak.

If students have trouble answering these questions, ask them what reading strategies they used and suggest they reread the selection.

> **Objectives**
> - Read literature independently and proficiently.
> - Apply information read to answer questions.
> - Evaluate reading strategies.

GRAB

Go Read a Book

Have students read a book or magazine of their own choosing for at least 20 minutes. Remind students to use the strategies on their Reading Strategies bookmark before and during reading to help them understand the text.

TIP Remember: The more students read, the better readers they become.

> **Objectives**
> - Read literature independently and proficiently.
> - Read a variety of texts for information and pleasure.

Explore "The Leak in the Dike"

Lesson Overview

🖥 〖Online〗 ④⓪ minutes

Check Your Reading	Comprehend "The Leak in the Dike"
Reading for Meaning	Identify Problem and Solution
	What Makes a Hero?

📄 〖Offline〗 ①⓪ minutes

Making Connections	What Peter Teaches Us
Beyond the Lesson	➕ OPTIONAL: Write a New Ending

Big Ideas

▸ To understand and interpret a story, readers need to understand and describe characters and what they do.

▸ Readers need to understand literary conflicts and their resolutions in order to analyze characters and themes.

〖Materials〗

Supplied

- "The Leak in the Dike," *K¹² Classics for Young Readers, Volume C,* pp. 126–133
- *K¹² Language Arts Activity Book,* pp. LC 109–111

Keywords

folktale – a story, which usually teaches a lesson important to a culture, that is passed down through many generations

hero – a character who must struggle to overcome problems in a story and whose actions and traits are admired by others

problem – an issue a character must solve in a story

solution – how a character solves a problem in a story

trait – a quality of a person or character

[Online] **40** minutes

Students will work **independently** to complete online Check Your Reading and Reading for Meaning activities.

Check Your Reading

Comprehend "The Leak in the Dike"

Students will answer questions about "The Leak in the Dike" to demonstrate their literal and inferential comprehension of the story.

Objectives

- Identify concrete answers to questions.
- Infer answers to questions.
- Apply information read to answer questions.
- Describe characters and their traits.

Reading for Meaning

Identify Problem and Solution

Students will identify the problems in the story "The Leak in the Dike" and how the main character, Peter, solves those problems.

What Makes a Hero?

Students will look at the character traits that make a hero in literature and examine the story "The Leak in the Dike" to learn how the main character, Peter, is a hero.

Objectives

- Define *problem*.
- Define the problem in a story.
- Define solution to the problem a character faces.
- Identify problems and solutions in a story.
- Define *hero*.
- Identify the hero of a story.
- Describe characters by what they do, what they say, or what others say about them.
- Describe characters and their traits.

 **Offline** ⑩ minutes

Work **together** with students to complete the offline Making Connections and Beyond the Lesson activities.

Making Connections

What Peter Teaches Us

Students will analyze the heroic qualities of the main character in "The Leak in the Dike" and identify the theme of the story. Turn to pages LC 109–111 in *K¹² Language Arts Activity Book*.

1. Have students read the directions.

2. Have them complete the Activity Book pages.

TIP Keep the Activity Book pages in a safe place for students to use later.

Objectives

- Describe characters by what they do, what they say, or what others say about them.
- Distinguish own opinion from that of the narrator or those of the characters.
- Determine the theme, moral, or lesson of a work of literature.
- Explain how theme, message, lesson, or moral is conveyed through details in a text.

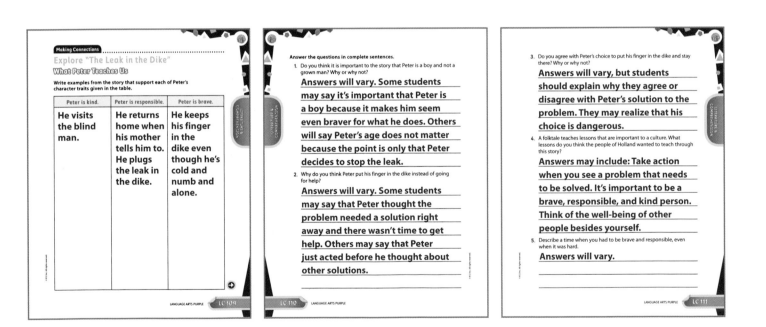

Beyond the Lesson

⊕ **OPTIONAL: Write a New Ending**

This activity is OPTIONAL. It is intended for students who have extra time and would benefit from imagining a new ending for "The Leak in the Dike." Feel free to skip this activity.

1. Have students tell how the story "The Leak in the Dike" ends. Peter calls for help, and in the morning a laborer finds him. Peter tells the laborer that he is holding back the water and asks the man to get help.

2. Tell students to imagine what they think might happen after Peter talks to the laborer. Have them consider these questions:

   ▸ Does the laborer go get help?
   ▸ Does the help come in time to keep the dike from breaking?
   ▸ What do Peter's mother and father do and say when they find out what has happened?

3. Have students write a new ending to the story that begins with Peter telling the laborer to get help. Tell them to make sure that the events in their new ending build on the plot, character traits, and theme of the original story.

4. Have students illustrate their story and then read it aloud to an audience.

Objectives

- Make connections between text and self, text and world, and text to text.
- Describe characters and their traits.
- Deliver a narrative presentation.
- Generate plausible alternative endings to plot.
- Create a visual.

Introduce "William Tell"

Lesson Overview

[Offline]   **50 minutes**

Get Ready	Lesson Introduction
	Heroes and Villains
	Book Walk
	Words to Know
Read	"William Tell"
GRAB	Go Read a Book

Content Background

This story takes place in the western European nation of Switzerland. William Tell is a national hero in Switzerland for his resistance to a ruthless tyrant from neighboring Austria.

Big Ideas

▸ Folktales are stories that are passed down from older people to younger people in order to teach important lessons or values.

▸ Active, strong readers employ reading strategies such as making connections between text and self, between and among texts, and between text and the real world.

▸ Folktales help readers understand a culture's values, hopes, and fears.

[Materials]

Supplied

● "William Tell," *K¹² Classics for Young Readers, Volume C*, pp. 134–139

● Reading Strategies bookmark

Also Needed

● globe

Story Synopsis

William Tell and his son Albert are captured by the tyrant Gessler who rules Switzerland. To save his own life and that of his son, Tell is forced by Gessler to shoot an apple off Albert's head from a great distance. Tell completes the feat, but then Gessler decides to put Tell in prison. On the way across a lake to the prison, Gessler, his soldiers, and Tell encounter a storm. The soldiers free Tell to steer the boat, and he escapes.

Keywords

folktale – a story, which usually teaches a lesson important to a culture, that is passed down through many generations

hero – a character who must struggle to overcome problems in a story and whose actions and traits are admired by others

setting – when and where a story takes place

villain – a bad or evil character who often works against the hero of a story

[Offline] 50 minutes

Work **together** with students to complete offline Get Ready, Read, and GRAB activities.

Get Ready

Lesson Introduction
Prepare students to read "William Tell."

1. Explain to students that before they read "William Tell," they will discuss with you

    ▸ What heroes and villains are
    ▸ The setting for the story
    ▸ Their predictions about the text
    ▸ Important words to know in the text

2. Tell students that while they read, you will check in to make sure they understand what they are reading.

3. Tell students that after they read, they will answer questions about the story.

> **Objectives**
> - Define *villain*.
> - Identify setting(s).
> - Use before-reading strategies.
> - Increase concept and content vocabulary.

Heroes and Villains
Review what heroes and villains are and discuss the setting of "William Tell." Gather the globe.

1. Have students tell what a **hero** is and give some qualities of a hero. Possible answers: a character who struggles to overcome problems in a story; a character who shows bravery, strength, honesty, responsibility, kindness, and leadership

2. Have students name a favorite hero from books or movies and explain why that character is a hero.

3. Tell students that the character who works against the hero is called the **villain**, or what most people know as the "bad guy." Have students name a villain they know who has fought against their favorite hero or another hero in a story.

4. Tell students that the story they will read has a hero and a villain. The story takes place long ago in the country of Switzerland. Help students find Switzerland on the globe.

Book Walk
Have students lead you through a Book Walk of "William Tell." Remind them to use the **title** and **illustrations** to make predictions about what will happen in the story.

Words to Know

Remind students that they will find the Words to Know at the bottoms of the pages in the selection.

Read

"William Tell"

Have students read "William Tell." Remind students to use the strategies on their Reading Strategies bookmark. For example, they may want to stop at the end of each page of the story and summarize what they just read.

⮌ **Learning Coach Check-In** This reading assignment should take about 20 minutes. After students finish reading, ask the following questions to assess their comprehension of the selection:

▸ What does Gessler make William Tell do? shoot an apple off Tell's son Albert's head

▸ How does William Tell escape? He jumps out of the boat and runs away before Gessler and the soldiers can chase him.

If students have trouble answering these questions, ask them what reading strategies they used and suggest they reread the selection.

Objectives
- Read literature independently and proficiently.
- Apply information read to answer questions.
- Evaluate reading strategies.

GRAB

Go Read a Book

Have students read a book or magazine of their own choosing for at least 20 minutes. Remind students to use the strategies on their Reading Strategies bookmark before and during reading to help them understand the text.

Objectives
- Read literature independently and proficiently.
- Read a variety of texts for information and pleasure.

Explore "William Tell"

Lesson Overview

🖥 [Online] — 40 minutes

Check Your Reading	Comprehend "William Tell"
Reading for Meaning	Choices and Consequences
	The Villain of the Story

📄 [Offline] — 10 minutes

Making Connections	The Hero vs. the Villain
Beyond the Lesson	⊕ OPTIONAL: Read Another William Tell Story

Big Ideas

▶ To understand and interpret a story, readers need to understand and describe characters and what they do.

▶ Readers need to understand literary conflicts and their resolutions in order to analyze characters and themes.

【Materials】

Supplied

- "William Tell," *K¹² Classics for Young Readers, Volume C,* pp. 134–139
- *K¹² Language Arts Activity Book,* pp. LC 113–116

Keywords

compare – to explain how two or more things are alike

contrast – to explain how two or more things are different

consequence – what happens because of an action or event

hero – a character who must struggle to overcome problems in a story and whose actions and traits are admired by others

trait – a quality of a person or character

villain – a bad or evil character who often works against the hero of a story

 **40 minutes**

Students will work **independently** to complete online Check Your Reading and Reading for Meaning activities.

Check Your Reading

Comprehend "William Tell"
Students will answer questions about "William Tell" to demonstrate their literal and inferential comprehension of the story.

Objectives
- Identify concrete answers to questions.
- Infer answers to questions.
- Apply information read to answer questions.
- Identify the hero of a story.

Reading for Meaning

Choices and Consequences
Students will learn how to identify the character traits of a hero in a story by looking at the character's choices and their consequences.

Objectives
- Identify choices that a character makes and their consequences.
- Identify character traits.
- Identify the villain of a story.

The Villain of the Story
Students will look at the traits and actions of the character Gessler in "William Tell" to identify him as the villain in the story.

〔Offline〕 ⏱ 10 minutes

Work **together** with students to complete the offline Making Connections and Beyond the Lesson activities.

Making Connections ....

The Hero vs. the Villain

Students will compare and contrast the hero and the villain in "William Tell." Turn to pages LC 113–116 in *K¹² Language Arts Activity Book*.

1. Have students read the directions.

2. Have them complete the Activity Book pages.

3. Make sure students' answers include examples from the story that support the character traits they identify.

TIP Keep the Activity Book pages in a safe place for students to use later.

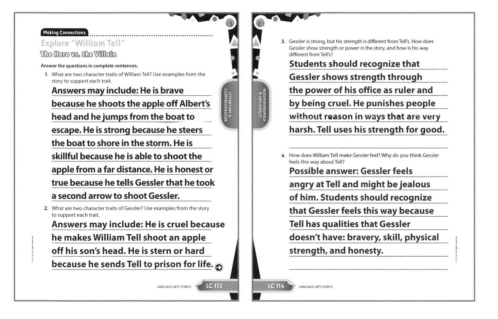

> **Objectives**
>
> - Describe characters by what they do, what they say, or what others say about them.
> - Compare and contrast characters in a literary selection.
> - Determine the theme, moral, or lesson of a work of literature.
> - Identify and use evidence from the text to support answers.
> - Make inferences using evidence from the text.

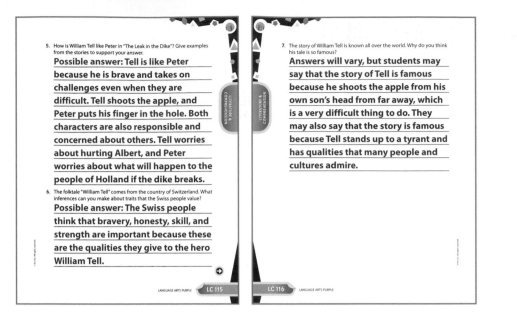

⊕ OPTIONAL: Read Another William Tell Story

This activity is OPTIONAL. It is intended for students who have extra time and would benefit from reading another version of the story of William Tell. Feel free to skip this activity.

1. Tell students that the story of William Tell is very famous. Tell them these examples of how the story has become part of many different cultures.

   ▶ The Italian composer Gioachino Rossini wrote an opera called *William Tell*. The opening piece of music, "The William Tell Overture," is very well known. The end of the overture became the theme for the famous movie and cartoon hero the Lone Ranger.

   ▶ The U.S. Air Force holds a William Tell competition to test its fighter pilots.

   ▶ There are many modern books that retell the story of William Tell. One book won the Newbery Award in 1952: *The Apple and the Arrow* by Mary and Conrad Buff.

2. Have students read the book *The Apple and the Arrow*. Discuss with students how the book is similar to and different from the folktale they read in this unit. For example, the name of Tell's son is Walter in the book, rather than Albert.

TIP If students are interested in music, have them listen to the overture from the opera *William Tell*, particularly the conclusion that may be most familiar to them. Discuss with students how the music reflects the plot of the story and the character traits of the hero William Tell.

Objectives

- Make connections between text and self, text and world, and text to text.
- Compare and contrast plot, setting, and character(s) of texts from different cultures.
- Compare and contrast the themes, settings, and plots of stories written by the same author about the same or similar characters.

Introduce "The Stone-Cutter"

Lesson Overview

[Offline]　　　　　　　　　　　50 minutes

Get Ready	Lesson Introduction
	How to Find Happiness
	Book Walk
	Words to Know
Read	"The Stone-Cutter"
GRAB	Go Read a Book

Big Ideas

▸ Folktales are stories that are passed down from older people to younger people in order to teach important lessons or values.

▸ Active, strong readers employ reading strategies such as making connections between text and self, between and among texts, and between text and the real world.

▸ Folktales help readers understand a culture's values, hopes, and fears.

[Materials]

Supplied

- "The Stone-Cutter," *K¹² Classics for Young Readers, Volume C,* pp. 140–151
- Reading Strategies bookmark

Also Needed

- globe

Story Synopsis

A stone-cutter named Taro is not happy in his work and asks the mountain spirit to make him a rich man. He is granted his wish but still is not happy. Taro continues to wish to be something greater but does not find happiness until he has been a prince, the sun, a cloud, and a stone. Finally Taro asks to be a man again and finds happiness as a stone-cutter once more.

Keywords

folktale – a story, which usually teaches a lesson important to a culture, that is passed down through many generations

setting – when and where a story takes place

[Offline] 50 minutes

Work **together** with students to complete offline Get Ready, Read, and GRAB activities.

Get Ready

Lesson Introduction

Prepare students to read "The Stone-Cutter."

1. Explain to students that before they read "The Stone-Cutter," they will discuss with you
   - ▶ What can make people happy
   - ▶ The setting for the story
   - ▶ Their predictions about the text
   - ▶ Important words to know in the text

2. Tell students that while they read, you will check in to make sure they understand what they are reading.

3. Tell students that after they read, they will answer questions about the story.

> **Objectives**
> - Connect text with prior knowledge.
> - Identify setting(s).
> - Use before-reading strategies.
> - Increase concept and content vocabulary.

How to Find Happiness

Discuss how people might find happiness in work and talk about the setting of the story. Gather the globe.

1. Tell students about something that is work that you enjoy, such as a professional job, a chore around the house, or a hobby that requires effort.

2. Have students tell about something they have to work at but still enjoy, such as an academic subject, a musical instrument, a sport, or a chore.

3. Ask students if they have ever wanted to change places with someone else and have them explain why. If they have never wanted to change places with someone, ask why they think a person might want to do this.

4. Tell students that they are going to read a **folktale** about a man who has trouble finding happiness in his work and wants to change places with someone else. Have students tell what a folktale is.

5. Have students find the story in the book. Have them use the first picture to describe the **setting**.

6. Tell students this story comes from the country of Japan, which is an island nation in Asia. Help students locate Japan on the globe.

Book Walk

Have students lead you through a Book Walk of "The Stone-Cutter." Remind them to use the **title** and **illustrations** to make predictions about what will happen in the story.

Words to Know

Remind students that they will find the Words to Know at the bottoms of the pages in the selection.

Read

"The Stone-Cutter"

Have students read "The Stone-Cutter." Remind students to use the strategies on their Reading Strategies bookmark. For example, they may want to reread parts of the story they find confusing.

➲ **Learning Coach Check-In** This reading assignment should take about 20 minutes. After students finish reading, ask the following questions to assess their comprehension of the selection:

▸ What are some of the reasons that Taro decides he doesn't like being a stone-cutter? Possible answers: It's hot; he has to get up early; he has to climb the mountain; he gets blisters; he gets cuts from the stone chips.

▸ What are some of the things that Taro wishes to become? a rich man, a prince, the sun, a cloud, a rock, a regular person

If students have trouble answering these questions, ask them what reading strategies they used and suggest they reread the selection.

Objectives

- Read literature independently and proficiently.
- Apply information read to answer questions.
- Evaluate reading strategies.

GRAB

Go Read a Book

Have students read a book or magazine of their own choosing for at least 20 minutes. Remind students to use the strategies on their Reading Strategies bookmark before and during reading to help them understand the text.

Objectives

- Read literature independently and proficiently.
- Read a variety of texts for information and pleasure.

Explore "The Stone-Cutter"

Lesson Overview

🖥 〔Online〕 ⏱40 minutes

Check Your Reading	Comprehend "The Stone-Cutter"
Reading for Meaning	Problem and Solution
	What Taro Learns

📄 〔Offline〕 ⏱10 minutes

Making Connections	The Lessons in the Tale
Beyond the Lesson	➕ OPTIONAL: Compare and Contrast Two Tales

〔Materials〕

Supplied
- "The Stone-Cutter," *K¹² Classics for Young Readers, Volume C,* pp. 140–151
- *K¹² Language Arts Activity Book,* pp. LC 117–120

Also Needed
- crayons

Big Ideas

▸ To understand and interpret a story, readers need to understand and describe characters and what they do.
▸ Readers need to understand literary conflicts and their resolutions in order to analyze characters and themes.

[Online] 40 minutes

Students will work **independently** to complete online Check Your Reading and Reading for Meaning activities.

Check Your Reading ....

Comprehend "The Stone-Cutter"

Students will answer questions about "The Stone-Cutter" to demonstrate their literal and inferential comprehension of the story.

> **Objectives**
> - Identify concrete answers to questions.
> - Apply information read to answer questions.

Reading for Meaning ....

Problem and Solution

Students will identify the problems in the story "The Stone-Cutter" and look at how the main character's solutions to his problems cause new problems.

What Taro Learns

Students will examine the lesson that the main character Taro learns when he tries to solve his problems in the story "The Stone-Cutter."

> **Objectives**
> - Identify problems and solutions in a story.
> - Describe characters by what they do, what they say, or what others say about them.
> - Determine theme, moral, or lesson of a work of literature.

[Offline] 🔟 minutes

Work **together** with students to complete the offline Making Connections and Beyond the Lesson activities.

Making Connections ••

The Lessons in the Tale
Students will identify the lessons in "The Stone-Cutter." Turn to pages LC 117–120 in *K¹² Language Arts Activity Book.*

1. Have students read the directions.

2. Have them complete the Activity Book pages.

3. After students write the lesson from "The Stone-Cutter" in their own words, remind them to illustrate their saying.

4. Have students share their lesson advertisement with someone else.

TIP Keep the Activity Book pages in a safe place for students to use later.

Objectives
- Describe characters by what they do, what they say, or what others say about them.
- Make inferences about characters using evidence from the text.
- Explain how theme, message, lesson, or moral is conveyed through details in a text.
- Recognize and explain the meaning of common idioms, adages, and proverbs.
- Write or draw a response that identifies a text-to-self, text-to-world, and/or text-to-text connection.

Making Connections
Explore "The Stone-Cutter"
The Lessons in the Tale

Answer the questions in complete sentences.

1. Taro wishes to be many things. Why does he keep making wishes? Explain your answer.
   Taro keeps wishing because there is always something more powerful than each thing Taro becomes.

2. What does Taro learn about being mighty?
   There is always something stronger than what he is. No one thing is mightier than everything else.

3. Taro makes many physical changes. His greatest change is how he feels. Describe the change in how Taro feels from the beginning of the story to the end.
   At the beginning of the story, Taro is happy being a stone-cutter. Then he becomes unhappy when he sees the rich man. He becomes more and more unhappy each time he changes and tries to become something more powerful. In the end, Taro is content just being a stone-cutter again.

4. Why do Taro's feelings change by the end of the story?
   Students should recognize that Taro has learned that he will never be happy trying to be something he is not and trying to be the most powerful thing there is. He learns to be content with what he has in life.

LANGUAGE ARTS PURPLE **LC 117**

LC 118 LANGUAGE ARTS PURPLE

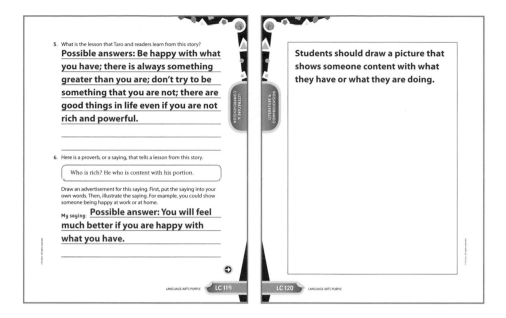

⊕ OPTIONAL: Compare and Contrast Two Tales

This activity is OPTIONAL. It is intended for students who have extra time and would benefit from reading another folktale with a lesson similar to the ones in "The Stone-Cutter." Feel free to skip this activity.

1. Have students read another folktale or fable with lessons similar to "The Stone-Cutter." Some possible tales include the following:

   ▶ "The Three Wishes"
   ▶ "The Fisherman and His Wife"
   ▶ "The Goose and the Golden Eggs"
   ▶ "King Midas"

2. Have students compare and contrast the tale with "The Stone-Cutter." Have them tell the similarities and differences in setting, plot, characters, problems and solutions, and lessons.

Objectives

- Make connections between text and self, text and world, and text to text.
- Compare text from different cultures and time periods.
- Compare and contrast the most important points presented by two texts on the same topic.

Introduce "Aladdin and the Wonderful Lamp"

Lesson Overview

[Offline]　　　　　　　　　　　**50** minutes

Get Ready	Lesson Introduction
	Identify Main Character and Setting
	Book Walk
	Words to Know
Read	"Aladdin and the Wonderful Lamp"
GRAB	Go Read a Book

Advance Preparation

The reading selection is a longer text than many others in this course. If students are struggling or reluctant readers, use the GRAB to continue the assigned reading.

Content Background

This story comes from a collection of tales titled *The Book of a Thousand and One Nights*, also known as the Arabian Nights. The collection is from the Middle East. "Aladdin" is set in Persia, which is the location of modern-day Iran.

Big Ideas

▸ Folktales are stories that are passed down from older people to younger people in order to teach important lessons or values.
▸ Active, strong readers employ reading strategies such as making connections between text and self, between and among texts, and between text and the real world.
▸ Folktales help readers understand a culture's values, hopes, and fears.

Materials

Supplied
- "Aladdin and the Wonderful Lamp," *K¹² Classics for Young Readers, Volume C*, pp. 152–177
- Reading Strategies bookmark

Also Needed
- globe

Story Synopsis

Aladdin is the son of a poor widow. One day an evil magician, pretending to be Aladdin's uncle, sends Aladdin underground to retrieve a magic lamp. Aladdin keeps the lamp, which contains a genie. Aladdin is granted wishes, which he uses to marry the sultan's daughter and build a palace for her. The magician returns and steals the lamp, the princess, and the palace. Aladdin uses a different genie to retrieve everything the magician has stolen and lives happily ever after.

Keywords

folktale – a story, which usually teaches a lesson important to a culture, that is passed down through many generations
main character – an important person, animal, or other being who is central to the plot
setting – when and where a story takes place

[Offline] 50 minutes

Work **together** with students to complete offline Get Ready, Read, and GRAB activities.

Get Ready ....

Lesson Introduction

Prepare students to read "Aladdin and the Wonderful Lamp"

1. Explain to students that before they read "Aladdin and the Wonderful Lamp," they will discuss with you

   ▸ The main character and the setting for the story
   ▸ Their predictions about the text
   ▸ Important words to know in the text

2. Tell students that while they read, you will check in to make sure they understand what they are reading.

3. Tell students that after they read, they will answer questions about the story.

Identify Main Character and Setting

Have students identify the main character and setting of the story. Gather the globe.

1. Tell students they are going to read a **folktale** about a **main character** named Aladdin. If students know a story of Aladdin, have them retell the version they know.

2. Tell students that the **setting** of the story is a place called Persia. Explain that Persia is not a country today, but it was located where the modern-day country of Iran is, in the Middle East. Show students Iran on the globe.

Book Walk

Have students lead you through a Book Walk of "Aladdin and the Wonderful Lamp." Remind them to use the **title** and **illustrations** to make predictions about what will happen in the story.

Words to Know

Remind students that they will find the Words to Know at the bottoms of the pages in the selection.

Read

"Aladdin and the Wonderful Lamp"

Have students read "Aladdin and the Wonderful Lamp." Remind students to use the strategies on their Reading Strategies bookmark. For example, they may need to use context clues to help them understand unfamiliar words.

⮑ **Learning Coach Check-In** This reading assignment should take about 20–25 minutes. After students finish reading, ask the following questions to assess their comprehension of the selection:

- ▶ What is the magician's plan for getting the lamp? He plans to send Aladdin into the tunnel, have Aladdin throw the lamp up to him, and then shut Aladdin underground.
- ▶ What happens instead? The magician shuts the door with Aladdin and the lamp trapped underground.
- ▶ What are some of the things that Aladdin has the Genie of the Lamp bring to him? Answers may include: food, forty baskets of jewels, a purple robe, a white horse, 10,000 gold pieces, a palace.

If students have trouble answering these questions, ask them what reading strategies they used and suggest they reread the selection.

Objectives
- Read literature independently and proficiently.
- Apply information read to answer questions.
- Evaluate reading strategies.

GRAB

Go Read a Book

Have students read a book or magazine of their own choosing for at least 20 minutes. Remind students to use the strategies on their Reading Strategies bookmark before and during reading to help them understand the text.

Objectives
- Read literature independently and proficiently.
- Read a variety of texts for information and pleasure.

Explore "Aladdin and the Wonderful Lamp"

Lesson Overview

🖥️ **【Online】**		**40** minutes
Check Your Reading	Comprehend "Aladdin and the Wonderful Lamp"	
Reading for Meaning	The Hero of the Tale	
	The Villain of the Tale	

📄 **【Offline】**		**10** minutes
Making Connections	The Hero vs. the Villain	
Beyond the Lesson	⊕ OPTIONAL: Compare and Contrast Two Aladdins	

Big Ideas

▸ To understand and interpret a story, readers need to understand and describe characters and what they do.

▸ Readers need to understand literary conflicts and their resolutions in order to analyze characters and themes.

【Materials】

Supplied

- "Aladdin and the Wonderful Lamp," *K¹² Classics for Young Readers, Volume C,* pp. 152–177
- *K¹² Language Arts Activity Book,* pp. LC 121–124

Keywords

folktale – a story, which usually teaches a lesson important to a culture, that is passed down through many generations

hero – a character who must struggle to overcome problems in a story and whose actions and traits are admired by others

problem – an issue a character must solve in a story

solution – how a character solves a problem in a story

trait – a quality of a person or character

villain – a bad or evil character who often works against the hero of a story

[Online] 40 minutes

Students will work **independently** to complete online Check Your Reading and Reading for Meaning activities.

Check Your Reading ....

Comprehend "Aladdin and the Wonderful Lamp"
Students will answer questions about "Aladdin and the Wonderful Lamp" to demonstrate their literal and inferential comprehension of the story.

Objectives
- Identify concrete answers to questions.
- Infer answers to questions.
- Apply information read to answer questions.

Reading for Meaning ....

The Hero of the Tale
Students will look at Aladdin's actions in the story "Aladdin and the Wonderful Lamp" to determine his character traits and recognize why he is the hero of the story.

The Villain of the Tale
Students will look at the actions of the magician to determine his character traits and identify why these traits make him the villain of "Aladdin and the Wonderful Lamp."

Objectives
- Define *hero*.
- Identify the hero of a story.
- Identify problems and solutions in a story.
- Describe characters by what they do, what they say, or what others say about them.
- Describe characters and their traits.
- Define *villain*.
- Identify the villain of a story.
- Identify character traits.

[Offline] ⏱ 10 minutes

Work **together** with students to complete the offline Making Connections and Beyond the Lesson activities.

Making Connections ●●

The Hero vs. the Villain

Students will compare and contrast the hero and the villain in "Aladdin and the Wonderful Lamp." Turn to pages LC 121–124 in *K¹² Language Arts Activity Book*.

1. Have students read the directions.

2. Have them complete the Activity Book pages.

TIP Keep the Activity Book pages in a safe place for students to use later.

Making Connections

Explore "Aladdin and the Wonderful Lamp"

The Hero vs. the Villain

Answer the questions in complete sentences.

1. What are two character traits of Aladdin? Use examples from the story to support each trait.

Answers may include: He is lucky because he accidentally learns there are genies in the lamp and the ring. He is generous because he shares his riches with his mother and wife. He is clever because he knows how to use the genie's powers to get the princess and to steal the lamp and his palace back from the magician.

LANGUAGE ARTS PURPLE | LC 121

---

2. What are two character traits of the magician? Use examples from the story to support each trait.

Answers may include: He is tricky because he lies and says he is Aladdin's uncle and later that he is a merchant trading new lamps. He is cruel because he plans to lock Aladdin in the tunnel. He is selfish and greedy because he steals the lamp, the palace, and the princess from Aladdin.

3. How are Aladdin and the magician similar?

Possible answer: Aladdin and the magician are similar because they both use tricks to get what they want.

LC 122 | LANGUAGE ARTS PURPLE

---

4. Aladdin is the hero and gets what he wants at the end of the story. The magician, who is the villain, fails. How are their traits responsible for what happens? Do you think this is a fair ending?

Answers may include: Aladdin is the hero because he uses tricks for good things, like love or helping others. The magician is the villain because he uses tricks for bad things, like getting all the riches and the princess for himself. Students should state their opinion about whether the ending is fair.

5. How does luck help Aladdin in this story? Describe two times when Aladdin is lucky.

Possible answers: Aladdin is lucky when he finds a genie in the magician's ring. He is lucky when he finds a genie in the magic lamp. He uses both genies to bring him things he wants, such as food, jewels, and a palace.

LANGUAGE ARTS PURPLE | LC 123

---

6. How is Aladdin rewarded for his character traits at the end of the story?

Possible answer: He becomes sultan. He is still married to the princess. He still has the magic ring and lamp.

7. What lessons do you think Aladdin learns?

Answers may include: Don't trust everyone. Be kind and giving, and you will be rewarded. Be smart, and you will be rewarded. Don't be afraid to ask for what you want.

8. What qualities were important to the people who told this tale?

Answers will vary, but students may say that the people who told this tale admired intelligence, kindness, and bravery because these are Aladdin's qualities. They may also say that being lucky was important to the people who told this tale.

LC 124 | LANGUAGE ARTS PURPLE

Objectives

- Describe characters by what they do, what they say, or what others say about them.
- Compare and contrast characters in a literary selection.
- Determine the theme, moral, or lesson of a work of literature.
- Explain how theme, message, lesson, or moral is conveyed through details in a text.
- State an opinion.
- Provide reasons that support an opinion.

Beyond the Lesson

⊕ OPTIONAL: Compare and Contrast Two Aladdins

This activity is OPTIONAL. It is intended for students who have extra time and would benefit from comparing the folktale "Aladdin and the Wonderful Lamp" to another story of Aladdin they have read or seen. Feel free to skip this activity.

1. Ask students if they have read another tale of Aladdin in a book or if they have seen a movie version of the story.

2. If students know another Aladdin story, have them summarize the tale.

3. Have students compare and contrast "Aladdin and the Wonderful Lamp" with the other version they have read or seen. Have them tell the similarities and differences in setting, plot, characters, problems and solutions, and lessons.

> **Objectives**
> - Make connections between text and self, text and world, and text to text.
> - Compare text from different cultures and time periods.
> - Compare and contrast the most important points and details on two texts on the same topic.

Reflections on Folktales from Many Lands (A)

Lesson Overview

[Offline]　　　　　　　　　　50 minutes

Get Ready	Lesson Introduction
	Review the Heroes of the Tales
Putting It All Together	Write an Acceptance Speech

Advance Preparation

Have students gather their completed analyses of the heroes of the tales on pages LC 109–111 (What Peter Teaches Us), 113–116 (The Hero vs. the Villain), 117–120 (The Lessons in the Tale), and 121–124 (The Hero vs. the Villain) in *K¹² Language Arts Activity Book*.

Big Ideas

- To understand and interpret a story, readers need to understand and describe characters and what they do.
- Competent writers rely on a repertoire of strategies when planning, composing, and revising their texts.

[Materials]

Supplied

- "The Leak in the Dike," "William Tell," "The Stone-Cutter," "Aladdin and the Wonderful Lamp," *K¹² Classics for Young Readers, Volume C*, pp. 126–177
- *K¹² Language Arts Activity Book*, pp. LC 109–111, 113–127

Keywords

hero – a character who must struggle to overcome problems in a story and whose actions and traits are admired by others

trait – a quality of a person or character

[Offline] 50 minutes

Work **together** with students to complete the offline Get Ready and Putting It All Together activities.

Get Ready

Lesson Introduction

Prepare students for assigning awards to the heroes of the folktales in this unit and writing an acceptance speech for one of the award winners. Explain to students that they are going to complete an activity in which they give awards to the heroes of the folktales they read in this unit. They will begin by discussing with you the actions and traits of the heroes of these tales.

> ### Objectives
> - Identify the hero of a story.
> - Describe characters and their traits.
> - Describe characters by what they do, what they say, or what others say about them.

Review the Heroes of the Tales

Review names of the heroes in the folktales in this unit and have students describe each one.

1. Have students name the **heroes** in the **folktales** in this unit: "The Leak in the Dike," "William Tell," "The Stone-Cutter," and "Aladdin and the Wonderful Lamp." Peter is the hero of "The Leak in the Dike"; William Tell is the hero of "William Tell"; Taro is the hero of "The Stone-Cutter"; Aladdin is the hero of "Aladdin and the Wonderful Lamp."

2. Have students describe each hero.

   ▸ Peter in "The Leak in the Dike" Answers may include: Peter is brave, responsible, and kind.
   ▸ William Tell in "William Tell" Answers may include: William Tell is brave, strong, skillful, and honest.
   ▸ Taro in "The Stone-Cutter" Answers may include: Taro is unhappy in each of his changes, but he is content at the end of the story.
   ▸ Aladdin in "Aladdin and the Wonderful Lamp" Answers may include: Aladdin is lucky, clever, and unafraid to ask for what he wants.

Putting It All Together

✏️ Write an Acceptance Speech

Students will demonstrate their understanding of the heroes in the folktales in this unit and the characteristics of those heroes. Gather the completed analyses of the heroes and turn to pages LC 125–127 in *K¹² Language Arts Activity Book*.

1. Have students read the directions. Remind them that they are to use their completed Activity Book pages about the folktales in the unit for ideas to complete this new activity.

2. Tell students they are going to complete this activity over two lessons.

   ▶ In this lesson, they will give an award to each hero in the unit. Then they will write an acceptance speech for one of the heroes.
   ▶ In the next lesson, they will deliver their acceptance speech to an audience.

   ➲ **Learning Coach Check-In** Check in with students after about 40 minutes to see if they have completed the assignment.

> **Objectives**
> - Describe characters by what they do, what they say, or what others say about them.
> - Identify descriptions that support comprehension.
> - Distinguish own opinion from that of the narrator or those of the characters.
> - Organize ideas.
> - Identify supporting information.
> - Write a speech.
> - Practice a presentation.

Making Connections

Explore "The Leak in the Dike"

What Peter Teaches Us

Write examples from the story that support each of Peter's character traits given in the table.

Peter is kind.	Peter is responsible.	Peter is brave.
He visits the blind man.	He returns home when his mother tells him to. He plugs the leak in the dike.	He keeps his finger in the dike even though he's cold and numb and alone.

LANGUAGE ARTS PURPLE LC 109

Answer the questions in complete sentences.

1. Do you think it is important to the story that Peter is a boy and not a grown man? Why or why not?

   Answers will vary. Some students may say it's important that Peter is a boy because it makes him seem even braver for what he does. Others will say Peter's age does not matter because the point is only that Peter decides to stop the leak.

2. Why do you think Peter put his finger in the dike instead of going for help?

   Answers will vary. Some students may say that Peter thought the problem needed a solution right away and there wasn't time to get help. Others may say that Peter just acted before he thought about other solutions.

LC 110 LANGUAGE ARTS PURPLE

---

3. Do you agree with Peter's choice to put his finger in the dike and stay there? Why or why not?

   Answers will vary, but students should explain why they agree or disagree with Peter's solution to the problem. They may realize that his choice is dangerous.

4. A folktale teaches lessons that are important to a culture. What lessons do you think the people of Holland wanted to teach through this story?

   Answers may include: Take action when you see a problem that needs to be solved. It's important to be a brave, responsible, and kind person. Think of the well-being of other people besides yourself.

5. Describe a time when you had to be brave and responsible, even when it was hard.

   Answers will vary.

LANGUAGE ARTS PURPLE LC 111

Making Connections

Explore "William Tell"
The Hero vs. the Villain

Answer the questions in complete sentences.

1. What are two character traits of William Tell? Use examples from the story to support each trait.

Answers may include: He is brave because he shoots the apple off Albert's head and he jumps from the boat to escape. He is strong because he steers the boat to shore in the storm. He is skillful because he is able to shoot the apple from a far distance. He is honest or true because he tells Gessler that he took a second arrow to shoot Gessler.

2. What are two character traits of Gessler? Use examples from the story to support each trait.

Answers may include: He is cruel because he makes William Tell shoot an apple off his son's head. He is stern or hard because he sends Tell to prison for life.

3. Gessler is strong, but his strength is different from Tell's. How does Gessler show strength or power in the story, and how is his way different from Tell's?

Students should recognize that Gessler shows strength through the power of his office as ruler and by being cruel. He punishes people without reason in ways that are very harsh. Tell uses his strength for good.

4. How does William Tell make Gessler feel? Why do you think Gessler feels this way about Tell?

Possible answer: Gessler feels angry at Tell and might be jealous of him. Students should recognize that Gessler feels this way because Tell has qualities that Gessler doesn't have: bravery, skill, physical strength, and honesty.

5. How is William Tell like Peter in "The Leak in the Dike"? Give examples from the stories to support your answer.

Possible answer: Tell is like Peter because he is brave and takes on challenges even when they are difficult. Tell shoots the apple, and Peter puts his finger in the hole. Both characters are also responsible and concerned about others. Tell worries about hurting Albert, and Peter worries about what will happen to the people of Holland if the dike breaks.

6. The folktale "William Tell" comes from the country of Switzerland. What inferences can you make about the traits that the Swiss people value?

Possible answer: The Swiss people think that bravery, honesty, skill, and strength are important because these are the qualities they give to the hero William Tell.

7. The story of William Tell is known all over the world. Why do you think his tale is so famous?

Answers will vary, but students may say that the story of Tell is famous because he shoots the apple from his own son's head from far away, which is a very difficult thing to do. They may also say that the story is famous because Tell stands up to a tyrant and has qualities that many people and cultures admire.

Making Connections

Explore "The Stone-Cutter"
The Lessons in the Tale

Answer the questions in complete sentences.

1. Taro wishes to be many things. Why does he keep making wishes? Explain your answer.

Taro keeps wishing because there is always something more powerful than each thing Taro becomes.

2. What does Taro learn about being mighty?

There is always something stronger than what he is. No one thing is mightier than everything else.

3. Taro makes many physical changes. His greatest change is how he feels. Describe the change in how Taro feels from the beginning of the story to the end.

At the beginning of the story, Taro is happy being a stone-cutter. Then he becomes unhappy when he sees the rich man. He becomes more and more unhappy each time he changes and tries to become something more powerful. In the end, Taro is content just being a stone-cutter again.

4. Why do Taro's feelings change by the end of the story?

Students should recognize that Taro has learned that he will never be happy trying to be something he is not and trying to be the most powerful thing there is. He learns to be content with what he has in life.

5. What is the lesson that Taro and readers learn from this story?

Possible answers: Be happy with what you have; there is always something greater than you are; don't try to be something that you are not; there are good things in life even if you are not rich and powerful.

6. Here is a proverb, or a saying, that tells a lesson from this story.

> Who is rich? He who is content with his portion.

Draw an advertisement for this saying. First, put the saying into your own words. Then, illustrate the saying. For example, you could show someone being happy at work or at home.

My saying: **Possible answer: You will feel much better if you are happy with what you have.**

Students should draw a picture that shows someone content with what they have or what they are doing.

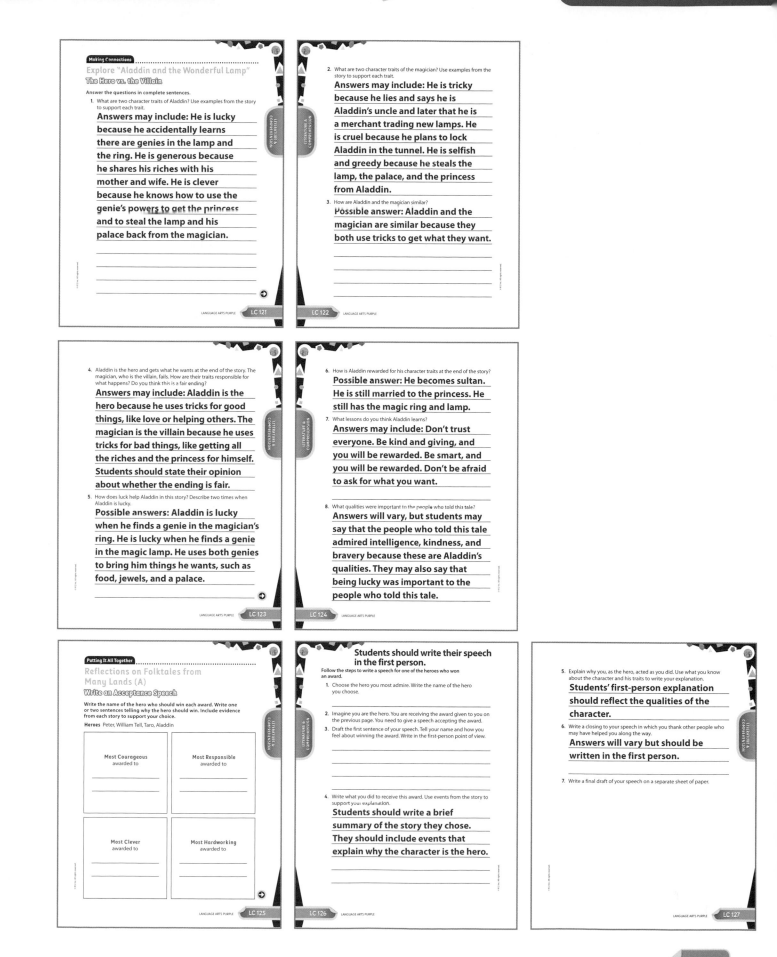

Making Connections

Explore "Aladdin and the Wonderful Lamp"
The Hero vs. the Villain

Answer the questions in complete sentences.

1. What are two character traits of Aladdin? Use examples from the story to support each trait.

Answers may include: He is lucky because he accidentally learns there are genies in the lamp and the ring. He is generous because he shares his riches with his mother and wife. He is clever because he knows how to use the genie's powers to get the princess and to steal the lamp and his palace back from the magician.

2. What are two character traits of the magician? Use examples from the story to support each trait.

Answers may include: He is tricky because he lies and says he is Aladdin's uncle and later that he is a merchant trading new lamps. He is cruel because he plans to lock Aladdin in the tunnel. He is selfish and greedy because he steals the lamp, the palace, and the princess from Aladdin.

3. How are Aladdin and the magician similar?

Possible answer: Aladdin and the magician are similar because they both use tricks to get what they want.

4. Aladdin is the hero and gets what he wants at the end of the story. The magician, who is the villain, fails. How are their traits responsible for what happens? Do you think this is a fair ending?

Answers may include: Aladdin is the hero because he uses tricks for good things, like love or helping others. The magician is the villain because he uses tricks for bad things, like getting all the riches and the princess for himself. Students should state their opinion about whether the ending is fair.

5. How does luck help Aladdin in this story? Describe two times when Aladdin is lucky.

Possible answers: Aladdin is lucky when he finds a genie in the magician's ring. He is lucky when he finds a genie in the magic lamp. He uses both genies to bring him things he wants, such as food, jewels, and a palace.

6. How is Aladdin rewarded for his character traits at the end of the story?

Possible answer: He becomes sultan. He is still married to the princess. He still has the magic ring and lamp.

7. What lessons do you think Aladdin learns?

Answers may include: Don't trust everyone. Be kind and giving, and you will be rewarded. Be smart, and you will be rewarded. Don't be afraid to ask for what you want.

8. What qualities were important to the people who told this tale?

Answers will vary, but students may say that the people who told this tale admired intelligence, kindness, and bravery because these are Aladdin's qualities. They may also say that being lucky was important to the people who told this tale.

Putting It All Together

Reflections on Folktales from Many Lands (A)
Write an Acceptance Speech

Write the name of the hero who should win each award. Write one or two sentences telling why the hero should win. Include evidence from each story to support your choice.

Heroes Peter, William Tell, Taro, Aladdin

| Most Courageous awarded to | Most Responsible awarded to |
| Most Clever awarded to | Most Hardworking awarded to |

Students should write their speech in the first person.

Follow the steps to write a speech for one of the heroes who won an award.

1. Choose the hero you most admire. Write the name of the hero you choose.

2. Imagine you are the hero. You are receiving the award given to you on the previous page. You need to give a speech accepting the award.

3. Draft the first sentence of your speech. Tell your name and how you feel about winning the award. Write in the first-person point of view.

4. Write what you did to receive this award. Use events from the story to support your explanation.

Students should write a brief summary of the story they chose. They should include events that explain why the character is the hero.

5. Explain why you, as the hero, acted as you did. Use what you know about the character and his traits to write your explanation.

Students' first-person explanation should reflect the qualities of the character.

6. Write a closing to your speech in which you thank other people who may have helped you along the way.

Answers will vary but should be written in the first person.

7. Write a final draft of your speech on a separate sheet of paper.

Reflections on Folktales from Many Lands (B)

Lesson Overview

📄 [Offline]   ⏱ 40 minutes

Get Ready	Lesson Introduction
	What Makes an Effective Speech?
Putting It All Together	Give an Effective Speech

🖥 [Online]   varies

More Practice	Review the Skills
Read	Read Fluently "The Brown Horse"
Performance Review	Fluency Check

[Materials]

Supplied

- "The Leak in the Dike," "William Tell," "The Stone-Cutter," "Aladdin and the Wonderful Lamp," *K¹² Classics for Young Readers, Volume C,* pp. 126–177
- *K¹² Language Arts Activity Book,* pp. LC 125–127, 129–130
- Putting It All Together Assessment Checklist (printout)
- "The Brown Horse" (printout)
- Fluency Performance Checklist (printout)

Also Needed

- stopwatch

Keywords

hero – a character who must struggle to overcome problems in a story and whose actions and traits are admired by others

trait – a quality of a person or character

Advance Preparation

Have students gather their completed hero awards and rough draft of an acceptance speech on pages LC 125–127 (Write an Acceptance Speech) in *K¹² Language Arts Activity Book*. Ideally students should present their speech to their peers, but if necessary you can have them present the speech to you.

Big Ideas

Good public speakers speak clearly, make eye contact, and use appropriate expression for their subject matter and audience.

[Offline] 40 minutes

Work **together** with students to complete the offline Get Ready and Putting It All Together activities.

Get Ready

Lesson Introduction

Prepare students for giving an acceptance speech on the part of one of the heroes from the unit readings. Tell students they are going to give their hero's acceptance speech. They will begin by discussing with you

- ▸ The awards they gave to the heroes
- ▸ Their favorite hero
- ▸ The qualities of an effective speech

> **Objectives**
> - Identify the hero of a story.
> - Describe characters and their traits.
> - Describe characters by what they do, what they say, or what others say about them.

What Makes an Effective Speech?

Discuss the heroes in the folktales from this unit and review the qualities of an effective speech.

1. Have students share the awards they gave the **heroes** of the stories.

2. Have them tell which hero is their favorite and why.

3. Remind students that they will be giving their acceptance speech as though they are one of the heroes from the unit. Review the qualities of an effective speech:

   - ▸ Speak clearly and loudly enough for the audience to hear, but not so loudly that you are shouting.
   - ▸ Make eye contact with the audience. Even if you are reading, look up often to speak to your audience directly.
   - ▸ Pause at the end of key ideas or sections of your speech to let the audience know when you've said something important or when you are switching to a new idea.
   - ▸ Use appropriate expression for the subject matter and audience. Your tone of voice and facial expressions should match the topic of the speech. For example, since this speech is for accepting an award, the hero should sound pleased and thankful.
   - ▸ Use language appropriate for your character and your audience. You are delivering a speech as a character. Speak in the way you think the character would speak.

Putting It All Together

Give an Effective Speech

Students will give an acceptance speech in the role of one of the heroes from this unit. Gather the rough draft of an acceptance speech and turn to pages LC 129 and 130 in *K¹² Language Arts Activity Book*.

1. Give students the Give an Effective Speech page and have them practice the speech on their own. Remind them to use the checklist as a guide for how they should present their speech.

2. If there are peers who will listen to the speech, give them the Tell Me About My Speech page.

3. Have students give their speech for the audience. If there are peers present, have them share their Tell Me About My Speech page with students.

4. When students have completed their speech, use the materials and instructions in the online lesson to evaluate students' work.

5. Enter the answers (Yes or No) for each line of the assessment checklist online.

TIP Students may want to cut out and hold up their award as they give their speech. They may also want to include a prop or a costume to help them play the part of the character.

Objectives

- Identify the hero of a story.
- Describe characters and their traits.
- Describe characters by what they do, what they say, or what others say about them.
- Speak clearly.
- Use public speaking techniques.
- Deliver a presentation as a response to literature.
- Use the first-person point of view.

Putting It All Together

Reflections on Folktales from Many Lands (B)

Give an Effective Speech

Follow this checklist to give your acceptance speech.

☐ Speak clearly and loudly so that everyone in the audience can hear you.

☐ Make eye contact. Look up often to address your audience directly.

☐ Pause at key points in your speech, such as after you've said something important or when you are switching to a new idea.

☐ Use a tone of voice, language, and facial expressions that fit your subject and audience.

☐ Use language that suits the character you are pretending to be.

LANGUAGE ARTS PURPLE — LC 129

Putting It All Together

Reflections on Folktales from Many Lands (B)

Tell Me About My Speech

Have another person listen to your acceptance speech and answer the questions.

1. Did the speaker speak as the character in the story?
   A. Yes   B. No

2. Was the speaker loud and clear?
   A. Yes   B. No

3. Did the speaker make eye contact with the audience?
   A. Yes   B. No

4. Did the speaker pause at key points in the speech?
   A. Yes   B. No

5. Were the speaker's manner, language, and tone appropriate to the subject and audience?
   A. Yes   B. No

6. How might the speaker improve next time?

   _____

   _____

   _____

   _____

   _____

LC 130 — LANGUAGE ARTS PURPLE

 **varies**

Students will work **independently** to complete the online More Practice activity.

More Practice

Review the Skills
If students scored less than 80 percent or had difficulty meeting the objectives of the Putting It All Together activity, have them go online for more practice.

Objectives
- Identify the hero of a story.
- Identify problem and solution.
- Identify choices that a character makes and their consequences.
- Determine the theme, moral, or lesson of a work of literature.

Read

Read Fluently "The Brown Horse"
Students will read aloud and record "The Brown Horse." The purpose of this activity is to assess students' oral reading and fluency. Have students read the passage aloud and record their reading. Note that this is a new passage to them, and there is no audio for them to hear a model reading. This will allow the recording to accurately reflect their fluency.

Objectives
- Read poetry and prose aloud.
- Read aloud grade-level text with appropriate automaticity, prosody, accuracy, and rate.

Performance Review

Fluency Check

Evaluate students' performance on the fluency reading. Gather the stopwatch and printout of "The Brown Horse."

1. Listen to students' recordings and use the Fluency Performance Checklist to review fluency and the printout to track performance.

2. Keep the completed checklist so you can review students' progress over time.

3. Follow the advice on the checklist regarding appropriate interventions for students who do not receive high scores on the Fluency Performance Checklist. If students aren't able to score above 12 points on the Fluency Performance Checklist, it is advisable to seek outside help from a teaching professional or reading specialist to improve students' reading fluency.

Reward: If students score 80 percent or more on the Putting It All Together activity and 18 or more on the Fluency Check, add a sticker for this unit on the My Accomplishments chart. If students did not score 80 percent or more on the Putting It All Together activity and 18 or more on the Fluency Check, work with them to revise their writing and practice their fluency until they attain those scores and then add a sticker to the My Accomplishments chart.

Objectives

- Read poetry and prose aloud.
- Read aloud grade-level text with appropriate automaticity, prosody, accuracy, and rate.

Critical Skills Practice 5

Unit Focus

In this unit, students will read nonfiction, poetry, fiction, and paired passages. They will review skills for answering multiple choice questions about those readings in a format similar to standardized tests. Students will also practice writing a response to a prompt.

Unit Plan		[Offline]	[Online]
Lesson 1	Nonfiction Passages (E)		50 minutes
Lesson 2	Poetry (C)		50 minutes
Lesson 3	Paired Passages (B)		50 minutes
Lesson 4	Fiction Passages (G)		50 minutes
Lesson 5	Write About Paired Passages	20 minutes	30 minutes
Lesson 6	Unit Checkpoint	50 minutes	varies
Lesson 7	Your Choice	50 minutes	

Nonfiction Passages (E)

Lesson Overview

Materials

Online — 50 minutes

Get Ready	Audience and Author's Purpose
Learn	Types of Questions
Try It	Practice Passage and Questions

Supplied

- Types of Questions (optional printout)
- Practice Passage and Questions (optional printout)

Big Ideas

- ▶ Narrative and expository text differ significantly—for example, in structure, content, and purpose.
- ▶ Readers need to synthesize, draw conclusions about, and interpret what they have read.
- ▶ Readers must understand the relationship between main idea and supporting details.

Keywords

audience – a writer's readers

author's purpose – the reason the author wrote a text: to entertain, to inform, to express an opinion, or to persuade

conclusion – a decision made about something not stated, using information provided and what is already known

main idea – the most important point the author makes; it may be stated or unstated

supporting details – the sentences that give more information about the main idea or topic sentence

 **50 minutes**

Students will work online to complete Get Ready, Learn, and Try It activities.

Get Ready

Audience and Author's Purpose

Students will review how to identify the intended audience for a text, the author's purpose or reason the author wrote the text, and the main idea.

Objectives
- Define *author's purpose*.
- Determine purpose and audience.
- Identify main idea.

Learn

Types of Questions

Students will learn how to answer questions related to a nonfiction passage by reading a work of nonfiction and working through several items.

TIP If students are not comfortable reading the passage for this activity online, print Types of Questions and have students read the printout.

Objectives
- Determine purpose and audience.
- Identify the main idea in a text.
- Recognize that details support the topic sentence.
- Identify the main idea and supporting details either stated or inferred.
- Draw conclusions from text.

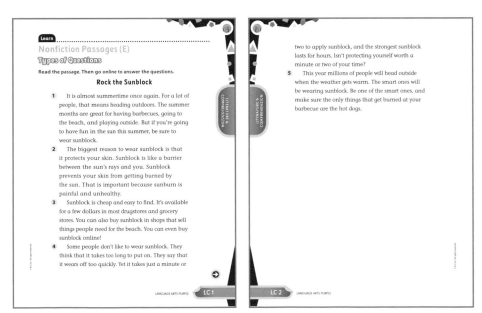

Try It

Practice Passage and Questions

Students will demonstrate their comprehension and ability to respond to questions similar to those found on standardized tests. They will read a nonfiction passage and answer multiple choice questions about it.

TIP If students are not comfortable reading the passage for this activity online, print Practice Passage and Questions and have students read the printout.

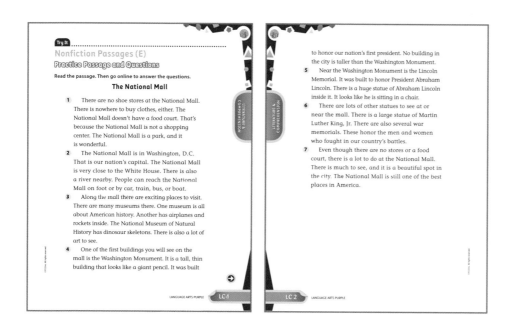

Try It

Nonfiction Passages (E)
Practice Passage and Questions

Read the passage. Then go online to answer the questions.

The National Mall

1. There are no shoe stores at the National Mall. There is nowhere to buy clothes, either. The National Mall doesn't have a food court. That's because the National Mall is not a shopping center. The National Mall is a park, and it is wonderful.

2. The National Mall is in Washington, D.C. That is our nation's capital. The National Mall is very close to the White House. There is also a river nearby. People can reach the National Mall on foot or by car, train, bus, or boat.

3. Along the mall there are exciting places to visit. There are many museums there. One museum is all about American history. Another has airplanes and rockets inside. The National Museum of Natural History has dinosaur skeletons. There is also a lot of art to see.

4. One of the first buildings you will see on the mall is the Washington Monument. It is a tall, thin building that looks like a giant pencil. It was built

to honor our nation's first president. No building in the city is taller than the Washington Monument.

5. Near the Washington Monument is the Lincoln Memorial. It was built to honor President Abraham Lincoln. There is a huge statue of Abraham Lincoln inside it. It looks like he is sitting in a chair.

6. There are lots of other statues to see at or near the mall. There is a large statue of Martin Luther King, Jr. There are also several war memorials. These honor the men and women who fought in our country's battles.

7. Even though there are no stores or a food court, there is a lot to do at the National Mall. There is much to see, and it is a beautiful spot in the city. The National Mall is still one of the best places in America.

LANGUAGE ARTS PURPLE **LC 1**

LC 2 LANGUAGE ARTS PURPLE

Poetry (C)

Lesson Overview

Online   **50** minutes

Get Ready	Figurative Language: Identify Similes
Learn	Types of Questions
Try It	Practice Poem and Questions

Big Ideas

▸ Poems are different from prose in structure and content. They are generally organized in lines and often contain rhymes.

▸ The use of imagery and sensory language creates detailed pictures in the reader's mind, so the reader can understand and appreciate the ideas and feelings the writer conveys.

Materials

Supplied

- Types of Questions (optional printout)
- Practice Poem and Questions (optional printout)

Keywords

figurative language – words that describe something by comparing it to something completely different
Example: Rain fell in buckets and the streets looked like rivers.

rhyme scheme – the pattern of rhymes made by the last sounds in the lines of a poem, shown by a different letter of the alphabet to represent each rhyme

simile – a comparison between two things using the word *like* or *as*
Example: I didn't hear him come in because he was as quiet as a mouse.

speaker – the narrator of a poem

theme – the author's message or big idea

[Online] 50 minutes

Students will work online to complete Get Ready, Learn, and Try It activities.

Get Ready

Figurative Language: Identify Similes

Students will review what figurative language is and focus on similes, figurative language that makes a comparison between two unlike things using the word *like* or *as*.

> **Objectives**
> - Define *figurative language*.
> - Distinguish between literal and figurative language.
> - Define *simile*.

Learn

Types of Questions

Students will learn how to answer questions related to poetry. They will read a poem and work through questions on rhyme scheme, speaker, figurative language, simile, and theme.

TIP If students are not comfortable reading the poem for this activity online, print Types of Questions and have students read the printout.

> **Objectives**
> - Identify rhyme scheme.
> - Identify speaker.
> - Distinguish between literal and figurative language.
> - Identify similes.
> - Identify theme.

Learn

Poetry (C)

Types of Questions

Read the poem. Then go online to answer the questions.

Arrival

by Emma Long

Our trip to Mars took one week.
Our leader's name was Captain Meek.
And when our ship at last did land,
It kicked up loads of dark red sand.

Down we stepped from our trusty craft,
And Captain Meek and I both laughed.
We were the first to walk on Mars.
Our faces lit up like shining stars.

We felt like Columbus when he did view
The New World he found in 1492.
Then, one by one, we hugged the crew.
And shouted out, "Dreams do come true!"

LANGUAGE ARTS PURPLE   LC 1

Try It

Practice Poem and Questions

Students will show their comprehension and ability to respond to questions based on poetry by reading a poem and then answering questions about it.

TIP If students are not comfortable reading the poem for this activity online, print Practice Poem and Questions and have students read the printout.

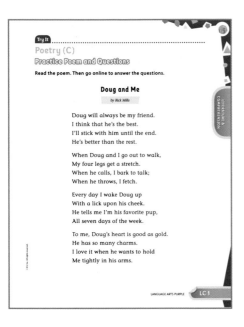

Objectives
- Identify rhyme scheme.
- Identify speaker.
- Distinguish between literal and figurative language.
- Identify similes.
- Identify theme.

Paired Passages (B)

Lesson Overview

[Online]   50 minutes

Get Ready	How to Make a Generalization
Learn	Types of Questions
Try It	Practice Passages and Questions

Big Ideas

- ▶ Nonfiction texts differ from fiction texts in that they describe real or true things in life, rather than things made up by the author.
- ▶ Readers must understand the relationship between main idea and supporting details.
- ▶ Signal words—such as *before, consequently, compare/contrast, therefore*—are a guide to understanding the relationship between and among ideas.

[Materials]

Supplied

- Types of Questions (optional printout)
- Practice Passages and Questions (optional printout)

Keywords

generalization – a statement meant to describe a whole group
Example: Everyone loves a parade.

 **50 minutes**

Students will work online to complete Get Ready, Learn, and Try It activities.

Get Ready

How to Make a Generalization

Students will learn what a generalization is and how to make a generalization about a text.

> **Objectives**
> - Define *generalization*.
> - Make generalizations from text.

Learn

Types of Questions

Students will learn how to answer questions related to paired nonfiction passages by reading paired passages and working through several items about both.

TIP If students are not comfortable reading the paired passages for this activity online, print Types of Questions and have students read the printout.

> **Objectives**
> - Identify problem and solution.
> - Identify cause and effect.
> - Compare and contrast using evidence from the text.
> - Identify opinions.
> - Make generalizations from text.

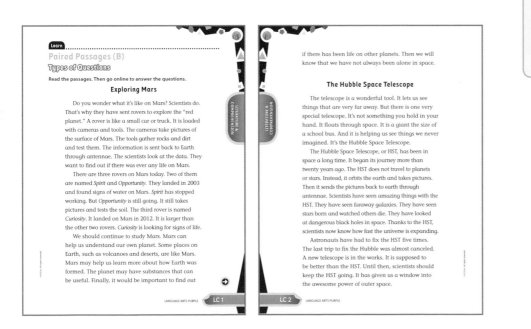

Learn

Paired Passages (B)

Types of Questions

Read the passages. Then go online to answer the questions.

Exploring Mars

Do you wonder what it's like on Mars? Scientists do. That's why they have sent rovers to explore the "red planet." A rover is like a small car or truck. It is loaded with cameras and tools. The cameras take pictures of the surface of Mars. The tools gather rocks and dirt and test them. The information is sent back to Earth through antennae. The scientists look at the data. They want to find out if there was ever any life on Mars.

There are three rovers on Mars today. Two of them are named *Spirit* and *Opportunity*. They landed in 2003 and found signs of water on Mars. *Spirit* has stopped working. But *Opportunity* is still going. It still takes pictures and tests the soil. The third rover is named *Curiosity*. It landed on Mars in 2012. It is larger than the other two rovers. *Curiosity* is looking for signs of life.

We should continue to study Mars. Mars can help us understand our own planet. Some places on Earth, such as volcanoes and deserts, are like Mars. Mars may help us learn more about how Earth was formed. The planet may have substances that can be useful. Finally, it would be important to find out

if there has been life on other planets. Then we will know that we have not always been alone in space.

The Hubble Space Telescope

The telescope is a wonderful tool. It lets us see things that are very far away. But there is one very special telescope. It's not something you hold in your hand. It floats through space. It is a giant the size of a school bus. And it is helping us see things we never imagined. It's the Hubble Space Telescope.

The Hubble Space Telescope, or HST, has been in space a long time. It began its journey more than twenty years ago. The HST does not travel to planets or stars. Instead, it orbits the earth and takes pictures. Then it sends the pictures back to earth through antennae. Scientists have seen amazing things with the HST. They have seen faraway galaxies. They have seen stars born and watched others die. They have looked at dangerous black holes in space. Thanks to the HST, scientists now know how fast the universe is expanding.

Astronauts have had to fix the HST five times. The last trip to fix the Hubble was almost canceled. A new telescope is in the works. It is supposed to be better than the HST. Until then, scientists should keep the HST going. It has given us a window into the awesome power of outer space.

LANGUAGE ARTS PURPLE   LC 1   LC 2   LANGUAGE ARTS PURPLE

Try It ∙∙∙

Practice Passages and Questions

Students will demonstrate their comprehension and ability to respond to questions based on paired nonfiction passages by reading paired passages and then answering questions about them.

TIP If students are not comfortable reading the paired passages for this activity online, print Practice Passages and Questions and have students read the printout.

Objectives
- Identify problem and solution.
- Identify cause and effect.
- Compare and contrast using evidence from the text.
- Identify opinions.
- Make generalizations from text.

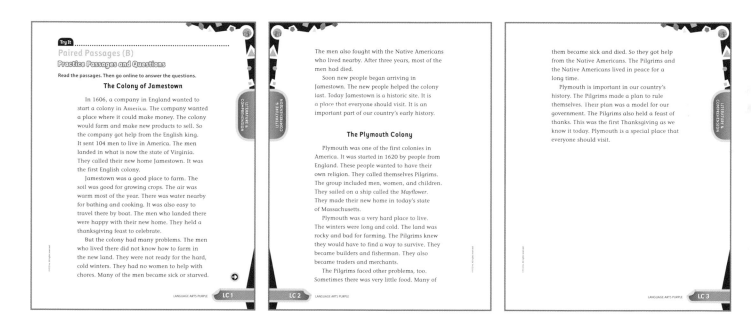

Paired Passages (B)
Practice Passages and Questions

Read the passages. Then go online to answer the questions.

The Colony of Jamestown

In 1606, a company in England wanted to start a colony in America. The company wanted a place where it could make money. The colony would farm and make new products to sell. So the company got help from the English king. It sent 104 men to live in America. They landed in what is now the state of Virginia. They called their new home Jamestown. It was the first English colony.

Jamestown was a good place to farm. The soil was good for growing crops. The air was warm most of the year. There was water nearby for bathing and cooking. It was also easy to travel there by boat. The men who landed there were happy with their new home. They held a thanksgiving feast to celebrate.

But the colony had many problems. The men who lived there did not know how to farm in the new land. They were not ready for the hard, cold winters. They had no women to help with chores. Many of the men became sick or starved.

The men also fought with the Native Americans who lived nearby. After three years, most of the men had died.

Soon new people began arriving in Jamestown. The new people helped the colony last. Today Jamestown is a historic site. It is a place that everyone should visit. It is an important part of our country's early history.

The Plymouth Colony

Plymouth was one of the first colonies in America. It was started in 1620 by people from England. These people wanted to have their own religion. They called themselves Pilgrims. The group included men, women, and children. They sailed on a ship called the *Mayflower*. They made their new home in today's state of Massachusetts.

Plymouth was a very hard place to live. The winters were long and cold. The land was rocky and bad for farming. The Pilgrims knew they would have to find a way to survive. They became builders and fisherman. They also became traders and merchants.

The Pilgrims faced other problems, too. Sometimes there was very little food. Many of

them became sick and died. So they got help from the Native Americans. The Pilgrims and the Native Americans lived in peace for a long time.

Plymouth is important in our country's history. The Pilgrims made a plan to rule themselves. Their plan was a model for our government. The Pilgrims also held a feast of thanks. This was the first Thanksgiving as we know it today. Plymouth is a special place that everyone should visit.

LANGUAGE ARTS PURPLE   LC 1

LC 2   LANGUAGE ARTS PURPLE

LANGUAGE ARTS PURPLE   LC 3

Fiction Passages (G)

Lesson Overview

[Online]   50 minutes

Get Ready	First-Person Narrator
Learn	Types of Questions
Try It	Practice Passages and Questions

Big Ideas

▶ The point of view that a story is told from determines how much information readers have about plot events and characters' feelings.

▶ Readers need to be able to sequence, summarize, and articulate the main idea.

▶ To understand and interpret a story, readers need to understand and describe characters and what they do.

[Materials]

Supplied

- Types of Questions (optional printout)
- Practice Passage and Questions (optional printout)

Keywords

author's purpose – the reason the author wrote a text: to entertain, to inform, to express an opinion, or to persuade

cause – the reason something happens

effect – the result of a cause

first-person point of view – the telling of a story by a character in that story, using pronouns such as *I*, *me*, and *we*

narrator – the teller of a story

sequence – the order in which things happen

third-person point of view – the telling of a story by someone outside of the action, using the third-person pronouns *he*, *she*, and *they*

trait – a quality of a person or character

[Online] 50 minutes

Students will work online to complete Get Ready, Learn, and Try It activities.

Get Ready

First-Person Narrator

Students will review how to identify a first-person narrator in a fiction passage and describe how the narrator's perspective affects the story.

Objectives
- Define *first-person point of view*.
- Define *third-person point of view*.
- Identify first person narrator(s).
- Describe the effect point of view has on a story.

Learn

Types of Questions

Students will learn how to answer questions related to a fiction passage by reading a passage and working through several items.

TIP If students are not comfortable reading the fiction passage for this activity online, print Types of Questions and have students read the printout.

Objectives
- Identify and infer cause-and-effect relationships and draw conclusions.
- Sequence events in a story.
- Identify character traits.
- Describe the effect point of view has on a story.
- Identify author's purpose.

Learn

Fiction Passages (G)

Types of Questions

Read the passage. Then go online to answer the questions.

What a Trip

I trip and bump into things all the time. I guess you could say I have a little trouble with balance. One time, though, I had a trip to remember.

It all started because my little sister left her ball on the kitchen floor. I didn't see the ball, and I stepped on it. That made me stumble, and I bumped into the table.

It was just bad luck that there was a chocolate milk shake on the edge of the table. In a flash, the milk shake spilled. I gasped, but that wasn't the end of it.

If the milk shake had just spilled on the floor, it wouldn't have been terrible. I could have mopped it up. The milk shake didn't just spill on the floor, though. It also spilled all over our dog, Walter.

Walter howled when the cold milk shake splashed on his back, and then he ran into the den. Of course, I chased him.

Walter must have thought we were playing a game. He wagged his tail, barked, and shook all over. You guessed it! Chocolate milk shake flew onto the walls, splashed the rug, and drizzled on the couch.

I guess that would not have been so bad, either. I could have wiped down the walls. I could have cleaned the rug and couch. The problem was that Dad was napping on the couch.

Needless to say, he wasn't napping anymore. The milk shake shower woke him up. His eyes were wide, and he started yelling and waving his arms. He jumped up like someone had poked him with a needle. He leaped to grab Walter. He didn't know that my sister's ball—the same one I slipped on—had rolled into the den.

Dad stepped on the ball, too. He stumbled just like I had stumbled. He bumped into the TV tray just like I had bumped into the kitchen table.

What were the chances that Dad would have left a big bowl of salsa on the edge of the tray? Why couldn't Walter have been anywhere else but under the tray when the salsa spilled? I guess dogs can be as accident-prone as people.

LC 1   LANGUAGE ARTS PURPLE   LC 2   LANGUAGE ARTS PURPLE

Try It ··

Practice Passage and Questions

Students will show their comprehension and ability to respond to questions based on a fiction passage by reading a fiction passage and then answering questions about it.

TIP If students are not comfortable reading the fiction passage for this activity online, print Practice Passage and Questions and have students read the printout.

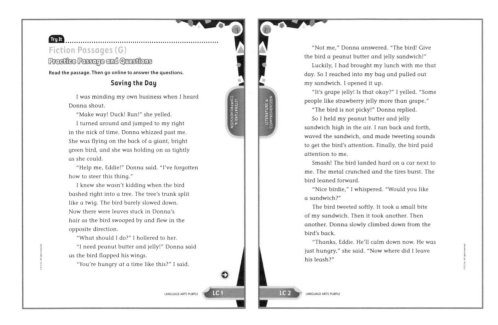

Try It ·····················

Fiction Passages (G)

Practice Passage and Questions

Read the passage. Then go online to answer the questions.

Saving the Day

I was minding my own business when I heard Donna shout.

"Make way! Duck! Run!" she yelled.

I turned around and jumped to my right in the nick of time. Donna whizzed past me. She was flying on the back of a giant, bright green bird, and she was holding on as tightly as she could.

"Help me, Eddie!" Donna said. "I've forgotten how to steer this thing."

I knew she wasn't kidding when the bird bashed right into a tree. The tree's trunk split like a twig. The bird barely slowed down. Now there were leaves stuck in Donna's hair as the bird swooped by and flew in the opposite direction.

"What should I do?" I hollered to her.

"I need peanut butter and jelly!" Donna said as the bird flapped his wings.

"You're hungry at a time like this?" I said.

"Not me," Donna answered. "The bird! Give the bird a peanut butter and jelly sandwich!"

Luckily, I had brought my lunch with me that day. So I reached into my bag and pulled out my sandwich. I opened it up.

"It's grape jelly! Is that okay?" I yelled. "Some people like strawberry jelly more than grape."

"The bird is not picky!" Donna replied.

So I held my peanut butter and jelly sandwich high in the air. I ran back and forth, waved the sandwich, and made tweeting sounds to get the bird's attention. Finally, the bird paid attention to me.

Smash! The bird landed hard on a car next to me. The metal crunched and the tires burst. The bird leaned forward.

"Nice birdie," I whispered. "Would you like a sandwich?"

The bird tweeted softly. It took a small bite of my sandwich. Then it took another. Then another. Donna slowly climbed down from the bird's back.

"Thanks, Eddie. He'll calm down now. He was just hungry," she said. "Now where did I leave his leash?"

LANGUAGE ARTS PURPLE | **LC 1**

LC 2 | LANGUAGE ARTS PURPLE

Write About Paired Passages

Lesson Overview

🖥 [Online] — 30 minutes

Get Ready	Questions That Require a Written Answer
Learn	Answer with a Compare-and-Contrast Paragraph

📄 [Offline] — 20 minutes

Try It	Read and Write a Response

Advance Preparation

For the Try It, students will write a response to an open-ended question, or writing prompt. You will evaluate this response using the tools provided in the online lesson or your own state's rubric. Print Read and Write a Response: Rubric and Sample Responses, which you will use to evaluate the open-ended response. You may wish to familiarize yourself with this tool in advance.

Big Ideas

▸ The study of writing models gives students opportunities to read, analyze, and emulate good writing.
▸ Writing helps build reading skills, and reading more helps improve writing skills.
▸ Writing is the communication of ideas in a structured, orderly form.

Materials

Supplied

- *K¹² Language Arts Activity Book*, pp. LC 131–134
- Answer with a Compare-and-Contrast Paragraph (optional printout)
- Read and Write a Response: Rubric and Sample Responses (printout)

Keywords

compare – to explain how two or more things are alike
contrast – to explain how two or more things are different

[Online] 30 minutes

Students will work online to complete Get Ready and Learn activities.

Get Ready

Questions That Require a Written Answer

Students will learn how to identify and respond to questions, similar to questions they might encounter on standardized tests, that call for written responses. They will also review how to compare and contrast two passages using details from the texts.

Objectives
- Compare and contrast literary elements in two or more literary selections.
- Compare and contrast using evidence from the text.
- Compare and contrast the most important points presented by two texts on the same topic.

Learn

Answer with a Compare-and-Contrast Paragraph

Students will compare and contrast two passages. They will learn how to analyze a question that is similar to questions they might encounter on standardized tests that require a written response.

TIP If students are not comfortable reading the passages for this activity online, print Answer with a Compare-and-Contrast Paragraph and have students read the printout.

Objectives
- Compare and contrast literary elements in two or more literary selections.
- Compare and contrast using evidence from the text.
- Write a paragraph that compares and contrasts two texts.

Learn

Write About Paired Passages
Answer with a Compare-and-Contrast Paragraph

Read the passages. Then go online to answer the question.

The Life of a Butterfly

All butterflies begin their lives as eggs. The eggs look like tiny beads. Each butterfly egg is about the size of the head of a pin. Female butterflies lay their eggs on the leaves and stems of plants. Each kind of butterfly has its own favorite kind of plant for its eggs. Monarch butterflies, for instance, like to lay their eggs on milkweed plants.

After a time, the young hatch from the eggs. The young are caterpillars, or larvae. Caterpillars come in all shapes and sizes. Monarch caterpillars have black, yellow, and white stripes. The caterpillars start eating right away. First they eat their own eggshells. Then they eat the nearby leaves. As they eat, they grow. A larva of a monarch can to be two thousand times as big as when it was born.

As a caterpillar grows, its skin becomes too tight. Then it molts, or sheds its old skin. Underneath, it has already grown a new skin. Most caterpillars molt four or five times. The last

LC 1

time the caterpillar molts, something different happens. The caterpillar settles on a leaf or twig. This time when it sheds its old skin, the caterpillar makes a hard shell. Scientists call this shell a chrysalis.

When the caterpillar goes into the chrysalis, it changes again. It becomes a pupa. Slowly the pupa develops wings. When the chrysalis finally cracks open, a fully formed butterfly comes out.

The Big Change

Monty was hungry. All he wanted to do was eat. He chewed through leaf after leaf, but it never seemed to be enough. He could finish a whole milkweed leaf in twenty minutes. That was a lot of leaf for a small caterpillar!

The days passed. Monty started to grow. His skin began to feel tight, like it was shrinking. Then one day Monty felt something funny. His skin had a little crack in it! Monty was worried. What did this mean? Then, suddenly, the crack began to get bigger. Monty's skin was falling away! Monty realized that he needed to crawl out. As he wriggled free, he noticed something different about himself. He had a bright, shiny

LC 2

new skin! Monty was relieved. Maybe he was supposed to lose his skin after all.

Monty lost his old skin a few more times. He began to get fatter and fatter. Then one day Monty started to feel very tired. He found a nice, firm branch and attached himself underneath a leaf. All Monty could think about was resting. Slowly, a new, hard shell began to form over him, but Marty was too tired to care. The weather was getting colder, and he was happy to have a cozy place to rest.

After a time, the cold months began to turn warmer. Spring was coming. Monty awakened from what seemed like a very long nap. He was still tired, but he had a feeling he had never felt before. There was something long and papery lying along his back. He struggled to free himself from the hard shell he had been sleeping in. As he popped out, something wonderful happened. The paper on his back unfolded. Monty gasped with delight when he realized he had wings! Monty had become a monarch butterfly.

LC 3

[Offline] 20 minutes

Work **together** with students to complete the Try It activity.

Try It

Read and Write a Response

Students will write a paragraph comparing and contrasting two passages. Turn to pages LC 131–134 in *K¹² Language Arts Activity Book*.

1. Have students carefully read the passages, directions, and prompt that requires a written response.

2. Tell students they are to write a paragraph comparing and contrasting two passages.

   ▸ Their paragraph should describe two ways that the passages are similar.
   ▸ Their paragraph should describe two ways that the passages are different.
   ▸ Their paragraph should include details from both passages and be written in students' own words.
   ▸ Their paragraph should be free of errors in grammar, usage, and mechanics.

3. Remind students that they should write in complete sentences, use good handwriting, and leave spaces between words so that others can read what they wrote.

4. Have students complete the Activity Book pages.

5. Use the Read and Write a Response: Rubric and Sample Responses to evaluate students' finished writing. You will be looking at students' writing to evaluate the following:

   ▸ **Purpose and Content:** The paragraph compares and contrasts the two passages. It describes two ways that the passages are similar and two ways that they are different. The paragraph provides details from each text to support the similarities and differences identified. The paragraph is mostly original and rarely repeats the words of the passages' authors.
   ▸ **Structure and Organization:** There is one paragraph. The paragraph explains similarities and differences together with supporting details, but ideas may not flow smoothly from similarities to differences.
   ▸ **Grammar and Mechanics:** Most sentences are complete, and there are a few errors in grammar, punctuation, and spelling.

Objectives

- Compare and contrast literary elements in two or more literary selections.
- Compare and contrast using evidence from the text.
- Write a paragraph that compares and contrasts two texts.

6. If students scored a 1 in any category, work with students to proofread and revise their work.

Write About Paired Passages
Read and Write a Response

Read the passages, and then write your response.

All About Big Brown Bats

Big brown bats are found all over the Americas. They can be found as far north as Canada and as far south as Central America. They live in cities and in forests, in mountains and in deserts. They find places to roost, or sleep, in trees, caves, mines, and buildings. They might even find a roosting place in the walls or attic of your house!

Big brown bats are not as big as they sound. The body of a big brown bat is about four inches long. The bats usually weigh less than an ounce. That's the weight of five quarters. They have long, brown, shiny fur and rounded ears. Their noses are wide and long, so they look like tiny dogs.

These bats are insectivores. That means they eat insects. Their favorite foods are beetles, but they eat other insects, too. They like to eat flying insects like moths, flies, wasps, and mosquitoes. This means that brown bats are very useful. They like to eat the bugs that humans think of as pests.

Like all bats, big brown bats hunt at night. How do they find their prey? They use echolocation. The bats send out sounds through their mouths and noses. The sounds make echoes. The bats use these echoes to tell where their prey is located. Humans cannot hear these sounds. But brown bats do make other sounds that people can hear, such as clicks and squeaks.

When winter comes, big brown bats hibernate. That means they go into a deep sleep. Then, when spring comes, the bats fly out to hunt again in the warmer weather.

Night of the Bats

Rita and her family had just moved to a farm in Virginia. Rita's parents were not farmers. They just liked the wide open spaces of the farm. They also loved the beautiful red barn that sat just across the yard from the house.

It was the first day in the new house. Rita and her brother Luke were exploring the pond on the farm. It was warm, but it was getting late. The sun was beginning to go down, and the air was getting cooler. Insects were buzzing all around.

Suddenly Rita noticed something flying over her head. It went past very quickly. Then it came by

again, dipping and turning sharply. It let out tiny little squeaks, almost like a mouse. Rita thought it was just a bird, so she looked away. Then the sky was filled with these small brown creatures. There were hundreds of them! They swarmed above Rita and Luke, diving and chirping. The children threw their arms over their heads and ran into the house.

"Mother! Hurry! Come see!" Rita shouted.

Rita's mother went to the door of the farmhouse. "Look at that," she said. "Those are brown bats. They must have been roosting in the barn."

"What?" Rita said with alarm. "Bats? I am never going outside again!"

Rita's mother put her arm around her daughter's shoulder. "Don't be silly, Rita," she said. "Bats won't hurt you. In fact, they are very good to have around."

Rita's mother explained how bats liked to eat the insects that bother people. They loved mosquitoes, flies, and wasps. She also told the children how bats use echolocation to find their prey. She said the bats were very good at flying around big objects. They rarely flew into people.

Rita felt a little better. But she knew it would take time to get used to so many flying, squeaky neighbors!

Describe two ways that these passages are similar and two ways they are different. Use details from both texts to support your answer.

Refer to the rubric and sample responses.

_____

_____

_____

_____

_____

_____

_____

_____

_____

_____

_____

_____

_____

_____

_____

_____

Unit Checkpoint

Lesson Overview

Offline — 50 minutes

Unit Checkpoint	Part 1: Nonfiction Passages
	Part 2: Poetry
	Part 3: Paired Passages
	Part 4: Fiction Passages
	Part 5: Write a Compare-and-Contrast Paragraph

Online — varies

More Practice	Review the Skills

Materials

Supplied

- K¹² Language Arts Assessments, pp. LC 61–76
- Write a Compare-and-Contrast Paragraph: Rubric and Sample Responses (printout)

Objectives

- Determine purpose and audience.
- Identify the topic sentence that expresses the main idea of a paragraph.
- Recognize that details support the topic sentence.
- Identify the author's message in a third-grade nonfiction passage.
- Draw conclusions from text.
- Identify rhyme scheme.
- Identify speaker.
- Distinguish between literal and figurative language.
- Identify similes.
- Identify theme.
- Identify problem and solution.
- Identify cause and effect.
- Compare and contrast using evidence from the text.
- Identify opinions.
- Make generalizations from text.
- Identify and infer cause-and-effect relationships and draw conclusions.
- Sequence events in a story.
- Identify character traits.
- Describe the effect point of view has on a story.
- Identify author's purpose.
- Compare and contrast literary elements in two or more literary selections.
- Compare and contrast the most important points and details on two texts on the same topic.

Unit Checkpoint

Explain to students that they are going to show what they have learned about reading and answering questions about nonfiction passages, poetry, and fiction passages, and about writing a compare-and-contrast paragraph.

1. Give students the Unit Checkpoint pages.

2. Read the directions together.

3. Use the Answer Key to score the Checkpoint, and then enter the results online.

4. Review each exercise with students. Work with students to correct any exercise that they missed.

Part 1: Nonfiction Passages
Have students read "Learn to Swim" and answer the questions.

Part 2: Poetry
Have students read "Rain in Summer" and answer the questions.

Part 3: Paired Passages
Have students read the "The Danger of Earthquakes" and "Deadly Hurricanes" and answer the questions.

Part 4: Fiction Passages
Have students read "The Metal Menace" and answer the questions.

Part 5: Write a Compare-and-Contrast Paragraph
Have students write a paragraph that compares and contrasts "Talking Turkey" and "In the Woods."

1. Direct students' attention to Part 5 of the Checkpoint and read the directions together, ensuring that students understand they are to write a paragraph that compares and contrasts "Talking Turkey" and "In the Woods."

2. Have students write their paragraph.

3. Use the Write a Compare-and-Contrast Paragraph: Rubric and Sample Responses to evaluate students' finished writing. You will be looking at students' writing to evaluate the following:

▸ **Purpose and Content:** The paragraph compares and contrasts the two passages. It describes two ways that the passages are similar and two ways that they are different. The paragraph provides details from each text to support the similarities and differences identified. The paragraph is mostly original and rarely repeats the words of the passages' authors.

▸ **Structure and Organization:** There is one paragraph. The paragraph explains similarities and differences together with supporting details, but ideas may not flow smoothly from similarities to differences.

▸ **Grammar and Mechanics:** Most sentences are complete, and there are a few errors in grammar, punctuation, and spelling.

4. If students scored a 1 in any category, work with them to proofread and revise their work.

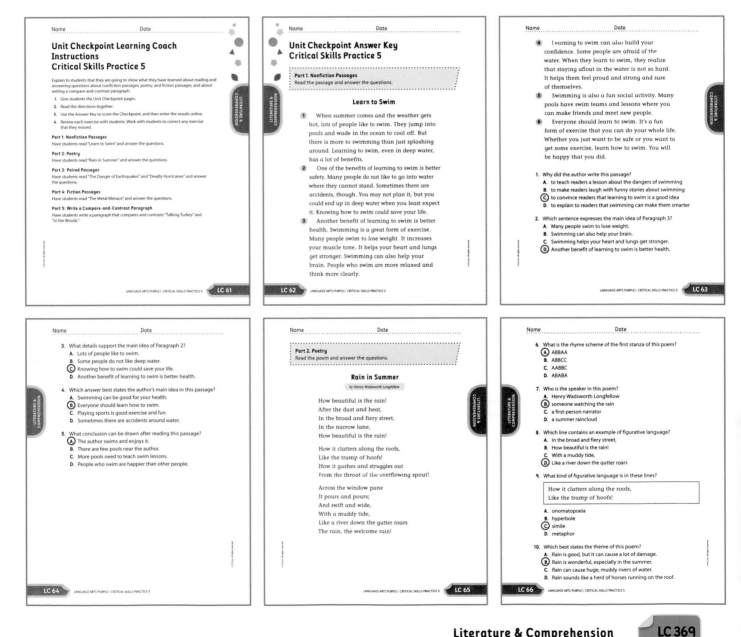

Name _____ Date _____

Part 3. Paired Passages
Read the two passages and answer the questions.

The Danger of Earthquakes

Earthquakes are a deadly force in nature. They can happen at almost any time and anywhere. They can destroy cities and towns. And we never know when they will strike.

Scientists know what causes earthquakes. Underneath the top layer of the earth are plates. These plates are like giant puzzle pieces. They are always moving and sliding against each other. Sometimes the plates get stuck. When they come loose, an earthquake happens.

Earthquakes do a lot of damage. They cause buildings to shake and crumble. They create huge cracks and holes in roads. They make bridges break and trees fall. Many people die every year from earthquakes.

There are ways to keep earthquakes from causing big problems. People have learned how to make buildings that will not break during an earthquake. Some buildings use stronger materials and sway when the earth moves. This keeps the buildings from falling down. These kinds of buildings should be built everywhere

around the world. We never know where an earthquake will strike.

Deadly Hurricanes

Hurricanes are some of the most powerful storms on earth. They can pack winds that blow up to 200 miles per hour. They can dump gallons of rain in just minutes. Hurricanes knock down buildings and trees. They cause flooding. They can leave people without power and without homes.

A hurricane is a giant storm. It forms over the ocean. Warm and cold air meet, and water from the ocean rises. The winds begin to swirl and pick up speed. Huge rain clouds form. Then the storm moves toward land. The storm brings powerful winds, rain, and waves of ocean water.

There are things that people can do to protect themselves from hurricanes. Buildings can be built high above the ground. This protects them against the high water that comes with hurricanes. Windows can be built with a special strong glass. Then the windows are less likely to be broken in high winds. High walls can prevent sea water from flooding towns. These are some steps that people should take wherever hurricanes may strike.

11. Which problem do both of these texts discuss?
    A. how to predict the next disaster
    B. how to make better tracking tools
    C. how to make buildings safer
    D. how to stop these events from happening

12. According to these passages, which is a possible effect of both a hurricane and an earthquake?
    A. They can knock down buildings.
    B. They can cause flooding.
    C. They can create holes in roads.
    D. They can make the ground shake.

13. How are these two texts similar?
    A. They predict where the next event will happen.
    B. They describe the damage from these natural events.
    C. They explain what people should do in an emergency.
    D. They tell interesting stories about famous disasters.

14. Which generalization can be made about both of these texts?
    A. All natural disasters cause people to die.
    B. No one should ever live where there are hurricanes.
    C. Most earthquakes can be predicted.
    D. Some events in nature can cause great harm.

15. What is the opinion of both authors about natural disasters?
    A. People should not live where natural disasters occur.
    B. People should build strong buildings where natural disasters occur.
    C. There is nothing that anyone can do about natural disasters.
    D. Scientists should worry about other problems on earth besides natural disasters.

Part 4. Fiction Passages
Read the passage and answer the questions.

The Metal Menace

I didn't know what to do. There seemed to be no stopping the giant robot. Where had this thing come from anyway? One minute everything in Milton was peaceful. The next minute people were running for their lives.

I didn't believe the robot existed when Mayor Dan first called me. Then I saw it for myself. It was as big as a skyscraper. And now the metal monster was heading straight for the city.

My superpowers were useless against the giant. I tried blasting it with my laser. The rays just bounced off the metal skin like drops of rain. The robot was smashing everything in sight. It pulled up trees like they were daisies. Every time it took a step it left a huge crater in the road. If it got to Milton, buildings would be crushed. People would be lost.

Just then my radio buzzed. "Marshall, are you there? What's happening?" It was Tracy, my partner. Tracy and I had been friends a long time. She took care of the business end of things. I took care of fighting crime.

"Yes, I'm here," I yelled into the radio. "Nothing seems to work against this thing! My laser is useless. And I don't want to fly too close. It has a mean left jab!"

"Where are you now? Where is it heading?" Tracy asked in a worried voice.

"It's heading right for the city. It's close to the stadium," I answered. And then it hit me. The stadium—it was a perfect. "Hold on, Tracy, I have a plan," I said.

"What? What plan? Marshall . . ." yelled Tracy as I turned off the radio. I didn't have time to explain. I had to move fast.

I flew to the nearest telephone pole. I blasted a wire with my laser. The wire dropped to the ground. I swooped down and picked up the end of the wire. Then I flew in quick, tight circles around the robot's feet. I held the end of the wire with all my strength and waited.

Just as I had hoped, the robot's feet got tangled in the wire. It swayed for a second. Then it dropped to the ground with an earth-shaking smash—right in the stadium parking lot. The fall knocked out the robot's computer. It was over.

I took a deep breath. Good thing there wasn't a game today!

16. Why do the rays from Marshall's laser bounce off the robot?
    A. Marshall's laser is not working correctly.
    B. Marshall does not take good aim at the robot.
    C. The robot blocks the rays with its arms.
    D. The robot's skin is made of tough metal.

17. What sequence of events is correct?
    A. The robot heads toward Milton; Marshall shoots the robot; Mayor Dan calls.
    B. Tracy calls; Marshall cuts a telephone wire; the robot falls.
    C. The robot pulls up trees; the robot nears the stadium; Marshall meets Tracy.
    D. The robot trips; Marshall shoots the robot; the robot smashes things.

18. Which character trait does Marshall have?
    A. helplessness
    B. fearfulness
    C. cleverness
    D. anger

19. How would the story be different if Tracy had told it?
    A. We would know where the robot came from.
    B. We would know what Mayor Dan was thinking.
    C. We would not know how Tracy felt about Marshall.
    D. We would not know how Marshall stopped the robot.

20. Why did the author write this story?
    A. to entertain readers with an exciting tale
    B. to inform readers about the dangers of science
    C. to show how to fight a robot
    D. to give his opinion about whether robots are real

Part 5. Write a Compare-and-Contrast Paragraph
Read the passages and then write your response.

Talking Turkey

At Thanksgiving, many people have turkey for dinner. The turkeys you eat come from farms. They have cousins who don't live on farms, though. Those are wild turkeys.

Wild turkeys have been in America for hundreds of years. The Native Americans ate them and used their feathers. The Pilgrims decided that turkeys would make good farm animals. That is how we ended up with turkeys on our dinner tables!

Wild turkeys can be found in much of the United States. They make their homes in woodlands. They look for food on the forest floor. Wild turkeys like to eat nuts, seeds, fruits, and insects. Sometimes they even eat salamanders!

Most people know turkeys by the big, red skin that hangs under their necks. This is called a wattle. It is found only on males. Male turkeys are also the only ones with big tail feathers. They fan these out to show off to the female turkeys. Wild turkeys can weigh between

5 and 18 pounds. Their wings can stretch almost 5 feet across!

The wild turkey is part of our country's history. Benjamin Franklin liked the turkey. He once said it would make a better national bird than the eagle. Maybe you think a turkey would look funny as our national symbol. But the wild turkey is a true American bird!

In the Woods

The ground crunched under Ming's feet. All around her birds twittered and chirped. Ming loved taking hikes with her father. She loved them time alone together. Sometimes they walked in silence. Other times they talked about things they saw in the woods.

On this day the trail was covered in shadows. It was early fall, so the trees still had all their leaves. Ming's father was walking in front as he always did. Ming was watching her feet. She didn't want to trip on any branches or rocks.

Suddenly Ming bumped into the back of her father. He had stopped walking. He turned around and looked down at her quietly. He had one finger pressed to his lips. Then he gently pulled Ming down behind a fallen tree.

"Do you see it?" Ming's father whispered in her ear. He was pointing over the tree trunk to a place down the trail. "It's a wild turkey."

Ming looked ahead. At first she didn't see anything. Then she saw movement. It was a large, round bird. Its feathers were a dark brown. Under the bird's chin was a pale red flap of skin. The bird had a funny, jerky way of walking. Every now and then it poked its head down at the ground.

"It's a boy turkey," said Ming's father. "See the red skin on its neck? That's a wattle. Only boy turkeys have that. He's looking for food on the ground."

Ming stared. She had never seen a live turkey before. She had only seen the ones her mother cooked at Thanksgiving. "I didn't know turkeys lived in the woods," Mind said.

"Only the wild ones do. The kinds of turkeys we eat come from farms. The Native Americans used to hunt wild turkeys. Some people still do today."

Ming and her father watched the turkey for a while until it moved away. Then they rose and continued on their walk. Ming hoped the turkey would find what he was looking for.

Name _____ Date _____

21.–23. Describe at least two ways that these passages are similar and at least two ways they are different. Use details from both texts to support your answer.

Use the rubric to score the response.
Enter the results online.

_____
_____
_____
_____
_____
_____
_____
_____
_____
_____
_____
_____
_____
_____
_____
_____
_____

LC 76 LANGUAGE ARTS PURPLE | CRITICAL SKILLS PRACTICE 5

〖 Online 〗 varies

Students will work **independently** to complete the online More Practice activity.

More Practice

Review the Skills

If students scored less than 80 percent or had difficulty meeting the objectives of the Unit Checkpoint, have them go online for more practice.

Reward: If students score 80 percent or more on the Unit Checkpoint, add a sticker for this unit on the My Accomplishments chart. If students did not score 80 percent or more, work with them to revise their work until they do score 80 percent.

Objectives
- Evaluate Unit Checkpoint results and choose activities for more practice.

Greek and Roman Myths

Unit Focus

In this unit, students will read ancient Greek and Roman myths. They will focus on the characteristics of a myth; the traits of characters, including important gods and goddesses; causes and their effects in myths; and themes and lessons of myths. Students will read these selections from *K¹² Classics for Young Readers, Volume C*:

▶ "Mount Olympus and Its Inhabitants"
▶ "The Naming of a Great City"
▶ "The Greater Gift"
▶ "The Story of Arachne"
▶ "The Story of Proserpina"
▶ "A Flight Through the Sky"

Students will compare and contrast the gods and goddesses and discuss them with their peers.

Unit Plan		〔Online〕	〔Offline〕
Lesson 1	Introduce "Mount Olympus and Its Inhabitants"		50 minutes
Lesson 2	Explore "Mount Olympus and Its Inhabitants"	40 minutes	10 minutes
Lesson 3	Introduce "The Naming of a Great City" and "The Greater Gift"		50 minutes
Lesson 4	Explore "The Naming of a Great City" and "The Greater Gift"	40 minutes	10 minutes
Lesson 5	Introduce "The Story of Arachne"		50 minutes
Lesson 6	Explore "The Story of Arachne"	40 minutes	10 minutes
Lesson 7	Introduce "The Story of Proserpina"		50 minutes
Lesson 8	Explore "The Story of Proserpina"	40 minutes	10 minutes
Lesson 9	Introduce "A Flight Through the Sky"		50 minutes
Lesson 10	Explore "A Flight Through the Sky"	40 minutes	10 minutes
Lesson 11	Reflections on Greek and Roman Myths	varies	50 minutes
Lesson 12	Your Choice		50 minutes

Introduce "Mount Olympus and Its Inhabitants"

Lesson Overview

[Offline]   **50** minutes

Get Ready	Lesson Introduction
	What Is a Myth?
	Book Walk
	Words to Know
Read	"Mount Olympus and Its Inhabitants"
GRAB	Go Read a Book

Advance Preparation

You may want to find peers to read the myths in this unit along with students so that they may participate in the discussion as part of the Reflections on Greek and Roman Myths lesson.

Content Background

The ancient Greeks created myths, or stories, about the gods and goddesses they believed controlled all aspects of life on earth. They ascribed human motivations, weaknesses, and other attributes to their gods, and they believed these gods at times interacted with or interfered in the lives of humankind. The myths explained natural phenomena and other happenings that the Greeks did not understand. The ancient Romans, who later conquered the Greeks, adopted this mythology. They believed in the same gods and goddesses as the Greeks, but gave them different names. Knowledge of these classic stories is important for cultural literacy and for a frame of reference for later readings that frequently allude to these stories.

Big Ideas

- ▸ Active, strong readers employ reading strategies such as making connections between text and the real world.
- ▸ Nonfiction texts differ from fiction texts in that they describe real or true things in life, rather than things made up by the author.
- ▸ Through reading diverse classic and contemporary literature as well as challenging informational texts in a range of subjects, students are expected to build knowledge, gain insights, explore possibilities, and broaden their perspective.
- ▸ Subject to debate and redefinition, there are works that merit the effort of interpretation.

[Materials]

Supplied

- "Mount Olympus and Its Inhabitants," *K¹² Classics for Young Readers, Volume C*, pp. 178–187
- Reading Strategies bookmark

Also Needed

- globe

Story Synopsis

This nonfiction text explains what an ancient Greek myth is and describes some of the most important gods and goddesses in Greek mythology.

Keywords

fiction – make-believe stories

myth – a story that explains how something came to be and that usually contains magical figures as characters

mythology – all the myths of one group of people

nonfiction – writings about true things

setting – when and where a story takes place

〖 Offline 〗 ⑤⓪ minutes

Work **together** with students to complete offline Get Ready, Read, and GRAB activities.

Get Ready ....

Lesson Introduction
Prepare students to read "Mount Olympus and Its Inhabitants."

1. Explain to students that before they read "Mount Olympus and Its Inhabitants," they will discuss with you

   ▸ What they remember about nonfiction texts
   ▸ What a myth is
   ▸ Their predictions about the text
   ▸ Important words to know in the text

2. Tell students that while they read, you will check in to make sure they understand what they are reading.

3. Tell students that after they read, they will answer questions about the text.

> ⭐ **Objectives**
> - Distinguish between fiction and nonfiction.
> - Define *myth*.
> - Identify setting.
> - Use text organizational features to locate and comprehend information (table of contents).
> - Use before-reading strategies.
> - Increase concept and content vocabulary.

What Is a Myth?
Review the differences between fiction and nonfiction and explain what a myth is. Gather the globe.

1. Have students tell what they remember about the differences between **fiction** and **nonfiction**. Fiction is writing about make-believe things. Fiction usually has characters, a plot, a setting, and conflicts or problems the characters must resolve. Nonfiction is writing about true things. Nonfiction includes facts, features such as graphs and headings, and main ideas and supporting details.

2. Tell students they are about to read a nonfiction text that that tells about fictional stories.

3. Ask students if they have ever heard of a **myth**. Have them define *myth*, or define it for them. A myth is a story that explains how something came to be. It usually contains magical figures as characters.

4. Tell students that many of the myths they will read about in this unit come from Greece. Help students find Greece on the globe.

5. Explain that the myths they will read came from the ancient Greeks. These were the people who lived in Greece thousands of years ago, before modern science and technology.

Book Walk

Have students lead you through a Book Walk of "Mount Olympus and Its Inhabitants." Remind them to use the **title** and **illustrations** to make predictions about what will happen in the text.

Words to Know

Before reading "Mount Olympus and Its Inhabitants," remind students that they will find the Words to Know at the bottoms of the pages in the selection.

Read

"Mount Olympus and Its Inhabitants"

Have students read "Mount Olympus and Its Inhabitants." Remind students to use the strategies on their Reading Strategies bookmark. For example, they may want to stop at the end of each page of the story and ask themselves questions about what they just read.

 Learning Coach Check-In This reading assignment should take about 15 minutes. After students finish reading, ask the following questions to assess their comprehension of the selection:

▸ How were the gods and goddesses of ancient Greece like people? Answers may include: They argued, they played tricks, and they fell in love.

▸ How were the gods and goddesses different from people? Answers may include: They could fly, they could change shapes, and they had magical powers.

If students have trouble answering these questions, ask them what reading strategies they used and suggest they reread the selection.

Objectives
- Read literature independently and proficiently.
- Apply information read to answer questions.
- Evaluate reading strategies.

GRAB

Go Read a Book

Have students read a book or magazine of their own choosing for at least 20 minutes. Remind students to use the strategies on their Reading Strategies bookmark before and during reading to help them understand the text.

TIP Remember: The more students read, the better readers they become.

Objectives
- Read literature independently and proficiently.
- Read a variety of texts for information and pleasure.

Explore "Mount Olympus and Its Inhabitants"

Lesson Overview

🖥 [Online] 40 minutes

Check Your Reading	Comprehend "Mount Olympus and Its Inhabitants"
Reading for Meaning	Understand Setting
	Meet the Gods and Goddesses

🗒 [Offline] 10 minutes

Making Connections	Describe Gods and Goddesses

Big Ideas

▸ Readers should be able to retell the story (or information) in their own words, not repeat what was written.

▸ To understand and interpret a story, readers need to understand and describe characters and what they do.

▸ Subject to debate and redefinition, there are works that merit the effort of interpretation.

[Materials]

Supplied

- "Mount Olympus and Its Inhabitants," *K¹² Classics for Young Readers, Volume C*, pp. 178–187
- *K¹² Language Arts Activity Book*, pp. LC 135–138

Keywords

myth – a story that explains how something came to be and that usually contains magical figures as characters

mythology – all the myths of one group of people

setting – when and where a story takes place

trait – a quality of a person or character

[Online] ⏱ 40 minutes

Students will work **independently** to complete online Check Your Reading and Reading for Meaning activities.

Check Your Reading ···

Comprehend "Mount Olympus and Its Inhabitants"
Students will answer questions about "Mount Olympus and Its Inhabitants" to demonstrate their literal and inferential comprehension of the story and to reinforce their knowledge of these important names and places.

Objectives
- Identify concrete answers to questions.
- Infer answers to questions.
- Apply information read to answer questions.
- Demonstrate knowledge of authors, characters, and events in significant works of literature.

Reading for Meaning ··

Understand Setting
Students will learn how Greece's location influenced the settings of the ancient Greek myths.

Meet the Gods and Goddesses
Students will identify the relationships among the important gods and goddesses in ancient Greek mythology, as well as some of their traits.

Objectives
- Identify setting.
- Describe setting.
- Use information from visuals to develop an understanding of the characters, setting, and plot.
- Demonstrate understanding of common features of legends, myths, folktales, fairy tales, and classic stories.
- Identify character traits.
- Demonstrate knowledge of authors, characters, and events in significant works of literature.

[Offline] ⑩ minutes

Work **together** with students to complete the offline Making Connections activity.

Making Connections ···

Describe Gods and Goddesses

Students will review the responsibilities and traits of some of the major Greek gods and goddesses and summarize "Mount Olympus and Its Inhabitants." Turn to pages LC 135–138 in *K¹² Language Arts Activity Book*.

1. Direct students' attention to the Activity Book pages and have them read the directions.

2. Have students complete the Activity Book pages.

TIP Keep the Activity Book pages in a safe place so students can refer to them later.

Objectives

- Demonstrate understanding of common features of legends, myths, folktales, fairy tales, and classic stories.
- Identify character traits.
- Demonstrate knowledge of authors, characters, and events in significant works of literature.
- Write a summary.
- Write a topic sentence introductory statement.
- Write a concluding statement.

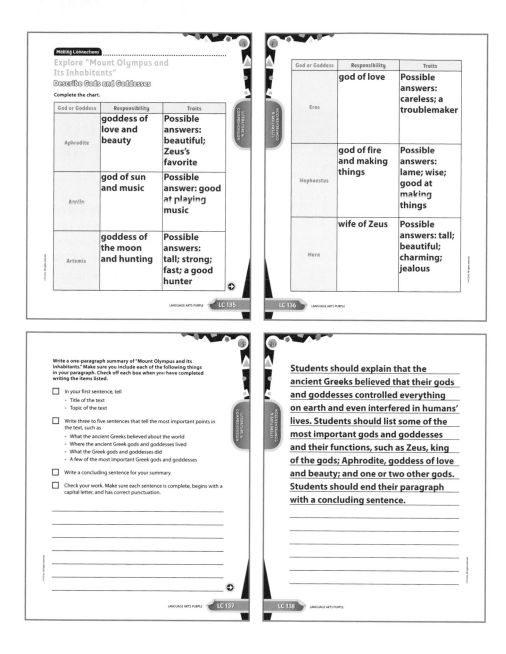

Making Connections

Explore "Mount Olympus and Its Inhabitants"

Describe Gods and Goddesses

Complete the chart.

God or Goddess	Responsibility	Traits
Aphrodite	goddess of love and beauty	Possible answers: beautiful; Zeus's favorite
Apollo	god of sun and music	Possible answer: good at playing music
Artemis	goddess of the moon and hunting	Possible answers: tall; strong; fast; a good hunter

God or Goddess	Responsibility	Traits
Eros	god of love	Possible answers: careless; a troublemaker
Hephaestus	god of fire and making things	Possible answers: lame; wise; good at making things
Hera	wife of Zeus	Possible answers: tall; beautiful; charming; jealous

LC 135

LC 136 LANGUAGE ARTS PURPLE

Write a one-paragraph summary of "Mount Olympus and Its Inhabitants." Make sure you include each of the following things in your paragraph. Check off each box when you have completed writing the items listed.

☐ In your first sentence, tell
  • Title of the text
  • Topic of the text

☐ Write three to five sentences that tell the most important points in the text, such as
  • What the ancient Greeks believed about the world
  • Where the ancient Greek gods and goddesses lived
  • What the Greek gods and goddesses did
  • A few of the most important Greek gods and goddesses

☐ Write a concluding sentence for your summary.

☐ Check your work. Make sure each sentence is complete, begins with a capital letter, and has correct punctuation.

LC 137

LC 138

Students should explain that the ancient Greeks believed that their gods and goddesses controlled everything on earth and even interfered in humans' lives. Students should list some of the most important gods and goddesses and their functions, such as Zeus, king of the gods; Aphrodite, goddess of love and beauty; and one or two other gods. Students should end their paragraph with a concluding sentence.

Introduce "The Naming of a Great City" and "The Greater Gift"

Lesson Overview

[Offline]   50 minutes

Get Ready	Lesson Introduction
	Review Myths and Drama
	Book Walk
	Words to Know
Read	"The Naming of a Great City" and "The Greater Gift"
GRAB	Go Read a Book

Big Ideas

▸ Active, strong readers employ reading strategies such as making connections between text and the real world.

▸ Through reading diverse classic and contemporary literature as well as challenging informational texts in a range of subjects, students are expected to build knowledge, gain insights, explore possibilities, and broaden their perspective.

[Materials]

Supplied

- "The Naming of a Great City," "The Greater Gift," *K¹² Classics for Young Readers, Volume C,* pp. 188–199
- Reading Strategies bookmark

Story Synopses

"The Naming of a Great City" is a myth that explains how the Greek city of Athens got its name. "The Greater Gift" is a play that tells the same story. In the myth, Poseidon and Athena each want to be the namesake of the ancient Greek city. Zeus holds a contest to see who brings the greater gift to the city. Poseidon brings a horse and promises power and glory in war. Athena brings an olive tree and promises peace and prosperity. Zeus chooses Athena's as the better gift, and thus the city is named for her.

Keywords

drama – another word for *play*

myth – a story that explains how something came to be and that usually contains magical figures as characters

[Offline] 50 minutes

Work **together** with students to complete offline Get Ready, Read, and GRAB activities.

Get Ready ....

Lesson Introduction

Prepare students to read "The Naming of a Great City" and "The Greater Gift."

1. Explain to students that before they read "The Naming of a Great City" and "The Greater Gift," they will discuss with you

   ▸ What they remember about myths and plays
   ▸ What they have learned about some of the major Greek gods and goddesses
   ▸ Their predictions about the text
   ▸ Important words to know in the text

2. Tell students that while they read, you will check in to make sure they understand what they are reading.

3. Tell students that after they read, they will answer questions about the text.

Review Myths and Drama

Review what a myth is and how it is different from a play, as well as the names and responsibilities of some of the major Greek gods and goddesses.

1. Have students tell what a **myth** is. a story that explains how something came to be and that usually contains magical figures as characters

2. Tell students they will read two myths: one in regular story form, and the other in the form of a **drama**. Have students tell what drama is and some of the elements of drama. *Drama* is another word for a play. Plays may include stage directions and lines for characters to say. They are meant to be acted out, not just read.

3. Tell students that the myths are about the ancient Greek gods Zeus, Athena, and Poseidon. Have students tell what they know about these gods. Answers may include: Zeus is the king of the gods; he is the most powerful. Athena is the goddess of wisdom. Poseidon is the god of the sea and Zeus's brother.

> ### Objectives
> - Define *myth*.
> - Define *drama*.
> - Use text organizational features to locate and comprehend information (table of contents).
> - Use before-reading strategies.
> - Increase concept and content vocabulary.

Book Walk

Have students lead you through a Book Walk of "The Naming of a Great City" and "The Greater Gift." Remind them to use the **title** and **illustrations** to make predictions about what will happen in the text.

Words to Know

Before reading "The Naming of a Great City" and "The Greater Gift," remind students that they will find the Words to Know at the bottoms of the pages in the selection.

Read

"The Naming of a Great City" and "The Greater Gift"

Have students read "The Naming of a Great City" and "The Greater Gift." Remind students to use the strategies on their Reading Strategies bookmark. For example, they may want to stop at the end of each page of the story and summarize what they have just read.

⮑ **Learning Coach Check-In** This reading assignment should take about 15 minutes. After students finish reading, ask the following questions to assess their comprehension of the selection:

► What gift does Poseidon bring to the city in the two stories? Possible answers: a horse; power and glory in war

► What gift does Athena bring? Possible answers: an olive tree; peace and prosperity

► Who is the city named for? Athena

If students have trouble answering these questions, ask them what reading strategies they used and suggest they reread the selection.

Objectives

- Read literature independently and proficiently.
- Apply information read to answer questions.
- Evaluate reading strategies.

GRAB

Go Read a Book

Have students read a book or magazine of their own choosing for at least 20 minutes. Remind students to use the strategies on their Reading Strategies bookmark before and during reading to help them understand the text.

Objectives

- Read literature independently and proficiently.
- Read a variety of texts for information and pleasure.

Explore "The Naming of a Great City" and "The Greater Gift"

Lesson Overview

🖥 [Online]   **40** minutes

Check Your Reading	Comprehend "The Naming of a Great City" and "The Greater Gift"
Reading for Meaning	The Theme of the Myths

📄 [Offline]   **10** minutes

Making Connections	Understand the Characters in Myths
Beyond the Lesson	➕ OPTIONAL: Act Out the Play

Big Ideas

- ▶ To understand and interpret a story, readers need to understand and describe characters and what they do.
- ▶ Readers need to understand literary conflicts and their resolutions in order to analyze characters and themes.

[Materials]

Supplied

- "The Naming of a Great City," "The Greater Gift," *K¹² Classics for Young Readers, Volume C*, pp. 188–199
- *K¹² Language Arts Activity Book*, pp. LC 139–142

Keywords

drama – another word for *play*

myth – a story that explains how something came to be and that usually contains magical figures as characters

plot – what happens in a story; the sequence of events

topic – the subject of a text

theme – the author's message or big idea

trait – a quality of a person or character

 **40 minutes**

Students will work **independently** to complete online Check Your Reading and Reading for Meaning activities.

Check Your Reading

Comprehend "The Naming of a Great City" and "The Greater Gift"
Students will answer questions about "The Naming of a Great City" and "The Greater Gift" to demonstrate their literal and inferential comprehension of the story.

Objectives
- Identify setting.
- Identify concrete answers to questions.
- Apply information read to answer questions.

Reading for Meaning

The Theme of the Myths
Students will review the plot of the myths "The Naming of a Great City" and "The Greater Gift" to determine the theme.

Objectives
- Define *topic*.
- Define *theme*.
- Distinguish between topic and theme.
- State the topic directly.
- Summarize the plot of a story.
- Determine the theme, moral, or lesson of a work of literature.

[Offline] 🔟 minutes

Work **together** with students to complete the offline Making Connections and Beyond the Lesson activities.

Making Connections •

Understand the Characters in Myths

Students will explore the character traits of Zeus, Poseidon, and Athena. Turn to pages 139–142 in *K¹² Language Arts Activity Book*.

1. Direct students' attention to the Activity Book pages and have them read the directions.

2. Have students complete the Activity Book pages.

TIP Keep the Activity Book pages in a safe place so students can refer to them later.

Objectives

- Demonstrate understanding of common features of legends, myths, folktales, fairy tales, and classic stories.
- Identify character traits.
- Compare and contrast literary elements in two or more literary selections.
- Compare and contrast using evidence from the text.
- Compare and contrast different versions of the same story.
- State an opinion.
- Provide reasons that support an opinion.

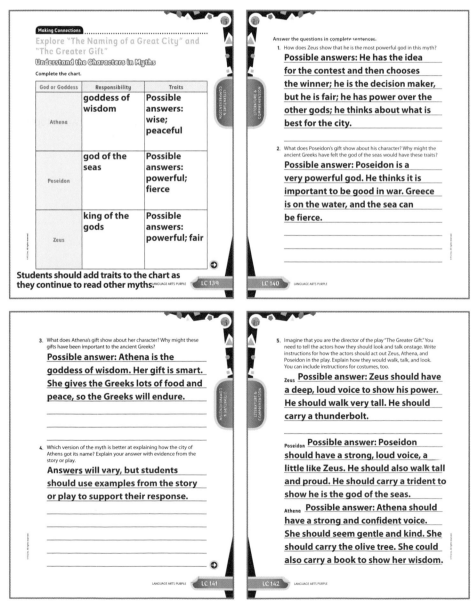

Beyond the Lesson

⊕ OPTIONAL: Act Out the Play

This activity is OPTIONAL. It is intended for students who have extra time and would benefit from acting out the play "The Greater Gift." Feel free to skip this activity.

1. If students have peers who are reading the myths along with them, have students and their peers act out the play "The Greater Gift." Tell them to use their characterizations from the Understand the Characters in Myths pages.

2. If students do not have peers who are reading the myths, have them do a dramatic reading of the play. Remind them to use different voices for the characters and use their Activity Book pages to help them choose the correct kind of voice for each role.

3. As students perform their roles, remind them not to read stage directions or the name of the character who is speaking.

4. Tell students to use props to represent the characters and the gifts.

TIP Students may need a reminder about how to read and stage drama. If they do, direct them to the online Reading for Meaning activity, Stage the Play, from the Explore "The Calabash Kids" lesson in the Stories That Teach unit.

Objectives

- Make inferences and draw conclusions about the structure and elements of drama.
- Explain the elements of plot, character, and dialogue.
- Describe characters by what they say, what they do, and what others say about them.
- Acknowledge differences among characters, including the use of a different voice for each character when reading dialogue aloud.

Introduce "The Story of Arachne"

Lesson Overview

[Offline] 50 minutes

Get Ready	Lesson Introduction
	Discuss Pride
	Book Walk
	Words to Know
Read	"The Story of Arachne"
GRAB	Go Read a Book

Advance Preparation

Gather completed page LC 139 (Understand the Characters in Myths chart) in *K¹² Language Arts Activity Book*.

Big Ideas

- ▶ Active, strong readers employ reading strategies such as making connections between text and the real world.
- ▶ Through reading diverse classic and contemporary literature as well as challenging informational texts in a range of subjects, students are expected to build knowledge, gain insights, explore possibilities, and broaden their perspective.

[Materials]

Supplied

- "The Story of Arachne," *K¹² Classics for Young Readers, Volume C*, pp. 200–203
- *K¹² Language Arts Activity Book* p. LC 139
- Reading Strategies bookmark

Story Synopsis

In this myth, a young woman named Arachne boasts that she is the best weaver in the world—even better than the goddess Athena. Athena challenges Arachne to a weaving contest. The one who loses may never weave again. Not surprisingly, Athena wins. The powerful goddess takes pity on Arachne and turns her into a spider, so she and her kind may continue to weave forever.

Keywords

myth – a story that explains how something came to be and that usually contains magical figures as characters

[Offline] 50 minutes

Work **together** with students to complete offline Get Ready, Read, and GRAB activities.

Get Ready

Lesson Introduction

Prepare students to read "The Story of Arachne."

1. Explain to students that before they read "The Story of Arachne," they will discuss with you

   ▸ The meaning of pride
   ▸ What they have learned about some of the major Greek gods and goddesses
   ▸ Their predictions about the text
   ▸ Important words to know in the text

2. Tell students that while they read, you will check in to make sure they understand what they are reading.

3. Tell students that after they read, they will answer questions about the text.

Discuss Pride

Discuss the meanings of the words *pride* and *arrogant*.

1. Ask students what pride is and have them give an example of something that they are proud of.

2. Ask students if there is ever a time when someone can be too proud. Have them give an example, either from real life or from a story, of what happens when someone is too proud.

3. Introduce the word *arrogant*. Explain that it is good to be proud of accomplishments, but a person who is too proud or overly boastful is arrogant. Provide an example sentence with the word *arrogant* and ask students to do the same. (Example: Susan showed that she was arrogant because she told everyone she met that she was the best piano player in her class and said that no one could play as well as she.)

4. Explain that students are about to read a myth about pride. Have students tell what they expect to find in an ancient Greek myth. Possible answers: gods, goddesses, themes about life, explanations of why things came to be

5. Explain that the goddess Athena is a character in the myth they are going to read. Tell students that if they find any new traits for the goddess as they read, they should add those traits to their description of Athena on their Understand the Characters in Myths chart.

> ### Objectives
> - Connect text with prior knowledge.
> - Use text organizational features to locate and comprehend information (table of contents).
> - Use before-reading strategies.
> - Increase concept and content vocabulary.

Book Walk

Have students lead you through a Book Walk of "The Story of Arachne." Remind them to use the **title** and **illustrations** to make predictions about what will happen in the text.

Words to Know

Before reading "The Story of Arachne," remind students that they will find the Words to Know at the bottoms of the pages in the selection.

Read

"The Story of Arachne"

Have students read "The Story of Arachne." Remind them to use the strategies on their Reading Strategies bookmark. For example, they may want to slow their reading if they find they are having trouble comprehending the story.

⊃ **Learning Coach Check-In** This reading assignment should take about 15 minutes. As students read, they should add new traits for Athena to their Understand the Characters in Myths chart. After students finish reading, ask the following questions to assess their comprehension of the selection:

▸ Why does Athena challenge Arachne to a weaving contest? Possible answer: Arachne has been boasting that she is better than Athena at weaving, and Athena wants to prove her wrong.

▸ What does Arachne become at the end of the myth? a spider

If students have trouble answering these questions, ask them what reading strategies they used and suggest they reread the selection.

> **Objectives**
> - Read literature independently and proficiently.
> - Apply information read to answer questions.
> - Evaluate reading strategies.

Making Connections

Explore "The Naming of a Great City" and "The Greater Gift"

Understand the Characters in Myths

Complete the chart.

God or Goddess	Responsibility	Traits
Athena	goddess of wisdom	Possible answers: wise; peaceful
Poseidon	god of the seas	Possible answers: powerful; fierce
Zeus	king of the gods	Possible answers: powerful; fair

Students should add traits to the chart as they continue to read other myths. LANGUAGE ARTS PURPLE   LC 139

GRAB

Go Read a Book

Have students read a book or magazine of their own choosing for at least 20 minutes. Remind students to use the strategies on their Reading Strategies bookmark before and during reading to help them understand the text.

Objectives

- Read literature independently and proficiently.
- Read a variety of texts for information and pleasure.

Explore "The Story of Arachne"

Lesson Overview

🖥 〖Online〗   40 minutes

Check Your Reading	Comprehend "The Story of Arachne"
Reading for Meaning	The Themes of the Myth

📄 〖Offline〗   10 minutes

Making Connections	Compare and Contrast Two Athenas
Beyond the Lesson	⊕ OPTIONAL: Greek Words in English

Advance Preparation

Gather completed page LC 139 (Understand the Characters in Myths chart) in *K¹² Language Arts Activity Book*.

Big Ideas

▸ To understand and interpret a story, readers need to understand and describe characters and what they do.
▸ Readers need to understand literary conflicts and their resolutions in order to analyze characters and themes.

〖Materials〗

Supplied

- "The Story of Arachne," *K¹² Classics for Young Readers, Volume C,* pp. 200–203
- *K¹² Language Arts Activity Book,* pp. LC 139, 143–145

Keywords

compare – to explain how two or more things are alike

contrast – to explain how two or more things are different

plot – what happens in a story; the sequence of events

theme – the author's message or big idea

trait – a quality of a person or character

 **40 minutes**

Students will work **independently** to complete online Check Your Reading and Reading for Meaning activities.

Check Your Reading

Comprehend "The Story of Arachne"
Students will answer questions about "The Story of Arachne" to demonstrate their literal and inferential comprehension of the story.

> ⭐ **Objectives**
> - Identify setting.
> - Identify concrete answers to questions.
> - Apply information read to answer questions.
> - Infer answers to questions.

Reading for Meaning

The Themes of the Myth
Students will identify the themes in "The Story of Arachne" by looking at the traits and actions of both Arachne and Athena. They will consider Arachne's arrogance and the compassion Athena demonstrates by finding a solution that allows Arachne to continue to weave, even though she has lost the contest.

TIP Students may have difficulty understanding that Athena actually shows compassion for Arachne in her decision to transform the girl into a spider. As necessary, help students see that the transformation allows Arachne to continue to weave, which is what she likes, but still proves Athena's superior power. Remind students that these stories were meant to be instructive.

> ⭐ **Objectives**
> - Determine the theme, moral, or lesson of a work of literature.
> - Identify character traits.

[Offline] 🕙 minutes

Work **together** with students to complete the offline Making Connections and Beyond the Lesson activities.

Making Connections ••

Compare and Contrast Two Athenas

Students will discuss what they added about the goddess Athena to their completed Understand the Characters in Myths chart and compare and contrast Athena in two myths to help them better understand the character. Turn to pages LC 143–145 in *K¹² Language Arts Activity Book*.

1. Have students tell what other trait or traits they added on the Understand the Characters in Myths chart to their description of Athena. Have them explain their answer. Possible answers for the chart: powerful, kind. Students may say that Athena shows she is powerful by beating Arachne in the weaving contest and turning her into a spider. They may say that Athena shows she is kind because she turns Arachne into a spider so she can still weave. Students may feel that Athena is cruel for turning Arachne into a spider. Help them understand that the ancient Greeks would not have had this same interpretation.

2. Direct students' attention to the new Activity Book pages and have them read the directions.

3. Have students complete the activity pages.

TIP Keep the Activity Book pages in a safe place so students can refer to them later.

> ### Objectives
> - Identify character traits.
> - Understand a variety of literature representing different cultures and traditions.
> - Compare and contrast characters from different stories.

Making Connections

Explore "The Naming of a Great City" and "The Greater Gift"

Understand the Characters in Myths

Complete the chart.

God or Goddess	Responsibility	Traits
Athena	goddess of wisdom	Possible answers: wise; peaceful
Poseidon	god of the seas	Possible answers: powerful; fierce
Zeus	king of the gods	Possible answers: powerful; fair

Students should add traits to the chart as they continue to read other myths. LANGUAGE ARTS PURPLE   LC 139

Making Connections

Explore "The Story of Arachne"

Compare and Contrast Two Athenas

In four paragraphs, compare and contrast the character of Athena in "The Naming of the City" and "The Greater Gift" with her character in "The Story of Arachne." Use this checklist to write your paragraphs.

☐ In you first paragraph, tell about a trait of Athena from the myths "The Naming of the City" and "The Greater Gift." Use examples from both myths to explain how she shows this trait.

☐ In your second paragraph, tell about another trait of Athena from the myth "The Story of Arachne." Use examples from the myth to explain how Athena shows this trait.

☐ In your third paragraph, compare and contrast the goddess Athena in the myths. Tell how she is the same and different. Use examples from the myths. Explain how one goddess could have more than one trait.

☐ In your fourth paragraph, tell why the Greeks might have described Athena in these ways. Explain what Athena's traits show about the ancient Greeks and what was important to them.

☐ Check that each sentence is complete, begins with a capital letter, and ends with an end mark.

LANGUAGE ARTS PURPLE   LC 143

Students' writing should include four paragraphs and follow the checklist. The writing should compare and contrast Athena in the three myths. For example, students might say that Athena is kind in all the myths because she helps people. They might say she is different in the myths because in "The Story of Arachne," Athena also hurts Arachne to prove Athena is more powerful.

LC 144   LANGUAGE ARTS PURPLE

Beyond the Lesson ....

⊕ OPTIONAL: Greek Words in English

This activity is OPTIONAL. It is intended for students who have extra time and would benefit from finding out the meaning of English words that have Greek roots.

1. Tell students that apart from *arachnid* and *arachnophobia*, there are many other words in English that come from ancient Greek words.

2. Give students the following list of Greek words and the English words that come from them. Have students look up the English words in a dictionary and write down the meaning. Then have them write a sentence for each word.

   ▸ Greek: *acros* means "high"
     English: *acrobat*
   ▸ Greek: *kardia* means "heart"
     English: *cardiology*
   ▸ Greek: *demos* means "people"
     English: *democracy*
   ▸ Greek: *geo* means "earth"
     English: *geography*
   ▸ Greek: *micros* means "small"
     English: *microscope*

Objectives

- Determine the meanings and pronunciations of unknown words by using dictionaries, glossaries, technology, and textual features, such as definitional footnotes or sidebars.
- Use search tools to locate information (for example, hyperlink).
- Determine the meaning of text-related words, including those related to mythology.

Introduce "The Story of Proserpina"

Lesson Overview

[Offline]   50 minutes

Get Ready	Lesson Introduction
	Review Roman Myths
	Book Walk
	Words to Know
Read	"The Story of Proserpina"
GRAB	Go Read a Book

Content Background

In the Greek version of this myth, the goddess Demeter makes things grow and the daughter she pines for is Persephone. The god of the underworld is known as Hades.

Big Ideas

▸ Active, strong readers employ reading strategies such as making connections between text and the real world.

▸ Through reading diverse classic and contemporary literature as well as challenging informational texts in a range of subjects, students are expected to build knowledge, gain insights, explore possibilities, and broaden their perspective.

[Materials]

Supplied
- "The Story of Proserpina," *K¹² Classics for Young Readers, Volume C,* pp. 204–213
- Reading Strategies bookmark

Also Needed
- globe

Story Synopsis
This Roman myth explains the changing of the seasons through the story of Proserpina, daughter of the goddess Ceres, who makes things grow. One day Pluto, god of the underworld, takes Proserpina and brings her back to his realm. Ceres warns the gods that if Proserpina is not returned to her, no plants will grow again. A compromise is reached, whereby Proserpina lives aboveground with Ceres for most of the year—the warm, growing months—but must live with Pluto during winter.

Keywords
myth – a story that explains how something came to be and that usually contains magical figures as characters
mythology – all the myths of one group of people
setting – when and where a story takes place

[Offline] 50 minutes

Work **together** with students to complete offline Get Ready, Read, and GRAB activities.

Get Ready

Lesson Introduction

Prepare students to read "The Story of Proserpina."

1. Explain to students that before they read "The Story of Proserpina," they will discuss with you

   ▸ The origin of ancient Roman gods
   ▸ Where Rome is on the globe
   ▸ Their predictions about the text
   ▸ Important words to know in the text

2. Tell students that while they read, you will check in to make sure they understand what they are reading.

3. Tell students that after they read, they will answer questions about the text.

> **Objectives**
> - Connect text with prior knowledge.
> - Identify setting.
> - Use text organizational features to locate and comprehend information (table of contents).
> - Use before-reading strategies.
> - Increase concept and content vocabulary.

Review Roman Myths

Discuss where the ancient Roman gods and goddesses came from and where Rome is located on a globe. Gather the globe.

1. Have students tell what group of people borrowed the mythology of the Greeks. the Romans

2. Remind students that the Romans changed the names of the Greek gods and goddesses. Tell them they are about to read a Roman myth in which the Roman names of the gods and goddesses are used. Provide them with examples.

   ▸ Hades, the god of the underworld, is Pluto in this story.
   ▸ Zeus, king of the gods, is Jupiter.
   ▸ Hermes, the messenger god, is Mercury.

3. Explain that the Romans lived in what is now the country of Italy. Help students find Italy and Rome on the globe. Point out that Greece and Italy share similar geography.

   ▸ Both Greece and Italy are peninsulas; a *peninsula* is land mostly surrounded by water.
   ▸ Both Greece and Rome have mountains. A famous mountain in Italy, which is also a volcano, is part of the setting of this story. It's called Mount Etna. Show students where Mount Etna is on the globe (on the island of Sicily).

4. Remind students that some myths explain how something happened or came to be. Have students tell what is explained in the myths "The Naming of the City" and "The Story of Arachne." "The Naming of the City" explains how Athens got its name; "The Story of Arachne" explains how spiders came to be.

5. Tell them to look for what this myth explains.

Book Walk

Have students lead you through a Book Walk of "The Story of Proserpina." Remind them to use the **title** and **illustrations** to make predictions about what will happen in the text.

Words to Know

Before reading "The Story of Proserpina," remind students that they will find the Words to Know at the bottoms of the pages in the selection.

Read

"The Story of Proserpina"

Have students read "The Story of Proserpina." Remind students to use the strategies on their Reading Strategies bookmark. For example, they may want to go back and reread parts of the story to help their comprehension.

⊃ **Learning Coach Check-In** This reading assignment should take about 15 minutes. After students finish reading, ask the following questions to assess their comprehension of the selection:

▸ Where does Pluto take Proserpina? to his kingdom, the underworld
▸ What compromise do the gods make at the end of the myth? Proserpina will live with her mother for part of the year, when things grow, and with Pluto for part of the year, when it's winter.

If students have trouble answering these questions, ask them what reading strategies they used and suggest they reread the selection.

Objectives
- Read literature independently and proficiently.
- Apply information read to answer questions.
- Evaluate reading strategies.

GRAB

Go Read a Book

Have students read a book or magazine of their own choosing for at least 20 minutes. Remind students to use the strategies on their Reading Strategies bookmark before and during reading to help them understand the text.

Objectives
- Read literature independently and proficiently.
- Read a variety of texts for information and pleasure.

Explore "The Story of Proserpina"

Lesson Overview

Online   40 minutes

Check Your Reading	Comprehend "The Story of Proserpina"
Reading for Meaning	What the Myth Explains
	The Themes of the Myth

Offline   10 minutes

| Making Connections | Analyze the Gods and the Setting |

Big Ideas

▸ To understand and interpret a story, readers need to understand and describe characters and what they do.
▸ Readers need to understand literary conflicts and their resolutions in order to analyze characters and themes.

Materials

Supplied

- "The Story of Proserpina," *K¹² Classics for Young Readers, Volume C,* pp. 204–213
- *K¹² Language Arts Activity Book,* pp. LC 147–150

Also Needed

- pencils, coloring, or crayons

Keywords

myth – a story that explains how something came to be and that usually contains magical figures as characters
plot – what happens in a story; the sequence of events
setting – when and where a story takes place
theme – the author's message or big idea
topic – the subject of a text
trait – a quality of a person or character

[Online] ④ minutes

Students will work **independently** to complete online Check Your Reading and Reading for Meaning activities.

Check Your Reading

Comprehend "The Story of Proserpina"
Students will answer questions about "The Story of Proserpina" to demonstrate their literal and inferential comprehension of the story.

Objectives
- Identify concrete answers to questions.
- Apply information read to answer questions.
- Infer answers to questions.

Reading for Meaning

What the Myth Explains
Students will examine what happens in "The Story of Proserpina" to determine that the topic of the myth is why the seasons change.

The Themes of the Myth
Students will identify the themes of the myth "The Story of Proserpina" by looking at the events in the plot and what the characters do and say.

Objectives
- Explain how the actions of characters contribute to the sequence of events.
- Demonstrate understanding of common features of legends, myths, folktales, fairy tales, and classic stories.
- Determine the theme, moral, or lesson of a work of literature.
- Distinguish between topic and theme.

 **Offline** **10** minutes

Work **together** with students to complete the offline Making Connections activity.

Making Connections

Analyze the Gods and the Setting

Students will describe the gods and the setting in the myth "The Story of Proserpina." Gather the coloring pencils or crayons, and turn to pages LC 147–150 in *K¹² Language Arts Activity Book*.

1. Direct students' attention to the Activity Book pages and have them read the directions.

2. Have students complete the Activity Book pages.

TIP Keep the Activity Book pages in a safe place so students can refer to them later.

Making Connections

Explore "The Story of Proserpina"

Analyze the Gods and the Setting

Complete the chart.

God or Goddess	Responsibility	Traits
Ceres (Demeter)	goddess of growing things	Possible answers: strong; powerful; brave; loving
Mercury (Hermes)	messenger to the gods	Possible answers: wise; fair; fast
Pluto (Hades)	god of the underworld	Possible answers: powerful; selfish; follows the laws

LC 147   LANGUAGE ARTS PURPLE

Answer the questions in complete sentences.

1. How is the earth like the underworld when Proserpina is with Pluto?

Possible answer: It is dark and cold. Everything is dead in winter, just like people are dead in the underworld.

2. How are the feelings of Pluto in the underworld similar to the feelings and ideas that might come with winter?

Possible answer: Pluto is very sad in the underworld, because there is no light or happiness there. His world is cold and seems dead. Winter is like this.

LC 148   LANGUAGE ARTS PURPLE

---

3. What is the earth like when Proserpina is with Ceres?

Possible answer: It is sunny and warm, and everything is growing.

4. How are Ceres's feelings when she is with Proserpina like the feelings and ideas that might come with the spring and summer?

Possible answer: Ceres feels happy, so she makes beautiful things grow. During spring and summer, everything seems alive and warm.

LC 149   LANGUAGE ARTS PURPLE

---

5. Draw a picture of winter or spring. Around your picture, write two or three words that you think of when you think of this time of year.

Students should draw a scene showing spring or winter and write two or three words that they associate with this season.

LC 150   LANGUAGE ARTS PURPLE

Introduce "A Flight Through the Sky"

Lesson Overview

Offline — 50 minutes

Get Ready	Lesson Introduction
	Think About Gods and Humans
	Book Walk
	Words to Know
Read	"A Flight Through the Sky"
GRAB	Go Read a Book

Big Ideas

▶ Active, strong readers employ reading strategies such as making connections between text and the real world.

▶ Through reading diverse classic and contemporary literature as well as challenging informational texts in a range of subjects, students are expected to build knowledge, gain insights, explore possibilities, and broaden their perspective.

▶ Subject to debate and redefinition, there are works that merit the effort of interpretation.

Materials

Supplied

- "A Flight Through the Sky," *K¹² Classics for Young Readers, Volume C,* pp. 214–219
- Reading Strategies bookmark

Story Synopsis

In this Greek myth, Daedalus is being held captive by a king because of his skills as a builder. Daedalus makes a plan to escape. He builds wings for himself and his son Icarus using wood and feathers held together with wax. As the pair escape, Icarus flies too close to the sun, the wax fastening the wings melts, and Icarus falls into the sea. The story can be read as a warning to children to be mindful of their parents, or as a warning to those who would choose to defy the gods or become godlike.

Keywords

myth – a story that explains how something came to be and that usually contains magical figures as characters

setting – when and where a story takes place

[Offline] 50 minutes

Work **together** with students to complete offline Get Ready, Read, and GRAB activities.

Get Ready

Lesson Introduction

Prepare students to read "A Flight Through the Sky."

1. Explain to students that before they read "A Flight Through the Sky," they will discuss with you

   ▸ The way ancient Greeks thought about gods, goddesses, and humans
   ▸ Their predictions about the text
   ▸ Important words to know in the text

2. Tell students that while they read, you will check in to make sure they understand what they are reading.

3. Tell students that after they read, they will answer questions about the text.

> **Objectives**
> - Demonstrate understanding of common features of legends, myths, folktales, fairy tales, and classic stories.
> - Use text organizational features to locate and comprehend information (table of contents).
> - Use before-reading strategies.
> - Increase concept and content vocabulary.

Think About Gods and Humans

Discuss how the ancient Greeks thought about gods and goddesses and their relationships with human beings.

1. Tell students they are going to read another myth from ancient Greece.

2. Review with students how the ancient Greeks thought about their gods and goddesses.

   ▸ What did the gods and goddesses do on earth? Possible answers: They controlled everything that happened; they were everywhere.
   ▸ How did the ancient Greeks believe that human beings were supposed to behave toward the gods and goddesses? Possible answer: People were supposed to listen to the gods and obey them. They were not supposed to try to be equal to the gods or better than the gods.
   ▸ What did the Greeks believe would happen to a person who tried to defy the gods or be like the gods? Give an example from one of the stories you read. Possible answer: The Greeks believed that people would be punished if they tried to disobey the gods or be like them. Arachne, who boasts she can weave better than Athena, loses a weaving contest and is turned into a spider.

3. Remind students to think about how the ancient Greeks thought of the gods and goddesses as they read the myth.

Book Walk

Have students lead you through a Book Walk of "A Flight Through the Sky." Remind them to use the **title** and **illustrations** to make predictions about what will happen in the text.

Words to Know

Before reading "A Flight Through the Sky," remind students that they will find the Words to Know at the bottoms of the pages in the selection.

 Read ●

"A Flight Through the Sky"

Have students read "A Flight Through the Sky." Remind students to use the strategies on their Reading Strategies bookmark. For example, they may want to stop and make inferences about the plot and the characters.

⊃ **Learning Coach Check-In** This reading assignment should take about 15 minutes. After students finish reading, ask the following questions to assess their comprehension of the selection:

> ▸ How does Daedalus plan to escape the island? He makes wings made of wood, feathers, and wax and plans to fly to freedom with his son Icarus.
> ▸ What happens to Icarus? He flies too close to the sun, so the wax melts and his wings fall apart. He falls into the sea.

If students have trouble answering these questions, ask them what reading strategies they used and suggest they reread the selection.

GRAB ●

Go Read a Book

Have students read a book or magazine of their own choosing for at least 20 minutes. Remind students to use the strategies on their Reading Strategies bookmark before and during reading to help them understand the text.

Objectives

- Read literature independently and proficiently.
- Apply information read to answer questions.
- Evaluate reading strategies.

Objectives

- Read literature independently and proficiently.
- Read a variety of texts for information and pleasure.

Explore "A Flight Through the Sky"

Lesson Overview

【Online 】 **40** minutes

Check Your Reading	Comprehend "A Flight Through the Sky"
Reading for Meaning	The Themes of the Myth

【Offline 】 **10** minutes

Making Connections	Write About the Myth

Big Ideas

- ▶ To understand and interpret a story, readers need to understand and describe characters and what they do.
- ▶ Readers need to understand literary conflicts and their resolutions in order to analyze characters and themes.

【Materials 】

Supplied

- "A Flight Through the Sky," *K¹² Classics for Young Readers, Volume C*, pp. 214–219
- *K¹² Language Arts Activity Book*, pp. LC 151–155

Also Needed

- pencils, coloring, or crayons

Keywords

myth – a story that explains how something came to be and that usually contains magical figures as characters

theme – the author's message or big idea

 **40 minutes**

Students will work **independently** to complete online Check Your Reading and Reading for Meaning activities.

Check Your Reading ....

Comprehend "A Flight Through the Sky"
Students will answer questions about "A Flight Through the Sky" to demonstrate their literal and inferential comprehension of the story.

Objectives
- Identify setting.
- Infer answers to questions.
- Identify problem and solution.

Reading for Meaning ....

The Themes of the Myth
Students will examine what happens to the characters in "A Flight Through the Sky" to determine the theme of the myth as understood by the ancient Greeks, as well as the lesson modern readers might learn from it.

Objectives
- Explain how the actions of characters contribute to the sequence of events.
- Demonstrate understanding of common features of legends, myths, folktales, fairy tales, and classic stories.
- Determine the theme, moral, or lesson of a work of literature.

[Offline] ⑩ minutes

Work **together** with students to complete the offline Making Connections activity.

Making Connections ●

Write About the Myth

Students will compare and contrast "A Flight Through the Sky" with "The Story of Arachne," as well as write a new ending for the story of Daedalus. Gather the coloring pencils or crayons, and turn to pages LC 151–155 in *K¹² Language Arts Activity Book*.

1. Direct students' attention to the Activity Book pages and have then read the directions.

2. Have students complete the Activity Book pages.

TIP Keep the Activity Book pages in a safe place so students can refer to them later.

Objectives

- Compare and contrast literary elements in two or more literary selections.
- Generate plausible alternative endings to plot.
- Demonstrate understanding of common features of legends, myths, folktales, fairy tales, and classic stories.
- Make connections between text and self, text and world, and text to text.

Making Connections

Explore "A Flight Through the Sky"

Write About the Myth

Answer the questions in complete sentences.

1. In two paragraphs, compare and contrast the myths "A Flight Through the Sky" and "The Story of Arachne."
   - In you first paragraph, tell how the two myths are similar. Use examples from the myths to support your ideas. Think about the characters and the themes.
   - In your second paragraph, tell how the two myths are different. Use examples from the myths to support your ideas. Think about the same topics for these differences as you did for similarities in your first paragraph.
   - Check that each sentence is complete, begins with a capital letter, and has an end mark.

LANGUAGE ARTS PURPLE **LC 151**

LC 152 LANGUAGE ARTS PURPLE

Some similarities students might include: Arachne and Daedalus are both proud and they both try to do something as well as the gods. Both characters get some reward for their skills, but they are both punished for their pride.

Some differences students might include: Arachne directly challenges the goddess Athena, while Daedalus does not challenge a god. Arachne boasts about doing something better than a goddess, while Daedalus tries to be like the gods. Daedalus harms his son through his actions, while Arachne only harms herself.

2. Write a new ending for the myth "A Flight Through the Sky." Write an ending that answers one of the following questions:
- What if Daedalus had decided to try to escape a different way?
- What if Daedalus had made the wings of another material?
- What if Daedalus and Icarus had flown away at night instead of during the day?
- What if Icarus had listened to his father?

Answers will vary, but students' new ending to the myth should tell what happens to Daedalus and Icarus.

3. Draw an illustration for your new ending.

Students should draw a scene showing their new ending.

Reflections on Greek and Roman Myths

Lesson Overview

📄 [Offline] **50** minutes

Get Ready	Lesson Introduction
	Who Is Your Favorite Character from the Myths?
Putting It All Together	Discuss the Gods and Goddesses and Write Your Own Myth

🖥 [Online] varies

More Practice	Review the Skills
Read	Read Fluently "The Story of Atalanta"
Performance Review	Fluency Check

📄 [Offline] varies

Beyond the Lesson	➕ OPTIONAL: Read More Myths

[Materials]

Supplied
- "Mount Olympus and Its Inhabitants," "The Naming of a Great City," "The Greater Gift," "The Story of Arachne," "The Story of Proserpina," "A Flight Through the Sky," *K¹² Classics for Young Readers, Volume C*, pp. 178–219
- *K¹² Language Arts Activity Book*, pp. LC 135–136, 139, 147, 157–162
- Putting It All Together Assessment Checklist (printout)
- "The Story of Atalanta" (printout)
- Fluency Performance Checklist (optional printout)

Also Needed
- pencils, coloring or crayons

Advance Preparation

Gather students' completed charts from pages LC 135–136 (Describe Gods and Goddesses), 139 (Understand the Characters in Myths), and 147 (Analyze the Gods and the Setting) in *K¹² Language Arts Activity Book*. If possible, gather peers to participate in the discussion as part of Putting It All Together.

Big Ideas

▶ Imaginative writing, in the form of stories and poems, allows writers to access their creativity while entertaining an audience.
▶ Good public speakers speak clearly, make eye contact, and use appropriate expression for their subject matter and audience.
▶ Fluent readers expend less energy on decoding and therefore have more energy for comprehension.
▶ Written words have a voice, or a sense that someone has written them.
▶ Writing requires organization and structure.
▶ To be effective communicators, writers and speakers should recognize and use complete sentences.

Keywords

compare – to explain how two or more things are alike
contrast – to explain how two or more things are different
myth – a story that explains how something came to be and that usually contains magical figures as characters
trait – a quality of a person or character

[Offline] 50 minutes

Work **together** with students to complete the offline Get Ready and Putting It All Together activities.

Get Ready

Lesson Introduction

Prepare students for discussing gods and goddesses and writing their own myth.

1. Explain to students that they will have a discussion with their peers about the gods and goddesses in the unit.

2. Tell students that before they have their discussion, they will discuss with you their favorite gods and goddesses.

3. Tell students that after the discussion, they will write their own myth.

> **Objectives**
> • Describe characters and their traits.

Who Is Your Favorite Character from the Myths?

Discuss students' favorite gods, goddesses, and human characters in the myths they read.

1. Have students tell which character—god, goddess, or human—from the myths is their favorite and explain why.

2. Tell students to use examples from the myths to describe the traits of the character.

Putting It All Together

✏ Discuss the Gods and Goddesses and Write Your Own Myth

Students will demonstrate their understanding of the gods and goddesses in the myths in this unit. Gather students' completed charts and the coloring pencils or crayons. Turn to pages LC 157–162 in *K¹² Language Arts Activity Book*.

1. Gather peers for a discussion about the gods and goddesses in the myths that students read. If this is not possible, you can have the discussion with students.

2. Have students read the Discuss the Gods and Goddesses pages.

3. Lead students in a discussion of the gods and goddesses. Tell them to use their charts on the gods and goddesses as talking points. Ask students the questions on the Discuss the Gods and Goddesses pages, and remind them to use evidence from the myths to support their answers.

4. Give students the Write Your Own Myth pages and coloring pencils or crayons, and have them read all the directions.

5. Have students complete the Activity Book pages. When they have completed the discussion and summary, use the materials and instructions in the online lesson to evaluate students' work.

6. Enter the answers (Yes or No) for each line of the assessment checklist online.

   ↻ **Learning Coach Check-In** Check in with students after about 20 minutes to see if they have completed the assignment.

TIP If you prefer, have students write their own myth first, and then hold the discussion.

Objectives

- Describe characters and their traits.
- Compare and contrast characters from different stories.
- Answer evaluative questions based on reading.
- Follow agreed-upon rules for discussions (for example, gaining the floor in respectful ways, listening to others with care, speaking one at a time about the topics and texts under discussion).
- Build on others' talk in conversations by linking their comments to the remarks of others.
- Speak clearly and at an appropriate pace for the type of communication.
- Contribute meaningfully to group discussions by being prepared, explaining one's own ideas, building upon others' comments, and asking questions.
- Determine the theme, moral, or lesson of a work of literature.
- Describe setting.
- Identify problem and solution.
- Identify cause and effect.
- Identify sensory language: vivid verbs.
- Create a visual.
- Apply the conventions of grammar, usage, mechanics, and spelling.

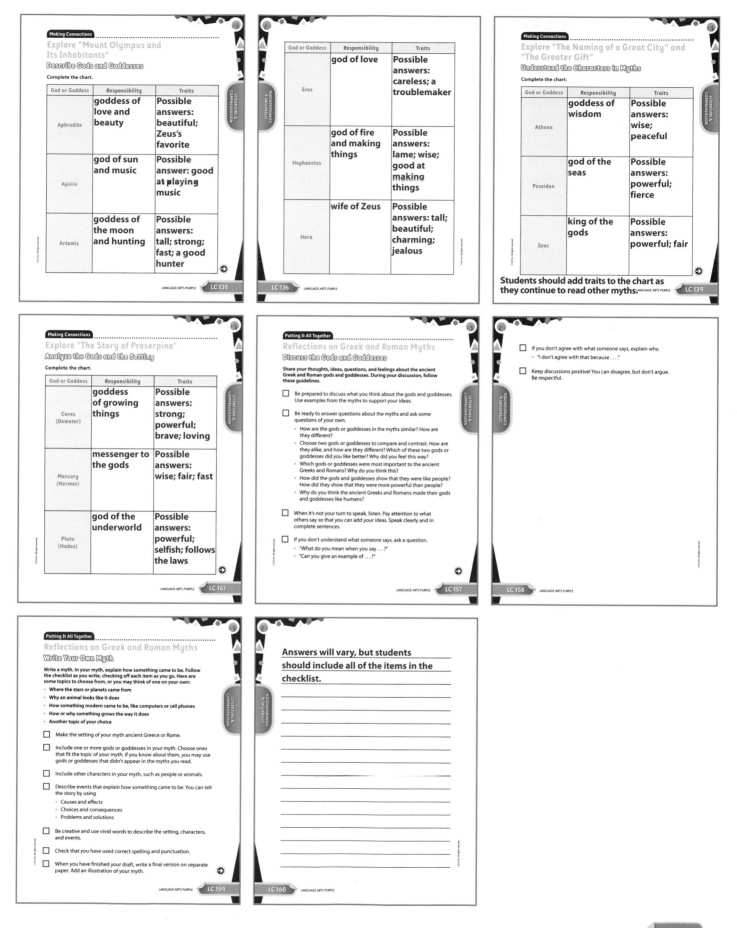

Making Connections

Explore "Mount Olympus and Its Inhabitants"
Describe Gods and Goddesses

Complete the chart.

God or Goddess	Responsibility	Traits
Aphrodite	goddess of love and beauty	Possible answers: beautiful; Zeus's favorite
Apollo	god of sun and music	Possible answer: good at playing music
Artemis	goddess of the moon and hunting	Possible answers: tall; strong; fast; a good hunter

LANGUAGE ARTS PURPLE LC 135

God or Goddess	Responsibility	Traits
Eros	god of love	Possible answers: careless; a troublemaker
Hephaestus	god of fire and making things	Possible answers: lame; wise; good at making things
Hera	wife of Zeus	Possible answers: tall; beautiful; charming; jealous

LC 136 LANGUAGE ARTS PURPLE

Making Connections

Explore "The Naming of a Great City" and "The Greater Gift"
Understand the Characters in Myths

Complete the chart.

God or Goddess	Responsibility	Traits
Athena	goddess of wisdom	Possible answers: wise; peaceful
Poseidon	god of the seas	Possible answers: powerful; fierce
Zeus	king of the gods	Possible answers: powerful; fair

Students should add traits to the chart as they continue to read other myths.
LANGUAGE ARTS PURPLE LC 139

Making Connections

Explore "The Story of Proserpina"
Analyze the Gods and the Setting

Complete the chart.

God or Goddess	Responsibility	Traits
Ceres (Demeter)	goddess of growing things	Possible answers: strong; powerful; brave; loving
Mercury (Hermes)	messenger to the gods	Possible answers: wise; fair; fast
Pluto (Hades)	god of the underworld	Possible answers: powerful; selfish; follows the laws

LANGUAGE ARTS PURPLE LC 147

Putting It All Together

Reflections on Greek and Roman Myths
Discuss the Gods and Goddesses

Share your thoughts, ideas, questions, and feelings about the ancient Greek and Roman gods and goddesses. During your discussion, follow these guidelines.

☐ Be prepared to discuss what you think about the gods and goddesses. Use examples from the myths to support your ideas.

☐ Be ready to answer questions about the myths and ask some questions of your own.
- How are the gods or goddesses in the myths similar? How are they different?
- Choose two gods or goddesses to compare and contrast. How are they alike, and how are they different? Which of these two gods or goddesses did you like better? Why did you feel this way?
- Which gods or goddesses were most important to the ancient Greeks and Romans? Why do you think this?
- How did the gods and goddesses show that they were like people? How did they show that they were more powerful than people?
- Why do you think the ancient Greeks and Romans made their gods and goddesses like humans?

☐ When it's not your turn to speak, listen. Pay attention to what others say so that you can add your ideas. Speak clearly and in complete sentences.

☐ If you don't understand what someone says, ask a question.
- "What do you mean when you say . . . ?"
- "Can you give an example of . . . ?"

LANGUAGE ARTS PURPLE LC 157

☐ If you don't agree with what someone says, explain why.
- "I don't agree with that because . . . ."

☐ Keep discussions positive! You can disagree, but don't argue. Be respectful.

LC 158 LANGUAGE ARTS PURPLE

Putting It All Together

Reflections on Greek and Roman Myths
Write Your Own Myth

Write a myth. In your myth, explain how something came to be. Follow the checklist as you write, checking off each item as you go. Here are some topics to choose from, or you may think of one on your own:
- Where the stars or planets came from
- Why an animal looks like it does
- How something modern came to be, like computers or cell phones
- How or why something grows the way it does
- Another topic of your choice

☐ Make the setting of your myth ancient Greece or Rome.

☐ Include one or more gods or goddesses in your myth. Choose ones that fit the topic of your myth. If you know about them, you may use gods or goddesses that didn't appear in the myths you read.

☐ Include other characters in your myth, such as people or animals.

☐ Describe events that explain how something came to be. You can tell the story by using
- Causes and effects
- Choices and consequences
- Problems and solutions

☐ Be creative and use vivid words to describe the setting, characters, and events.

☐ Check that you have used correct spelling and punctuation.

☐ When you have finished your draft, write a final version on separate paper. Add an illustration of your myth.

LANGUAGE ARTS PURPLE LC 159

Answers will vary, but students should include all of the items in the checklist.

LC 160 LANGUAGE ARTS PURPLE

[Online] varies

Students will work **independently** to complete the online More Practice activity.

More Practice

Review the Skills

If students scored less than 80 percent or had difficulty meeting the objectives of the Putting It All Together activity, have them go online for more practice.

> **Objectives**
> - Describe characters and their traits.

Read

Read Fluently "The Story of Atalanta"

Students will read aloud and record a passage. The purpose of this activity is to assess students' oral reading and fluency. Have students read the passage aloud and record their reading. Note that this is a new passage to them, and there is no audio for them to hear a model reading. This will allow the recording to accurately reflect their fluency.

> **Objectives**
> - Read poetry and prose aloud.
> - Read aloud grade-level text with appropriate automaticity, prosody, accuracy, and rate.

Performance Review

Fluency Check

Evaluate students' performance on the fluency reading.

1. Listen to students' recordings and use the Fluency Performance Checklist to review fluency and track performance.

2. Keep the completed checklist so you can review students' progress over time.

3. Follow the advice on the checklist regarding appropriate interventions for students who do not receive high scores on the Fluency Performance Checklist. If students aren't able to score above 12 points on the Fluency Performance Checklist, it is advisable to seek outside help from a teaching professional or reading specialist to improve students' reading fluency.

> **Objectives**
> - Read poetry and prose aloud.
> - Read aloud grade-level text with appropriate automaticity, prosody, accuracy, and rate.

 Reward: If students score 80 percent or more on the Putting It All Together activity and 18 or more on the Fluency Check, add a sticker for this unit on the My Accomplishments chart. If students did not score 80 percent or more on the Putting It All Together activity and 18 or more on the Fluency Check, work with them to revise their writing and practice their fluency until they attain those scores and then add a sticker to the My Accomplishments chart.

[Offline] varies

Work **together** with students to complete the optional Beyond the Lesson activity.

Beyond the Lesson

⊕ OPTIONAL: Read More Myths

This activity is OPTIONAL. It is intended for students who have extra time and would benefit from reading other ancient Greek and Roman myths.

1. Ask students if they would like to read other ancient Greek and Roman myths, and if so, why.

2. Have students read more Greek and Roman myths. They can read new ones, or they can read different versions of the myths in this unit. Students can find the myths online or in library books.

3. Discuss the new myths.

   ▸ Which myth did you like the best? Why?
   ▸ Which myth did you like the least? Why?
   ▸ How are these myths similar to the ones you read in this unit? How are they different?
   ▸ Did you learn about any new gods or goddesses? Who are they, and what are they like?
   ▸ What did the myths explain for ancient Greeks and Romans?

Objectives

- Demonstrate understanding of common features of legends, myths, folktales, fairy tales, and classic stories.
- Make connections between text and self, text and world, and text to text.
- Read a variety of texts for information and pleasure.
- Compare and contrast literary elements in two or more literary selections.
- Compare and contrast the most important points and details on two texts on the same topic.
- Demonstrate knowledge of authors, characters, and events in significant works of literature.

UNIT OVERVIEW | *The Glory of Greece*

Unit Focus

In this unit, students will learn about ancient Greece and review skills required for reading nonfiction. They will read *The Glory of Greece* by Beth Zemble and John Holdren, which includes the following chapters:

▶ "Why Study Ancient Greece?"
▶ "The Land and Seas"
▶ "Many Gods and Goddesses"
▶ "A Land of City–States"
▶ "A Day with a Boy in Athens"
▶ "Art and Architecture"
▶ "Going to the Theater"
▶ "The Olympic Games"
▶ "Great Thinkers"
▶ "How We Know, What We Owe"

Unit Plan		〖Online〗	〖Offline〗
Lesson 1	Introduce *The Glory of Greece* (A)		50 minutes
Lesson 2	Explore *The Glory of Greece* (A)	40 minutes	10 minutes
Lesson 3	Introduce *The Glory of Greece* (B)		50 minutes
Lesson 4	Explore *The Glory of Greece* (B)	40 minutes	10 minutes
Lesson 5	Introduce *The Glory of Greece* (C)		50 minutes
Lesson 6	Explore *The Glory of Greece* (C)	40 minutes	10 minutes
Lesson 7	Introduce *The Glory of Greece* (D)		50 minutes
Lesson 8	Explore *The Glory of Greece* (D)	40 minutes	10 minutes
Lesson 9	Reflections on *The Glory of Greece* (A)		50 minutes
Lesson 10	Reflections on *The Glory of Greece* (B)	varies	50 minutes
Lesson 11	Your Choice		50 minutes

Introduce *The Glory of Greece* (A)

Lesson Overview

[Offline] **50** minutes

Get Ready	Lesson Introduction
	What Do You Know About Ancient Greece?
	Book Walk
	Words to Know
Read	Introduction and Chapters 1 and 2
GRAB	Go Read a Book

Big Ideas

- ► Comprehension is facilitated when readers connect new information to information previously learned.
- ► Nonfiction texts differ from fiction texts in that they describe real or true things in life, rather than things made up by the author.
- ► Through reading diverse classic and contemporary literature as well as challenging informational texts in a range of subjects, students are expected to build knowledge, gain insight, explore possibilities, and broaden their perspective.

[Materials]

Supplied

- *The Glory of Greece* by Beth Zemble and John Holdren
- *K¹² Language Arts Activity Book*, p. LC 163
- **Reading Strategies bookmark**

Chapter Synopses

The Introduction explains that ancient Greek civilization is important because of the many cultural achievements the Greeks contributed to human society. "The Land and Seas" describes how geography affected the ancient Greeks' livelihoods. "Many Gods and Goddesses" explains the Greek belief in gods and goddesses, as well as the myths they told to explain events in nature and human life.

Keywords

caption – writing printed with a picture that describes or explains the picture

glossary – a list of important terms and their meanings that is usually found in the back of a book

heading – a title within the body of a text that tells the reader something important about a section of the text

sidebar – a short text within a larger text that tells something related but not necessary to the main story

[Offline] 50 minutes

Work **together** with students to complete offline Get Ready, Read, and GRAB activities.

Get Ready

Lesson Introduction

Prepare students to read the Introduction and the first two chapters of *The Glory of Greece*.

1. Tell students that they are going to read a short chapter book titled *The Glory of Greece*. Today they will read the Introduction and the first two chapters of the book.

2. Explain to students that before they read, they will discuss with you

   ▶ What they remember about nonfiction texts
   ▶ What they know about ancient Greece
   ▶ Their predictions about the text
   ▶ Important words to know in the text

3. Tell students that while they read, you will check in to make sure they understand what they are reading.

4. Tell students that after they read, they will answer questions about the text.

What Do You Know About Ancient Greece?

Review the features of nonfiction texts and what students know about ancient Greece. Turn to page LC 163 in *K¹² Language Arts Activity Book*.

1. Have students tell what they know about **nonfiction**. Nonfiction is writing about true things; nonfiction texts contain facts.

2. Have students tell some of the features they might find in a nonfiction text, such as pictures with captions.

3. Tell students that *The Glory of Greece* is a nonfiction book about ancient Greece.

4. Have students find the **table of contents** in *The Glory of Greece*. Explain that the letters stand for the page numbers of the Introduction.

5. Tell students that Chapter 2 is about the ancient Greek gods, goddesses, and myths, which they may know something about already. Tell them that they will need to read carefully in this chapter for the parts of the text that are nonfiction and those that are **fiction**.

> ## Objectives
> - Identify features of a nonfiction text.
> - Connect text to prior knowledge.
> - Use a graphic organizer to organize information.
> - Use text organizational features to locate and comprehend information (table of contents).
> - Use before-reading strategies.
> - Distinguish between fiction and nonfiction.
> - Increase concept and content vocabulary.
> - Determine the meanings and pronunciations of unknown words by using dictionaries, glossaries, technology and textual features, such as definitional footnotes or sidebars.

6. Have students write two things they know about ancient Greece in the first column of the Know-Learn-Wonder chart, particularly something they remember about the ancient Greek gods and myths.

7. Tell students they will complete the chart and answer the questions in the next lesson.

TIP Keep students' KLW chart in a safe place so they can refer to it later.

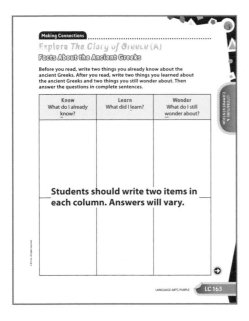

Book Walk

Have students lead you through a Book Walk of the Introduction and the first two chapters of *The Glory of Greece*. Remind them to use the **chapter titles** and **illustrations** to make predictions about what the text will be about.

Words to Know

Before students read the Introduction and the first two chapters of *The Glory of Greece*, explain the words to know and the Let's Say It! feature in the book.

1. Tell students that the words to know are the boldfaced terms in the book that can be found in the glossary. They should use the glossary definitions as they read so that they can understand the text.

2. Turn to "Let's Say It!" on page 56. Have students read the section. Check that they understand the pronunciation guide by having them say the example word *Acropolis* aloud.

3. Turn to page 5. Have students locate the Let's Say It! feature at the bottom of the page and say the words aloud.

Read

Introduction and Chapters 1 and 2

Have students read the Introduction and Chapters 1 and 2. Remind them to use the strategies on their Reading Strategies bookmark. For example, they may want to stop at the end of each page of the text and ask themselves questions about what they just read.

➲ **Learning Coach Check-In** This reading assignment should take about 15 minutes. After students finish reading, ask the following questions to assess their comprehension of the selection:

► What is one way that the land of Greece affected the way people lived there in ancient times? Possible answers: The land was hilly and rocky, so the ancient Greeks grew crops that grew well in that kind of soil, such as grains, grapes, and olives, and they raised sheep and goats; many people lived by the sea instead of in the mountains and therefore had jobs on the water, such as fisherman and sailor.

► Why did the ancient Greeks leave gifts for the gods and goddesses? They left gifts to honor the gods and keep them happy, because they believed that if the gods were happy, things would go well for people. If the gods were unhappy, then people would suffer.

If students have trouble answering these questions, ask them what reading strategies they used and suggest they reread the selection.

Objectives
- Read literature independently and proficiently.
- Apply information read to answer questions.
- Evaluate reading strategies.

GRAB

Go Read a Book

Have students read a book or magazine of their own choosing for at least 20 minutes. Remind students to use the strategies on their Reading Strategies bookmark before and during reading to help them understand the text.

TIP Remember: The more students read, the better readers they become.

Objectives
- Read literature independently and proficiently.
- Read a variety of texts for information and pleasure.

Explore *The Glory of Greece* (A)

Lesson Overview

🖥 [Online]   40 minutes

Check Your Reading	Comprehend Introduction and Chapters 1 and 2
Reading for Meaning	All About the Ancient Greeks
	Make Generalizations About Ancient Greek Religion

📄 [Offline]   10 minutes

Making Connections	Facts About the Ancient Greeks
Beyond the Lesson	⊕ OPTIONAL: Learn More About the Trojan War

Advance Preparation

Gather students' partially completed KLW chart on page LC 163 (Facts About the Ancient Greeks) in *K¹² Language Arts Activity Book*.

Big Ideas

- Narrative and expository text differ significantly—for example, in structure, content, and purpose.
- Readers need to synthesize, draw conclusions about, and interpret what they have read.

[Materials]

Supplied

- *The Glory of Greece* by Beth Zemble and John Holdren

- *K¹² Language Arts Activity Book*, pp. LC 163–164

Keywords

caption – writing printed with a picture that describes or explains the picture

generalization – a statement meant to describe a whole group
Example: Everyone loves a parade.

heading – a title within the body of a text that tells the reader something important about a section of the text

map key – a guide to what the symbols on a map mean

sidebar – a short text within a larger text that tells something related but not necessary to the main story

time line – a line showing dates and events in the order that they happened

 **40 minutes**

Students will work **independently** to complete online Check Your Reading and Reading for Meaning activities.

Check Your Reading

Comprehend Introduction and Chapters 1 and 2
Students will answer questions about the Introduction and Chapters 1 and 2 to demonstrate their literal and inferential comprehension of the text.

Objectives
- Identify concrete answers to questions.
- Apply information read to answer questions.
- Demonstrate knowledge of authors, characters, and events in significant works of literature.
- Determine the meanings and pronunciations of unknown words by using dictionaries, glossaries, technology and textual features, such as definitional footnotes or sidebars.

Reading for Meaning

All About the Ancient Greeks
Students will review some of the features of nonfiction texts and use the features in the book *The Glory of Greece* to locate important information.

Make Generalizations About Ancient Greek Religion
Students will learn how to identify and make generalizations to help them understand the Greek belief in gods and goddesses.

Objectives
- Identify features of nonfiction text.
- Use text organizational features to locate and comprehend information (table of contents, glossary, chapter, index, title, author, illustrator, caption).
- Identify generalizations and evidence that supports them in a text.
- Make generalizations from text.
- Recognize words that signal transitions.

[Offline] 🔟 minutes

Work **together** with students to complete the offline Making Connections and Beyond the Lesson activities.

Making Connections

Facts About the Ancient Greeks

Students will tell what they learned and what they would still like to know about the ancient Greeks after reading this section of *The Glory of Ancient Greece*. Gather students' partially completed Activity Book pages.

1. Direct students' attention to the Activity Book pages and have them read the directions.

2. Repeat to students the directions that they should write two facts they learned about the ancient Greeks in the second column of the KLW chart and two things they still wonder about the ancient Greeks in the third column.

3. Have students complete the Activity Book pages.

TIP Keep the Activity Book pages in a safe place so students can refer to them later.

Objectives
- Use a graphic organizer to organize information.
- Make inferences using evidence from the text.

Making Connections

Explore *The Glory of Greece* (A)

Facts About the Ancient Greeks

Before you read, write two things you already know about the ancient Greeks. After you read, write two things you learned about the ancient Greeks and two things you still wonder about. Then answer the questions in complete sentences.

Know What do I already know?	Learn What did I learn?	Wonder What do I still wonder about?

Students should write two items in each column. Answers will vary.

LANGUAGE ARTS PURPLE — LC 163

1. Why did the Greeks think their gods and goddesses were like people?
   Answers will vary, but students may say that having the gods and goddesses look and act like people helped the Greeks understand the gods better and imagine what they were like.

2. Why might the Greeks have believed that the Trojan War started because of a fight over a woman?
   Answers will vary, but students may say that fighting over a woman was something that happened among people, too, so this reason made sense to the Greeks and was something they could understand and relate to.

LC 164 — LANGUAGE ARTS PURPLE

Beyond the Lesson

⊕ OPTIONAL: Learn More About the Trojan War

This activity is OPTIONAL. It is intended for students who have extra time and would benefit from learning more about the major characters and events in the story of the Trojan War. Feel free to skip this activity.

1. Have students use library books or the Internet to learn more about the Trojan War, including the major heroes on both sides and some of the stories told about the war. Possible websites are listed in the online lesson.

2. Have students write a short summary of one important event or story from the war, such as the story of the Trojan horse, the death of the Greek hero Patroclus (puh-TROH-kluhs), the death of the Greek hero Achilles, or other stories.

Objectives

- Use search tools to locate information (for example, hyperlink).
- Make connections between text and self, text and world, and text to text.
- Summarize the plot of a story.

Introduce *The Glory of Greece* (B)

Lesson Overview

[Offline]   **50** minutes

Get Ready	Lesson Introduction
	Daily Life in Ancient Greece
	Book Walk
	Words to Know
Read	Chapters 3 and 4
GRAB	Go Read a Book

Big Ideas

▸ Active, strong readers employ reading strategies such as making connections between text and self, between and among texts, and between text and the real world.

▸ Nonfiction texts differ from fiction texts in that they describe real or true things in life, rather than things made up by the author.

▸ Through reading diverse classic and contemporary literature as well as challenging informational texts in a range of subjects, students are expected to build knowledge, gain insights, explore possibilities, and broaden their perspective.

[Materials]

Supplied

- *The Glory of Greece* by Beth Zemble and John Holdren
- *K¹² Language Arts Activity Book*, p. LC 165
- Reading Strategies bookmark

Chapter Synopses

"A Land of City–States" describes the two best known Greek city–states, Sparta and Athens. Sparta valued war and success in battle, while Athens valued wisdom and beauty. Athens was also the home of democracy, and the chapter describes some of the ways the Athenians ruled themselves. "A Day with a Boy in Athens" describes a day in the life of a fictional Athenian boy, Nestor, as he makes his way from home to school through the agora.

Keywords

fact – something that can be proven true
fiction – make-believe stories
nonfiction – writings about true things

Offline 50 minutes

Work **together** with students to complete offline Get Ready, Read, and GRAB activities.

Get Ready

Lesson Introduction

Prepare students to read Chapters 3 and 4 of *The Glory of Greece*.

1. Tell students that they are going to read the next two chapters of *The Glory of Greece*.

2. Explain to students that before they read Chapters 3 and 4, they will discuss with you

   ▶ What their own daily life is like
   ▶ What they know about daily life in ancient Greece
   ▶ Their predictions about the text
   ▶ Important words to know in the text

3. Tell students that while they read, you will check in to make sure they understand what they are reading.

4. Tell students that after they read, they will answer questions about the text.

> **Objectives**
> - Connect text with prior knowledge.
> - Distinguish between fiction and nonfiction.
> - Use a graphic organizer to organize information.
> - Use before-reading strategies.
> - Increase concept and content vocabulary.
> - Determine the meanings and pronunciations of unknown words by using dictionaries, glossaries, technology and textual features, such as definitional footnotes or sidebars.

Daily Life in Ancient Greece

Discuss what modern daily life is like to help students connect their own experiences with the descriptions of daily life in *The Glory of Greece*. Turn to page LC 165 in *K¹² Language Arts Activity Book*.

1. Have students describe some of the things they do every day. If necessary, prompt them with questions about what they do in the morning, afternoon, and evening.

2. Have students tell some of the things they do for fun and to describe some of the things their parents or other family members do.

3. Tell students that the next two chapters in the book describe what life was like in ancient Greece.

4. Tell students that Chapter 4 contains a **fiction** story within the text. Remind them that sometimes fiction contains **facts**. Have students give an example of a fictional story that contains facts. Answers may include the Tornado Chase cartoon from the magazine *K¹² World: Weather or Not*.

5. Have students write two things they know about the way the ancient Greeks lived in the first column of the KLW chart on page LC 165.

6. Tell students they will complete the chart and answer the questions in the next lesson.

TIP Keep students' KLW chart in a safe place so they can refer to it later.

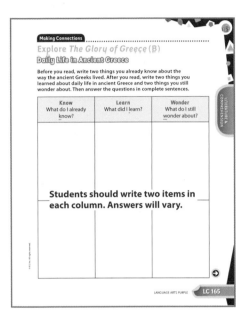

Book Walk

Have students lead you through a Book Walk of Chapters 3 and 4 of *The Glory of Greece*. Remind them to use the **chapter titles** and **illustrations** to make predictions about what the text will be about.

Words to Know

Before students read Chapters 3 and 4 of *The Glory of Greece*, remind them that the Words to Know in this book are boldfaced terms. The definitions can be found in the glossary. The Let's Say It! feature gives pronunciation guides for some words in the text. Students can refer to page 56 for more on the pronunciation key.

Read

Chapters 3 and 4

Have students read Chapters 3 and 4. Remind them to use the strategies on their Reading Strategies bookmark. For example, they may want to stop at the end of each page of the text and summarize what they just read.

➲ **Learning Coach Check-In** This reading assignment should take about 15–20 minutes. After students finish reading, ask the following questions to assess their comprehension of the selection:

▸ What was Sparta known for? What was Athens known for? Possible answers: Sparta was known for its citizens' skill in sports and battle; Athens was known for its people's skill in building, creating art, debate, and democracy.

▸ What are some of the ways that Nestor's life is like your own? Answers will vary, but students may say that Nestor's life is like their own because he studies some of the same subjects, lives with his parents and sister, eats some of the same foods, shops in a market, and likes sports.

If students have trouble answering these questions, ask them what reading strategies they used and suggest they reread the selection.

Objectives
- Read literature independently and proficiently.
- Apply information read to answer questions.
- Evaluate reading strategies.

GRAB

Go Read a Book

Have students read a book or magazine of their own choosing for at least 20 minutes. Remind students to use the strategies on their Reading Strategies bookmark before and during reading to help them understand the text.

Objectives
- Read literature independently and proficiently.
- Read a variety of texts for information and pleasure.

Explore *The Glory of Greece* (B)

Lesson Overview

🖥 [Online]   40 minutes

Check Your Reading	Comprehend Chapters 3 and 4
Reading for Meaning	Sparta and Athens
	Daily Life in Athens

📄 [Offline]   10 minutes

Making Connections	Daily Life in Ancient Greece
Beyond the Lesson	➕ OPTIONAL: Ancient Life vs. Modern Life
	➕ OPTIONAL: Learn More About Life in Ancient Greece

Materials

Supplied

- *The Glory of Greece* by Beth Zemble and John Holdren
- *K¹² Language Arts Activity Book*, pp. LC 165–167

Also Needed

- pencils, coloring, or crayons (optional)
- glue (optional)

Advance Preparation

Gather students' partially completed KLW chart on page LC 165 (Daily Life in Ancient Greece) in *K¹² Language Arts Activity Book*.

Big Ideas

► Narrative and expository text differ significantly—for example, in structure, content, and purpose.
► Readers need to synthesize, draw conclusions about, and interpret what they have read.

Keywords

compare – to explain how two or more things are alike

conclusion – a decision made about something not stated, using information provided and what is already known

contrast – to explain how two or more things are different

fact – something that can be proven true

fiction – make-believe stories

inference – a guess that readers make using the clues that authors give them in a piece of writing

nonfiction – writings about true things

 **40 minutes**

Students will work **independently** to complete online Check Your Reading and Reading for Meaning activities.

Check Your Reading ....

Comprehend Chapters 3 and 4
Students will answer questions about Chapters 3 and 4 to demonstrate their literal and inferential comprehension of the text.

Objectives
- Identify concrete answers to questions.
- Apply information read to answer questions.
- Use graphics to answer a question.

Reading for Meaning ....

Sparta and Athens
Students will compare and contrast Athens and Sparta to learn how the two ancient Greek city–states were alike and different.

Daily Life in Athens
Students will identify facts in the fictional story contained in Chapter 4, and use facts from the story to make inferences and draw conclusions about life in ancient Athens.

Objectives
- Compare and contrast using evidence from the text.
- Identify supporting details.
- Demonstrate knowledge of authors, characters, and events in significant works of literature.
- Distinguish between fiction and nonfiction.
- Identify facts.
- Draw conclusions using evidence from text.
- Make inferences using evidence from the text.

[Offline] ⑩ minutes

Work **together** with students to complete the offline Making Connections and Beyond the Lesson activities.

Making Connections

Daily Life in Ancient Greece

Students will tell what they learned and what they would still like to know about the ancient Greeks after reading this section of *The Glory of Ancient Greece*. Gather students' partially completed Activity Book pages.

1. Direct students' attention to the Activity Book pages and have them read the directions.

2. Repeat to students the directions that they should write two facts they learned about daily life in ancient Greece in the second column of the chart and two things they still wonder about in the third column.

3. Have students complete the Activity Book pages.

TIP Keep the Activity Book pages in a safe place so students can refer to them later.

> **Objectives**
> - Make inferences and draw conclusions.
> - Compare and contrast using evidence from the text.

Making Connections

Explore *The Glory of Greece* (B)
Daily Life in Ancient Greece

Before you read, write two things you already know about the way the ancient Greeks lived. After you read, write two things you learned about daily life in ancient Greece and two things you still wonder about. Then answer the questions in complete sentences.

Know What do I already know?	Learn What did I learn?	Wonder What do I still wonder about?
Students should write two items in each column. Answers will vary.		

LANGUAGE ARTS PURPLE **LC 165**

---

1. Athens and Sparta were in a very long war with each other. Sparta won. Does this surprise you? Why or why not?

Answers will vary, but some students may say that this does not surprise them because Spartans spent more time preparing for war than Athenians.

2. Why didn't the Athenians allow women and slaves to become citizens and vote?

Answers will vary, but students may say that the Athenians thought women and slaves were not equal to free men and thus could not have the right to choose Athenian leaders.

LC 166 LANGUAGE ARTS PURPLE

---

3. Why did the Athenians choose democracy rather than being ruled by a king? Think about what you learned about the Athenians.

Answers will vary, but students may say that the Athenians loved wisdom and debate. In a democracy, people think and talk about issues, which was important to the Athenians. They also are able to vote, which requires thought.

4. Why did the Spartans believe in the idea of "win or die"? What does this idea say about them?

Answers will vary, but students may say that the Spartans thought war was very important, so winning was the only outcome the Spartans would accept. If soldiers couldn't win a war, they should at least die trying. This idea says that the Spartans were probably very fierce fighters who did not give up easily.

LANGUAGE ARTS PURPLE **LC 167**

Beyond the Lesson ....

➕ OPTIONAL: Ancient Life vs. Modern Life

This activity is OPTIONAL. It is intended for students who have extra time and would benefit from comparing their own lives to that of the fictional character Nestor in *The Glory of Greece*. Feel free to skip this activity. Gather the coloring pencils or crayons and glue.

1. Tell students that they are going to make a minibook comparing ancient Greek life and modern life.

2. Give students two sheets of paper. Have students fold each sheet in half, bringing the two short sides of the paper together to make a crease across the center.

3. Have students hold one sheet lengthwise, so that the crease runs vertically. Tell them to write about life in ancient Greece on this paper.

   ▸ On the left side of the crease, have students write a one-paragraph summary of Nestor's life. Tell them to use facts from Chapter 4 in their summary.
   ▸ On the right side of the crease, have students draw a picture of an aspect of Nestor's life.

4. Have students hold the second sheet lengthwise, so that the crease runs vertically. Tell them to write about modern life on this paper.

   ▸ On the left side of the crease, have students write a one-paragraph summary of their own daily lives. Tell them to use facts in their summary.
   ▸ On the right side of the crease, have students draw a picture of an aspect of their daily life.

5. Have students glue the back of their picture of Nestor's life to the back of their summary of modern life, to make a book.

6. Tell students to write a title on the cover of the book, "Ancient Life vs. Modern Life." Encourage students to share the book with others.

(TIP) If students would like to make a longer book, have them write separate facts about ancient and modern life on multiple sheets of paper that they fold. Have them draw a picture of each fact. Then have them glue the pages together to make a longer book.

_____

➕ OPTIONAL: Learn More About Life in Ancient Greece

This activity is OPTIONAL. It is intended for students who have extra time and would benefit from learning more about what life was like in ancient Greece. Feel free to skip this activity.

1. Have students learn more about life in ancient Greece by using the library or Internet to research one or more of the following topics:

   ▸ Life for girls and women
   ▸ Life for slaves
   ▸ What school was like for boys
   ▸ The Peloponnesian War

2. Have students write a brief summary of what they discover. Tell them to include facts from their research.

Objectives

- Use search tools to locate information (for example, hyperlink).
- Make connections between text and self, text and world, and text to text.
- Recognize and explain the meaning of common idioms, adages, and proverbs.
- Determine the meaning of text-related words, including those related to mythology.

Introduce *The Glory of Greece* (C)

Lesson Overview

[Offline] ⬛ 50 minutes

Get Ready	Lesson Introduction
	Gifts from the Ancient Greeks
	Book Walk
	Words to Know
Read	Chapters 5–7
GRAB	Go Read a Book

Big Ideas

▸ Active, strong readers employ reading strategies such as making connections between text and self, between and among texts, and between text and the real world.

▸ Nonfiction texts differ from fiction texts in that they describe real or true things in life, rather than things made up by the author.

▸ Through reading diverse classic and contemporary literature as well as challenging informational texts in a range of subjects, students are expected to build knowledge, gain insights, explore possibilities, and broaden their perspective.

Materials

Supplied

- *The Glory of Greece* by Beth Zemble and John Holdren
- *K¹² Language Arts Activity Book*, p. LC 169
- Reading Strategies bookmark

Chapter Synopses

"Art and Architecture" describes some of the elements of ancient Greek buildings, statues, and pottery that are still with us today. "Going to the Theater" describes what it was like to go to a play in ancient Greece and what elements of Greek drama are part of modern drama. "The Olympic Games" is all about the origins of the Olympics and what the games were like in ancient times.

Keywords

fact – something that can be proven true

[Offline] 50 minutes

Work **together** with students to complete offline Get Ready, Read, and GRAB activities.

Get Ready

Lesson Introduction

Prepare students to read Chapters 5–7 of *The Glory of Greece*.

1. Tell students that they are going to read the next three chapters of *The Glory of Greece*.

2. Explain to students that before they read Chapters 5–7 of the book they will discuss with you

   ▸ What they have learned about the ancient Greeks so far
   ▸ Their predictions about the text
   ▸ Important words to know in the text

3. Tell students that while they read, you will check in to make sure they understand what they are reading.

4. Tell students that after they read, they will answer questions about the text.

> ⭐ **Objectives**
> - Connect text with prior knowledge.
> - Use a graphic organizer to organize information.
> - Use before-reading strategies.
> - Increase concept and content vocabulary.
> - Determine the meanings and pronunciations of unknown words by using dictionaries, glossaries, technology and textual features, such as definitional footnotes or sidebars.

Gifts from the Ancient Greeks

Discuss what modern daily life is like to help students connect their experiences with the descriptions of daily life in *The Glory of Greece*. Turn to page LC 169 in *K¹² Language Arts Activity Book*.

1. Ask students what they learned about ancient Greek life that is still part of life today. Give students an example: We still read the myths of the ancient Greeks. Possible answers: democracy; juries; assemblies; school subjects such as math and science; open-air markets; statues and buildings built by the ancient Greeks

2. Tell students that the next three chapters in the book describe more things that the ancient Greeks contributed to modern life.

3. Have students write two things they know about any of the following topics in the first column of the KLW chart on page LC 169:

   ▸ Ancient Greek art and architecture, including statues, buildings, and pottery
   ▸ Theater in ancient Greece
   ▸ The original Olympic Games in ancient Greece

4. Tell students they will finish the chart and write the paragraph in the next lesson.

TIP Keep students' KLW chart in a safe place so they can refer to it later.

Making Connections

Explore *The Glory of Greece* (C)

The Influence of the Greeks

Before you read, write two things you already know about ancient Greek art, architecture, theater, or the Olympics. After you read, write two things you learned about these topics and two things you still wonder about. Then complete the assignment.

Know What do I already know?	Learn What did I learn?	Wonder What do I still wonder about?

Students should write two items in each column. Answers will vary.

LANGUAGE ARTS PURPLE | LC 169

Book Walk

Have students lead you through a Book Walk of Chapters 5–7 of *The Glory of Greece*. Remind them to use the **chapter titles** and **illustrations** to make predictions about what the text will be about.

Words to Know

Before students read Chapters 5–7 of *The Glory of Greece*, remind them that in this book the Words to Know are boldfaced terms, and the definitions can be found in the glossary. The Let's Say It! feature gives pronunciation guides for some words in the text. Students can refer to page 56 for more on the pronunciation key.

Read

Chapters 5–7

Have students read Chapters 5–7. Remind them to use the strategies on their Reading Strategies bookmark. For example, they may want to stop at the end of each page of the text and ask and answer a question about what they have just read.

⟳ **Learning Coach Check-In** This reading assignment should take about 15 minutes. After students finish reading, ask the following questions to assess their comprehension of the selection:

▸ What are two things that the ancient Greeks put on their buildings that we can see on buildings today? Possible answers: white marble; wide steps; tall columns

▸ What was an ancient Greek theater like? Describe it. Greek theaters were large and outdoors. They looked like modern stadiums. Each theater was shaped like a semicircle with the stage at the bottom and in the center. The seats were in long rows, like bleachers, that rose high above the stage. The shape of the theater helped the audience see and hear the actors.

▸ What kinds of events were held during the ancient Olympic Games? Possible answers: foot races including relays; chariot races; javelin and discus throwing; wrestling; jumping; pankration (which combined boxing and wrestling); pentathlon

If students have trouble answering these questions, ask them what reading strategies they used and suggest they reread the selection.

Objectives
- Read literature independently and proficiently.
- Apply information read to answer questions.
- Evaluate reading strategies.

GRAB

Go Read a Book

Have students read a book or magazine of their own choosing for at least 20 minutes. Remind students to use the strategies on their Reading Strategies bookmark before and during reading to help them understand the text.

Objectives
- Read literature independently and proficiently.
- Read a variety of texts for information and pleasure.

Explore *The Glory of Greece* (C)

Lesson Overview

[Online]   **40** minutes

Check Your Reading	Comprehend Chapters 5–7
Reading for Meaning	Understand the Visuals
	Idioms from Ancient Greece

[Offline]   **10** minutes

Making Connections	The Influence of the Greeks
Beyond the Lesson	✚ OPTIONAL: Make a Greek Drama Mask
	✚ OPTIONAL: The History of the Marathon

Advance Preparation

Gather students' partially completed KLW chart on page LC 169 (The Influence of the Greeks) in *K¹² Language Arts Activity Book*.

Big Ideas

▶ Readers should pay close attention to the visual elements (for example, illustrations) that accompany a story to help create and describe the meaning of a text.

▶ Active, strong readers employ reading strategies such as making connections between text and self, between and among texts, and between text and the real world.

▶ Writers must be able to articulate a main idea and support it with appropriate details.

▶ Readers should be able to retell the story (or information) in their own words, not repeat what was written.

▶ Writing requires organization and structure.

Materials

Supplied

- *The Glory of Greece* by Beth Zemble and John Holdren
- *K¹² Language Arts Activity Book*, pp. LC 169–170

Also Needed

- pencils, coloring, or crayons (optional)
- glue (optional)

Keywords

caption – writing printed with a picture that describes or explains the picture

compare – to explain how two or more things are alike

contrast – to explain how two or more things are different

idiom – a group of words that does not actually mean what it says; for example, *raining cats and dogs; a month of Sundays*

supporting details – the sentences that give information about the main idea or topic sentence

 **40 minutes**

Students will work **independently** to complete online Check Your Reading and Reading for Meaning activities.

Check Your Reading

Comprehend Chapters 5–7

Students will answer questions about Chapters 5–7 to demonstrate their literal and inferential comprehension of the text.

> **⭐ Objectives**
> - Identify concrete answers to questions.
> - Infer answers to questions.
> - Apply information read to answer questions.
> - Use graphics and visuals to comprehend meaning and answer questions (diagrams, charts, captions).

Reading for Meaning

Understand the Visuals

Students will use the visuals, captions, and text from Chapters 5–7 of *The Glory of Greece* to learn how ancient Greek culture influenced aspects of modern culture.

Idioms from Ancient Greece

Students will learn words, sayings, and idioms that were inspired by ancient Greek myths and culture.

> **⭐ Objectives**
> - Use graphics and visuals to comprehend meaning and answer questions (diagrams, charts, captions).
> - Compare and contrast using evidence from the text.
> - Recognize and explain the meaning of common idioms, adages, and proverbs.
> - Determine the meaning of text-related words, including those related to mythology.

[Offline] 🔟 minutes

Work **together** with students to complete the offline Making Connections and Beyond the Lesson activities.

Making Connections ....

The Influence of the Greeks

Students will tell what they learned and what they would still like to know about the ancient Greeks after reading this section of the book. They will also write a paragraph comparing an aspect of ancient Greek culture with modern times. Gather students' partially completed Activity Book pages.

1. Direct students' attention to the Activity Book pages and have them read the directions.

2. Repeat to students the directions that they should write in the second column of the chart two facts they learned about art, architecture, theater, or the Olympics in ancient Greece and two things they still wonder about life in ancient Greece in the third column.

3. Have students complete the Activity Book pages.

TIP Keep the Activity Book pages in a safe place so students can refer to them later.

> ### Objectives
> - Compare and contrast using evidence from the text.
> - Identify supporting details.
> - Recount key (supporting) details.

Making Connections

Explore *The Glory of Greece* (C)

The Influence of the Greeks

Before you read, write two things you already know about ancient Greek art, architecture, theater, or the Olympics. After you read, write two things you learned about these topics and two things you still wonder about. Then complete the assignment.

| Know
What do I already know? | Learn
What did I learn? | Wonder
What do I still wonder about? |
|---|---|---|
| | | |

Students should write two items in each column. Answers will vary.

LANGUAGE ARTS PURPLE   **LC 169**

Choose one of the topics from this lesson: art, architecture, theater, or the Olympics. Write a paragraph comparing and contrasting your topic in ancient Greek times and in modern times.

- First write a sentence that introduces your topic.
- Next tell two ways the topic is the same today as in ancient times. Support your thoughts with evidence from *The Glory of Greece* and what you already know.
- Then write two ways it is different. Use evidence from the text and your own knowledge to support your ideas.
- Finally, write a concluding sentence.

Students should choose one of the categories from this lesson's reading—art, architecture, theater, or the Olympics—and compare and contrast that aspect of culture in ancient Greece and today. They should include two ways their topic is similar and two ways it is different from then to now. They should support their ideas with evidence from the text.

LC 170   LANGUAGE ARTS PURPLE

Beyond the Lesson •••

⊕ OPTIONAL: Make a Greek Drama Mask

This activity is OPTIONAL. It is intended for students who have extra time and would benefit from making their own version of a Greek drama mask. Feel free to skip this activity.

1. Have students make a mask for a tragedy or a comedy. They can draw the mask on construction paper, or cut out a mask from cardboard and add color with markers or colored paper.

2. Tell students to make sure the expression on the face of the mask shows a feeling that would go with either tragedy or comedy.

⊕ OPTIONAL: The History of the Marathon

This activity is OPTIONAL. It is intended for students who have extra time and would benefit from learning more about how the first marathon started in ancient Greece. Feel free to skip this activity.

1. Tell students that another famous athletic event also came from ancient Greece: the marathon.

2. Have students research the history of the marathon using the library or the Internet.

3. Have students make a poster advertising the marathon to runners in ancient Greek times. Tell students to include on the poster information about where the race will take place, how long it is, and who may compete.

> **Objectives**
> - Make connections between text and self, text and world, and text to text.
> - Use search tools to locate information (for example, hyperlink).

Introduce *The Glory of Greece* (D)

Lesson Overview

【 Offline 】 **50** minutes

Get Ready	Lesson Introduction
	Think About Thinking
	Book Walk
	Words to Know
Read	Chapter 8 and Conclusion
GRAB	Go Read a Book

Big Ideas

▸ Active, strong readers employ reading strategies such as making connections between text and self, between and among texts, and between text and the real world.

▸ Nonfiction texts differ from fiction texts in that they describe real or true things in life, rather than things made up by the author.

▸ Through reading diverse classic and contemporary literature as well as challenging informational texts in a range of subjects, students are expected to build knowledge, gain insights, explore possibilities, and broaden their perspective.

【 Materials 】

Supplied

- *The Glory of Greece* by Beth Zemble and John Holdren
- *K¹² Language Arts Activity Book*, p. LC 171
- Reading Strategies bookmark

Chapter Synopses

"Great Thinkers" introduces the three greatest ancient Greek philosophers: Socrates, Plato, and Aristotle. It also tells about Hippocrates, considered the father of modern medicine. "How We Know, What We Owe" explains how modern archaeologists learn about ancient Greek culture by studying artifacts and ruins.

Keywords

nonfiction – writings about true things

Offline 50 minutes

Work **together** with students to complete offline Get Ready, Read, and GRAB activities.

Get Ready

Lesson Introduction

Prepare students to read Chapter 8 and the Conclusion of *The Glory of Greece.*

1. Tell students that they are going to finish reading *The Glory of Greece.*
2. Explain to students that before they read Chapter 8 and the Conclusion of the book, they will discuss with you
   - What a philosopher is and what they know about philosophers
   - Their predictions about the text
   - Important words to know in the text
3. Tell students that while they read, you will check in to make sure they understand what they are reading.
4. Tell students that after they read, they will answer questions about the book.

Objectives

- Connect text with prior knowledge.
- Use a graphic organizer to organize information.
- Use before-reading strategies.
- Increase concept and content vocabulary.
- Determine the meanings and pronunciations of unknown words by using dictionaries, glossaries, technology and textual features, such as definitional footnotes or sidebars.

Think About Thinking

Explain what a philosopher is and ask what students know about famous philosophers. Turn to page LC 171 in K^{12} *Language Arts Activity Book.*

1. Have students tell some of the things that ancient Greeks contributed to modern life and culture, such as certain kinds of architecture and the Olympics.
2. Ask students if they know what a philosopher is. If they do not, explain that a philosopher is someone who thinks about important ideas, human behavior, and life.
3. Tell students that some of the most important philosophers in history were ancient Greeks, including Socrates, Plato, and Aristotle, among others. Chapter 8 is about Socrates, Plato, and Aristotle, and also includes Hippocrates, considered the father of medicine.
4. Tell them that the Conclusion is about how people know about the ancient Greeks, using artifacts, ruins, and stories.

5. Have students write two things they know about either the ancient Greek philosophers or how people study ancient cultures in the first column of the KLW chart on page LC 171.

6. Tell students they will finish the chart and write their paragraph in the next lesson.

TIP Keep students' KLW chart in a safe place so they can refer to it later.

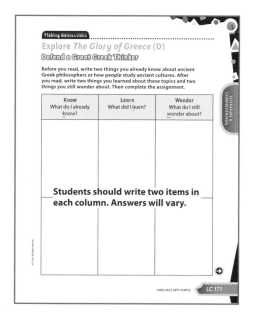

Book Walk

Have students lead you through a Book Walk of Chapter 8 and the Conclusion of *The Glory of Greece*. Remind them to use the **chapter titles** and **illustrations** to make predictions about what the text will be about.

Words to Know

Before students read Chapter 8 and the Conclusion of *The Glory of Greece*, remind students that the Words to Know in this book are the boldfaced terms. The definitions can be found in the glossary. The Let's Say It! feature gives pronunciation guides for some words in the text. Students can refer to page 56 for more on the pronunciation key.

Read

Chapter 8 and Conclusion

Have students read Chapter 8 and the Conclusion. Remind them to use the strategies on their Reading Strategies bookmark. For example, they may want to stop at the end of each page of the text and reread anything they did not understand.

⮑ **Learning Coach Check-In** This reading assignment should take about 15 minutes. After students finish reading, ask the following questions to assess their comprehension of the selection:

▸ What are the names of the three famous Greek philosophers? Socrates, Plato, and Aristotle

▸ What is one thing that archaeologists use to learn about the past and ancient Greece? Possible answers: artifacts; ruins; myths and stories

If students have trouble answering these questions, ask them what reading strategies they used and suggest they reread the selection.

Objectives

- Read literature independently and proficiently.
- Apply information read to answer questions.
- Evaluate reading strategies.

GRAB

Go Read a Book

Have students read a book or magazine of their own choosing for at least 20 minutes. Remind students to use the strategies on their Reading Strategies bookmark before and during reading to help them understand the text.

Objectives

- Read literature independently and proficiently.
- Read a variety of texts for information and pleasure.

Explore *The Glory of Greece* (D)

Lesson Overview

	Online	**40** minutes

Check Your Reading	Comprehend Chapter 8 and Conclusion

Reading for Meaning	The Great Greek Thinkers
	Why We Learn About the Past

Offline		**10** minutes

Making Connections	Defend a Great Greek Thinker

Materials

Supplied

- *The Glory of Greece* by Beth Zemble and John Holdren
- *K¹² Language Arts Activity Book*, pp. LC 171–173

Keywords

conclusion – a decision made about something not stated, using information provided and what is already known

inference – a guess that readers make using the clues that authors give them in a piece of writing

Advance Preparation

Gather students' partially completed KLW chart on page LC 171 (Defend a Great Greek Thinker) in *K¹² Language Arts Activity Book*.

Big Ideas

- ▶ Active, strong readers employ reading strategies such as making connections between text and self, between and among texts, and between text and the real world.
- ▶ Readers need to synthesize, draw conclusions about, and interpret what they have read.
- ▶ Writers must be able to articulate a main idea and support it with appropriate details.
- ▶ Readers should be able to retell the story (or information) in their own words, not repeat what was written.
- ▶ Writing requires organization and structure.

[Online] 40 minutes

Students will work **independently** to complete online Check Your Reading and Reading for Meaning activities.

Check Your Reading . . . .

Comprehend Chapter 8 and Conclusion

Students will answer questions about Chapter 8 and the Conclusion to demonstrate their literal and inferential comprehension of the text.

Objectives
- Identify concrete answers to questions.
- Apply information read to answer questions.
- Use text features to locate information.

Reading for Meaning . . . .

The Great Greek Thinkers

Students will make inferences and draw conclusions about why the great Greek thinkers were important and why we still study their ideas today.

Objectives
- Draw conclusions using evidence from text.
- Make inferences using evidence from the text.

Why We Learn About the Past

Students will examine the legacy of ancient Greeks and the many important ideas, stories, and objects they left behind to understand why we study this influential culture.

[Offline] ⑩ minutes

Work **together** with students to complete the offline Making Connections activity.

Making Connections ●●

Defend a Great Greek Thinker

Students will tell what they learned and what they would still like to know about the ancient Greeks after reading this section of the book. They will also write a paragraph in which they defend a Greek philosopher. Gather students' partially completed Activity Book pages.

1. Direct students' attention to the Activity Book pages and have them read the directions.

2. Repeat to students the directions that they should write in the second column of the chart two facts they learned about the Greek philosophers or how we learn about the ancient Greeks and two things they still wonder about ancient Greece in the third column.

3. Have students complete the Activity Book pages.

TIP Keep the Activity Book pages in a safe place so students can refer to them later.

Objectives

- Recount key (supporting) details.
- Recognize author's opinion and distinguish it from own.
- State an opinion related to topic.
- Give reasons for opinion.
- Write a paragraph.
- Write an introductory statement.
- Write a concluding statement.

Making Connections ....
Explore *The Glory of Greece* (D)
Defend a Great Greek Thinker

Before you read, write two things you already know about ancient Greek philosophers or how people study ancient cultures. After you read, write two things you learned about these topics and two things you still wonder about. Then complete the assignment.

Know What do I already know?	Learn What did I learn?	Wonder What do I still wonder about?

Students should write two items in each column. Answers will vary.

LANGUAGE ARTS PURPLE · LC 171

Write a paragraph defending one of the great Greek thinkers from people who are afraid of his ideas.

- Choose one of the great ancient Greek thinkers as your subject: Socrates, Plato, Aristotle, or Hippocrates.
- Imagine that this man is on trial. The Greeks are afraid of his ideas and want to put him in jail.
- Write a paragraph using the first-person point of view.
- Start your paragraph with an introductory statement telling who you are defending and why.
- Write a paragraph in which you defend this thinker. Imagine that you agree with his ideas. Explain why his ideas are important and why he should be free to teach. Use examples from the *The Glory of Greece* to support your argument.
- End your paragraph with a concluding sentence urging the Greek jury to set your great thinker free.

Students should defend one of the great thinkers using the first-person point of view. Their paragraph should have an introductory sentence. The writing should state why the thinker's ideas are important and the argument should be supported with evidence from the text. The paragraph should end with a concluding statement pleading for the great thinker's freedom.

LC 172 · LANGUAGE ARTS PURPLE

Reflections on *The Glory of Greece* (A)

Lesson Overview

[Offline]		50 minutes
Get Ready	**Lesson Introduction**	
	Review Facts and Opinions About Ancient Greece	
Putting It All Together	**Create a Presentation**	

[Materials]

Supplied
- *The Glory of Greece* by Beth Zemble and John Holdren
- *K¹² Language Arts Activity Book,* pp. LC 163, 165, 169, 171, 175–180

Keywords

fact – something that can be proven true

main idea – the most important point the author makes; it may be stated or unstated

opinion – something that a person thinks or believes, but which cannot be proven to be true

supporting details – the sentences that give information about the main idea or topic sentence

topic – the subject of a text

Advance Preparation

Gather students' completed KLW charts on pages LC 163 (Facts About the Ancient Greeks), 165 (Daily Life in Ancient Greece), 169 (The Influence of the Greeks), and 171 (Defend a Great Greek Thinker) in *K¹² Language Arts Activity Book.*

Big Ideas

- ▶ Readers need to synthesize, draw conclusions about, and interpret what they have read.
- ▶ Competent writers rely on a repertoire of strategies when planning, composing, and revising their texts.
- ▶ Writers must be able to articulate a main idea and support it with appropriate details.
- ▶ Readers should be able to retell the story (or information) in their own words, not repeat what was written.
- ▶ Writing requires organization and structure.

[Offline] 50 minutes

Work **together** with students to complete the offline Get Ready and Putting It All Together activities.

Get Ready

Lesson Introduction

Prepare students to give a presentation about ancient Greece using the information they gathered from the book *The Glory of Greece* and information they research on their own.

1. Explain to students that they are going to use the information they collected in their KLW charts to prepare a speech. The speech will be about

   ▸ Life in ancient Greece
   ▸ How some ancient Greek ideas are still important today
   ▸ Students' opinion on whether or not it is important to learn about ancient Greece

2. Tell students they will also research one of their "wonder" questions, or think of another question they still have about ancient Greece, and include that information in the speech as well.

> **Objectives**
> - Recount key (supporting) details.
> - Recognize author's opinion and distinguish it from own.
> - State an opinion related to topic.

Review Facts and Opinions About Ancient Greece

Review some of the facts about ancient Greece from the book *The Glory of Greece* and discuss the authors' opinion about studying this culture.

1. Have students tell some of the **facts** they learned about ancient Greece. If students need prompting, have them look at the **table of contents** in *The Glory of Greece* to remind them of the major **topics** in the book. Then have them tell at least one fact about each topic.

2. Ask students what they think is the authors' opinion about studying ancient Greece. Tell them to give supporting details from the text to support their idea about the authors' opinion. Possible answer: The authors think ancient Greece was an important culture that people should learn about.

3. Ask students whether or not they agree with the authors about the importance of studying ancient Greece, and tell them to explain their answer.

Putting It All Together

Create a Presentation

Students will demonstrate their understanding of what they have learned about ancient Greece. Gather the completed KLW charts and turn to pages LC 175–180 in *K¹² Language Arts Activity Book*.

1. Give students the Activity Book pages that they will use to create their presentation. Have them read all the directions and use their KLW charts for ideas.

2. Tell students that they are going to complete this activity over two days.

   ▸ In **this lesson**, students will complete only Steps 1–7 only. They will write a draft of their presentation.

   ▸ In **the next lesson**, they will finish writing a draft of their presentation and complete Steps 8–11. Students will develop a visual aid and add it to their presentation. Then they will complete their final draft, practice their presentation, and present it to an audience.

   ⊃ **Learning Coach Check-In** Check in with students after about 40 minutes to see if they have completed the assignment.

TIP Students may want to finish more of the presentation than recommended in the lesson. Allow them to work at their own pace.

Objectives
- Identify descriptions that support comprehension.
- Identify main idea and supporting details in a text.
- State an opinion related to topic.
- Organize ideas.
- Write a speech.

Putting It All Together

Reflections on *The Glory of Greece* (A)

Create a Presentation

Give a speech about ancient Greece. Your presentation will include your opinion on why we should study this culture and its people. Before you begin, read the instructions all the way through. Then follow the steps.

1. What is the purpose of your presentation? Your purpose may be to inform, to entertain, to express emotions, or to persuade. You may have more than one purpose.

2. Who is your audience? Are you presenting to people who have read the book or know about ancient Greece? What kind of language will you use with them?

3. Write Part 1, the introduction, of your presentation. In it, tell
   - Where Greece is and what the land is like
   - When ancient Greece was at its height

   Students should write a brief paragraph that includes facts from their KLW chart on these topics.

---

4. Write Part 2 of your presentation. Choose one of the topics from your KLW charts, such as facts about the ancient Greeks or daily life.
   - Write a main idea about your topic.
   - Use two details from your KLW chart to support the main idea.

   Students should write a brief paragraph that describes one of the topics from the KLW charts, such as Greek religion or daily life, and provide two supporting details from the chart.

5. Write Part 3 of your presentation. Choose another topic from your KLW charts, such as art, architecture, the Olympics, or the great thinkers.
   - Write a main idea about this topic.
   - Use two details from your KLW chart to support the main idea.

   Students should write a brief paragraph that describes a different topic from the KLW charts and provide two supporting details from the chart.

---

6. Write Part 4 of your presentation. Choose one of the questions that you still have about ancient Greece (the questions you wrote in the third column of your KLW charts). Research the answer to the question and write about it.
   - Use the library, an encyclopedia, or a reliable source on the Internet to find information to answer your question.
   - Write a main idea about your topic. This should be the answer to your question.
   - Use two details from your research to support the main idea.

   Students should write a brief paragraph about one of the questions they still have about ancient Greece. They should use library books, an encyclopedia, or the Internet to find information about the topic. Then they should write a main idea and two supporting details based on their research.

---

7. Write Part 5, the conclusion, of your presentation. In the conclusion
   - Tell how the ideas from the Greeks are still important to us today.
   - Give your opinion about whether or not we should study the ancient Greeks and their ideas. Explain why you think so.

   Students should write a brief conclusion that explains how the ideas in their presentation are still important to modern society and tells whether or not we should study the ancient Greeks and why.

---

8. Add interest to your presentation by creating at least two visual aids. You can
   - Draw your own visual aids on paper.
   - Create another kind of display.
   - Use a multimedia program to make slides or create another visual that goes with your presentation.

   Put important points from your presentation on different slides or pages. Use the space below to draw what your visual aids might look like or write notes about what you would like to create.

---

9. Make a final draft of your presentation.
   - Write the important points from your draft on note cards or on slides in a multimedia presentation.
   - Create your visuals using art supplies or a computer.

10. Practice your presentation several times in front of a mirror or to a pretend audience. Try to look up frequently to make eye contact, and memorize as many points as you can.

11. Deliver your presentation to your audience. Remember to look at your audience and speak in a clear voice that is easy to hear. Emphasize important points and be enthusiastic about your ideas.

Reflections on *The Glory of Greece* (B)

Lesson Overview

Offline		**50** minutes
Get Ready	Lesson Introduction	
	What Makes an Effective Presentation?	
Putting It All Together	Give a Presentation	

Online		varies
More Practice	Review the Skills	
Read	Read Fluently "Sparta and Athens"	
Performance Review	Fluency Check	

Advance Preparation

Gather students' partially completed presentation on pages LC 175–180 (Create a Presentation) in *K¹² Language Arts Activity Book*. Ideally students should give their presentation to their peers, but if necessary you can have them present to you.

Big Ideas

Good public speakers speak clearly, make eye contact, and use appropriate expression for their subject matter and audience.

Materials

Supplied

- *The Glory of Greece* by Beth Zemble and John Holdren
- *K¹² Language Arts Activity Book*, pp. LC 175–182
- Putting It All Together Assessment Checklist (printout)
- "Sparta and Athens" (printout)
- Fluency Performance Checklist (printout)

Keywords

fact – something that can be proven true

main idea – the most important point the author makes; it may be stated or unstated

opinion – something that a person thinks or believes, but which cannot be proven to be true

supporting details – the sentences that give information about the main idea or topic sentence

topic – the subject of a text

[Offline] 50 minutes

Work **together** with students to complete the offline Get Ready and Putting It All Together activities.

Get Ready ....

Lesson Introduction

Prepare students for giving their presentation on ancient Greece. Tell students they are going to give their presentation on ancient Greece. They will begin by discussing with you

- ► What topics they decided to cover in their presentation
- ► The qualities of an effective presentation

> **Objectives**
> - State an opinion related to topic.
> - State the topic directly.

What Makes an Effective Presentation?

Discuss the topics students chose for their presentation and review the qualities of an effective presentation.

1. Have students tell what topics about ancient Greece they decided to include in their presentation and why.

2. Have students tell what their opinion is about whether it is important to study ancient Greece.

3. Review with students the qualities of an effective presentation:

   - ► Speak clearly and loudly enough for the audience to hear, but not so loudly that you are shouting.
   - ► Make eye contact with the audience. Even if you are reading, look up once in a while to address your audience directly.
   - ► Pause at the end of key ideas or sections of your presentation to let the audience know when you've said something important or when you are switching to a new idea.
   - ► Use appropriate expression for the subject matter and audience. Your tone of voice and facial expressions should match the topic of the presentation. For example, since you are presenting factual information, your tone and facial expressions should be serious and informative.
   - ► Use language appropriate for your purpose and your audience. You are delivering information about ancient Greece. Choose words that are formal and factual, but don't be too formal if you are presenting to a younger audience.
   - ► Make sure your visuals are interesting to look at and help the audience understand the information you are presenting.

Putting It All Together

Give a Presentation

Students will complete their presentation and use a checklist to give a presentation on ancient Greece. Gather students' partially completed presentation and turn to pages LC 181 and 182 in *K¹² Language Arts Activity Book*.

1. Have students complete Steps 8–11 of the Create a Presentation pages.

2. Give students the checklist on page LC 181.

3. Have them practice the presentation on their own. Remind them to use the checklist as a guide for how they should deliver their presentation.

4. If there are peers who will listen to the presentation, give them page LC 182 (Tell Me About My Presentation). (Additional copies of this form can be printed from the online lesson.)

5. Have students give their presentation for the audience. If there are peers present, have them share their form.

6. When students have completed their presentation, use the materials and instructions in the online lesson to evaluate students' work.

7. Enter the answers (Yes or No) for each line of the assessment checklist online.

➲ **Learning Coach Check-In** Check in with students after about 30 minutes to see if they have completed the presentation and are ready to share it with the audience.

Objectives

- State an opinion related to topic.
- State the topic directly.
- Use search tools to locate information (for example, hyperlink).
- Practice a presentation.
- Deliver a presentation.
- Speak clearly at an understandable pace.
- Uses public speaking techniques.
- Create a visual.

Putting It All Together

Reflections on *The Glory of Greece* (A)

Create a Presentation

Give a speech about ancient Greece. Your presentation will include your opinion on why we should study this culture and its people. Before you begin, read the instructions all the way through. Then follow the steps.

1. What is the purpose of your presentation? Your purpose may be to inform, to entertain, to express emotions, or to persuade. You may have more than one purpose.

2. Who is your audience? Are you presenting to people who have read the book or know about ancient Greece? What kind of language will you use with them?

3. Write Part 1, the introduction, of your presentation. In it, tell
   - Where Greece is and what the land is like
   - When ancient Greece was at its height

   Students should write a brief paragraph that includes facts from their KLW chart on these topics.

LANGUAGE ARTS PURPLE **LC 175**

---

4. Write Part 2 of your presentation. Choose one of the topics from your KLW charts, such as facts about the ancient Greeks or daily life.
   - Write a main idea about your topic.
   - Use two details from your KLW chart to support the main idea.

   Students should write a brief paragraph that describes one of the topics from the KLW charts, such as Greek religion or daily life, and provide two supporting details from the chart.

5. Write Part 3 of your presentation. Choose another topic from your KLW charts, such as art, architecture, the Olympics, or the great thinkers.
   - Write a main idea about this topic.
   - Use two details from your KLW chart to support the main idea.

   Students should write a brief paragraph that describes a different topic from the KLW charts and provide two supporting details from the chart.

LC 176 LANGUAGE ARTS PURPLE

---

6. Write Part 4 of your presentation. Choose one of the questions that you still have about ancient Greece (the questions you wrote in the third column of your KLW charts). Research the answer to the question and write about it.
   - Use the library, an encyclopedia, or a reliable source on the Internet to find information to answer your question.
   - Write a main idea about your topic. This should be the answer to your question.
   - Use two details from your research to support the main idea.

   Students should write a brief paragraph about one of the questions they still have about ancient Greece. They should use library books, an encyclopedia, or the Internet to find information about the topic. Then they should write a main idea and two supporting details based on their research.

LANGUAGE ARTS PURPLE **LC 177**

---

7. Write Part 5, the conclusion, of your presentation. In the conclusion
- Tell how the ideas from the Greeks are still important to us today.
- Give your opinion about whether or not we should study the ancient Greeks and their ideas. Explain why you think so.

Students should write a brief conclusion that explains how the ideas in their presentation are still important to modern society and tells whether or not we should study the ancient Greeks and why.

8. Add interest to your presentation by creating at least two visual aids. You can
- Draw your own visual aids on paper.
- Create another kind of display.
- Use a multimedia program to make slides or create another visual that goes with your presentation.

Put important points from your presentation on different slides or pages. Use the space below to draw what your visual aids might look like or write notes about what you would like to create.

9. Make a final draft of your presentation.
- Write the important points from your draft on note cards or on slides in a multimedia presentation.
- Create your visuals using art supplies or a computer.

10. Practice your presentation several times in front of a mirror or to a pretend audience. Try to look up frequently to make eye contact, and memorize as many points as you can.

11. Deliver your presentation to your audience. Remember to look at your audience and speak in a clear voice that is easy to hear. Emphasize important points and be enthusiastic about your ideas.

Putting It All Together

Reflections on *The Glory of Greece* (B)
Effective Presentation Checklist

Follow these steps to give an effective presentation.

☐ Speak up so that your audience can hear and understand you.

☐ Make eye contact. Look up now and then to address your audience directly.

☐ Pause at certain points in your speech, such as after you've said something important or when you switch to a new idea.

☐ Use a tone of voice and facial expression that suits your subject and audience.

☐ Use language that suits your purpose and your audience.

☐ Make sure your visuals are interesting to look at and help the audience understand your topic.

Putting It All Together

Reflections on *The Glory of Greece* (B)
Tell Me About My Presentation

Have another person listen to your presentation and answer the questions.

1. Did the speaker speak loudly and clearly?
   A. Yes   **B.** No

2. Did the speaker make eye contact with the audience?
   A. Yes   **B.** No

3. Did the speaker pause at the end of key ideas or sections of the presentation?
   A. Yes   **B.** No

4. Did the speaker use appropriate expression for the subject matter and audience?
   A. Yes   **B.** No

5. How could the speaker improve his or her public speaking techniques next time?

 **varies**

Students will work **independently** to complete the online More Practice activity.

More Practice

Review the Skills

If students scored less than 80 percent or had difficulty meeting the objectives of the Putting It All Together activity, have them go online for more practice.

> **Objectives**
> - Use text organizational features to locate and comprehend information (table of contents, glossary, chapter, index, title, author, illustrator, caption).
> - Make generalizations from text.
> - Compare and contrast using evidence from the text.
> - Identify facts.
> - Identify supporting details.
> - Distinguish between fiction and nonfiction.
> - Use graphics and visuals to comprehend meaning and answer questions (diagrams, charts, captions).

Read

Read Fluently "Sparta and Athens"

Students will read aloud and record a passage. The purpose of this activity is to assess students' oral reading and fluency. Have students read the passage aloud and record their reading. Note that this is a new passage to them, and there is no audio for them to hear a model reading. This will allow the recording to accurately reflect their fluency.

> **Objectives**
> - Read poetry and prose aloud.
> - Read aloud grade-level text with appropriate automaticity, prosody, accuracy, and rate.

Performance Review

Fluency Check

Evaluate students' performance on the fluency reading.

1. Listen to students' recordings and use the Fluency Performance Checklist to review fluency and track performance.

2. Keep the completed checklist so you can review students' progress over time.

3. Follow the advice on the checklist regarding appropriate interventions for students who do not receive high scores on the Fluency Performance Checklist. If students aren't able to score above 12 points on the Fluency Performance Checklist, it is advisable to seek outside help from a teaching professional or reading specialist to improve students' reading fluency.

Reward: If students score 80 percent or more on the Putting It All Together activity and 18 or more on the Fluency Check, add a sticker for this unit on the My Accomplishments chart. If students did not score 80 percent or more on the Putting It All Together activity and 18 or more on the Fluency Check, work with them to revise their writing.

Objectives

- Read poetry and prose aloud.

- Read aloud grade-level text with appropriate automaticity, prosody, accuracy, and rate.

Semester Review and Checkpoint

Unit Focus

In this unit, students will review what they have learned about reading and understanding poetry, fiction, nonfiction, and directions. They will also review specific details from works they have studied that have cultural or historical significance. Then they will complete the Semester Checkpoint to demonstrate their skills in comprehending literature, nonfiction, and practical writing.

Unit Plan		[Online]	[Offline]
Lesson 1	Semester Review	35 minutes	15 minutes
Lesson 2	Semester Checkpoint (A)	50 minutes	
Lesson 3	Semester Checkpoint (B)	varies	50 minutes

Semester Review

Lesson Overview

Online	35 minutes
Reading for Meaning	Review the Elements of Literature
	Practice Responding to Literature

Offline	15 minutes
Making Connections	Practice Responding in Writing

Materials

Supplied
- *K¹² Language Arts Activity Book*, pp. LC 183–191

Content Background

The Semester Review and Checkpoint marks the end of this program. If students are not able to score above 70 percent on the Semester Checkpoint, Learning Coaches should seek assistance from a teaching professional.

Online 35 minutes

Students will work **independently** to complete online Reading for Meaning activities.

Reading for Meaning ....

Review the Elements of Literature

Students will play a game to help them review the elements of fiction, nonfiction, poetry, and directions.

_____

Practice Responding to Literature

Students will help the K[12] characters properly analyze and answer questions about a fiction passage, a nonfiction passage, and paired passages.

> ⭐ **Objectives**
> • Complete a Semester Review on the elements of literature and responding to literature, nonfiction, and practical writing.

[Offline] 15 minutes

Work **together** with students to complete the offline Making Connections activity.

Making Connections

Practice Responding in Writing

Students will review how to write responses to fiction passages, nonfiction passages, poems, and paired passages. Turn to pages LC 183–191 in *K¹² Language Arts Activity Book*.

1. Direct students' attention to the Activity Book pages and have them read the directions.

2. Have students complete the Activity Book pages.

3. Go over students' answers with them to make sure they understand how to respond to paired passages.

Objectives

- Differentiate among various literary genres.
- Summarize a work of literature and maintain accurate sequence.
- Write a summary.
- Identify problems and solutions in a story.
- Demonstrate understanding of common features of legends, myths, folktales, fairy tales, and classic stories.
- Determine the theme, moral, or lesson of a work of literature.
- Use graphics to answer a question.
- Identify main idea and supporting details in a text.
- Identify author's purpose.
- Identify rhyme scheme in a poem.
- Identify speaker.
- Identify personification.
- Compare and contrast literary elements in two or more literary selections.
- Follow directions to complete a task.
- State an opinion related to a topic.
- Apply the conventions of grammar, usage, mechanics, and spelling.

Semester Review
Practice Responding in Writing

Read the passages and answer the questions.

Clytie

Clytie was a water goddess who lived in a river near the great sea. She loved the sun god Apollo, who drove the chariot of the sun.

Day after day, Clytie stood on the bank of her river home and watched for Apollo's chariot to come up in the east. All day, she stood and watched him driving across the sky. In the evening, when the sun went down, she stood looking after him.

Sadly for Clytie, Apollo did not care for her. The god of the sun ignored her as he rode his chariot across the sky.

For nine long days, Clytie stood there. All that time, she ate nothing but dewdrops, and every day she grew paler and thinner.

At last the gods took pity on her. They changed her into a beautiful flower.

Her feet became roots in the ground. Her body changed to a green stem, and her golden hair turned to yellow petals.

But Clytie still kept her face turned toward Apollo as he crossed the sky. So it came to pass that people named her Sunflower.

LC 183

---

1. What type of writing is "Clytie"?
   a myth

2. Write a brief summary of "Clytie."
   Students should write two to three sentences telling the main events of the story in sequence.

3. What problem does Clytie have in the story?
   She loves the god Apollo, but he doesn't love her.

4. How does Clytie try to solve her problem?
   She sits and watches Apollo for nine days.

5. What new problem does Clytie's solution cause?
   She gets thinner and paler.

6. How is Clytie's problem finally solved?
   The gods turn her into a sunflower.

7. What does the story explain?
   how sunflowers came to be

LC 184

All About Sunflowers

One of the most interesting flowers in the world is the sunflower. Sunflowers are very easy to recognize by their shape. The flowers have a ring of bright yellow petals around a brown-black center. The stalks are thick and light green, and the leaves are shaped like hearts.

Sunflowers come in many different sizes. The most magnificent is the giant sunflower. It may grow to be ten to fifteen feet tall. Taller than a basketball hoop! Other sunflowers are much smaller. They grow to be only three feet tall.

The name *sunflower* comes from two qualities of the plant. First, the head of the flower looks like a sun. Second, young sunflowers turn to follow the sun as it moves across the sky. You can't see the flowers moving while it happens. But when you look at a sunflower at different times of the day, you can tell the head has moved!

Sunflowers are not just beautiful. They are also useful. The center of a sunflower head produces seeds. After the

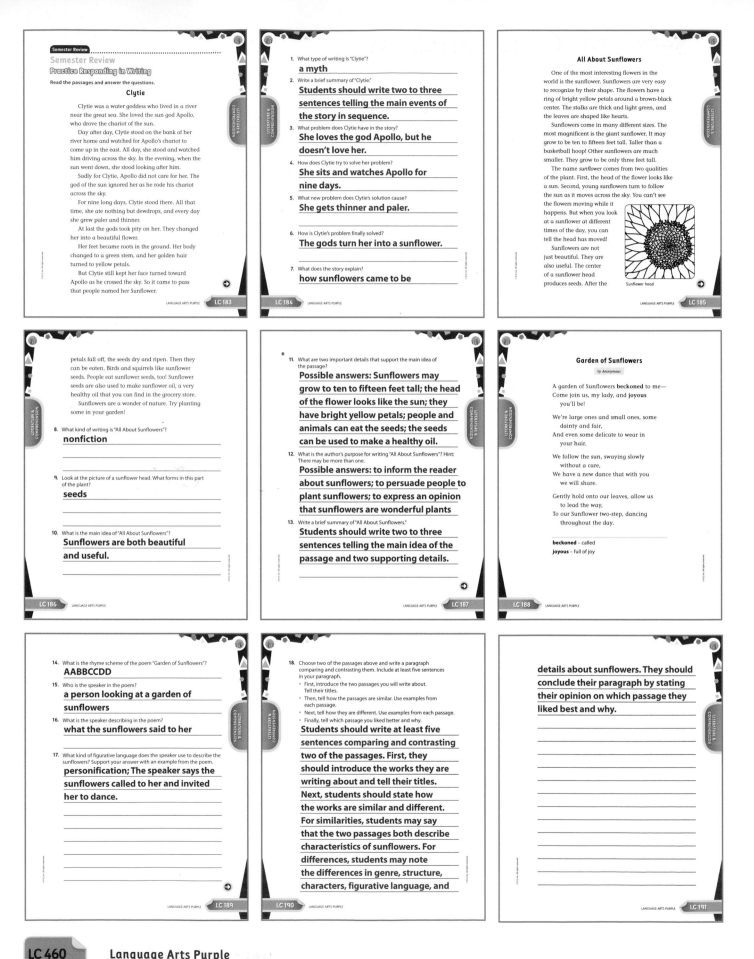

Sunflower head

LC 185

---

petals fall off, the seeds dry and ripen. Then they can be eaten. Birds and squirrels like sunflower seeds. People eat sunflower seeds, too! Sunflower seeds are also used to make sunflower oil, a very healthy oil that you can find in the grocery store.

Sunflowers are a wonder of nature. Try planting some in your garden!

8. What kind of writing is "All About Sunflowers"?
   nonfiction

9. Look at the picture of a sunflower head. What forms in this part of the plant?
   seeds

10. What is the main idea of "All About Sunflowers"?
    Sunflowers are both beautiful and useful.

LC 186

---

11. What are two important details that support the main idea of the passage?
    Possible answers: Sunflowers may grow to ten to fifteen feet tall; the head of the flower looks like the sun; they have bright yellow petals; people and animals can eat the seeds; the seeds can be used to make a healthy oil.

12. What is the author's purpose for writing "All About Sunflowers"? Hint: There may be more than one.
    Possible answers: to inform the reader about sunflowers; to persuade people to plant sunflowers; to express an opinion that sunflowers are wonderful plants

13. Write a brief summary of "All About Sunflowers."
    Students should write two to three sentences telling the main idea of the passage and two supporting details.

LC 187

Garden of Sunflowers
by Anonymous

A garden of Sunflowers **beckoned** to me—
Come join us, my lady, and **joyous**
    you'll be!

We're large ones and small ones, some
    dainty and fair,
And even some delicate to wear in
    your hair.

We follow the sun, swaying slowly
    without a care,
We have a new dance that with you
    we will share.

Gently hold onto our leaves, allow us
    to lead the way,
To our Sunflower two-step, dancing
    throughout the day.

beckoned – called
joyous – full of joy

LC 188

---

14. What is the rhyme scheme of the poem "Garden of Sunflowers"?
    AABBCCDD

15. Who is the speaker in the poem?
    a person looking at a garden of sunflowers

16. What is the speaker describing in the poem?
    what the sunflowers said to her

17. What kind of figurative language does the speaker use to describe the sunflowers? Support your answer with an example from the poem.
    personification; The speaker says the sunflowers called to her and invited her to dance.

LC 189

---

18. Choose two of the passages above and write a paragraph comparing and contrasting them. Include at least five sentences in your paragraph.
    • First, introduce the two passages you will write about. Tell their titles.
    • Then, tell how the passages are similar. Use examples from each passage.
    • Next, tell how they are different. Use examples from each passage.
    • Finally, tell which passage you liked better and why.
    Students should write at least five sentences comparing and contrasting two of the passages. First, they should introduce the works they are writing about and tell their titles. Next, students should state how the works are similar and different. For similarities, students may say that the two passages both describe characteristics of sunflowers. For differences, students may note the differences in genre, structure, characters, figurative language, and

LC 190

---

details about sunflowers. They should conclude their paragraph by stating their opinion on which passage they liked best and why.

LC 191

Semester Checkpoint (A)

Lesson Overview

[Online]   **50** minutes

Semester Checkpoint	Questions About Literature
	Questions About a Fiction Passage
	Questions About a Nonfiction Passage
	Questions About a Poem
	Questions About Directions

Content Background

Students complete the Semester Checkpoint over two days. This part of the Checkpoint is completed online. The next part is completed offline.

[Materials]

Supplied

- Questions About a Fiction Passage (optional printout)
- Questions About a Nonfiction Passage (optional printout)
- Questions About a Poem (optional printout)
- Questions About Directions (optional printout)

[Online] 50 minutes

Students will work **independently** to complete the online part of the Semester Checkpoint.

Semester Checkpoint

Questions About Literature

Students will answer multiple choice questions about the elements of fiction, nonfiction, poetry, and practical or technical text. Questions will assess their knowledge of key terms and the names of significant characters and events in literature.

Questions About a Fiction Passage

Students will read a fiction passage and answer multiple choice questions about the text.

TIP If students are not comfortable reading the passage for this activity online, print Questions About a Fiction Passage and have students read the printout.

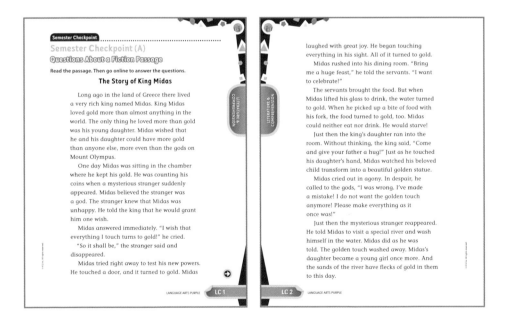

Objectives

- Complete a Semester Checkpoint on the elements of literature and responding to literature, nonfiction, and practical writing.

Questions About a Nonfiction Passage

Students will read a nonfiction passage and answer multiple choice questions about the text.

TIP If students are not comfortable reading the passage for this activity online, print Questions About a Nonfiction Passage and have students read the printout.

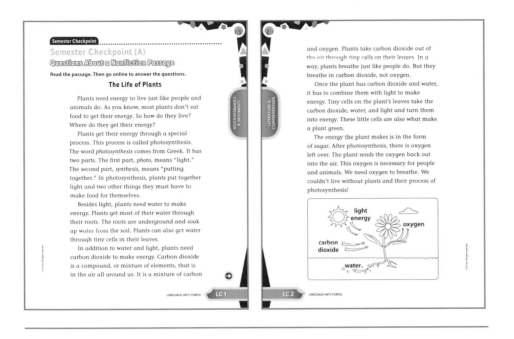

Questions About a Poem

Students will answer questions about a poem.

TIP If students are not comfortable reading the passage for this activity online, print Questions About a Poem and have students read the printout.

Questions About Directions

Students will answer questions about a recipe.

TIP If students are not comfortable reading the passage for this activity online, print Questions About Directions and have students read the printout.

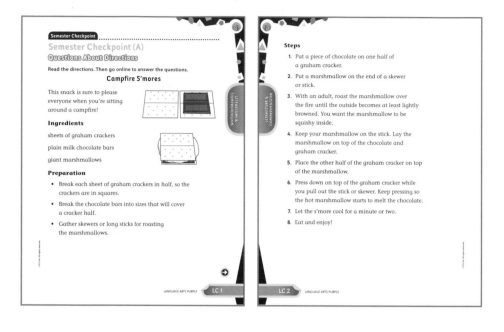

Semester Checkpoint

Semester Checkpoint (A)

Questions About Directions

Read the directions. Then go online to answer the questions.

Campfire S'mores

This snack is sure to please everyone when you're sitting around a campfire!

Ingredients

sheets of graham crackers

plain milk chocolate bars

giant marshmallows

Preparation

- Break each sheet of graham crackers in half, so the crackers are in squares.
- Break the chocolate bars into sizes that will cover a cracker half.
- Gather skewers or long sticks for roasting the marshmallows.

Steps

1. Put a piece of chocolate on one half of a graham cracker.
2. Put a marshmallow on the end of a skewer or stick.
3. With an adult, roast the marshmallow over the fire until the outside becomes at least lightly browned. You want the marshmallow to be squishy inside.
4. Keep your marshmallow on the stick. Lay the marshmallow on top of the chocolate and graham cracker.
5. Place the other half of the graham cracker on top of the marshmallow.
6. Press down on top of the graham cracker while you pull out the stick or skewer. Keep pressing so the hot marshmallow starts to melt the chocolate.
7. Let the s'more cool for a minute or two.
8. Eat and enjoy!

LC 1

LC 2   LANGUAGE ARTS PURPLE

Semester Checkpoint (B)

Lesson Overview

Offline	50 minutes
Semester Checkpoint	Respond in Writing

Online	varies
More Practice	Review the Skills
Read	Read Fluently "The Travels of Odysseus"
Performance Review	Fluency Check

Materials

Supplied

- *K¹² Language Arts Assessments*, pp. LC 77–88
- Semester Checkpoint Assessment Checklist (printout)
- "The Travels of Odysseus" (printout)
- Fluency Performance Checklist (printout)

Also Needed

- stopwatch

Content Background

This Semester Checkpoint marks the end of this program. If students are not able to score above 70 percent on the Semester Checkpoint, Learning Coaches should seek assistance from a teaching professional.

【Offline】 ⏱ 15 minutes

Work **together** with students to complete the offline part of the Semester Checkpoint.

Semester Checkpoint •••

Respond in Writing

Explain that students are going to show what they have learned about comparing and contrasting reading selections.

1. Give students the Semester Checkpoint pages.

2. Read the directions together.

3. Use the Answer Key to score the Checkpoint and the Semester Checkpoint Assessment Checklist to evaluate students' response to Questions 20–25. Then enter the results online.

4. Review each exercise with students. Work with students to correct any exercise they missed.

_____

Part 1: "The Story of Prometheus"
Have students read the passage and answer the questions.

_____

Part 2: "What Is Fire?"
Have students read the passage and answer the questions.

_____

Part 3: "Fire"
Have students read the poem and answer the questions.

_____

Part 4: Respond in Writing
Have students write a paragraph comparing and contrasting two of the three Checkpoint passages.

⭐ **Objectives**

- Differentiate among various literary genres.
- Summarize a work of literature and maintain accurate sequence.
- Write a summary.
- Identify problems and solutions in a story.
- Demonstrate understanding of common features of legends, myths, folktales, fairy tales, and classic stories.
- Determine the theme, moral, or lesson of a work of literature.
- Identify choices that a character makes and their consequences.
- Use graphics to answer a question.
- Identify main idea and supporting details in a text.
- Identify author's purpose.
- Identify rhyme scheme in a poem.
- Identify speaker.
- Identify similes.
- Identify personification.
- Identify metaphor.
- Follow directions to complete a task.
- Compare and contrast literary elements in two or more literary selections.
- State an opinion related to a topic.
- Apply the conventions of grammar, usage, mechanics, and spelling.

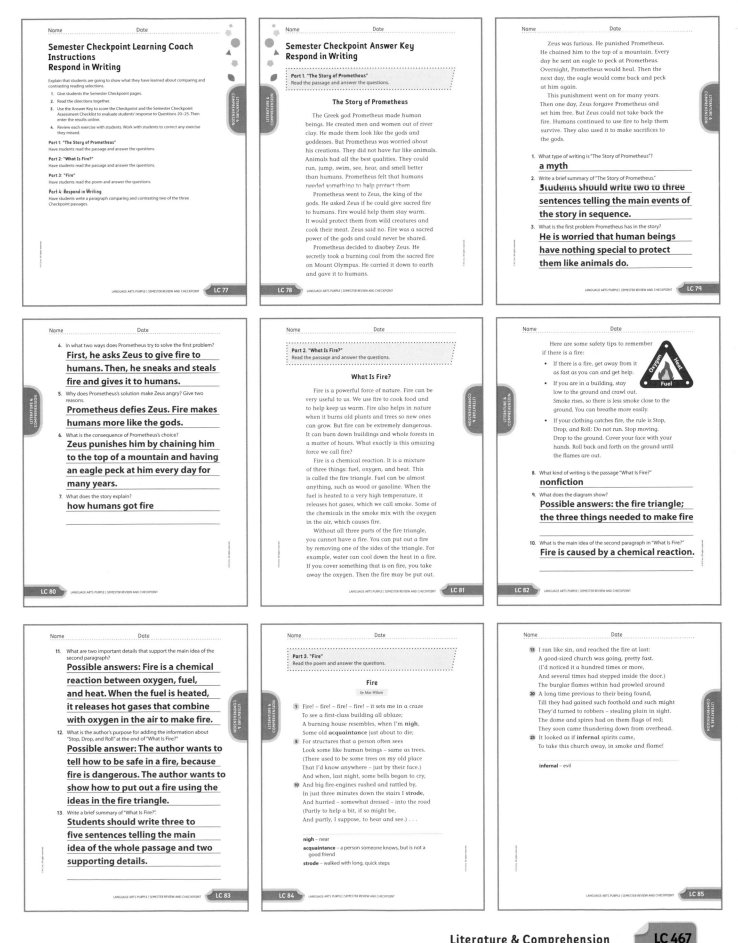

Panel LC 77:

Name_____ Date_____

Semester Checkpoint Learning Coach Instructions
Respond in Writing

Explain that students are going to show what they have learned about comparing and contrasting reading selections.

1. Give students the Semester Checkpoint pages.
2. Read the directions together.
3. Use the Answer Key to score the Checkpoint and the Semester Checkpoint Assessment Checklist to evaluate students' response to Questions 20–25. Then enter the results online.
4. Review each exercise with students. Work with students to correct any exercise they missed.

Part 1: "The Story of Prometheus"
Have students read the passage and answer the questions.

Part 2: "What Is Fire?"
Have students read the passage and answer the questions.

Part 3: "Fire"
Have students read the poem and answer the questions.

Part 4: Respond in Writing
Have students write a paragraph comparing and contrasting two of the three Checkpoint passages.

LANGUAGE ARTS PURPLE | SEMESTER REVIEW AND CHECKPOINT **LC 77**

Panel LC 78:

Name_____ Date_____

Semester Checkpoint Answer Key
Respond in Writing

Part 1. "The Story of Prometheus"
Read the passage and answer the questions.

The Story of Prometheus

The Greek god Prometheus made human beings. He created men and women out of river clay. He made them look like the gods and goddesses. But Prometheus was worried about his creations. They did not have fur like animals. Animals had all the best qualities. They could run, jump, swim, see, hear, and smell better than humans. Prometheus felt that humans needed something to help protect them

Prometheus went to Zeus, the king of the gods. He asked Zeus if he could give sacred fire to humans. Fire would help them stay warm. It would protect them from wild creatures and cook their meat. Zeus said no. Fire was a sacred power of the gods and could never be shared.

Prometheus decided to disobey Zeus. He secretly took a burning coal from the sacred fire on Mount Olympus. He carried it down to earth and gave it to humans.

LC 78 LANGUAGE ARTS PURPLE | SEMESTER REVIEW AND CHECKPOINT

Panel LC 79:

Name_____ Date_____

Zeus was furious. He punished Prometheus. He chained him to the top of a mountain. Every day he sent an eagle to peck at Prometheus. Overnight, Prometheus would heal. Then the next day, the eagle would come back and peck at him again.

This punishment went on for many years. Then one day, Zeus forgave Prometheus and set him free. But Zeus could not take back the fire. Humans continued to use fire to help them survive. They also used it to make sacrifices to the gods.

1. What type of writing is "The Story of Prometheus"?
   a myth

2. Write a brief summary of "The Story of Prometheus."
   Students should write two to three sentences telling the main events of the story in sequence.

3. What is the first problem Prometheus has in the story?
   He is worried that human beings have nothing special to protect them like animals do.

LANGUAGE ARTS PURPLE | SEMESTER REVIEW AND CHECKPOINT **LC 79**

Panel LC 80:

Name_____ Date_____

4. In what two ways does Prometheus try to solve the first problem?
   First, he asks Zeus to give fire to humans. Then, he sneaks and steals fire and gives it to humans.

5. Why does Prometheus's solution make Zeus angry? Give two reasons.
   Prometheus defies Zeus. Fire makes humans more like the gods.

6. What is the consequence of Prometheus's choice?
   Zeus punishes him by chaining him to the top of a mountain and having an eagle peck at him every day for many years.

7. What does the story explain?
   how humans got fire

LC 80 LANGUAGE ARTS PURPLE | SEMESTER REVIEW AND CHECKPOINT

Panel LC 81:

Name_____ Date_____

Part 2. "What Is Fire?"
Read the passage and answer the questions.

What Is Fire?

Fire is a powerful force of nature. Fire can be very useful to us. We use fire to cook food and to help keep us warm. Fire also helps in nature when it burns old plants and trees so new ones can grow. But fire can be extremely dangerous. It can burn down buildings and whole forests in a matter of hours. What exactly is this amazing force we call fire?

Fire is a chemical reaction. It is a mixture of three things: fuel, oxygen, and heat. This is called the fire triangle. Fuel can be almost anything, such as wood or gasoline. When the fuel is heated to a very high temperature, it releases hot gases, which we call smoke. Some of the chemicals in the smoke mix with the oxygen in the air, which causes fire.

Without all three parts of the fire triangle, you cannot have a fire. You can put out a fire by removing one of the sides of the triangle. For example, water can cool down the heat in a fire. If you cover something that is on fire, you take away the oxygen. Then the fire may be put out.

LANGUAGE ARTS PURPLE | SEMESTER REVIEW AND CHECKPOINT **LC 81**

Panel LC 82:

Name_____ Date_____

Here are some safety tips to remember if there is a fire:

- If there is a fire, get away from it as fast as you can and get help.
- If you are in a building, stay low to the ground and crawl out. Smoke rises, so there is less smoke close to the ground. You can breathe more easily.
- If your clothing catches fire, the rule is Stop, Drop, and Roll: Do not run. Stop moving. Drop to the ground. Cover your face with your hands. Roll back and forth on the ground until the flames are out.

8. What kind of writing is the passage "What Is Fire?"
   nonfiction

9. What does the diagram show?
   Possible answers: the fire triangle; the three things needed to make fire

10. What is the main idea of the second paragraph in "What Is Fire?"
    Fire is caused by a chemical reaction.

LC 82 LANGUAGE ARTS PURPLE | SEMESTER REVIEW AND CHECKPOINT

Panel LC 83:

Name_____ Date_____

11. What are two important details that support the main idea of the second paragraph?
    Possible answers: Fire is a chemical reaction between oxygen, fuel, and heat. When the fuel is heated, it releases hot gases that combine with oxygen in the air to make fire.

12. What is the author's purpose for adding the information about "Stop, Drop, and Roll" at the end of "What Is Fire?"
    Possible answer: The author wants to tell how to be safe in a fire, because fire is dangerous. The author wants to show how to put out a fire using the ideas in the fire triangle.

13. Write a brief summary of "What Is Fire?"
    Students should write three to five sentences telling the main idea of the whole passage and two supporting details.

LANGUAGE ARTS PURPLE | SEMESTER REVIEW AND CHECKPOINT **LC 83**

Panel LC 84:

Name_____ Date_____

Part 3. "Fire"
Read the poem and answer the questions.

Fire
by Max Wilson

1 Fire! – fire! – fire! – fire! – it sets me in a craze
   To see a first-class building all ablaze;
   A burning house resembles, when I'm **nigh**,
   Some old **acquaintance** just about to die;
5 For structures that a person often sees
   Look some like human beings – same as trees.
   (There used to be some trees on my old place
   That I'd know anywhere – just by their face.)
   And when, last night, some bells began to cry,
10 And big fire-engines rushed and rattled by,
   In just three minutes down the stairs I **strode**,
   And hurried – somewhat dressed – into the road
   (Partly to help a bit, if so might be,
   And partly, I suppose, to hear and see.) . . .

nigh – near
acquaintance – a person someone knows, but is not a good friend
strode – walked with long, quick steps

LC 84 LANGUAGE ARTS PURPLE | SEMESTER REVIEW AND CHECKPOINT

Panel LC 85:

Name_____ Date_____

15 I ran like sin, and reached the fire at last:
   A good-sized church was going, pretty fast.
   (I'd noticed it a hundred times or more,
   And several times had stepped inside the door.)
   The burglar flames within had prowled around
20 A long time previous to their being found,
   Till they had gained such foothold and such might
   They'd turned to robbers – stealing plain in sight.
   The dome and spires had on them flags of red;
   They soon came thundering down from overhead.
25 It looked as if **infernal** spirits came,
   To take this church away, in smoke and flame!

infernal – evil

LANGUAGE ARTS PURPLE | SEMESTER REVIEW AND CHECKPOINT **LC 85**

Name _____ Date _____

14. What is the rhyme scheme of the first six lines of the poem "Fire"?

AABBCC

15. What is the speaker in the poem doing?

watching a fire

16. What type of figurative language is contained in the line "I ran like sin"?

simile

17. What kind of figurative language is contained in the line "last night, some bells began to cry"?

personification

18. In the second stanza of the poem, the speaker uses an extended metaphor. How does the speaker use a metaphor to describe the flames in the church?

Possible answer: He compares the flames to a burglar or robbers that steal the parts of the church by burning them down.

19. Read this line from the poem.

> The dome and spires had on them flags of red;

What kind of figurative language is this, and what two things is the speaker comparing?

metaphor; He's comparing the flames with red flags.

Name _____ Date _____

Part 4. Respond in Writing
Write a paragraph comparing and contrasting two passages.

20.–25. Choose two of the three passages about fire. Write a paragraph comparing and contrasting them. Include at least five sentences in your paragraph.

- First, tell the titles of both passages and tell what type of writing each one is.
- Then, tell how the passages are similar.
- Next, tell how they are different.
- Finally, tell which passage you liked better and why.

Use the rubric to score the paragraph. Enter the results online.

_____

_____

_____

_____

_____

_____

_____

_____

_____

Online   varies

Review students' performance on the Read activities from the semester. Students will work **independently** to complete the online More Practice and Read activities.

More Practice

Review the Skills

If students scored less than 80 percent on or had difficulty meeting the objectives of the Semester Checkpoint, have them go online for more practice.

If students are not able to score above 70 percent on the Semester Checkpoint, Learning Coaches should seek assistance from a teaching professional.

Objectives
- Evaluate Checkpoint results and choose activities to review.

Read

Read Fluently "The Travels of Odysseus"

Students will read aloud and record a passage. The purpose of this activity is to assess students' oral reading and fluency. Have students read the passage aloud and record their reading. Note that this is a new passage to them, and there is no audio for them to hear a model reading. This will allow the recording to accurately reflect their fluency.

Objectives
- Read poetry and prose aloud.
- Read aloud grade-level text with appropriate automaticity, prosody, accuracy, and rate.

Performance Review

Fluency Check

Evaluate students' performance on the fluency reading. Gather the stopwatch and printout of "The Travels of Odysseus."

1. Listen to students' recordings and use the Fluency Performance Checklist to review fluency and the printout to track performance.

2. Keep the completed checklist so you can review students' progress over time.

3. Follow the advice on the checklist regarding appropriate interventions for students who do not receive high scores on the Fluency Performance Checklist. If students aren't able to score above 12 points on the Fluency Performance Checklist, it is advisable to seek outside help from a teaching professional or reading specialist to improve students' reading fluency.

Reward: If students score 80 percent or more on the Semester Checkpoint and 18 or more on the Fluency Check, add a sticker for this unit on the My Accomplishments chart. If students did not score 80 percent or more on the Semester Checkpoint and 18 or more on the Fluency Check, work with them to revise their work and practice their fluency until they attain those scores and then add a sticker to the My Accomplishments chart.

Objectives

- Read poetry and prose aloud.
- Read aloud grade-level text with appropriate automaticity, prosody, accuracy, and rate.

Writing Skills

UNIT OVERVIEW — Quotations and Short Research Project

Unit Focus

In the grammar part of the unit, students will learn about recognizing and writing quotations. They will

▶ Learn that writers use quotation marks around the exact words that someone wrote or spoke.
▶ Learn the role played by speaker tags.
▶ Learn how to properly capitalize a quotation.
▶ Learn how to use commas correctly with quotations.

In the composition part of the unit, students will complete a short research project on a famous person. They will

▶ Use their journal to freewrite.
▶ Choose a famous person as a subject for a short research project.
▶ Research and take notes on their subject.
▶ Keep track of their sources.
▶ Present their finished short research project to an audience.

Unit Plan		Online	Offline
Lesson 1	Quotation Marks and Journal Entry	20 minutes	25 minutes
Lesson 2	Capital Letters in Quotations and Model Short Research Project	25 minutes	20 minutes
Lesson 3	Commas in Quotations and Choose Your Topic	20 minutes	25 minutes
Lesson 4	Take Notes About Your Topic	15 minutes	30 minutes
Lesson 5	Organize Your Project (A)	15 minutes	30 minutes
Lesson 6	Organize Your Project (B)		45 minutes
Lesson 7	Unit Review and Complete Your Short Research Project	20 minutes	25 minutes
Lesson 8	Unit Checkpoint and Present Your Project	20 minutes	25 minutes

Quotation Marks and Journal Entry

Lesson Overview

[Online]   **20** minutes

GUM (Grammar, Usage, and Mechanics)	Quotation Marks

[Offline]   **25** minutes

Composition	Journal: Write About a Project
Beyond the Lesson	⊕ OPTIONAL: Journal: Freewrite on a Topic

Advance Preparation

To prepare for the GUM portion of this lesson, review Quotation Marks in the *Grammar Reference Guide* (linked in the online lesson) to familiarize yourself with the topic.

Big Ideas

- Journal writing is a form of freewriting. It is an opportunity to get ideas on paper without regard for correctness of the language or the format of a piece of writing.
- To improve, writers require frequent practice.

[Materials]

Supplied

- *K¹² My Journal*, pp. 30–31
- *Grammar Reference Guide* Online Book (optional)

Keywords

dialogue – the words spoken between two or more people

quotation – a report of exact words spoken or written, usually placed within quotation marks

quotation marks – punctuation that encloses a quotation, or the exact words of a speaker or writer

speaker tag – the part of a dialogue that identifies who is speaking

 **20** minutes

Students will work online **independently** to complete an activity on recognizing quotations, using quotation marks, and understanding the purpose of speaker tags. Help students locate the online activity.

GUM (Grammar, Usage, and Mechanics)

Quotation Marks
Students will learn about the purpose of quotations, how to use quotation marks, and the role of speaker tags. They will then practice identifying quotations and speakers and recognizing when a quotation is written correctly.

Objectives
- Recognize that quotation marks are used around the exact words of an author or speaker.

 **25** minutes

Work **together** with students to complete the offline Composition and Beyond the Lesson activities.

Composition

🖉 **Journal: Write About a Project**
Students will respond to a journal prompt by writing about a project that they have completed and the experience of doing it. Gather *K¹² My Journal* and have students turn to pages 30 and 31.

Objectives
- Respond to a journal prompt.
- Freewrite about a topic.

1. Tell students they are going to write in their journal about a project they have completed and how working on the project made them feel. To help students think of projects they have done and what their experiences were like, ask them to think about their answers to the following questions.

   ▶ Have you ever drawn a poster, completed a mobile, or made something with your hands? What did you do? What materials did you use? Why did you create what you did?

   ▶ Have you ever taken an arts and crafts class? What did you make in the class? Did you give what you made to someone else or did you keep it for yourself? If you gave it to someone else, whom did you give it to, and how did that person feel to receive it?

   ▶ How do you feel after you've worked to make something? Do you like to be able to hold and touch things that you've made? How can projects give us ways to feel proud of ourselves?

2. Have students respond to the prompt in their journal. Encourage them to write in complete sentences, although it is not a requirement when they are freewriting in their journal.

TIP Students should write for about 25 minutes. Freewriting allows students to use their imagination to write what they want without worrying about being graded, so encourage them to keep writing for the entire time. If students have trouble writing for 25 minutes, use the prompting questions or have them list ideas or words. If they want to keep writing beyond the suggested time limit, praise them for their enthusiasm and offer to let them complete their entry later in the day as a reward.

A Finished Project Date _____

What is one project you have completed?
What did you like about doing it?

_____
_____
_____
_____
_____
_____
_____
_____
_____
_____
_____
_____
_____
_____
_____

30

Beyond the Lesson

⊕ OPTIONAL: Journal: Freewrite on a Topic

This activity is OPTIONAL. It is intended for students who have extra time and would benefit from extra practice. Feel free to skip this activity. Gather *K¹² My Journal*.

1. Have students either respond to a prompt in Thoughts and Experiences (pages 50–93) or write about their own topic on the next available page in Ideas (pages 96–139).

2. Encourage students to explore their thoughts and write as much as they want. There are no rules. If students wish, ideas can be fleshed out into a more developed composition at a later time.

TIP Studies show that students who write more frequently become better writers.

Objectives
- Respond to a journal prompt.
- Freewrite about a topic.

Capital Letters in Quotations and Model Short Research Project

Lesson Overview

【Online】 25 minutes

Skills Update	Quotation Marks
GUM (Grammar, Usage, and Mechanics)	Capital Letters in Quotations
Composition	Explore a Model Form for a Short Research Project

【Offline】 20 minutes

Composition	Respond to the Model Form for a Short Research Project

【Materials】

Supplied

- *K¹² Language Arts Activity Book*, pp. WS 119–121
- *Grammar Reference Guide* Online Book (optional)

Keywords

quotation – a report of exact words spoken or written, usually placed within quotation marks

quotation marks – punctuation that encloses a quotation, or the exact words of a speaker or writer

speaker tag – the part of a dialogue that identifies who is speaking

Advance Preparation

To prepare for the GUM portion of this lesson, review Capitalization (Other Uses of Capital Letters) in the *Grammar Reference Guide* (linked in the online lesson) to familiarize yourself with the topic. In this lesson, students begin to accumulate documents they will need as they work on their short research project. You might want to provide students with a folder, large envelope, or box in which to keep these documents. **Note:** The Web addresses in the online Composition activity and on pages WS 119 and 120 (Model Form for a Short Research Project) in *K¹² Language Arts Activity Book* are fictitious. Each is only an example and should not be used for students' research.

Big Ideas

Following a specific organizational structure is a useful tool for novice writers; however, writers require the freedom and flexibility to follow their ideas to completion.

[Online] ⏱ 25 minutes

Students will work online to review quotation marks, to learn how to properly use capital letters in quotations, and to read and explore a model short research project. Help students locate the online activities.

Skills Update

Quotation Marks

Students will review how to recognize quotations by completing Skills Update exercises. Sit with students as they do this activity and note if they answer correctly.

⤷ **Learning Coach Check-In** How did students do on the Skills Update?

▸ **All answers correct:** Great! Skip the review screen and go on to the next activity.

▸ **Any answers incorrect:** Take a few minutes to review quotation marks now. Use the link on the screen after the Skills Update to take another look at the online activity or review Quotation Marks in the *Grammar Reference Guide* together.

TIP This activity will require extra time if students need to review quotation marks. Take the extra 5–10 minutes to review now because new skills build on what students have already learned.

> **Objectives**
> • Recognize that quotation marks are used around the exact words of an author or speaker.

GUM (Grammar, Usage, and Mechanics)

Capital Letters in Quotations

Students will learn how to use capital letters in quotations. Then they will practice identifying capitalization errors in sentences with quotations and correctly complete sentences with quotations.

> **Objectives**
> • Use a capital letter to begin a quotation.

Composition

Explore a Model Form for a Short Research Project

By reading and exploring a model form for a short research project, students will learn what a short research project is and the type of work it takes to complete one.

TIP If students are not comfortable reading the model form for a short research project for this activity online, they may read the model on pages WS 119 and 120 in *K¹² Language Arts Activity Book*.

> **Objectives**
> • Describe the elements of a short research project.

Offline **20** minutes

Work **together** with students to complete the offline Composition activity.

Composition ....

Respond to the Model Form for a Short Research Project

Students will review what they learned about the model form for a short research project. Turn to pages WS 119–121 in *K¹² Language Arts Activity Book*.

1. Have students reread Rosa's model form for her short research project about a famous person. Tell students that the Web address in the model is only an example and should not be used for their research.

2. Have students complete the Activity Book page about Rosa's form. Provide support as necessary. Students should refer to Rosa's completed form as needed.

TIP Keep Rosa's form in a safe place so students can refer to it later.

Objectives

- Describe the elements of a short research project.

Composition
Capital Letters in Quotations and
Model Short Research Project
Model Form for a Short Research Project
Use Rosa's form for a short research project as you work through
the lessons in the unit.

Short Research Project

Name of Topic ___ Sally Ride

Date of Birth ___ May 26, 1951

Place of Birth ___ Los Angeles, California

Two reasons this person is important

1. Was the first woman to become an astronaut (1983).

2. Wrote books on space, and worked to teach young people, especially girls, about science (1989–2012).

What someone else said or wrote about this person ___
President Ronald Reagan (he called after Sally Ride's first trip to space):
"You were the best person for the job."

LANGUAGE ARTS PURPLE   WS 119

WS 120   LANGUAGE ARTS PURPLE

Two qualities this person showed in his or her life ___
courage and intelligence

The most interesting fact I learned ___ Sally Ride trained for more than
five years for her first trip into space (1978–1983).

Where I found my facts

1. "Sally Ride." Encyclopedia America. Print.

2. "Sally Ride." American Heroes.
http://www.americanheroes.gov/Bios/htmlbios/ride-sk.model
(January 28, 2012).

Composition
Capital Letters in Quotations and
Model Short Research Project
Respond to the Model Form for a Short Research Project

Answer the questions about Rosa's form.

1. Who is the topic of Rosa's short research project?
Sally Ride

2. Where was that person born?
Los Angeles, California

3. Who said the quotation that Rosa used?
President Ronald Reagan

4. What is the name of the book where Rosa found some of the information?
Encyclopedia America

5. What is the name of the website where Rosa found some of the information?
American Heroes

6. If Rosa wanted to learn more about her topic, what might she do?
Go to the library to find other books or articles about Sally Ride.

LANGUAGE ARTS PURPLE   WS 121

Commas in Quotations and Choose Your Topic

Lesson Overview

🖥 Online — 20 minutes

Skills Update	Capital Letters in Quotations
GUM (Grammar, Usage, and Mechanics)	Commas in Quotations
Composition	Rosa Chooses a Topic

📄 Offline — 25 minutes

Composition	Choose Your Topic

Materials

Supplied
- *K¹² Language Arts Activity Book*, pp. WS 123–124
- *Grammar Reference Guide* Online Book (optional)

Keywords

quotation – a report of exact words spoken or written, usually placed within quotation marks

quotation marks – punctuation that encloses a quotation, or the exact words of a speaker or writer

speaker tag – the part of a dialogue that identifies who is speaking

Advance Preparation

To prepare for the GUM portion of this lesson, review Quotation Marks in the *Grammar Reference Guide* (linked in the online lesson) to familiarize yourself with the topic. In the Composition portion of this lesson, students will begin a short research project in which they research information about a famous person's life. They should use an encyclopedia as one source and a website as another source. Website guidance and suggestions are provided in the online lesson. Before directing students to any website, be sure to first visit it yourself and become familiar with its content. **Note:** The Web addresses in the online Composition activity are fictitious. Each is only an example and should not be used for students' research.

Big Ideas

- ▸ Writing requires thought and planning.
- ▸ Following a specific organizational structure is a useful tool for novice writers; however, writers require the freedom and flexibility to follow their ideas to completion.

 **20 minutes**

Students will work online to review the correct use of capital letters in quotations, to complete an activity on commas in quotations, and to learn how to choose a topic for their short research project. Help students locate the online activities.

Skills Update

Capital Letters in Quotations

Students will review how to use capital letters in quotations by completing Skills Update exercises. Sit with students as they do this activity and note if they answer correctly.

⮑ **Learning Coach Check-In** How did students do on the Skills Update?

▸ **All answers correct:** Great! Skip the review screen and go on to the next activity.

▸ **Any answers incorrect:** Take a few minutes to review capital letters in quotations now. Use the link on the screen after the Skills Update to take another look at the online activity or review Capitalization (Other Uses of Capital Letters) in the *Grammar Reference Guide* together.

TIP This activity will require extra time if students need to review capital letters in quotations. Take the extra 5–10 minutes to review now because new skills build on what students have already learned.

> **Objectives**
> • Use a capital letter to begin a quotation.

GUM (Grammar, Usage, and Mechanics)

Commas in Quotations

Students will learn how to use commas in sentences with quotations. Then they will answer questions about using commas in sentences with quotations.

> **Objectives**
> • Use a comma to separate a quotation from the speaker tag.

Composition

Rosa Chooses a Topic

By watching Rosa learn about several possible topics for her short research project and then choosing one, students will learn how to select one topic from many possible options as they begin their own short research project.

> **Objectives**
> • Choose a topic for a short research project.
> • Gather information from print and digital sources.

[Offline] 25 minutes

Work **together** with students to complete the offline Composition activity.

Composition ....

Choose Your Topic

Students will learn about choosing a topic for their short research project. To do so, they should visit a website that contains reliable and age-appropriate information about the lives of notable historical figures. The online lesson provides website suggestions and guidance.

Students may also read about the lives of notable historical figures at a different credible website that they find with your help. Be sure to remind them that sites created and maintained by government organizations, by universities, and by other accredited groups are the ones most likely to contain accurate information. *Wikipedia* and websites whose content is not developed—and rigorously checked—by experts are not reliable sources.

After students read about several historical figures, they will answer several questions to help them choose one to be the subject of their short research project. Turn to pages WS 123 and 124 in *K¹² Language Arts Activity Book*.

1. Tell students they will investigate some important Americans as possible topics for their short research project. Provide support as necessary, helping students navigate the website or websites and encouraging them to think about people and subjects that interest them. Remind students that during this stage, they may consider many possible topics.

2. Have students complete the Activity Book pages.

TIP Keep students' completed Activity Book pages in a safe place so they can refer to them later.

> **Objectives**
> - Choose a topic for a short research project.
> - Gather information from print and digital sources.

Composition ....
Commas in Quotations and
Choose Your Topic
Choose Your Topic

Follow the steps to choose a topic for your short research project. Fill in the information and then answer the last question.

1. **Go to a website** where you can read about the lives of important people in history. Suggestions for websites are included in the online lesson, so ask your Learning Coach for help.

   If you choose to use a different website, be sure that the site has accurate information. The most reliable sites are usually created by the U.S. government or universities. These websites end in .gov or .edu.

2. Once you find a site with reliable information, **read about the lives** of several important people. As you find people whose lives interest you, **write down their names.**

3. Which one of these people would you most like to be the topic of your short research project? To help you choose, **ask yourself these questions:**
   - Do I already know a lot about any of the people on this list?
   - Which person led the most interesting life or lived during the most interesting time?
   - Who accomplished the most impressive things?
   - Who do I most want to learn more about?

4. **Cross off the names** of those people you have decided not to choose as your topic. **Circle the name** of the person you selected.

LANGUAGE ARTS PURPLE **WS 123**

WS 124 LANGUAGE ARTS PURPLE

5. **Write the name of the website and Web address** where you found information about your topic.

6. Why did you choose this person for your short research project?
   Answers will vary.

Take Notes About Your Topic

Lesson Overview

🖥 [Online]   15 minutes

Skills Update	Commas in Quotations
Composition	Rosa Takes Notes for a Short Research Project

📄 [Offline]   30 minutes

Composition	Take Notes for Your Short Research Project

[Materials]

Supplied
- *K¹² Language Arts Activity Book*, pp. WS 123–126
- *Grammar Reference Guide* Online Book (optional)

Also Needed
- encyclopedia or other print reference

Advance Preparation

To prepare for the Composition portion of this lesson, familiarize yourself with the website that students have selected as their online source of information about their topic. They should have written down the name and Web address of this site on completed pages WS 123 and 124 (Choose Your Topic) in *K¹² Language Arts Activity Book*. With students, visit a library to help them find a print source about their topic, such as an encyclopedia or other book. **Note:** The Web addresses in the online Composition activity are fictitious. Each is only an example and should not be used for students' research.

Big Ideas

- ▶ Writing requires thought and planning.
- ▶ Following a specific organizational structure is a useful tool for novice writers; however, writers require the freedom and flexibility to follow their ideas to completion.

[Online] ⓰ minutes

Students will work online to review how to use commas in quotations and to learn how to take notes for a short research project. Help students locate the online activities.

Skills Update

Commas in Quotations

Students will review how to use commas in quotations by completing Skills Update exercises. Sit with students as they do this activity and note if they answer correctly.

➲ **Learning Coach Check-In** How did students do on the Skills Update?

- ▸ **All answers correct:** Great! Skip the review screen and go on to the next activity.
- ▸ **Any answers incorrect:** Take a few minutes to review the rules about commas in quotations now. Use the link on the screen after the Skills Update to take another look at the online activity or review Quotation Marks in the *Grammar Reference Guide* together.

TIP This activity will require extra time if students need to review the rules on using commas in quotations. Take the extra 5–10 minutes to review now.

> **Objectives**
> - Use a comma to separate a quotation from the speaker tag.

Composition

Rosa Takes Notes for a Short Research Project

By watching Rosa research and take notes on the topic of her short research project, students will learn how to research and take notes on the topic of their own project.

> **Objectives**
> - Gather information from print and digital sources.
> - Take brief notes on sources.
> - Sort evidence into provided categories.

[Offline] 🕥 minutes

Work **together** with students to complete the offline Composition activity.

Composition ···

Take Notes for Your Short Research Project

Students will research and take notes on the topic of their short research project about the life of a famous person. Gather students' completed Choose Your Topic activity pages and turn to pages WS 125 and 126 in *K¹² Language Arts Activity Book*.

1. Have students complete the Activity Book pages by researching and taking notes about the person who is the subject of their short research project. Students should start with the website that has information about the person who is their topic. They should read about the person online and record important information about his or her life and accomplishments. Provide support as necessary.

2. Once students have used the website to take notes about their topic, have them use an encyclopedia or other print source to find additional information. Remind students to write down both of their sources on the form, along with the dates of key information. Students do not need to use complete sentences on the form, but they should copy quotations exactly and use quotation marks correctly.

TIP Keep students' completed form in a safe place so they can refer to it later.

> **Objectives**
> - Gather information from print and digital sources.
> - Take brief notes on sources.
> - Sort evidence into provided categories.

Organize Your Project (A)

Lesson Overview

🖥 **[Online]**   **15** minutes

Composition	Rosa Organizes Her Short Research Project

📄 **[Offline]**   **30** minutes

Composition	Organize Your Short Research Project

[Materials]

Supplied
- *K¹² Language Arts Activity Book*, pp. WS 125–133

Also Needed
- students' project materials

Advance Preparation

Gather pages WS 125 and 126 (Take Notes for Your Short Research Project, students' form with their notes about their topic) in *K¹² Language Arts Activity Book*. In this lesson, students will choose a presentation option for their short research project and gather materials for the project. You may want to read the project options on pages WS 127–133 in the Activity Book in advance to get an idea of what materials will be needed for each option.

Big Ideas

- ▶ Writing requires thought and planning.
- ▶ Following a specific organizational structure is a useful tool for novice writers; however, writers require the freedom and flexibility to follow their ideas to completion.

[Online] ⑮ minutes

Students will work online **independently** to learn how to organize a short research project. Help students locate the online activity.

Composition

Rosa Organizes Her Short Research Project

By watching Rosa learn about some options for organizing the information in her short research project, students will learn how to begin organizing the information in their own project.

> **Objectives**
> • Create a short research project.

[Offline] ㉚ minutes

Work **together** with students to complete the offline Composition activity.

Composition

Organize Your Short Research Project

Students will learn about three options for organizing the information in their short research project and presenting what they have learned. Turn to pages WS 127–133 in *K¹² Language Arts Activity Book* and gather students' completed form.

1. Have students read all the directions, consider each of the options for organizing their information and presenting it, and then choose one. Provide support as necessary.

2. Once students have chosen how they want to organize and present their information, encourage them to begin to work on their project, using the directions on the Activity Book pages to guide them. Students should refer to their notes form as needed.

3. If students have not finished taking notes, encourage them to do so before they choose a means of presentation. They will also have the next lesson to work on their presentation. However, by the end of this lesson, students should have at least chosen a project option and gathered the necessary materials.

> **Objectives**
> • Create a short research project.

Composition

Take Notes About Your Topic

Take Notes for Your Short Research Project

Take notes from a website that has information about the person you chose as the topic for your short research project. Also use an encyclopedia or other print source to find more information. Be sure to write down important dates in the person's life.

Short Research Project

Name of Topic _____

Date of Birth _____

Place of Birth _____

Two reasons this person is important _____

_____

_____

What someone else said or wrote about this person _____

_____

Answers will vary.

Two qualities this person showed in his or her life _____

_____

The most interesting fact I learned _____

_____

Where I found my facts

1. _____

_____

_____

2. _____

_____

_____

Composition

Organize Your Project (A)

Organize Your Short Research Project

Organize your short research project so that you can present it to others. Read the instructions for all three project choices, and select the one that you like best. Use your completed take-notes form.

Choice 1: Time Line

Sample

Sally Ride: Astronaut
courage / intelligence

| 1978 Sally was accepted into the space program. | | 2012 Sally died in San Diego, California. |

| 1951 Sally Ride was born in Los Angeles, California. | 1983 Sally became the first American woman to go into space. | 2001 Sally started a company to teach young girls about math and science. |

"You were the best person for the job." -Ronald Reagan
http://www.americanheroes.gov/Bios/htmlbios/ride-sk.model
Encyclopedia America

Materials
large sheet of paper or poster board
markers or crayons

Directions

☐ Place the paper or poster board on its side. **Write the name** of the person you researched and **what he or she did** along the long edge.

☐ Under the person's name, **write two qualities** that this person showed in his or her life.

☐ **Draw a line** across the middle of the paper.

☐ On the far left end of the line, **write the year** in which this person was born.

☐ Under the year, **write a short sentence** that gives the person's name and tells where he or she was born.

☐ Continue to **write important dates** in this person's life, in order, on top of the line. Under each date, briefly describe the important event or achievement that happened then. If necessary, explain why each event or achievement was important.

☐ Under the time line, **write what another person said or wrote** about the person you researched. Remember to use quotation marks.

☐ At the very bottom of the paper or poster board, **write where you found your information.**

Presentation

1. Share your time line with someone.

2. **Briefly explain who you researched** and describe the person using the two words written on the top of your time line.

3. **Discuss the person's life and achievements** in order. Use the time line to remind you of important dates and accomplishments.

4. **Tell what was said or written** about the person you researched and **what you learned** by completing this project.

5. Remember to speak slowly, clearly, and in complete sentences.

Choice 2: Box Biography

Materials
empty box, such as a cereal or shoe box
markers or crayons
several sheets of paper
scissors, safety
tape or glue

Directions

☐ **Cut the paper sheets** to fit over the six sides of the box.

☐ Decide which side of the box will be the front. On the piece of paper that fits that side, **write the name of the person** you researched and **draw a picture** of him or her.

☐ On the second piece of paper, **write when and where** the person was born.

☐ On the third piece of paper, **write two reasons** that the person you researched is important.

☐ On the fourth piece of paper, **write what another person said or wrote** about the person you researched. Remember to use quotation marks.

☐ On the fifth piece of paper, **write two qualities** that this person showed in his or her life.

☐ On the sixth piece of paper, **write the most interesting fact** you learned from your research, as well as the **two sources** you used to find information.

☐ **Glue or tape the pieces of paper** to the sides of the box, placing the paper with the name and picture of your person on the front.

Presentation

1. Share your box biography with someone.

2. **Name who you researched** and **show the picture** on the front of the box.

3. **Discuss the information** on each side of the box. As you talk, **turn the box** to show each side of your project.

4. Remember to speak slowly, clearly, and in complete sentences.

Choice 3: Poster

Materials
large sheet of paper or poster board
markers or crayons

Directions

☐ In the middle of the paper or poster board, **draw a picture** of the person you researched. Show the person doing what he or she is best known for.

☐ **Write the person's name** above the picture.

☐ On the right side of the picture, **write the two qualities** that this person showed in his or her life.

☐ On the left side of the picture, **write what another person said or wrote** about the person you researched. Remember to use quotation marks.

☐ Under the picture, **write at least three sentences about the person** you researched. Include information about the reasons that this person is important and the most interesting fact you learned.

☐ **Write the two sources** you used in your research at the bottom of the paper or poster board.

Presentation

1. Share your poster with someone.

2. **Name who you researched** and **show the picture** you drew. Explain what the person is doing in the picture and why you chose to draw it as you did.

3. **Discuss the person's life and achievements.** Explain how the person showed the **qualities you wrote** on the right side of the picture. Talk about the **quotation on the left side** of the picture.

4. **Tell what you wrote below the picture.** Explain why the person's accomplishments matter and discuss the most interesting fact you learned. **Point out where you found your information,** as well.

5. Remember to speak slowly, clearly, and in complete sentences.

Writing Skills **WS 301**

Organize Your Project (B)

Lesson Overview

📋 **[Offline]**	⏱ **45** minutes
Composition	**Continue Your Short Research Project**

Materials

Supplied
- *K¹² Language Arts Activity Book*, pp. WS 125–133

Also Needed
- students' short research project

Advance Preparation

Gather pages WS 125–126 (Take Notes for Your Short Research Project, students' form with their notes about their topic) and WS 127–133 (Organize Your Short Research Project, project instructions) in *K¹² Language Arts Activity Book*. Also gather students' partially completed short research project, if begun.

Big Ideas

▸ Writing requires thought and planning.
▸ Following a specific organizational structure is a useful tool for novice writers; however, writers require the freedom and flexibility to follow their ideas to completion.

[Offline] 45 minutes

Work **together** with students to complete the offline Composition activity.

Continue Your Short Research Project
Students will continue to work on their short research project. (They should have gathered their materials in the previous lesson and may have even begun to work on it.) If students complete the project during this lesson, they should begin to practice presenting it.

⮑ **Learning Coach Check-In** How are students progressing on their project? As students work on their short research project, make sure they are on track. Help them avoid errors before it is too late to fix them by making sure they understand the project instructions and are following them correctly.

☆ **Objectives**
- Create a short research project.

Composition

Take Notes About Your Topic
Take Notes for Your Short Research Project

Take notes from a website that has information about the person you chose as the topic for your short research project. Also use an encyclopedia or other print source to find more information. Be sure to write down important dates in the person's life.

Short Research Project

Name of Topic _____

Date of Birth _____

Place of Birth _____

Two reasons this person is important _____

_____

_____

What someone else said or wrote about this person _____

_____

_____

Answers will vary.

Two qualities this person showed in _____

_____

The most interesting fact I learned _____

_____

Where I found my facts

1. _____

_____

2. _____

_____

Composition

Organize Your Project (A)
Organize Your Short Research Project

Organize your short research project so that you can present it to others. Read the instructions for all three project choices, and select the one that you like best. Use your completed take-notes form.

Choice 1: Time Line

Sample

Sally Ride: Astronaut
courage / intelligence

1978	2012
Sally was accepted into the space program.	Sally died in San Diego, California.

1951	1983	2001
Sally Ride was born in Los Angeles, California.	Sally became the first American woman to go into space.	Sally started a company to teach young girls about math and science.

"You were the best person for the job." -Ronald Reagan
http://www.americanheroes.gov/Bios/htmlbios/ride-sk.model
Encyclopedia America

Materials

large sheet of paper or poster board
markers or crayons

Directions

☐ Place the paper or poster board on its side. **Write the name** of the person you researched and **what he or she did** along the long edge.

☐ Under the person's name, **write two qualities** that this person showed in his or her life.

☐ **Draw a line** across the middle of the paper.

☐ On the far left end of the line, **write the year** in which this person was born.

☐ Under the year, **write a short sentence** that gives the person's name and tells where he or she was born.

☐ Continue to **write important dates** in this person's life, in order, on top of the line. Under each date, briefly describe the important event or achievement that happened then. If necessary, explain why each event or achievement was important.

☐ Under the time line, **write what another person said or wrote** about the person you researched. Remember to use quotation marks.

☐ At the very bottom of the paper or poster board, **write where you found your information.**

Presentation

1. Share your time line with someone.

2. **Briefly explain who you researched** and describe the person using the two words written on the top of your time line.

3. **Discuss the person's life and achievements** in order. Use the time line to remind you of important dates and accomplishments.

4. **Tell what was said or written** about the person you researched and **what you learned** by completing this project.

5. Remember to speak slowly, clearly, and in complete sentences.

Choice 2: Box Biography

Materials

empty box, such as a cereal or shoe box
markers or crayons
several sheets of paper
scissors, safety
tape or glue

Directions

☐ **Cut the paper sheets** to fit over the six sides of the box.

☐ Decide which side of the box will be the front. On the piece of paper that fits that side, **write the name of the person** you researched and **draw a picture** of him or her.

☐ On the second piece of paper, **write when and where** the person was born.

☐ On the third piece of paper, **write two reasons** that the person you researched is important.

☐ On the fourth piece of paper, **write what another person said or wrote** about the person you researched. Remember to use quotation marks.

☐ On the fifth piece of paper, **write two qualities** that this person showed in his or her life.

☐ On the sixth piece of paper, **write the most interesting fact** you learned from your research, as well as the **two sources** you used to find information.

☐ **Glue or tape the pieces of paper** to the sides of the box, placing the paper with the name and picture of your person on the front.

Presentation

1. Share your box biography with someone.

2. **Name who you researched** and show the **picture** on the front of the box.

3. **Discuss the information** on each side of the box. As you talk, **turn the box** to show each side of your project.

4. Remember to speak slowly, clearly, and in complete sentences.

Choice 3: Poster

Materials

large sheet of paper or poster board
markers or crayons

Directions

☐ In the middle of the paper or poster board, **draw a picture** of the person you researched. Show the person doing what he or she is best known for.

☐ **Write the person's name** above the picture.

☐ On the right side of the picture, **write the two qualities** that this person showed in his or her life.

☐ On the left side of the picture, **write what another person said or wrote** about the person you researched. Remember to use quotation marks.

☐ Under the picture, **write at least three sentences about the person** you researched. Include information about the reasons that this person is important and the most interesting fact you learned.

☐ **Write the two sources** you used in your research at the bottom of the paper or poster board.

Presentation

1. Share your poster with someone.

2. **Name who you researched** and **show the picture** you drew. Explain what the person is doing in the picture and why you chose to draw it as you did.

3. **Discuss the person's life and achievements.** Explain how the person showed the **qualities you wrote** on the right side of the picture. Talk about the **quotation on the left side** of the picture.

4. **Tell what you wrote below the picture.** Explain why the person's accomplishments matter and discuss the most interesting fact you learned. **Point out where you found your information,** as well.

5. Remember to speak slowly, clearly, and in complete sentences.

Writing Skills WS 303

Unit Review and Complete Your Short Research Project

Lesson Overview

🖥 〔Online〕 ⓴ minutes

Unit Review	Quotations
More Practice	Quotations

▤ 〔Offline〕 ㉕ minutes

Composition	Complete Your Short Research Project

〔Materials〕

Supplied

- *K¹² Language Arts Activity Book*, pp. WS 125–133
- *Grammar Reference Guide* Online Book (optional)

Also Needed

- students' short research project

Keywords

quotation – a report of exact words spoken or written, usually placed within quotation marks

quotation marks – punctuation that enclose a quotation, or the exact words of a speaker or writer

speaker tag – the part of a dialogue that identifies who is speaking

Advance Preparation

Gather pages WS 125–126 (Take Notes for Your Short Research Project, students' form with their notes about their topic) and 127–133 (Organize Your Short Research Project, project instructions) in *K¹² Language Arts Activity Book*. Also gather students' short research project.

Big Ideas

▸ Writing requires thought and planning.
▸ Following a specific organizational structure is a useful tool for novice writers; however, writers require the freedom and flexibility to follow their ideas to completion.

〔Online〕 20 minutes

Students will work online to review the grammar, usage, and mechanics skills learned in the unit. Help students locate the online activities.

Unit Review ·

Quotations

To review for the Unit Checkpoint, students will review what they have learned about quotations, including how to identify and correctly write quotations, how to use capital letters in quotations, and how to use commas with quotations.

TIP A full list of objectives covered in the Unit Review can be found in the online lesson.

> **Objectives**
> • Complete a review of grammar, usage, and mechanics skills.

More Practice ·

Quotations

Go over students' results on the Unit Review and, if necessary, have them complete the appropriate review activities listed in the table online. Help students locate the activities and provide support as needed.

TIP The time students need to complete this activity will vary. Set aside enough time for students to complete all review activities, if they need to do so.

> **Objectives**
> • Evaluate Unit Review results and choose activities for more practice.

〔Offline〕 25 minutes

Work **together** with students to complete the offline Composition activity.

Composition ·

Complete Your Short Research Project

Have students finish creating their short research project, if they have not already, and practice presenting it, using the presentation guidelines in the project instructions. Remind students that they will share their project. Provide support as necessary.

TIP If possible, record students practicing their presentation. Watching themselves often helps students improve.

> **Objectives**
> • Create a short research project.

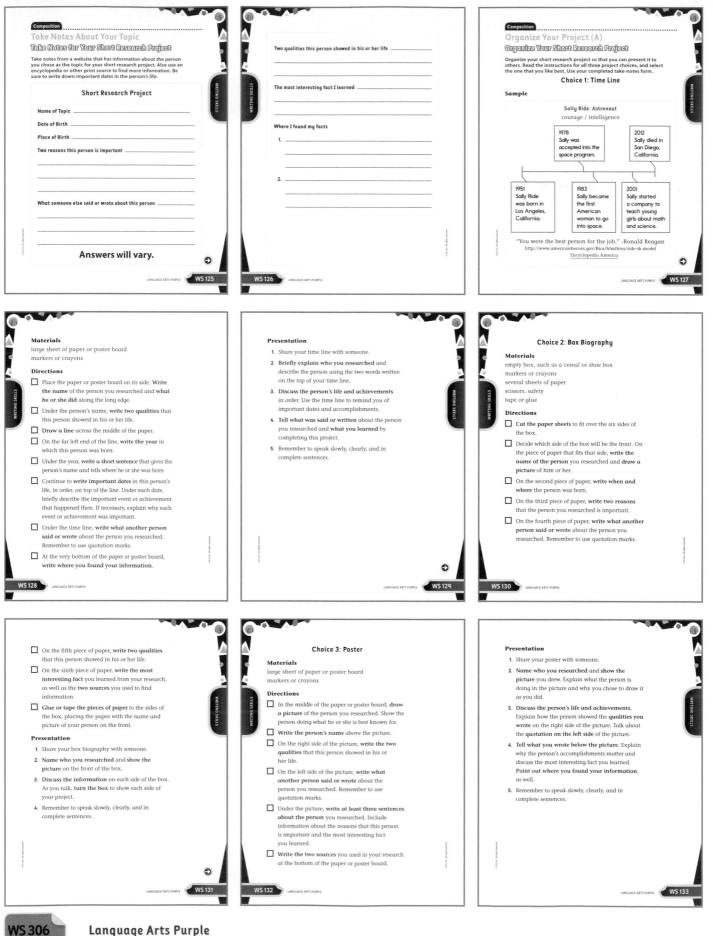

Composition
Take Notes About Your Topic
Take Notes for Your Short Research Project

Take notes from a website that has information about the person you chose as the topic for your short research project. Also use an encyclopedia or other print source to find more information. Be sure to write down important dates in the person's life.

Short Research Project

Name of Topic _____

Date of Birth _____

Place of Birth _____

Two reasons this person is important _____

_____

_____

What someone else said or wrote about this person _____

_____

_____

Answers will vary.

WS 125

Two qualities this person showed in his or her life _____

_____

_____

The most interesting fact I learned _____

_____

_____

Where I found my facts

1. _____

_____

_____

2. _____

_____

_____

WS 126

Composition
Organize Your Project (A)
Organize Your Short Research Project

Organize your short research project so that you can present it to others. Read the instructions for all three project choices, and select the one that you like best. Use your completed take-notes form.

Choice 1: Time Line

Sample

Sally Ride: Astronaut
courage / intelligence

| 1978 Sally was accepted into the space program. | | 2012 Sally died in San Diego, California. |

| 1951 Sally Ride was born in Los Angeles, California. | 1983 Sally became the first American woman to go into space. | 2001 Sally started a company to teach young girls about math and science. |

"You were the best person for the job." -Ronald Reagan
http://www.americanheroes.gov/Bios/htmlbios/ride-sk.model
Encyclopedia America

WS 127

Materials

large sheet of paper or poster board
markers or crayons

Directions

☐ Place the paper or poster board on its side. **Write the name** of the person you researched and **what he or she did** along the long edge.

☐ Under the person's name, **write two qualities** that this person showed in his or her life.

☐ **Draw a line** across the middle of the paper.

☐ On the far left end of the line, **write the year** in which this person was born.

☐ Under the year, **write a short sentence** that gives the person's name and tells where he or she was born.

☐ Continue to **write important dates** in this person's life, in order, on top of the line. Under each date, briefly describe the important event or achievement that happened then. If necessary, explain why each event or achievement was important.

☐ Under the time line, **write what another person said or wrote** about the person you researched. Remember to use quotation marks.

☐ At the very bottom of the paper or poster board, **write where you found your information.**

WS 128

Presentation

1. Share your time line with someone.

2. **Briefly explain who you researched** and describe the person using the two words written on the top of your time line.

3. **Discuss the person's life and achievements** in order. Use the time line to remind you of important dates and accomplishments.

4. **Tell what was said or written** about the person you researched and **what you learned** by completing this project.

5. Remember to speak slowly, clearly, and in complete sentences.

WS 129

Choice 2: Box Biography

Materials

empty box, such as a cereal or shoe box
markers or crayons
several sheets of paper
scissors, safety
tape or glue

Directions

☐ **Cut the paper sheets** to fit over the six sides of the box.

☐ Decide which side of the box will be the front. On the piece of paper that fits that side, **write the name of the person** you researched and **draw a picture** of him or her.

☐ On the second piece of paper, **write when and where** the person was born.

☐ On the third piece of paper, **write two reasons** that the person you researched is important.

☐ On the fourth piece of paper, **write what another person said or wrote** about the person you researched. Remember to use quotation marks.

WS 130

☐ On the fifth piece of paper, **write two qualities** that this person showed in his or her life.

☐ On the sixth piece of paper, **write the most interesting fact** you learned from your research, as well as the **two sources** you used to find information.

☐ **Glue or tape the pieces of paper** to the sides of the box, placing the paper with the name and picture of your person on the front.

Presentation

1. Share your box biography with someone.

2. **Name who you researched** and **show the picture** on the front of the box.

3. **Discuss the information** on each side of the box. As you talk, **turn the box** to show each side of your project.

4. Remember to speak slowly, clearly, and in complete sentences.

WS 131

Choice 3: Poster

Materials

large sheet of paper or poster board
markers or crayons

Directions

☐ In the middle of the paper or poster board, **draw a picture** of the person you researched. Show the person doing what he or she is best known for.

☐ **Write the person's name** above the picture.

☐ On the right side of the picture, **write the two qualities** that this person showed in his or her life.

☐ On the left side of the picture, **write what another person said or wrote** about the person you researched. Remember to use quotation marks.

☐ Under the picture, **write at least three sentences about the person** you researched. Include information about the reasons that this person is important and the most interesting fact you learned.

☐ **Write the two sources** you used in your research at the bottom of the paper or poster board.

WS 132

Presentation

1. Share your poster with someone.

2. **Name who you researched** and **show the picture** you drew. Explain what the person is doing in the picture and why you chose to draw it as you did.

3. **Discuss the person's life and achievements.** Explain how the person showed the **qualities you wrote** on the right side of the picture. Talk about the **quotation on the left side** of the picture.

4. **Tell what you wrote below the picture.** Explain why the person's accomplishments matter and discuss the most interesting fact you learned. **Point out where you found your information,** as well.

5. Remember to speak slowly, clearly, and in complete sentences.

WS 133

Unit Checkpoint and Present Your Project

Lesson Overview

🖥️ **〖Online〗**		**20 minutes**
Unit Checkpoint	Quotations	

📄 **〖Offline〗**		**25 minutes**
More Practice	Quotations	
Write Now	Present Your Project	

Advance Preparation

Gather pages WS 125 and 126 (Take Notes for Your Research Project, students' form with their notes about their topic) in *K¹² Language Arts Activity Book* and students' completed short research project, which they will present today.

Big Ideas

- ► Writing requires thought and planning.
- ► Following a specific organizational structure is a useful tool for novice writers; however, writers require the freedom and flexibility to follow their ideas to completion.

〖 Materials 〗

Supplied

- *K¹² Language Arts Activity Book*, pp. WS 125–126
- *Grammar Reference Guide* Online Book (optional)
- Short Research Project: Rubric (printout)
- Quotations (optional printout)
- Capital Letters in Quotations (optional printout)
- Commas in Quotations (optional printout)

Also Needed

- students' short research project

Keywords

quotation – a report of exact words spoken or written, usually placed within quotation marks

quotation marks – punctuation that encloses a quotation, or the exact words of a speaker or writer

speaker tag – the part of a dialogue that identifies who is speaking

⟦ Online ⟧ ⓴ minutes

Students will work online **independently** to complete the Unit Checkpoint. Help students locate the Unit Checkpoint and provide support as necessary.

Unit Checkpoint ···

Quotations

Students will complete an online Unit Checkpoint about quotations, including how to identify and correctly write quotations, how to use capital letters in quotations, and how to use commas with quotations. If necessary, read the directions to students.

TIP A full list of objectives covered in the Unit Checkpoint can be found in the online lesson.

Objectives
- Complete a Unit Checkpoint on grammar, usage, and mechanics skills.

⟦ Offline ⟧ ㉕ minutes

Work **together** with students to complete the offline More Practice and Write Now activities.

More Practice ···

Quotations

Go over students' results on the Unit Checkpoint and, if necessary, print out and have them complete the appropriate activity pages listed in the table online. Students can complete all necessary pages now or, if more time is needed, they can spread them out over the next few days. They can also review the appropriate sections of the *Grammar Reference Guide* with you. If students scored less than 80 percent on the Unit Checkpoint, you may want them to retake the Checkpoint after completing the additional activity pages.

TIP The time students need to complete this activity will vary. Set aside enough time for students to complete some or all activity pages and to retake the Unit Checkpoint, if they need to do so. Students may retake the Unit Checkpoint immediately, but having them complete the activity pages and then retake it might be more effective.

Objectives
- Evaluate Unit Checkpoint results and choose activities for more practice.

More Practice

Improve Your Skills
Quotations

Choose the answer.

1. Which sentence has a quotation?
   A. Let's talk tomorrow.
   B. I will write you a letter.
   C. You told me the truth.
   D. "Try the cheese," I said. *(circled)*

2. Which sentence is a quotation?
   A. Harry said the house was empty.
   B. "The flowers in the garden are lovely." *(circled)*
   C. We asked Miss Davis to help us.
   D. Are there any elephants in China?

3. Read this passage.

> Cara and Ryan looked at the menu. It was already past lunchtime, and Cara's stomach grumbled. Ryan looked up.
> "What are you going to order?" Ryan asked.
> "I think I'm going to get the chicken," Cara replied.
> "That sounds tasty, so I'll try it, too."

Who says the final line above?
   A. Ryan *(circled)*
   B. Cara
   C. It's impossible to know.

WS 1

4. Which sentence is written correctly?
   A. "Mary said, It's very cold outside."
   B. Mary said, "It's very cold outside.
   C. Mary said, "It's very cold outside." *(circled)*
   D. "Mary said," It's very cold outside.

WS 2

More Practice

Improve Your Skills
Capital Letters in Quotations

Complete each exercise.

1. Circle the underlined word in the sentence that should be capitalized.
   "what is your phone number?" the cashier asked.

2. Circle the underlined word in the sentence that should be capitalized.
   A farmer once told me, "pigs are as smart as dogs."

3. Which answer choice correctly completes the sentence?
   "_____ laugh!" Vern said.
   A. don't
   B. DON'T
   C. do not
   D. Don't *(circled)*

4. Which answer choice correctly completes the sentence?
   Trevor asked, "_____ at the door?"
   A. Who's *(circled)*
   B. who is
   C. WHO'S
   D. who's

WS 1

More Practice

Improve Your Skills
Commas in Quotations

Choose the answer.

1. Where does the comma belong in the sentence?
   Jack told his mother "I bought some magic beans."
   A. After *Jack*
   B. After *mother* *(circled)*
   C. After *bought*
   D. After *beans*

2. Where does the comma belong in the sentence?
   "That's my favorite song" Annabel replied.
   A. After *That's*
   B. After *favorite*
   C. After *song* *(circled)*
   D. After *replied*

3. Which sentence is written correctly?
   A. Diego called out "Is anybody home?"
   B. Diego called, out "Is anybody home?"
   C. Diego called out "Is anybody home,"
   D. Diego called out, "Is anybody home?" *(circled)*

4. Which sentence is written correctly?
   A. "My cousin got married in June," Fiona said. *(circled)*
   B. "My cousin got married in June" Fiona said.
   C. "My cousin got married in June" Fiona said,
   D. "My cousin got married in June" Fiona, said.

WS 1

Write Now

•••

Present Your Project

Students will present their short research project about a famous person. Have them gather their project and form.

1. Explain to students that they will finish their short research project by completing the last stage of the process—publishing their work.
   Say: Publishing your work, in this case, means making a presentation in which you share your work with others.

   ▸ To be ready to publish your short research project, you should have finished creating your project and be ready to present and explain it to others.

   ▸ The final project and presentation should be your best effort and should not have any errors.

2. Tell students that they should use a clear speaking voice when presenting their project and speak in complete sentences as they explain their work. Students should refer to their project and form during their presentation as needed.

3. Use the materials and instructions in the online lesson to evaluate students' finished project and presentation. You will be looking at students' work to evaluate the following:

   ▸ **Purpose and Content:** The project focuses on the life and accomplishments of one person. It displays three or four key facts about the person's life and achievements, one or two words that accurately describe the person, and a quotation that someone else said or wrote about the person. No more than one irrelevant detail is included in the project.

   ▸ **Presentation and Organization:** The presentation is well organized and touches on all but one element of the completed research form, as illustrated in the project. With perhaps one exception, the student speaks clearly and slowly enough for audience members to understand the key details of the presentation.

   ▸ **Grammar and Mechanics:** With a few exceptions, the student speaks in complete sentences while presenting the project. On the project itself, the student may have made an error or two in using quotation marks, capital letters, and commas for the words that someone else said or wrote.

4. Enter students' scores online for each rubric category.

Objectives
- Present a short research project.
- Speak in complete sentences to provide requested detail or clarification.

5. If students' project and presentation scored a 1 in any category, discuss with them how their work might be revised. Students do not need to actually make the revisions, unless they can be made easily without major **rework** to the project.

 TIP Tell students that producing a project that is ready to publish **and share with** others is a great accomplishment. Let students know that the effort they put in to complete and present their project is something to be proud of.

Reward: When students score 80 percent or above on the Unit Checkpoint and they've completed their short research project presentation, add a sticker for this unit on the My Accomplishments chart.

Composition

Take Notes About Your Topic

Take Notes for Your Short Research Project

Take notes from a website that has information about the person you chose as the topic for your short research project. Also use an encyclopedia or other print source to find more information. Be sure to write down important dates in the person's life.

Short Research Project

Name of Topic _____

Date of Birth _____

Place of Birth _____

Two reasons this person is important _____

_____

_____

What someone else said or wrote about this person _____

_____

_____

Answers will vary.

WS 125   LANGUAGE ARTS PURPLE

Two qualities this person showed in his or her life _____

_____

The most interesting fact I learned _____

_____

Where I found my facts

1. _____

_____

_____

2. _____

_____

_____

WS 126   LANGUAGE ARTS PURPLE

Critical Skills Practice 4

Unit Focus

In this unit, students will learn how to answer multiple choice questions about

- ► Reference works
- ► Author's purpose
- ► Main ideas and supporting details

Students will also learn how to recognize and respond to writing prompts. Finally, they will write a response to a writing prompt.

Unit Plan		Offline	Online
Lesson 1	Research Skills		45 minutes
Lesson 2	Writing Strategies (A)		45 minutes
Lesson 3	Writing Strategies (B)		45 minutes
Lesson 4	Writing Prompts		45 minutes
Lesson 5	Unit Checkpoint	45 minutes	varies

Research Skills

Lesson Overview

	Online	45 minutes
Get Ready	References	
Learn	Questions About References	
Try It	Answer Questions About References	

Materials

There are no materials to gather for this lesson.

Keywords

reference – a work that contains useful information for a writer such as an encyclopedia, a dictionary, or a website

Big Ideas

Practice answering the kinds of questions often found on standardized tests can make taking the tests less stressful for students.

 Online 45 minutes

Students will work online **independently** to complete Get Ready, Learn, and Try It activities. Help students locate the online activities.

Get Ready

References
Students will review what a reference is and some key references that writers and readers use often.

Objectives
• Define *reference*.

Learn

Questions About References

Students will learn how to answer questions about references by working through several exercises.

Objectives
- Identify and select the best reference source.

Try It

Answer Questions About References

Students will show their comprehension and ability to respond to questions about references.

Objectives
- Identify and select the best reference source.

Writing Strategies (A)

Lesson Overview

Online		45 minutes
Get Ready	Purposes for Writing	
Learn	Questions About Purposes for Writing	
Try It	Answer Questions About Purposes for Writing	

Materials

There are no materials to gather for this lesson.

Keywords

author's purpose – the reason the author wrote a text: to entertain, to inform, to express an opinion, or to persuade

Big Ideas

Practice answering the kinds of questions often found on standardized tests can make taking the tests less stressful for students.

Online 45 minutes

Students will work online **independently** to complete Get Ready, Learn, and Try It activities. Help students locate the online activities.

Get Ready

Purposes for Writing

Students will review the meaning of author's purpose, as well as three main purposes for a piece of writing: to entertain, to inform, and to persuade. They will also go over some common examples of writing created for each of these purposes.

Objectives
• Define *author's purpose*.

Learn

Questions About Purposes for Writing

Students will learn how to answer questions about identifying the purpose of a passage by reading and working through several exercises.

Objectives
- Identify purpose for writing.

Try It

Answer Questions About Purposes for Writing

Students will show their comprehension and ability to respond to questions about identifying the purpose of a passage.

Objectives
- Identify purpose for writing.

Writing Strategies (B)

Lesson Overview

Online   **45** minutes

Get Ready	Main Ideas and Supporting Details
Learn	Questions About Main Ideas and Supporting Details
Try It	Answer Questions About Main Ideas and Supporting Details

[Materials]

There are no materials to gather for this lesson.

Keywords

main idea – the most important point of the paragraph

supporting details – the sentences that give information about the main idea or topic sentence

Big Ideas

Practice answering the kinds of questions often found on standardized tests can make taking the tests less stressful for students.

[Online] **45** minutes

Students will work online **independently** to complete Get Ready, Learn, and Try It activities. Help students locate the online activities.

Get Ready

Main Ideas and Supporting Details

Students will review what is meant by the terms *main idea* and *supporting details*. Then they will go over the relationship between a paragraph's main idea and its supporting details.

Objectives

- Define *main idea*.
- Define *supporting details*.

Learn

Questions About Main Ideas and Supporting Details

Students will learn how to answer questions about main ideas and supporting details by reading and working through several exercises.

Objectives

- Identify the main idea and supporting details.
- Organize text using main idea and supporting details.

Try It

Answer Questions About Main Ideas and Supporting Details

Students will show their comprehension and ability to respond to questions about main ideas and supporting details.

Objectives

- Identify the main idea and supporting details.
- Organize text using main idea and supporting details.

Writing Prompts

Lesson Overview

Online   **45** minutes

Get Ready	Recognize Writing Prompts
Learn	How to Respond to a Writing Prompt
Try It	Review How to Respond to a Writing Prompt

Materials

There are no materials to gather for this lesson.

Keywords

narrative – a kind of writing that tells a story

writing prompt – a sentence or sentences that ask for a particular kind of writing

Big Ideas

Practice answering the kinds of questions often found on standardized tests can make taking the tests less stressful for students.

Online **45** minutes

Students will work online **independently** to complete Get Ready, Learn, and Try It activities. Help students locate the online activities.

Get Ready

Recognize Writing Prompts

Students will review what writing prompts are and how to know what a prompt requires in terms of the type of writing and how much to write. They will also go over the importance of planning and reviewing a response to a writing prompt.

Objectives

- Recognize a writing prompt that calls for a narrative response.

Learn

How to Respond to a Writing Prompt

Students will learn how to respond to a writing prompt by exploring one student's effort to do so and answering questions about how she did it.

Objectives

- Recognize a writing prompt that calls for a narrative response.
- Determine how to respond to a writing prompt.

Try It

Review How to Respond to a Writing Prompt

Students will show their comprehension of how to respond to a writing prompt by answering several questions about the steps to take when they have to respond to a writing prompt.

Objectives

- Recognize a writing prompt that calls for a narrative response.
- Determine how to respond to a writing prompt.

Unit Checkpoint

Lesson Overview

Offline	45 minutes
Unit Checkpoint	Critical Skills Practice 4

Online	varies
More Practice	Critical Skills Practice 4

Materials

Supplied

- *K¹² Language Arts Assessments*, pp. WS 25–34
- Writing Prompt: Rubric and Sample Responses (printout)

Objectives

- Identify and select the best reference source.
- Identify purpose for writing.
- Identify the main idea and supporting details.
- Organize text using main idea and supporting details.
- Recognize a writing prompt that calls for a narrative response.
- Write a response to a writing prompt.
- Write sentences and paragraphs that develop a central idea, consider purpose and audience, and use the writing process.
- Use an appropriate organizational pattern in writing.
- Write a narrative with a beginning, middle, and end.

Offline 45 minutes

Unit Checkpoint

Critical Skills Practice 4

Explain that students are going to show what they have learned about references, author's purpose, main ideas and supporting details, and writing prompts.

1. Give students the Unit Checkpoint pages.

2. Read the directions together. Have students complete the Checkpoint on their own.

3. Use the Answer Key to score the Checkpoint and then enter the results online.

4. Review each exercise with students. Work with students to correct any exercise they missed.

Parts 1–3: References, Author's Purpose, and Main Ideas and Supporting Details

Have students spend about 15 minutes answering the questions about references, author's purpose, and main ideas and supporting details.

Part 4: Respond to a Writing Prompt

Have students respond to the writing prompt. Tell students they have 30 minutes to complete their response.

1. Direct students' attention to Part 4 of the Checkpoint and read the directions together, ensuring that students understand they are to write a response to the writing prompt.

2. Remind students that they should write their response in complete sentences, use good handwriting, and leave spaces between words so that others can read what they wrote.

3. Have students write their response to the writing prompt.

4. Use the Writing Prompt: Rubric and Sample Responses to evaluate students' finished writing. You will be looking at students' writing to evaluate the following:

   ▸ **Purpose and Content:** The response focuses on a time when someone the student knows surprised him or her. It describes what happened, tells who was involved, and explains why the student was surprised. It contains no more than two irrelevant facts or details.

   ▸ **Structure and Organization:** The response shows some organization and evidence of planning and revising. With perhaps one exception, it describes events in chronological order. The response is at least one paragraph in length.

   ▸ **Grammar and Mechanics:** The response has been proofread, and three or four errors remain in grammar and mechanics.

5. If students' writing scored a 1 in any category, work with them to revise and proofread their work.

 Reward: If students score 80 percent or more on the Unit Checkpoint, add a sticker for this unit on the My Accomplishments chart. If students did not score 80 percent or more, work with them to revise their work until they do score 80 percent.

Name _____ Date _____

Unit Checkpoint Learning Coach Instructions
Critical Skills Practice 4

Explain that students are going to show what they have learned about references, author's purpose, main ideas and supporting details, and writing prompts.

1. Give students the Unit Checkpoint pages.

2. Read the directions together. Have students complete the Checkpoint on their own.

3. Use the Answer Key to score the Checkpoint and then enter the results online.

4. Review each exercise with students. Work with students to correct any exercise they missed.

Parts 1–3. References, Author's Purpose, and Main Ideas and Supporting Details
Have students spend about 15 minutes answering the questions about references, author's purpose, and main ideas and supporting details.

Part 4. Respond to a Writing Prompt
Have students respond to the writing prompt. Tell students they have 30 minutes to complete their response.

1. Direct students' attention to Part 4 of the Checkpoint and read the directions together, ensuring that students understand they are to write a response to the writing prompt.

2. Remind students that they should write their response in complete sentences, use good handwriting, and leave spaces between words so that others can read what they wrote.

3. Have students write their response to the writing prompt.

4. Use the Writing Prompt: Rubric and Sample Responses to evaluate students' finished writing. You will be looking at students' writing to evaluate the following:

   • **Purpose and Content:** The response focuses on a time when someone the student knows surprised him or her. It describes what happened, tells who was involved, and explains why the student was surprised. It contains no more than two irrelevant facts or details.

LANGUAGE ARTS PURPLE | CRITICAL SKILLS PRACTICE 4   **WS 25**

Name _____ Date _____

• **Structure and Organization:** The response shows some organization and evidence of planning and revising. With perhaps one exception, it describes events in chronological order. The response is at least one paragraph in length.

• **Grammar and Mechanics:** The response has been proofread, and three or four errors remain in grammar and mechanics.

5. If students' writing scored a 1 in any category, work with them to revise and proofread their work.

WS 26   LANGUAGE ARTS PURPLE | CRITICAL SKILLS PRACTICE 4

Name _____ Date _____

Unit Checkpoint Answer Key
Critical Skills Practice 4

Part 1. References
Read and answer each question.

1. Which source would be best to use to find the meaning of the word *density*?
   A. atlas
   B. encyclopedia
   C. thesaurus
   (D) dictionary

2. Read this sentence.

   > Jake made a poor decision.

   Which resource should the writer use to find a word that means almost the same thing as *poor*, but that helps tell readers that Jake's decision was very, very poor?
   A. dictionary
   (B) thesaurus
   C. atlas
   D. encyclopedia

3. Carter wants to learn more about ancient Rome. Where would he find the most information on this subject?
   (A) encyclopedia article on ancient Rome
   B. dictionary entry for *Rome*
   C. atlas with maps of Rome
   D. thesaurus entry for the word *ancient*

LANGUAGE ARTS PURPLE | CRITICAL SKILLS PRACTICE 4   **WS 27**

Name _____ Date _____

4. Janice wants to find out who the city council members are in her hometown. Which reference would give her the most information?
   A. encyclopedia entry on local government
   B. atlas with a map of the city
   (C) city council's website
   D. dictionary entry for the word *council*

5. Lena is writing a report on Spain. Which reference would make it easiest for her to see which countries are near Spain?
   (A) atlas
   B. dictionary
   C. thesaurus
   D. encyclopedia

Part 2. Author's Purpose
Read and answer each question.

6. Read this passage.

   > Fresh berries are great, but they can spoil and get moldy before you have a chance to eat them. Follow these helpful steps so that moldy berries become a memory.
   > 1. Mix one part vinegar with ten parts water.
   > 2. Put the berries into the mixture and swirl them around.
   > 3. Drain and rinse the berries with fresh water.
   > 4. Place the berries in the refrigerator.

   Why did the author probably write this passage?
   (A) to teach people a simple way to keep berries fresh
   B. to convince readers that fresh berries taste best
   C. to remind readers that vinegar has many uses
   D. to tell readers what kinds of berries to buy

WS 28   LANGUAGE ARTS PURPLE | CRITICAL SKILLS PRACTICE 4

Name _____ Date _____

7. Read this passage.

   > *Clumsy* might as well be Frank's middle name. He's always tripping and bumping into things. So no one was surprised when Frank did not see the water on the ground and slipped. He didn't fall though. He just flung his arms wildly to keep his balance. He shouted and groaned. His knees wobbled. His ankles buckled. He looked like an ostrich on ice skates, and he felt very silly. But he kept a smile on his face, and everyone had a good laugh.

   Why did the author most likely write this passage?
   A. to warn readers to be careful around Frank
   (B) to entertain readers with a story about a funny event
   C. to convince readers that water can be dangerous
   D. to teach readers how to keep their balance if they ever slip

LANGUAGE ARTS PURPLE | CRITICAL SKILLS PRACTICE 4   **WS 29**

Name _____ Date _____

8. Read this passage.

   > If you are going to get a dog, do not go to a pet store. Instead, go to an animal shelter. At a shelter, you can adopt a dog rather than buy one. Adoption is better than buying for a couple of reasons. The most important reason is adoption saves the life of an animal. Another reason is that adopting a dog is much cheaper than buying one. So, when you want a dog, take my advice, and go to a shelter.

   Which best describes why the author wrote this passage?
   A. to scare readers so that they do not want to get a pet anymore
   B. to persuade readers that having a pet is a major responsibility
   C. to teach readers how the pet adoption process works
   (D) to convince readers that adopting a dog is better than buying one from a pet store

9. Read this passage.

   > The 1984 Summer Olympics were held in Los Angeles, California. Carl Lewis, an American sprinter, won four gold medals. Mary Lou Retton showed off her amazing gymnastic skills. And a young Michael Jordan led the men's basketball team to a gold medal.

   What is the author's main purpose in writing this passage?
   A. to persuade readers that the Summer Olympics are better than the Winter Olympics
   B. to entertain readers with an exciting story about an athletic event
   (C) to teach readers some things about the 1984 Summer Olympics
   D. to convince readers that Carl Lewis was a better athlete than Michael Jordan

WS 30   LANGUAGE ARTS PURPLE | CRITICAL SKILLS PRACTICE 4

Name _____ Date _____

Part 3. Main Ideas and Supporting Details
Read and answer each question.

10. Which sentence states the main idea of this paragraph?

    > *The Last Hero* is easily the best movie to come out this year. The film is full of exciting twists and thrilling turns. In addition, the actors who star in the movie are all excellent. Lastly, the movie just looks amazing. Let me tell you more!

    (A) *The Last Hero* is easily the best movie to come out this year.
    B. The film is full of exciting twists and thrilling turns.
    C. In addition, the actors who star in the movie are all excellent.
    D. Lastly, the movie just looks amazing.

11. Based on the supporting details, which sentence states the main idea that belongs at the start of this paragraph?

    > _____. Jane Gallagher plays the main character in *The Last Hero*. She may look sweet and small, but she knows how to be strong, too. Ray Wilkins plays the villain, but he shows the thoughtful side of the bad guy. Finally, six-year-old Timmy Radley steals the show with his charm. Radley will win some awards for his acting.

    A. The action keeps going until the credits roll at the end of the film.
    (B) The acting in the film is great.
    C. All of my friends have toys from *The Last Hero*.
    D. The only problem with the movie is its title.

LANGUAGE ARTS PURPLE | CRITICAL SKILLS PRACTICE 4   **WS 31**

Name _____ Date _____

12. Based on the main idea, which supporting detail belongs in this paragraph?

    > Of course, *The Last Hero* looks terrific. Watching it is a feast for the eyes. _____ The 3-D effects make it feel like you are a part of the action.

    (A) The colors are so bright and vivid that they almost jump off the screen.
    B. Even actors with small parts are great in this movie.
    C. I was shocked by the movie's surprise ending.
    D. No one else in my family has seen the movie yet.

13. Which supporting detail does **not** belong in this paragraph?

    > If you only see one movie this year, make it *The Last Hero*. You will see more action than you've ever seen. You will watch great actors. You will even be wowed by the beauty of the movie. You should also see *Green Yellow Red*, because that's good, too. So go get your ticket today!

    A. You will see more action than you've ever seen.
    B. You will watch great actors.
    C. You will even be wowed by the beauty of the movie.
    (D) You should also see *Green Yellow Red*, because that's good, too.

WS 32   LANGUAGE ARTS PURPLE | CRITICAL SKILLS PRACTICE 4

Name _____ Date _____

Part 4. Respond to a Writing Prompt
Follow the directions to write a response to the prompt.

14.–16. Read the writing prompt. Then write your response on the lines.

> Tell a story about a time when someone you know did something to surprise you. Write at least one paragraph and include details about what happened, who was involved, and why you were surprised.
>
> You have **30 minutes** to complete this writing assignment. Before you begin, write down the most important ideas you want to include. After you have finished your response, read what you have written. Then make changes and correct mistakes in the time you have left.

Refer to the rubric and sample responses to evaluate.

_____

_____

_____

_____

_____

_____

LANGUAGE ARTS PURPLE | CRITICAL SKILLS PRACTICE 4   **WS 33**

 **varies**

Work **together** with students to complete the online More Practice activity.

More Practice

Critical Skills Practice 4

Go over students' results on the Unit Checkpoint. If necessary, have students complete the appropriate review activities listed in the table online. Help students locate the activities and provide support as needed.

TIP The time students need to complete this activity will vary. Set aside enough time for students to complete all review activities, if they need to do so.

Objectives
- Evaluate Unit Checkpoint results and choose activities for more practice.

Pronouns and Book Review

Unit Focus

In the grammar part of the unit, students will learn about pronouns. They will

- ► Learn what a personal pronoun is.
- ► Learn which pronouns are singular and which are plural and how to use them in sentences.
- ► Learn the difference between subject and object pronouns, as well as when to use each.
- ► Learn how to identify and use possessive pronouns correctly.
- ► Learn about reflexive and intensive pronouns and practice using them.

In the composition part of the unit, students will write a book review. They will

- ► Use their journal to freewrite.
- ► List the books they've read recently and brainstorm pros and cons for each book before deciding which one to review.
- ► Use a story map to plan a review.
- ► Review what a summary is and what belongs in one.
- ► Write a book review of at least three paragraphs.
- ► Revise, proofread, and write a clean copy of their book review.

Unit Plan		**Online**	**Offline**
Lesson 1	Singular Personal Pronouns and Journal Entry	30 minutes	15 minutes
Lesson 2	Plural Personal Pronouns and Model Book Review	30 minutes	15 minutes
Lesson 3	Subject Pronouns and Choose Your Book to Review	30 minutes	15 minutes
Lesson 4	Pronouns After Action Verbs and Plan Your Book Review	25 minutes	20 minutes
Lesson 5	Possessive Pronouns and Review Summaries	30 minutes	15 minutes
Lesson 6	Possessive Pronouns and Write Your Summary	20 minutes	25 minutes
Lesson 7	Draft Your Book Review	20 minutes	25 minutes
Lesson 8	Pronouns with –self	30 minutes	15 minutes
Lesson 9	Revise Your Book Review	20 minutes	25 minutes
Lesson 10	Unit Review and Proofread Your Book Review	20 minutes	25 minutes
Lesson 11	Unit Checkpoint and Publish Your Book Review	20 minutes	25 minutes

Singular Personal Pronouns and Journal Entry

Lesson Overview

🖥 〔Online〕 **30** minutes

GUM (Grammar, Usage, and Mechanics)	Singular Personal Pronouns

📄 〔Offline〕 **15** minutes

Composition	Journal: Write About a Great Book
Beyond the Lesson	⊕ **OPTIONAL:** Journal: Freewrite on a Topic

〔Materials〕

Supplied
- *K¹² My Journal*, pp. 32–33
- *Grammar Reference Guide* Online Book (optional)

Keywords

personal pronoun – a word that takes the place of one or more nouns; the personal pronouns are *I, me, you, he, him, she, her, it, we, us, they,* and *them*

Advance Preparation

To prepare for the GUM portion of this lesson, review Pronouns (Personal Pronouns) in the *Grammar Reference Guide* (linked in the online lesson) to familiarize yourself with the topic.

Big Ideas

- ► Using pronouns to take the place of some nouns helps writers avoid repetition.
- ► Journal writing is a form of freewriting. It is an opportunity to get ideas on paper without regard for correctness of the language or the format of a piece of writing.
- ► To improve, writers require frequent practice.

 **30 minutes**

Students will work online **independently** to complete an activity on singular personal pronouns. Help students locate the online activity.

GUM (Grammar, Usage, and Mechanics)

Singular Personal Pronouns
Students will learn to identify the singular personal pronouns and practice using them to take the place of nouns in sentences.

Objectives
- Identify and use singular personal pronouns.

 **15 minutes**

Work **together** with students to complete the offline Composition and Beyond the Lesson activities.

Composition

Journal: Write About a Great Book
Students will respond to a journal prompt by writing about their favorite book from the past year and explaining why they liked that book so much. Gather *K¹² My Journal* and have students turn to pages 32 and 33.

Objectives
- Respond to a journal prompt.
- Freewrite about a topic.

1. Tell students they are going to write in their journal about the book that they most enjoyed reading in the last year. To help students think of several books that they've read, ask them to think about their answers to the following questions.

   ▸ What are some books that you've read recently? Which books did you enjoy? What were some reasons that you enjoyed these books?
   ▸ Did any of these books make you laugh? Were they exciting? Did they make you think about things in new ways? Did you feel as though you understood the characters in any of these books especially well?
   ▸ Which main characters were the most like you? What stories told of events that are similar to ones that you have experienced? What books made you want to read more works by the same author?

2. Have students respond to the prompt in their journal. Encourage them to write in complete sentences, although it is not a requirement when they are freewriting in their journal.

TIP Students should write for about 15 minutes. Freewriting allows students to use their imagination to write what they want without worrying about being graded, so encourage them to keep writing for the entire time. If students have trouble writing for 15 minutes, use the prompting questions in Step 1 or have them list ideas or words. If they want to keep writing beyond the suggested time limit, praise them for their enthusiasm and offer to let them complete their entry later in the day as a reward.

Book of the Year   Date _____

Which book is the best one you read this year? Why?

_____
_____
_____
_____
_____
_____
_____
_____
_____
_____
_____
_____
_____

WRITING SKILLS

32

Beyond the Lesson

✏️ ✚ **OPTIONAL: Journal: Freewrite on a Topic**

This activity is OPTIONAL. It is intended for students who have extra time and would benefit from extra practice. Feel free to skip this activity. Gather *K¹² My Journal*.

1. Have students either respond to a prompt in Thoughts and Experiences (pages 50–93) or write about their own topic on the next available page in Ideas (pages 96–139).

2. Encourage students to explore their thoughts and write as much as they want. There are no rules. If students wish, ideas can be fleshed out into a more developed composition at a later time.

TIP Studies show that students who write more frequently become better writers.

> **Objectives**
> - Respond to a journal prompt.
> - Freewrite about a topic.

Plural Personal Pronouns and Model Book Review

Lesson Overview

💻 [Online] 30 minutes

Skills Update	Singular Personal Pronouns
GUM (Grammar, Usage, and Mechanics)	Plural Personal Pronouns
Composition	Explore a Model Book Review

📄 [Offline] 15 minutes

Composition	Respond to the Model Book Review

[Materials]

Supplied
- *K¹² Language Arts Activity Book*, pp. WS 135–138
- *Grammar Reference Guide* Online Book (optional)

Keywords

book review – a piece of writing that gives an opinion about a book and tells about it

personal pronoun – a word that takes the place of one or more nouns; the personal pronouns are *I, me, you, he, him, she, her, it, we, us, they,* and *them*

Advance Preparation

To prepare for the GUM portion of this lesson, review Pronouns (Personal Pronouns) in the *Grammar Reference Guide* (linked in the online lesson) to familiarize yourself with the topic. In this lesson, students begin to accumulate documents they will need as they work on their book review. You might want to provide students with a folder or large envelope in which to keep these documents.

Big Ideas

- Book reviews allow writers to share information about books they have read with audiences who want to know more about the books. Book reviews often include a summary or analysis of the content, an opinion about the book, and a recommendation to readers.
- Using pronouns to take the place of some nouns helps writers avoid repetition.

[Online] ③⓪ minutes

Students will work online to review singular personal pronouns, to learn about plural personal pronouns, and to read and explore a model book review. Help students locate the online activities.

Skills Update ....

Singular Personal Pronouns

Students will review how to use singular personal pronouns by completing Skills Update exercises. Sit with students as they do this activity and note if they answer correctly.

> ➲ **Learning Coach Check-In**   How did students do on the Skills Update?

> ► **All answers correct:** Great! Skip the review screen and go on to the next activity.
> ► **Any answers incorrect:** Take a few minutes to review singular personal pronouns now. Use the link on the screen after the Skills Update to take another look at the online activity or review Pronouns (Personal Pronouns) in the *Grammar Reference Guide* together.

TIP This activity will require extra time if students need to review singular personal pronouns. Take the extra 5–10 minutes to review now because new skills build on what students have already learned.

Objectives
• Identify and use singular personal pronouns.

GUM (Grammar, Usage, and Mechanics) ....

Plural Personal Pronouns

Students will learn to identify the plural personal pronouns and practice using them to take the place of nouns in sentences.

Objectives
• Identify and use plural personal pronouns.

Composition ....

Explore a Model Book Review

By reading and exploring Alexander's model book review, students will learn what a book review is, what belongs in one, and how one is organized.

TIP Seeing a final version of a book review helps students see the goal of this unit. It will be easier for them to understand each step in the process if they know how the steps result in a finished product. If students are not comfortable reading the model book review for this activity online, they may read the model on pages WS 135 and 136 in *K¹² Language Arts Activity Book*.

Objectives
• Describe the elements of a book review.

⟦ Offline ⟧ 🕒 minutes

Work **together** with students to complete the offline Composition activity.

Composition ....

Respond to the Model Book Review

Students will review what they learned about the model book review. Gather pages WS 135–138 in *K¹² Language Arts Activity Book*.

1. Have students reread Alexander's model book review.

2. Have them complete the Activity Book pages about Alexander's review. Provide support as necessary, encouraging students to write in complete sentences. Students should refer to Alexander's review as needed.

TIP Keep Alexander's review in a safe place so students can refer to it later.

> **Objectives**
> - Describe the elements of a book review.
> - Respond to a book review.

Composition

Plural Personal Pronouns and
Model Book Review

Model Book Review

Use Alexander's book review as you work through the lessons
in this unit.

The Long Walk Home ← title

Ribsy is a book by Beverly Cleary.
It is about a dog named Ribsy. Ribsy
belongs to a boy named Henry
Huggins. The story takes place
around the city where Henry and
Ribsy live. It tells how Ribsy gets lost
and finds his way home to Henry. — basic information

Ribsy first gets lost at a shopping
center. A family named the Dingleys
takes him to their house. They give
him a bath. Yet Ribsy wants to be
with Henry again. Henry misses
Ribsy, too. Soon Ribsy runs away from
the Dingleys. An older woman takes
care of him for a while. Then he stays
in a school. Later Ribsy runs onto the
field at a football game. His picture
gets in the newspaper where Henry
sees it. He finds out that Ribsy is with — summary

WS 135   LANGUAGE ARTS PURPLE

WS 136   LANGUAGE ARTS PURPLE

a boy named Joe Saylor. Yet before
Henry can get Ribsy, he runs away
again! This time Ribsy meets a boy
named Larry. Larry hides Ribsy on the
fire escape of his apartment building.
Luckily, Henry and his parents see
Ribsy there. They get him down and
take him home. — summary

Ribsy is a great book. It is funny
and exciting. I did not know what — opinion
was going to happen. Anyone who — recommendation
likes action and dogs will like Ribsy.

Composition

Plural Personal Pronouns and
Model Book Review

Respond to the Model Book Review

Answer the questions about Alexander's book review.

1. Where does Ribsy take place?
   in the city where Henry and Ribsy live

2. According to Paragraph 1 of the model book review, what is Ribsy about?
   Ribsy gets lost and has to find his way home.

3. Where is the first place that Ribsy goes after he gets lost?
   the Dingleys' house

4. Who hides Ribsy on the fire escape just before Henry and his family come to take Ribsy home?
   a boy named Larry

5. Why does Alexander say he likes this book?
   because it's funny and exciting and because he didn't know what was going to happen

WS 137   LANGUAGE ARTS PURPLE

WS 138   LANGUAGE ARTS PURPLE

6. Who does Alexander think should read Ribsy?
   anyone who likes action and dogs

7. Did reading Alexander's book review make you want to read Ribsy? Tell why or why not.
   Answers will vary.

Subject Pronouns and Choose Your Book to Review

Lesson Overview

🖥 [Online]　　30 minutes

Skills Update	Plural Personal Pronouns
GUM (Grammar, Usage, and Mechanics)	Subject Pronouns
Composition	Alexander Chooses a Book to Review

📄 [Offline]　　15 minutes

Composition	Choose a Book to Review

Advance Preparation

To prepare for the GUM portion of this lesson, review Subject and Object Pronouns (Subject Pronouns) in the *Grammar Reference Guide* (linked in the online lesson) to familiarize yourself with the topic.

Big Ideas

- Book reviews allow writers to share information about books they have read with audiences who want to know more about the books. Book reviews often include a summary or analysis of the content, an opinion about the book, and a recommendation to readers.
- Using pronouns to take the place of some nouns helps writers avoid repetition.

 **Online** **30** minutes

Students will work online to review plural personal pronouns, to learn about subject pronouns, and to find out how to choose a book to review. Help students locate the online activities.

Skills Update

Plural Personal Pronouns

Students will review how to use plural personal pronouns by completing Skills Update exercises. Sit with students as they do this activity and note if they answer correctly.

> ↻ **Learning Coach Check-In**   How did students do on the Skills Update?

> ▸ **All answers correct:** Great! Skip the review screen and go on to the next activity.
> ▸ **Any answers incorrect:** Take a few minutes to review plural personal pronouns now. Use the link on the screen after the Skills Update to take another look at the online activity or review Pronouns (Personal Pronouns) in the *Grammar Reference Guide* together.

TIP This activity will require extra time if students need to review plural personal pronouns. Take the extra 5–10 minutes to review now because new skills build on what students have already learned.

> **Objectives**
> • Identify and use plural personal pronouns.

GUM (Grammar, Usage, and Mechanics)

Subject Pronouns

Students will learn how to use pronouns as the subjects of sentences.

> **Objectives**
> • Identify and use subject pronouns.

Composition

Alexander Chooses a Book to Review

By watching Alexander list the pros and cons of several books he's read and ultimately how he chooses one to review, students will learn how to do the same to choose the book they want to review.

> **Objectives**
> • Brainstorm books to review.
> • Determine pros and cons of each book.
> • Choose a book to review.

⟦ Offline ⟧ ⏱ 15 minutes

Work **together** with students to complete the offline Composition activity.

Composition

Choose a Book to Review

Students will choose a book to review. Turn to pages WS 139 and 140 in *K¹² Language Arts Activity Book*.

1. Have students complete the table on the first page to list books they might like to review. Provide support as necessary, encouraging students to think about the pros and cons of each book and to write down what they liked and didn't like about each one.

2. Once students have filled out the table, have them answer the questions on the second page. Students should begin to rule out books based on their preferences and their answers to the questions. Remind them that there is no wrong choice when it comes to which book to review. Any book that they've read can be the subject of a review.

3. Have students circle their choice book to review.

TIP Keep students' completed form in a safe place so they can refer to it later.

> **Objectives**
> - Brainstorm books to review.
> - Determine pros and cons of each book.
> - Choose a book to review.

Composition

Subject Pronouns and Choose Your Book to Review

Choose a Book to Review

It's time to choose a book to review. Begin by filling in the table with books you've recently read.

Book Title	What You Liked	What You Disliked

LANGUAGE ARTS PURPLE   WS 139

Now ask yourself these questions to narrow your choices and decide which book to review.   **Answers will vary.**

1. Which book told a story that kept you interested?

2. Did that book teach you something?

3. Would you like to read other books by the same author?

4. Which book did you have the most fun reading?

5. Which book would you like to tell others about?

Think about your answers and circle your choice of a book to review.

WS 140   LANGUAGE ARTS PURPLE

Pronouns After Action Verbs and Plan Your Book Review

Lesson Overview

🖥 〖 Online 〗   ⏱ 25 minutes

Skills Update	Subject Pronouns
GUM (Grammar, Usage, and Mechanics)	Pronouns After Action Verbs
Composition	Alexander Plans His Book Review

▤ 〖 Offline 〗   ⏱ 20 minutes

Composition	Plan Your Book Review

〖 Materials 〗

Supplied

- *K¹² Language Arts Activity Book*, p. WS 141
- *Grammar Reference Guide* Online Book (optional)

Also Needed

- students' chosen book

Keywords

action verb – a word that shows action

book review – a piece of writing that gives an opinion about a book and tells about it

Advance Preparation

To prepare for the GUM portion of this lesson, review Subject and Object Pronouns (Object Pronouns) in the *Grammar Reference Guide* (linked in the online lesson) to familiarize yourself with the topic.

Big Ideas

- ▸ Book reviews allow writers to share information about books they have read with audiences who want to know more about the books. Book reviews often include a summary or analysis of the content, an opinion about the book, and a recommendation to readers.
- ▸ Using pronouns to take the place of some nouns helps writers avoid repetition.

[Online] 25 minutes

Students will work online to review subject pronouns, to learn about pronouns after action verbs, and to see how Alexander planned his book review. Help students locate the online activities.

Skills Update ....

Subject Pronouns

Students will review how to use subject pronouns by completing Skills Update exercises. Sit with students as they do this activity and note if they answer correctly.

> ⟳ **Learning Coach Check-In** How did students do on the Skills Update?

> ▸ **All answers correct:** Great! Skip the review screen and go on to the next activity.

> ▸ **Any answers incorrect:** Take a few minutes to review subject pronouns now. Use the link on the screen after the Skills Update to take another look at the online activity or review Subject and Object Pronouns (Subject Pronouns) in the *Grammar Reference Guide* together.

TIP This activity will require extra time if students need to review subject pronouns. Take the extra 5–10 minutes to review now because new skills build on what students have already learned.

> **Objectives**
> • Identify and use subject pronouns.

GUM (Grammar, Usage, and Mechanics) ....

Pronouns After Action Verbs

Students will learn which pronouns can be used after action verbs and practice using these pronouns.

> **Objectives**
> • Identify and use pronouns after action verbs.

Composition ....

Alexander Plans His Book Review

By watching Alexander use a story map to begin planning his book review, students will learn how to use a story map to begin planning their own book review.

> **Objectives**
> • Use a story map to plan.

[Offline] 20 minutes

Work **together** with students to complete the offline Composition activity.

Composition

Plan Your Book Review

Students will use a story map, or graphic organizer, to plan the first and third paragraphs of their book review. Turn to page WS 141 in *K¹² Language Arts Activity Book*.

Have students complete only the first and third boxes on the Activity Book page to plan the first and third paragraphs of their book review. (Students will complete the second box of the story map during another lesson.) Provide support as necessary, encouraging students to include all the information for those two boxes on the story map. Remind students that it is not necessary to write in complete sentences on the story map.

TIP Keep students' story map in a safe place so they can add to it later.

Objectives
• Use a story map to plan.

Possessive Pronouns and Review Summaries

Lesson Overview

🖥 〖Online〗   **30** minutes

Skills Update	Pronouns After Action Verbs
GUM (Grammar, Usage, and Mechanics)	Possessive Pronouns
Composition	Review Summaries

📄 〖Offline〗   **15** minutes

Composition	What Belongs in a Summary?

〖Materials〗

Supplied
- *K¹² Language Arts Activity Book*, pp. WS 143–144
- *Grammar Reference Guide* Online Book (optional)

Also Needed
- students' chosen book

Keywords

possessive pronoun – the form of a pronoun that shows ownership

summary – a short retelling that includes only the most important ideas or events of a text

Advance Preparation

To prepare for the GUM portion of this lesson, review Pronouns (Possessive Pronouns) in the *Grammar Reference Guide* (linked in the online lesson) to familiarize yourself with the topic.

Big Ideas

► Book reviews allow writers to share information about books they have read with audiences who want to know more about the books. Book reviews often include a summary or analysis of the content, an opinion about the book, and a recommendation to readers.

► Explicit instruction in how to summarize a text is an important element in learning to write well.

► Using pronouns to take the place of some nouns helps writers avoid repetition.

[Online] 30 minutes

Students will work online to review pronouns after action verbs, to learn about possessive pronouns, and to review the characteristics of an effective summary. Help students locate the online activities.

Skills Update

Pronouns After Action Verbs

Students will review how to use pronouns after action verbs by completing Skills Update exercises. Sit with students as they do this activity and note if they answer correctly.

⟳ **Learning Coach Check-In**   How did students do on the Skills Update?

> ▸ **All answers correct:** Great! Skip the review screen and go on to the next activity.
> ▸ **Any answers incorrect:** Take a few minutes to review pronouns after action verbs now. Use the link on the screen after the Skills Update to take another look at the online activity or review Subject and Object Pronouns (Object Pronouns) in the *Grammar Reference Guide* together.

TIP This activity will require extra time if students need to review pronouns after action verbs. Take the extra 5–10 minutes to review now because new skills build on what students have already learned.

> **Objectives**
> • Identify and use pronouns after action verbs.

GUM (Grammar, Usage, and Mechanics)

Possessive Pronouns

Students will learn about some of the pronouns that can show ownership and practice using those pronouns. Note that the possessive pronouns *my, your, his, her, its, our,* and *their* are sometimes called *possessive adjectives*. However, this program refers to them as *possessive pronouns*.

> **Objectives**
> • Identify and use possessive pronouns in sentences.

Composition

Review Summaries

By reviewing what a summary is and learning what kind of information belongs in a summary, students will be prepared to plan a summary.

> **Objectives**
> • Define *summary*.
> • Determine what kind of information belongs in a summary.

[Offline] 🕐 15 minutes

Work **together** with students to complete the offline Composition activity.

Composition

What Belongs in a Summary?

Students will practice writing a summary of a short passage. This practice will help prepare students to write a summary of the book they chose for their book review. Turn to pages WS 143 and 144 in *K¹² Language Arts Activity Book*.

1. Have students complete the Activity Book pages. The sentences they underline should convey the most important information or describe the most important events in the passage. Be sure students understand that the sentences they choose should be the ones that will best help them write a summary of the passage.

2. Remind students that their summary should be in their own words and follow the same sequence as the passage. Provide support as necessary, reminding students that summaries are meant to be short. If the summary is as long as or longer than the original passage, encourage students to revise it.

> **Objectives**
> - Define *summary*.
> - Determine what kind of information belongs in a summary.

Possessive Pronouns and Write Your Summary

Lesson Overview

Online   20 minutes

Skills Update	Possessive Pronouns
GUM (Grammar, Usage, and Mechanics)	Possessive Pronouns
Composition	Alexander Writes a Summary

Offline   25 minutes

Composition	Write Your Summary

Materials

Supplied
- *K¹² Language Arts Activity Book*, p. WS 141
- *Grammar Reference Guide* Online Book (optional)

Also Needed
- students' chosen book

Keywords

possessive pronoun – the form of a pronoun that shows ownership

summary – a short retelling that includes only the most important ideas or events of a text

Advance Preparation

To prepare for the GUM portion of this lesson, review Pronouns (Possessive Pronouns) in the *Grammar Reference Guide* (linked in the online lesson) to familiarize yourself with the topic. Gather page WS 141 (Plan Your Book Review, students' partially completed story map) in *K¹² Language Arts Activity Book*.

Big Ideas

► Book reviews allow writers to share information about books they have read with audiences who want to know more about the books. Book reviews often include a summary or analysis of the content, an opinion about the book, and a recommendation to readers.

► Explicit instruction in how to summarize a text is an important element in learning to write well.

► Using pronouns to take the place of some nouns helps writers avoid repetition.

Online — 20 minutes

Students will work online to review some possessive pronouns, to learn about more possessive pronouns, and to review the characteristics of an effective summary. Help students locate the online activities.

Skills Update

Possessive Pronouns

Students will review how to use some possessive pronouns by completing Skills Update exercises. Sit with students as they do this activity and note if they answer correctly.

➲ **Learning Coach Check-In** How did students do on the Skills Update?

▸ **All answers correct:** Great! Skip the review screen and go on to the next activity.

▸ **Any answers incorrect:** Take a few minutes to review possessive pronouns now. Use the link on the screen after the Skills Update to take another look at the online activity or review Pronouns (Possessive Pronouns) in the *Grammar Reference Guide* together.

TIP This activity will require extra time if students need to review possessive pronouns. Take the extra 5–10 minutes to review now because new skills build on what students have already learned.

> **Objectives**
> - Identify and use possessive pronouns in sentences.

GUM (Grammar, Usage, and Mechanics)

Possessive Pronouns

Students will learn about some of the pronouns that can show ownership and practice using those pronouns.

> **Objectives**
> - Identify and use possessive pronouns in sentences.

Composition

Alexander Writes a Summary

By watching Alexander summarize events from *Ribsy* on his story map, students will learn how to summarize events from their book on their story map.

> **Objectives**
> - Choose information for a summary.
> - Write a summary.

⟦ Offline ⟧ 25 minutes

Work **together** with students to complete the offline Composition activity.

Composition ....

Write Your Summary

Students will plan the second paragraph, or summary, of their book review. Have students gather their partially completed story map.

1. Have students complete the story map by filling in the second box to plan the second paragraph of their book review.

2. Remind students that the second paragraph will be where they summarize their book, so they should only include the most important events and ideas from the book in this section. Encourage students to write in complete sentences as they summarize the book they have chosen.

TIP Keep students' completed story map in a safe place so they can refer to it later.

Composition ....

Pronouns After Action Verbs and
Plan Your Book Review

Plan Your Book Review   **Answers will vary.**

Complete the story map to plan your book review.

Title and Author _____

┌─────────────────────────────────────┐
│   Main Characters, Setting, and Description │
│   │
│   │
└─────────────────────────────────────┘
                    ↓
┌─────────────────────────────────────┐
│   Book Summary   │
│   │
│   │
└─────────────────────────────────────┘
                    ↓
┌─────────────────────────────────────┐
│   My Opinion, Reasons, and Recommendation │
│   │
│   │
└─────────────────────────────────────┘

LANGUAGE ARTS PURPLE   **WS 141**

> **Objectives**
> - Choose information for a summary.
> - Write a summary.

Draft Your Book Review

Lesson Overview

💻 〔Online〕 ⏱20 minutes

Skills Update	Possessive Pronouns
Composition	Alexander Drafts His Book Review

📄 〔Offline〕 ⏱25 minutes

Composition	Write Your Draft
Peer Interaction	➕ OPTIONAL: Tell Me About My Book Review

Materials

Supplied
- *K¹² Language Arts Activity Book*, pp. WS 135–136, 141, 145–149
- Book Review: Feedback Sheet (printout)
- drafting page (optional printout)

Also Needed
- students' chosen book

Keywords
book review – a piece of writing that gives an opinion about a book and tells about it

summary – a short retelling that includes only the most important ideas or events of a text

Advance Preparation

Gather pages WS 135 and 136 (Model Book Review) and 141 (Plan Your Book Review, students' completed story map) in *K¹² Language Arts Activity Book*. Print the Book Review: Feedback Sheet from the online lesson.

Big Ideas

- Book reviews allow writers to share information about books they have read with audiences who want to know more about the books. Book reviews often include a summary or analysis of the content, an opinion about the book, and a recommendation for readers.
- Explicit instruction in how to summarize a text is an important element in learning to write well.

Online · 20 minutes

Students will work online to review possessive pronouns and to learn how to draft a book review. Help students locate the online activities. Note that this lesson does not contain any new Grammar, Usage, and Mechanics activities so that students can concentrate on writing their draft.

Skills Update

Possessive Pronouns

Students will review how to use some possessive pronouns by completing Skills Update exercises. Sit with students as they do this activity and note if they answer correctly.

➲ **Learning Coach Check-In**   How did students do on the Skills Update?

▸ **All answers correct:** Great! Skip the review screen and go on to the next activity.

▸ **Any answers incorrect:** Take a few minutes to review possessive pronouns now. Use the link on the screen after the Skills Update to take another look at the online activity or review Pronouns (Possessive Pronouns) in the *Grammar Reference Guide* together.

TIP This activity will require extra time if students need to review possessive pronouns. Take the extra 5–10 minutes to review now because new skills build on what students have already learned.

Objectives
- Identify and use possessive pronouns in sentences.

Composition

Alexander Drafts His Book Review

By watching how Alexander drafts his book review, students will learn how to draft their own book review.

Objectives
- Write a book review.
- Use a summary in the book review.
- Use temporal words and phrases to signal event order.

[Offline] 25 minutes

Work **together** with students to complete the offline Composition and Peer Interaction activities.

Composition ·

Write Your Draft

Students chose a book to review and planned each section of it with a story map. They will now draft their book review. Have students gather the model book review and their completed story map. Turn to pages WS 145–148 in *K¹² Language Arts Activity Book*.

1. Help students start drafting by reminding them to refer to Alexander's model book review and their story map as necessary. The model and their story map will help students remember what elements to include in their writing and in what order.

2. Remind students that a draft does not have to be perfect. It's just a first try at putting ideas on paper.

3. Have students use the lined Activity Book pages to begin drafting their book review. Students should write only in the white rows, because the purple rows will be used for making revisions to the draft later. If needed, additional drafting pages can be printed from the online lesson.

   ⊃ **Learning Coach Check-In**   When students have finished their draft, read and review it using the Book Review: Feedback Sheet, but do not go over the feedback sheet with students now. The notes you take on this sheet will guide your feedback to students as they revise their draft in a later lesson. Keep the feedback sheet in a safe place until students are ready to revise their draft.

TIP Keep students' drafting pages in a safe place so students can continue working on them later. If students want to use a reference material such as the *Grammar Reference Guide* or a dictionary while drafting, suggest that they wait until they are revising or proofreading. Looking up information while drafting can interfere with students' flow of ideas.

> **Objectives**
> - Write a book review.
> - Use a summary in the book review.
> - Use temporal words and phrases to signal event order.

Composition

Plural Personal Pronouns and Model Book Review

Model Book Review

Use Alexander's book review as you work through the lessons in this unit.

The Long Walk Home ←——— title

Ribsy is a book by Beverly Cleary. It is about a dog named Ribsy. Ribsy belongs to a boy named Henry Huggins. The story takes place around the city where Henry and Ribsy live. It tells how Ribsy gets lost and finds his way home to Henry.]——— basic information

Ribsy first gets lost at a shopping center. A family named the Dingleys takes him to their house. They give him a bath. Yet Ribsy wants to be with Henry again. Henry misses Ribsy, too. Soon Ribsy runs away from the Dingleys. An older woman takes care of him for a while. Then he stays in a school. Later Ribsy runs onto the field at a football game. His picture gets in the newspaper where Henry sees it. He finds out that Ribsy is with]——— summary

---

a boy named Joe Saylor. Yet before Henry can get Ribsy, he runs away again! This time Ribsy meets a boy named Larry. Larry hides Ribsy on the fire escape of his apartment building. Luckily, Henry and his parents see Ribsy there. They get him down and take him home.]——— summary

Ribsy is a great book. It is funny ←——— opinion and exciting. I did not know what was going to happen. Anyone who ←——— recommendation likes action and dogs will like Ribsy.

Composition

Pronouns After Action Verbs and Plan Your Book Review

Plan Your Book Review   **Answers will vary.**

Complete the story map to plan your book review.

Title and Author
_____

┌─────────────────────────────────────┐
│ Main Characters, Setting, and Description │
│   │
│   │
└─────────────────────────────────────┘
                  ↓
┌─────────────────────────────────────┐
│   Book Summary   │
│   │
│   │
└─────────────────────────────────────┘
                  ↓
┌─────────────────────────────────────┐
│ My Opinion, Reasons, and Recommendation │
│   │
│   │
└─────────────────────────────────────┘

Composition

Draft Your Book Review

Write Your Draft

Read the assignment. Use your story map to help you write the first draft of your book review. Write only on the white rows. You will use the purple rows for revisions later.

> Write a book review about a book you have read in the past year.
> * Begin with a title that gives a hint about the book.
> * Write the name of the book, the author, the main characters, the setting, and the basic plot in the first paragraph.
> * Write a summary of the book in the second paragraph. Use words and phrases that show the order in which events happen.
> * Include your opinion and recommendation to readers in the third paragraph.

Start here ▶

Peer Interaction

✚ OPTIONAL: Tell Me About My Book Review

This activity is OPTIONAL. It is intended for students who have extra time and would benefit from extra practice. Feel free to skip this activity.

Students can benefit from exchanging book reviews with another student. Each writer should receive feedback. To complete this optional activity, turn to page WS 149 in *K¹² Language Arts Activity Book*. (Additional copies of the Peer Interaction Form can be printed from the online lesson.)

1. Have students exchange drafts with other students.

2. Have students use the Activity Book page to provide others with feedback about their writing.

TIP In the upcoming revising lesson, students may use the feedback provided from other students to improve their book review.

Objectives
- Use guidance from adults and peers to revise writing.
- Collaborate with peers on writing projects.

Peer Interaction
Draft Your Book Review
Tell Me About My Book Review

Have another person read your book review and answer the questions.
Answers will vary.

1. What is the name of the book that the student wrote about, and who is the author?

2. Does the student tell the main characters, the setting, and a brief plot description in the first paragraph? If not, what is missing?

3. Does the second paragraph include a summary of the book? In what order are the events in the summary?

4. Write one word or phrase that the student uses to show order of events.

5. Does the student give an opinion of the book in the third paragraph? What is the student's opinion?

6. Would you like to read this book? Why or why not?

LANGUAGE ARTS PURPLE   **WS 149**

Pronouns with –*self*

Lesson Overview

Online	30 minutes
GUM (Grammar, Usage, and Mechanics)	Pronouns That End in –*self* or –*selves*

Offline	15 minutes
GUM (Grammar, Usage, and Mechanics)	Pronouns That End in –*self* or –*selves*

[Materials]

Supplied
- *K¹² Language Arts Activity Book*, pp. WS 151–152
- *Grammar Reference Guide* Online Book (optional)
- Book Review: Feedback Sheet (printout)

Also Needed
- students' chosen book

Advance Preparation

To prepare for the GUM portion of this lesson, review Pronouns (Reflexive Pronouns; Intensive Pronouns) in the *Grammar Reference Guide* (linked in the online lesson) to familiarize yourself with the topic. If you have not already completed the Book Review: Feedback Sheet, do so during this lesson while students work independently. You will need to share this form with students in the next lesson.

Big Ideas

Using pronouns to take the place of some nouns helps writers avoid repetition.

[Online] 30 minutes

Students will work online **independently** to learn about pronouns that end in –*self* or –*selves*. Help students locate the online activity.

GUM (Grammar, Usage, and Mechanics)

Pronouns That End in –*self* or –*selves*
Students will learn about pronouns that end in –*self* and –*selves* and practice using those pronouns. Pronouns that end in –*self* or –*selves* are called either *reflexive pronouns* or *intensive pronouns*, depending on their use in a sentence. However, this program does not use these terms with students.

> ⭐ **Objectives**
> - Identify and use pronouns that end in –*self* or –*selves*.

[Offline] 15 minutes

Work **together** with students to complete the offline GUM activity.

GUM (Grammar, Usage, and Mechanics) ●

Pronouns That End in *–self* **or** *–selves*

Students will demonstrate their understanding of pronouns that end in *–self* or *–selves* by answering several questions about them. Turn to pages WS 151 and 152 in *K¹² Language Arts Activity Book.*

1. Have students complete the Activity Book pages. Review their responses with them.

2. As necessary, remind students that the word that a pronoun ending in *–self* or *–selves* refers to or replaces dictates which pronoun to use. For instance, the correct answer to the first question is *himself* because the pronoun replaces *Bob*.

> ### Objectives
> • Identify and use pronouns that end in *–self* or *–selves*.

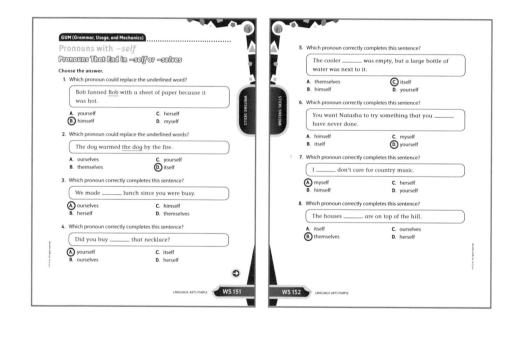

Revise Your Book Review

Lesson Overview

🖥 [Online]   20 minutes

Skills Update	Pronouns That End in *-self* or *-selves*
Composition	Alexander Revises with a Checklist

📄 [Offline]   25 minutes

Composition	Revise with a Checklist

[Materials]

Supplied

- *K¹² Language Arts Activity Book*, pp. WS 145–149, 153
- *Grammar Reference Guide* Online Book (optional)
- Book Review: Feedback Sheet (printout)
- drafting page (optional printout)

Advance Preparation

Gather pages WS 145–148 (Write Your Draft, students' draft of their book review) and 149 (Tell Me About My Book Review, if completed) in *K¹² Language Arts Activity Book* and the completed Book Review: Feedback Sheet. You will review the feedback with students.

Big Ideas

- ▸ Book reviews allow writers to share information about books they have read with audiences who want to know more about the books. Book reviews often include a summary or analysis of the content, an opinion about the book, and a recommendation to readers.
- ▸ Explicit instruction in how to summarize a text is an important element in learning to write well.
- ▸ Using pronouns to take the place of some nouns helps writers avoid repetition.

[Online] ⏱ 20 minutes

Students will work online to review pronouns that end in *–self* or *–selves* and to learn how to revise a book review. Help students locate the online activities. Note that this lesson does not contain any new Grammar, Usage, and Mechanics activities so that students can concentrate on revising their draft.

Skills Update

Pronouns That End in *–self* or *–selves*

Students will review how to use pronouns that end in *–self* or *–selves* by completing Skills Update exercises. Sit with students as they do this activity and note if they answer correctly.

> ⮑ **Learning Coach Check-In** How did students do on the Skills Update?
>
> ▸ **All answers correct:** Great! Skip the review screen and go on to the next activity.
>
> ▸ **Any answers incorrect:** Take a few minutes to review pronouns that end in *–self* or *–selves* now. Use the link on the screen after the Skills Update to take another look at the online activity or review Pronouns (Reflexive Pronouns; Intensive Pronouns) in the *Grammar Reference Guide* together.

TIP This activity will require extra time if students need to review pronouns that end in *–self* or *–selves*. Take the extra 5–10 minutes to review now because new skills build on what students have already learned.

> **Objectives**
> - Identify and use pronouns that end in *–self* or *–selves*.

Composition

Alexander Revises with a Checklist

By watching how Alexander revises his book review draft, students will learn how to revise their own draft.

> **Objectives**
> - Revise a book review.
> - Revise for complete information.
> - Revise for order of ideas.

〖 Offline 〗 ㉕ minutes

Work **together** with students to complete the offline Composition activity.

Composition

Revise with a Checklist

Students will revise their book review. Have them gather their book review draft and any completed Peer Interaction forms. Turn to page WS 153 in K^{12} *Language Arts Activity Book* and gather the Book Review: Feedback Sheet that you filled out.

> ### Objectives
> - Revise a book review.
> - Revise for complete information.
> - Revise for order of ideas.

1. Use the Book Review: Feedback Sheet to guide your discussion with students.

   ▸ Tell students the strengths of their book review. Provide positive comments about the ideas, language, details, or other elements of the review that you enjoyed.

   ▸ Walk through the Purpose and Content and Structure and Organization sections of the feedback sheet with students. Do not address your comments in the Grammar and Mechanics section at this time. You can work with students on grammar and mechanics when they proofread. Providing these corrections now may distract students from the real work of revising for content and structure.

   ▸ As you go through the feedback sheet with students, encourage them to actively revise their draft based on your feedback. Reassure students that it's okay to remove ideas or sentences from their review. Doing so may help their review be more accurate and succinct, even if something they cut was included in their story map.

   ▸ As students revise their draft, have them use the purple rows to mark their revisions.

2. Once you've reviewed your comments on the first two sections of the feedback sheet with students, have them review their draft once more, using the revision checklist on the Activity Book page. Students should check off each box on the checklist as they complete each item.

3. If students received feedback from peers, discuss with them how they might use it to improve their book review. Help students decide what peer feedback would be useful to include in their revisions.

4. If students' revised book review has many changes that make the review difficult to read and understand, encourage them to make a clean copy before they proofread in the next lesson. Additional drafting pages can be printed from the online lesson.

 TIP Keep students' revised book review in a safe place so they can refer to it later.

Composition

Draft Your Book Review

Write Your Draft

Read the assignment. Use your story map to help you write the first draft of your book review. Write only on the white rows. You will use the purple rows for revisions later.

Write a book review about a book you have read in the past year.

- Begin with a title that gives a hint about the book.
- Write the name of the book, the author, the main characters, the setting, and the basic plot in the first paragraph.
- Write a summary of the book in the second paragraph. Use words and phrases that show the order in which events happen.
- Include your opinion and recommendation to readers in the third paragraph.

Start here ▶

LANGUAGE ARTS PURPLE **WS 145**

Peer Interaction

Draft Your Book Review

Tell Me About My Book Review

Have another person read your book review and answer the questions. **Answers will vary.**

1. What is the name of the book that the student wrote about, and who is the author?

2. Does the student tell the main characters, the setting, and a brief plot description in the first paragraph? If not, what is missing?

3. Does the second paragraph include a summary of the book? In what order are the events in the summary?

4. Write one word or phrase that the student uses to show order of events.

5. Does the student give an opinion of the book in the third paragraph? What is the student's opinion?

6. Would you like to read this book? Why or why not?

LANGUAGE ARTS PURPLE **WS 149**

Composition

Revise Your Book Review

Revise with a Checklist

Follow this checklist as you revise your book review. Check off each box after you complete each item.

- ☐ Name the book's title and author in the first paragraph of the review.
- ☐ Include the names of major characters, describe the setting, and briefly explain what the book is about in the first paragraph.
- ☐ Summarize the book's major events in the second paragraph.
- ☐ Describe events from the book in the correct order in the second paragraph.
- ☐ Include an opinion and a recommendation about the book in the third paragraph.
- ☐ Order your opinion, reasons, and recommendation correctly in the third paragraph.
- ☐ Include all important ideas and details in the review.

Students should check off each box after they complete each item.

LANGUAGE ARTS PURPLE **WS 153**

Unit Review and Proofread Your Book Review

Lesson Overview

🖥 [Online] ⏱ 20 minutes

Unit Review	Pronouns
More Practice	Pronouns
Composition	Alexander Proofreads with a Checklist

📄 [Offline] ⏱ 25 minutes

Composition	Proofread with a Checklist

Advance Preparation

Gather pages WS 145–148 (Write Your Draft, students' draft of their book review) in *K¹² Language Arts Activity Book* and the completed Book Review: Feedback Sheet. If students' revised book review has many changes that make it difficult to read and understand, you may want to encourage them to make a clean copy before they proofread in this lesson. Additional drafting pages can be printed from the online lesson.

Big Ideas

Book reviews allow writers to share information about books they have read with audiences who want to know more about the books. Book reviews often include a summary or analysis of the content, an opinion about the book, and a recommendation to readers.

[Materials]

Supplied

- *K¹² Language Arts Activity Book*, pp. WS 145–148, 154
- *Grammar Reference Guide* Online Book (optional)
- Book Review: Feedback Sheet (printout)
- drafting page (optional printout)

Also Needed

- students' chosen book

Keywords

action verb – a word that shows action

book review – a piece of writing that gives an opinion about a book and tells about it

personal pronoun – a word that takes the place of one or more nouns; the personal pronouns are *I, me, you, he, him, she, her, it, we, us, they,* and *them*

possessive pronoun – the form of a pronoun that shows ownership

subject pronoun – a pronoun used as a subject or predicate nominative

summary – a short retelling that includes only the most important ideas or events of a text

[Online] ⓩ minutes

Students will work online to review the grammar, usage, and mechanics skills learned in the unit and to learn how to proofread a book review. Help students locate the online activities.

Unit Review ....

Pronouns

To review for the Unit Checkpoint, students will review what they have learned about pronouns, including how to use singular and plural personal pronouns, subject pronouns, pronouns after action verbs, possessive pronouns, and pronouns that end in –*self* or –*selves*.

TIP A full list of objectives covered in the Unit Review can be found in the online lesson.

> **Objectives**
> • Complete a review of grammar, usage, and mechanics skills.

More Practice ....

Pronouns

Go over students' results on the Unit Review and, if necessary, have them complete the appropriate review activities listed in the table online. Help students locate the activities. Provide support as needed.

TIP The time students need to complete this activity will vary. Set aside enough time for students to complete all review activities, if they need to do so.

> **Objectives**
> • Evaluate Unit Review results and choose activities for more practice.

Composition ....

Alexander Proofreads with a Checklist

By watching how Alexander proofreads his book review draft, students will learn how to proofread their own book review draft.

> **Objectives**
> • Proofread the book review.

[Offline] (25) minutes

Work **together** with students to complete the offline Composition activity.

Composition ....

Proofread with a Checklist

Students will proofread their book review. Have them gather their book review draft.
Turn to page WS 154 in *K¹² Language Arts Activity Book* and gather the Book Review:
Feedback Sheet that you filled out.

> ### Objectives
> - Proofread the book review.

1. If students did not do so in advance, have them make a clean copy of their draft, if necessary, before they proofread it. Additional drafting pages can be printed from the online lesson.

2. Review with students your comments in the Grammar and Mechanics section of the feedback sheet. As you go through the feedback sheet with students, encourage them to use the purple rows on their drafting pages to actively mark changes based on your feedback.

3. Once you've reviewed your comments in the Grammar and Mechanics section of the feedback sheet with students, have them review their draft once more using the proofreading checklist. Students should check the boxes on the checklist as they complete the items.

TIP Keep students' proofread book review in a safe place so they can refer to it later.

Composition

Draft Your Book Review

Write Your Draft

Read the assignment. Use your story map to help you write the first draft of your book review. Write only on the white rows. You will use the purple rows for revisions later.

> Write a book review about a book you have read in the past year.
> - Begin with a title that gives a hint about the book.
> - Write the name of the book, the author, the main characters, the setting, and the basic plot in the first paragraph.
> - Write a summary of the book in the second paragraph. Use words and phrases that show the order in which events happen.
> - Include your opinion and recommendation to readers in the third paragraph.

Start here ▶

LANGUAGE ARTS PURPLE **WS 145**

Composition

Unit Review and Proofread Your Book Review

Proofread with a Checklist

Follow this checklist as you proofread your book review. Check off each box after you complete each item.

- ☐ Capitalize the book's title.
- ☐ Underline the book's title.
- ☐ Capitalize the names of all characters.
- ☐ Use pronouns correctly.
- ☐ Begin every sentence with a capital letter.
- ☐ End every sentence with the correct punctuation mark.
- ☐ Fix sentence fragments.
- ☐ Correct spelling mistakes.

Students should check off each box after they complete each item.

WS 154 LANGUAGE ARTS PURPLE

Unit Checkpoint and Publish Your Book Review

Lesson Overview

[Online]	20 minutes
Unit Checkpoint	Pronouns

[Offline]	25 minutes
More Practice	Pronouns
Write Now	Publish Your Book Review
More Practice	Book Review

Advance Preparation

Gather pages WS 145–148 (Write Your Draft, students' draft of their book review) in *K¹² Language Arts Activity Book*, which students should have revised and proofread.

Big Ideas

Book reviews allow writers to share information about books they have read with audiences who want to know more about the books. Book reviews often include a summary or analysis of the content, an opinion about the book, and a recommendation to readers.

[Materials]

Supplied

- *K¹² Language Arts Activity Book*, pp. WS 145–148, 155–158
- *Grammar Reference Guide* Online Book (optional)
- Book Review: Rubric and Sample Responses (printout)
- Singular Personal Pronouns (optional printout)
- Plural Personal Pronouns (optional printout)
- Subject Pronouns (optional printout)
- Pronouns After Action Verbs (optional printout)
- Possessive Pronouns (optional printout)
- Pronouns That End in *–self* or *–selves* (optional printout)
- lined writing page (optional printout)

Also Needed

- students' chosen book

 **20 minutes**

Students will work online **independently** to complete the Unit Checkpoint. Help students locate the Unit Checkpoint and provide support as necessary.

Unit Checkpoint

Pronouns

Students will complete an online Unit Checkpoint about pronouns, including how to use singular and plural personal pronouns, subject pronouns, pronouns after action verbs, possessive pronouns, and pronouns that end in –*self* or –*selves*. If necessary, read the directions to students.

TIP A full list of objectives covered in the Unit Checkpoint can be found in the online lesson.

> **Objectives**
> • Complete a Unit Checkpoint on grammar, usage, and mechanics skills.

 **25 minutes**

Work **together** with students to complete the offline More Practice and Write Now activities.

More Practice

Pronouns

Go over students' results on the Unit Checkpoint and, if necessary, print out and have them complete the appropriate activity pages listed in the table online. Students can complete all necessary pages now or, if more time is needed, they can spread them out over the next few days. They can also review the appropriate sections of the *Grammar Reference Guide* with you. If students scored less than 80 percent on the Unit Checkpoint, you may want them to retake the Checkpoint after completing the additional activity pages.

TIP The time students need to complete this activity will vary. Set aside enough time for students to complete some or all activity pages and to retake the Unit Checkpoint, if they need to do so. Students may retake the Unit Checkpoint immediately, but having them complete the activity pages and then retake it might be more effective.

> **Objectives**
> • Evaluate Unit Checkpoint results and choose activities for more practice.

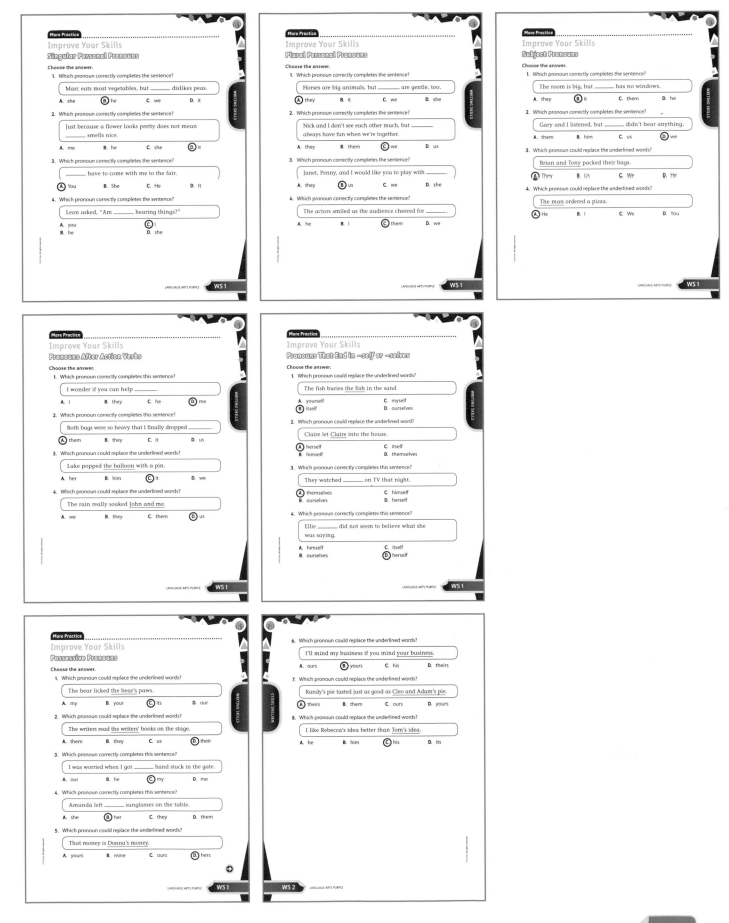

More Practice

Improve Your Skills
Singular Personal Pronouns

Choose the answer.

1. Which pronoun correctly completes the sentence?

   Marc eats most vegetables, but _____ dislikes peas.

   A. she   **B. he**   C. we   D. it

2. Which pronoun correctly completes the sentence?

   Just because a flower looks pretty does not mean _____ smells nice.

   A. me   B. he   C. she   **D. it**

3. Which pronoun correctly completes the sentence?

   _____ have to come with me to the fair.

   A. You   B. She   C. He   D. It

4. Which pronoun correctly completes the sentence?

   Leon asked, "Am _____ hearing things?"

   A. you   **C. I**
   B. he   D. she

LANGUAGE ARTS PURPLE   WS 1

More Practice

Improve Your Skills
Plural Personal Pronouns

Choose the answer.

1. Which pronoun correctly completes the sentence?

   Horses are big animals, but _____ are gentle, too.

   A. they   B. it   C. we   D. she

2. Which pronoun correctly completes the sentence?

   Nick and I don't see each other much, but _____ always have fun when we're together.

   A. they   B. them   **C. we**   D. us

3. Which pronoun correctly completes the sentence?

   Janet, Penny, and I would like you to play with _____.

   A. they   **B. us**   C. we   D. she

4. Which pronoun correctly completes the sentence?

   The actors smiled as the audience cheered for _____.

   A. he   B. I   **C. them**   D. we

LANGUAGE ARTS PURPLE   WS 1

More Practice

Improve Your Skills
Subject Pronouns

Choose the answer.

1. Which pronoun correctly completes the sentence?

   The room is big, but _____ has no windows.

   A. they   **B. it**   C. them   D. he

2. Which pronoun correctly completes the sentence?

   Gary and I listened, but _____ didn't hear anything.

   A. them   B. him   C. us   **D. we**

3. Which pronoun could replace the underlined words?

   Brian and Tony packed their bags.

   A. They   B. Us   C. We   D. He

4. Which pronoun could replace the underlined words?

   The man ordered a pizza.

   A. He   B. I   C. We   D. You

LANGUAGE ARTS PURPLE   WS 1

More Practice

Improve Your Skills
Pronouns After Action Verbs

Choose the answer.

1. Which pronoun correctly completes this sentence?

   I wonder if you can help _____.

   A. I   B. they   C. he   **D. me**

2. Which pronoun correctly completes this sentence?

   Both bags were so heavy that I finally dropped _____.

   A. them   B. they   C. it   D. us

3. Which pronoun could replace the underlined words?

   Luke popped the balloon with a pin.

   A. her   B. him   **C. it**   D. we

4. Which pronoun could replace the underlined words?

   The rain really soaked John and me.

   A. we   B. they   C. them   **D. us**

LANGUAGE ARTS PURPLE   WS 1

More Practice

Improve Your Skills
Pronouns That End in –self or –selves

Choose the answer.

1. Which pronoun could replace the underlined words?

   The fish buries the fish in the sand

   A. yourself   C. myself
   B. itself   D. ourselves

2. Which pronoun could replace the underlined word?

   Claire let Claire into the house.

   A. herself   C. itself
   B. himself   D. themselves

3. Which pronoun correctly completes this sentence?

   They watched _____ on TV that night.

   A. themselves   C. himself
   B. ourselves   D. herself

4. Which pronoun correctly completes this sentence?

   Ellie _____ did not seem to believe what she was saying.

   A. himself   C. itself
   B. ourselves   **D. herself**

LANGUAGE ARTS PURPLE   WS 1

More Practice

Improve Your Skills
Possessive Pronouns

Choose the answer.

1. Which pronoun could replace the underlined words?

   The bear licked the bear's paws.

   A. my   B. your   **C. its**   D. our

2. Which pronoun could replace the underlined words?

   The writers read the writers' books on the stage.

   A. them   B. they   C. us   **D. their**

3. Which pronoun correctly completes this sentence?

   I was worried when I got _____ hand stuck in the gate.

   A. our   B. he   **C. my**   D. me

4. Which pronoun correctly completes this sentence?

   Amanda left _____ sunglasses on the table.

   A. she   **B. her**   C. they   D. them

5. Which pronoun could replace the underlined words?

   That money is Donna's money.

   A. yours   B. mine   C. ours   **D. hers**

LANGUAGE ARTS PURPLE   WS 1

---

6. Which pronoun could replace the underlined words?

   I'll mind my business if you mind your business.

   A. ours   **B. yours**   C. his   D. theirs

7. Which pronoun could replace the underlined words?

   Randy's pie tasted just as good as Cleo and Adam's pie.

   A. theirs   B. them   C. ours   D. yours

8. Which pronoun could replace the underlined words?

   I like Rebecca's idea better than Tom's idea.

   A. he   B. him   **C. his**   D. its

WS 2   LANGUAGE ARTS PURPLE

Write Now ●

◯▷ **Publish Your Book Review**

Students will publish their book review. Have them gather their proofread draft. Turn to pages WS 155–158 in *K¹² Language Arts Activity Book*.

Objectives
- Make a clean copy of a book review.

1. Explain to students that they will finish their book review by completing the last stage of the writing process—publishing their work.
   Say: Publishing your writing means making a clean and final copy that is ready for sharing with others.

   ▸ To be ready to publish your book review, you should have finished revising and proofreading your draft.
   ▸ The final copy should be your best effort and should not have any errors.

2. Explain that the final copy should be written clearly and neatly on clean sheets of paper. Tell students that they should use good handwriting and leave spaces between words so that others can read what they wrote.

3. Have students use the lined Activity Book pages to write their final copy. If needed, additional lined writing pages can be printed from the online lesson.

4. Use the materials and instructions in the online lesson to evaluate students' finished writing. You will be looking at students' writing to evaluate the following:

   ▸ **Purpose and Content:** The review focuses on one book and tells most of the important elements and events from the book. The review includes only two of the following: informs the readers, shares an opinion, and gives a recommendation.
   ▸ **Structure and Organization:** The review has been revised. The first paragraph lists four of the following: the book's title, author, main characters, setting, and brief plot description. The second paragraph summarizes the events in chronological order. The third paragraph includes comments from the reviewer. One paragraph may be out of order.
   ▸ **Grammar and Mechanics:** The review has been proofread. Only two or three errors in grammar and mechanics remain. The book's title may not be capitalized or underlined correctly.

5. Enter students' scores online for each rubric category.

6. If students' writing scored a 1 in any category, work with them to revise and proofread their work.

TIP Tell students that producing a piece of writing that is ready to publish and share with others is a great accomplishment. Let students know that the effort they put in to publish a book review is something to be proud of. Keep students' book review in a safe place for future reference.

More Practice

Book Review

If students' writing did not meet objectives, have them complete the appropriate review activities listed in the table online. Follow the online instructions to help students revise and edit their work. Impress upon students that revising makes their work better. Writing is a process, and each time they revise their book review they are improving their writing. Always begin with something positive to say. For example, if students made up a title for their book review, you might say that the title made you want to read the book review.

Help students locate the activities and provide support as needed.

Objectives
- Revise a book review.

Reward: When students score 80 percent or above on the Unit Checkpoint and their writing is Level 2 or higher on the Book Review grading rubric, add a sticker for this unit on the My Accomplishments chart.

Book Review Presentation

Unit Focus

In this Composition unit, students will create a project that is related to a book review and give a presentation. They will

- ▸ Use their journal to freewrite.
- ▸ Choose an important scene from the book that they reviewed to represent with a project.
- ▸ Select one of several possible projects to complete.
- ▸ Work independently on their project, making certain that it shows the key elements of the scene, such as the main characters, setting, and important plot events.

- ▸ Learn how to give a presentation that includes reading their book review aloud and explaining their project.
- ▸ Practice their presentation.
- ▸ Deliver their presentation.

Unit Plan		**⟦Online⟧**	**⟦Offline⟧**
Lesson 1	Consider Media to Use and Journal Entry	**30** minutes	**15** minutes
Lesson 2	Plan Your Project	**20** minutes	**25** minutes
Lesson 3	Work on Your Project (A)	**25** minutes	**20** minutes
Lesson 4	Work on Your Project (B)		**45** minutes
Lesson 5	Practice Your Presentation	**15** minutes	**30** minutes
Lesson 6	Present Your Book Review Project		**45** minutes

Consider Media to Use and Journal Entry

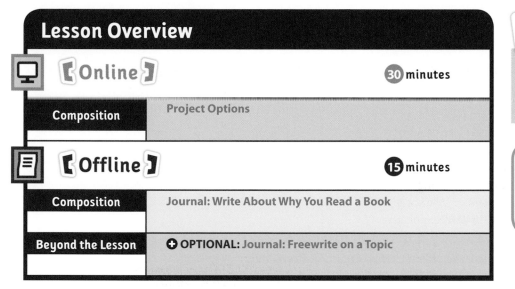

Lesson Overview		
Online		**30** minutes
Composition	Project Options	
Offline		**15** minutes
Composition	Journal: Write About Why You Read a Book	
Beyond the Lesson	⊕ OPTIONAL: Journal: Freewrite on a Topic	

Materials

Supplied
- *K¹² My Journal,* pp. 34–35

Keywords

media – all the ways by which something can be shown, shared, or expressed

Big Ideas

- Book reviews allow writers to share information about books they have read with audiences who want to know more about the books. Book reviews often include a summary or analysis of the content, an opinion about the book, and a recommendation to readers.
- To be effective communicators, writers and speakers should recognize and use complete sentences.
- Journal writing is a form of freewriting. It is an opportunity to get ideas on paper without regard for correctness of the language or for the format of a piece of writing.
- To improve, writers require frequent practice.

 **30** minutes

Students will work online **independently** to find out about the options for this unit's project. Help students locate the online activity.

Composition

Project Options

Students will learn about the different projects that they may choose to enhance their book review.

Objectives
- Examine media options for illustration.

 **15** minutes

Work **together** with students to complete the offline Composition and Beyond the Lesson activities.

Composition

✏ Journal: Write About Why You Read a Book

Students will respond to a journal prompt by writing about some of the things that can influence them to read a particular book. Gather *K¹² My Journal* and have students turn to pages 34 and 35.

Objectives
- Respond to a journal prompt.
- Freewrite about a topic.

1. Tell students they are going to write in their journal about what makes them want to read a book. To help students think of several reasons for reading a book, ask them to think about their answers to the following questions.

   ▸ Have you ever decided to read a book because someone else recommended it? What book did you read? Who recommended it? Why was that person's recommendation enough to make you read the book?

   ▸ Has seeing a picture on a book's cover or on a poster ever made you want to read a particular book? When did this happen? What was it that sparked your interest?

   ▸ If you want to convince someone else to read a book, what might you do? Would you talk about the book? Would you show an illustration of the book? Would you mention what someone else has said about a book? Why do you think these methods often work?

2. Have students respond to the prompt in their journal. Encourage them to write in complete sentences, although it is not a requirement when they are freewriting in their journal.

TIP Students should write for about 15 minutes. Freewriting allows students to use their imagination to write what they want without worrying about being graded, so encourage them to keep writing for the entire time. If students have trouble writing for 15 minutes, use the prompting questions in Step 1 or have them list ideas or words. If they want to keep writing beyond the suggested time limit, praise them for their enthusiasm and offer to let them complete their entry later in the day as a reward.

Why Read a Book?   Date _____

What makes you want to read a book? How can you convince someone else to read the same book?

_____
_____
_____
_____
_____
_____
_____
_____
_____
_____
_____
_____
_____

34

Beyond the Lesson ....

✏ ✚ **OPTIONAL:** Journal: Freewrite on a Topic

This activity is OPTIONAL. It is intended for students who have extra time and would benefit from extra practice. Feel free to skip this activity. Gather *K¹² My Journal.*

1. Have students either respond to a prompt in Thoughts and Experiences (pages 50–93) or write about their own topic on the next available page in Ideas (pages 96–139).

2. Encourage students to explore their thoughts and write as much as they want. There are no rules. If students wish, ideas can be fleshed out into a more developed composition at a later time.

TIP Studies show that students who write more frequently become better writers.

Objectives
- Respond to a journal prompt.
- Freewrite about a topic.

Plan Your Project

Lesson Overview

🖥 **[Online]** ⓴ minutes

| Composition | Explore a Model Book Review Project |

📄 **[Offline]** ㉕ minutes

| Composition | Choose a Scene and Project |

Supplied
- *K¹² Language Arts Activity Book*, pp. WS 159–165
- Book Review Project Directions (printout)
- Accordion Book Template (optional printout)
- Pop-Up Book Template (optional printout)
- Mobile Template (optional printout)
- Slide Show Template (optional printout)

Also Needed
- students' chosen book

Advance Preparation

In this lesson, students begin to accumulate documents and materials they will need as they work on their book review project and presentation. You might want to provide students with a folder, large envelope, or a box in which to keep these documents and materials. Gather the book students chose to review and print the Book Review Project Directions from the online lesson.

[Online] ⓴ minutes

Students will work online **independently** to explore a model book review project and learn the first steps Alexander took when he began to work on it. Help students locate the online activity.

Composition •••

Explore a Model Book Review Project

By exploring a model book review project, students will learn what steps are necessary to produce their book review project.

TIP If students are not comfortable reading the model book review project planning form for this activity online, they may read the model on pages WS 159–161 in *K¹² Language Arts Activity Book*.

⭐ **Objectives**
- Choose media.
- Gather materials for a project.

【 Offline 】 ㉕ minutes

Work **together** with students to complete the offline Composition activity.

Composition ··

Choose a Scene and Project

Students will choose a scene and option for their book review project, and then gather project materials. Turn to pages WS 159–165 in *K¹² Language Arts Activity Book*. Gather the book students chose to review and the Book Review Project Directions, which you should have printed from the online lesson.

> **Objectives**
> • Choose media.
> • Gather materials for a project.

1. Have students read Alexander's model book review project planning form.

2. Have students complete their planning form on the Activity Book pages. They should refer to Alexander's planning form and the book they reviewed as needed. They will need to read the Book Review Project Directions to help make their project choice. Provide support as necessary.

3. Once students have chosen a project, work with them to gather the necessary materials. Project templates can be printed from the online lesson.

TIP Keep students' completed planning form and the project directions in a safe place so students can refer to them later.

Panel 1 (WS 159)

Composition

Plan Your Project
Model Book Review Project Planning Form

Use Alexander's model planning form to help you as you complete your own planning form.

Follow the directions to choose a scene.
- Think about the book that you reviewed. List three important scenes on the Scene 1, Scene 2, and Scene 3 lines.
- List the characters, setting, and events in each scene.
  Are the main characters a part of each scene?
  Can you draw each setting to show how it affects events?
  Are the events in each scene important?
- Choose a scene that includes main characters, a setting you can easily draw, and important events. Circle it. Cross out the other two scenes.

Scene 1 ~~Ribsy goes into the wrong car in the shopping center.~~

Characters Ribsy, who is a main character

Setting the parking lot of a shopping center — not easy to draw to show how it affects events

Events Ribsy gets into the wrong car — it's important because it is how Ribsy gets lost.

Panel 2 (WS 160)

Scene 2 ~~Ribsy runs onto the football field.~~

Characters Ribsy, who is a main character, and Joe Saylor, who is not really a main character

Setting a football stadium — I could draw this, but it would have to be a really big drawing.

Events Ribsy runs onto the field — it's important because Joe Saylor says he owns Ribsy, but Ribsy's picture ends up in the newspaper.

Scene 3 (Henry finally finds Ribsy.)

Characters Henry, his parents, Larry, Ribsy — so the two main characters (Henry and Ribsy) are in the scene

Setting Larry's apartment building and fire escape — very easy to draw and shows how Ribsy can be seen

Events Henry and his family see Ribsy, but Ribsy can't get down, so Mr. Huggins rescues Ribsy — it's important because it's how Ribsy and Henry finally get back together.

Panel 3 (WS 161)

Answer the questions to explain your choice.

1. Why did you decide not to use the scenes you crossed out?
   The first scene only has Ribsy in it. It would also be hard to draw the parking lot, and not very much action happens in the scene. The second scene doesn't have Henry either, and I think a football stadium is too big to draw.

2. Why did you decide on the scene you circled? Henry and Ribsy are both in this scene, and the setting really affects what happens. Also, the events in this scene are some of the most important ones in the book.

Look at the project choices on the Book Review Project Directions. Which project would work best with the scene you've chosen? Choose a project and answer the questions.

3. What project will you do? the mobile

4. Why did you choose this project? It will let me show the main characters and the setting really well. Also, there are two events, so I can draw each one on its own piece of the mobile. Finally, I like the idea of making something that moves and that doesn't look like the other projects.

Panel 4 (WS 163)

Composition

Plan Your Project
Choose a Scene and Project

Follow the directions to choose a scene.
- Think about the book that you reviewed. List three important scenes on the Scene 1, Scene 2, and Scene 3 lines.
- List the characters, setting, and events in each scene.
  Are the main characters a part of each scene?
  Can you draw each setting to show how it affects events?
  Are the events in each scene important?
- Choose a scene that includes main characters, a setting you can easily draw, and important events. Circle it. Cross out the other two scenes.

Scene 1 _____

Characters _____

Setting _____

Events _____

Panel 5 (WS 164)

Scene 2 _____

Characters _____

Setting _____

Events _____

Scene 3 _____

Characters _____

Setting _____

Events _____

Panel 6 (WS 165)

Answer the questions to explain your choice.

1. Why did you decide not to use the scenes you crossed out?
   _____

2. Why did you decide on the scene you circled? _____

Look at the project choices on the Book Review Project Directions. Which project would work best with the scene you've chosen? Choose a project and answer the questions.

3. What project will you do? _____

4. Why did you choose this project? _____

Answers will vary.

Work on Your Project (A)

Lesson Overview

🖥 **〔Online〕**		**25** minutes
Composition	Alexander Begins His Project	

📄 **〔Offline〕**		**20** minutes
Composition	Begin Your Project	

Advance Preparation

Gather the Book Review Project Directions and the corresponding project template (both printable from the online lesson), as well as the book that students reviewed.

 **〔Online〕** **25** minutes

Students will work online **independently** to learn how Alexander began his book review project. Help students locate the online activity.

Composition ....

Alexander Begins His Project
By exploring the steps that Alexander took to begin working on his book review project, students will learn the steps they should take as they begin to work on their own project.

> **Objectives**
> - Develop a project.
> - Use a visual display to enhance facts or details.

[Offline] 20 minutes

Work **together** with students to complete the offline Composition activity.

Composition ....

Begin Your Project

Students will take notes on the scene that their book review project will show and then start to make their project. Gather the book students chose to review and turn to page WS 167 in *K¹² Language Arts Activity Book.*

1. Have students complete the Activity Book page, making sure that they first reread the scene in the book that they plan to show with their project. Provide support as necessary.

2. Guide students to begin making their project by following the Book Review Project Directions. Print the corresponding project template from the online lesson if you have not done so already.

TIP Keep the Activity Book page and project materials in a safe place so students can refer to them as they work on their project.

↪ **Learning Coach Check-In** How are students progressing on their project? As students work on their book review project, make sure they are on track. Help them avoid errors before it is too late to fix them by making sure they understand the project instructions and are following them correctly.

> **Objectives**
> - Develop a project.
> - Use a visual display to enhance facts or details.

Composition ....

Work on Your Project (A)

Begin Your Project

In the book you reviewed, reread the scene that you've chosen to show in your project. As you read, think about the characters, setting, and events in the scene. Then answer the questions.

Who are the characters in the scene? _____

How do they feel? _____

What is the setting of the scene? _____

How does the setting affect the action? _____

What events happen in the scene? _____

Why are these events important? _____

Answers will vary.

LANGUAGE ARTS PURPLE   **WS 167**

Work on Your Project (B)

Lesson Overview

[Offline]   **45** minutes

Composition	Finish Your Project

Advance Preparation

Gather page WS 167 (Begin Your Project, students' completed planning form) in *K¹² Language Arts Activity Book*. Also gather students' partially completed book review project and anything they may need to complete it, such as the Book Review Project Directions and the corresponding project template (both printable from the online lesson), as well as the book that students' reviewed.

[Materials]

Supplied
- *K¹² Language Arts Activity Book*, p. WS 167
- Book Review Project Directions (printout)
- Accordion Book Template (optional printout)
- Pop-Up Book Template (optional printout)
- Mobile Template (optional printout)
- Slide Show Template (optional printout)

Also Needed
- students' chosen book
- students' book review project

 **45** minutes

Work **together** with students to complete the offline Composition activity.

Composition

Finish Your Project

Students will continue to work to complete their book review project. Gather students' partially completed project, the Book Review Project Directions, the book students chose to review, and students' completed planning form.

1. Guide students to continue working on their project by using their planning form and by following the directions on the Book Review Project Directions.

2. As necessary, help students put the finishing touches on their project and complete any tasks related to assembling their project.

Objectives
- Develop a project.
- Use a visual display to enhance facts or details.

Composition

Work on Your Project (A)

Begin Your Project

In the book you reviewed, reread the scene that you've chosen to show in your project. As you read, think about the characters, setting, and events in the scene. Then answer the questions.

Who are the characters in the scene? _____

How do they feel? _____

What is the setting of the scene? _____

How does the setting affect the action? _____

What events happen in the scene? _____

Why are these events important? _____

Answers will vary.

LANGUAGE ARTS PURPLE | WS 167

Practice Your Presentation

Lesson Overview

Online	**15** minutes
Composition	Explore a Model Book Review Presentation

Offline	**30** minutes
Composition	Practice Your Presentation with a Checklist

Materials

Supplied
- *K¹² Language Arts Activity Book*, pp. WS 155–158, 168
- Book Review Presentation: Feedback Sheet (printout)

Also Needed
- students' book review project

Advance Preparation

Gather pages WS 155–158 (Publish Your Book Review, students' completed book review) in *K¹² Language Arts Activity Book* and their completed book review project. Print the Book Review Presentation: Feedback Sheet from the online lesson.

 **15** minutes

Students will work online to watch a model book review presentation. Help students locate the online activity.

Composition

Explore a Model Book Review Presentation
By watching and discussing a model book review presentation, students will get an idea of how to deliver their own presentation. Watch the model video with students and discuss the questions about the model together.

Objectives
- Develop a project.
- Use a visual display to enhance facts or details.
- Practice a presentation.

Offline · 30 minutes

Work **together** with students to complete the offline Composition activity.

Composition

Practice Your Presentation with a Checklist

Students will practice delivering their book review presentation. Gather students' completed book review and project, and turn to page WS 168 in *K¹² Language Arts Activity Book*. You will also need the Book Review Presentation: Feedback Sheet, printable from the online lesson.

1. Have students read over the presentation checklist.

2. Guide students to deliver their presentation several times, standing in front of a mirror and reading their book review aloud before explaining the project they completed. After each practice run, encourage students to consult the items on the checklist and discuss the guiding questions with you to help improve the presentation.

3. Remind students that the more they practice, the more comfortable they will be and the better their presentation will be. If possible, offer to help students record themselves delivering the presentation so that they can both see and hear the strengths and weaknesses of their effort.

4. After students have practiced their presentation several times, complete the Book Review Presentation: Feedback Sheet and discuss it with students. Help students understand ways they can improve their presentation.

TIP Keep the presentation checklist in a safe place so students can refer to it later. If students would benefit from seeing the model book review presentation again, you can access the video in the online lesson.

Objectives
- Develop a project.
- Use a visual display to enhance facts or details.
- Practice a presentation.

Write Now

Unit Checkpoint and Publish Your Book Review

Publish Your Book Review

Write the final copy of your book review in your best handwriting. Write the title of your book review on the first line.

LANGUAGE ARTS PURPLE WS 155

Composition

Practice Your Presentation

Practice Your Presentation with a Checklist

Follow the steps in the checklist as you practice your book review presentation.

1. Read your book review aloud.
   - Speak at an appropriate pace—not too fast or too slow.
   - Use a friendly voice and speak loudly.
   - Speak with enthusiasm and expression.
2. Talk about your project.
   - Look at your audience as much as possible.
   - Tell what scene your project shows.
   - Explain who the characters are and how they feel.
   - State where the scene takes place and what events happen.
   - Describe why the scene is important and why you chose it.
3. Practice the presentation so you know what to say.

Ask yourself the following questions after you practice your presentation. Then give the presentation again. Try to improve your performance.

1. Did you look at your audience? About how many times?
2. Did you lose your place or forget any points? How can you keep that from happening?
3. How long was your presentation? Did you speak too slowly or too quickly?
4. Does your description of your project make sense? Do you need to say more about it and what it shows?

WS 168 LANGUAGE ARTS PURPLE

Present Your Book Review Project

Lesson Overview

[Offline]		**45** minutes
Write Now	**Deliver Your Book Review Presentation**	

[Materials]

Supplied
- *K¹² Language Arts Activity Book*, pp. WS 155–158, 168
- Book Review Presentation: Rubric (printout)

Also Needed
- students' book review project

Advance Preparation

Gather pages WS 155–158 (Publish Your Book Review, students' completed book review) and 168 (Practice Your Presentation with a Checklist) in *K¹² Language Arts Activity Book*. Also gather students' completed book review project.

Big Ideas

- Book reviews allow writers to share information about books they have read with audiences who want to know more about the books. Book reviews often include a summary or analysis of the content, an opinion about the book, and a recommendation to readers.
- To be effective communicators, writers and speakers should recognize and use complete sentences.

[Offline] **45** minutes

Work **together** with students to complete the offline Write Now activity.

Write Now

Deliver Your Book Review Presentation

Students will deliver their book review presentation. Have them gather the final draft of their book review, their book review project, and the presentation checklist.

1. Remind students that they will read their book review aloud and then present their completed project.
   Say: To be ready to give your presentation, your project must be finished and you should also have practiced your presentation several times. Today's presentation should be your best effort. Review the presentation checklist one last time before giving your presentation.

Objectives
- Share the book review and project.
- Speak clearly at an understandable pace.
- Speak in complete sentences.

2. Explain that students will not be graded on the artistic quality of their project, but on how well they present it and how well they followed the directions.

3. Use the materials and instructions in the online lesson to evaluate the presentation. You will evaluate the following:

   ▸ **Purpose and Content:** The presentation includes both a book review and a project that shows an important scene from the book. The student followed the directions in creating the project. The project shows the scene's most important characters, its setting, and some key plot events of the scene. The student states the reasons for choosing and depicting this scene.

   ▸ **Structure and Organization:** The presentation begins with the book review and then moves to the project. The description of the project starts with the student telling about the characters and the setting before explaining the plot events. The plot events are described in mostly chronological order.

   ▸ **Grammar and Mechanics:** The student speaks mostly in complete sentences and makes eye contact at several points during the presentation. The student speaks clearly, but sometimes speaks too quickly, too slowly, too loudly, or too softly.

4. Enter students' scores online for each rubric category.

5. If students' presentation scored a 1 in any category, discuss with them how their work might be revised. Students do not need to actually make the revisions, unless they can be made easily without major rework to the project.

6. If possible, find a way to allow students to share their presentation with others, such as family members who live far away. For example, you might make a videotape of students' presentation and have students address an envelope and mail the recording. Or you could have students deliver their presentation by video conferencing over a mobile device, such as a cell phone or tablet, or via an Internet program.

TIP Tell students that completing a project and presenting it to others is a great accomplishment. Let students know that the effort they put in to creating a book review project and presentation is something to be proud of.

Reward: When students have completed their book review project presentation, add a sticker for this unit on the My Accomplishments chart.

Unit Checkpoint and Publish Your Book Review

Publish Your Book Review

Write the final copy of your book review in your best handwriting. Write the title of your book review on the first line.

_____

_____

_____

_____

_____

_____

_____

_____

_____

_____

_____

Practice Your Presentation

Practice Your Presentation with a Checklist

Follow the steps in the checklist as you practice your book review presentation.

1. Read your book review aloud.
   - Speak at an appropriate pace—not too fast or too slow.
   - Use a friendly voice and speak loudly.
   - Speak with enthusiasm and expression.

2. Talk about your project.
   - Look at your audience as much as possible.
   - Tell what scene your project shows.
   - Explain who the characters are and how they feel.
   - State where the scene takes place and what events happen.
   - Describe why the scene is important and why you chose it.

3. Practice the presentation so you know what to say.

Ask yourself the following questions after you practice your presentation. Then give the presentation again. Try to improve your performance.

1. Did you look at your audience? About how many times?

2. Did you lose your place or forget any points? How can you keep that from happening?

3. How long was your presentation? Did you speak too slowly or too quickly?

4. Does your description of your project make sense? Do you need to say more about it and what it shows?

Agreement and Plan a Research Report

Unit Focus

In the grammar part of the unit, students will learn about subject–verb agreement and pronoun–antecedent agreement. They will

- Learn that singular subjects must be paired with singular verbs and plural subjects must be paired with plural verbs.
- Recognize subject–verb agreement in both simple and compound sentences.
- Learn that pronouns must agree with their antecedents in both number and gender.
- Recognize pronoun–antecedent agreement in sentences.

In the composition part of the unit, students will develop an outline for a research report on one of the 50 states in the United States. They will

- Use their journal to freewrite.
- Select a state to learn more about.
- Find and use digital and print sources with information about their topic.
- Take notes on their topic.
- Organize their notes.
- Create an outline for their research report.

Unit Plan		[Online]	[Offline]
Lesson 1	Subject–Verb Agreement and Journal Entry	30 minutes	15 minutes
Lesson 2	Subject–Verb Agreement and Model Research Report	30 minutes	15 minutes
Lesson 3	Pronoun–Antecedent Agreement and Choose a Topic	30 minutes	15 minutes
Lesson 4	Pronoun–Antecedent Agreement and Find Sources	30 minutes	15 minutes
Lesson 5	Take Notes About Your Research Topic (A)	25 minutes	20 minutes
Lesson 6	Take Notes About Your Research Topic (B)		45 minutes
Lesson 7	Take Notes About Your Research Topic (C)		45 minutes
Lesson 8	Organize Your Notes	15 minutes	30 minutes
Lesson 9	Use an Outline	15 minutes	30 minutes
Lesson 10	Unit Review	45 minutes	
Lesson 11	Unit Checkpoint	45 minutes	varies

Subject–Verb Agreement and Journal Entry

Lesson Overview

Online	30 minutes
GUM (Grammar, Usage, and Mechanics)	Subject–Verb Agreement in Simple Sentences

Offline	15 minutes
Composition	Journal: Write About What Interests You
Beyond the Lesson	⊕ OPTIONAL: Journal: Freewrite on a Topic

Materials

Supplied
- *K¹² My Journal*, pp. 36–37
- *Grammar Reference Guide* Online Book (optional)

Keywords

subject–verb agreement – the way a subject and verb match when both are singular or both are plural

Advance Preparation

To prepare for the GUM portion of this lesson, review Agreement (Subject and Verb Agreement) in the *Grammar Reference Guide* (linked in the online lesson) to familiarize yourself with the topic.

Big Ideas

▸ Journal writing is a form of freewriting. It is an opportunity to get ideas on paper without regard for the correctness of the language or the format of a piece of writing.
▸ To improve, writers require frequent practice.

[Online] 30 minutes

Students will work online **independently** to complete an activity on subject–verb agreement. Help students locate the online activity.

GUM (Grammar, Usage, and Mechanics) •••

Subject–Verb Agreement in Simple Sentences

Students will learn that subject–verb agreement means pairing singular subjects with singular verbs and plural subjects with plural verbs. Students will practice recognizing and creating subject–verb agreement in simple sentences.

Objectives
- Use a verb that agrees with its subject.

[Offline] 15 minutes

Work **together** with students to complete the offline Composition and Beyond the Lesson activities.

Composition ••

Journal: Write About What Interests You

Students will respond to a journal prompt by writing about some topics that interest them and that they would like to learn more about. Gather *K¹² My Journal* and have students turn to pages 36 and 37.

Objectives
- Respond to a journal prompt.
- Freewrite about a topic.

1. Tell students they are going to write in their journal about some topics and subjects that they find interesting. To help students think of several such topics, ask them to think about their answers to the following questions.

   ▸ What is something that you wish you knew how to do? Why do you wish you knew how to do it? How would knowing how to do this thing make you happier or give you satisfaction? What is it about this thing that you find interesting?

   ▸ Are there subjects that you don't fully understand that you'd like to learn more about? Which subjects? How might you begin to learn more about them?

   ▸ Is there a topic that you have a lot of questions about? Do you ever seek out answers to your questions?

   ▸ Are there books, magazines, television shows, or movies on a certain topic that you always want to watch and usually enjoy? What is that topic?

2. Have students respond to the prompt in their journal. Encourage students to write in complete sentences, although it is not a requirement when they are freewriting in their journal.

TIP Students should write for about 15 minutes. Freewriting allows students to use their imagination to write what they want without worrying about being graded, so encourage them to keep writing for the entire time. If students have trouble writing for 15 minutes, use the prompting questions in Step 1 or have them list ideas or words. If they want to keep writing beyond the suggested time limit, praise them for their enthusiasm and offer to let them complete their entry later in the day as a reward.

Become an Expert　　Date _____

What are some topics you'd like to know more about?
If you could be an expert in any of these topics, which
one would you choose?

_____

_____

_____

_____

_____

_____

_____

_____

_____

_____

_____

_____

36

Beyond the Lesson

⊕ OPTIONAL: Journal: Freewrite on a Topic

This activity is OPTIONAL. It is intended for students who have extra time and would benefit from extra practice. Feel free to skip this activity. Gather *K¹² My Journal*.

1. Have students either respond to a prompt in Thoughts and Experiences (pages 50–93) or write about their own topic on the next available page in Ideas (pages 96–139).

2. Encourage students to explore their thoughts and write as much as they want. There are no rules. If students wish, ideas can be fleshed out into a more developed composition at a later time.

TIP Studies show that students who write more frequently become better writers.

Objectives
- Respond to a journal prompt.
- Freewrite about a topic.

Subject–Verb Agreement and Model Research Report

Lesson Overview

🖥 Online — 30 minutes

Skills Update	Subject–Verb Agreement in Simple Sentences
GUM (Grammar, Usage, and Mechanics)	Subject–Verb Agreement in Compound Sentences
Composition	Explore a Model Research Report

📄 Offline — 15 minutes

Composition	Respond to the Model Research Report

Materials

Supplied
- *K¹² Language Arts Activity Book*, pp. WS 169–175
- *Grammar Reference Guide* Online Book (optional)

Keywords

audience – a writer's readers

compound sentence – a sentence that has at least two independent parts

purpose – the reason for writing

research report – a type of essay based mainly on the author's research

subject–verb agreement – the way a subject and verb match when both are singular or both are plural

tone – the writer's attitude toward the topic or subject

Advance Preparation

To prepare for the GUM portion of this lesson, review Agreement (Subject and Verb Agreement) in the *Grammar Reference Guide* (linked in the online lesson) to familiarize yourself with the topic. In this lesson, students begin to accumulate documents they will need as they work on their research report. You might want to provide students with a folder or large envelope in which to keep these documents.

Big Ideas

To write a strong research report, one should be able to follow an interest to its conclusion.

[Online] ③⓪ minutes

Students will work online to review subject–verb agreement in simple sentences, to learn about subject–verb agreement in compound sentences, and to read and explore a model research report. Help students locate the online activities.

Skills Update ....

Subject–Verb Agreement in Simple Sentences
Students will review subject–verb agreement in simple sentences by completing Skills Update exercises. Sit with students as they do this activity and note if they answer correctly.

⊃ **Learning Coach Check-in** How did students do on the Skills Update?

- ▸ **All answers correct:** Great! Skip the review screen and go on to the next activity.
- ▸ **Any answers incorrect:** Take a few minutes to review subject–verb agreement in simple sentences now. Use the link on the screen after the Skills Update to take another look at the online activity or review Agreement (Subject and Verb Agreement) in the *Grammar Reference Guide* together.

(TIP) This activity will require extra time if students need to review subject–verb agreement in simple sentences. Take the extra 5–10 minutes to review now because new skills build on what students have already learned.

Objectives
- Use a verb that agrees with its subject.

GUM (Grammar, Usage, and Mechanics) ....

Subject–Verb Agreement in Compound Sentences
Students will learn about subject–verb agreement in compound sentences and practice recognizing and creating subject–verb agreement in compound sentences.

Objectives
- Use a verb that agrees with its subject.

Composition

Explore a Model Research Report

By reading and exploring a model research report, students will learn what a research report is, how one is structured, and what type of information belongs in one. They will also learn about purpose, audience, and the appropriate tone and language for a research report.

TIP Seeing a final version of a research report helps students see the goal of this unit. It will be easier for them to understand each step in the process if they know how the steps result in a finished product. If students are not comfortable reading the model research report for this activity online, they may read the model on pages WS 169–171 in *K¹² Language Arts Activity Book*.

Objectives
- Describe the elements of a research report.
- Respond to a research report.
- Identify purpose and audience.
- Identify words and phrases that reveal the tone of a text.

[Offline] 15 minutes

Word **together** with students to complete the offline Composition activity.

Composition

Respond to the Model Research Report

Students will review what they learned about the model research report. Turn to pages WS 173–175 in *K¹² Language Arts Activity Book*.

1. Have students reread Winnie's research report on pages WS 169–171.

2. Have students complete the Activity Book pages about Winnie's research report. Provide support as necessary, encouraging students to write in complete sentences. Students should refer to Winnie's research report as needed.

TIP Keep Winnie's research report in a safe place so students can refer to it later.

Objectives
- Describe the elements of a research report.
- Respond to a research report.
- Identify purpose and audience.
- Identify words and phrases that reveal the tone of a text.

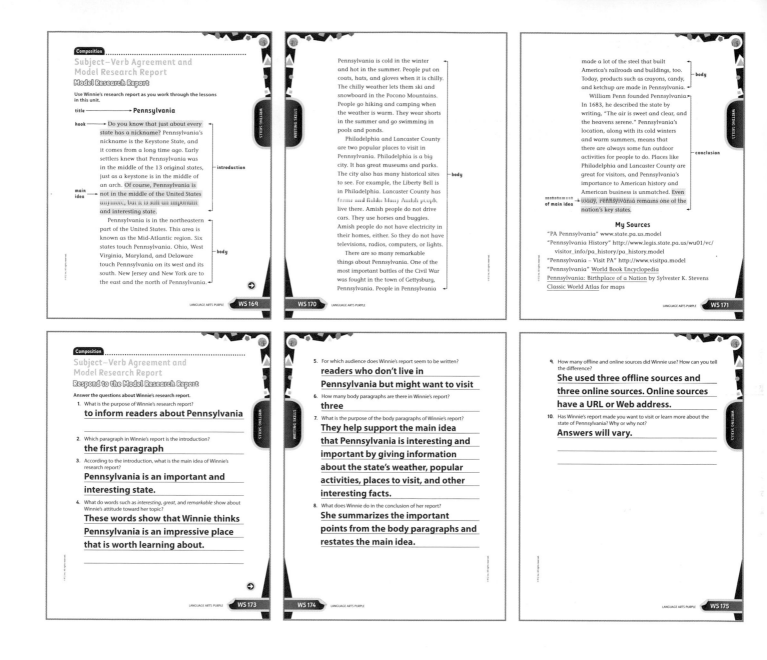

Composition

Subject–Verb Agreement and Model Research Report
Model Research Report

Use Winnie's research report as you work through the lessons in this unit.

title → **Pennsylvania**

hook → Do you know that just about every state has a nickname? Pennsylvania's nickname is the Keystone State, and it comes from a long time ago. Early settlers knew that Pennsylvania was in the middle of the 13 original states, just as a keystone is in the middle of an arch.

main idea → Of course, Pennsylvania is not in the middle of the United States anymore, but it is still an important and interesting state. —introduction

Pennsylvania is in the northeastern part of the United States. This area is known as the Mid-Atlantic region. Six states touch Pennsylvania. Ohio, West Virginia, Maryland, and Delaware touch Pennsylvania on its west and its south. New Jersey and New York are to the east and the north of Pennsylvania. —body

LANGUAGE ARTS PURPLE **WS 169**

Pennsylvania is cold in the winter and hot in the summer. People put on coats, hats, and gloves when it is chilly. The chilly weather lets them ski and snowboard in the Pocono Mountains. People go hiking and camping when the weather is warm. They wear shorts in the summer and go swimming in pools and ponds.

Philadelphia and Lancaster County are two popular places to visit in Pennsylvania. Philadelphia is a big city. It has great museums and parks. The city also has many historical sites to see. For example, the Liberty Bell is in Philadelphia. Lancaster County has farms and fields. Many Amish people live there. Amish people do not drive cars. They use horses and buggies. Amish people do not have electricity in their homes, either. So they do not have televisions, radios, computers, or lights. —body

There are so many remarkable things about Pennsylvania. One of the most important battles of the Civil War was fought in the town of Gettysburg, Pennsylvania. People in Pennsylvania

WS 170 LANGUAGE ARTS PURPLE

---

made a lot of the steel that built America's railroads and buildings, too. Today, products such as crayons, candy, and ketchup are made in Pennsylvania. —body

William Penn founded Pennsylvania. In 1683, he described the state by writing, "The air is sweet and clear, and the heavens serene." Pennsylvania's location, along with its cold winters and warm summers, means that there are always some fun outdoor activities for people to do. Places like Philadelphia and Lancaster County are great for visitors, and Pennsylvania's importance to American history and American business is unmatched. Even —conclusion

restatement of main idea → today, Pennsylvania remains one of the nation's key states.

My Sources
"PA Pennsylvania" www.state.pa.us.model
"Pennsylvania History" http://www.legis.state.pa.us/wu01/vc/ visitor_info/pa_history/pa_history.model
"Pennsylvania – Visit PA" http://www.visitpa.model
"Pennsylvania" World Book Encyclopedia
Pennsylvania: Birthplace of a Nation by Sylvester K. Stevens
Classic World Atlas for maps

LANGUAGE ARTS PURPLE **WS 171**

Composition

Subject–Verb Agreement and Model Research Report
Respond to the Model Research Report

Answer the questions about Winnie's research report.

1. What is the purpose of Winnie's research report?
to inform readers about Pennsylvania

2. Which paragraph in Winnie's report is the introduction?
the first paragraph

3. According to the introduction, what is the main idea of Winnie's research report?
Pennsylvania is an important and interesting state.

4. What do words such as *interesting*, *great*, and *remarkable* show about Winnie's attitude toward her topic?
These words show that Winnie thinks Pennsylvania is an impressive place that is worth learning about.

LANGUAGE ARTS PURPLE **WS 173**

---

5. For which audience does Winnie's report seem to be written?
readers who don't live in Pennsylvania but might want to visit

6. How many body paragraphs are there in Winnie's report?
three

7. What is the purpose of the body paragraphs of Winnie's report?
They help support the main idea that Pennsylvania is interesting and important by giving information about the state's weather, popular activities, places to visit, and other interesting facts.

8. What does Winnie do in the conclusion of her report?
She summarizes the important points from the body paragraphs and restates the main idea.

WS 174 LANGUAGE ARTS PURPLE

---

9. How many offline and online sources did Winnie use? How can you tell the difference?
She used three offline sources and three online sources. Online sources have a URL or Web address.

10. Has Winnie's report made you want to visit or learn more about the state of Pennsylvania? Why or why not?
Answers will vary.

LANGUAGE ARTS PURPLE **WS 175**

Pronoun–Antecedent Agreement and Choose a Topic

Lesson Overview

🖥 [Online]   **30** minutes

Skills Update	Subject–Verb Agreement in Compound Sentences
GUM (Grammar, Usage, and Mechanics)	Pronoun and Antecedent Agreement
Composition	Winnie Chooses a Topic

🗐 [Offline]   **15** minutes

Composition	Choose Your Topic

[Materials]

Supplied

- *K¹² Language Arts Activity Book*, pp. WS 177–178
- *Grammar Reference Guide* Online Book (optional)

Keywords

antecedent – the noun or pronoun that a pronoun points back to

research report – a type of essay based mainly on the author's research

Advance Preparation

To prepare for the GUM portion of this lesson, review Agreement (Pronoun and Antecedent Agreement) in the *Grammar Reference Guide* (linked in the online lesson) to familiarize yourself with the topic.

Big Ideas

To write a strong research report, one should be able to follow an interest to its conclusion.

[Online] ⏱ 30 minutes

Students will work online to review subject–verb agreement in compound sentences, to learn about pronoun and antecedent agreement, and to find out how to choose a topic for their research report. Help students locate the online activities.

Skills Update

Subject–Verb Agreement in Compound Sentences

Students will review subject–verb agreement in compound sentences by completing Skills Update exercises. Sit with students as they do this activity and note if they answer correctly.

➲ **Learning Coach Check-In** How did students do on the Skills Update?

> ▸ **All answers correct:** Great! Skip the review screen and go on to the next activity.
>
> ▸ **Any answers incorrect:** Take a few minutes to review subject–verb agreement in compound sentences now. Use the link on the screen after the Skills Update to take another look at the online activity or review Agreement (Subject and Verb Agreement) in the *Grammar Reference Guide* together.

TIP This activity will require extra time if students need to review subject–verb agreement in compound sentences. Take the extra 5–10 minutes to review now because new skills build on what students have already learned.

> **Objectives**
> • Use a verb that agrees with its subject.

GUM (Grammar, Usage, and Mechanics)

Pronoun and Antecedent Agreement

Students will learn about agreement of pronouns and antecedents and practice recognizing and creating agreement between a pronoun and its antecedent.

> **Objectives**
> • Use a pronoun that agrees with the noun to which it refers.

Composition

Winnie Chooses a Topic

By watching Winnie answer several questions about states and ultimately choose a state to be the topic of her research report, students will learn how to do the same.

> **Objectives**
> • Brainstorm topics for a research report.
> • Recall information from experiences.
> • Choose a topic for a research report.

〖 Offline 〗 ⓯ minutes

Work **together** with students to complete the offline Composition activity.

Composition •••

Choose Your Topic

Students will answer several questions about different states, consider which state or states most interest them, and ultimately choose one to be the topic of their research report. Turn to pages WS 177 and 178 in *K¹² Language Arts Activity Book*.

1. Have students complete the Activity Book pages to choose a topic for their research report. Provide support as necessary, encouraging students to think about their answers to the questions and why they might like to learn about some states more than others.

2. Remind students that there is no wrong choice when it comes to choosing a state to research. Any state that they choose can be the subject of a research report. Consider telling students that the more interested they are in a state, the better their report is likely to be because they will enjoy learning about a state that interests them. That enjoyment generally translates to improved results.

TIP Keep students' completed form in a safe place so they can refer to it later.

> ### Objectives
> - Brainstorm topics for a research report.
> - Recall information from experiences.
> - Choose a topic for a research report.

Composition

Pronoun–Antecedent Agreement and Choose a Topic

Choose Your Topic   **Answers will vary.**

Answer the questions to choose a state as the topic of your research report.

1. Which states other than your own have you visited?

2. Which states would you visit if you could? Why?

3. Do you have family members or friends who live in other states? If so, which states?

4. Think about the characters in stories and books you've read, and in TV shows and movies you've seen. Which states do these characters live in?

5. Look over your answers to Questions 1–4. Which state would you like to learn more about for your research report?

6. Why did you choose this state?

LANGUAGE ARTS PURPLE   **WS 177**

WS 178   LANGUAGE ARTS PURPLE

 WS 390   **Language Arts Purple**

Pronoun–Antecedent Agreement and Find Sources

Lesson Overview

🖥 [Online]　30 minutes

Skills Update	Pronoun and Antecedent Agreement
GUM (Grammar, Usage, and Mechanics)	Pronoun and Antecedent Agreement
Composition	Winnie Finds Sources

📄 [Offline]　15 minutes

Composition	Find Your Sources

Materials

Supplied

- *K¹² Language Arts Activity Book*, pp. WS 179–181
- *Grammar Reference Guide* Online Book (optional)

Keywords

antecedent – the noun or pronoun that a pronoun points back to

atlas – a book of maps

encyclopedia – a reference work made up of articles on many topics, usually in alphabetical order

search engine – software that searches for websites, usually by keywords

URL – the Internet address of a website; stands for *uniform resource locator*

website – a place on the Internet devoted to a specific organization, group, or individual

Advance Preparation

To prepare for the GUM portion of this lesson, review Agreement (Pronoun and Antecedent Agreement) in the *Grammar Reference Guide* (linked in the online lesson) to familiarize yourself with the topic. In the Composition portion of the lesson, students will find sources for their research report. Students should use both online and print sources. When students work online, supervise their searches so that you can be sure they choose reliable websites. In addtion, plan a trip to the library so that students can locate print sources—a book, an encyclopedia, and an atlas—for the topic of their research report.

Big Ideas

Understanding appropriate resources to use makes a research task easier.

 **30 minutes**

Students will work online to review pronoun and antecedent agreement concerning gender, to learn about pronoun and antecedent agreement concerning number, and to learn how to find and record sources of information for their research report. Help students locate the online activities.

Skills Update ....

Pronoun and Antecedent Agreement
Students will review pronoun and antecedent agreement concerning gender by completing Skills Update exercises. Sit with students as they do this activity and note if they answer correctly.

⮑ **Learning Coach Check-In** How did students do on the Skills Update?

▶ **All answers correct:** Great! Skip the review screen and go on to the next activity.

▶ **Any answers incorrect:** Take a few minutes to review pronoun and antecedent agreement concerning gender now. Use the link on the screen after the Skills Update to take another look at the online activity or review Agreement (Pronoun and Antecedent Agreement) in the *Grammar Reference Guide* together.

TIP This activity will require extra time if students need to review pronoun and antecedent agreement concerning gender. Take the extra 5–10 minutes to review now because new skills build on what students have already learned.

> **Objectives**
> - Use a pronoun that agrees with the noun to which it refers.

GUM (Grammar, Usage, and Mechanics) ....

Pronoun and Antecedent Agreement
Students will learn about pronoun and antecedent agreement concerning number, and they will practice recognizing and creating agreement between pronouns and their antecedents.

> **Objectives**
> - Use a pronoun that agrees with the noun to which it refers.

Composition ....

Winnie Finds Sources
By watching Winnie search for sources of information about the state she has chosen and use a form to keep track of the sources she finds, students will learn how to do the same as they look for online and print sources for their research report.

> **Objectives**
> - Recognize the purpose of an encyclopedia.
> - Recognize the purpose of an atlas.
> - Use a print source to find information.
> - Use a digital source to find information.

[Offline] ⏱ 15 minutes

Work **together** with students to complete the offline Composition activity.

Composition •••

Find Your Sources

Students will search for both print and digital sources that have information about the state they have chosen and record important details about these sources on a form. Turn to pages WS 179–181 in *K¹² Language Arts Activity Book*.

1. Work with students to help them complete the Activity Book pages. Help them find both digital and print sources for their research report. Provide support as necessary, encouraging students to be sure to include at least one website, one encyclopedia, and one atlas among their sources. A trip to the library may be needed. (Note that the form has space for seven sources, but seven is not a requirement.)

2. Remind students that all websites are not equally reliable. To be sure that the information on a website is credible and trustworthy, it is best to use sites whose authorship can be checked and verified. Sites with Web addresses ending in .gov or .edu are generally credible and trustworthy. As necessary, tell students that Wikipedia.org is not a reliable source of information because anyone can add or edit information.

TIP Keep students' completed list of sources in a safe place so they can refer to it later.

Objectives

- Recognize the purpose of an encyclopedia.
- Recognize the purpose of an atlas.
- Use a print source to find information.
- Use a digital source to find information.

Take Notes About Your Research Topic (A)

Lesson Overview

🖥 [Online]   25 minutes

Skills Update	Pronoun and Antecedent Agreement
Composition	Winnie Takes Notes

📄 [Offline]   20 minutes

Composition	Take Notes

[Materials]

Supplied
- *K¹² Language Arts Activity Book*, pp. WS 179–181, 183–184
- *Grammar Reference Guide* Online Book (optional)

Also Needed
- index cards

Advance Preparation

Gather pages WS 179–181 (Find Your Sources) in *K¹² Language Arts Activity Book*. To prepare for the Composition portion of this lesson, gather at least 15 index cards. Write the following labels at the top of at least three cards each: General Information; Location and Climate; Outdoor Activities; Popular Places to Visit; Interesting Facts.

Big Ideas

- ▸ Writers must be able to articulate a main idea and support it with appropriate details.
- ▸ Following a specific organizational structure is a useful tool for novice writers; however, writers require the freedom and flexibility to follow their ideas to completion.

[Online] (25) minutes

Students will work online to review pronoun and antecedent agreement concerning number and to learn how to use their sources and index cards to take notes on the topic of their research report. Help students locate the online activities.

Skills Update ....

Pronoun and Antecedent Agreement

Students will review pronoun and antecedent agreement concerning number by completing Skills Update exercises. Sit with students as they do this activity and note if they answer correctly.

> ⟳ **Learning Coach Check-In** How did students do on the Skills Update?
>
> ▸ **All answers correct:** Great! Skip the review screen and go on to the next activity.
>
> ▸ **Any answers incorrect:** Take a few minutes to review pronoun and antecedent agreement concerning number now. Use the link on the screen after the Skills Update to take another look at the online activity or review Agreement (Pronoun and Antecedent Agreement) in the *Grammar Reference Guide* together.

TIP This activity will require extra time if students need to review pronoun and antecedent agreement concerning number. Take the extra 5–10 minutes to review now because new skills build on what students have already learned.

Objectives
- Use a pronoun that agrees with the noun to which it refers.

Composition ....

Winnie Takes Notes

By watching Winnie use her sources and index cards to take notes on the topic of her research report, students will learn how to do the same as they begin to do research and take notes on their topic.

Objectives
- Take brief notes on sources.

〖 Offline 〗 ⓴ minutes

Work **together** with students to complete the offline Composition activity.

Composition ....

Take Notes

Students will begin to do research and take notes on the topic of their research report. Have them gather their completed sources form. Turn to pages WS 183 and 184 in *K¹² Language Arts Activity Book*.

> **Objectives**
> • Take brief notes on sources.

1. Give students the index cards you labeled and guide them through the directions on the Activity Book page. Tell them that they will use the sources from their completed sources form and the index cards to take notes on the topic of their research report.

2. Help students locate the sources they listed on their sources form. Tell them to take their time reading from their sources and taking notes about important information. Guide students to watch for information that relates to the labels on their note cards. Warn them to avoid jotting down information unrelated to the labels, because such notes will not be useful to them when they write their research report.

3. As students take notes on the index cards, remind them to keep notes from their sources separate. That is, students should not write notes from multiple sources on the same card because they may later get confused about which source a piece of information came from.

4. Remind students that, as they take notes, they do not need to write in complete sentences or use proper punctuation. Their focus should be on gathering information that is important enough to be included in their research report.

5. So that students do not unintentionally plagiarize, caution them to use their own words as they take notes. However, if students find a quotation they might like to use in their report, they should copy the information word for word, including the punctuation, and place quotation marks around it.

6. Let students know that they will have more time in upcoming lessons to take notes on the topic of their research report. They will not, and should not, finish taking notes today.

7. As necessary, provide students with additional index cards.

TIP Keep students' completed sources form and note cards in a safe place so they can refer to them later.

Pronoun–Antecedent Agreement and Find Sources

Find Your Sources

Search for sources of information about the state you chose for your research report. Use the Internet and go to a library. For each source you find, fill out one section on the form as follows:

- For print sources (a book, an entry in an encyclopedia, an atlas, a magazine or newspaper article), write the title, author, and notes about each source.
- For online sources (websites), write the name, URL, and notes about each source.

Example

Online or Print _online_

Name or Title _PA Pennsylvania_

URL or Author _www.state.pa.us.model_

Notes _lots of info about state history and things to do for fun_

Source #1

Online or Print _____

Name or Title _____

URL or Author _____

Notes _____

Source #2

Online or Print _____

Name or Title _____

URL or Author _____

Notes _____

Source #3

Online or Print _____

Name or Title _____

URL or Author _____

Notes _____

Source #4

Online or Print _____

Name or Title _____

URL or Author _____

Notes _____

Source #5

Online or Print _____

Name or Title _____

URL or Author _____

Notes _____

Source #6

Online or Print _____

Name or Title _____

URL or Author _____

Notes _____

Source #7

Online or Print _____

Name or Title _____

URL or Author _____

Notes _____

Take Notes About Your Research Topic (A)

Take Notes

Follow the directions to take notes about your research topic.

1. Gather your completed sources form and the prepared index cards. If the cards still need to be labeled, **write the following labels** at the top of at least three cards each:
   - General Information
   - Location and Climate
   - Outdoor Activities
   - Popular Places to Visit
   - Interesting Facts
2. Return to a source you listed on your sources form and **read about your state**. As you read, look for information that relates to the labels on your note cards.
3. When you read something important, find the correct note card and **write down the key information**. Write information from just one source per card.
4. For each note card that you complete, **write down the number of the source you used** to find the information in case you need to return to it later. If it is a print source, write down chapter or page numbers, too.
5. **Continue to read and take notes** from all of your sources. Make more note cards when you need to. It is better to have too many notes than too few. Keep your note cards together in a safe place.
6. **Turn over this page** to see two sample note cards.

Note card for an online source

Outdoor Activities

- skiing and snowboarding in the Pocono Mountains
- hiking and camping
- swimming in pools and ponds
- polka dancing
- boating and fishing

Source # 1

Note card for a print source

Location and Climate

- Mid-Atlantic region
- PA bordered by NY, NJ, DE, MD, WV, and OH
- looks like a rectangle
- has lots of rivers

Source #6, pages 60 and 71

Take Notes About Your Research Topic (B)

Lesson Overview

⊟ [**Offline**]   **45** minutes

Composition	Take Notes

[Materials]

Supplied
- *K¹² Language Arts Activity Book*, pp. WS 179–181, 183–184

Also Needed
- index cards
- students' completed note cards

Advance Preparation

Gather pages WS 179–181 (Find Your Sources) and 183–184 (Take Notes) in *K¹² Language Arts Activity Book*. Also gather students' completed note cards and extra blank index cards. If students need additional index cards, label the cards for them as needed.

Big Ideas

▸ Writers must be able to articulate a main idea and support it with appropriate details.
▸ Following a specific organizational structure is a useful tool for novice writers; however, writers require the freedom and flexibility to follow their ideas to completion.

[Offline] **45** minutes

Work **together** with students to complete the offline Composition activity.

Composition ....

Take Notes

Students will continue to research and take notes on the topic of their research report. Have them gather their completed sources form and any completed note cards.

1. Remind students to follow the directions on page WS 181 in *K¹² Language Arts Activity Book* as they continue to take notes.

⭐ **Objectives**
- Take brief notes on sources.

2. Let students know that they will have more time in upcoming lessons to take notes on their topic. They will not, and should not, finish taking notes today.

3. As necessary, provide students with additional index cards.

TIP Keep students' completed sources form and note cards in a safe place so they can refer to them later.

Composition

Pronoun-Antecedent Agreement and Find Sources

Find Your Sources

Search for sources of information about the state you chose for your research report. Use the Internet and go to a library. For each source you find, fill out one section on the form as follows:

- For print sources (a book, an entry in an encyclopedia, an atlas, a magazine or newspaper article), write the title, author, and notes about each source.
- For online sources (websites), write the name, URL, and notes about each source.

Example

Online or Print _online_

Name or Title _PA Pennsylvania_

URL or Author _www.state.pa.us.model_

Notes _lots of info about state history and things to do for fun_

Source #1

Online or Print _____

Name or Title _____

URL or Author _____

Notes _____

Source #2

Online or Print _____

Name or Title _____

URL or Author _____

Notes _____

Source #3

Online or Print _____

Name or Title _____

URL or Author _____

Notes _____

Source #4

Online or Print _____

Name or Title _____

URL or Author _____

Notes _____

Source #5

Online or Print _____

Name or Title _____

URL or Author _____

Notes _____

Source #6

Online or Print _____

Name or Title _____

URL or Author _____

Notes _____

Source #7

Online or Print _____

Name or Title _____

URL or Author _____

Notes _____

Composition

Take Notes About Your Research Topic (A)

Take Notes

Follow the directions to take notes about your research topic.

1. Gather your completed sources form and the prepared index cards. If the cards still need to be labeled, **write the following labels** at the top of at least three cards each:
- General Information
- Location and Climate
- Outdoor Activities
- Popular Places to Visit
- Interesting Facts

2. Return to a source you listed on your sources form and **read about your state**. As you read, look for information that relates to the labels on your note cards.

3. When you read something important, find the correct note card and **write down the key information**. Write information from just one source per card.

4. For each note card that you complete, **write down the number of the source you used** to find the information in case you need to return to it later. If it is a print source, write down chapter or page numbers, too.

5. **Continue to read and take notes** from all of your sources. Make more note cards when you need to. It is better to have too many notes than too few. Keep your note cards together in a safe place.

6. **Turn over this page** to see two sample note cards.

Note card for an online source

Outdoor Activities
- skiing and snowboarding in the Pocono Mountains
- hiking and camping
- swimming in pools and ponds
- polka dancing
- boating and fishing

Source # 1

Note card for a print source

Location and Climate
- Mid-Atlantic region
- PA bordered by NY, NJ, DE, MD, WV, and OH
- looks like a rectangle
- has lots of rivers

Source #6, pages 60 and 71

Take Notes About Your Research Topic (C)

Lesson Overview

[Offline]	**45** minutes
Composition	Take Notes

Materials

Supplied
- *K¹² Language Arts Activity Book*, pp. WS 179–181, 183–184

Also Needed
- index cards
- students' completed note cards

Advance Preparation

Gather pages WS 179–181 (Find Your Sources) and 183–184 (Take Notes) in *K¹² Language Arts Activity Book*. Also gather students' completed note cards and extra blank index cards. If students need additional index cards, label the cards for them as needed.

Big Ideas

- ▸ Writers must be able to articulate a main idea and support it with appropriate details.
- ▸ Following a specific organizational structure is a useful tool for novice writers; however, writers require the freedom and flexibility to follow their ideas to completion.

[Offline] **45** minutes

Work **together** with students to complete the offline Composition activity.

Composition ....

Take Notes

Students will finish researching and taking notes on the topic of their research report. Have them gather their completed sources form and any completed note cards.

1. Remind students to follow the directions on page WS 183 in *K¹² Language Arts Activity Book* as they continue to take notes.

> **Objectives**
> - Take brief notes on sources.

2. Let students know that they should finish taking notes today. As necessary, provide students with additional index cards.

3. Make sure students have completed at least three cards per label so that they have enough information to write their report.

TIP Keep students' completed sources form and note cards in a safe place so they can refer to them later.

Composition

Pronoun–Antecedent Agreement and Find Sources

Find Your Sources

Search for sources of information about the state you chose for your research report. Use the Internet and go to a library. For each source you find, fill out one section on the form as follows:

- For print sources (a book, an entry in an encyclopedia, an atlas, a magazine or newspaper article), write the title, author, and notes about each source.
- For online sources (websites), write the name, URL, and notes about each source.

Example

Online or Print   online

Name or Title   PA Pennsylvania

URL or Author   www.state.pa.us.model

Notes   lots of info about state history and things to do for fun

Source #1

Online or Print _____

Name or Title _____

URL or Author _____

Notes _____

Source #2

Online or Print _____

Name or Title _____

URL or Author _____

Notes _____

Source #3

Online or Print _____

Name or Title _____

URL or Author _____

Notes _____

Source #4

Online or Print _____

Name or Title _____

URL or Author _____

Notes _____

Source #5

Online or Print _____

Name or Title _____

URL or Author _____

Notes _____

Source #6

Online or Print _____

Name or Title _____

URL or Author _____

Notes _____

Source #7

Online or Print _____

Name or Title _____

URL or Author _____

Notes _____

Composition

Take Notes About Your Research Topic (A)

Take Notes

Follow the directions to take notes about your research topic.

1. Gather your completed sources form and the prepared index cards. If the cards still need to be labeled, **write the following labels** at the top of at least three cards each:
   - General Information
   - Location and Climate
   - Outdoor Activities
   - Popular Places to Visit
   - Interesting Facts

2. Return to a source you listed on your sources form and **read about your state**. As you read, look for information that relates to the labels on your note cards.

3. When you read something important, find the correct note card and **write down the key information**. Write information from just one source per card.

4. For each note card that you complete, **write down the number of the source you used** to find the information in case you need to return to it later. If it is a print source, write down chapter or page numbers, too.

5. **Continue to read and take notes** from all of your sources. Make more note cards when you need to. It is better to have too many notes than too few. Keep your note cards together in a safe place.

6. **Turn over this page** to see two sample note cards.

Note card for an online source

Outdoor Activities

- skiing and snowboarding in the Pocono Mountains
- hiking and camping
- swimming in pools and ponds
- polka dancing
- boating and fishing

Source # 1

Note card for a print source

Location and Climate

- Mid-Atlantic region
- PA bordered by NY, NJ, DE, MD, WV, and OH
- looks like a rectangle
- has lots of rivers

Source #6, pages 60 and 71

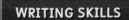

Organize Your Notes

Lesson Overview

🖥️ **【Online 】**		**15** minutes
Composition	Winnie Organizes Her Notes	
📑 **【Offline 】**		**30** minutes
Composition	Put Your Notes in Order	

【 Materials 】

Supplied
- *K¹² Language Arts Activity Book*, pp. WS 185–188

Also Needed
- students' completed note cards

Advance Preparation

Gather students' completed note cards.

Big Ideas

- Writers must be able to articulate a main idea and support it with appropriate details.
- Following a specific organizational structure is a useful tool for novice writers; however, writers require the freedom and flexibility to follow their ideas to completion.

[Online] ⑮ minutes

Students will work online **independently** to learn how to use their completed note cards and a form to organize the information they've gathered during their research. Help students locate the online activity.

Composition ··

Winnie Organizes Her Notes
By watching how Winnie transfers information from her note cards to a form, students will learn how to do the same to organize their own notes.

> **Objectives**
> • Sort evidence into provided categories.

[Offline] ㉚ minutes

Work **together** with students to complete the offline Composition activity.

Composition ··

Put Your Notes in Order
Students will complete a form designed to help them organize the information they gathered in their research. Have students gather their completed note cards. Turn to pages WS 185–188 in K^{12} *Language Arts Activity Book*.

1. Have students complete the Activity Book pages to organize the notes they took about the state they chose. Provide support as necessary.

2. Let students know that, in their research report, they probably won't use every note they took. Tell them to think about which details and facts are important to someone who wants to learn about the state. Only these details and facts should be included on the form.

> **Objectives**
> • Sort evidence into provided categories.

3. Emphasize to students the importance of keeping track of their sources on this organizing form.

TIP Keep students' completed form in a safe place so they can refer to it later.

Composition

Organize Your Notes

Put Your Notes in Order

Use your note cards to help you complete this form and organize the information you gathered about your research topic.

State you researched _____

Notes about general information

1. What general information about the state should people know?
   _____
   _____
   _____

2. Where you found your information
   _____
   _____
   _____

Notes about location, climate, and activities

1. What part of the United States best describes the state's location?
   _____

2. Which states border the state you chose?
   _____

WS 185

---

3. What is the weather like in the winter?
   _____

4. What outdoor activities could someone do in the winter?
   _____

5. What is the weather like in the summer?
   _____

6. What outdoor activities could someone do in the summer?
   _____

7. Where you found your information
   _____
   _____
   _____

Notes about popular places to visit

1. What are two popular places to visit in this state?
   _____
   _____

WS 186

---

2. Describe the first place.
   _____
   _____
   _____
   _____
   _____

3. Describe the second place.
   _____
   _____
   _____
   _____

4. Where you found your information
   _____
   _____
   _____

WS 187

Notes about other interesting facts

1. What are some interesting historical facts about the state?
   _____
   _____
   _____
   _____

2. What are some interesting facts about the state today?
   _____
   _____
   _____
   _____

3. Where you found your information
   _____
   _____
   _____
   _____

WS 188

Use an Outline

Lesson Overview

🖥️ **[Online]**		**15** minutes
Composition	Winnie Uses an Outline	
📄 **[Offline]**		**30** minutes
Composition	Outline Your Research Report	

[Materials]

Supplied
- *K¹² Language Arts Activity Book*, pp. WS 185–193

Advance Preparation

Gather completed pages WS 185–188 (Put Your Notes in Order) in *K¹² Language Arts Activity Book*.

Big Ideas

▸ Writers must be able to articulate a main idea and support it with appropriate details.

▸ Following a specific organizational structure is a useful tool for novice writers; however, writers require the freedom and flexibility to follow their ideas to completion.

[Online] 15 minutes

Students will work online **independently** to learn how to use the form on which they organized their notes to help them create an outline for their research report. Help students locate the online activity.

Composition ....

Winnie Uses an Outline
By watching Winnie use the form on which she organized her notes to help her create an outline for her research report, students will learn how to do the same as they create an outline for their report.

> ⭐ **Objectives**
> - Use an outline to organize information.

〔 Offline 〕 **30** minutes

Work **together** with students to complete the offline Composition activity.

Composition ....

Outline Your Research Report

Students will create an outline for their research report. Have them gather their Put Your Notes in Order form. Turn to pages WS 189–193 in *K¹² Language Arts Activity Book*.

⭐ **Objectives**
- Use an outline to organize information.

1. Have students complete the Activity Book pages to create an outline for a five-paragraph research report. Guide them to use the form on which they organized their notes to help them complete the outline. Provide support as necessary, pointing out to students that the outline does not need to be created with complete sentences or perfect grammar. The focus is on placing important ideas where they belong in the outline. Students may expand upon sections of the outline as necessary.

2. Encourage students to take some time to consider all that they have learned about their state and all the information that will be included in the three body paragraphs of the research report. Guide students to develop a main idea statement that tells what their research report will show about their state. Remind them that the main idea should be a general statement that will appear in the introduction to the report. They will support the main idea statement with facts and details in the body paragraphs. Make sure students know that they will also write the same main idea in different words in the conclusion.

TIP Keep students' completed outline in a safe place so they can refer to it later.

➲ **Learning Coach Check-In** How does the outline look? Review students' outline to make sure they've included all necessary, relevant information from their notes. If they've left out information, included irrelevant facts, or placed information in a section where it does not belong, help them revise their outline. A solid outline will be critical when students draft their report in later lessons.

Composition

Organize Your Notes
Put Your Notes in Order

Use your note cards to help you complete this form and organize the information you gathered about your research topic.

State you researched _____

Notes about general information

1. What general information about the state should people know?
   _____
   _____
   _____

2. Where you found your information
   _____
   _____
   _____

Notes about location, climate, and activities

1. What part of the United States best describes the state's location?
   _____

2. Which states border the state you chose?
   _____

---

3. What is the weather like in the winter?
   _____

4. What outdoor activities could someone do in the winter?
   _____

5. What is the weather like in the summer?
   _____

6. What outdoor activities could someone do in the summer?
   _____

7. Where you found your information
   _____

Notes about popular places to visit

1. What are two popular places to visit in this state?
   _____
   _____

---

2. Describe the first place.
   _____
   _____
   _____
   _____

3. Describe the second place.
   _____
   _____
   _____
   _____

4. Where you found your information
   _____
   _____
   _____

Notes about other interesting facts

1. What are some interesting historical facts about the state?
   _____
   _____
   _____

2. What are some interesting facts about the state today?
   _____
   _____
   _____

3. Where you found your information
   _____
   _____
   _____

Composition

Use an Outline
Outline Your Research Report

Use the notes you organized to create an outline for your research report.

Paragraph 1: Introduction

A. Main idea of research report _____
   _____

B. General information _____
   _____
   _____
   _____

Paragraph 2: Location and climate

A. Region of the United States and bordering states _____
   _____
   _____

B. Winter weather _____
   1. Clothing _____
   2. Outdoor activities _____
      _____

C. Summer weather _____
   1. Clothing _____
   2. Outdoor activities _____
      _____

Paragraph 3: Popular places to visit

A. Name of first place to visit _____
   1. Description _____
      _____
   2. Reason for being popular _____
      _____

B. Name of second place to visit _____
   1. Description _____
      _____
   2. Reason for being popular _____
      _____

Paragraph 4: Other interesting facts

A. Historical facts about the state _____
   _____
   _____
   _____

B. Current facts about the state _____
   _____
   _____
   _____

Paragraph 5: Conclusion

A. Short summary _____
   _____
   _____
   _____

B. Restatement of main idea _____
   _____

Unit Review

Lesson Overview

Online   **45** minutes

Unit Review	Agreement
More Practice	Agreement

Materials

Supplied
- *Grammar Reference Guide* Online Book (optional)

Keywords

antecedent – the noun or pronoun that a pronoun points back to

compound sentence – a sentence that has at least two independent parts

subject–verb agreement – the way a subject and verb match when both are singular or both are plural

Online   **45** minutes

Students will work online **independently** to review the grammar, usage, and mechanics skills learned in the unit. Help students locate the online activity.

Unit Review

Agreement

Students will review what they have learned about subject–verb agreement and pronoun–antecedent agreement for the Unit Checkpoint.

TIP A full list of objectives covered in the Unit Review can be found in the online lesson.

Objectives
- Complete a review of grammar, usage, and mechanics skills.

More Practice

Agreement

Go over students' results on the Unit Review and, if necessary, have students complete the appropriate review activities listed in the table online. Help students locate the activities. Provide support as needed.

TIP The time students need to complete this activity will vary. Set aside enough time for students to complete all review activities, if they need to do so.

Objectives
- Evaluate Unit Review results and choose activities for more practice.

Unit Checkpoint

<table>
<tr><td colspan="3">Lesson Overview</td></tr>
<tr><td colspan="2">【Online】</td><td>45 minutes</td></tr>
<tr><td>Unit Checkpoint</td><td colspan="2">Agreement</td></tr>
<tr><td colspan="2">【Offline】</td><td>varies</td></tr>
<tr><td>More Practice</td><td colspan="2">Agreement</td></tr>
</table>

【Materials】

Supplied

- *Grammar Reference Guide* Online Book (optional)
- Subject–Verb Agreement in Simple Sentences (optional printout)
- Subject–Verb Agreement in Compound Sentences (optional printout)
- Pronoun and Antecedent Agreement (A) (optional printout)
- Pronoun and Antecedent Agreement (B) (optional printout)

Keywords

antecedent – the noun or pronoun that a pronoun points back to

compound sentence – a sentence that has at least two independent parts

subject–verb agreement – the way a subject and verb match when both are singular or both are plural

[Online] ⓸⓹ minutes

Students will work online **independently** to complete the Unit Checkpoint. Help students locate the online checkpoint.

Unit Checkpoint

Agreement

Students will complete an online Unit Checkpoint about subject–verb agreement and agreement of pronouns and their antecedents. If necessary, read the directions to students.

TIP A full list of objectives covered in the Unit Checkpoint can be found in the online lesson.

> ★ **Objectives**
> • Complete a Unit Checkpoint on grammar, usage, and mechanics skills.

[Offline] varies

Work **together** with students to complete the offline More Practice activity.

More Practice

Agreement

Go over students' results on the Unit Checkpoint and, if necessary, print out and have them complete the appropriate practice pages listed in the table online. Students can complete all necessary pages now or, if more time is needed, they can spread them out over the next few days. They can also review the appropriate sections of the *Grammar Reference Guide* with you. If students scored less than 80 percent on the Unit Checkpoint, you may want them to retake the Checkpoint after completing the additional activity pages.

TIP The time students need to complete this activity will vary. Set aside enough time for students to complete some or all activity pages and to retake the Unit Checkpoint, if they need to do so. Students may retake the Unit Checkpoint immediately, but having them complete the practice pages and then retake it might be more effective.

> ★ **Objectives**
> • Evaluate Unit Checkpoint results and choose activities for more practice.

 Reward: When students score 80 percent or above on the Unit Checkpoint, add a sticker for this unit on the My Accomplishments chart.

More Practice
Improve Your Skills
Subject–Verb Agreement in Simple Sentences

Choose the answer.

1. Which verb correctly completes this sentence?

   The police officer _____ the lost dog.

   A. help   B. find   C. return   **D. rescues**

2. Which verb correctly completes this sentence?

   Snowflakes _____ on the pond.

   A. blows   B. falls   **C. melt**   D. lands

3. Which verb correctly completes this sentence?

   Michael and Dora _____ the fair.

   A. visit   B. _____   C. _____   D. likes

4. Which sentence is correct?
   A. Shiny silver coins shakes in his pocket.
   B. The shop on the corner sell cakes and pies.
   C. A loud bang in the street wake Jimmy.
   D. Soft evening breezes from the north cool the house.

5. Which sentence is correct?
   A. Sugary snacks and juice causes cavities.
   B. The long-haired princess in the story live in a tower.
   C. Jack and Emily take piano lessons.
   D. The curtain close at the end of the play.

LANGUAGE ARTS PURPLE   **WS 1**

More Practice
Improve Your Skills
Subject–Verb Agreement in Compound Sentences

Choose the answer.

1. Which verb correctly completes this sentence?

   The bus driver stands, and he _____ everyone to be quiet.

   A. tells   C. want
   B. ask   D. make

2. Which verb correctly completes this sentence?

   Five runners start the race, but only two people _____ it.

   A. stops   C. ends
   B. enjoys   **D. finish**

3. Which verbs can correctly complete this sentence?

   The trains _____ at the station, and the passengers _____ aboard.

   A. arrive, climb   C. arrive, climbs
   B. arrives, climbs   D. arrives, climb

4. Which sentence is correct?
   A. Alex makes lunch for Joe, but Joe shares with me.
   B. Alex make lunch for Joe, but Joe share with me.
   C. Alex make lunch for Joe, but Joe shares with me.
   D. Alex makes lunch for Joe, but Joe share with me.

LANGUAGE ARTS PURPLE   **WS 1**

---

5. Which sentence is correct?
   A. Both hotels offer cable TV, but only one serve breakfast.
   B. Both hotels offers cable TV, but only one serves breakfast.
   C. Both hotels offer cable TV, but only one serves breakfast.
   D. Both hotels offers cable TV, but only one serve breakfast.

WS 2   LANGUAGE ARTS PURPLE

More Practice
Improve Your Skills
Pronoun and Antecedent Agreement (A)

Choose the answer.

1. Which pronoun correctly completes this sentence?

   The prince takes off _____ crown.

   A. its   C. their
   B. his   D. her

2. Which pronoun correctly completes this sentence?

   Lisa had never been in a snowball fight, so _____ was excited.

   A. it   **C. she**
   B. he   D. him

3. Which pronoun correctly completes this sentence?

   My alarm clock beeped until I finally got up and turned _____ off.

   A. it   C. he
   B. her   D. him

4. Which pronoun correctly completes this sentence?

   The reptile house at the zoo is neat, but _____ big snakes can scare younger children.

   A. him   C. her
   B. his   **D. its**

LANGUAGE ARTS PURPLE   **WS 1**

---

5. Which pronoun correctly completes this sentence?

   Ms. Turner spent _____ Sunday at the mall.

   A. his   C. my
   B. your   **D. her**

WS 2   LANGUAGE ARTS PURPLE

More Practice
Improve Your Skills
Pronoun and Antecedent Agreement (B)

Choose the answer.

1. Which pronoun correctly completes this sentence?

   I will brush _____ teeth before bed.

   A. they   **C. my**
   B. our   D. their

2. Which pronoun correctly completes this sentence?

   Sweet potatoes and yams look alike, but _____ are not the same food.

   A. they   C. she
   B. it   D. he

3. Which pronoun correctly completes this sentence?

   You and Joanna can help _____ to a glass of water.

   A. herself   C. itself
   B. yourselves   D. himself

4. Which pronoun correctly completes this sentence?

   The rivers twist and turn, but _____ water doesn't flow uphill.

   A. his   **C. their**
   B. its   D. her

LANGUAGE ARTS PURPLE   **WS 1**

---

5. Which pronoun correctly completes this sentence?

   Bobby twisted _____ ankle playing soccer.

   A. our   C. their
   B. his   D. them

WS 2   LANGUAGE ARTS PURPLE

UNIT OVERVIEW Adjectives and Write a Research Report

Unit Focus

In the grammar part of the unit, students will learn about adjectives. They will

- Learn that adjectives are words that are used to describe someone or something.
- Practice recognizing and using adjectives correctly.
- Replace weak adjectives with strong adjectives to make sentences more vivid and memorable.
- Learn about articles and how they function.
- Learn what demonstrative and limiting adjectives are and practice using both.
- Form and use adjectives to make comparisons.

In the composition part of the unit, students will write a research report. They will

- Use their journal to freewrite.
- Use the outline they completed in the Agreement and Plan a Research Report unit to guide them as they draft a report that contains an introduction, multiple body paragraphs, and a conclusion.
- Revise and proofread their research report.
- Make a final clean copy of their research report.

Unit Plan		**〖Online〗**	**〖Offline〗**
Lesson 1	Descriptive Adjectives and Journal Entry	25 minutes	20 minutes
Lesson 2	Strong Adjectives and Start Your Research Report Draft	25 minutes	20 minutes
Lesson 3	Articles and Work on Your Research Report Draft	25 minutes	20 minutes
Lesson 4	Work on Your Research Report Draft	5 minutes	40 minutes
Lesson 5	Complete Your Research Report Draft	20 minutes	25 minutes
Lesson 6	Other Adjectives	30 minutes	15 minutes
Lesson 7	Compare with Adjectives and Revise Your Research Report (A)	25 minutes	20 minutes
Lesson 8	Compare with Adjectives and Revise Your Research Report (B)	25 minutes	20 minutes
Lesson 9	Proofread Your Research Report	20 minutes	25 minutes
Lesson 10	Unit Review and Publish Your Research Report	20 minutes	25 minutes
Lesson 11	Unit Checkpoint and Publish Your Research Report	20 minutes	25 minutes

Descriptive Adjectives and Journal Entry

Lesson Overview

💻 **【Online】**		**25** minutes
GUM (Grammar, Usage, and Mechanics)	Descriptive Adjectives	
📄 **【Offline】**		**20** minutes
Composition	Journal: Write About the Topic of Your Research Report	
Beyond the Lesson	➕ OPTIONAL: Journal: Freewrite on a Topic	

【Materials】

Supplied

- K⁷ My Journal, pp. 38–39
- Grammar Reference Guide Online Book (optional)

Keywords

adjective – a word that describes a noun or a pronoun

Advance Preparation

To prepare for the GUM portion of this lesson, review Adjectives (Descriptive Adjectives) in the *Grammar Reference Guide* (linked in the online lesson) to familiarize yourself with the topic.

Big Ideas

- ► Journal writing is a form of freewriting. It is an opportunity to get ideas on paper without regard for the correctness of the language or the format of a piece of writing.
- ► To improve, writers require frequent practice.
- ► The use of descriptive adjectives can turn an ordinary piece of writing into one that enables the audience to form clear mental pictures of a scene.

 **25 minutes**

Students will work online **independently** to complete an activity on recognizing and using descriptive adjectives. Help students locate the online activity.

GUM (Grammar, Usage, and Mechanics)

Descriptive Adjectives
Students will learn what descriptive adjectives are and how adjectives can improve writing to make a text more interesting. They will then practice identifying and using descriptive adjectives in sentences.

> **Objectives**
> - Recognize descriptive words known as adjectives.
> - Recognize that adjectives describe nouns.
> - Use adjectives to describe someone or something.

 **20 minutes**

Work **together** with students to complete the offline Composition and Beyond the Lesson activities.

Composition

Journal: Write About the Topic of Your Research Report
Students will respond to a journal prompt by writing about the topic of their research report. Gather *K¹² My Journal* and have students turn to pages 38 and 39.

1. Tell students they are going to write in their journal about the topic of their research report. To help students think of ways to explain and describe their topic, ask them to think about their answers to the following questions.

   ▶ What state are you writing about? What are some important pieces of information that you've learned about this state? What is the one thing that you found most interesting about your state? Was there anything that you learned that surprised you? What was it?

   ▶ How would you describe your state to someone who knows very little about it? What words would you use to make others understand why your state is special, or different, or worth learning about?

> **Objectives**
> - Respond to a journal prompt.
> - Freewrite about a topic.

2. Have students respond to the prompt in their journal. Encourage them to write in complete sentences, although it is not a requirement when they are freewriting in their journal.

TIP Students should write for about 20 minutes. Freewriting allows students to use their imagination to write what they want without worrying about being graded, so encourage them to keep writing for the entire time. If students have trouble writing for 20 minutes, use the prompting questions in Step 1 or have them list ideas or words. If they want to keep writing beyond the suggested time limit, praise them for their enthusiasm and offer to let them complete their entry later in the day as a reward.

Research Report Topic   Date _____

What is the topic of your research report?
What adjectives describe the topic?

_____

_____

_____

_____

_____

_____

_____

_____

_____

_____

_____

_____

38

Beyond the Lesson

OPTIONAL: Journal: Freewrite on a Topic

This activity is OPTIONAL. It is intended for students who have extra time and would benefit from extra practice. Feel free to skip this activity. Gather *K¹² My Journal*.

1. Have students either respond to a prompt in Thoughts and Experiences (pages 50–93) or write about their own topic on the next available page in Ideas (pages 96–139).

2. Encourage students to explore their thoughts and write as much as they want. There are no rules. If students wish, ideas can be fleshed out into a more developed composition at a later time.

TIP Studies show that students who write more frequently become better writers.

Objectives
- Respond to a journal prompt.
- Freewrite about a topic.

Strong Adjectives and Start Your Research Report Draft

Lesson Overview

💻 [Online] ⏱ 25 minutes

Skills Update	Descriptive Adjectives
GUM (Grammar, Usage, and Mechanics)	Strong Adjectives
Composition	Winnie Drafts Her Introduction

📄 [Offline] ⏱ 20 minutes

Composition	Write Your Draft

[Materials]

Supplied

- *K¹² Language Arts Activity Book*, pp. WS 169–171, 189–193, 195–200
- *Grammar Reference Guide* Online Book (optional)
- drafting page (optional printout)

Keywords

adjective – a word that describes a noun or a pronoun

research report – a type of essay based mainly on the author's research

Advance Preparation

To prepare for the GUM portion of this lesson, review Adjectives (Descriptive Adjectives) in the *Grammar Reference Guide* (linked in the online lesson) to familiarize yourself with the topic. In this lesson, students continue to accumulate documents they will need as they work on their research report. Add these documents to those you have already collected. Gather pages WS 169–171 (Model Research Report) and 189–193 (Outline Your Research Report, students' completed outline) in *K¹² Language Arts Activity Book*.

Big Ideas

- ▸ Replacing weak adjectives with strong adjectives makes writing precise and specific.
- ▸ To write a strong research report, one should be able to follow an interest to its conclusion.
- ▸ Writers must be able to articulate a main idea and support it with appropriate details.
- ▸ Writing varies by purpose and audience. The specific reason for writing and the writer's intended readers (audience) determine the correct form and language to use.

⟦Online⟧ 25 minutes

Students will work online to review descriptive adjectives, to learn about using strong adjectives, and to examine how to use an outline to help them begin to draft a research report. Help students locate the online activities.

Skills Update ···

Descriptive Adjectives

Students will review how to identify and use descriptive adjectives by completing Skills Update exercises. Sit with students as they do this activity and note if they answer correctly.

⟳ **Learning Coach Check-In** How did students do on the Skills Update?

▸ **All answers correct:** Great! Skip the review screen and go on to the next activity.

▸ **Any answers incorrect:** Take a few minutes to review descriptive adjectives now. Use the link on the screen after the Skills Update to take another look at the online activity or review Adjectives (Descriptive Adjectives) in the *Grammar Reference Guide* together.

TIP This activity will require extra time if students need to review descriptive adjectives. Take the extra 5–10 minutes to review now because new skills build on what students have already learned.

> **Objectives**
> - Recognize descriptive words known as adjectives.
> - Recognize that adjectives describe nouns.
> - Use adjectives to describe someone or something.

GUM (Grammar, Usage, and Mechanics) ·······························

Strong Adjectives

Students will learn that strong adjectives make sentences more vivid and interesting than bland adjectives. They will then practice identifying and using strong adjectives and replacing bland adjectives with strong ones.

> **Objectives**
> - Use adjectives to describe someone or something.
> - Replace ordinary adjectives with specific adjectives.

Composition ···

Winnie Drafts Her Introduction

By exploring how Winnie uses a completed outline to help draft the introduction to her research report, students will learn how to begin drafting their own research report.

> **Objectives**
> - Write a research report.
> - Write an introduction to a research report.

〔 Offline 〕 🕐 20 minutes

Work **together** with students to complete the offline Composition activity.

Composition ··

Write Your Draft

Students will begin to draft their research report. Gather the model research report and students' completed outline. Turn to pages WS 195–200 in *K¹² Language Arts Activity Book*.

1. Have students use their outline and follow the directions on the drafting pages to begin writing their research report. Provide support as necessary, encouraging students to write in complete sentences.

2. Guide students to begin their introduction with a hook; name their topic early in the first paragraph; include background, or general, information; and end the introduction with a statement of the main idea of the report. Encourage students to refer to Winnie's research report as needed.

TIP Keep the drafting pages in a safe place so students can return to them later as they continue to write.

> **Objectives**
> - Write a research report.
> - Write an introduction to a research report.

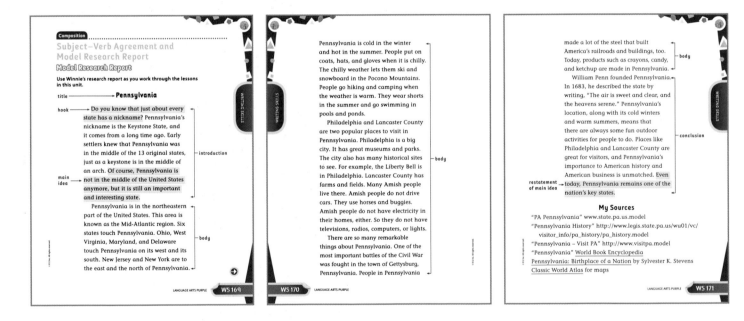

Composition

Use an Outline
Outline Your Research Report

Use the notes you organized to create an outline for your research report.

Paragraph 1: Introduction

A. Main idea of research report _____

_____

B. General information _____

_____

_____

_____

_____

Paragraph 2: Location and climate

A. Region of the United States and bordering states _____

_____

_____

B. Winter weather _____

1. Clothing _____

2. Outdoor activities _____

_____

C. Summer weather _____

1. Clothing _____

2. Outdoor activities _____

_____

_____

Paragraph 3: Popular places to visit

A. Name of first place to visit _____

1. Description _____

_____

_____

2. Reason for being popular _____

_____

_____

B. Name of second place to visit _____

1. Description _____

_____

_____

2. Reason for being popular _____

_____

_____

Paragraph 4: Other interesting facts

A. Historical facts about the state _____

_____

_____

_____

B. Current facts about the state _____

_____

_____

_____

Paragraph 5: Conclusion

A. Short summary _____

_____

_____

_____

_____

B. Restatement of main idea _____

_____

_____

Composition

Strong Adjectives and Start Your Research Report Draft
Write Your Draft

Read the assignment. Use your outline to help you write the first draft of your research report. Write only on the white rows. You will use the purple rows when you revise later.

> Write a research report on the state that you chose.
> - Begin with an introduction. It should name the topic and state the main idea.
> - Include three body paragraphs. Each should focus on one important part of the topic.
> - End with a conclusion. It should include a summary of the report's facts and details and restate the main idea in different words.
> - List the sources where you found the information for the report.

Start here ▸

Articles and Work on Your Research Report Draft

Lesson Overview

[Online]   25 minutes

Skills Update	Strong Adjectives
GUM (Grammar, Usage, and Mechanics)	Articles
Composition	Winnie Drafts Her Body Paragraphs

[Offline]   20 minutes

Composition	Write Your Draft

[Materials]

Supplied

- *K¹² Language Arts Activity Book*, pp. WS 169–171, 189–193, 195–200
- *Grammar Reference Guide* Online Book (optional)
- drafting page (optional printout)

Keywords

article – the adjective *a*, *an*, or *the*

research report – a type of essay based mainly on the author's research

transition – a word or phrase that connects ideas

Advance Preparation

To prepare for the GUM portion of this lesson, review Adjectives (Articles) in the *Grammar Reference Guide* (linked in the online lesson) to familiarize yourself with the topic. Gather pages WS 169–171 (Model Research Report), 189–193 (Outline Your Research Report, students' completed outline), and 195–200 (Write Your Draft, students' partially completed research report draft) in *K¹² Language Arts Activity Book*.

Big Ideas

- ▶ To write a strong research report, one should be able to follow an interest to its conclusion.
- ▶ Writers must be able to articulate a main idea and support it with appropriate details.
- ▶ Writing varies by purpose and audience. The specific reason for writing and the writer's intended readers (audience) determine the correct form and language to use.

[Online] 25 minutes

Students will work online to review strong adjectives, to learn about using articles, and to examine how to use an outline to help them draft the body paragraphs of a research report. Help students locate the online activities.

Skills Update

Strong Adjectives

Students will review how to identify and use strong adjectives by completing Skills Update exercises. Sit with students as they do this activity and note if they answer correctly.

⊃ **Learning Coach Check-In** How did students do on the Skills Update?

▸ **All answers correct:** Great! Skip the review screen and go on to the next activity.

▸ **Any answers incorrect:** Take a few minutes to review strong adjectives now. Use the link on the screen after the Skills Update to take another look at the online activity or review Adjectives (Descriptive Adjectives) in the *Grammar Reference Guide* together.

TIP This activity will require extra time if students need to review strong adjectives. Take the extra 5–10 minutes to review now because new skills build on what students have already learned.

Objectives
- Use adjectives to describe someone or something.
- Replace ordinary adjectives with specific adjectives.

GUM (Grammar, Usage, and Mechanics)

Articles

Students will learn what articles are and how to use them correctly in sentences. They will then practice choosing the correct articles to use.

Objectives
- Use *the*, *a*, and *an* correctly.

Composition

Winnie Drafts Her Body Paragraphs

By exploring how Winnie uses a completed outline to help her draft the body paragraphs of her research report, students will learn how to draft the body paragraphs for their research report.

Objectives
- Write a research report.
- Write a new paragraph for each new idea.
- Develop the topic with facts, definitions, and details.
- Group related information together.
- Use linking words and phrases to connect ideas within categories of information.

[Offline] 20 minutes

Work **together** with students to complete the offline Composition activity.

Composition ....

Write Your Draft

Students will continue to draft their research report by beginning to write their body paragraphs. Gather the model research report, students' completed outline, and students' partially completed draft.

1. Have students use their outline to continue writing their research report by focusing on the body paragraphs. Provide support as necessary, encouraging students to write in complete sentences.

2. Guide students to maintain the order of the outline in their draft, keep related ideas and information together, leave out details that do not support the main idea of the report, and use transitions appropriately. Encourage students to refer to Winnie's research report as needed.

TIP Keep the drafting pages in a safe place so students can return to them later as they continue to write.

Objectives

- Write a research report.
- Write a new paragraph for each new idea.
- Develop a topic with facts, definitions, and details.
- Group related information together.
- Use linking words and phrases to connect ideas within categories of information.

Composition

Use an Outline
Outline Your Research Report

Use the notes you organized to create an outline for your research report.

Paragraph 1: Introduction

A. Main idea of research report _____

_____

B. General information _____

_____

_____

_____

_____

Paragraph 2: Location and climate

A. Region of the United States and bordering states _____

_____

_____

B. Winter weather _____

1. Clothing _____

2. Outdoor activities _____

_____

C. Summer weather _____

1. Clothing _____

2. Outdoor activities _____

_____

_____

Paragraph 3: Popular places to visit

A. Name of first place to visit _____

1. Description _____

_____

2. Reason for being popular _____

_____

B. Name of second place to visit _____

1. Description _____

_____

2. Reason for being popular _____

_____

Paragraph 4: Other interesting facts

A. Historical facts about the state _____

_____

_____

_____

B. Current facts about the state _____

_____

_____

_____

Paragraph 5: Conclusion

A. Short summary _____

_____

_____

_____

_____

B. Restatement of main idea _____

_____

_____

Composition

Strong Adjectives and Start Your Research Report Draft
Write Your Draft

Read the assignment. Use your outline to help you write the first draft of your research report. Write only on the white rows. You will use the purple rows when you revise later.

> Write a research report on the state that you chose.
> * Begin with an introduction. It should name the topic and state the main idea.
> * Include three body paragraphs. Each should focus on one important part of the topic.
> * End with a conclusion. It should include a summary of the report's facts and details and restate the main idea in different words.
> * List the sources where you found the information for the report.

_____

Start here ►

_____

_____

_____

Work on Your Research Report Draft

Lesson Overview

🖥 **[Online]**		**5** minutes
Skills Update	Articles	

📄 **[Offline]**		**40** minutes
Composition	Write Your Draft	

Materials

Supplied

- *K¹² Language Arts Activity Book,* pp. WS 169–171, 189–193, 195–200
- *Grammar Reference Guide* Online Book (optional)
- drafting page (optional printout)

Keywords

research report – a type of essay based mainly on the author's research

transition – a word or phrase that connects ideas

Advance Preparation

Gather pages WS 169–171 (Model Research Report), 189–193 (Outline Your Research Report, students' completed outline), and 195–200 (Write Your Draft, students' partially completed research report draft) in *K¹² Language Arts Activity Book.*

Big Ideas

- To write a strong research report, one should be able to follow an interest to its conclusion.
- Writers must be able to articulate a main idea and support it with appropriate details.
- Writing varies by purpose and audience. The specific reason for writing and the writer's intended readers (audience) determine the correct form and language to use.

[Online] 5 minutes

Students will work online to review articles. Help students locate the online activity.

Skills Update ....

Articles

Students will review how to identify and use articles by completing Skills Update exercises. Sit with students as they do this activity and note if they answer correctly.

⟳ **Learning Coach Check-In** How did students do on the Skills Update?

> ▸ **All answers correct:** Great! Skip the review screen and go on to the next activity.
>
> ▸ **Any answers incorrect:** Take a few minutes to review articles now. Use the link on the screen after the Skills Update to take another look at the online activity or review Adjectives (Articles) in the *Grammar Reference Guide* together.

(TIP) This activity will require extra time if students need to review articles. Take the extra 5–10 minutes to review now because new skills build on what students have already learned.

> **Objectives**
> • Use *the*, *a*, and *an* correctly.

[Offline] 40 minutes

Work **together** with students to complete the offline Composition activity.

Composition ....

Write Your Draft

Students will continue to draft their research report by writing the body paragraphs. Gather the model research report, students' completed outline, and students' partially completed draft.

1. Have students use their outline to continue writing their research report by focusing on the body paragraphs. Provide support as necessary, encouraging students to write in complete sentences.

2. Guide students to maintain the order of the outline in their draft, keep related ideas and information together, leave out details that do not support the main idea of the report, and use transitions appropriately. Encourage students to refer to Winnie's research report as needed.

3. Encourage students to do their best to complete the three body paragraphs today.

(TIP) Keep the drafting pages in a safe place so students can return to them later as they continue to write.

> **Objectives**
> • Write a research report.
> • Write a new paragraph for each new idea.
> • Develop a topic with facts, definitions, and details.
> • Group related information together.
> • Use linking words and phrases to connect ideas within categories of information.

Composition

Subject–Verb Agreement and Model Research Report

Model Research Report

Use Winnie's research report as you work through the lessons in this unit.

title ──────► **Pennsylvania**

hook ──────► Do you know that just about every state has a nickname? Pennsylvania's nickname is the Keystone State, and it comes from a long time ago. Early settlers knew that Pennsylvania was in the middle of the 13 original states, just as a keystone is in the middle of an arch. Of course, Pennsylvania is ── introduction

main idea ──► not in the middle of the United States anymore, but it is still an important and interesting state.

Pennsylvania is in the northeastern part of the United States. This area is known as the Mid-Atlantic region. Six states touch Pennsylvania. Ohio, West Virginia, Maryland, and Delaware touch Pennsylvania on its west and its south. New Jersey and New York are to the east and the north of Pennsylvania. ── body

---

Pennsylvania is cold in the winter and hot in the summer. People put on coats, hats, and gloves when it is chilly. The chilly weather lets them ski and snowboard in the Pocono Mountains. People go hiking and camping when the weather is warm. They wear shorts in the summer and go swimming in pools and ponds.

Philadelphia and Lancaster County are two popular places to visit in Pennsylvania. Philadelphia is a big city. It has great museums and parks. The city also has many historical sites to see. For example, the Liberty Bell is in Philadelphia. Lancaster County has farms and fields. Many Amish people live there. Amish people do not drive cars. They use horses and buggies. Amish people do not have electricity in their homes, either. So they do not have televisions, radios, computers, or lights. ── body

There are so many remarkable things about Pennsylvania. One of the most important battles of the Civil War was fought in the town of Gettysburg, Pennsylvania. People in Pennsylvania

---

made a lot of the steel that built America's railroads and buildings, too. Today, products such as crayons, candy, and ketchup are made in Pennsylvania. ── body

William Penn founded Pennsylvania. In 1683, he described the state by writing, "The air is sweet and clear, and the heavens serene." Pennsylvania's location, along with its cold winters and warm summers, means that there are always some fun outdoor activities for people to do. Places like Philadelphia and Lancaster County are great for visitors, and Pennsylvania's importance to American history and American business is unmatched. Even ── conclusion

restatement of main idea ──► today, Pennsylvania remains one of the nation's key states.

My Sources

"PA Pennsylvania" www.state.pa.us.model
"Pennsylvania History" http://www.legis.state.pa.us/wu01/vc/visitor_info/pa_history/pa_history.model
"Pennsylvania – Visit PA" http://www.visitpa.model
"Pennsylvania" World Book Encyclopedia
Pennsylvania: Birthplace of a Nation by Sylvester K. Stevens
Classic World Atlas for maps

Composition

Use an Outline

Outline Your Research Report

Use the notes you organized to create an outline for your research report.

Paragraph 1: Introduction

A. Main idea of research report _____

B. General information _____
_____
_____
_____
_____
_____

Paragraph 2: Location and climate

A. Region of the United States and bordering states _____
_____
_____
_____

B. Winter weather _____

  1. Clothing _____

  2. Outdoor activities _____

C. Summer weather _____

  1. Clothing _____

  2. Outdoor activities _____
_____
_____

Paragraph 3: Popular places to visit

A. Name of first place to visit _____

  1. Description _____
_____

  2. Reason for being popular _____
_____

B. Name of second place to visit _____

  1. Description _____
_____

  2. Reason for being popular _____
_____

Paragraph 4: Other interesting facts

A. Historical facts about the state _____
_____
_____
_____

B. Current facts about the state _____
_____
_____
_____

Paragraph 5: Conclusion

A. Short summary _____
_____
_____
_____

B. Restatement of main idea _____
_____

Composition

Strong Adjectives and Start Your Research Report Draft

Write Your Draft

Read the assignment. Use your outline to help you write the first draft of your research report. Write only on the white rows. You will use the purple rows when you revise later.

> Write a research report on the state that you chose.
> - Begin with an introduction. It should name the topic and state the main idea.
> - Include three body paragraphs. Each should focus on one important part of the topic.
> - End with a conclusion. It should include a summary of the report's facts and details and restate the main idea in different words.
> - List the sources where you found the information for the report.

Start here ▶

Complete Your Research Report Draft

Lesson Overview

🖥 **[Online]**   **20** minutes

Composition	Winnie Drafts Her Conclusion

📃 **[Offline]**   **25** minutes

Composition	Write Your Draft
Peer Interaction	⊕ OPTIONAL: Tell Me About My Research Report

[Materials]

Supplied

- *K¹² Language Arts Activity Book*, pp. WS 169–171, 189–193, 195–200
- Research Report: Feedback Sheet (printout)
- drafting page (optional printout)

Keywords

research report – a type of essay based mainly on the author's research

transition – a word or phrase that connects ideas

Advance Preparation

Gather pages WS 169–171 (Model Research Report), 189–193 (Outline Your Research Report, students' completed outline), and 195–200 (Write Your Draft, students' partially completed research report draft) in *K¹² Language Arts Activity Book*. Print the Research Report: Feedback Sheet from the online lesson.

Big Ideas

- To write a strong research report, one should be able to follow an interest to its conclusion.
- Writers must be able to articulate a main idea and support it with appropriate details.
- Writing varies by purpose and audience. The specific reason for writing and the writer's intended readers (audience) determine the correct form and language to use.

 **20 minutes**

Students will work online **independently** to learn how to draft a conclusion to a research report. Help students locate the online activity. Note that this lesson does not contain any new Grammar, Usage, and Mechanics activities so that students can concentrate on completing their draft.

Composition ....

Winnie Drafts Her Conclusion

By watching how Winnie drafts the conclusion to her research report, students will learn how to draft the conclusion to their own report.

Objectives
- Write a research report.
- Write a new paragraph for each new idea.
- Develop a topic with facts, definitions, and details.
- Group related information together.
- Use linking words and phrases to connect ideas within categories of information.
- Provide a concluding statement or section.

 **25 minutes**

Work **together** with students to complete the offline Composition activity.

Composition ....

Write Your Draft

Students will continue to draft their research report by writing their conclusion. If students have not yet finished drafting their body paragraphs, have them complete that section of their report before drafting their conclusion. Gather the model research report, students' completed outline, and students' partially completed draft.

1. Have students use their outline and follow the directions on the drafting pages to continue writing their research report by focusing on the conclusion. Provide support as necessary, encouraging students to write in complete sentences.

Objectives
- Write a research report.
- Write a new paragraph for each new idea.
- Develop a topic with facts, definitions, and details.
- Group related information together.
- Use linking words and phrases to connect ideas within categories of information.
- Provide a concluding statement or section.

2. Guide students to use transitions appropriately, sum up the most important points from the body of the report in order, and conclude their report with a restatement of the main idea. Encourage students to refer to Winnie's research report as needed.

3. Encourage students to do their best to complete their research report draft today.

   ⮌ **Learning Coach Check-In** When students have finished their draft, read and review it using the Research Report: Feedback Sheet, but do not go over the feedback sheet with students now. The notes you take on this sheet will guide your feedback to students as they revise their draft in a later lesson. Keep the feedback sheet in a safe place until students are ready to revise their draft.

   TIP Keep students' drafting pages in a safe place so they can refer to them later.

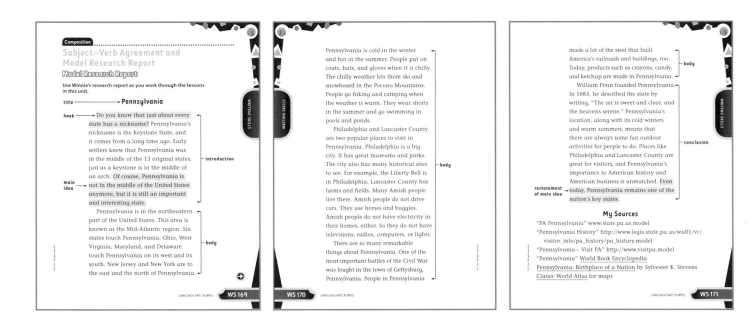

Composition

Subject–Verb Agreement and Model Research Report

Model Research Report

Use Winnie's research report as you work through the lessons in this unit.

title ⟶ **Pennsylvania**

hook ⟶ Do you know that just about every state has a nickname? Pennsylvania's nickname is the Keystone State, and it comes from a long time ago. Early settlers knew that Pennsylvania was in the middle of the 13 original states, just as a keystone is in the middle of an arch. Of course, Pennsylvania is | introduction

main idea ⟶ not in the middle of the United States anymore, but it is still an important and interesting state.

Pennsylvania is in the northeastern part of the United States. This area is known as the Mid-Atlantic region. Six states touch Pennsylvania. Ohio, West Virginia, Maryland, and Delaware touch Pennsylvania on its west and its south. New Jersey and New York are to the east and the north of Pennsylvania. | body

WS 169 LANGUAGE ARTS PURPLE

WS 170 LANGUAGE ARTS PURPLE

Pennsylvania is cold in the winter and hot in the summer. People put on coats, hats, and gloves when it is chilly. The chilly weather lets them ski and snowboard in the Pocono Mountains. People go hiking and camping when the weather is warm. They wear shorts in the summer and go swimming in pools and ponds.

Philadelphia and Lancaster County are two popular places to visit in Pennsylvania. Philadelphia is a big city. It has great museums and parks. The city also has many historical sites to see. For example, the Liberty Bell is in Philadelphia. Lancaster County has farms and fields. Many Amish people live there. Amish people do not drive cars. They use horses and buggies. Amish people do not have electricity in their homes, either. So they do not have televisions, radios, computers, or lights. | body

There are so many remarkable things about Pennsylvania. One of the most important battles of the Civil War was fought in the town of Gettysburg, Pennsylvania. People in Pennsylvania

made a lot of the steel that built America's railroads and buildings, too. Today, products such as crayons, candy, and ketchup are made in Pennsylvania. | body

William Penn founded Pennsylvania. In 1683, he described the state by writing, "The air is sweet and clear, and the heavens serene." Pennsylvania's location, along with its cold winters and warm summers, means that there are always some fun outdoor activities for people to do. Places like Philadelphia and Lancaster County are great for visitors, and Pennsylvania's importance to American history and American business is unmatched. Even | conclusion

restatement of main idea ⟶ today, Pennsylvania remains one of the nation's key states.

My Sources

"PA Pennsylvania" www.state.pa.us.model
"Pennsylvania History" http://www.legis.state.pa.us/wu01/vc/visitor_info/pa_history/pa_history.model
"Pennsylvania – Visit PA" http://www.visitpa.model
"Pennsylvania" World Book Encyclopedia
Pennsylvania: Birthplace of a Nation by Sylvester K. Stevens
Classic World Atlas for maps

LANGUAGE ARTS PURPLE **WS 171**

Composition

Use an Outline
Outline Your Research Report

Use the notes you organized to create an outline for your research report.

Paragraph 1: Introduction

A. Main idea of research report _____

_____

B. General information _____

_____

_____

_____

Paragraph 2: Location and climate

A. Region of the United States and bordering states _____

_____

_____

B. Winter weather

1. Clothing _____

2. Outdoor activities _____

C. Summer weather

1. Clothing _____

2. Outdoor activities _____

_____

Paragraph 3: Popular places to visit

A. Name of first place to visit _____

1. Description _____

_____

2. Reason for being popular _____

B. Name of second place to visit _____

1. Description _____

_____

2. Reason for being popular _____

_____

Paragraph 4: Other interesting facts

A. Historical facts about the state _____

_____

_____

B. Current facts about the state _____

_____

_____

_____

Paragraph 5: Conclusion

A. Short summary _____

_____

_____

_____

_____

B. Restatement of main idea _____

_____

_____

Composition

Strong Adjectives and Start Your Research Report Draft
Write Your Draft

Read the assignment. Use your outline to help you write the first draft of your research report. Write only on the white rows. You will use the purple rows when you revise later.

Write a research report on the state that you chose.

- Begin with an introduction. It should name the topic and state the main idea.
- Include three body paragraphs. Each should focus on one important part of the topic.
- End with a conclusion. It should include a summary of the report's facts and details and restate the main idea in different words.
- List the sources where you found the information for the report.

Start here ▶

Peer Interaction

⊕ OPTIONAL: Tell Me About My Research Report

This activity is OPTIONAL. It is intended for students who have extra time and would benefit from extra practice. Feel free to skip this activity.

Students can benefit from exchanging research reports with another student. Each writer should receive feedback. To complete this optional activity, turn to pages WS 201 and 202 in *K¹² Language Arts Activity Book*. (Additional copies of the Peer Interaction form can be printed from the online lesson.)

1. Have students exchange drafts with other students.

2. Have students use the Activity Book pages to provide others with feedback about their writing.

TIP In the upcoming revising lesson, students may use the feedback provided from other students to improve their research report.

Objectives

- Use guidance from adults and peers to revise writing.
- Collaborate with peers on writing projects.

Peer Interaction

Complete Your Research Report Draft

Tell Me About My Research Report

Have another person read your research report and answer the questions. **Answers will vary.**

1. Which state is the research report about?

2. What is the main idea of the report?

3. Are the main idea and some general background facts in the introduction?

4. What is one fact or detail about the state's location and climate? Is it in the first body paragraph? If not, where is it?

5. What is one fact or detail about places to visit? Is it in the second body paragraph? If not, where is it?

6. What is an interesting historical or current fact about the state? Is it in the third body paragraph? If not, where is it?

7. Does the student restate the main idea of the report in the conclusion?

WS 201   LANGUAGE ARTS PURPLE

WS 202   LANGUAGE ARTS PURPLE

Other Adjectives

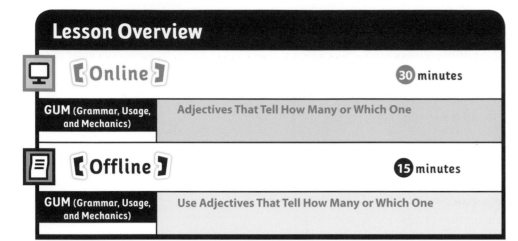

Lesson Overview

🖥	**[Online]**	**30** minutes
GUM (Grammar, Usage, and Mechanics)	Adjectives That Tell How Many or Which One	

📄	**[Offline]**	**15** minutes
GUM (Grammar, Usage, and Mechanics)	Use Adjectives That Tell How Many or Which One	

[Materials]

Supplied
- *K¹² Language Arts Activity Book,* pp. WS 203–204
- *Grammar Reference Guide* Online Book (optional)
- Research Report: Feedback Sheet (printout)

Advance Preparation

To prepare for the GUM portion of this lesson, review Adjectives (Limiting Adjectives; Demonstrative Adjectives) in the *Grammar Reference Guide* (linked in the online lesson) to familiarize yourself with the topic. If you have not already completed the Research Report: Feedback Sheet, do so during this lesson while students work independently. You will need to share this form with students in the next lesson.

 **[Online]** **30** minutes

Students will work online **independently** to learn about limiting adjectives and demonstrative adjectives. Help students locate the online activity.

GUM (Grammar, Usage, and Mechanics) ....

Adjectives That Tell How Many or Which One
Students will learn about limiting adjectives and demonstrative adjectives. Limiting adjectives, such as *seven, two, few,* and *several,* describe nouns and pronouns by telling how many people, places, things, or ideas there are. Demonstrative pronouns—*this, that, these,* and *those*—describe nouns by telling which ones a writer or speaker is referring to. However, we will not be using the terms *limiting adjectives* and *demonstrative adjectives* with students.

> ⭐ **Objectives**
> - Use limiting adjectives.
> - Use *this, that, these,* and *those.*

[Offline] 🕐 15 minutes

Work **together** with students to complete the offline GUM activity.

GUM (Grammar, Usage, and Mechanics) ●●

Use Adjectives That Tell How Many or Which One

Students will demonstrate their understanding of limiting and demonstrative adjectives by answering several questions about them. Turn to pages WS 203 and 204 in *K¹² Language Arts Activity Book*.

1. Have students complete the Activity Book pages.

2. As necessary, explain to students that adjectives that tell how many must agree in number with the noun that they are describing. For instance, the correct answer to the first question is *one* because the noun *card* is singular.

3. As necessary, explain to students that adjectives that tell which one must agree in number with the noun that they are describing. For instance, the correct answer to the seventh question is *those* because the noun *bowls* is plural. Also remind students that *this* and *these* usually refer to objects that are nearby, while *that* and *those* refer to objects that are farther away. In many cases, *this/that* and *these/those* are used in the same sentences to distinguish between objects or groups of objects based on their proximity to the speaker.

> **⭐ Objectives**
> - Use limiting adjectives.
> - Use *this, that, these,* and *those.*

GUM (Grammar, Usage, and Mechanics) ●●●●●●●●●●●●●●●●●●

Other Adjectives

Use Adjectives That Tell How Many or Which One

Choose the answer.

1. Which adjective completes this sentence **and** tells how many?

   Choose _____ card from the deck.

   A. this   C. four
   (B) one   D. that

2. Which adjective completes this sentence **and** tells how many?

   _____ artifacts from ancient Rome are on display at the museum.

   (A) Many   C. Those
   B. Interesting   D. Everyday

3. Which adjective completes this sentence **and** tells how many?

   I drew all _____ pictures myself.

   A. one   **(C) three**
   B. these   D. those

4. Which adjective completes this sentence **and** tells how many?

   Chicago is bigger than _____ cities, but not all cities.

   A. all   C. this
   (B) some   D. these

5. Which adjective completes this sentence **and** tells which one?

   Can you hand me _____ hammer on the work bench?

   A. two   **(C) that**
   B. our   D. those

6. Which adjective completes this sentence **and** tells which one?

   A dove does not look like _____ red bird at all.

   A. big   C. young
   (B) this   D. one

7. Which adjective completes this sentence **and** tells which one?

   These dishes are clean, but _____ bowls are still dirty.

   (A) those   C. that
   B. this   D. some

8. Which adjective completes this sentence **and** tells which one?

   If _____ shoes fit me, I will buy them.

   A. two   C. this
   B. all   **(D) these**

Compare with Adjectives and Revise Your Research Report (A)

Lesson Overview

💻 Online — 25 minutes

Skills Update	Adjectives That Tell How Many or Which One
GUM (Grammar, Usage, and Mechanics)	Use Adjectives to Compare
Composition	Winnie Revises Her Draft for Ideas, Content, and Language

📄 Offline — 20 minutes

Composition	Revise with a Checklist

Materials

Supplied

- *K¹² Language Arts Activity Book*, pp. WS 195–202, 205
- *Grammar Reference Guide* Online Book (optional)
- **Research Report: Feedback Sheet** (printout)

Advance Preparation

To prepare for the GUM portion of this lesson, review Using Adjectives and Adverbs (Comparative and Superlative Forms of Adjectives) in the *Grammar Reference Guide* (linked in the online lesson) to familiarize yourself with the topic. Gather pages WS 195–200 (Write Your Draft, students' draft of their research report) and 201–202 (Tell Me About My Research Report, if completed) in *K¹² Language Arts Activity Book* and the completed Research Report: Feedback Sheet. You will review the feedback with students.

Big Ideas

- ▶ Adjectives and adverbs can be used to compare two or more objects.
- ▶ Writers must be able to articulate a main idea and support it with appropriate details.
- ▶ Writing varies by purpose and audience. The specific reason for writing and the writer's intended readers (audience) determine the correct form and language to use.
- ▶ Revision is best accomplished through discrete, focused tasks.
- ▶ Good writers carefully check their work for errors.

[Online] 25 minutes

Students will work online to review limiting and demonstrative adjectives, to learn about using adjectives to compare nouns, and to learn how to revise a research report to improve its ideas, content, and language. Help students locate the online activities.

Skills Update ....

Adjectives That Tell How Many or Which One
Students will review how to use limiting and demonstrative adjectives by completing Skills Update exercises. Sit with students as they do this activity and note if they answer correctly.

⟳ **Learning Coach Check-In**   How did students do on the Skills Update?

▸ **All answers correct:** Great! Skip the review screen and go on to the next activity.

▸ **Any answers incorrect:** Take a few minutes to review limiting and demonstrative adjectives now. Use the link on the screen after the Skills Update to take another look at the online activity or review Adjectives (Limiting Adjectives; Demonstrative Adjectives) in the *Grammar Reference Guide* together.

(TIP) This activity will require extra time if students need to review limiting and demonstrative adjectives. Take the extra 5–10 minutes to review now because new skills build on what students have already learned.

> **Objectives**
> • Use limiting adjectives.
> • Use *this, that, these,* and *those.*

GUM (Grammar, Usage, and Mechanics) ....

Use Adjectives to Compare
Students will learn about adding *–er* or *–est* to some adjectives to compare nouns.

> **Objectives**
> • Add *–er* and *–est* to some adjectives to show comparisons.

Composition ....

Winnie Revises Her Draft for Ideas, Content, and Language
By watching how Winnie revises her research report draft to improve ideas, content, and language, students will learn how to revise their own draft.

> **Objectives**
> • Revise a research report.
> • Revise for ideas and content.
> • Revise for formal language.

[Offline] ⏱ 20 minutes

Work **together** with students to complete the offline Composition activity.

Composition ....

Revise with a Checklist

Students will begin to revise their research report. In this lesson, students will focus on improving the ideas, content, and language in their draft. They will focus on improving the structure and organization of their draft in another lesson. Have them gather their research report draft and any completed Peer Interaction forms. Turn to pages WS 205 in *K¹² Language Arts Activity Book* and gather the Research Report: Feedback Sheet that you filled out.

> **Objectives**
> * Revise a research report.
> * Revise for ideas and content.
> * Revise for formal language.

1. Use the Research Report: Feedback Sheet to guide your discussion with students.

   ▸ Tell students the strengths of their research report. Provide positive comments about the ideas, content, and language that you enjoyed.

   ▸ Walk through the Purpose and Content section of the feedback sheet with students. Do not address your comments in the Structure and Organization section or the Grammar and Mechanics section at this time. You can work with students on structure and organization in the next lesson and on grammar and mechanics when they proofread. Providing these corrections at this time may distract students from the real work of revising for ideas, content, and language.

   ▸ As you go through the feedback sheet with students, encourage them to actively revise their draft based on your feedback. Reassure students that it's okay to remove ideas or sentences from their report. Doing so may help their report become more accurate and succinct, even if something they cut was included in their outline. Likewise, reassure students that it is okay to add an idea or sentence if it is relevant and important to the points that they are trying to make.

   ▸ As students revise their draft, have them use the purple rows to mark their revisions.

2. Once you've reviewed your comments on the first section of the feedback sheet with students, have them review their draft once more, using the revision checklist on the Activity Book page. For this lesson, students should use the items under Ideas, Content, and Language on the checklist. Students should check off the boxes on the checklist as they complete the items.

3. If students received feedback from peers, discuss with them how they might use it to improve their research report. Help students decide what peer feedback would be useful to include in their revisions.

TIP Keep students' revised research report in a safe place so they can refer to it later.

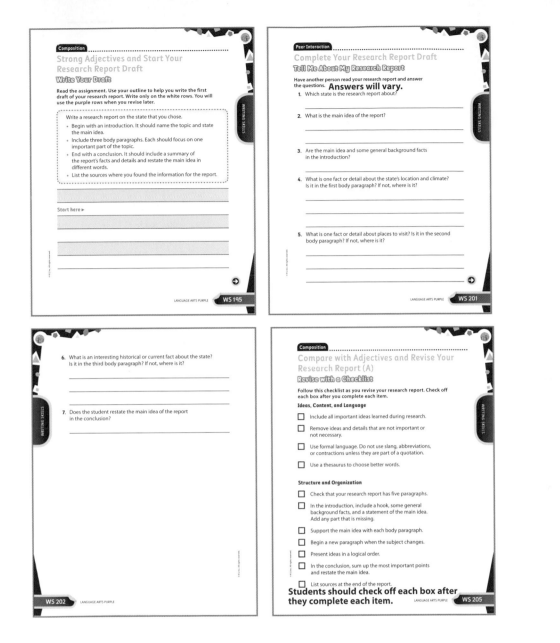

Composition

Strong Adjectives and Start Your Research Report Draft

Write Your Draft

Read the assignment. Use your outline to help you write the first draft of your research report. Write only on the white rows. You will use the purple rows when you revise later.

Write a research report on the state that you chose.

- Begin with an introduction. It should name the topic and state the main idea.
- Include three body paragraphs. Each should focus on one important part of the topic.
- End with a conclusion. It should include a summary of the report's facts and details and restate the main idea in different words.
- List the sources where you found the information for the report.

Start here ▶

Peer Interaction

Complete Your Research Report Draft

Tell Me About My Research Report

Have another person read your research report and answer the questions. **Answers will vary.**

1. Which state is the research report about?

2. What is the main idea of the report?

3. Are the main idea and some general background facts in the introduction?

4. What is one fact or detail about the state's location and climate? Is it in the first body paragraph? If not, where is it?

5. What is one fact or detail about places to visit? Is it in the second body paragraph? If not, where is it?

6. What is an interesting historical or current fact about the state? Is it in the third body paragraph? If not, where is it?

7. Does the student restate the main idea of the report in the conclusion?

Composition

Compare with Adjectives and Revise Your Research Report (A)

Revise with a Checklist

Follow this checklist as you revise your research report. Check off each box after you complete each item.

Ideas, Content, and Language

☐ Include all important ideas learned during research.

☐ Remove ideas and details that are not important or not necessary.

☐ Use formal language. Do not use slang, abbreviations, or contractions unless they are part of a quotation.

☐ Use a thesaurus to choose better words.

Structure and Organization

☐ Check that your research report has five paragraphs.

☐ In the introduction, include a hook, some general background facts, and a statement of the main idea. Add any part that is missing.

☐ Support the main idea with each body paragraph.

☐ Begin a new paragraph when the subject changes.

☐ Present ideas in a logical order.

☐ In the conclusion, sum up the most important points and restate the main idea.

☐ List sources at the end of the report.

Students should check off each box after they complete each item.

Compare with Adjectives and Revise Your Research Report (B)

Lesson Overview

[Online] 25 minutes

Skills Update	Use Adjectives to Compare
GUM (Grammar, Usage, and Mechanics)	Adjectives with *More* and *Most*
Composition	Winnie Revises Her Draft for Structure and Organization

[Offline] 20 minutes

Composition	Revise with a Checklist

[Materials]

Supplied

- *K¹² Language Arts Activity Book*, pp. WS 195–202, 205
- *Grammar Reference Guide* Online Book (optional)
- Research Report: Feedback Sheet (printout)
- drafting page (optional printout)

Advance Preparation

To prepare for the GUM portion of this lesson, review Using Adjectives and Adverbs (Comparative and Superlative Forms of Adjectives) in the *Grammar Reference Guide* (linked in the online lesson) to familiarize yourself with the topic. Gather pages WS 195–200 (Write Your Draft, students' draft of their research report), 201–202 (Tell Me About My Research Report, if completed), and 205 (Revise with a Checklist) in *K¹² Language Arts Activity Book* and the completed Research Report: Feedback Sheet. You will review the feedback for structure and organization with students.

Big Ideas

- Adjectives and adverbs can be used to compare two or more objects.
- Writers must be able to articulate a main idea and support it with appropriate details.
- Writing varies by purpose and audience. The specific reason for writing and the writer's intended readers (audience) determine the correct form and language to use.
- Revision is best accomplished through discrete, focused tasks.
- Good writers carefully check their work for errors.

[Online] ⓟ minutes

Students will work online to review comparative and superlative forms of adjectives, to learn about using the words *more* and *most* with some adjectives to compare nouns, and to learn how to revise a research report to improve its structure and organization. Help students locate the online activities.

Skills Update

Use Adjectives to Compare

Students will review how to use adjectives that end in *–er* and *–est* to make comparisons by completing Skills Update exercises. Sit with students as they do this activity and note if they answer correctly.

➲ **Learning Coach Check-In** How did students do on the Skills Update?

▶ **All answers correct:** Great! Skip the review screen and go on to the next activity.

▶ **Any answers incorrect:** Take a few minutes to review how to use adjectives that end in *–er* and *–est* to make comparisons now. Use the link on the screen after the Skills Update to take another look at the online activity or review Using Adjectives and Adverbs (Comparative and Superlative Forms of Adjectives) in the *Grammar Reference Guide* together.

(TIP) This activity will require extra time if students need to review how to use adjectives that end in *–er* and *–est* to make comparisons. Take the extra 5–10 minutes to review now because new skills build on what students have already learned.

> **Objectives**
> - Add *–er* and *–est* to some adjectives to show comparisons.

GUM (Grammar, Usage, and Mechanics)

Adjectives with *More* and *Most*

Students will learn about using the words *more* and *most* with some adjectives to compare nouns.

> **Objectives**
> - Use *more* and *most* with some adjectives and adverbs to show comparisons.

Composition

Winnie Revises Her Draft for Structure and Organization

By watching how Winnie revises her research report draft to improve its structure and organization, students will learn how to revise their own draft.

> **Objectives**
> - Revise a research report.
> - Revise for structure.
> - Revise for organization.

[Offline] ⏱ 20 minutes

Work **together** with students to complete the offline Composition activity.

Composition

Revise with a Checklist

Students will continue to revise their research report. They will focus on improving the structure and organization of their draft. Have them gather their research report draft, any completed Peer Interaction forms, and their checklist. Gather the Research Report: Feedback Sheet that you filled out.

> **Objectives**
> - Revise a research report.
> - Revise for structure.
> - Revise for organization.

1. Use the Research Report: Feedback Sheet to guide your discussion with students.

   ▶ Tell students the strengths of their research report. Provide positive comments about the elements related to the report's structure and organization that you enjoyed.

   ▶ Walk through the Structure and Organization section of the feedback sheet with students. Do not address your comments in the Grammar and Mechanics section at this time. You can work with students on grammar and mechanics when they proofread. Providing these corrections at this time may distract students from the real work of revising for structure and organization.

   ▶ As you go through the feedback sheet with students, encourage them to actively revise their draft based on your feedback. Reassure students that it's okay to reorganize ideas or restructure sections of the report. Doing so may help their report be more ordered and easy to follow.

   ▶ As students revise their draft, have them use the purple rows to mark their revisions.

2. Once you've reviewed your comments on the second section of the feedback sheet with students, have them review their draft once more, using the revision checklist on the Activity Book page. For this lesson, students should use the items under Structure and Organization on the checklist. Students should check off the boxes on the checklist as they complete the items.

3. If students received feedback from peers, discuss with them how they might use it to improve their research report. Help students decide what peer feedback would be useful to include in their revisions.

4. If students' revised research report has many changes that make the report difficult to read and understand, encourage them to make a clean copy before they proofread in a later lesson. Additional drafting pages can be printed from the online lesson.

TIP Keep students' revised research report in a safe place so they can refer to it later.

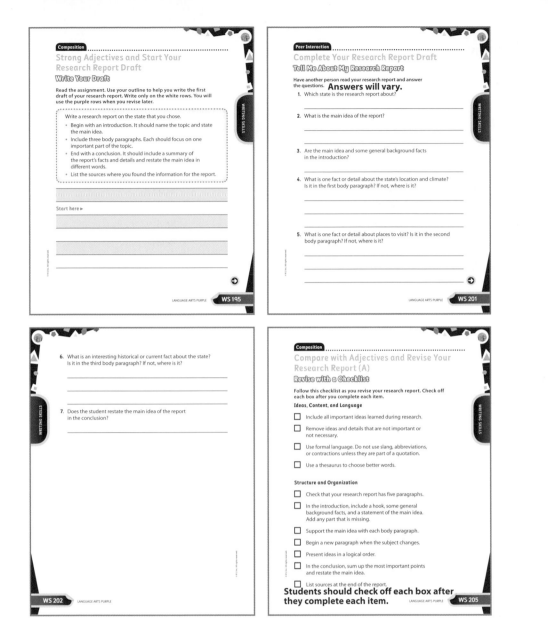

Composition

Strong Adjectives and Start Your Research Report Draft

Write Your Draft

Read the assignment. Use your outline to help you write the first draft of your research report. Write only on the white rows. You will use the purple rows when you revise later.

> Write a research report on the state that you chose.
> - Begin with an introduction. It should name the topic and state the main idea.
> - Include three body paragraphs. Each should focus on one important part of the topic.
> - End with a conclusion. It should include a summary of the report's facts and details and restate the main idea in different words.
> - List the sources where you found the information for the report.

Start here ▶

Peer Interaction

Complete Your Research Report Draft

Tell Me About My Research Report

Have another person read your research report and answer the questions. **Answers will vary.**

1. Which state is the research report about?

2. What is the main idea of the report?

3. Are the main idea and some general background facts in the introduction?

4. What is one fact or detail about the state's location and climate? Is it in the first body paragraph? If not, where is it?

5. What is one fact or detail about places to visit? Is it in the second body paragraph? If not, where is it?

---

6. What is an interesting historical or current fact about the state? Is it in the third body paragraph? If not, where is it?

7. Does the student restate the main idea of the report in the conclusion?

Composition

Compare with Adjectives and Revise Your Research Report (A)

Revise with a Checklist

Follow this checklist as you revise your research report. Check off each box after you complete each item.

Ideas, Content, and Language

- ☐ Include all important ideas learned during research.
- ☐ Remove ideas and details that are not important or not necessary.
- ☐ Use formal language. Do not use slang, abbreviations, or contractions unless they are part of a quotation.
- ☐ Use a thesaurus to choose better words.

Structure and Organization

- ☐ Check that your research report has five paragraphs.
- ☐ In the introduction, include a hook, some general background facts, and a statement of the main idea. Add any part that is missing.
- ☐ Support the main idea with each body paragraph.
- ☐ Begin a new paragraph when the subject changes.
- ☐ Present ideas in a logical order.
- ☐ In the conclusion, sum up the most important points and restate the main idea.
- ☐ List sources at the end of the report.

Students should check off each box after they complete each item.

Proofread Your Research Report

Lesson Overview

[Online]   20 minutes

Skills Update	Adjectives with *More* and *Most*
Composition	Winnie Proofreads with a Checklist

[Offline]   25 minutes

| Composition | Proofread with a Checklist |

Materials

Supplied

- *K¹² Language Arts Activity Book*, pp. WS 195–200, 206
- *Grammar Reference Guide* Online Book (optional)
- Research Report: Feedback Sheet (printout)
- drafting page (optional printout)

Advance Preparation

Gather pages WS 195–200 (Write Your Draft, students' draft of their research report) in *K¹² Language Arts Activity Book* and the completed Research Report: Feedback Sheet. If students' revised research report has many changes that make it difficult to read and understand, you may want to encourage them to make a clean copy before they proofread in this lesson. Additional drafting pages can be printed from the online lesson.

Big Ideas

Good writers carefully check their work for errors.

〔Online〕 ㉂ minutes

Students will work online to review comparative and superlative forms of adjectives and to learn how to proofread a research report. Help students locate the online activities.

Skills Update ....

Adjectives with *More* and *Most*

Students will review how to use *more* and *most* with some adjectives to make comparisons by completing Skills Update exercises. Sit with students as they do this activity and note if they answer correctly.

⮕ **Learning Coach Check-In** How did students do on the Skills Update?

  ▸ **All answers correct:** Great! Skip the review screen and go on to the next activity.

  ▸ **Any answers incorrect:** Take a few minutes to review how to use *more* and *most* with some adjectives to make comparisons now. Use the link on the screen after the Skills Update to take another look at the online activity or review Using Adjectives and Adverbs (Comparative and Superlative Forms of Adjectives) in the *Grammar Reference Guide* together.

TIP This activity will require extra time if students need to review how to use *more* and *most* with some adjectives to make comparisons. Take the extra 5–10 minutes to review now because new skills build on what students have already learned.

> **Objectives**
> • Use *more* and *most* with some adjectives and adverbs to show comparisons.

Composition ....

Winnie Proofreads with a Checklist

By watching how Winnie proofreads her research report, students will learn how to proofread their own draft.

> **Objectives**
> • Proofread a research report.
> • Proofread for use of quotation marks.
> • Proofread for spelling.

[Offline] 25 minutes

Work **together** with students to complete the offline Composition activity.

Composition

Proofread with a Checklist

Students will proofread their research report. Have them gather their revised research report draft. Turn to page WS 206 in *K¹² Language Arts Activity Book* and gather the Research Report: Feedback Sheet that you filled out.

1. Review your comments in the Grammar and Mechanics section of the feedback sheet with students. As you go through the feedback sheet, encourage students to use the purple rows on their drafting pages to actively mark changes based on your feedback.

2. Once you've reviewed your comments in the Grammar and Mechanics section of the feedback sheet, have students review their draft once more using the proofreading checklist. Students should check off the boxes on the checklist as they complete the items.

3. If students' revised research report has many changes that make the report difficult to read and understand, encourage them to make a clean copy before they proofread. Additional drafting pages can be printed from the online lesson.

TIP Keep students' proofread research report in a safe place so they can refer to it later.

Objectives

- Proofread a research report.
- Proofread for use of quotation marks.
- Proofread for spelling.

Composition

Strong Adjectives and Start Your Research Report Draft

Write Your Draft

Read the assignment. Use your outline to help you write the first draft of your research report. Write only on the white rows. You will use the purple rows when you revise later.

Write a research report on the state that you chose.

- Begin with an introduction. It should name the topic and state the main idea.
- Include three body paragraphs. Each should focus on one important part of the topic.
- End with a conclusion. It should include a summary of the report's facts and details and restate the main idea in different words.
- List the sources where you found the information for the report.

Start here ▸

LANGUAGE ARTS PURPLE **WS 195**

Composition

Proofread Your Research Report

Proofread with a Checklist

Follow this checklist as you proofread your research report. Check off each box as you complete each item.

- ☐ Use linking words and phrases to connect ideas.
- ☐ Capitalize proper nouns, including the names of people and places.
- ☐ Begin each sentence with a capital letter.
- ☐ End each sentence with the correct punctuation mark.
- ☐ Put quotations marks around words that someone wrote or said.
- ☐ Use a dictionary to check spelling of words you don't know.
- ☐ Replace weak adjectives with strong ones. Replace general adjectives with specific ones.

Students should check off each box after they complete each item.

WS 206 LANGUAGE ARTS PURPLE

Unit Review and Publish Your Research Report

Lesson Overview

🖥 [Online]   20 minutes

Unit Review	Adjectives
More Practice	Adjectives

📄 [Offline]   25 minutes

Write Now	Publish Your Research Report

Advance Preparation

Gather pages WS 195–200 (Write Your Draft, students' draft of their research report) in *K¹² Language Arts Activity Book*, which students should have revised and proofread.

Big Ideas

To write a strong research report, one should be able to follow an interest to its conclusion.

[Materials]

Supplied

- *K¹² Language Arts Activity Book*, pp. WS 195–200, 207–212
- *Grammar Reference Guide* Online Book (optional)
- lined writing page (optional printout)

Keywords

adjective – a word that describes a noun or a pronoun

article – the adjective *a, an,* or *the*

research report – a type of essay based mainly on the author's research

transition – a word or phrase that connects ideas

[Online] 20 minutes

Students will work online to review the grammar, usage, and mechanics skills learned in the unit. Help students locate the online activities.

Unit Review

Adjectives

Students will review what they have learned about adjectives. This activity will check students' ability to identify and use descriptive adjectives, to replace weak adjectives with strong adjectives, to use articles, to identify and use adjectives that tell how many or which ones, and to use adjectives to compare nouns in order to review for the Unit Checkpoint.

TIP A full list of objectives covered in the Unit Review can be found in the online lesson.

Objectives
- Complete a review of grammar, usage, and mechanics skills.

More Practice

Adjectives

Go over students' results on the Unit Review and, if necessary, have students complete the appropriate review activities listed in the table online. Help students locate the activities. Provide support as needed.

TIP The time students need to complete this activity will vary. Set aside enough time for students to complete all review activities, if they need to do so.

Objectives
- Evaluate Unit Review results and choose activities for more practice.

[Offline] 25 minutes

Work **together** with students to complete the offline Write Now activity.

Write Now

✏️ **Publish Your Research Report**

Students will begin making a clean, final copy of their research report. Have them gather their proofread draft. Turn to pages WS 207–212 in *K¹² Language Arts Activity Book*.

> **Objectives**
> • Make a clean copy of a research report.

1. Explain to students that they will finish their research report by completing the last stage of the writing process—publishing their work.
   Say: Publishing your writing means making a clean and final copy that is ready for sharing with others.

   ▸ To be ready to publish your research report, you should have finished revising and proofreading your draft.
   ▸ The final copy should be your best effort and should not have any errors.

2. Explain that the final copy should be written clearly and neatly on clean sheets of paper. Tell students that they should use good handwriting and leave spaces between words so that others can read what they wrote.

3. Have students use the lined Activity Book pages to write their final copy. If needed, additional lined writing pages can be printed from the online lesson. Since the research report is lengthy, students may complete their clean copy in the next lesson, and you will evaluate it then.

TIP Tell students that producing a piece of writing that is ready to publish and share with others is a great accomplishment. Let students know that the effort they put in to writing and publishing a research report is something to be proud of.

Composition
Strong Adjectives and Start Your Research Report Draft
Write Your Draft

Read the assignment. Use your outline to help you write the first draft of your research report. Write only on the white rows. You will use the purple rows when you revise later.

Write a research report on the state that you chose.
• Begin with an introduction. It should name the topic and state the main idea.
• Include three body paragraphs. Each should focus on one important part of the topic.
• End with a conclusion. It should include a summary of the report's facts and details and restate the main idea in different words.
• List the sources where you found the information for the report.

Start here ▸

LANGUAGE ARTS PURPLE   WS 195

Write Now
Unit Review and Publish Your Research Report
Publish Your Research Report

Write the final copy of your research report in your best handwriting. Write the title of your research report on the first line.
Refer to the rubric and sample responses.

LANGUAGE ARTS PURPLE   WS 207

Unit Checkpoint and Publish Your Research Report

ING SKILLS

Lesson Overview

Online — 20 minutes

Unit Checkpoint	Adjectives

Offline — 25 minutes

More Practice	Adjectives
Write Now	Publish Your Research Report
More Practice	Research Report

Advance Preparation

Gather pages WS 207–212 (Publish Your Research Report, students' partially completed clean copy of their research report) in *K¹² Language Arts Activity Book*.

Materials

Supplied

- *K¹² Language Arts Activity Book*, pp. WS 207–212
- *Grammar Reference Guide* Online Book (optional)
- Descriptive Adjectives (optional printout)
- Strong Adjectives (optional printout)
- Articles (optional printout)
- Adjectives That Tell How Many or Which Ones (optional printout)
- Use Adjectives to Compare (optional printout)
- Adjectives with *More* and *Most* (optional printout)
- Research Report: Rubric and Sample Responses (printout)
- lined writing page (optional printout)

Keywords

adjective – a word that describes a noun or a pronoun

article – the adjective *a*, *an*, or *the*

research report – a type of essay based mainly on the author's research

transition – a word or phrase that connects ideas

WS 448   Language Arts Purple

[Online] 🔟 minutes

Students will work online **independently** to complete the Unit Checkpoint. Help students locate the Unit Checkpoint and provide support as necessary.

Unit Checkpoint •••

Adjectives

Students will complete an online Unit Checkpoint about adjectives. If necessary, read the directions to students.

TIP A full list of objectives covered in the Unit Checkpoint can be found in the online lesson.

> **Objectives**
> • Complete a Unit Checkpoint on grammar, usage, and mechanics skills.

[Offline] 🟤 minutes

Work **together** with students to complete the offline More Practice and Write Now activities.

More Practice •••

Adjectives

Go over students' results on the Unit Checkpoint and, if necessary, print and have them complete the appropriate practice pages listed in the table online. Students can complete all necessary pages now or, if more time is needed, they can spread them out over the next few days. They can also review the appropriate sections of the *Grammar Reference Guide* with you. If students scored less than 80 percent on the Unit Checkpoint, you may want them to retake the Checkpoint after completing the additional activity pages.

> **Objectives**
> • Evaluate Unit Checkpoint results and choose activities for more practice.

TIP The time students need to complete this activity will vary. Set aside enough time for students to complete some or all activity pages and to retake the Unit Checkpoint, if they need to do so. Students may retake the Unit Checkpoint immediately, but having them complete the practice pages and then retake it might be more effective.

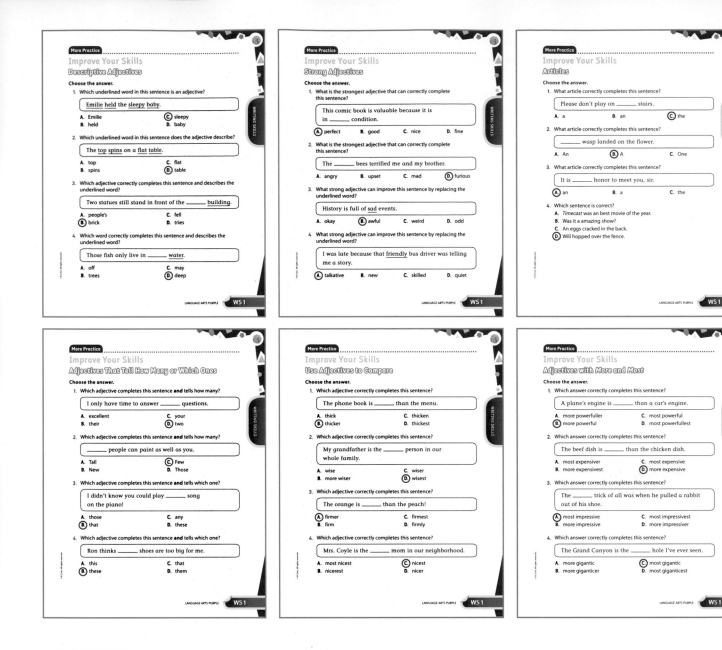

More Practice

Improve Your Skills
Descriptive Adjectives

Choose the answer.

1. Which underlined word in this sentence is an adjective?

   Emilie held the sleepy baby.

   A. Emilie   C. sleepy
   B. held   D. baby

2. Which underlined word in this sentence does the adjective describe?

   The top spins on a flat table.

   A. top   C. flat
   B. spins   D. table

3. Which adjective correctly completes this sentence and describes the underlined word?

   Two statues still stand in front of the _____ building.

   A. people's C. fell
   B. brick   D. tries

4. Which word correctly completes this sentence and describes the underlined word?

   Those fish only live in _____ water.

   A. off   C. may
   B. trees   D. deep

LANGUAGE ARTS PURPLE   WS 1

More Practice

Improve Your Skills
Strong Adjectives

Choose the answer.

1. What is the strongest adjective that can correctly complete this sentence?

   This comic book is valuable because it is in _____ condition.

   A. perfect   B. good   C. nice   D. fine

2. What is the strongest adjective that can correctly complete this sentence?

   The _____ bees terrified me and my brother.

   A. angry   B. upset   C. mad   D. furious

3. What strong adjective can improve this sentence by replacing the underlined word?

   History is full of sad events.

   A. okay   B. awful   C. weird   D. odd

4. What strong adjective can improve this sentence by replacing the underlined word?

   I was late because that friendly bus driver was telling me a story.

   A. talkative   B. new   C. skilled   D. quiet

LANGUAGE ARTS PURPLE   WS 1

More Practice

Improve Your Skills
Articles

Choose the answer.

1. What article correctly completes this sentence?

   Please don't play on _____ stairs.

   A. a   B. an   C. the

2. What article correctly completes this sentence?

   _____ wasp landed on the flower.

   A. An   B. A   C. One

3. What article correctly completes this sentence?

   It is _____ honor to meet you, sir.

   A. an   B. a   C. the

4. Which sentence is correct?

   A. *Timecast* was an best movie of the year.
   B. Was it a amazing show?
   C. An eggs cracked in the back.
   D. Will hopped over the fence.

LANGUAGE ARTS PURPLE   WS 1

More Practice

Improve Your Skills
Adjectives That Tell How Many or Which Ones

Choose the answer.

1. Which adjective completes this sentence and tells how many?

   I only have time to answer _____ questions.

   A. excellent   C. your
   B. their   D. two

2. Which adjective completes this sentence and tells how many?

   _____ people can paint as well as you.

   A. Tall   C. Few
   B. New   D. Those

3. Which adjective completes this sentence and tells which one?

   I didn't know you could play _____ song on the piano!

   A. those   C. any
   B. that   D. these

4. Which adjective completes this sentence and tells which one?

   Ron thinks _____ shoes are too big for me.

   A. this   C. that
   B. these   D. them

LANGUAGE ARTS PURPLE   WS 1

More Practice

Improve Your Skills
Use Adjectives to Compare

Choose the answer.

1. Which adjective correctly completes this sentence?

   The phone book is _____ than the menu.

   A. thick   C. thicken
   B. thicker D. thickest

2. Which adjective correctly completes this sentence?

   My grandfather is the _____ person in our whole family.

   A. wise   C. wiser
   B. more wiser   D. wisest

3. Which adjective correctly completes this sentence?

   The orange is _____ than the peach!

   A. firmer   C. firmest
   B. firm   D. firmly

4. Which adjective correctly completes this sentence?

   Mrs. Coyle is the _____ mom in our neighborhood.

   A. most nicest   C. nicest
   B. nicerest   D. nicer

LANGUAGE ARTS PURPLE   WS 1

More Practice

Improve Your Skills
Adjectives with More and Most

Choose the answer.

1. Which answer correctly completes this sentence?

   A plane's engine is _____ than a car's engine.

   A. more powerfuller   C. most powerful
   B. more powerful   D. most powerfullest

2. Which answer correctly completes this sentence?

   The beef dish is _____ than the chicken dish.

   A. most expensiver   C. most expensive
   B. more expensivest D. more expensive

3. Which answer correctly completes this sentence?

   The _____ trick of all was when he pulled a rabbit out of his shoe.

   A. most impressive   C. most impressivest
   B. more impressive   D. more impressiver

4. Which answer correctly completes this sentence?

   The Grand Canyon is the _____ hole I've ever seen.

   A. more gigantic   C. most gigantic
   B. more giganticer   D. most giganticest

LANGUAGE ARTS PURPLE   WS 1

Write Now

Publish Your Research Report

Students will finish publishing their research report. Have them gather their partially completed clean copy.

1. Explain to students that they should finish the clean copy of their research report. If needed, additional lined writing pages can be printed from the online lesson.

Objectives
- Make a clean copy of a research report.

2. Use the materials and instructions in the online lesson to evaluate students' finished writing. You will be looking at students' writing to evaluate the following:

   ▸ **Purpose and Content:** The report focuses on one state. With one or two exceptions, it contains facts and information in the body paragraphs that support a main idea, expressed in the introduction. The facts and information in the report come from credible sources, and there are few unimportant or irrelevant details. The conclusion sums up most of the key points and restates the main idea. The language is formal with only one or two uses of slang, contractions, and abbreviations.

   ▸ **Structure and Organization:** The report has been revised. It has an introductory paragraph, three body paragraphs, and a concluding paragraph. With one or two exceptions, the ideas are presented in logical order. Some transitions effectively connect ideas, and the sources are listed at the end of the report.

   ▸ **Grammar and Mechanics:** The report has been proofread, and no more than three or four errors remain. Most sentences are complete, proper nouns are capitalized, quotations are punctuated properly, and, with perhaps one exception, place names are spelled correctly. Where possible, the report generally uses strong, specific adjectives rather than weak ones.

3. Enter students' scores online for each rubric category.

4. If students' writing scored a 1 in any category, work with them to revise and proofread their work.

5. Suggest that students share their research report with an audience—people they think might want to learn more about the state they chose.

TIP Tell students that producing a piece of writing that is ready to publish and share with others is a great accomplishment. Let students know that the effort they put in to writing and publishing a research report is something to be proud of.

Write Now

Unit Review and Publish Your Research Report

Publish Your Research Report

Write the final copy of your research report in your best handwriting. Write the title of your research report on the first line.

Refer to the rubric and sample responses.

LANGUAGE ARTS PURPLE WS 207

More Practice

Research Report

If students' writing did not meet objectives, have them complete the appropriate review activities listed in the table online. Follow the online instructions to help students revise and edit their work. Impress upon students that revising makes their work better. Writing is a process, and each time they revise their research report they are improving their writing. Always begin with something positive to say. If there is one fact that really helps support the main idea, for example, mention it and say how this fact strengthened the report.

Help students locate the activities and provide support as needed.

Reward: When students score 80 percent or above on the Unit Checkpoint and their writing is Level 2 or higher on the Research Report grading rubric, add a sticker for this unit on the My Accomplishments chart.

⭐ **Objectives**
- Revise a research report.

UNIT OVERVIEW Adverbs and Research Report Presentation

Unit Focus

In the grammar part of the unit, students will learn about adverbs. They will

- Learn that adverbs are words that describe verbs.
- Learn about adverbs of manner, adverbs of time, and adverbs of place.
- Practice recognizing and using different types of adverbs correctly.
- Learn how to use adverbs to make comparisons.
- Recognize when to use an adverb and when to use an adjective in a sentence.

This is the third of three units in which students plan, write, and present a research report of at least five paragraphs. In this unit, students will plan and give a presentation based on their research report. They will

- Use their journal to freewrite.
- Choose the most important point from each paragraph in their report to include in their presentation.
- Select media to accompany their presentation.
- Learn how to give an effective presentation.
- Practice their presentation.
- Deliver their presentation.

Unit Plan		[Online]	[Offline]
Lesson 1	Adverbs and Journal Entry	25 minutes	20 minutes
Lesson 2	Compare with Adverbs and Plan Your Presentation	25 minutes	20 minutes
Lesson 3	Choose Media for Your Presentation	30 minutes	15 minutes
Lesson 4	Presentation Skills	30 minutes	15 minutes
Lesson 5	Practice Your Presentation		45 minutes
Lesson 6	Unit Review and Practice Your Presentation	15 minutes	30 minutes
Lesson 7	Unit Checkpoint and Deliver Your Presentation	15 minutes	30 minutes

Adverbs and Journal Entry

Lesson Overview

 **[Online]**		**25** minutes
GUM (Grammar, Usage, and Mechanics)	Adverbs That Tell How, When, and Where	
[Offline]		**20** minutes
Composition	Journal: Write About Speaking in Front of a Group	
Beyond the Lesson	⊕ OPTIONAL: Journal: Freewrite on a Topic	

Materials

Supplied

- *K¹² My Journal*, pp. 40–41
- *Grammar Reference Guide* Online Book (optional)

Keywords

adverb – a word that describes a verb, an adjective, or another adverb

adverb of manner – an adverb that answers the question, "How?"

adverb of place – an adverb that answers the question, "Where?"

adverb of time – an adverb that answers the question, "When?"

verb – a word that shows action or a state of being

Advance Preparation

To prepare for the GUM portion of this lesson, review Adverbs (Adverbs of Time, Space, Manner, and Degree) in the *Grammar Reference Guide* (linked in the online lesson) to familiarize yourself with the topic.

Big Ideas

- ▶ Journal writing is a form of freewriting. It is an opportunity to get ideas on paper without regard for the correctness of the language or the format of a piece of writing.
- ▶ To improve, writers require frequent practice.
- ▶ Using a wide range of adverbs allows a writer to convey specific information about how, when, where, or why an action occurs.

Online ⏱ 25 minutes

Students will work online **independently** to complete an activity on recognizing and using adverbs. Help students locate the online activity.

GUM (Grammar, Usage, and Mechanics) ···

Adverbs That Tell How, When, and Where

Students will learn what adverbs are and how adverbs can make a text more interesting by describing how, when, or where an action happens. They will then practice identifying and using adverbs in sentences.

> ★ **Objectives**
> - Recognize descriptive words called adverbs.
> - Recognize that adverbs describe verbs.
> - Identify adverbs that tell how.
> - Identify adverbs that tell when.
> - Identify adverbs that tell where.

Offline ⏱ 20 minutes

Work **together** with students to complete the offline Composition and Beyond the Lesson activities.

Composition ···

 **Journal: Write About Speaking in Front of a Group**

Students will respond to a journal prompt by writing about speaking in front of a group of people. Gather *K¹² My Journal* and have students turn to pages 40 and 41.

> ★ **Objectives**
> - Respond to a journal prompt.
> - Freewrite about a topic.

1. Tell students that they are going to write in their journal about speaking in front of a group of people. To help students think of what to say about their experiences with public speaking, ask them to think about their answers to the following questions.

   ▸ When have you spoken in front of a group in the past? Why were you speaking to the group? Were you speaking because you wanted to or because you had to? How did the purpose for speaking affect how much you enjoyed speaking in front of a group?

   ▸ Did you prepare what you were going to say to the group before you began talking? If so, how did you prepare? Did you practice your speech? If you did not prepare, why not? Do you think you would have enjoyed the experience more or less if you had practiced what you were going to say? Why?

   ▸ What words would you use to describe how you felt before, during, and after speaking to a group?

2. Have students respond to the prompt in their journal. Encourage students to write in complete sentences, although it is not a requirement when they are freewriting in their journal.

TIP Students should write for about 20 minutes. Freewriting allows students to use their imagination to write what they want without worrying about being graded, so encourage them to keep writing for the entire time. If students have trouble writing for 20 minutes, use the prompting questions in Step 1or have them list ideas or words. If they want to keep writing beyond the suggested time limit, praise them for their enthusiasm and offer to let them complete their entry later in the day as a reward.

Speak to a Group   Date _____

Do you like to speak in front of a group?
Explain why or why not.

_____

_____

_____

_____

_____

_____

_____

_____

_____

_____

_____

_____

_____

40

Beyond the Lesson

OPTIONAL: Journal: Freewrite on a Topic

This activity is OPTIONAL. It is intended for students who have extra time and would benefit from extra practice. Feel free to skip this activity. Gather *K¹² My Journal*.

1. Have students either respond to a prompt in Thoughts and Experiences (pages 50–93) or write about their own topic on the next available page in Ideas (pages 96–139).

2. Encourage students to explore their thoughts and write as much as they want. There are no rules. If students wish, ideas can be fleshed out into a more developed composition at a later time.

TIP Studies show that students who write more frequently become better writers.

Objectives
- Respond to a journal prompt.
- Freewrite about a topic.

Compare with Adverbs and Plan Your Presentation

Lesson Overview

🖥️ [Online] 25 minutes

Skills Update	Adverbs That Tell How, When, and Where
GUM (Grammar, Usage, and Mechanics)	Compare with Adverbs
Composition	Winnie Plans Her Presentation

📄 [Offline] 20 minutes

Composition	Plan Your Presentation

[Materials]

Supplied
- *K¹² Language Arts Activity Book*, pp. WS 213–214
- *Grammar Reference Guide* Online Book (optional)

Also Needed
- students' research report

Keywords

adverb – a word that describes a verb, an adjective, or another adverb

media – all the ways by which something can be shown, shared, or expressed

verb – a word that shows action or a state of being

Advance Preparation

To prepare for the GUM portion of this lesson, review Using Adjectives and Adverbs (Comparative and Superlative Forms of Adverbs) in the *Grammar Reference Guide* (linked in the online lesson) to familiarize yourself with the topic. In this lesson, students begin to accumulate documents and materials they will need as they work on their presentation. You might want to provide students with a folder or large envelope and a box in which to keep these documents and materials. Gather students' completed research report.

Big Ideas

Adjectives and adverbs can be used to compare two or more objects.

[Online] 25 minutes

Students will work online to review adverbs that tell how, when, and where; to learn about using adverbs to make comparisons; and to examine how to begin planning their research report presentation. Help students locate the online activities.

Skills Update

Adverbs That Tell How, When, and Where
Students will review identifying adverbs that tell how, when, and where by completing Skills Update exercises. Sit with students as they do this activity and note if they answer correctly.

⮑ **Learning Coach Check-In** How did students do on the Skills Update?

  ▸ **All answers correct:** Great! Skip the review screen and go on to the next activity.
  ▸ **Any answers incorrect:** Take a few minutes to review adverbs that tell how, when, and where now. Use the link on the screen after the Skills Update to take another look at the online activity or review Adverbs (Adverbs of Time, Space, Manner, and Degree) in the *Grammar Reference Guide* together.

TIP This activity will require extra time if students need to review adverbs that tell how, when, and where. Take the extra 5–10 minutes to review now because new skills build on what students have already learned.

Objectives
- Recognize descriptive words called adverbs.
- Recognize that adverbs describe verbs.
- Identify adverbs that tell how.
- Identify adverbs that tell when.
- Identify adverbs that tell where.

GUM (Grammar, Usage, and Mechanics)

Compare with Adverbs
Students will learn that adverbs can be used to compare actions. They will then practice using adverbs to make comparisons by adding the words *more* or *most* or the suffixes *–er* or *–est* to them. They will also practice determining whether a sentence calls for an adverb or an adjective, based on what word is described.

Objectives
- Identify and use adverbs that show comparisons.
- Use *more* and *most* with some adjectives and adverbs to show comparisons.
- Recognize that adjectives describe nouns and adverbs describe verbs.

Composition

Winnie Plans Her Presentation
By exploring how Winnie uses a planning form to help her choose which points from her research report to include in her presentation, students will learn how to begin planning their own presentation.

Objectives
- Choose points from a research report to use in a presentation.

Writing Skills WS 459

[Offline] ⏱ 20 minutes

Work **together** with students to complete the offline Composition activity.

Composition ....

Plan Your Presentation

Students will begin to plan their research report presentation. Turn to pages WS 213 and 214 in *K¹² Language Arts Activity Book*.

1. Have students gather their completed research report.

2. Have students use their completed report and follow the directions on the Activity Book pages to plan the points they will talk about in their research report presentation. They should not complete the Media to Use column yet; they will do so in the next lesson.

3. In their plan, guide students to include the main point from each paragraph of their report. Encourage them to write their points on their planning form in new ways—that is, they should not just transfer sentences from their report to their form. Students should try to combine details from multiple sentences in a paragraph to express one key point on their planning form. Provide support as necessary.

TIP Keep the planning form in a safe place so students can return to it later as they continue to plan and practice their presentation.

> **Objectives**
> - Choose points from a research report to use in a presentation.

Choose Media for Your Presentation

Lesson Overview

🖥️ **【Online】**		**30** minutes
Skills Update	Compare with Adverbs	
Composition	Winnie Chooses Media	

📄 **【Offline】**		**15** minutes
Composition	Choose Media	

Advance Preparation

Gather pages WS 213 and 214 (Plan Your Presentation, students' partially completed planning form) in *K¹² Language Arts Activity Book*. Also gather students' research report.

【Materials】

Supplied
- *K¹² Language Arts Activity Book*, pp. WS 213–214
- *Grammar Reference Guide* Online Book (optional)

Also Needed
- students' research report

Keywords

media – all the ways by which something can be shown, shared, or expressed

[Online] 30 minutes

Students will work online to review using adverbs to make comparisons and to examine how to choose media to include in their research report presentation. Help students locate the online activities.

Skills Update

Compare with Adverbs

Students will review how to use adverbs to make comparisons by completing Skills Update exercises. Sit with students as they do this activity and note if they answer correctly.

⊃ **Learning Coach Check-In** How did students do on the Skills Update?

▸ **All answers correct:** Great! Skip the review screen and go on to the next activity.

▸ **Any answers incorrect:** Take a few minutes now to review using adverbs to make comparisons. Use the link on the screen after the Skills Update to take another look at the online activity or review Using Adjectives and Adverbs (Comparative and Superlative Forms of Adverbs) in the *Grammar Reference Guide* together.

TIP This activity will require extra time if students need to review using adverbs to make comparisons. Take the extra 5–10 minutes to review now because new skills build on what students have already learned.

Objectives
- Identify and use adverbs that show comparisons.
- Use *more* and *most* with some adjectives and adverbs to show comparisons.
- Recognize that adjectives describe nouns and adverbs describe verbs.

Composition

Winnie Chooses Media

By exploring how Winnie uses a planning form to help her choose media to include in her research report presentation, students will learn how to choose media for their own presentation.

Objectives
- Choose media for a presentation.
- Include illustrations when useful.
- Report on a topic with appropriate facts and relevant details.

[Offline] **15** minutes

Work **together** with students to complete the offline Composition activity.

Composition ....

Choose Media

Students will continue to plan their research report presentation by choosing media. Gather students' completed research report and their partially completed planning form.

1. Have students use their completed report and follow the directions on the planning form to continue planning their presentation by filling in the Media to Use column.

2. Encourage students to think about media that relates to the points that they plan to make in their presentation. They should consider everything from pictures and graphics to relevant songs and video. Students should write down their ideas and eventually decide on one or two pieces of media to find for their presentation. Once they have chosen media, guide them to look for that media. This may mean searching online or going to the local library, or it may mean making the media themselves. If students want to search online, help them find appropriate websites. Remind students to note on their planning form the sources of any media they intend to use. Provide support as necessary.

TIP Keep the planning form in a safe place so students can return to it later as they continue to plan and practice their presentation.

> **Objectives**
> - Choose media for a presentation.
> - Include illustrations when useful.
> - Report on a topic with appropriate facts and relevant details.

Presentation Skills

Lesson Overview

【Online 】   **30** minutes

Composition	Winnie Reviews Presentation Skills

【Offline 】   **15** minutes

Composition	Presentation Guidelines

Advance Preparation

Gather pages WS 213 and 214 (Plan Your Presentation, students' completed planning form) in *K¹² Language Arts Activity Book* and students' research report.

【Materials 】

Supplied
- *K¹² Language Arts Activity Book*, pp. WS 213–216

Also Needed
- students' research report

Keywords

audience – a writer's readers

pace – the speed, and the change of speeds, of a speaker's delivery

tone – a speaker's attitude as shown by his or her voice

volume – how loud or soft a speaker's voice is

 **30** minutes

Students will work online **independently** to learn about important skills related to giving an effective presentation. Help students locate the online activity.

Composition

Winnie Reviews Presentation Skills
By exploring how Winnie practices her presentation, students will learn about the skills they will need to master as they practice giving their own presentation.

> **Objectives**
> • Review the elements of a presentation.

Offline **15** minutes

Work **together** with students to complete the offline Composition activity.

Composition

Presentation Guidelines
Students will review guidelines for giving a successful presentation. Gather students' completed research report and their planning form, and turn to pages WS 215 and 216 in *K12 Language Arts Activity Book*.

> **Objectives**
> • Review the elements of a presentation.

1. Have students review the guidelines for a successful presentation. Provide support as necessary, encouraging students to ask questions about elements that they do not understand.

2. With their planning forms in hand, have students begin to practice their presentation. To simulate having an audience, encourage students to deliver their presentation while standing in front of a mirror. Remind them that it is okay to make mistakes and that they should not grow frustrated. A good presentation is the product of practice and rehearsal.

3. After students finish giving their presentation for the first time, guide them to answer the questions on the second page of the guidelines. Encourage students to answer each question aloud. Tell them to be as honest as possible as they consider what they did well and what still needs work.

4. Tell students they will have more opportunities to practice their presentation.

TIP Keep the research report, planning form, and guidelines in a safe place so students can return to them whenever they practice their presentation.

Composition

Compare with Adverbs and Plan Your Presentation

Plan Your Presentation

Use this form to plan your research report presentation. Follow these directions to decide what to include.

- Points to Talk About: List five points that you will talk about in your presentation. Include one main point from each of your five paragraphs.
- Media to Use: List ideas for media you could show during your presentation. Write each idea next to the point you would use it with. When choosing media, think about what the media will help you show. Then circle the one or two media choices you most want to use, and write their sources.

Title of presentation _____

Points to Talk About	Media to Use

Students should list topics and choose one.

1. _____   1. _____
   _____   Source _____
   _____   _____
2. _____   2. _____
   _____   Source _____
   _____   _____

LANGUAGE ARTS PURPLE   **WS 213**

Points to Talk About	Media to Use

3. _____   3. _____
   _____   Source _____
   _____   _____
4. _____   4. _____
   _____   Source _____
   _____   _____
5. _____   5. _____
   _____   Source _____
   _____   _____

WS 214   LANGUAGE ARTS PURPLE

Composition

Presentation Skills

Presentation Guidelines

Follow these guidelines as you practice your research report presentation.

- Talk about each of your points and why each one is important.
- Use your planning form to help you remember what points to make, but do not read directly from the form or from your report.
- Pronounce each word clearly as you speak.
- Speak with enthusiasm and expression.
- Speak at an appropriate pace: not too fast or too slow.
- Speak with a pleasing volume: not too loud or too soft.
- Show confidence in your knowledge of your topic.
- Stand up straight.
- Look at your audience as much as possible.
- Direct your audience's attention to the media you have chosen.
- Practice the presentation so you know what to say.

LANGUAGE ARTS PURPLE   **WS 215**

Ask yourself the following questions after you practice your presentation. Then give the presentation again. Try to improve your performance.

1. Did you talk about each point on your planning form? Did you explain why each point is important? Did you lose your place or forget any points? How can you keep that from happening?
2. Did you read directly from your research report or planning form? If so, how can you keep from reading?
3. Did you speak clearly? Did you stumble on any words or phrases? If so, which ones? How can you stop yourself from doing so again?
4. Was your tone appropriate? Did you sound enthusiastic?
5. Did you speak too slowly or too quickly? If so, how can you improve your pace?
6. Did you speak too loudly or too quietly? If so, how can you make sure to maintain a proper volume?
7. Did you sound confident in your knowledge? If not, how can you become more confident?
8. Did you stand up straight? If not, how can you remember to do so?
9. Did you look up at your audience? About how many times?
10. Did you show the media you chose? Do you need to say more about your media and what it shows?

WS 216   LANGUAGE ARTS PURPLE

Practice Your Presentation

Lesson Overview

[Offline]		45 minutes
Composition	Use Guidelines to Practice Your Presentation	
Peer Interaction	⊕ OPTIONAL: Tell Me About My Presentation	

[Materials]

Supplied
- *K¹² Language Arts Activity Book*, pp. WS 213–217
- Research Report Presentation: Feedback Sheet (printout)

Also Needed
- students' chosen media

Advance Preparation

Gather pages WS 213–214 (Plan Your Presentation, students' completed planning form) and WS 215–216 (Presentation Guidelines) in *K¹² Language Arts Activity Book*. Also gather students' chosen media and print the Research Report Presentation: Feedback Sheet from the online lesson.

[Offline] 45 minutes

Work **together** with students to complete the offline Composition and Peer Interaction activities.

Composition

Use Guidelines to Practice Your Presentation

Students will practice giving their research report presentation. Gather students' completed planning form, the presentation guidelines, students' chosen media, and the Research Report Presentation: Feedback Sheet.

Objectives
- Practice a presentation.

1. Have students consult their presentation guidelines and continue to practice giving their presentation.

2. Remind students that the more they practice, the more comfortable they will be and the better their presentation will be. If possible, offer to record students as they practice giving the presentation so that they can both see and hear the strengths and weaknesses of their effort.

3. After students have practiced their presentation several times, complete the Research Report Presentation: Feedback Sheet. You will discuss it with students in the next lesson.

TIP Keep the planning form, presentation guidelines, media, and completed feedback sheet in a safe place for students to use later.

Compare with Adverbs and Plan Your Presentation

Plan Your Presentation

Use this form to plan your research report presentation. Follow these directions to decide what to include.

- Points to Talk About: List five points that you will talk about in your presentation. Include one main point from each of your five paragraphs.
- Media to Use: List ideas for media you could show during your presentation. Write each idea next to the point you would use it with. When choosing media, think about what the media will help you show. Then circle the one or two media choices you most want to use, and write their sources.

Title of presentation _____

Points to Talk About	Media to Use

Students should list topics and choose one.

1. _____   1. _____
   _____   _____
   _____   Source _____
   _____   _____
2. _____   2. _____
   _____   _____
   _____   Source _____
   _____   _____

WRITING SKILLS

LANGUAGE ARTS PURPLE · **WS 213**

WRITING SKILLS

Points to Talk About	Media to Use

3. _____   3. _____
   _____   _____
   _____   Source _____
   _____   _____
4. _____   4. _____
   _____   _____
   _____   Source _____
   _____   _____
5. _____   5. _____
   _____   _____
   _____   Source _____
   _____   _____

WS 214 · LANGUAGE ARTS PURPLE

Presentation Skills

Presentation Guidelines

Follow these guidelines as you practice your research report presentation.

- Talk about each of your points and why each one is important.
- Use your planning form to help you remember what points to make, but do not read directly from the form or from your report.
- Pronounce each word clearly as you speak.
- Speak with enthusiasm and expression.
- Speak at an appropriate pace: not too fast or too slow.
- Speak with a pleasing volume: not too loud or too soft.
- Show confidence in your knowledge of your topic.
- Stand up straight.
- Look at your audience as much as possible.
- Direct your audience's attention to the media you have chosen.
- Practice the presentation so you know what to say.

WRITING SKILLS

LANGUAGE ARTS PURPLE · **WS 215**

WRITING SKILLS

Ask yourself the following questions after you practice your presentation. Then give the presentation again. Try to improve your performance.

1. Did you talk about each point on your planning form? Did you explain why each point is important? Did you lose your place or forget any points? How can you keep that from happening?
2. Did you read directly from your research report or planning form? If so, how can you keep from reading?
3. Did you speak clearly? Did you stumble on any words or phrases? If so, which ones? How can you stop yourself from doing so again?
4. Was your tone appropriate? Did you sound enthusiastic?
5. Did you speak too slowly or too quickly? If so, how can you improve your pace?
6. Did you speak too loudly or too quietly? If so, how can you make sure to maintain a proper volume?
7. Did you sound confident in your knowledge? If not, how can you become more confident?
8. Did you stand up straight? If not, how can you remember to do so?
9. Did you look up at your audience? About how many times?
10. Did you show the media you chose? Do you need to say more about your media and what it shows?

WS 216 · LANGUAGE ARTS PURPLE

Peer Interaction

⊕ OPTIONAL: Tell Me About My Presentation

This activity is OPTIONAL. It is intended for students who have extra time and would benefit from extra practice. Feel free to skip this activity.

Students can benefit from practicing their presentations for one another. Each student should receive feedback. To complete this optional activity, turn to page WS 217 in *K¹² Language Arts Activity Book*. (Additional copies of the Peer Interaction form can be printed from the online lesson.)

1. Have students give their presentation for another student by video conferencing over a mobile device, such as a cell phone or tablet, or via an Internet program.

2. Have students use the Activity Book page to collaborate and provide one another with feedback about their video presentation.

TIP Students may use the feedback provided from other students to improve their research report presentation.

Objectives

- Use guidance from adults and peers to revise writing.
- Collaborate with peers on writing projects.

Peer Interaction

Practice Your Presentation

Tell Me About My Presentation

Have another person watch and listen to your presentation and answer the questions. **Answers will vary.**

1. Which state is the presentation about?

2. Does the speaker include only the most interesting points about this state? If not, which points are less interesting than others?

3. What media does the speaker include in the presentation? How do the media relate to the points being made?

4. Does the speaker make eye contact and have good posture? If not, how can the speaker improve?

5. Did you learn interesting information about the state? If not, what could the speaker do to make the presentation better?

LANGUAGE ARTS PURPLE | **WS 217**

Unit Review and Practice Your Presentation

Lesson Overview

💻 [Online]   15 minutes

Unit Review	Adverbs
More Practice	Adverbs

📄 [Offline]   30 minutes

Composition	Use Guidelines to Practice Your Presentation

Advance Preparation

Gather pages WS 213–214 (Plan Your Presentation, students' completed planning form) and 215–216 (Presentation Guidelines) in *K¹² Language Arts Activity Book*. Also gather students' chosen media and the completed Research Report Presentation: Feedback Sheet.

[Materials]

Supplied

- *K¹² Language Arts Activity Book*, pp. WS 213–216
- *Grammar Reference Guide* Online Book (optional)
- **Research Report Presentation: Feedback Sheet** (printout)

Also Needed

- student's chosen media

Keywords

adverb – a word that describes a verb, an adjective, or another adverb

adverb of manner – an adverb that answers the question, "How?"

adverb of place – an adverb that answers the question, "Where?"

adverb of time – an adverb that answers the question, "When?"

audience – a writer's readers

media – all the ways by which something can be shown, shared, or expressed

pace – the speed, and the change of speeds, of a speaker's delivery

tone – a speaker's attitude as shown by his or her voice

verb – a word that shows action or a state of being

[Online] 15 minutes

Students will work online to review the grammar, usage, and mechanics skills learned in the unit. Help students locate the online activities.

Unit Review ••

Adverbs

To review for the Unit Checkpoint, students will review what they have learned about adverbs, including how to recognize them and the verbs they describe; how to identify adverbs of manner, time, and place; how to use adverbs to make comparisons; and whether to use an adverb or an adjective in a sentence.

TIP A full list of objectives covered in the Unit Review can be found in the online lesson.

> **Objectives**
> • Complete a review of grammar, usage, and mechanics skills.

More Practice ••

Adverbs

Go over students' results on the Unit Review and, if necessary, have students complete the appropriate review activities listed in the table online. Help students locate the activities. Provide support as needed.

TIP The time students need to complete this activity will vary. Set aside enough time for students to complete all review activities, if they need to do so.

> **Objectives**
> • Evaluate Unit Review results and choose activities for more practice.

[Offline] 30 minutes

Work **together** with students to complete the offline Composition activity.

Composition ••

Use Guidelines to Practice Your Presentation

Students will continue to practice their research report presentation. Gather students' completed planning form, the presentation guidelines, students' chosen media, and your completed Research Report Presentation: Feedback Sheet.

> **Objectives**
> • Practice a presentation.

1. Review with students your comments in each section of the feedback sheet. As you go through the feedback sheet with students, encourage them to ask questions and take notes on how to improve their presentation based on your feedback.

2. Once you've reviewed your comments in each section of the feedback sheet with students, have them review their planning form and guidelines once more before practicing the presentation again. Students should ask themselves the questions in the guidelines after they've finished each practice run.

TIP Keep students' planning form and media in a safe place so they can refer to them during their final presentation.

Composition

Compare with Adverbs and Plan Your Presentation

Plan Your Presentation

Use this form to plan your research report presentation. Follow these directions to decide what to include.

- Points to Talk About: List five points that you will talk about in your presentation. Include one main point from each of your five paragraphs.
- Media to Use: List ideas for media you could show during your presentation. Write each idea next to the point you would use it with. When choosing media, think about what the media will help you show. Then circle the one or two media choices you most want to use, and write their sources.

Title of presentation _____

Points to Talk About	Media to Use

Students should list topics and choose one.

1. _____   1. _____
   Source _____

2. _____   2. _____
   Source _____

WS 213   LANGUAGE ARTS PURPLE

Points to Talk About	Media to Use

3. _____   3. _____
   Source _____

4. _____   4. _____
   Source _____

5. _____   5. _____
   Source _____

WS 214   LANGUAGE ARTS PURPLE

Composition

Presentation Skills

Presentation Guidelines

Follow these guidelines as you practice your research report presentation.

- Talk about each of your points and why each one is important.
- Use your planning form to help you remember what points to make, but do not read directly from the form or from your report.
- Pronounce each word clearly as you speak.
- Speak with enthusiasm and expression.
- Speak at an appropriate pace: not too fast or too slow.
- Speak with a pleasing volume: not too loud or too soft.
- Show confidence in your knowledge of your topic.
- Stand up straight.
- Look at your audience as much as possible.
- Direct your audience's attention to the media you have chosen.
- Practice the presentation so you know what to say.

WS 215   LANGUAGE ARTS PURPLE

Ask yourself the following questions after you practice your presentation. Then give the presentation again. Try to improve your performance.

1. Did you talk about each point on your planning form? Did you explain why each point is important? Did you lose your place or forget any points? How can you keep that from happening?
2. Did you read directly from your research report or planning form? If so, how can you keep from reading?
3. Did you speak clearly? Did you stumble on any words or phrases? If so, which ones? How can you stop yourself from doing so again?
4. Was your tone appropriate? Did you sound enthusiastic?
5. Did you speak too slowly or too quickly? If so, how can you improve your pace?
6. Did you speak too loudly or too quietly? If so, how can you make sure to maintain a proper volume?
7. Did you sound confident in your knowledge? If not, how can you become more confident?
8. Did you stand up straight? If not, how can you remember to do so?
9. Did you look up at your audience? About how many times?
10. Did you show the media you chose? Do you need to say more about your media and what it shows?

WS 216   LANGUAGE ARTS PURPLE

Unit Checkpoint and Deliver Your Presentation

Lesson Overview

🖥	**⟦Online⟧**		ⓕ minutes
	Unit Checkpoint	Adverbs	

📄	**⟦Offline⟧**		㉚ minutes
	More Practice	Adverbs	
	Write Now	Give Your Research Report Presentation	

Advance Preparation

Gather pages WS 213–214 (Plan Your Presentation, students' completed planning form) and 215–216 (Presentation Guidelines) in *K¹² Language Arts Activity Book.* Also gather students' chosen media.

⟦ Materials ⟧

Supplied

- *K¹² Language Arts Activity Book*, pp. WS 213–216
- *Grammar Reference Guide* Online Book (optional)
- Adverbs That Tell How, When, and Where (optional printout)
- Compare with Adverbs (optional printout)
- Research Report Presentation: Rubric (printout)

Also Needed

- students' chosen media

Keywords

adverb – a word that describes a verb, an adjective, or another adverb

adverb of manner – an adverb that answers the question, "How?"

adverb of place – an adverb that answers the question, "Where?"

adverb of time – an adverb that answers the question, "When?"

audience – a writer's readers

media – all the ways by which something can be shown, shared, or expressed

pace – the speed, and the change of speeds, of a speaker's delivery

tone – a speaker's attitude as shown by his or her voice

verb – a word that shows action or a state of being

[Online] ⑮ minutes

Students will work online **independently** to complete the Unit Checkpoint. Help students locate the Unit Checkpoint and provide support as necessary.

Unit Checkpoint ••

Adverbs

Students will complete an online Unit Checkpoint about adverbs, including how to recognize them and the verbs they describe; how to identify adverbs of manner, time, and place; how to use adverbs to make comparisons; and whether to use an adverb or an adjective in a sentence. If necessary, read the directions to students.

TIP A full list of objectives covered in the Unit Checkpoint can be found in the online lesson.

> **Objectives**
> • Complete a Unit Checkpoint on grammar, usage, and mechanics skills.

[Offline] ㉚ minutes

Work **together** with students to complete the offline More Practice and Write Now activities.

More Practice ••

Adverbs

Go over students' results on the Unit Checkpoint and, if necessary, print and have them complete the appropriate practice pages listed in the table online. Students can complete all necessary pages now or, if more time is needed, they can spread them out over the next few days. They can also review the appropriate sections of the *Grammar Reference Guide* with you. If students scored less than 80 percent on the Unit Checkpoint, you may want them to retake the Checkpoint after completing the additional activity pages.

> **Objectives**
> • Evaluate Unit Checkpoint results and choose activities for more practice.

TIP The time students need to complete this activity will vary. Set aside enough time for students to complete some or all activity pages and to retake the Unit Checkpoint, if they need to do so. Students may retake the Unit Checkpoint immediately, but having them complete the practice pages and then retake it might be more effective.

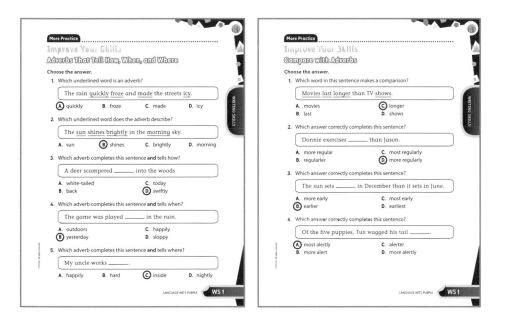

Write Now

Give Your Research Report Presentation

Students will give their research report presentation. Gather their planning form and media, as well as the presentation guidelines.

1. Explain to students that they will finish this unit by giving a presentation about their state and showing their media.
   Say: To be ready to give your presentation, you should have practiced several times talking about your state and describing the media you chose. Today's presentation should be your best effort. Review the presentation guidelines one last time before giving your presentation.

Objectives
- Deliver a presentation.
- Speak clearly at an understandable pace.
- Speak in complete sentences to provide requested detail or clarification.
- Ask and answer questions about information from a speaker.

2. Use the materials and instructions in the online lesson to evaluate students' presentation. You will be watching and listening to the presentation to evaluate the following:

   ▸ **Purpose and Content:** The presentation focuses on one key point from four of the report's five paragraphs and shows some related media. The student followed the directions in developing and practicing the presentation. With perhaps one exception, the presentation includes the report's most important and interesting points.

   ▸ **Structure and Organization:** The presentation includes points in mostly the same order that they appeared in the research report. The student shows the media at the proper time in the presentation. With perhaps one exception, the beginning of the presentation includes the point made by the main idea of the report, the middle of the presentation includes points from the body paragraphs, and the end of the presentation includes points from the conclusion.

   ▸ **Speaking Skills:** The student mostly speaks in complete sentences and makes eye contact at several points during the presentation. The student mostly speaks clearly, rarely speaks too quickly or too slowly, and uses an appropriate volume. With perhaps one or two exceptions, the student speaks with confidence and enthusiasm and stands up straight throughout most of the presentation.

3. Enter students' scores online for each rubric category.

4. If students' presentation scored a 1 in any category, discuss with them how their presentation might be improved. However, students do not need to actually give their presentation again.

5. If you wish, videotape students' presentation to share with others. Help students share the presentation, if possible.

6. If others watch and listen to students' presentation, encourage them to ask questions for clarification or for more details.

TIP Tell students that giving a presentation is a great accomplishment. Let students know that the effort they put in to doing this unit's assignment is something to be proud of.

Reward: When students score 80 percent or above on the Unit Checkpoint and they have completed their research report presentation, add a sticker for this unit on the My Accomplishments chart.

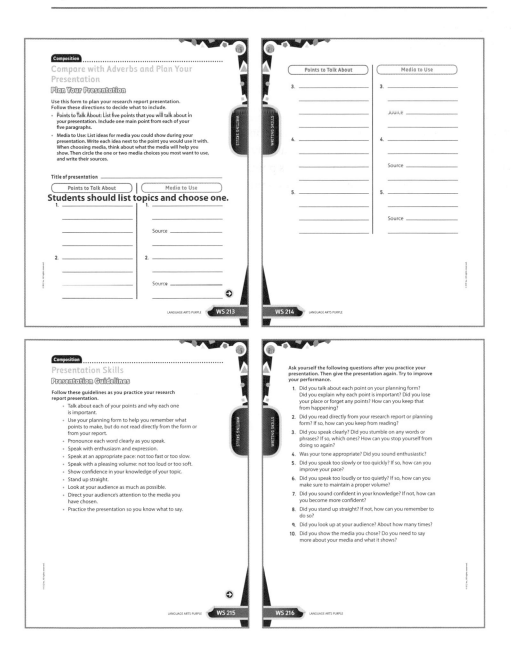

Composition

Compare with Adverbs and Plan Your Presentation

Plan Your Presentation

Use this form to plan your research report presentation. Follow these directions to decide what to include.

- Points to Talk About: List five points that you will talk about in your presentation. Include one main point from each of your five paragraphs.
- Media to Use: List ideas for media you could show during your presentation. Write each idea next to the point you would use it with. When choosing media, think about what the media will help you show. Then circle the one or two media choices you most want to use, and write their sources.

Title of presentation _____

Points to Talk About	Media to Use
Students should list topics and choose one.	
1. _____	1. _____
_____	Source _____
2. _____	2. _____
_____	Source _____

WS 213 LANGUAGE ARTS PURPLE

Points to Talk About	Media to Use
3. _____	3. _____
_____	_____
_____	Source _____
4. _____	4. _____
_____	_____
_____	Source _____
5. _____	5. _____
_____	_____
_____	Source _____

WS 214 LANGUAGE ARTS PURPLE

Composition

Presentation Skills

Presentation Guidelines

Follow these guidelines as you practice your research report presentation.

- Talk about each of your points and why each one is important.
- Use your planning form to help you remember what points to make, but do not read directly from the form or from your report.
- Pronounce each word clearly as you speak.
- Speak with enthusiasm and expression.
- Speak at an appropriate pace: not too fast or too slow.
- Speak with a pleasing volume: not too loud or too soft.
- Show confidence in your knowledge of your topic.
- Stand up straight.
- Look at your audience as much as possible.
- Direct your audience's attention to the media you have chosen.
- Practice the presentation so you know what to say.

WS 215 LANGUAGE ARTS PURPLE

Ask yourself the following questions after you practice your presentation. Then give the presentation again. Try to improve your performance.

1. Did you talk about each point on your planning form? Did you explain why each point is important? Did you lose your place or forget any points? How can you keep that from happening?

2. Did you read directly from your research report or planning form? If so, how can you keep from reading?

3. Did you speak clearly? Did you stumble on any words or phrases? If so, which ones? How can you stop yourself from doing so again?

4. Was your tone appropriate? Did you sound enthusiastic?

5. Did you speak too slowly or too quickly? If so, how can you improve your pace?

6. Did you speak too loudly or too quietly? If so, how can you make sure to maintain a proper volume?

7. Did you sound confident in your knowledge? If not, how can you become more confident?

8. Did you stand up straight? If not, how can you remember to do so?

9. Did you look up at your audience? About how many times?

10. Did you show the media you chose? Do you need to say more about your media and what it shows?

WS 216 LANGUAGE ARTS PURPLE

Capital Letters, Punctuation, and Forms

Unit Focus

In the grammar part of the unit, students will learn about using capital letters and punctuation correctly. They will

▶ Learn that a proper noun must always begin with a capital letter.

▶ Learn the abbreviations for the names of days and months and the titles of people.

▶ Learn when to use commas after beginning words and phrases in sentences.

▶ Learn to use commas with words or phrases in a series.

In this unit, students will focus on filling out a variety of forms. They will

▶ Use their journal to freewrite.

▶ Read and respond to a model form.

▶ Learn how to fill out an invitation form.

▶ Learn how to fill out an application.

▶ Learn how to fill out a schedule.

▶ Proofread one form that they filled out.

Unit Plan		〖Online〗	〖Offline〗
Lesson 1	Proper Nouns and Journal Entry	25 minutes	20 minutes
Lesson 2	Abbreviations and Model Form	30 minutes	15 minutes
Lesson 3	Beginning Words and an Invitation Form	25 minutes	20 minutes
Lesson 4	Words in a Series and Library Card Application	25 minutes	20 minutes
Lesson 5	Unit Review and a Schedule	25 minutes	20 minutes
Lesson 6	Unit Checkpoint and Proofread a Form	30 minutes	15 minutes

Proper Nouns and Journal Entry

Lesson Overview

🖥️ **【Online】**   **25** minutes

GUM (Grammar, Usage, and Mechanics)	Proper Nouns

📝 **【Offline】**   **20** minutes

Composition	Journal: Write About Forms You've Filled Out
Beyond the Lesson	⊕ OPTIONAL: Journal: Freewrite on a Topic

【Materials】

Supplied
- *K⁷ My Journal*, pp. 42–45
- *Grammar Reference Guide* **Online Book** (optional)

Keywords

proper noun – the name of a particular person, place, thing, or idea; proper nouns begin with a capital letter

Advance Preparation

To prepare for the GUM portion of this lesson, review Capital Letters in the *Grammar Reference Guide* (linked in the online lesson) to familiarize yourself with the topic.

Big Ideas

▶ Knowing how to fill in forms is a skill necessary for both young people, who may want to get a library card, and adults, who may want to apply for a job.

▶ Journal writing is a form of freewriting. It is an opportunity to get ideas on paper without regard for the correctness of the language or the format of a piece of writing.

▶ To improve, writers require frequent practice.

[Online] 25 minutes

Students will work online **independently** to complete an activity on recognizing and writing proper nouns. Help students locate the online activity.

GUM (Grammar, Usage, and Mechanics)

Proper Nouns
Students will review what a proper noun is and that it always begins with a capital letter. They will then practice identifying and capitalizing proper nouns.

Objectives
• Use a capital letter to begin a proper noun.

[Offline] 20 minutes

Work **together** with students to complete the offline Composition and Beyond the Lesson activities.

Composition

 **Journal: Write About Forms You've Filled Out**
Students will respond to a journal prompt by writing about forms they've filled out. Gather *K¹² My Journal* and have students turn to pages 42 and 43.

Objectives
• Respond to a journal prompt.
• Freewrite about a topic.

1. Tell students that they are going to write in their journal about forms they've filled out. To help students think of what to say about their experiences with filling out forms, ask them to think about their answers to the following questions.

   ▸ When have you joined an organization or a team? What paperwork did you have to fill out? What information did you have to give to the league, the coach, or the leaders of the organization you wished to join?
   ▸ Have you ever applied for anything? Did you write down the information that was needed yourself, or did someone else do it for you? What problems did you face in completing the paperwork?

2. Have students respond to the prompt in their journal. Encourage them to write in complete sentences, although it is not a requirement when they are freewriting in their journal.

TIP Students should write for about 20 minutes. Freewriting allows students to use their imagination to write what they want without worrying about being graded, so encourage them to keep writing for the entire time. If students have trouble writing for 20 minutes, use the prompting questions in Step 1 or have them list ideas or words. If they want to keep writing beyond the suggested time limit, praise them for their enthusiasm and offer to let them complete their entry later in the day as a reward.

Forms　　　　　　　Date _____

WRITING SKILLS

What kinds of forms have you filled out? What was the most difficult one to do? Why?

_____
_____
_____
_____
_____
_____
_____
_____
_____
_____
_____
_____
_____
_____

42

Beyond the Lesson ●

✏️ ➕ OPTIONAL: Journal: Freewrite on a Topic

This activity is OPTIONAL. It is intended for students who have extra time and would benefit from extra practice. Feel free to skip this activity. Gather *K¹² My Journal*.

1. Have students either respond to a prompt in Thoughts and Experiences (pages 50–93) or write about their own topic on the next available page in Ideas (pages 96–139).

2. Encourage students to explore their thoughts and write as much as they want. There are no rules. If students wish, ideas can be fleshed out into a more developed composition at a later time.

TIP Studies show that students who write more frequently become better writers.

> **Objectives**
> - Respond to a journal prompt.
> - Freewrite about a topic.

Abbreviations and Model Form

Lesson Overview

🖥 [Online]   30 minutes

Skills Update	Proper Nouns
GUM (Grammar, Usage, and Mechanics)	Abbreviations and Initials
Composition	Explore a Model Form

📄 [Offline]   15 minutes

Composition	Respond to a Model Form

[Materials]

Supplied
- *K¹² Language Arts Activity Book*, pp. WS 219, 221
- *Grammar Reference Guide* Online Book (optional)

Keywords

abbreviation – the shortened form of a word or phrase

Advance Preparation

To prepare for the GUM portion of this lesson, review Capitalization (Names and Initials; Other Uses of Capital Letters) and Punctuation (Other Uses of the Period) in the *Grammar Reference Guide* (linked in the online lesson) to familiarize yourself with the topics.

Big Ideas

Knowing how to fill in forms is a skill necessary for both young people, who may want to get a library card, and adults, who may want to apply for a job.

〔Online〕 ③⓿ minutes

Students will work online to review proper nouns; to learn how to write the abbreviations of months, days, titles, and initials; and to examine how to complete a form. Help students locate the online activities.

Skills Update ••

Proper Nouns
Students will review how to correctly write proper nouns by completing Skills Update exercises. Sit with students as they do this activity and note if they answer correctly.

⊃ **Learning Coach Check-In** How did students do on the Skills Update?

▸ **All answers correct:** Great! Skip the review screen and go on to the next activity.

▸ **Any answers incorrect:** Take a few minutes to review proper nouns now. Use the link on the screen after the Skills Update to take another look at the online activity or review Capital Letters in the *Grammar Reference Guide* together.

(TIP) This activity will require extra time if students need to review proper nouns. Take the extra 5–10 minutes to review now because new skills build on what students have already learned.

> **Objectives**
> • Use a capital letter to begin a proper noun.

GUM (Grammar, Usage, and Mechanics) •••••••••••••••••••••••••••••••

Abbreviations and Initials
Students will learn that the names of months and days, as well as common titles, can be abbreviated. They will learn these abbreviations and practice using them. They will also learn what initials are and how to correctly write them.

> **Objectives**
> • Capitalize and punctuate abbreviations and initials correctly.

Composition ••

Explore a Model Form
By exploring how one writer fills out a form, students will learn how to fill out forms of their own.

(TIP) Seeing a final version of a form helps students see the goal of this unit. It will be easier for them to understand how to complete a form if they see a finished product. If students are not comfortable reading the model form for this activity online, they may read the model on page WS 219 in *K¹² Language Arts Activity Book*.

> **Objectives**
> • Describe the kind of information on a form.
> • Respond to questions about a form.

❲ Offline ❳ 🕙 minutes

Work **together** with students to complete the offline Composition activity.

Composition ....

Respond to a Model Form

Students will review what they learned about the model form. Turn to pages WS 219 and 221 in *K¹² Language Arts Activity Book*.

1. Have students reread the model form on page WS 219.

2. Have students complete the Activity Book page about Emily's form. Provide support as necessary, encouraging students to write in complete sentences. Students should refer to Emily's form as needed.

Objectives
- Describe the kind of information on a form.
- Respond to questions about a form.

Composition ....
Abbreviations and Model Form
Model Form

Read Emily's form.

Sandycove Soccer Stars – Player Application
Please fill out in blue or black ink. Return to Coach Morris by Aug. 31.

A. Name Emily Gold	**B.** Address 419 Price Street, Sandycove, ME 03902		
C. Gender ☐ Male ☒ Female	**D.** Birthday 4/30/2005	**E.** Phone number 207-555-1013	**F.** E-mail address egold1@scove. net
G. I give permission for my child to play on the Sandycove Soccer Stars team. *Judy Gold*		**H.** Today's date 8/15/2013	

LANGUAGE ARTS PURPLE **WS 219**

Composition ....
Abbreviations and Model Form
Respond to the Model Form

Answer the questions about Emily's form.

1. What is the purpose of the form?
   to sign up for a soccer team

2. Why did Emily use a blue pen when filling out this form?
   The directions say to use blue or black ink.

3. According to the form, what street does Emily live on?
   Price Street

4. According to the form, when is Emily's birthday?
   April 30, 2005

5. When does this form have to be returned to Coach Morris?
   by August 31

6. Who signed Emily's form in Box G?
   her mom, Judy Gold

7. Do you think you would have been able to fill out this form if you were signing up to play soccer in Sandycove? Who would you have had help you complete the form?
   Answers will vary.

LANGUAGE ARTS PURPLE **WS 221**

Beginning Words and an Invitation Form

Lesson Overview

Online — 25 minutes

Skills Update	Abbreviations and Initials
GUM (Grammar, Usage, and Mechanics)	Beginning Words
Composition	Invitations

Offline — 20 minutes

Composition	Fill Out an Invitation

Materials

Supplied

- K¹² *Language Arts Activity Book*, p. WS 223
- *Grammar Reference Guide* Online Book (optional)

Advance Preparation

To prepare for the GUM portion of this lesson, review Commas (After Introductory Words, Phrases, and Clauses) in the *Grammar Reference Guide* (linked in the online lesson) to familiarize yourself with the topic. In this lesson, students begin to accumulate forms they complete in the lessons in this unit. You might want to provide students with a folder or large envelope in which to keep these forms.

Big Ideas

Knowing how to fill in forms is a skill necessary for both young people, who may want to get a library card, and adults, who may want to apply for a job.

 ⏱ **25 minutes**

Students will work online to review abbreviations and initials, to learn about beginning words and phrases at the start of sentences, and to find out how to fill out invitation forms. Help students locate the online activities.

Skills Update ·

Abbreviations and Initials

Students will review abbreviations and initials by completing Skills Update exercises. Sit with students as they do this activity and note if they answer correctly.

⟳ **Learning Coach Check-In** How did students do on the Skills Update?

- ▸ **All answers correct:** Great! Skip the review screen and go on to the next activity.
- ▸ **Any answers incorrect:** Take a few minutes to review abbreviations and initials now. Use the link on the screen after the Skills Update to take another look at the online activity or review Capitalization (Names and Initials; Other Uses of Capital Letters) and Punctuation (Other Uses of the Period) in the *Grammar Reference Guide* together.

⒯⒤⒫ This activity will require extra time if students need to review abbreviations and initials. Take the extra 5–10 minutes to review now because new skills build on what students have already learned.

> **Objectives**
> - Capitalize and punctuate abbreviations and initials correctly.

GUM (Grammar, Usage, and Mechanics) ·

Beginning Words

Students will learn about using commas after words and phrases that serve as introductions or transitions at the beginnings of sentences.

> **Objectives**
> - Use a comma after a transitional word or phrase.

Composition ·

Invitations

By reviewing a completed invitation form, students will learn how to complete an invitation form of their own.

> **Objectives**
> - Recognize the kind of information in an invitation form.
> - Fill out an invitation form.

[Offline] 20 minutes

Work **together** with students to complete the offline Composition activity.

Composition

Fill Out an Invitation

Students will fill out an invitation form. Turn to page WS 223 in *K¹² Language Arts Activity Book*.

1. Have students complete the Activity Book page to fill out an invitation to a party of their choosing. Provide support as necessary, encouraging students to think about what belongs in each part of the form.

2. Remind students that there is no wrong choice when it comes to the purpose for the invitation or when or where the party is to be held. Any event or party that they choose can be the subject of an invitation, and any correctly written date or time is acceptable.

TIP Keep students' completed form in a safe place so they can refer to it later.

Objectives

- Recognize the kind of information in an invitation form.
- Fill out an invitation form.

Words in a Series and Library Card Application

Lesson Overview

Online — 25 minutes

Skills Update	Beginning Words
GUM (Grammar, Usage, and Mechanics)	Words in a Series
Composition	Applications

Offline — 20 minutes

Composition	Fill Out an Application

Materials

Supplied

- *K¹² Language Arts Activity Book*, p. WS 225
- *Grammar Reference Guide* Online Book (optional)

Advance Preparation

To prepare for the GUM portion of this lesson, review Commas (For Items in a Series) in the *Grammar Reference Guide* (linked in the online lesson) to familiarize yourself with the topic.

Big Ideas

Knowing how to fill in forms is a skill necessary for both young people, who may want to get a library card, and adults, who may want to apply for a job.

[Online] 25 minutes

Students will work online to review how to punctuate beginning words and phrases, to learn about using commas with items in series, and to find out how to fill out a library card application. Help students locate the online activities.

Skills Update

Beginning Words

Students will review using commas after beginning words and phrases by completing Skills Update exercises. Sit with students as they do this activity and note if they answer correctly.

⮑ **Learning Coach Check-In** How did students do on the Skills Update?

  ▸ **All answers correct:** Great! Skip the review screen and go on to the next activity.
  ▸ **Any answers incorrect:** Take a few minutes to review using commas after beginning words and phrases now. Use the link on the screen after the Skills Update to take another look at the online activity or review Commas (After Introductory Words, Phrases, and Clauses) in the *Grammar Reference Guide* together.

TIP This activity will require extra time if students need to review using commas after beginning words and phrases. Take the extra 5–10 minutes to review now because new skills build on what students have already learned.

Objectives
• Use a comma after a transitional word or phrase.

GUM (Grammar, Usage, and Mechanics)

Words in a Series

Students will learn about using commas when writing words and phrases in a series.

Objectives
• Use commas to separate words in a series.

Composition

Applications

By reviewing a completed application for a library card, students will learn how to complete an application of their own.

Objectives
• Recognize the kind of information in a library card application.
• Fill out a library card application.

[Offline] 20 minutes

Work **together** with students to complete the offline Composition activity.

Composition

Fill Out an Application

Students will fill out a library card application. Turn to page WS 225 in *K¹² Language Arts Activity Book.*

1. Have students complete the Activity Book page. Provide support as necessary, encouraging students to think about each element of the form and what belongs there.

2. Remind students to read the instructions on the form and follow them. They should use their own name, address, and contact information when filling out the form.

TIP Keep students' completed application in a safe place so they can refer to it later.

Objectives

- Recognize the kind of information in a library card application.
- Fill out a library card application.

Unit Review and a Schedule

Lesson Overview

🖥 [Online]   25 minutes

Skills Update	Words in a Series
Unit Review	Capital Letters and Punctuation
More Practice	Capital Letters and Punctuation
Composition	Schedules

📄 [Offline]   20 minutes

Composition	Fill Out a Schedule

[Materials]

Supplied
- K™ Language Arts Activity Book, p. WS 227
- *Grammar Reference Guide* Online Book (optional)

Keywords

abbreviation – the shortened form of a word or phrase

proper noun – the name of a particular person, place, thing, or idea; proper nouns begin with a capital letter

Big Ideas

Knowing how to fill in forms is a skill necessary for both young people, who may want to get a library card, and adults, who may want to apply for a job.

 **25 minutes**

Students will work online to review using commas to separate words and phrases in a series; to review the grammar, usage, and mechanics skills learned in the unit; and to find out how to fill out a schedule. Help students locate the online activities.

Skills Update

Words in a Series

Students will review using commas to separate words and phrases in a series by completing Skills Update exercises. Sit with students as they do this activity and note if they answer correctly.

⊃ **Learning Coach Check-In** How did students do on the Skills Update?

- ▸ **All answers correct:** Great! Skip the review screen and go on to the next activity.
- ▸ **Any answers incorrect:** Take a few minutes to review using commas to separate words and phrases in a series now. Use the link on the screen after the Skills Update to take another look at the online activity or review Commas (For Items in a Series) in the *Grammar Reference Guide* together.

TIP This activity will require extra time if students need to review using commas to separate words and phrases in a series. Take the extra 5–10 minutes to review now because new skills build on what students have already learned.

> **Objectives**
> - Use commas to separate words in a series.

Unit Review

Capital Letters and Punctuation

Students will review what they have learned about capital letters and punctuation for the Unit Checkpoint.

TIP A full list of objectives covered in the Unit Review can be found in the online lesson.

> **Objectives**
> - Complete a review of grammar, usage, and mechanics skills.

More Practice

Capital Letters and Punctuation

Go over students' results on the Unit Review and, if necessary, have students complete the appropriate review activities listed in the table online. Help students locate the activities. Provide support as needed.

TIP The time students need to complete this activity will vary. Set aside enough time for students to complete all review activities, if they need to do so.

> **Objectives**
> - Evaluate Unit Review results and choose activities for more practice.

Composition

Schedules
By reviewing a completed schedule, students will learn how to complete a daily schedule of their own.

[Offline] 20 minutes

Work **together** with students to complete the offline Composition activity.

Composition

Fill Out a Schedule
Students will fill out a daily schedule. Turn to page WS 227 in *K¹² Language Arts Activity Book*.

1. Have students complete the Activity Book page. Provide support as necessary, encouraging students to think about each element of the form and what belongs there.

2. Remind students to fill out something for each box on the schedule. They should use their actual chores and activities to fill in the schedule. Encourage students to decorate their schedule with tiny drawings or stickers related to the activities and chores they list.

TIP Keep students' completed schedule in a safe place so they can refer to it later.

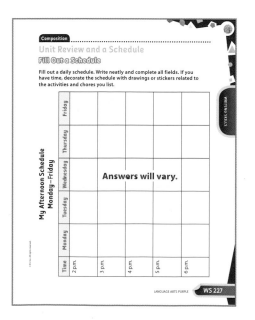

Unit Checkpoint and Proofread a Form

Lesson Overview

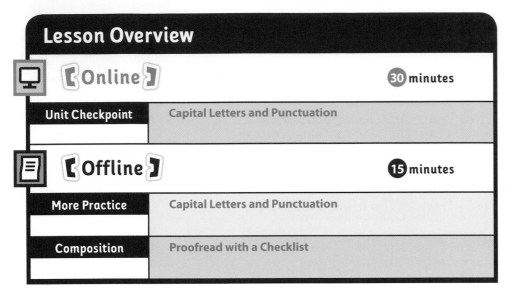

Online		30 minutes
Unit Checkpoint	Capital Letters and Punctuation	
Offline		15 minutes
More Practice	Capital Letters and Punctuation	
Composition	Proofread with a Checklist	

Materials

Supplied
- *K¹² Language Arts Activity Book*, pp. WS 223, 225, 227, 229
- *Grammar Reference Guide* Online Book (optional)
- Proper Nouns (optional printout)
- Abbreviations and Initials (optional printout)
- Beginning Words (optional printout)
- Words in a Series (optional printout)
- Forms: Feedback Sheet (printout)

Keywords

abbreviation – the shortened form of a word or phrase

proper noun – the name of a particular person, place, thing, or idea; proper nouns begin with a capital letter

Advance Preparation

Gather students' completed forms on pages WS 223 (Fill Out an Invitation), 225 (Fill Out an Application), and 227 (Fill Out a Schedule) in *K¹² Language Arts Activity Book*. Print the Forms: Feedback Sheet from the online lesson.

Online 30 minutes

Students will work online **independently** to complete the Unit Checkpoint. Help students locate the Unit Checkpoint and provide support as necessary.

Unit Checkpoint

Capital Letters and Punctuation
Students will complete an online Unit Checkpoint about capital letters and punctuation. If necessary, read the directions to students.

TIP A full list of objectives covered in the Unit Checkpoint can be found in the online lesson.

Objectives
- Complete a Unit Checkpoint on grammar, usage, and mechanics skills.

〔 Offline 〕 15 minutes

Work **together** with students to complete the offline More Practice and Composition activities.

More Practice

Capital Letters and Punctuation

Go over students' results on the Unit Checkpoint and, if necessary, print out and have them complete the appropriate practice pages listed in the table online. Students can complete all necessary pages now or, if more time is needed, they can spread them out over the next few days. They can also review the appropriate sections of the *Grammar Reference Guide* with you. If students scored less than 80 percent on the Unit Checkpoint, you may want them to retake the Checkpoint after completing the additional activity pages.

TIP The time students need to complete this activity will vary. Set aside enough time for students to complete some or all activity pages and to retake the Unit Checkpoint, if they need to do so. Students may retake the Unit Checkpoint immediately, but having them complete the practice pages and then retake it might be more effective.

> **Objectives**
> - Evaluate Unit Checkpoint results and choose activities for more practice.

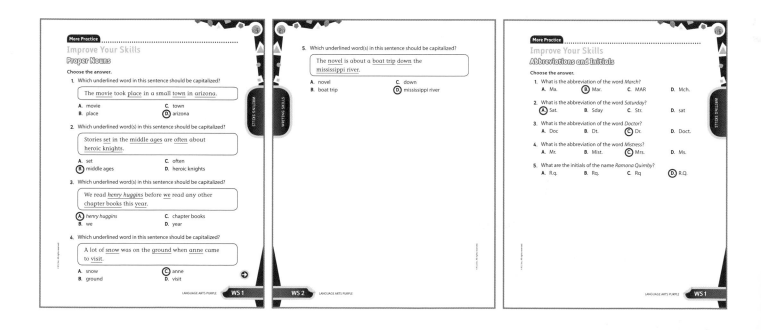

More Practice

Improve Your Skills

Proper Nouns

Choose the answer.

1. Which underlined word in this sentence should be capitalized?

   The movie took place in a small town in arizona.

   A. movie   C. town
   B. place   **D. arizona**

2. Which underlined word(s) in this sentence should be capitalized?

   Stories set in the middle ages are often about heroic knights.

   A. set   C. often
   B. middle ages   D. heroic knights

3. Which underlined word(s) in this sentence should be capitalized?

   We read henry huggins before we read any other chapter books this year.

   A. henry huggins   C. chapter books
   B. we   D. year

4. Which underlined word in this sentence should be capitalized?

   A lot of snow was on the ground when anne came to visit.

   A. snow   **C. anne**
   B. ground   D. visit

LANGUAGE ARTS PURPLE   **WS 1**

5. Which underlined word(s) in this sentence should be capitalized?

   The novel is about a boat trip down the mississippi river.

   A. novel   C. down
   B. boat trip   **D. mississippi river**

WS 2   LANGUAGE ARTS PURPLE

More Practice

Improve Your Skills

Abbreviations and Initials

Choose the answer.

1. What is the abbreviation of the word *March*?
   A. Ma.   **B. Mar.**   C. MAR   D. Mch.

2. What is the abbreviation of the word *Saturday*?
   A. Sat.   B. Sday   C. Str.   D. sat

3. What is the abbreviation of the word *Doctor*?
   A. Doc   B. Dt.   **C. Dr.**   D. Doct.

4. What is the abbreviation of the word *Mistress*?
   A. Mr.   B. Mist.   **C. Mrs.**   D. Ms.

5. What are the initials of the name *Ramona Quimby*?
   A. R.q.   B. Rq.   C. Rq   **D. R.Q.**

LANGUAGE ARTS PURPLE   **WS 1**

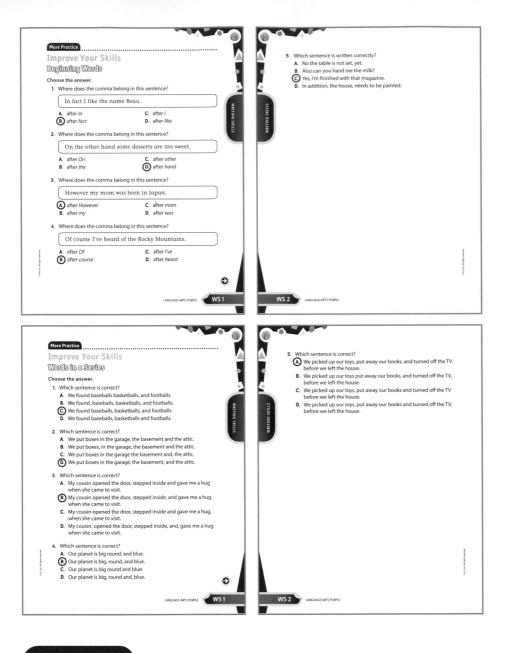

More Practice

Improve Your Skills
Beginning Words

Choose the answer.

1. Where does the comma belong in this sentence?

   In fact I like the name Beau.

   A. after *In*   C. after *I*
   B. after *fact* ●   D. after *like*

2. Where does the comma belong in this sentence?

   On the other hand some desserts are too sweet.

   A. after *On*   C. after *other*
   B. after *the*   D. after *hand* ●

3. Where does the comma belong in this sentence?

   However my mom was born in Japan.

   A. after *However* ●   C. after *mom*
   B. after *my*   D. after *was*

4. Where does the comma belong in this sentence?

   Of course I've heard of the Rocky Mountains.

   A. after *Of*   C. after *I've*
   B. after *course* ●   D. after *heard*

LANGUAGE ARTS PURPLE   WS 1

---

5. Which sentence is written correctly?
   A. No the table is not set, yet.
   B. Also can you hand me the milk?
   C. Yes, I'm finished with that magazine. ●
   D. In addition, the house, needs to be painted.

WS 2   LANGUAGE ARTS PURPLE

More Practice

Improve Your Skills
Words in a Series

Choose the answer.

1. Which sentence is correct?
   A. We found baseballs basketballs, and footballs.
   B. We found, baseballs, basketballs, and footballs.
   C. We found baseballs, basketballs, and footballs. ●
   D. We found baseballs, basketballs and footballs.

2. Which sentence is correct?
   A. We put boxes in the garage, the basement and the attic.
   B. We put boxes, in the garage, the basement and the attic.
   C. We put boxes in the garage the basement and, the attic.
   D. We put boxes in the garage, the basement, and the attic. ●

3. Which sentence is correct?
   A. My cousin opened the door, stepped inside and gave me a hug when she came to visit.
   B. My cousin opened the door, stepped inside, and gave me a hug when she came to visit. ●
   C. My cousin opened the door, stepped inside and gave me a hug, when she came to visit.
   D. My cousin, opened the door, stepped inside, and, gave me a hug when she came to visit.

4. Which sentence is correct?
   A. Our planet is big round, and blue.
   B. Our planet is big, round, and blue. ●
   C. Our planet is big round and blue.
   D. Our planet is big, round and, blue.

LANGUAGE ARTS PURPLE   WS 1

---

5. Which sentence is correct?
   A. We picked up our toys, put away our books, and turned off the TV before we left the house. ●
   B. We picked up our toys put away our books, and turned off the TV, before we left the house.
   C. We picked up our toys, put away our books and turned off the TV before we left the house.
   D. We picked up our toys, put away our books and turned off the TV, before we left the house.

WS 2   LANGUAGE ARTS PURPLE

Composition

Proofread with a Checklist

Students will choose one form that they filled out in this unit to proofread and make corrections to. Have them gather their completed forms and the proofreading checklist on page WS 229 of *K¹² Language Arts Activity Book*. Also gather the Forms: Feedback Sheet, which you should have printed.

1. Using the proofreading checklist, review with students the form that they chose. Have them make corrections to the form based on the items on the checklist.

2. When students have finished proofreading their form, review it using the Forms: Feedback Sheet.

Objectives
- Proofread the forms.
- Proofread for errors in capitalization.
- Proofread for errors in abbreviations.

3. Review with students your comments in the feedback sheet. If students' forms were unsatisfactory in multiple areas (if the answers to more than three of the Yes/No questions are "No," for instance), work with them to revise and improve their work.

Reward: When students score 80 percent or above on the Unit Checkpoint and any necessary revisions to their form are complete, add a sticker for this unit on the My Accomplishments chart.

Composition

Beginning Words and an Invitation Form
Fill Out an Invitation

Fill out the party invitation. Write the reason for the party on the first line. Then write when and where the party will be. List yourself as the host and give your own phone number or e-mail address for people to respond to the invitation.

You're invited to
Answers will vary.

Date _____

Time _____

Address _____

_____

_____

Host _____

RSVP _____

LANGUAGE ARTS PURPLE | WS 223

Composition

Words in a Series and Library Card Application
Fill Out an Application

Fill out the library card application. Follow the instructions on the form, print neatly, and complete all fields.

Uptown Library
123 Beech Street
York, ME 03909
Phone:(123) 555-1234
www.upl.lib.me.us.model

Complete the library card form below. Then sign the form and return it to the Circulation Desk.

Answers will vary.

First Name _____ Last Name _____

Street Address _____ Apartment Number _____

City/Town _____ State _____ Zip Code _____

E-mail _____ Birth Date _____

If the applicant is under 18, a parent or guardian should fill out the remainder of this form.

Parent/Guardian _____ Workplace _____

Child's School _____ Child's Grade _____

Signature _____

LANGUAGE ARTS PURPLE | WS 225

Composition

Unit Review and a Schedule
Fill Out a Schedule

Fill out a daily schedule. Write neatly and complete all fields. If you have time, decorate the schedule with drawings or stickers related to the activities and chores you list.

My Afternoon Schedule Monday–Friday

Time	Monday	Tuesday	Wednesday	Thursday	Friday
2 p.m.					
3 p.m.					
4 p.m.		**Answers will vary.**			
5 p.m.					

LANGUAGE ARTS PURPLE | WS 227

Composition

Unit Checkpoint and Proofread a Form
Proofread with a Checklist

Follow this checklist as you proofread one of the forms that you filled out. Check off each box after you complete each item.

☐ Follow the directions on the form.

☐ Write neatly.

☐ Fill in every field on the form.

☐ Check that all information on the form is correct.

☐ Correctly abbreviate the names of months and days, as well as the titles of people.

☐ Capitalize all proper nouns.

Students should check off each box after they complete each item.

LANGUAGE ARTS PURPLE | WS 229

UNIT OVERVIEW Verb Tense and Plan a Short Story

Unit Focus

In the grammar part of the unit, students will learn about verbs and verb tenses. They will

▸ Learn about the principal parts of verbs.
▸ Identify and use present tense verbs.
▸ Identify and use future tense verbs.
▸ Identify regular past tense verbs and form them by adding *–ed* or *–d* to the present form.
▸ Identify and use irregular past tense verbs.

In the composition part of the unit, students will develop a plan for writing a short story. They will

▸ Use their journal to freewrite.
▸ Read a model short story.
▸ Brainstorm a topic for their short story.
▸ Choose a setting for their short story.
▸ Create characters for their short story.
▸ Develop a plot for their short story.
▸ Create a story plan that includes details about setting, characters, and plot and that will serve as a writing aid for their short story.
▸ Learn to write dialogue and practice writing dialogue.
▸ Improve and correct their story plan.

Unit Plan		〔Online〕	〔Offline〕
Lesson 1	Principal Parts of Verbs and Journal Entry	25 minutes	20 minutes
Lesson 2	Present Tense Verbs and Model Short Story	25 minutes	20 minutes
Lesson 3	Future Tense Verbs and Brainstorm Story Ideas	25 minutes	20 minutes
Lesson 4	Past Tense Verbs and Choose a Setting for Your Story	25 minutes	20 minutes
Lesson 5	Irregular Past Tense Verbs and Choose Characters for Your Story	25 minutes	20 minutes
Lesson 6	Irregular Past Tense Verbs and Choose a Plot for Your Story	25 minutes	20 minutes
Lesson 7	Plan Your Story	20 minutes	25 minutes
Lesson 8	Focus on Dialogue	20 minutes	25 minutes
Lesson 9	Unit Review and Write Dialogue	25 minutes	20 minutes
Lesson 10	Unit Checkpoint and Review Your Story Plan	25 minutes	20 minutes

Principal Parts of Verbs and Journal Entry

Lesson Overview

Online — 25 minutes

GUM (Grammar, Usage, and Mechanics)	Principal Parts of Verbs

Offline — 20 minutes

Composition	Journal: Write About a Character You'd Like to Meet
Beyond the Lesson	⊕ OPTIONAL: Journal: Freewrite on a Topic

Materials

Supplied
- *K⁽⁾ My Journal*, pp. 44–45
- *Grammar Reference Guide* **Online Book (optional)**

Keywords

irregular verb – a verb that does not add –*d* or –*ed* to the present form to make the past and the past participle

principal part – one of four basic verb forms—present, present participle, past, and past participle

regular verb – a verb that adds –*d* or –*ed* to the present form to make the past and the past participle

tense – the time that verbs show, such as present, future, or past

Advance Preparation

To prepare for the GUM portion of this lesson, review Principal Parts of Verbs (Regular Verbs; Irregular Verbs) in the *Grammar Reference Guide* (linked in the online lesson) to familiarize yourself with the topic.

Big Ideas

- Knowing how to form different verb tenses and when to use them helps writers and speakers express their ideas in a logical manner.
- Journal writing is a form of freewriting. It is an opportunity to get ideas on paper without regard for the correctness of the language or the format of a piece of writing.
- To improve, writers require frequent practice.

 **25** minutes

Students will work online **independently** to complete an activity on the principal parts of verbs. Help students locate the online activity.

GUM (Grammar, Usage, and Mechanics)

Principal Parts of Verbs
Students will learn that the basic forms of verbs are called principal parts. They will learn how to write the principal parts of regular and irregular verbs, and they will practice identifying and using the present, past, and past participle forms of regular and irregular verbs.

> **Objectives**
> * Identify and use the principal parts of regular verbs.
> * Identify and use the principal parts of irregular verbs.

 **20** minutes

Work **together** with students to complete the offline Composition and Beyond the Lesson activities.

Composition

Journal: Write About a Character You'd Like to Meet
Students will respond to a journal prompt by writing about a character they would like to meet from a work of fiction. Gather K^{12} *My Journal* and have students turn to pages 44 and 45.

> **Objectives**
> * Respond to a journal prompt.
> * Freewrite about a topic.

1. Tell students they are going to write in their journal about a fictional character that they have read about. To help students think of an appropriate one, ask them to think about their answers to the following questions.

   ▸ What are some of the books and stories that you've read during the past year? Who were the main characters? Who were some of the other memorable characters?

   ▸ Did any of these characters seem especially interesting, funny, or neat to you? If so, which ones? What qualities drew you to this character or these characters?

   ▸ Would you rather meet a character who is like you, with experiences similar to your own, or one who is different from you, with very different experiences? Why?

   ▸ What would you like to do with a character you met? How do you think that character would feel about you?

2. Have students respond to the prompt in their journal. Encourage students to write in complete sentences, although it is not a requirement when they are freewriting in their journal.

TIP Students should write for about 20 minutes. Freewriting allows students to use their imagination to write what they want without worrying about being graded, so encourage them to keep writing for the entire time. If students have trouble writing for 20 minutes, use the prompting questions in Step 1 or have them list ideas or words. If they want to keep writing beyond the suggested time limit, praise them for their enthusiasm and offer to let them complete their entry later in the day as a reward.

> **Meet a Book Character**   Date _____
>
> If you could meet any book character, who would it be? Why?
>
> _____
> _____
> _____
> _____
> _____
> _____
> _____
> _____
> _____
> _____
> _____
> _____
> _____
>
> 44

Beyond the Lesson

⊕ OPTIONAL: Journal: Freewrite on a Topic

This activity is OPTIONAL. It is intended for students who have extra time and would benefit from extra practice. Feel free to skip this activity. Gather *K¹² My Journal.*

1. Have students either respond to a prompt in Thoughts and Experiences (pages 50–93) or write about their own topic on the next available page in Ideas (pages 96–139).

2. Encourage students to explore their thoughts and write as much as they want. There are no rules. If students wish, ideas can be fleshed out into a more developed composition at a later time.

TIP Studies show that students who write more frequently become better writers.

> **Objectives**
> - Respond to a journal prompt.
> - Freewrite about a topic.

Present Tense Verbs and Model Short Story

Lesson Overview

Online — 25 minutes

Skills Update	Principal Parts of Verbs
GUM (Grammar, Usage, and Mechanics)	Present Tense Verbs
Composition	Explore a Model Short Story

Offline — 20 minutes

Composition	Respond to the Model Short Story

Materials

Supplied
- *K¹² Language Arts Activity Book*, pp. WS 231–236
- *Grammar Reference Guide* Online Book (optional)

Keywords

character – a person or animal in a story

dialogue – the words spoken between two or more people

plot – what happens in a story; the sequence of events

present tense – the verb form that tells what is happening now

setting – when and where a story takes place

tense – the time that verbs show, such as present, future, or past

Advance Preparation

To prepare for the GUM portion of this lesson, review Verb Tense (Present Tense) in the *Grammar Reference Guide* (linked in the online lesson) to familiarize yourself with the topic. In this lesson, students begin to accumulate documents they will need as they work on their short story. You might want to provide students with a folder or large envelope in which to keep these documents.

Big Ideas

- Imaginative writing, in the form of stories and poems, allows writers to access their creativity while entertaining an audience.
- Knowing how to form different verb tenses and when to use them helps writers and speakers express their ideas in a logical manner.

[Online] 🕐 **25** minutes

Students will work online to review the principal parts of verbs, to learn about present tense verbs, and to read and explore a model short story. Help students locate the online activities.

Skills Update

Principal Parts of Verbs

Students will review the principal parts of verbs by completing Skills Update exercises. Sit with students as they do this activity and note if they answer correctly.

⮞ **Learning Coach Check-In** How did students do on the Skills Update?

▸ **All answers correct:** Great! Skip the review screen and go on to the next activity.

▸ **Any answers incorrect:** Take a few minutes to review the principal parts of verbs now. Use the link on the screen after the Skills Update to take another look at the online activity or review Principal Parts of Verbs (Regular Verbs; Irregular Verbs) in the *Grammar Reference Guide* together.

TIP This activity will require extra time if students need to review the principal parts of verbs. Take the extra 5–10 minutes to review now because new skills build on what students have already learned.

> **Objectives**
> - Identify and use the principal parts of regular verbs.
> - Identify and use the principal parts of irregular verbs.

GUM (Grammar, Usage, and Mechanics)

Present Tense Verbs

Students will learn about verbs in the present tense and practice identifying and using present tense verbs in sentences.

> **Objectives**
> - Identify and use present tense.

Composition

Explore a Model Short Story

By reading and exploring a model short story, students will learn about some key elements of any short story. These elements include characters, setting, plot, dialogue, and length.

TIP Seeing a final version of a short story helps students see the goal of this composition assignment. It will be easier for them to understand each stage in the process if they know how the steps result in a finished product. If students are not comfortable reading the model short story for this activity online, they may read the model on pages WS 231–233 in *K¹² Language Arts Activity Book*.

> **Objectives**
> - Describe the elements of a short story.
> - Respond to a short story.

[Offline] 20 minutes

Work **together** with students to complete the offline Composition activity.

Composition ....

Respond to the Model Short Story

Students will review what they learned about the model short story. Turn to pages WS 235 and 236 in *K¹² Language Arts Activity Book*.

1. Have students reread Serena's short story on pages WS 231–233.

2. Have students complete the Activity Book pages about Serena's short story. Provide support as necessary, encouraging students to write in complete sentences. Students should refer to Serena's short story as needed.

TIP Keep Serena's short story in a safe place so students can refer to it later.

Objectives

- Describe the elements of a short story.
- Respond to a short story.

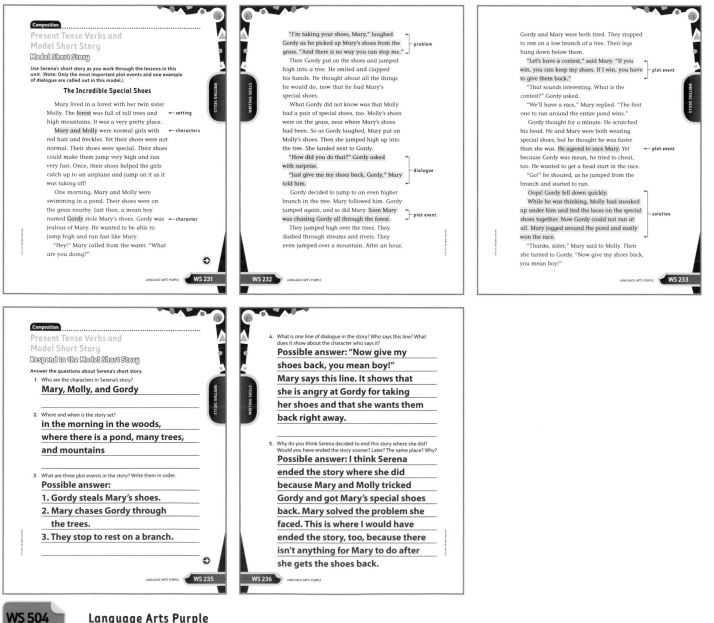

Future Tense Verbs and Brainstorm Story Ideas

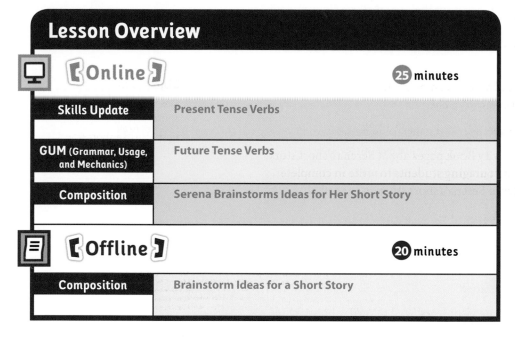

Lesson Overview

Online — 25 minutes

Skills Update	Present Tense Verbs
GUM (Grammar, Usage, and Mechanics)	Future Tense Verbs
Composition	Serena Brainstorms Ideas for Her Short Story

Offline — 20 minutes

Composition	Brainstorm Ideas for a Short Story

Materials

Supplied
- *K⁽¹⁾ Language Arts Activity Book*, pp. WS 237–239
- *Grammar Reference Guide* Online Book (optional)

Keywords

future tense – a form of a verb that names an action that will happen later

plot – what happens in a story; the sequence of events

Advance Preparation

To prepare for the GUM portion of this lesson, review Verb Tense (Future Tense) in the *Grammar Reference Guide* (linked in the online lesson) to familiarize yourself with the topic.

Big Ideas

▸ Knowing how to form different verb tenses and when to use them helps writers and speakers express their ideas in a logical manner.
▸ Imaginative writing, in the form of stories and poems, allows writers to access their creativity while entertaining an audience.
▸ Writers use various methods to plan, and novices should use what works for them: freewriting, listing, graphic organizers, or other methods.
▸ Engaging students in prewriting activities improves the quality of writing.

 **25 minutes**

Students will work online to review present tense verbs, to learn about future tense verbs, and to find out how to brainstorm ideas for their short story. Help students locate the online activities.

Skills Update

Present Tense Verbs
Students will review present tense verbs by completing Skills Update exercises. Sit with students as they do this activity and note if they answer correctly.

> **Learning Coach Check-In** How did students do on the Skills Update?

> ▸ **All answers correct:** Great! Skip the review screen and go on to the next activity.
> ▸ **Any answers incorrect:** Take a few minutes to review present tense verbs now. Use the link on the screen after the Skills Update to take another look at the online activity or review Verb Tense (Present Tense) in the *Grammar Reference Guide* together.

TIP This activity will require extra time if students need to review present tense verbs. Take the extra 5–10 minutes to review now because new skills build on what students have already learned.

Objectives
• Identify and use present tense.

GUM (Grammar, Usage, and Mechanics)

Future Tense Verbs
Students will learn about verbs in the future tense and practice identifying and using future tense verbs in sentences.

Objectives
• Identify and use future tense.

Composition

Serena Brainstorms Ideas for Her Short Story
By watching Serena think about ideas for her short story and ultimately choose one, students will learn how to do the same.

Objectives
• Brainstorm ideas for an imaginative story.
• Choose an idea for a story.

⟦ Offline ⟧ ⏱ 20 minutes

Work **together** with students to complete the offline Composition activity.

Composition ···

Brainstorm Ideas for a Short Story

Students will think about ideas for their short story, considering aspects of each idea and which one most interests them, and ultimately choose one. Turn to pages WS 237–239 in *K¹² Language Arts Activity Book.*

1. Have students complete the Activity Book pages to choose an idea for their short story. Provide support as necessary, encouraging students to think about their answers to the questions and why they might enjoy writing a story about one idea more than others.

2. Remind students that there is no wrong choice when it comes to which idea to choose. Tell them that the more interested they are in an idea, the better their story is likely to be, because they will enjoy developing and expanding upon an idea that interests them. That enjoyment generally translates to improved results.

TIP Keep students' completed brainstorming form in a safe place so they can refer to it later.

> ⭐ **Objectives**
> - Brainstorm ideas for an imaginative story.
> - Choose an idea for a story.

Composition

Future Tense Verbs and
Brainstorm Story Ideas

Brainstorm Ideas for a Short Story

Brainstorm ideas for your short story. Answer Questions 1–4 to begin. **Answers will vary.**

1. Do you want to write a funny story about people who are like your friends or family?

2. Do you want to write a scary story about places or people that are unusual and frightening?

3. Do you want to write a sad story about characters who face a difficult and upsetting problem?

4. Do you want to write an exciting story about characters who have a thrilling adventure?

WS 237 · LANGUAGE ARTS PURPLE

Use your imagination to think about story ideas. Write down four short story ideas in the boxes. Include some key plot events and the problem that your characters will face.

Idea 1

Idea 2

Idea 3

WS 238 · LANGUAGE ARTS PURPLE

Idea 4

Answer Questions 5–8 to choose one of your ideas for your short story.

5. Which story's characters seem least interesting to you? Cross off that story idea.

6. Are any stories too complicated to tell in two or three pages? Cross off those story ideas.

7. Do any of the stories seem too much like another story you have read or a TV show or movie you have seen? If so, cross them off.

8. Which story's characters are most interesting to you? What story would be most fun to write? What story already has you imagining some settings, characters, and important events? Circle that idea.

LANGUAGE ARTS PURPLE · WS 239

Past Tense Verbs and Choose a Setting for Your Story

Lesson Overview

💻 [Online]   25 minutes

Skills Update	Future Tense Verbs
GUM (Grammar, Usage, and Mechanics)	Past Tense Verbs
Composition	Serena Chooses a Setting for Her Story

▤ [Offline]   20 minutes

Composition	Choose a Setting for Your Story

[Materials]

Supplied
- *K¹² Language Arts Activity Book*, pp. WS 241–242
- *Grammar Reference Guide* Online Book (optional)

Keywords

past tense – the form of the verb that tells what has already happened

regular verb – a verb that adds *–d* or *–ed* to the present form to make the past and the past participle

setting – when and where a story takes place

Advance Preparation

To prepare for the GUM portion of this lesson, review Verb Tense (Past Tense) in the *Grammar Reference Guide* (linked in the online lesson) to familiarize yourself with the topic.

Big Ideas

- ► Knowing how to form different verb tenses and when to use them helps writers and speakers express their ideas in a logical manner.
- ► Imaginative writing, in the form of stories and poems, allows writers to access their creativity while entertaining an audience.
- ► Writers use various methods to plan, and novices should use what works for them: freewriting, listing, graphic organizers, or other methods.
- ► Engaging students in prewriting activities improves the quality of writing.

[Online] 25 minutes

Students will work online to review future tense verbs, to learn about regular past tense verbs, and to find out how to choose a setting for their short story. Help students locate the online activities.

Skills Update

Future Tense Verbs

Students will review future tense verbs by completing Skills Update exercises. Sit with students as they do this activity and note if they answer correctly.

⟳ **Learning Coach Check-In** How did students do on the Skills Update?

> ▸ **All answers correct:** Great! Skip the review screen and go on to the next activity.

> ▸ **Any answers incorrect:** Take a few minutes to review future tense verbs now. Use the link on the screen after the Skills Update to take another look at the online activity or review Verb Tense (Future Tense) in the *Grammar Reference Guide* together.

TIP This activity will require extra time if students need to review future tense verbs. Take the extra 5–10 minutes to review now because new skills build on what students have already learned.

Objectives
- Identify and use future tense.

GUM (Grammar, Usage, and Mechanics)

Past Tense Verbs

Students will learn how to form regular verbs in the past tense and practice identifying and using past tense verbs in sentences.

Objectives
- Identify and use past tense.

Composition

Serena Chooses a Setting for Her Story

By watching Serena decide when and where her short story will take place, students will learn how to do the same.

Objectives
- Choose a setting for a story.

[Offline] 20 minutes

Work **together** with students to complete the offline Composition activity.

Composition

Choose a Setting for Your Story

Students will answer questions to help them decide when and where the action of their short story will take place. Turn to pages WS 241 and 242 in *K¹² Language Arts Activity Book*.

1. Have students complete the Activity Book pages to choose a setting for their short story. Provide support as necessary, encouraging students to think about their answers to the questions and why they might enjoy writing a story that takes place in one time or place rather than another.

2. Remind students that there is no wrong choice when it comes to when and where to set their story. Any time or place that they can imagine could be a viable setting for their short story. Tell students that a story's setting can have a major influence on its plot, so they would be wise to consider how the setting they choose might affect the action of their story.

TIP Keep students' completed setting form in a safe place so they can refer to it later.

Objectives
- Choose a setting for a story.

Composition

Past Tense Verbs and Choose a Setting for Your Story

Choose a Setting for Your Story

Answer the questions to choose a setting for your short story.

1. What is your story going to be about? **Answers will vary.**

2. When will your story take place? (Check one.)
   ☐ long ago
   ☐ in the present time
   ☐ in the future

3. In what time of day will your story take place? (Check one.)
   ☐ morning   ☐ evening
   ☐ afternoon   ☐ night

4. Where will the action of your story begin?

5. Will the action of your story happen in more than one place? If so, describe all of the places where the action of your story is likely to happen.

6. How might the setting affect what happens in your story?

LANGUAGE ARTS PURPLE **WS 241**   **WS 242** LANGUAGE ARTS PURPLE

Irregular Past Tense Verbs and Choose Characters for Your Story

Lesson Overview

🖥 〖Online〗   25 minutes

Skills Update	Past Tense Verbs
GUM (Grammar, Usage, and Mechanics)	Irregular Past Tense Verbs
Composition	Serena Chooses Characters for Her Story

📄 〖Offline〗   20 minutes

Composition	Choose Characters for Your Story

〖Materials〗

Supplied

- *K¹¹ Language Arts Activity Book*, pp. WS 243–245
- *Grammar Reference Guide* Online Book (optional)

Keywords

character – a person or animal in a story

irregular verb – a verb that does not add –d or –ed to the present form to make the past and the past participle

past tense – the form of the verb that tells what has already happened

Advance Preparation

To prepare for the GUM portion of this lesson, review Verb Tense (Past Tense) in the *Grammar Reference Guide* (linked in the online lesson) to familiarize yourself with the topic.

Big Ideas

- ▸ Knowing how to form different verb tenses and when to use them helps writers and speakers express their ideas in a logical manner.
- ▸ Imaginative writing, in the form of stories and poems, allows writers to access their creativity while entertaining an audience.
- ▸ Writers use various methods to plan, and novices should use what works for them: freewriting, listing, graphic organizers, or other methods.
- ▸ Engaging students in prewriting activities improves the quality of writing.

 **25 minutes**

Students will work online to review regular past tense verbs, to learn about some irregular past tense verbs, and to find out how to choose characters for their short story. Help students locate the online activities.

Skills Update

Past Tense Verbs

Students will review regular past tense verbs by completing Skills Update exercises. Sit with students as they do this activity and note if they answer correctly.

> ➲ **Learning Coach Check-In** How did students do on the Skills Update?

> ▸ **All answers correct:** Great! Skip the review screen and go on to the next activity.

> ▸ **Any answers incorrect:** Take a few minutes to review regular past tense verbs now. Use the link on the screen after the Skills Update to take another look at the online activity or review Verb Tense (Past Tense) in the *Grammar Reference Guide* together.

TIP This activity will require extra time if students need to review regular past tense verbs. Take the extra 5–10 minutes to review now because new skills build on what students have already learned.

Objectives
• Identify and use past tense.

GUM (Grammar, Usage, and Mechanics)

Irregular Past Tense Verbs

Students will learn about irregular verbs in the past tense and practice identifying and using two types of irregular past tense verbs in sentences.

Objectives
• Identify and use past tense.

Composition

Serena Chooses Characters for Her Story

By watching Serena name and describe characters for her short story, students will learn how to do the same.

Objectives
• Choose characters for a story.
• Describe each character.

【Offline】 20 minutes

Work **together** with students to complete the offline Composition activity.

Composition

Choose Characters for Your Story

Students will choose and name the characters in their short story and describe those characters. Turn to pages WS 243–245 in *K¹² Language Arts Activity Book*.

1. Have students complete the Activity Book pages to choose characters for their short story. Provide support as necessary, encouraging students to think about what each character is like, how the characters are different from one another, and how the characters feel about each other.

2. Remind students that there are no wrong choices when it comes to choosing characters for their story. Any people or animals that they can imagine could be characters in their tale. Consider telling students that a story's characters do not always have to like one another or want the same things, so they might consider choosing characters who will be in conflict or competition with each other.

3. If students want their story to have more than four characters, it is okay. But let them know that the more characters they have, the more difficult it will be to develop them all and give all of them attention in their short story.

TIP Keep students' completed characters form in a safe place so they can refer to it later.

Composition
Irregular Past Tense Verbs and Choose Characters for Your Story

Choose Characters for Your Story

Choose characters for your short story. Write each character's name, a description of the character, and how this character feels about the others.

Character 1

Name _____

Description _____

_____

How this character feels about other characters _____

LANGUAGE ARTS PURPLE **WS 243**

Character 2

Name _____

Description _____

_____

How this character feels about other characters _____

_____

Character 3

Name _____

Description _____

_____

How this character feels about other characters _____

WS 244 LANGUAGE ARTS PURPLE

Character 4

Name _____

Description _____

_____

How this character feels about other characters _____

_____

Character 5

Name _____

Description _____

_____

How this character feels about other characters _____

LANGUAGE ARTS PURPLE **WS 245**

Irregular Past Tense Verbs and Choose a Plot for Your Story

Lesson Overview

Online   25 minutes

Skills Update	Irregular Past Tense Verbs
GUM (Grammar, Usage, and Mechanics)	Irregular Past Tense Verbs
Composition	Serena Develops the Plot of Her Story

Offline   20 minutes

Composition	Develop the Plot of Your Story

Materials

Supplied
- *K¹² Language Arts Activity Book*, pp. WS 247–248
- *Grammar Reference Guide* Online Book (optional)

Keywords
irregular verb – a verb that does not add *–d or –*ed to the present form to make the past and the past participle

past tense – the form of the verb that tells what has already happened

plot – what happens in a story; the sequence of events

Advance Preparation

To prepare for the GUM portion of this lesson, review Verb Tense (Past Tense) in the *Grammar Reference Guide* (linked in the online lesson) to familiarize yourself with the topic.

Big Ideas

▶ Knowing how to form different verb tenses and when to use them helps writers and speakers express their ideas in a logical manner.
▶ Imaginative writing, in the form of stories and poems, allows writers to access their creativity while entertaining an audience.
▶ Writers use various methods to plan, and novices should use what works for them: freewriting, listing, graphic organizers, or other methods.
▶ Engaging students in prewriting activities improves the quality of writing.

[Online] (25) minutes

Students will work online to review some irregular past tense verbs, to learn about other irregular past tense verbs, and to find out how to develop the plot of their short story. Help students locate the online activities.

Skills Update ●●

Irregular Past Tense Verbs

Students will review irregular past tense verbs by completing Skills Update exercises. Sit with students as they do this activity and note if they answer correctly.

> **Learning Coach Check-In** How did students do on the Skills Update?

> ▸ **All answers correct:** Great! Skip the review screen and go on to the next activity.

> ▸ **Any answers incorrect:** Take a few minutes to review irregular past tense verbs now. Use the link on the screen after the Skills Update to take another look at the online activity or review Verb Tense (Past Tense) in the *Grammar Reference Guide* together.

TIP This activity will require extra time if students need to review irregular past tense verbs. Take the extra 5–10 minutes to review now because new skills build on what students have already learned.

> **Objectives**
> • Identify and use past tense.

GUM (Grammar, Usage, and Mechanics) ●●●●●●●●●●●●●●●●●●●●●●●●●●●●●●●●●●●●●●

Irregular Past Tense Verbs

Students will learn about irregular verbs in the past tense and practice identifying and using two types of irregular past tense verbs in sentences.

> **Objectives**
> • Identify and use past tense.

Composition ●●

Serena Develops the Plot of Her Story

By watching Serena develop the plot of her short story, students will learn how to do the same.

> **Objectives**
> • Organize an event sequence that unfolds naturally.

 **20** minutes

Work **together** with students to complete the offline Composition activity.

Composition

Develop the Plot of Your Story

Students will develop the plot of their short story. Turn to pages WS 247 and 248 in *K¹² Language Arts Activity Book*.

1. Have students complete the Activity Book pages to decide what happens in their short story. Provide support as necessary, encouraging students to think about one main problem the main character will face, what events lead to the problem, what events will happen because of the problem, and what happens to allow the character to solve the problem.

2. Remind students that the plot of a story *must* include at least one problem. The attempts of the main character to solve the problem will make up many of the events in the story's plot. Any events that they can imagine could be part of their story's plot, provided these events are logically connected to one another or to the problem of the story, the characters, and the setting. Consider telling students that a story's plot is a bit like a chain. Each event is like a link that is connected to what came before it and what comes after it.

3. Tell students that this plan is something that they can and will make changes and improvements to before they begin writing.

TIP Keep students' completed plot form in a safe place so they can refer to it later.

> **Objectives**
> * Organize an event sequence that unfolds naturally.

Composition

Irregular Past Tense Verbs and
Choose a Plot for Your Story
Develop the Plot of Your Story Answers will vary.

Answer the questions to develop the plot of your short story.

1. What is the problem that the main character faces?

2. What leads to the problem?

3. What are three things that the main character of your story will do after the problem arises?

4. How will the main character solve the problem?

5. What will the final events in your short story be?

LANGUAGE ARTS PURPLE **WS 247**

WS 248 LANGUAGE ARTS PURPLE

Plan Your Story

Lesson Overview

🖥️ Online — 20 minutes

Skills Update	Irregular Past Tense Verbs
Composition	Serena Plans Her Story

📄 Offline — 25 minutes

Composition	Plan Your Story

Materials

Supplied

- *K¹² Language Arts Activity Book,* pp. WS 241–251
- *Grammar Reference Guide* Online Book (optional)

Keywords

character – a person or animal in a story

plot – what happens in a story; the sequence of events

setting – when and where a story takes place

Advance Preparation

Gather pages WS 241–248 (students' completed Choose a Setting for Your Story, Choose Characters for Your Story, and Develop the Plot of Your Story forms) in *K¹² Language Arts Activity Book*. Students will use these pages as they put together a plan for their short story.

Big Ideas

- ▸ Imaginative writing, in the form of stories and poems, allows writers to access their creativity while entertaining an audience.
- ▸ Writers use various methods to plan, and novices should use what works for them: freewriting, listing, graphic organizers, or other methods.
- ▸ Engaging students in prewriting activities improves the quality of writing.

 **20 minutes**

Students will work online to review irregular past tense verbs and to learn how to use their setting, characters, and plot forms to create a plan for their short story. Help students locate the online activities.

Skills Update

Irregular Past Tense Verbs

Students will review irregular past tense verbs by completing Skills Update exercises. Sit with students as they do this activity and note if they answer correctly.

⮑ **Learning Coach Check-In** How did students do on the Skills Update?

▸ **All answers correct:** Great! Skip the review screen and go on to the next activity.

▸ **Any answers incorrect:** Take a few minutes to review irregular past tense verbs now. Use the link on the screen after the Skills Update to take another look at the online activity or review Verb Tense (Past Tense) in the *Grammar Reference Guide* together.

TIP This activity will require extra time if students need to review irregular past tense verbs. Take the extra 5–10 minutes to review now because new skills build on what students have already learned.

> **Objectives**
> • Identify and use past tense.

Composition

Serena Plans Her Story

By watching Serena use a graphic organizer to plan her short story, students will learn how to do the same.

> **Objectives**
> • Use a graphic organizer to plan a story.

 **25 minutes**

Work **together** with students to complete the offline Composition activity.

Composition

Plan Your Story

Students will develop a plan for each part of their short story. Have them gather their completed setting, characters, and plot forms, and turn to pages WS 249–251 in *K¹² Language Arts Activity Book*.

> **Objectives**
> • Use a graphic organizer to plan a story.

1. Guide students to follow the directions on the Activity Book pages to complete their Plan Your Story form. Tell them that they will use what they wrote on their setting, characters, and plot forms to plan the beginning, middle, and end of their short story.

2. As necessary, work with students to help them locate details about setting, characters, and plot and to use those details to decide what happens in each part of the story, where the action takes place, and which characters are involved. Tell them that they do not need to have every character involved in every event or part of the story. Remind them that their story may have more than one setting. Stress that the events of the plot will and should be affected by the setting and the characters. For instance, a character cannot get sunburned if the story takes place at night.

3. Remind students that, as they plan their story, they do not need to write in complete sentences or use proper punctuation. The goal is for them to organize their ideas.

4. Let students know that they will have time in the upcoming lessons to change and improve their story plan. They should understand that the form they complete today is not the final plan for their story.

TIP Keep students' completed story plan in a safe place so they can refer to it later.

Composition

Past Tense Verbs and Choose a Setting for Your Story

Choose a Setting for Your Story

Answer the questions to choose a setting for your short story.

1. What is your story going to be about? **Answers will vary.**

_____

_____

_____

2. When will your story take place? (Check one.)
   ☐ long ago
   ☐ in the present time
   ☐ in the future

3. In what time of day will your story take place? (Check one.)
   ☐ morning   ☐ evening
   ☐ afternoon   ☐ night

4. Where will the action of your story begin?

_____

_____

_____

---

5. Will the action of your story happen in more than one place? If so, describe all of the places where the action of your story is likely to happen.

_____

_____

_____

6. How might the setting affect what happens in your story?

_____

_____

_____

_____

_____

_____

_____

_____

Composition

Irregular Past Tense Verbs and Choose Characters for Your Story

Choose Characters for Your Story

Choose characters for your short story. Write each character's name, a description of the character, and how this character feels about the others.

Character 1

Name _____

Description _____

_____

_____

How this character feels about other characters _____

_____

_____

Character 2

Name _____

Description _____

_____

_____

How this character feels about other characters _____

_____

_____

Character 3

Name _____

Description _____

_____

_____

How this character feels about other characters _____

_____

_____

Character 4

Name _____

Description _____

_____

_____

How this character feels about other characters _____

_____

_____

Character 5

Name _____

Description _____

_____

_____

How this character feels about other characters _____

_____

_____

Composition

Irregular Past Tense Verbs and
Choose a Plot for Your Story

Develop the Plot of Your Story **Answers will vary.**

Answer the questions to develop the plot of your short story.

1. What is the problem that the main character faces?

_____

_____

2. What leads to the problem?

_____

_____

_____

3. What are three things that the main character of your story will do after the problem arises?

_____

_____

_____

_____

4. How will the main character solve the problem?

_____

_____

_____

5. What will the final events in your short story be?

_____

_____

_____

_____

Composition

Plan Your Story

Plan Your Story **Answers will vary.**

Make a plan for your short story. Describe the setting, characters, and plot events for the beginning, middle, and end of your story.

Beginning
Setting
Characters
Plot Events (Include the problem.)

Middle
Setting
Characters
Plot Events

End
Setting
Characters
Plot Events (Include the solution.)

Focus on Dialogue

Lesson Overview

🖥️	**〔Online〕**	**20** minutes
Composition	Review Dialogue	
📄	**〔Offline〕**	**25** minutes
Composition	Explore Dialogue	

〔Materials〕

Supplied
- *K¹² Language Arts Activity Book*, pp. WS 253–256
- *Grammar Reference Guide* Online Book (optional)

Keywords

dialogue – the words spoken between two or more people

Big Ideas

▸ Imaginative writing, in the form of stories and poems, allows writers to access their creativity while entertaining an audience.

▸ Using quotations, the exact words of the speaker, enhances writing. Rather than reporting what a speaker says in conversation, a good writer allows the audience to read the character's words.

▸ Writers use various methods to plan, and novices should use what works for them: freewriting, listing, graphic organizers, or other methods.

▸ Engaging students in prewriting activities improves the quality of writing.

[Online] 🕙 minutes

Students will work online **independently** to learn about dialogue: how to write it, its characteristics, and how it can be used effectively. Help students locate the online activity.

Composition ....

Review Dialogue
Students will review the rules for writing dialogue, as well as some of the characteristics of well-written dialogue.

> ⭐ **Objectives**
> - Use quotation marks around a speaker's exact words.
> - Begin a new paragraph each time the speaker changes.
> - Write dialogue.
> - Recognize differences between spoken language and written language.

[Offline] 🕙 minutes

Work **together** with students to complete the offline Composition activity.

Composition ....

Explore Dialogue
Students will review what they know about dialogue and practice writing dialogue. Turn to pages WS 253–256 in *K¹² Language Arts Activity Book*.

1. Have students complete the Activity Book pages to review and practice writing dialogue. Provide support as necessary, encouraging students to think about proper format, as well as how people truly speak.

> ⭐ **Objectives**
> - Use quotation marks around a speaker's exact words.
> - Begin a new paragraph each time the speaker changes.
> - Write dialogue.
> - Recognize differences between spoken language and written language.

2. Remind students that dialogue can and should include contractions, informal words and phrases, and fragments if that is how the character speaking would talk. Guide students to also think about how a character's words can reveal that character's traits or feelings.

Composition

Focus on Dialogue
Explore Dialogue

Complete each exercise to show what you know about dialogue.

1. Place quotation marks around the dialogue.

> Mike asked,**"**Did anyone leave a jacket at my house?**"**

2. Underline the sentences that should be in another paragraph. Then write that paragraph. Remember to indent the first word.

> Sasha looked left and right. There were no boats at the docks. There were no people around, either. The whole place was strangely still. It was as if everyone had simply decided to vanish without a trace. <u>"Hello?" Sasha called out. "Is anyone here?"</u>

"Hello?" Sasha called out. "Is anyone here?"

---

3. Rewrite these sentences containing dialogue correctly.

> "Hey, Joe," Lisa said. "Hi, Lisa," said Joe. "What's new?" asked Lisa.

"Hey, Joe," Lisa said.

"Hi, Lisa," said Joe.

"What's new?" asked Lisa.

4. Which of the following statements about dialogue are true? Choose all correct answers.

- (A) Dialogue can have contractions.
- (B) Dialogue can have informal words and phrases.
- (C) Dialogue can be made up of sentence fragments.
- D. Dialogue should have only complete sentences.

---

5. Gale and Todd are about your age. They play on the same soccer team, and they are at soccer practice. Rewrite the dialogue between Gale and Todd so that it is more realistic.

> "Gale," said Todd, "will you please kick the soccer ball to me?"
> "I will," Gale said. "Are you prepared?"
> "I am prepared," Todd replied. "Just do not kick the soccer ball over my head!"
> "I will not. I promise."

Possible answer:

"Gale," said Todd, "kick the ball to me, will ya?"

"Okay," Gale said. "You ready?"

"I'm ready," Todd replied. "Just don't kick it over my head!"

"I won't. I promise."

---

6. Imagine this situation.

> Rob and Sue are both eating lunch. As they finish their sandwiches, they notice that there is only one apple. Rob and Sue both want the apple. Yet they like one another and are both very generous people.

Write dialogue for both Rob and Sue in which they talk about who will eat the apple. Remember, as you write, that Rob and Sue are friends and neither of them is a selfish person.

Possible answer:

"Hey, Sue," Rob said. "You want that apple?"

"Yeah, why?" Sue asked. "Do you want it, too?"

"Sort of," Rob replied. "But you can have it. Really. I don't mind."

"No, you have it, Rob. I don't want it that much."

"How about we split it?" Rob said with a smile.

Unit Review and Write Dialogue

Lesson Overview

🖥 [Online] — 25 minutes

Unit Review	Verb Tense
More Practice	Verb Tense
Composition	Serena Writes Dialogue

📄 [Offline] — 20 minutes

Composition	Write Dialogue for Your Story

Advance Preparation

Gather pages WS 243–245 (Choose Characters for Your Story, students' completed characters form) and 249–251 (Plan Your Story, students' initial story plan) in *K¹² Language Arts Activity Book*.

[Materials]

Supplied

- *K¹² Language Arts Activity Book*, pp. WS 243–245, 249–251, 257–259
- *Grammar Reference Guide* Online Book (optional)

Keywords

dialogue – the words spoken between two or more people

future tense – a form of a verb that names an action that will happen later

irregular verb – a verb that does not add –*d* or –*ed* to the present form to make the past and the past participle

past tense – the form of the verb that tells what has already happened

present tense – the verb form that tells what is happening now

principal part – one of four basic verb forms—present, present participle, past, and past participle

regular verb – a verb that adds –*d* or –*ed* to the present form to make the past and the past participle

tense – the time that verbs show, such as present, future, or past

[Online] 25 minutes

Students will work online **independently** to review the grammar, usage, and mechanics skills learned in the unit and to see how to use a story plan to begin to write dialogue for the characters in a short story. Help students locate the online activities.

Unit Review

Verb Tense

Students will review what they have learned about principal parts of verbs, present tense verbs, future tense verbs, regular past tense verbs, and irregular past tense verbs to review for the Unit Checkpoint.

TIP A full list of objectives covered in the Unit Review can be found in the online lesson.

Objectives
- Complete a review of grammar, usage, and mechanics skills.

More Practice

Verb Tense

Go over students' results on the Unit Review and, if necessary, have students complete the appropriate review activities listed in the table online. Help students locate the activities. Provide support as needed.

TIP The time students need to complete this activity will vary. Set aside enough time for students to complete all review activities, if they need to do so.

Objectives
- Evaluate Unit Review results and choose activities for more practice.

Composition

Serena Writes Dialogue

By watching Serena practice writing dialogue between the characters she created and based on the situations she's imagined, students will learn how to do the same as they prepare to write dialogue between the characters in their own short story.

Objectives
- Use quotation marks around a speaker's exact words.
- Begin a new paragraph each time the speaker changes.
- Write dialogue.

[Offline] 20 minutes

Work **together** with students to complete the offline Composition activity.

Composition ....

Write Dialogue for Your Story

Students will write dialogue for the characters in their short story. Have students gather their story plan and characters form, and turn to pages WS 257–259 in *K¹² Language Arts Activity Book*.

1. Have students complete the Activity Book pages to begin writing dialogue between the characters in their short story. Provide support as necessary, encouraging students to use their story plan to help them know the situation that characters face, which characters are present, and the events that they might talk about. Their characters form might remind them how characters in their story feel about each other, which can influence dialogue.

2. Remind students that not all characters should speak alike and that dialogue is informal and therefore can have contractions, informal words, and sentence fragments—if such ways of speaking are realistic for the character and the situation in the story.

3. Tell students that they do not have to try to write all the dialogue for their story now. The purpose of this activity is to give students some practice in writing dialogue between some of their characters.

TIP Keep students' completed dialogue form in a safe place so they can refer to it later.

> ### Objectives
> - Use quotation marks around a speaker's exact words.
> - Begin a new paragraph each time the speaker changes.
> - Write dialogue.

Composition

Irregular Past Tense Verbs and Choose Characters for Your Story

Choose Characters for Your Story

Choose characters for your short story. Write each character's name, a description of the character, and how this character feels about the others.

Character 1

Name _____

Description _____

_____

How this character feels about other characters _____

_____

Character 2

Name _____

Description _____

_____

How this character feels about other characters _____

Character 3

Name _____

Description _____

_____

How this character feels about other characters _____

Character 4

Name _____

Description _____

_____

How this character feels about other characters _____

Character 5

Name _____

Description _____

_____

How this character feels about other characters _____

Composition

Plan Your Story

Plan Your Story   **Answers will vary.**

Make a plan for your short story. Describe the setting, characters, and plot events for the beginning, middle, and end of your story.

Beginning

Setting

↓

Characters

↓

Plot Events (Include the problem.)

Middle

Setting

↓

Characters

↓

Plot Events

End

Setting

↓

Characters

↓

Plot Events (Include the solution.)

Composition

Unit Review and Write Dialogue

Write Dialogue for Your Story

Practice writing some dialogue that your characters might speak in the beginning, middle, and end of your short story. The dialogue should sound realistic, show some character traits, and move the plot of your story forward.   **Answers will vary.**

Beginning

Character 1 _____

Character 2 _____

Situation _____

Dialogue _____

Middle

Character 1 _____

Character 2 _____

Situation _____

Dialogue _____

End

Character 1 _____

Character 2 _____

Situation _____

Dialogue _____

Unit Checkpoint and Review
Your Story Plan

Lesson Overview

🖥️ **⟦ Online ⟧**		**25** minutes
Unit Checkpoint	Verb Tense	

📄 **⟦ Offline ⟧**		**20** minutes
More Practice	Verb Tense	
Composition	Revise Your Story Plan with a Checklist	

Advance Preparation

Gather pages WS 249–251 (Plan Your Story, students' story plan) in *K¹² Language Arts Activity Book*.

⟦ Materials ⟧

Supplied

- *K¹² Language Arts Activity Book*, pp. WS 249–251, 261
- *Grammar Reference Guide* Online Book (optional)
- Principal Parts of Verbs (optional printout)
- Present Tense Verbs (optional printout)
- Future Tense Verbs (optional printout)
- Past Tense Verbs (optional printout)
- Irregular Past Tense Verbs (optional printout)
- Story Plan (optional printout)

Keywords

dialogue – the words spoken between two or more people

future tense – a form of a verb that names an action that will happen later

irregular verb – a verb that does not add –d or –ed to the present form to make the past and the past participle

past tense – the form of the verb that tells what has already happened

present tense – the verb form that tells what is happening now

principal part – one of four basic verb forms—present, present participle, past, and past participle

regular verb – a verb that adds –d or –ed to the present form to make the past and the past participle

tense – the time that verbs show, such as present, future, or past

[Online] ⏱️25 minutes

Students will work online **independently** to complete the Unit Checkpoint. Help students locate the Unit Checkpoint and provide support as necessary.

Unit Checkpoint ....

Verb Tense

Students will complete an online Unit Checkpoint about principal parts of verbs, present tense verbs, future tense verbs, regular past tense verbs, and irregular past tense verbs. If necessary, read the directions to students.

TIP A full list of objectives covered in the Unit Checkpoint can be found in the online lesson.

> **Objectives**
> • Complete a Unit Checkpoint on grammar, usage, and mechanics skills.

[Offline] ⏱️20 minutes

Work **together** with students to complete the offline More Practice and Composition activities.

More Practice ....

Verb Tense

Go over students' results on the Unit Checkpoint and, if necessary, print out and have them complete the appropriate practice pages listed in the table online. Students can complete all necessary pages now or, if more time is needed, they can spread them out over the next few days. They can also review the appropriate sections of the *Grammar Reference Guide* with you. If students scored less than 80 percent on the Unit Checkpoint, you may want them to retake the Checkpoint after completing the additional activity pages.

TIP The time students need to complete this activity will vary. Set aside enough time for students to complete some or all activity pages and to retake the Unit Checkpoint, if they need to do so. Students may retake the Unit Checkpoint immediately, but having them complete the practice pages and then retake it might be more effective.

> **Objectives**
> • Evaluate Unit Checkpoint results and choose activities for more practice.

More Practice

Improve Your Skills
Principal Parts of Verbs

Choose the answer.

1. Which underlined word is the present part of a verb?

   The wheels squeak, but Anna fixed the handlebars of her bike.

   (A) squeak   B. fixed   C. bike

2. Which word is the past participle of the verb that completes the sentence?

   Larry has _____ to help many times.

   A. offer   B. offering   (C) offered

3. Choose the principal part of the underlined verb.

   Todd knew that his babysitter would let him eat cake.

   A. present   (B) past   C. past participle

4. Which word is the past part of the verb that completes the sentence?

   I'm sorry to tell you that I _____ your shirt.

   A. shrink   (B) shrank   C. shrunk

WRITING SKILLS

LANGUAGE ARTS PURPLE   **WS 1**

More Practice

Improve Your Skills
Present Tense Verbs

Choose the answer.

1. Which underlined word (or words) is a present tense verb?

   I will open your suitcase and I will see what you have packed, but first I need some water.

   A. will open   C. packed
   B. will see   (D) need

2. Which underlined word (or words) is a present tense verb?

   Miss Williams met Hank before, and she knows his brothers, but tomorrow she will spend the entire day with him.

   A. met   C. will spend
   (B) knows   D. with

3. Which is the present tense verb that completes the sentence?

   An apple _____ to the ground.

   A. fall   C. falling
   B. fell   (D) falls

WRITING SKILLS

LANGUAGE ARTS PURPLE   **WS 1**   →

---

4. Which is the present tense verb that completes the sentence?

   Two tall ladders _____ against the side of the building.

   (A) rest   C. rested
   B. rests   D. will rest

5. Which is the present tense verb that completes the sentence?

   Several runners _____ to warm up for the race.

   A. begins   (C) begin
   B. will begin   D. began

WRITING SKILLS

WS 2   LANGUAGE ARTS PURPLE

More Practice

Improve Your Skills
Future Tense Verbs

Complete each exercise.

1. Choose the future tense verb in the sentence.

   The guard will unlock the gate once he has talked to you and realizes that you live nearby.

   (A) will unlock   C. realizes
   B. has talked   D. live

2. Choose the future tense verb in the sentence.

   I laughed and shouted, "You will pay for playing that trick on me!"

   A. laughed   (C) will pay
   B. shouted   D. for playing

3. Which is the future tense verb that completes the sentence?

   Linda _____ the paper so it looks like a bird.

   A. folds   (C) will fold
   B. folded   D. has folded

4. Which is the future tense verb that completes the sentence?

   The crayons _____ if you leave them near the heater.

   A. melt   C. have melted
   (B) will melt   D. melts

WRITING SKILLS

LANGUAGE ARTS PURPLE   **WS 1**   →

---

5. Write the future tense of the verb *catch* to complete the sentence.

   The ball is rolling toward me, so I **will catch** it.

WRITING SKILLS

WS 2   LANGUAGE ARTS PURPLE

More Practice

Improve Your Skills
Past Tense Verbs

Choose the answer.

1. Which underlined word in this sentence is a past tense verb?

   Today, the king and queen laugh and smile, but yesterday they ruled an unhappy kingdom.

   A. laugh   (C) ruled
   B. smile   D. unhappy

2. Which underlined word in this sentence is a past tense verb?

   "Can you push the bed against the wall and sweep the floor after I wash the windows?" Gerry asked.

   A. push   C. wash
   B. sweep   (D) asked

3. Which is the past tense verb that completes the sentence?

   Gram _____ Katie climb onto the swing.

   (A) helped   C. helping
   B. helps   D. help

4. Which is the past tense verb that completes the sentence?

   The flowers on the table _____ because not enough water was in the vase.

   A. droop   C. will droop
   (B) drooped   D. droops

WRITING SKILLS

LANGUAGE ARTS PURPLE   **WS 1**

More Practice

Improve Your Skills
Irregular Past Tense Verbs

Choose the answer.

1. Which underlined word in this sentence is an irregular past tense verb?

   I dropped the box on my foot when the doorbell rang because I was so surprised to see you.

   A. dropped   C. surprised
   (B) rang   D. see

2. Which is the past tense verb that completes the sentence?

   The girls _____ downstairs and hid from their brother.

   A. creep   C. creept
   B. creeped   (D) crept

3. Which underlined word in this sentence is an irregular past tense verb?

   The shoes you bought look like they belong in that store we visited in Baltimore.

   (A) bought   C. belong
   B. look   D. visited

4. Which is the past tense verb that completes the sentence?

   Fiona _____ a picture of a red bird with yellow wings.

   A. drawed   C. drewed
   B. drawn   (D) drew

WRITING SKILLS

LANGUAGE ARTS PURPLE   **WS 1**

Composition

Revise Your Story Plan with a Checklist

Students will revise their story plan. They will focus on improving and adding to their ideas about the setting, characters, and plot events in each part of their short story. Have students gather their story plan, and turn to page WS 261 in *K¹² Language Arts Activity Book*.

1. Tell students to use the checklist to revise their story plan. Students should check off each box on the checklist as they complete the items.

2. If students make so many improvements and additions to their story plan that the plan becomes difficult to read, print a new story plan form from the online lesson and have them write a clean version of their plan.

   ⊃ Learning Coach Check-In Once students have finished revising their story plan, check to make sure that their plan includes a setting for each section of the story, the names of characters involved in each part of the action, and a series of logically connected events that include a problem for the story's main character to face and try to solve.

   TIP Keep students' revised story plan in a safe place so they can refer to it later.

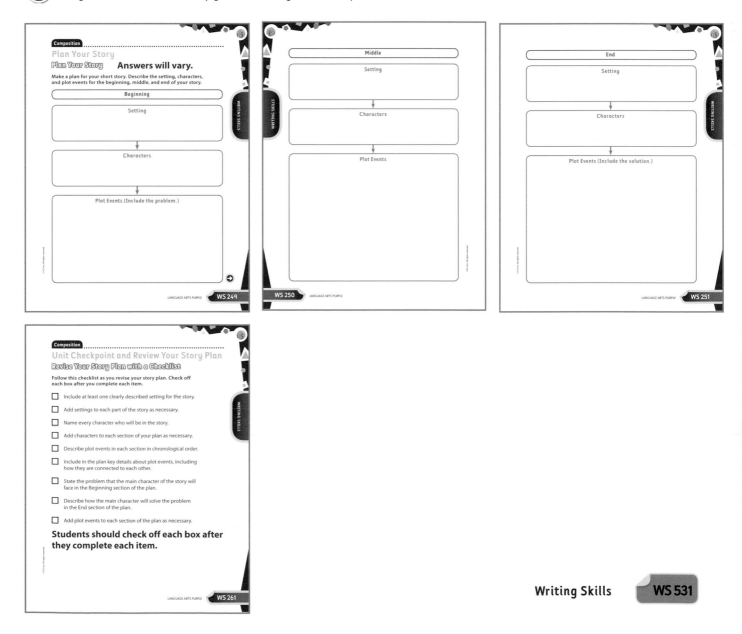

UNIT OVERVIEW Some Parts of Speech and Write a Short Story

Unit Focus

In the grammar part of the unit, students will learn about some important parts of speech. They will

▸ Learn how to identify prepositions and prepositional phrases.
▸ Learn to identify and use interjections.
▸ Review how to differentiate between adverbs and adjectives to learn how to use *good* and *well* correctly.
▸ Learn to identify double negatives and fix double negatives in sentences.

In the composition part of the unit, students will write a short story. They will

▸ Use their journal to freewrite.
▸ Use the plan they completed in the Verb Tense and Plan a Short Story unit to guide them as they draft a short story that contains a beginning, middle, and end; characters who face problems and seek solutions; and descriptions and dialogue that highlight characters' traits, emotions, and actions.
▸ Revise and proofread their short story.
▸ Make a final clean copy of their short story.

Unit Plan		Online	Offline
Lesson 1	Prepositions & Prepositional Phrases and Journal Entry	25 minutes	20 minutes
Lesson 2	Interjections and Draft Your Story	25 minutes	20 minutes
Lesson 3	*Good & Well* and Draft Your Story	25 minutes	20 minutes
Lesson 4	Double Negatives and Draft Your Story	25 minutes	20 minutes
Lesson 5	Unit Review and Draft Your Story	25 minutes	20 minutes
Lesson 6	Unit Checkpoint and Draft Your Story	20 minutes	25 minutes
Lesson 7	Revise Your Story (A)	20 minutes	25 minutes
Lesson 8	Revise Your Story (B)	20 minutes	25 minutes
Lesson 9	Proofread Your Story	20 minutes	25 minutes
Lesson 10	Publish Your Story (A)		45 minutes
Lesson 11	Publish Your Story (B)		45 minutes

WS 532   **Language Arts Purple**

Prepositions & Prepositional Phrases and Journal Entry

Lesson Overview

【Online 】 **25** minutes

| **GUM** (Grammar, Usage, and Mechanics) | Prepositions and Prepositional Phrases |

【Offline 】 **20** minutes

| **Composition** | Journal: Write About Your Short Story |
| **Beyond the Lesson** | ➕ OPTIONAL: Journal: Freewrite on a Topic |

【 Materials 】

Supplied
- *K¹¹ My Journal*, pp. 46–47
- *Grammar Reference Guide* Online Book (optional)

Keywords

preposition – a word that begins a phrase that ends with a noun or a pronoun *Examples:* In the phrases "over the bridge" and "to me," the words *over* and *to* are prepositions.

prepositional phrase – a group of words that begins with a preposition and usually ends with the noun or a pronoun that is the object of the preposition

Advance Preparation

To prepare for the GUM portion of this lesson, review Prepositions (Prepositional Phrases) in the *Grammar Reference Guide* (linked in the online lesson) to familiarize yourself with the topic.

Big Ideas

- ▶ Using prepositional phrases and varying their placement in sentences adds details and interest to writing.
- ▶ Journal writing is a form of freewriting. It is an opportunity to get ideas on paper without regard for the correctness of the language or the format of a piece of writing.
- ▶ To improve, writers require frequent practice.

[Online] ⓔ minutes

Students will work online **independently** to complete an activity on identifying prepositions and prepositional phrases. Help students locate the online activity.

GUM (Grammar, Usage, and Mechanics) ·

Prepositions and Prepositional Phrases

Students will learn what prepositions are and that prepositions begin prepositional phrases, which add details to sentences. Then they will practice identifying both prepositions and prepositional phrases.

> **Objectives**
> - Identify prepositions.
> - Identify prepositional phrases.

[Offline] ⓔ minutes

Work **together** with students to complete the offline Composition and Beyond the Lesson activities.

Composition ·

✏ Journal: Write About Your Short Story

Students will respond to a journal prompt by writing about their short story and the process of planning it. Gather *K¹² My Journal* and have students turn to pages 46 and 47.

> **Objectives**
> - Respond to a journal prompt.
> - Freewrite about a topic.

1. Tell students that they are going to write in their journal about the short story they have been planning, focusing on what they've enjoyed about the planning process and what parts of the process have proven challenging. To help students think of both what's been enjoyable and what's been a struggle in this process, ask them to think about their answers to the following questions.

   ▸ What elements of the story were the most fun to plan? Did you like coming up with characters? Did you like deciding what their traits would be and how they would feel about one another? Was planning the plot enjoyable? Was it fun to imagine when and where your story might take place as you chose a setting?

   ▸ Which parts of your story plan do you feel are the strongest? Why?

   ▸ What elements of your story plan did you have the most difficulty with? Was it tough to decide on a setting or come up with plot events? Were some characters harder to imagine than others? How hard or easy was it to write dialogue for your characters?

   ▸ Which parts of your story plan do you feel are the weakest? Why? How might you improve these parts of your story as you begin drafting?

2. Have students respond to the prompt in their journal. Encourage students to write in complete sentences, although it is not a requirement when they are freewriting in their journal.

TIP Students should write for about 20 minutes. Freewriting allows students to use their imagination to write what they want without worrying about being graded, so encourage them to keep writing for the entire time. If students have trouble writing for 20 minutes, use the prompting questions in Step 1 or have them list ideas or words. If they want to keep writing beyond the suggested time limit, praise them for their enthusiasm and offer to let them complete their entry later in the day as a reward.

Reflect on Your Short Story   Date _____

WRITING SKILLS

What parts of your short story are you happy with? What parts of it need more work?

_____

_____

_____

_____

_____

_____

_____

_____

_____

_____

_____

_____

46

Beyond the Lesson

◖▬▬◗ ✚ **OPTIONAL: Journal: Freewrite on a Topic**

This activity is OPTIONAL. It is intended for students who have extra time and would benefit from extra practice. Feel free to skip this activity. Gather *K¹² My Journal*.

1. Have students either respond to a prompt in Thoughts and Experiences (pages 50–93) or write about their own topic on the next available page in Ideas (pages 96–139).

2. Encourage students to explore their thoughts and write as much as they want. There are no rules. If students wish, ideas can be fleshed out into a more developed composition at a later time.

TIP Studies show that students who write more frequently become better writers.

Objectives
- Respond to a journal prompt.
- Freewrite about a topic.

Interjections and Draft Your Story

Lesson Overview

🖥 [Online] **25** minutes

Skills Update	Prepositions and Prepositional Phrases
GUM (Grammar, Usage, and Mechanics)	Interjections
Composition	Serena Writes the Beginning of Her Story

📄 [Offline] **20** minutes

Composition	Write Your Short Story Draft

[Materials]

Supplied

- *K¹² Language Arts Activity Book*, pp. WS 231–233, 249–251, 263–268
- *Grammar Reference Guide* Online Book (optional)
- drafting page (optional printout)

Keywords

character – a person or animal in a story
interjection – a word (or words) that expresses strong feeling
setting – when and where a story takes place

Advance Preparation

To prepare for the GUM portion of this lesson, review Conjunctions and Interjections (Interjections) in the *Grammar Reference Guide* (linked in the online lesson) to familiarize yourself with the topic. In this lesson, students continue to accumulate documents they will need as they work on their short story. Add these documents to those they have already been collecting. Gather pages WS 231–233 (Model Short Story) and 249–251 (Plan Your Story, students' completed story plan) in *K¹² Language Arts Activity Book*.

Big Ideas

- Imaginative writing, in the form of stories and poems, allows writers to access their creativity while entertaining an audience.
- The writing process is fluid and recursive. Writers make improvements to their drafts as needed.
- Written work is not perfect in its first version. First efforts are called drafts, and they are not meant to be final.

Online   25 minutes

Students will work online to review prepositions and prepositional phrases, to learn about interjections, and to explore how to begin to write a short story. Help students locate the online activities.

Skills Update

Prepositions and Prepositional Phrases

Students will review prepositions and prepositional phrases by completing Skills Update exercises. Sit with students as they do this activity and note if they answer correctly.

> **Learning Coach Check-In** How did students do on the Skills Update?

> ▸ **All answers correct:** Great! Skip the review screen and go on to the next activity.

> ▸ **Any answers incorrect:** Take a few minutes to review prepositions and prepositional phrases now. Use the link on the screen after the Skills Update to take another look at the online activity or review Prepositions (Prepositional Phrases) in the *Grammar Reference Guide* together.

TIP This activity will require extra time if students need to review prepositions and prepositional phrases. Take the extra 5–10 minutes to review now because new skills build on what students have already learned.

> **Objectives**
> * Identify prepositions.
> * Identify prepositional phrases.

GUM (Grammar, Usage, and Mechanics)

Interjections

Students will learn about interjections and practice identifying and using interjections.

> **Objectives**
> * Identify and use interjections.

Composition

Serena Writes the Beginning of Her Story

By examining how Serena begins her short story, students will learn about introducing characters, establishing setting, and developing the early part of a story's plot. They will also see how Serena presents the problem that her main character faces in the story.

> **Objectives**
> * Write a short story.
> * Write the beginning of a story.
> * Establish a situation in a story.
> * Introduce the characters in a story.

 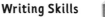

⟦ Offline ⟧ 🔟 minutes

Work **together** with students to complete the offline Composition activity.

Composition ....

Write Your Short Story Draft

Students will begin to draft their short story. Have them gather the model short story and their completed story plan, and turn to pages WS 263–268 in *K¹² Language Arts Activity Book*.

1. Have students use their plan and follow the directions on the Activity Book page to begin drafting their short story. Provide support as necessary, encouraging students to write in complete sentences.

2. Remind students to begin their story with a few paragraphs that introduce the main characters, establish the setting, give readers an idea of the characters' relationships with one another, and present the problem that the main character or characters face. Unlike previous writing assignments, there is no requirement for the number of paragraphs to write. The more dialogue that is included, the more paragraphs there will be. Encourage students to rely on their story plan, especially the beginning section, and to refer to Serena's short story as needed.

TIP Keep students' drafting pages in a safe place so they can return to them later as they continue to write.

> **⭐ Objectives**
> - Write a short story.
> - Write the beginning of a story.
> - Establish a situation in a story.
> - Introduce the characters in a story.

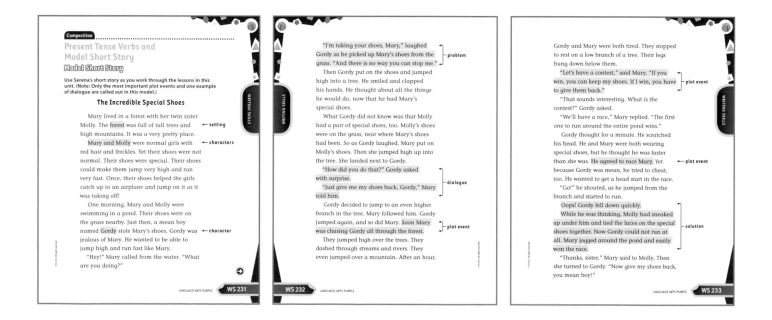

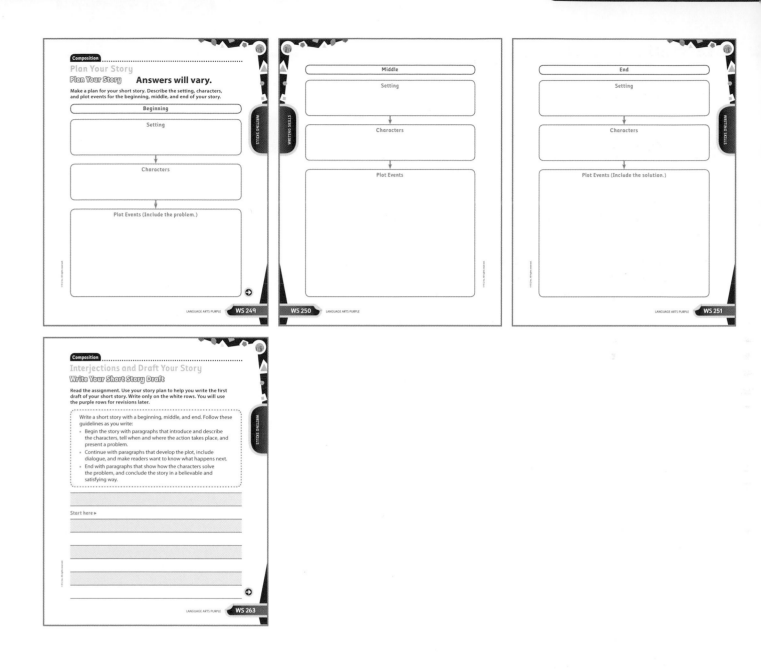

Composition

Plan Your Story

Plan Your Story   **Answers will vary.**

Make a plan for your short story. Describe the setting, characters, and plot events for the beginning, middle, and end of your story.

Beginning

Setting

↓

Characters

↓

Plot Events (Include the problem.)

LANGUAGE ARTS PURPLE   **WS 249**

Middle

Setting

↓

Characters

↓

Plot Events

WS 250   LANGUAGE ARTS PURPLE

End

Setting

↓

Characters

↓

Plot Events (Include the solution.)

LANGUAGE ARTS PURPLE   **WS 251**

Composition

Interjections and Draft Your Story

Write Your Short Story Draft

Read the assignment. Use your story plan to help you write the first draft of your short story. Write only on the white rows. You will use the purple rows for revisions later.

Write a short story with a beginning, middle, and end. Follow these guidelines as you write:

- Begin the story with paragraphs that introduce and describe the characters, tell when and where the action takes place, and present a problem.
- Continue with paragraphs that develop the plot, include dialogue, and make readers want to know what happens next.
- End with paragraphs that show how the characters solve the problem, and conclude the story in a believable and satisfying way.

Start here ▶

LANGUAGE ARTS PURPLE   **WS 263**

Writing Skills   **WS 539**

Good & Well and Draft Your Story

Lesson Overview

💻 [Online]   25 minutes

Skills Update	Interjections
GUM (Grammar, Usage, and Mechanics)	*Good* and *Well*
Composition	Serena Begins to Write the Middle of Her Story

📄 [Offline]   20 minutes

Composition	Write Your Short Story Draft

[Materials]

Supplied

- *K¹² Language Arts Activity Book*, pp. WS 231–233, 249–251, 263–268
- *Grammar Reference Guide* Online Book (optional)
- drafting page (optional printout)

Advance Preparation

In this lesson, students will continue to work on their short story. Gather pages WS 231–233 (Model Short Story), 249–251 (Plan Your Story, students' completed story plan), and 263–268 (Write Your Short Story Draft, students' partially completed draft) in *K¹² Language Arts Activity Book*.

Big Ideas

▸ Imaginative writing, in the form of stories and poems, allows writers to access their creativity while entertaining an audience.

▸ The writing process is fluid and recursive. Writers make improvements to their drafts as needed.

▸ Written work is not perfect in its first version. First efforts are called drafts, and they are not meant to be final.

▸ Using quotations, the exact words of the speaker, enhances writing. Rather than reporting what a speaker says in conversation, a good writer allows the audience to read the character's words.

▸ Dialogue adds realism and interest to a story.

[Online] 🕐 25 minutes

Students will work online to review interjections, to learn about distinguishing between adverbs and adjectives and to use *good* and *well* correctly, and to see how to work on the middle section of a short story. Help students locate the online activities.

Skills Update

Interjections
Students will review interjections by completing Skills Update exercises. Sit with students as they do this activity and note if they answer correctly.

> ⟳ **Learning Coach Check-In** How did students do on the Skills Update?

> ▸ **All answers correct:** Great! Skip the review screen and go on to the next activity.
> ▸ **Any answers incorrect:** Take a few minutes to review interjections now. Use the link on the screen after the Skills Update to take another look at the online activity or review Conjunctions and Interjections (Interjections) in the *Grammar Reference Guide* together.

TIP This activity will require extra time if students need to review interjections. Take the extra 5–10 minutes to review now because new skills build on what students have already learned.

Objectives
- Identify and use interjections.

GUM (Grammar, Usage, and Mechanics)

Good* and *Well
Students will learn about distinguishing between adjectives and adverbs and practice using *good* and *well* correctly in sentences.

Objectives
- Distinguish between adverbs and adjectives.
- Use *good* and *well* in sentences.

Composition

Serena Begins to Write the Middle of Her Story
By examining how Serena continues to work on her short story, students will learn about using dialogue; describing the thoughts, feelings, and actions of characters; and using words and phrases to signal the order of events in a story.

Objectives
- Draft the middle of a story.
- Use dialogue and descriptions of actions, thoughts, and feelings to develop characters.
- Use temporal words and phrases to signal event order.

[Offline] 20 minutes

Work **together** with students to complete the offline Composition activity.

Composition ....

Write Your Short Story Draft

Students will continue to draft their short story by focusing on the middle section of their story. Have students gather their completed story plan, as well as the model short story and their drafting pages.

1. Have students use their plan and follow the directions on the drafting pages to continue writing their short story, focusing on the middle of the story. Provide support as necessary, encouraging students to write in complete sentences.

2. Remind students to maintain the order of the story plan in their draft; incorporate dialogue; describe how characters think, feel, and act; and use words and phrases to signal the order of events. Encourage them to refer to Serena's short story as needed.

TIP Keep students' drafting pages in a safe place so they can return to them as they continue to write.

Objectives

- Draft the middle of a story.
- Use dialogue and descriptions of actions, thoughts, and feelings to develop characters.
- Use temporal words and phrases to signal event order.

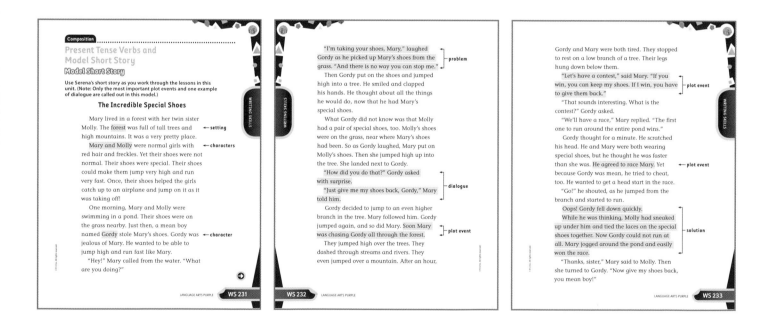

Composition

Plan Your Story

Plan Your Story   Answers will vary.

Make a plan for your short story. Describe the setting, characters, and plot events for the beginning, middle, and end of your story.

Beginning

Setting

Characters

Plot Events (Include the problem.)

Middle

Setting

Characters

Plot Events

End

Setting

Characters

Plot Events (Include the solution.)

Composition

Interjections and Draft Your Story

Write Your Short Story Draft

Read the assignment. Use your story plan to help you write the first draft of your short story. Write only on the white rows. You will use the purple rows for revisions later.

> Write a short story with a beginning, middle, and end. Follow these guidelines as you write:
> - Begin the story with paragraphs that introduce and describe the characters, tell when and where the action takes place, and present a problem.
> - Continue with paragraphs that develop the plot, include dialogue, and make readers want to know what happens next.
> - End with paragraphs that show how the characters solve the problem, and conclude the story in a believable and satisfying way.

Start here ▶

Double Negatives and Draft Your Story

Lesson Overview

Online — 25 minutes

Skills Update	*Good* and *Well*
GUM (Grammar, Usage, and Mechanics)	Double Negatives
Composition	Serena Continues to Write Her Short Story

Offline — 20 minutes

Composition	Write Your Short Story Draft

Materials

Supplied

- *K¹² Language Arts Activity Book,* pp. WS 231–233, 249–251, 263–268
- *Grammar Reference Guide* Online Book (optional)
- drafting page (optional printout)

Keywords

double negative – the incorrect use of two negative words in a sentence

Advance Preparation

In this lesson, students will continue to work on their short story. Gather pages WS 231–233 (Model Short Story), 249–251 (Plan Your Story, students' completed story plan), and 263–268 (Write Your Short Story Draft, students' partially completed draft) in *K¹² Language Arts Activity Book.*

Big Ideas

- ▶ Imaginative writing, in the form of stories and poems, allows writers to access their creativity while entertaining an audience.
- ▶ The writing process is fluid and recursive. Writers make improvements to their drafts as needed.
- ▶ Written work is not perfect in its first version. First efforts are called drafts, and they are not meant to be final.
- ▶ Using quotations, the exact words of the speaker, enhances writing. Rather than reporting what a speaker says in conversation, a good writer allows the audience to read the character's words.
- ▶ Dialogue adds realism and interest to a story.

[Online] 25 minutes

Students will work online to review how to correctly use *good* and *well*, to learn about double negatives, and to see how to continue to work on the middle section of a short story. Help students locate the online activities.

Skills Update

****

Good and Well

Students will review how to use *good* and *well* correctly by completing Skills Update exercises. Sit with students as they do this activity and note if they answer correctly.

➲ **Learning Coach Check-In** How did students do on the Skills Update?

▸ **All answers correct:** Great! Skip the review screen and go on to the next activity.

▸ **Any answers incorrect:** Take a few minutes to review using *good* and *well* correctly now. Use the link on the screen after the Skills Update to take another look at the online activity together.

TIP This activity will require extra time if students need to review using *good* and *well* correctly. Take the extra 5–10 minutes to review now because new skills build on what students have already learned.

> **Objectives**
> - Distinguish between adverbs and adjectives.
> - Use *good* and *well* in sentences.

GUM (Grammar, Usage, and Mechanics)

****

Double Negatives

Students will learn about double negatives and practice identifying and fixing double negatives in sentences.

> **Objectives**
> - Identify double negatives in sentences.
> - Fix double negatives in sentences.

Composition

****

Serena Continues to Write Her Short Story

By watching Serena continue to work on her short story, students will learn how to finish the middle section of their own story.

> **Objectives**
> - Draft the middle of a story.
> - Use dialogue and descriptions of actions, thoughts, and feelings to develop characters.
> - Use temporal words and phrases to signal event order.

[Offline] 20 minutes

Work **together** with students to complete the offline Composition activity.

Composition

Write Your Short Story Draft

Students will continue to draft their short story by working on the middle section of their story. Have students gather their completed story plan, as well as the model short story and their drafting pages.

1. Have students use their plan and follow the directions on the drafting pages to continue writing their short story, focusing on the middle section of the story. Provide support as necessary, encouraging students to write in complete sentences.

2. Remind students to maintain the order of the story plan in their draft; incorporate dialogue; describe how characters think, feel, and act; and use words and phrases to signal the order of events. Remind students that this section of the story should *not* include the solution to the problem that the main character faces. However, this section should set up the conclusion and the solution to the problem. Encourage students to refer to Serena's short story as needed.

TIP Keep students' drafting pages in a safe place so they can return to them later as they continue to write.

> ### Objectives
> - Draft the middle of a story.
> - Use dialogue and descriptions of actions, thoughts, and feelings to develop characters.
> - Use temporal words and phrases to signal event order.

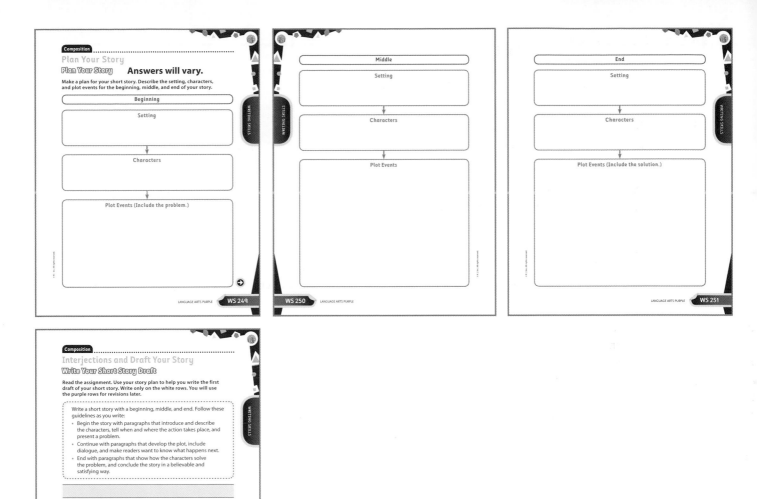

Composition

Plan Your Story

Plan Your Story Answers will vary.

Make a plan for your short story. Describe the setting, characters, and plot events for the beginning, middle, and end of your story.

Beginning

Setting

↓

Characters

↓

Plot Events (Include the problem.)

Middle

Setting

↓

Characters

↓

Plot Events

End

Setting

↓

Characters

↓

Plot Events (Include the solution.)

Composition

Interjections and Draft Your Story

Write Your Short Story Draft

Read the assignment. Use your story plan to help you write the first draft of your short story. Write only on the white rows. You will use the purple rows for revisions later.

> Write a short story with a beginning, middle, and end. Follow these guidelines as you write:
> - Begin the story with paragraphs that introduce and describe the characters, tell when and where the action takes place, and present a problem.
> - Continue with paragraphs that develop the plot, include dialogue, and make readers want to know what happens next.
> - End with paragraphs that show how the characters solve the problem, and conclude the story in a believable and satisfying way.

Start here ▶

Unit Review and Draft Your Story

Lesson Overview

💻 [Online]   25 minutes

Skills Update	Double Negatives
Unit Review	Some Parts of Speech
More Practice	Some Parts of Speech
Composition	Serena Finishes Writing Her Short Story

📝 [Offline]   20 minutes

Composition	Write Your Short Story Draft

Advance Preparation

In this lesson, students will continue to work on their short story. Gather pages WS 231–233 (Model Short Story), 249–251 (Plan Your Story, students' completed story plan), and 263–268 (Write Your Short Story Draft, students' partially completed draft) in *K¹² Language Arts Activity Book*.

Big Ideas

- ▶ Imaginative writing, in the form of stories and poems, allows writers to access their creativity while entertaining an audience.
- ▶ The writing process is fluid and recursive. Writers make improvements to their drafts as needed.
- ▶ Written work is never perfect in its first version. First efforts are called drafts, and they are not meant to be final.
- ▶ Using quotations, the exact words of the speaker, enhances writing. Rather than reporting what a speaker says in conversation, a good writer allows the audience to read the character's words.
- ▶ Dialogue adds realism and interest to a story.

[Materials]

Supplied
- *K¹² Language Arts Activity Book,* pp. WS 231–233,
- drafting page (optional printout)

Keywords

double negative – the incorrect use of two negative words in a sentence

interjection – a word (or words) that expresses strong feeling

preposition – a word that begins a phrase that ends with a noun or pronoun *Examples:* In the phrases "over the bridge" and "to me," the words *over* and *to* are prepositions.

prepositional phrase – a group of words that begins with a preposition and usually ends with the noun or a pronoun that is the object of the preposition

[Online] **25** minutes

Students will work online to review double negatives; to review the grammar, usage, and mechanics skills learned in the unit; and to see how to begin working on the ending of a short story. Help students locate the online activities.

Skills Update

Double Negatives

Students will review double negatives by completing Skills Update exercises. Sit with students as they do this activity and note if they answer correctly.

⊃ **Learning Coach Check-In** How did students do on the Skills Update?

▸ **All answers correct:** Great! Skip the review screen and go on to the next activity.

▸ **Any answers incorrect:** Take a few minutes to review double negatives now. Use the link on the screen after the Skills Update to take another look at the online activity together.

TIP This activity will require extra time if students need to review double negatives. Take the extra 5–10 minutes to review now because new skills build on what students have already learned.

> **Objectives**
> - Identify double negatives in sentences.
> - Fix double negatives in sentences.

Unit Review

Some Parts of Speech

Students will review what they have learned about some parts of speech. Exercises in this activity will check their ability to identify prepositions and prepositional phrases, to identify and use interjections, to distinguish between adverbs and adjectives and to use *good* and *well* correctly, and to identify and fix double negatives in sentences to review for the Unit Checkpoint.

TIP A full list of objectives covered in the Unit Review can be found in the online lesson.

> **Objectives**
> - Complete a review of grammar, usage, and mechanics skills.

More Practice

Some Parts of Speech

Go over students' results on the Unit Review and, if necessary, have students complete the appropriate review activities listed in the table online. Help students locate the activities. Provide support as needed.

TIP The time students need to complete this activity will vary. Set aside enough time for students to complete all review activities, if they need to do so.

> **Objectives**
> - Evaluate Unit Review results and choose activities for more practice.

Composition ···

Serena Finishes Writing Her Short Story
By watching Serena continue to work on her short story, students will learn how to write the ending of their own story.

> ⭐ **Objectives**
> • Write a conclusion to a story.

 **20** minutes

Work **together** with students to complete the offline Composition activity.

Composition ···

Write Your Short Story Draft
Students will continue to draft their short story by finishing the middle section and then beginning to work on the final section of their story. Have students gather their completed story plan, as well as the model short story and their drafting pages.

1. Have students use their plan and follow the directions on the drafting pages to continue writing their short story, focusing on finishing the middle section and starting the end section, or conclusion. Provide support as necessary, encouraging students to write in complete sentences.

2. Remind students to maintain the order of the story plan in their draft. In the final section of their story, students should work to show how the main character solves the problem and to tie up any loose ends. Encourage students to refer to Serena's short story as needed.

3. Tell students that they do not have to finish their short story today. They will have time in the next lesson to continue to work on the ending.

TIP Keep students' drafting pages in a safe place so they can return to them as they continue to write.

> ⭐ **Objectives**
> • Draft the middle of a story.
> • Use dialogue and descriptions of actions, thoughts, and feelings to develop characters.
> • Use temporal words and phrases to signal event order.
> • Write a conclusion to a story.

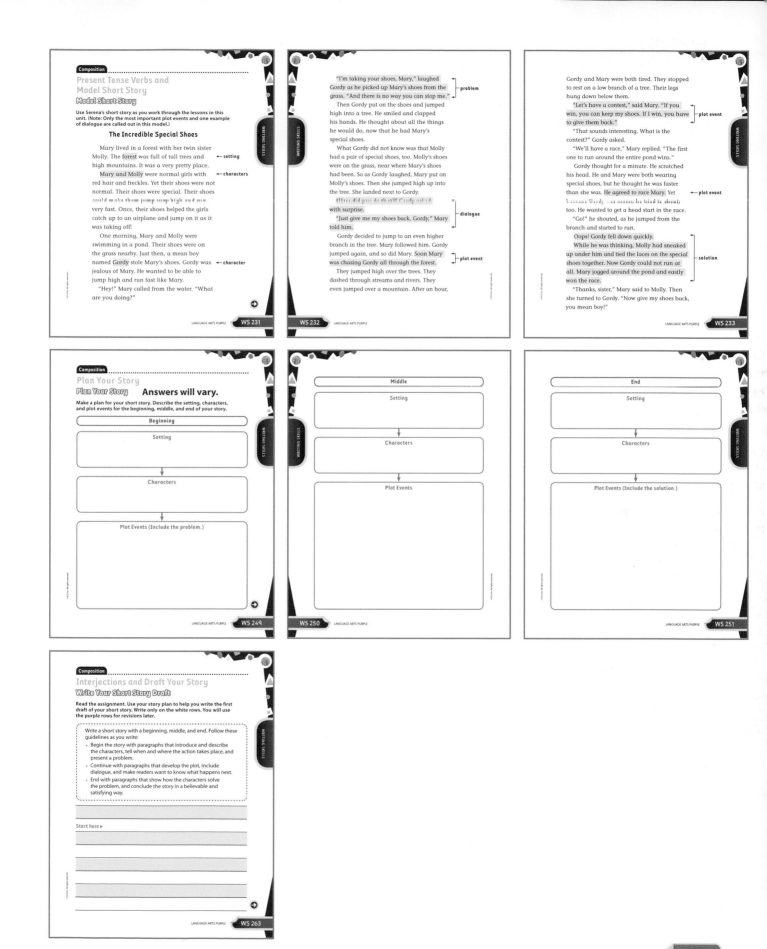

Composition

Present Tense Verbs and Model Short Story

Model Short Story

Use Serena's short story as you work through the lessons in this unit. (Note: Only the most important plot events and one example of dialogue are called out in this model.)

The Incredible Special Shoes

Mary lived in a forest with her twin sister Molly. The forest was full of tall trees and high mountains. It was a very pretty place. ← setting

Mary and Molly were normal girls with red hair and freckles. Yet their shoes were not normal. Their shoes were special. Their shoes could make them jump very high and run very fast. Once, their shoes helped the girls catch up to an airplane and jump on it as it was taking off! ← characters

One morning, Mary and Molly were swimming in a pond. Their shoes were on the grass nearby. Just then, a mean boy named Gordy stole Mary's shoes. Gordy was jealous of Mary. He wanted to be able to jump high and run fast like Mary. ← character

"Hey!" Mary called from the water. "What are you doing?"

WS 231

"I'm taking your shoes, Mary," laughed Gordy as he picked up Mary's shoes from the grass. "And there is no way you can stop me." ← problem

Then Gordy put on the shoes and jumped high into a tree. He smiled and clapped his hands. He thought about all the things he would do, now that he had Mary's special shoes.

What Gordy did not know was that Molly had a pair of special shoes, too. Molly's shoes were on the grass, near where Mary's shoes had been. So as Gordy laughed, Mary put on Molly's shoes. Then she jumped high up into the tree. She landed next to Gordy.

"How did you do that?" Gordy asked with surprise. ← dialogue

"Just give me my shoes back, Gordy," Mary told him.

Gordy decided to jump to an even higher branch in the tree. Mary followed him. Gordy jumped again, and so did Mary. Soon Mary was chasing Gordy all through the forest. ← plot event

They jumped high over the trees. They dashed through streams and rivers. They even jumped over a mountain. After an hour,

WS 232

Gordy and Mary were both tired. They stopped to rest on a low branch of a tree. Their legs hung down below them.

"Let's have a contest," said Mary. "If you win, you can keep my shoes. If I win, you have to give them back." ← plot event

"That sounds interesting. What is the contest?" Gordy asked.

"We'll have a race," Mary replied. "The first one to run around the entire pond wins."

Gordy thought for a minute. He scratched his head. He and Mary were both wearing special shoes, but he thought he was faster than she was. He agreed to race Mary. Yet [unclear] Gordy was going to try to cheat, too. He wanted to get a head start in the race. ← plot event

"Go!" he shouted, as he jumped from the branch and started to run.

Oops! Gordy fell down quickly.

While he was thinking, Molly had sneaked up under him and tied the laces on the special shoes together. Now Gordy could not run at all. Mary jogged around the pond and easily won the race. ← solution

"Thanks, sister," Mary said to Molly. Then she turned to Gordy. "Now give my shoes back, you mean boy!"

WS 233

Composition

Plan Your Story

Plan Your Story   Answers will vary.

Make a plan for your short story. Describe the setting, characters, and plot events for the beginning, middle, and end of your story.

Beginning

Setting

Characters

Plot Events (Include the problem.)

WS 249

Middle

Setting

Characters

Plot Events

WS 250

End

Setting

Characters

Plot Events (Include the solution.)

WS 251

Composition

Interjections and Draft Your Story

Write Your Short Story Draft

Read the assignment. Use your story plan to help you write the first draft of your short story. Write only on the white rows. You will use the purple rows for revisions later.

Write a short story with a beginning, middle, and end. Follow these guidelines as you write:
- Begin the story with paragraphs that introduce and describe the characters, tell when and where the action takes place, and present a problem.
- Continue with paragraphs that develop the plot, include dialogue, and make readers want to know what happens next.
- End with paragraphs that show how the characters solve the problem, and conclude the story in a believable and satisfying way.

Start here ►

WS 263

Unit Checkpoint and Draft Your Story

Lesson Overview

💻 Online — 20 minutes

Unit Checkpoint	Some Parts of Speech

📄 Offline — 25 minutes

More Practice	Some Parts of Speech
Composition	Write Your Short Story Draft

Advance Preparation

In this lesson, students will continue to work on their short story. They should finish drafting their story in this lesson. Gather pages WS 231–233 (Model Short Story), 249–251 (Plan Your Story, students' completed story plan), and 263–268 (Write Your Short Story Draft, students' partially completed draft) in *K¹² Language Arts Activity Book*.

Big Ideas

▸ Imaginative writing, in the form of stories and poems, allows writers to access their creativity while entertaining an audience.

▸ The writing process is fluid and recursive. Writers make improvements to their drafts as needed.

▸ Written work is not perfect in its first version. First efforts are called drafts, and they are not meant to be final.

▸ Using quotations, the exact words of the speaker, enhances writing. Rather than reporting what a speaker says in conversation, a good writer allows the audience to read the character's words.

▸ Dialogue adds realism and interest to a story.

Materials

Supplied

- *K¹² Language Arts Activity Book*, pp. WS 231–233, 249–251, 263–268
- *Grammar Reference Guide* Online Book (optional)
- **Prepositions and Prepositional Phrases** (optional printout)
- **Interjections** (optional printout)
- *Good* and *Well* (optional printout)
- **Double Negatives** (optional printout)
- **drafting page** (optional printout)

Keywords

double negative – the incorrect use of two negative words in a sentence

interjection – a word (or words) that expresses strong feeling

preposition – a word that begins a phrase that ends with a noun or pronoun *Examples:* In the phrases "over the bridge" and "to me," the words *over* and *to* are prepositions.

prepositional phrase – a group of words that begins with a preposition and usually ends with the noun or a pronoun that is the object of the preposition

[Online] 20 minutes

Students will work online **independently** to complete the Unit Checkpoint. Help students locate the Unit Checkpoint and provide support as necessary.

Unit Checkpoint ....

Some Parts of Speech

Students will complete an online Unit Checkpoint about some parts of speech. Exercises in this checkpoint will check students' ability to identify prepositions and prepositional phrases, to identify and use interjections, to distinguish between adverbs and adjectives and use *good* and *well* correctly, and to identify and fix double negatives in sentences. If necessary, read the directions to students.

TIP A full list of objectives covered in the Unit Checkpoint can be found in the online lesson.

> **Objectives**
> * Complete a Unit Checkpoint on grammar, usage, and mechanics skills.

[Offline] 25 minutes

Work **together** with students to complete the offline More Practice and Composition activities.

More Practice ....

Some Parts of Speech

Go over students' results on the Unit Checkpoint and, if necessary, print out and have them complete the appropriate practice pages listed in the table online. Students can complete all necessary pages now or, if more time is needed, they can spread them out over the next few days. They can also review the appropriate sections of the *Grammar Reference Guide* with you. If students scored less than 80 percent on the Unit Checkpoint, you may want them to retake the Checkpoint after completing the additional activity pages.

TIP The time students need to complete this activity will vary. Set aside enough time for students to complete some or all activity pages and to retake the Unit Checkpoint, if they need to do so. Students may retake the Unit Checkpoint immediately, but having them complete the practice pages and then retake it might be more effective.

> **Objectives**
> * Evaluate Unit Checkpoint results and choose activities for more practice.

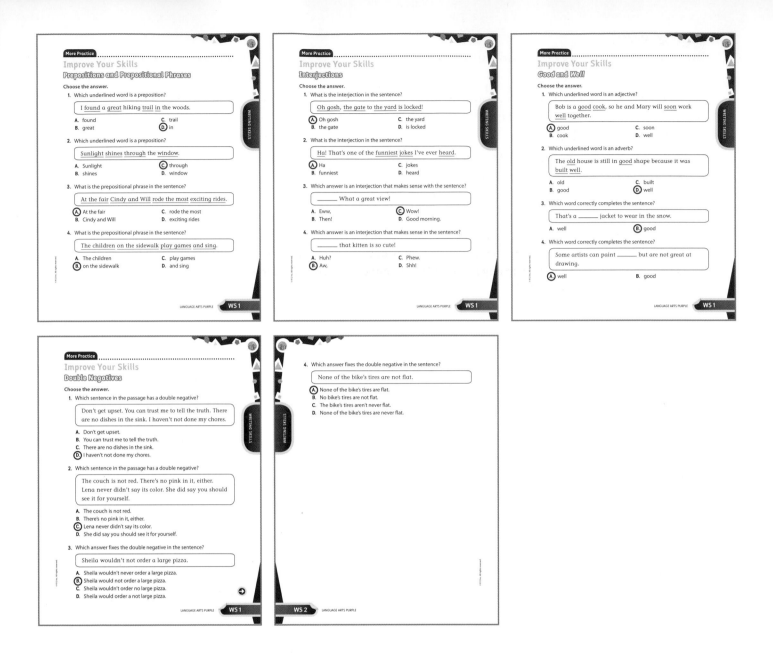

More Practice

Improve Your Skills
Prepositions and Prepositional Phrases

Choose the answer.

1. Which underlined word is a preposition?

> I found a great hiking trail in the woods.

A. found
B. great
C. trail
D. in

2. Which underlined word is a preposition?

> Sunlight shines through the window.

A. Sunlight
B. shines
C. through
D. window

3. What is the prepositional phrase in the sentence?

> At the fair Cindy and Will rode the most exciting rides.

A. At the fair
B. Cindy and Will
C. rode the most
D. exciting rides

4. What is the prepositional phrase in the sentence?

> The children on the sidewalk play games and sing.

A. The children
B. on the sidewalk
C. play games
D. and sing

More Practice

Improve Your Skills
Interjections

Choose the answer.

1. What is the interjection in the sentence?

> Oh gosh, the gate to the yard is locked!

A. Oh gosh
B. the gate
C. the yard
D. is locked

2. What is the interjection in the sentence?

> Ha! That's one of the funniest jokes I've ever heard.

A. Ha
B. funniest
C. jokes
D. heard

3. Which answer is an interjection that makes sense with the sentence?

> _____ What a great view!

A. Eww,
B. Then!
C. Wow!
D. Good morning.

4. Which answer is an interjection that makes sense in the sentence?

> _____ that kitten is so cute!

A. Huh?
B. Aw,
C. Phew.
D. Shh!

More Practice

Improve Your Skills
Good and Well

Choose the answer.

1. Which underlined word is an adjective?

> Bob is a good cook, so he and Mary will soon work well together.

A. good
B. cook
C. soon
D. well

2. Which underlined word is an adverb?

> The old house is still in good shape because it was built well.

A. old
B. good
C. built
D. well

3. Which word correctly completes the sentence?

> That's a _____ jacket to wear in the snow.

A. well
B. good

4. Which word correctly completes the sentence?

> Some artists can paint _____ but are not great at drawing.

A. well
B. good

More Practice

Improve Your Skills
Double Negatives

Choose the answer.

1. Which sentence in the passage has a double negative?

> Don't get upset. You can trust me to tell the truth. There are no dishes in the sink. I haven't not done my chores.

A. Don't get upset.
B. You can trust me to tell the truth.
C. There are no dishes in the sink.
D. I haven't not done my chores.

2. Which sentence in the passage has a double negative?

> The couch is not red. There's no pink in it, either. Lena never didn't say its color. She did say you should see it for yourself.

A. The couch is not red.
B. There's no pink in it, either.
C. Lena never didn't say its color.
D. She did say you should see it for yourself.

3. Which answer fixes the double negative in the sentence?

> Sheila wouldn't not order a large pizza.

A. Sheila wouldn't never order a large pizza.
B. Sheila would not order a large pizza.
C. Sheila wouldn't order no large pizza.
D. Sheila would order a not large pizza.

4. Which answer fixes the double negative in the sentence?

> None of the bike's tires are not flat.

A. None of the bike's tires are flat.
B. No bike's tires are not flat.
C. The bike's tires aren't never flat.
D. None of the bike's tires are never flat.

Composition

Write Your Short Story Draft

Students will finish drafting their short story by completing the final section of the story. Have students gather their completed story plan, as well as the model short story and their drafting pages.

1. Have students use their plan and follow the directions on the drafting pages to finish writing their short story, focusing on completing the story today. Provide support as necessary, encouraging students to write in complete sentences.

2. Remind students to maintain the order of the story plan in their draft. In this final section of their story, they should work to show how the main character solves the problem and to tie up any loose ends. Encourage students to refer to Serena's short story as needed.

TIP Keep students' drafting pages in a safe place so they can return to them as they revise and proofread their work.

Objectives
- Write a conclusion to a story.

Composition

Present Tense Verbs and Model Short Story

Model Short Story

Use Serena's short story as you work through the lessons in this unit. (Note: Only the most important plot events and one example of dialogue are called out in this model.)

The Incredible Special Shoes

Mary lived in a forest with her twin sister Molly. The forest was full of tall trees and high mountains. It was a very pretty place. ← setting

Mary and Molly were normal girls with ← characters red hair and freckles. Yet their shoes were not normal. Their shoes were special. Their shoes could make them jump very high and run very fast. Once, their shoes helped the girls catch up to an airplane and jump on it as it was taking off!

One morning, Mary and Molly were swimming in a pond. Their shoes were on the grass nearby. Just then, a mean boy named Gordy stole Mary's shoes. Gordy was ← character jealous of Mary. He wanted to be able to jump high and run fast like Mary.

"Hey!" Mary called from the water. "What are you doing?"

LANGUAGE ARTS PURPLE WS 231

"I'm taking your shoes, Mary," laughed Gordy as he picked up Mary's shoes from the grass. "And there is no way you can stop me." ⎤ problem

Then Gordy put on the shoes and jumped high into a tree. He smiled and clapped his hands. He thought about all the things he would do, now that he had Mary's special shoes.

What Gordy did not know was that Molly had a pair of special shoes, too. Molly's shoes were on the grass, near where Mary's shoes had been. So as Gordy laughed, Mary put on Molly's shoes. Then she jumped high up into the tree. She landed next to Gordy.

"How did you do that?" Gordy asked with surprise. ⎤ dialogue

"Just give me my shoes back, Gordy," Mary told him. ⎦

Gordy decided to jump to an even higher branch in the tree. Mary followed him. Gordy jumped again, and so did Mary. Soon Mary was chasing Gordy all through the forest. ⎦ plot event

They jumped high over the trees. They dashed through streams and rivers. They even jumped over a mountain. After an hour,

WS 232 LANGUAGE ARTS PURPLE

Gordy and Mary were both tired. They stopped to rest on a low branch of a tree. Their legs hung down below them.

"Let's have a contest," said Mary. "If you win, you can keep my shoes. If I win, you have ⎤ plot event to give them back." ⎦

"That sounds interesting. What is the contest?" Gordy asked.

"We'll have a race," Mary replied. "The first one to run around the entire pond wins."

Gordy thought for a minute. He scratched his head. He and Mary were both wearing special shoes, but he thought he was faster than she was. He agreed to race Mary. Yet ← plot event because Gordy was mean, he tried to cheat, too. He wanted to get a head start in the race.

"Go!" he shouted, as he jumped from the branch and started to run.

Oops! Gordy fell down quickly.

While he was thinking, Molly had sneaked up under him and tied the laces on the special ⎤ solution shoes together. Now Gordy could not run at all. Mary jogged around the pond and easily won the race. ⎦

"Thanks, sister," Mary said to Molly. Then she turned to Gordy. "Now give me my shoes back, you mean boy!"

LANGUAGE ARTS PURPLE WS 233

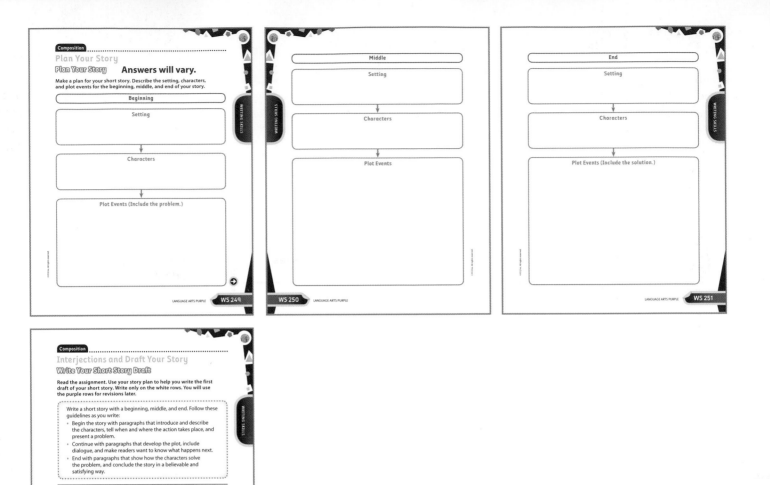

Composition

Plan Your Story

Plan Your Story   Answers will vary.

Make a plan for your short story. Describe the setting, characters, and plot events for the beginning, middle, and end of your story.

Beginning

Setting

Characters

Plot Events (Include the problem.)

Middle

Setting

Characters

Plot Events

End

Setting

Characters

Plot Events (Include the solution.)

LANGUAGE ARTS PURPLE **WS 249**

WS 250 LANGUAGE ARTS PURPLE

LANGUAGE ARTS PURPLE **WS 251**

Composition

Interjections and Draft Your Story

Write Your Short Story Draft

Read the assignment. Use your story plan to help you write the first draft of your short story. Write only on the white rows. You will use the purple rows for revisions later.

Write a short story with a beginning, middle, and end. Follow these guidelines as you write:

- Begin the story with paragraphs that introduce and describe the characters, tell when and where the action takes place, and present a problem.
- Continue with paragraphs that develop the plot, include dialogue, and make readers want to know what happens next.
- End with paragraphs that show how the characters solve the problem, and conclude the story in a believable and satisfying way.

Start here ▶

LANGUAGE ARTS PURPLE **WS 263**

Revise Your Story (A)

Lesson Overview

Online — 20 minutes

| Composition | Serena Revises Her Story for Details |

Offline — 25 minutes

| Composition | Revise with a Checklist |

Materials

Supplied

- *K¹² Language Arts Activity Book*, pp. WS 263–269
- Short Story: Feedback Sheet (printout)
- drafting page (optional printout)

Advance Preparation

In this lesson, students will begin to revise their short story. Gather pages WS 263–268 (Write Your Short Story Draft, students' completed draft) in *K¹² Language Arts Activity Book*. Print the Short Story: Feedback Sheet from the online lesson.

Big Ideas

- ▸ Imaginative writing, in the form of stories and poems, allows writers to access their creativity while entertaining an audience.
- ▸ The writing process is fluid and recursive. Writers make improvements to their drafts as needed.
- ▸ Written work is not perfect in its first version. First efforts are called drafts, and they are not meant to be final.
- ▸ Good writers carefully check their work for errors.

[Online] ⏱ 20 minutes

Students will work online **independently** to learn how to revise a short story by adding or improving ideas and details that make characters more believable and the plot easier to understand. Help students locate the online activity.

Composition ....

Serena Revises Her Story for Details

By watching how Serena revises her short story draft to improve or add details related to character, setting, and plot, as well as remove unnecessary or irrelevant details, students will learn how to begin revising their own draft.

> **Objectives**
> * Revise a story.
> * Add content to strengthen a story.

[Offline] ⏱ 25 minutes

Work **together** with students to complete the offline Composition activity.

Composition ....

Revise with a Checklist

Students will begin to revise their short story. They will focus only on improving or adding details and ideas that make their characters more believable and the plot easier to understand. In the next lesson, they will focus on improving the organization and language of their draft. Gather students' completed short story draft and the Short Story: Feedback Sheet that you should have printed from the online lesson. Students should read their stories aloud, and you should base your feedback on what you hear.

> **Objectives**
> * Revise a story.
> * Add content to strengthen a story.

1. Before students begin reading aloud, read over the feedback sheet so that you are familiar with what you should be listening for. As students read aloud, think about how they might add or improve details to make their characters more believable and the plot of the story more understandable. Fill out the Short Story: Feedback Sheet as students read. Use the comments section to make notes about the strengths of their story and to include suggestions for improvement.

2. In this lesson, use the Ideas and Details section of the Feedback Sheet to guide you in your discussion with students. For instance, you might point out a moment in which the main character is strangely passive or overly calm considering the situation and help students understand that the events of the plot would likely make the character more active or excited. Similarly, you might focus student attention on an instance in which one of the characters says or does something that does not fit with how he or she has been portrayed to that point and suggest that students really think about the character's traits and feelings as they revise. (In the next lesson, you will discuss with students the Language and Organization section of the feedback sheet.)

3. Encourage students to actively revise their draft based on your feedback. Reassure students that it's okay to remove ideas or sentences from their story. Doing so may help their story become more powerful, even if something they cut was included in their story plan. Likewise, reassure students that it is okay (even necessary) to add ideas and details that will make their story more interesting and their characters more lifelike.

4. As students revise their draft, have them use the purple rows to mark their revisions.

5. Once you've discussed the first draft with students, have them review their draft once more, using the first part of the revising checklist on page WS 269 in *K¹² Language Arts Activity Book*. Students should check off each box on the checklist as they complete the Ideas and Details items.

TIP Keep students' revised short story and revising checklist in a safe place so that they can refer to them later.

Composition

Interjections and Draft Your Story

Write Your Short Story Draft

Read the assignment. Use your story plan to help you write the first draft of your short story. Write only on the white rows. You will use the purple rows for revisions later.

Write a short story with a beginning, middle, and end. Follow these guidelines as you write:
- Begin the story with paragraphs that introduce and describe the characters, tell when and where the action takes place, and present a problem.
- Continue with paragraphs that develop the plot, include dialogue, and make readers want to know what happens next.
- End with paragraphs that show how the characters solve the problem, and conclude the story in a believable and satisfying way.

Start here ➤

Composition

Revise Your Story (A)

Revise with a Checklist

Follow this checklist as you revise the draft of your short story. Check off each box after you complete each item.

Ideas and Details

☐ Focus your story on a character who faces a problem.

☐ Give good descriptions of characters and their traits.

☐ Include the setting and key details that make the plot interesting.

☐ Remove unnecessary details from the story, such as details that are out of place or don't help the plot.

Language and Organization

☐ Write a story with a beginning, middle, and end.

☐ Arrange plot events in a logical order.

☐ Include words and phrases that show when events happen.

☐ Use dialogue that reveals important information about characters and plot.

☐ Use informal language for dialogue to make the characters sound real.

☐ Conclude your story in a satisfying way.

Students should check off each box after they complete each item.

Revise Your Story (B)

Lesson Overview

🖥	**[Online]**	**20** minutes
Composition	Serena Revises Her Story for Organization and Language	

📄	**[Offline]**	**25** minutes
Composition	Revise with a Checklist	

[Materials]

Supplied

- *K¹² Language Arts Activity Book*, pp. WS 263–269
- Short Story: Feedback Sheet (printout)
- drafting page (optional printout)

Advance Preparation

In this lesson, students will continue to revise their short story. Gather pages WS 263–268 (Write Your Short Story Draft, students' completed draft) and 269 (Revise with a Checklist) in *K¹² Language Arts Activity Book*. Also gather the completed Short Story: Feedback Sheet.

Big Ideas

▸ Imaginative writing, in the form of stories and poems, allows writers to access their creativity while entertaining an audience.

▸ The writing process is fluid and recursive. Writers make improvements to their drafts as needed.

▸ Written work is not perfect in its first version. First efforts are called drafts, and they are not meant to be final.

▸ Good writers carefully check their work for errors.

[Online] 🔟 minutes

Students will work online **independently** to learn how to revise a short story by improving its organization to make the plot more logical and its language to make dialogue more realistic. Help students locate the online activity.

Composition ·

Serena Revises Her Story for Organization and Language
By watching how Serena revises her short story draft to improve its organization, as well as to make the dialogue sound more realistic, students will learn how to finish revising their own draft.

> **Objectives**
> - Revise a story.
> - Revise a story for organization.
> - Revise a story for language and word choice.

[Offline] 🔠 minutes

Work **together** with students to complete the offline Composition activity.

Composition ·

Revise with a Checklist
Students will continue to revise their short story. They will focus on improving the organization of their story to make the plot more logical and improving the language to make dialogue more realistic. Gather students' short story draft, the revising checklist, and your completed Short Story: Feedback Sheet.

> **Objectives**
> - Revise a story.
> - Revise a story for organization.
> - Revise a story for language and word choice.

1. Use the Language and Organization section of the feedback sheet to guide you as you discuss with students the strengths of the beginning, middle, and end of their story and the dialogue among characters. Then focus on some areas of organization and language that could be improved. For example, mention those parts of the story where you think events happen in an illogical order or characters speak in unrealistic ways. Talk with students how moving plot events or details around will make their work stronger. You might also focus students' attention on an instance in which one of the characters speaks in a way that is overly formal or unlike the way people really talk to each other.

2. Once you've discussed students' draft with them, have them review it once more, using the second part of the revising checklist. Students should check off each box on the checklist as they complete the Language and Organization items.

3. If students' revised short story has many changes that make the story difficult to read and understand, encourage them to make a clean copy before they proofread in a later lesson. Additional drafting pages can be printed from the online lesson.

TIP Keep students' revised short story in a safe place so they can refer to it later.

Composition

Interjections and Draft Your Story

Write Your Short Story Draft

Read the assignment. Use your story plan to help you write the first draft of your short story. Write only on the white rows. You will use the purple rows for revisions later.

Write a short story with a beginning, middle, and end. Follow these guidelines as you write:
- Begin the story with paragraphs that introduce and describe the characters, tell when and where the action takes place, and present a problem.
- Continue with paragraphs that develop the plot, include dialogue, and make readers want to know what happens next.
- End with paragraphs that show how the characters solve the problem, and conclude the story in a believable and satisfying way.

Start here ▶

LANGUAGE ARTS PURPLE **WS 263**

Composition

Revise Your Story (A)

Revise with a Checklist

Follow this checklist as you revise the draft of your short story. Check off each box after you complete each item.

Ideas and Details

☐ Focus your story on a character who faces a problem.

☐ Give good descriptions of characters and their traits.

☐ Include the setting and key details that make the plot interesting.

☐ Remove unnecessary details from the story, such as details that are out of place or don't help the plot.

Language and Organization

☐ Write a story with a beginning, middle, and end.

☐ Arrange plot events in a logical order.

☐ Include words and phrases that show when events happen.

☐ Use dialogue that reveals important information about characters and plot.

☐ Use informal language for dialogue to make the characters sound real.

☐ Conclude your story in a satisfying way.

Students should check off each box after they complete each item.

LANGUAGE ARTS PURPLE **WS 269**

Proofread Your Story

Lesson Overview

🖥️	**[Online]**		**20** minutes
Composition		Serena Proofreads Her Story	

📄	**[Offline]**		**25** minutes
Composition		Proofread with a Checklist	

[Materials]

Supplied

- *K¹² Language Arts Activity Book*, pp. WS 263–268, 270
- *Grammar Reference Guide* Online Book (optional)
- drafting page (optional printout)

Advance Preparation

In this lesson, students will proofread their short story. Gather pages WS 263–268 (Write Your Short Story Draft, students' revised draft) in *K¹² Language Arts Activity Book*. If students' revised short story has many changes that make it difficult to read and understand, you may want to encourage them to make a clean copy before they proofread in this lesson. Additional drafting pages can be printed from the online lesson.

Big Ideas

- ▸ Imaginative writing, in the form of stories and poems, allows writers to access their creativity while entertaining an audience.
- ▸ The writing process is fluid and recursive. Writers make improvements to their drafts as needed.
- ▸ Written work is not perfect in its first version. First efforts are called drafts, and they are not meant to be final.
- ▸ Using quotations, the exact words of the speaker, enhances writing. Rather than reporting what a speaker says in conversation, a good writer allows the audience to read the character's words.
- ▸ Good writers carefully check their work for errors.

〔Online〕 ⑳ minutes

Students will work online **independently** to learn how to proofread a short story. Help students locate the online activity.

Composition ....

Serena Proofreads Her Story
By watching how Serena proofreads her short story, students will learn how to proofread their own draft.

> **Objectives**
> - Proofread a story.
> - Proofread for quotation marks.
> - Proofread for commas.
> - Proofread for capital letters.

〔Offline〕 ㉕ minutes

Work **together** with students to complete the offline Composition activity.

Composition ....

Proofread with a Checklist
Students will proofread their short story. Have them gather their revised short story draft. Turn to page WS 270 in *K¹² Language Arts Activity Book*.

1. Have students review their draft using the proofreading checklist. Students should check off each box on the checklist as they complete each item. If necessary, tell students to use the purple rows on their drafting pages to actively mark changes.

> **Objectives**
> - Proofread a story.
> - Proofread for quotation marks.
> - Proofread for commas.
> - Proofread for capital letters.

2. If students' revised short story has many changes that make the story difficult to read and understand, encourage them to make a clean copy before they proofread. Additional drafting pages can be printed from the online lesson.

 TIP Keep students' proofread short story in a safe place so they can refer to it later.

Composition

Interjections and Draft Your Story
Write Your Short Story Draft

Read the assignment. Use your story plan to help you write the first draft of your short story. Write only on the white rows. You will use the purple rows for revisions later.

> Write a short story with a beginning, middle, and end. Follow these guidelines as you write:
> * Begin the story with paragraphs that introduce and describe the characters, tell when and where the action takes place, and present a problem.
> * Continue with paragraphs that develop the plot, include dialogue, and make readers want to know what happens next.
> * End with paragraphs that show how the characters solve the problem, and conclude the story in a believable and satisfying way.

Start here ►

LANGUAGE ARTS PURPLE **WS 263**

Composition

Proofread Your Story
Proofread with a Checklist

Follow this checklist as you proofread the draft of your short story. Check off each box after you complete each item.

☐ Capitalize proper nouns, including the names of people and places.

☐ Begin each sentence with a capital letter.

☐ End each sentence with the correct punctuation mark.

☐ Place quotations marks around the exact words of characters.

☐ Begin a new paragraph each time a different character begins to speak.

☐ Use commas correctly.

☐ Use interjections to express strong feelings.

☐ Avoid double negatives.

☐ Use a dictionary to check the spellings of any words you don't know.

Students should check off each box after they complete each item.

WS 270 LANGUAGE ARTS PURPLE

Publish Your Story (A)

Lesson Overview

Offline	45 minutes
Write Now	Publish Your Short Story

Materials

Supplied
- *K¹² Language Arts Activity Book*, pp. WS 263–268, 271–276
- lined writing page (optional printout)

Advance Preparation

Gather pages WS 263–268 (Write Your Short Story Draft, students' draft of their short story) in *K¹² Language Arts Activity Book*, which students should have revised and proofread.

Big Ideas

Imaginative writing, in the form of stories and poems, allows writers to access their creativity while entertaining an audience.

[Offline] (45) minutes

Work **together** with students to complete the offline Write Now activity.

Write Now ....

✏️ **Publish Your Short Story**

Students will begin to publish their short story. Have them gather their proofread draft. Turn to pages WS 271–276 in *K¹² Language Arts Activity Book*.

1. Explain to students that they will finish their short story by completing the last stage of the writing process—publishing their work.
   Say: Publishing your writing means making a clean and final copy that is ready for sharing with others.

   ▸ To be ready to publish your short story, you should have finished revising and proofreading your draft.
   ▸ The final copy should be your best effort and should not have any errors.

2. Explain that the final copy should be written clearly and neatly on clean sheets of paper. Tell students that they should use good handwriting and leave spaces between words so that others can read what they have written.

3. Have students use the lined Activity Book pages to write their final copy. If needed, additional lined writing pages can be printed from the online lesson. Since the short story is lengthy, students will complete their clean copy in the next lesson, and you will evaluate it then.

Composition
Interjections and Draft Your Story
Write Your Short Story Draft

Read the assignment. Use your story plan to help you write the first draft of your short story. Write only on the white rows. You will use the purple rows for revisions later.

Write a short story with a beginning, middle, and end. Follow these guidelines as you write:
• Begin the story with paragraphs that introduce and describe the characters, tell when and where the action takes place, and present a problem.
• Continue with paragraphs that develop the plot, include dialogue, and make readers want to know what happens next.
• End with paragraphs that show how the characters solve the problem, and conclude the story in a believable and satisfying way.

Start here ▸

LANGUAGE ARTS PURPLE **WS 263**

Write Now
Publish Your Story (A)
Publish Your Short Story

Make a clean copy of your finished short story, which you have revised and proofread.

Refer to the rubric and sample responses.

LANGUAGE ARTS PURPLE **WS 271**

Publish Your Story (B)

Lesson Overview

📄 [Offline]　　　　　　　　45 minutes

Write Now	Publish Your Short Story
More Practice	Short Story

[Materials]

Supplied
- *K¹² Language Arts Activity Book*, pp. WS 263–268, 271–276
- Short Story: Rubric and Sample Responses (printout)
- lined writing page (optional printout)

Advance Preparation

Gather pages WS 263–268 (Write Your Short Story Draft, students' draft of their short story) and 271–276 (Publish Your Short Story, students' partially completed clean copy of their short story) in *K¹² Language Arts Activity Book*.

Big Ideas

Imaginative writing, in the form of stories and poems, allows writers to access their creativity while entertaining an audience.

〔 Offline 〕 45 minutes

Work **together** with students to complete the offline Write Now and More Practice activities.

Write Now ·

✏️ **Publish Your Short Story**

Students will finish publishing their short story. Have them gather their draft and their partially completed clean copy.

> **Objectives**
> • Publish a short story.

1. Explain to students that they should finish the clean copy of their short story. If needed, additional lined writing pages can be printed from the online lesson.

2. Use the materials and instructions in the online lesson to evaluate students' finished writing. You will be looking at students' writing to evaluate the following:

   ▶ **Ideas and Details:** The story focuses on characters who have distinct traits and who, in almost all instances, behave in ways that are consistent with those traits. The relationships between characters are expressed or suggested to readers. With one or two exceptions, the story provides clear descriptions of setting and plot events. The story contains few unnecessary or irrelevant details.

   ▶ **Language and Organization:** The story has been revised. There is a problem that the main character faces, and it is presented in the beginning section of the story. In the middle section, the character makes attempts to solve the problem. In the final section, the problem is solved, and some resolution occurs. With one or two exceptions, plot events are logically connected. The story contains dialogue that is usually realistic and mirrors real speech.

   ▶ **Grammar and Mechanics:** The story has been proofread using a checklist, and four to six errors remain in grammar, usage, or mechanics.

3. Enter students' scores online for each rubric category.

4. If students' writing scored a 1 in any category, work with them to revise and proofread their work.

5. Make suggestions for ways that students can share their short story with an audience.

- ► Have students read their story aloud to people they think might enjoy hearing a creative tale.
- ► Suggest that students make their short story into a book. They can type their story, leaving spaces for illustrations. Then they can draw pictures of the main characters and events. When it is completed, they can share their book with siblings or friends.
- ► Give students the option of turning their story into a play with some of their peers.
- ► Send the short story as an e-mail attachment to relatives who might enjoy having their own copy to read.

TIP Tell students that producing a piece of writing that is ready to publish and share with others is a great accomplishment. Let students know that the effort they put in to writing and publishing a short story is something to be proud of.

Composition

Interjections and Draft Your Story

Write Your Short Story Draft

Read the assignment. Use your story plan to help you write the first draft of your short story. Write only on the white rows. You will use the purple rows for revisions later.

Write a short story with a beginning, middle, and end. Follow these guidelines as you write:
- Begin the story with paragraphs that introduce and describe the characters, tell when and where the action takes place, and present a problem.
- Continue with paragraphs that develop the plot, include dialogue, and make readers want to know what happens next.
- End with paragraphs that show how the characters solve the problem, and conclude the story in a believable and satisfying way.

Start here ►

LANGUAGE ARTS PURPLE **WS 263**

Write Now

Publish Your Story (A)

Publish Your Short Story

Make a clean copy of your finished short story, which you have revised and proofread.

Refer to the rubric and sample responses.

LANGUAGE ARTS PURPLE **WS 271**

More Practice

Short Story

If students' writing did not meet objectives, have them complete the appropriate review activities listed in the table online. Follow the online instructions to help students revise and edit their work. Impress upon students that revising makes their work better. Writing is a process, and each time they revise their short story they are improving their writing. Always begin with something positive to say. If there is a character trait that students have described that really helps bring that figure to life, for example, mention it and say how this element strengthened the story.

Help students locate the activities and provide support as needed.

Reward: When students score 80 percent or above on the Unit Checkpoint and their writing is Level 2 or higher on the Short Story grading rubric, add a sticker for this unit on the My Accomplishments chart.

Objectives
- Revise a story.

Semester Review and Checkpoint

Unit Focus

In this unit, students will review what they have learned about quotations, references, pronouns, agreement, adjectives, adverbs, capital letters and punctuation, verb tense, and parts of speech. They will

▶ Complete two review activities containing multiple choice questions about the skills taught this semester.

▶ Return to activities from different units, as necessary, to do more practice on these skills.

▶ Complete two checkpoints that test their ability to answer questions on the grammar, usage, mechanics, and critical skills taught during this semester.

Unit Plan　〔Online〕

Lesson 1	Semester Review: Quotations, References, Pronouns, Agreement, and Adjectives	45 minutes
Lesson 2	Semester Checkpoint: Quotations, References, Pronouns, Agreement, and Adjectives	45 minutes
Lesson 3	Semester Review: Adverbs, Capital Letters & Punctuation, Verb Tense, and Some Parts of Speech	45 minutes
Lesson 4	Semester Checkpoint: Adverbs, Capital Letters & Punctuation, Verb Tense, and Some Parts of Speech	45 minutes

Semester Review: Quotations, References, Pronouns, Agreement, and Adjectives

Lesson Overview

🖥 **⟦ Online ⟧**   **45** minutes

Semester Review	Quotations, References, Pronouns, Agreement, and Adjectives
More Practice	Quotations, References, Pronouns, Agreement, and Adjectives

⟦ Online ⟧ **45** minutes

Students will work online **independently** to review the grammar, usage, mechanics, and critical skills from this semester. Help students locate the online activities.

Semester Review

Quotations, References, Pronouns, Agreement, and Adjectives
Students will review what they have learned about quotations, references, pronouns, agreement, and adjectives to review for the Semester Checkpoint.

TIP A full list of objectives covered in the Semester Review can be found in the online lesson.

Objectives
- Complete a Semester Review of grammar, usage, mechanics, and critical skills.

More Practice

Quotations, References, Pronouns, Agreement, and Adjectives
Go over students' results on the Semester Review and, if necessary, have them complete the appropriate review activities listed in the table online. Help students locate the activities and provide support as needed.

TIP The time students need to complete this activity will vary. Set aside enough time for students to complete all review activities, if they need to do so.

Objectives
- Evaluate Semester Review results and choose activities for more practice.

Semester Checkpoint: Quotations, References, Pronouns, Agreement, and Adjectives

Materials

There are no materials to gather for this lesson.

Lesson Overview

Online   45 minutes

Semester Checkpoint	Quotations, References, Pronouns, Agreement, and Adjectives
More Practice	Quotations, References, Pronouns, Agreement, and Adjectives

Online   45 minutes

Students will work online to complete the Semester Checkpoint and More Practice activities. Help students locate the activities and provide support as necessary.

Semester Checkpoint

Quotations, References, Pronouns, Agreement, and Adjectives
Students will complete an online Semester Checkpoint about quotations, references, pronouns, subject–verb agreement, pronoun–antecedent agreement, and identifying and using adjectives.

TIP A full list of objectives covered in the Semester Checkpoint can be found in the online lesson.

Objectives
- Complete a Semester Checkpoint on grammar, usage, mechanics, and critical skills.

More Practice

Quotations, References, Pronouns, Agreement, and Adjectives
Go over students' results on the Semester Checkpoint and, if necessary, have them complete the appropriate review activities listed in the table online. If students scored less than 80 percent on the Semester Checkpoint, you may want them to retake the checkpoint after completing the review activities.

TIP The time students need to complete this activity will vary. Set aside enough time for students to review and retake the Semester Checkpoint, if they need to do so. Students may retake the Semester Checkpoint immediately, but having them review and then retake it might be more effective.

Objectives
- Evaluate Semester Checkpoint results and choose activities for more practice.

Semester Review: Adverbs, Capital Letters & Punctuation, Verb Tense, and Some Parts of Speech

Lesson Overview

[Online]   **45** minutes

Semester Review	Adverbs, Capital Letters & Punctuation, Verb Tense, and Some Parts of Speech
More Practice	Adverbs, Capital Letters & Punctuation, Verb Tense, and Some Parts of Speech

[Online]   **45** minutes

Students will work online **independently** to review grammar, usage, and mechanics skills from this semester. Help students locate the online activities.

Semester Review ···

Adverbs, Capital Letters & Punctuation, Verb Tense, and Some Parts of Speech

Students will review what they have learned about adverbs, capital letters and punctuation, verb tense, and some parts of speech to review for the Semester Checkpoint.

TIP A full list of objectives covered in the Semester Review can be found in the online lesson.

Objectives
- Complete a Semester Review of grammar, usage, and mechanics skills.

More Practice ···

Adverbs, Capital Letters & Punctuation, Verb Tense, and Some Parts of Speech

Go over students' results on the Semester Review and, if necessary, have them complete the appropriate review activities listed in the table online. Help students locate the activities and provide support as needed.

TIP The time students need to complete this activity will vary. Set aside enough time for students to complete all review activities, if they need to do so.

Objectives
- Evaluate Semester Review results and choose activities for more practice.

[Materials]

There are no materials to gather for this lesson.

Semester Checkpoint: Adverbs, Capital Letters & Punctuation, Verb Tense, and Some Parts of Speech

Materials

There are no materials to gather for this lesson.

Lesson Overview

Online   45 minutes

Semester Checkpoint	Adverbs, Capital Letters & Punctuation, Verb Tense, and Some Parts of Speech
More Practice	Adverbs, Capital Letters & Punctuation, Verb Tense, and Some Parts of Speech

Online   45 minutes

Students will work online to complete the Semester Checkpoint and More Practice activities. Help students locate the activities and provide support as necessary.

Semester Checkpoint

Adverbs, Capital Letters & Punctuation, Verb Tense, and Some Parts of Speech

Students will complete an online Semester Checkpoint about adverbs, capital letters and punctuation, verb tense, and some parts of speech.

TIP A full list of objectives covered in the Semester Checkpoint can be found in the online lesson.

Objectives

- Complete a Semester Checkpoint on grammar, usage, and mechanics skills.

More Practice

Adverbs, Capital Letters & Punctuation, Verb Tense, and Some Parts of Speech

Go over students' results on the Semester Checkpoint and, if necessary, have them complete the appropriate review activities listed in the table online. If students scored less than 80 percent on the Semester Checkpoint, you may want them to retake the checkpoint after completing the review activities.

 The time students need to complete this activity will vary. Set aside enough time for students to review and retake the Semester Checkpoint, if they need to do so. Students may retake the Semester Checkpoint immediately, but having them review and then retake it might be more effective.

Reward: When students score 80 percent or above on both Semester Checkpoints, add a sticker for this unit on the My Accomplishments chart.

Objectives

- Evaluate Semester Checkpoint results and choose activities for more practice.

K¹² Language Arts Purple Keywords

abbreviation – the shortened form of a word or phrase

abstract noun – a word that names an idea

action verb – a word that shows action

adage – a saying that contains a lot of ideas in very few words, or embodies an idea using a metaphor
Example The early bird catches the worm.

adjective – a word that describes a noun or a pronoun

adverb – a word that describes a verb, an adjective, or another adverb

adverb of manner – an adverb that answers the question, "How?"

adverb of place – an adverb that answers the question, "Where?"

adverb of time – an adverb that answers the question, "When?"

alliteration – the use of words with the same or close to the same beginning sounds

almanac – a book that comes out each year with facts about many topics

alphabetical order – a sequence according to position in the alphabet; for example, in alphabetical order, *at* comes before *bat*, which comes before *cat*

antecedent – the noun or pronoun that a pronoun points back to

antonym – a word that means the opposite of another word

article – the adjective *a*, *an*, or *the*

atlas – a book of maps

audience – a writer's readers

author – a writer

author's purpose – the reason the author wrote a text: to entertain, to inform, to express an opinion, or to persuade

autobiography – the story of a person's life written by that person

being verb – a verb that does not express action; for example, *am*, *is*, *are*, *was*, *were*

bibliography card – a note card on which one writes the source of a fact

biography – the story of someone's life written by another person

body – the main text of a piece of writing

body (of a friendly letter) – the main text of a friendly letter

book review – a piece of writing that gives an opinion about a book and tells about it

brainstorming – before writing, a way for the writer to come up with ideas

business letter – a letter written to an organization or a person at a business

call number – a number given to each item held by a library

caption – writing printed with a picture that describes or explains the picture

card catalog – usually offered online, a record of a library's holdings in alphabetical order by title, author, and subject

case – the form of a noun or pronoun based on its use in a sentence

cause – the reason something happens

character – a person or animal in a story

chronological order – a way to organize that puts details in time order

citation – a note that says where the author found a specific piece of information

clarity – of writing, the quality of being clear and easy to understand

clause – a group of words that has a subject and a verb

climax – the turning point in a story

closing (of a business letter) – the part of a business letter that follows the body text, containing a phrase such as "Sincerely" or "Yours truly"

closing (of a friendly letter) – the part of a friendly letter that follows the body; for example, *Your friend* or *Love*

cluster – a type of graphic organizer in which words and phrases about a topic are jotted down and connected

coherence – of writing, the smooth connection of ideas in a paragraph or essay

collective noun – a word that means a group of things but is usually singular

comma mistake – a mistake that occurs when two sentences are joined only with a comma

command – a kind of sentence that gives an order or makes a request

common noun – a word that names any person, place, thing, or idea

comparative form – the form of an adjective or adverb used to compare two things

compare – to explain how two or more things are alike

comparison – a look at how two things are alike

complement – a word that completes the meaning of a verb

complete predicate – the verb in a sentence and all the words that belong with and describe the verb

complete sentence – a group of words that tells a complete thought

complete subject – the part of the sentence that tells whom or what the sentence is about

complex sentence – a sentence that has one independent part and at least one dependent part

compound antecedent – two or more words a pronoun points back to

compound noun – a noun made up of two or more words

compound predicate – two or more predicates that have the same subject

compound sentence – a sentence that has at least two independent parts

compound subject – two or more subjects that have the same predicate

compound verb – two or more verbs with the same subject

compound word – a word made from two smaller words

comprehension – understanding

computer catalog – an online record of a library's holdings; also *card catalog*

concluding sentence – the last sentence of a paragraph; often summarizes the paragraph

conclusion – a decision made about something not stated, using information provided and what is already known (Literature & Comprehension)

conclusion – the final paragraph of a written work (Writing Skills: Composition)

concrete noun – a word that names a physical person, place, or thing

conflict – a problem or issue that a character faces in a story

conjunction – a word used to join parts of a sentence, such as *and*, *but*, and *or*

consequence – what happens because of an action or event

content – the information or ideas in a piece of writing

context clue – a word or phrase in a text that helps you figure out the meaning of an unknown word

contraction – a shortened word or words where an apostrophe replaces missing letters

contrast – to explain how two or more things are different

coordinating conjunction – one of seven words—*and*, *but*, *for*, *nor*, *or*, *so*, *yet*—that connect two independent clauses

couplet – two successive lines of poetry that work together and often rhyme

declarative sentence – a group of words that makes a statement

definition – a statement that tells what a word means

demonstrative adjective – one of four describing words—*this*, *that*, *these*, *those*—that point out an object or objects

dependent clause – a group of words that has a subject and a verb but cannot stand alone as a sentence

dependent part – about a sentence, a group of words that has a subject and verb but cannot stand on its own as a sentence

description – writing that uses words that show how something looks, sounds, feels, tastes, or smells.
Example: The sky is a soft, powdery blue, and the golden sun feels warm on my face.

descriptive adjective – a word that describes a noun or a pronoun

detail – a fact or description that tells more about a topic

diagram – a drawing or design that shows how pieces of information are related

dialect – a way of speaking that is particular to a certain group of people, place, or time

dialogue – the words that characters say in a written work (Literature & Comprehension)

dialogue – the words spoken between two or more people (Writing Skills: Grammar, Usage, & Mechanics)

dictionary – a reference work made up of words with their definitions, in alphabetical order

direct quotation – the exact words of a speaker or writer

domain name – the part of an Internet address stating the site's general type, such as .com, .org, .edu, or .gov.

double negative – the incorrect use of two negative words in a sentence

draft – an early effort at a piece of writing, not the finished work

drafting – of writing, the stage or step of the process in which the writer first writes the piece

drama – another word for *play*

effect – the result of a cause

encyclopedia – a reference work made up of articles on many topics, usually in alphabetical order

evidence – a specific detail, such as a fact or expert opinion, that supports a reason

example – a specific instance of something, used to illustrate an idea

exclamation – a kind of sentence that shows strong feeling

exclamatory sentence – a group of words that shows strong feeling

fable – a story that teaches a lesson and may contain animal characters

fact – something that can be proven true

fairy tale – a folktale with magical elements

fantasy – a story with characters, settings, or other elements that could not really exist

feedback – information given to help improve a piece of writing

fiction – make-believe stories

fictional narrative – a term often used for *short story*

figurative language – words that describe something by comparing it to something completely different
Example: Rain fell in buckets and the streets looked like rivers.

first-person narrator – a narrator who tells a story from the first-person point of view

first-person point of view – the telling of a story by a character in that story, using pronouns such as *I*, *me*, and *we*

focus – the direction or emphasis of a piece of writing; writing with a focus sticks to the main idea and does not include lots of ideas that are unrelated

folktale – a story, which usually teaches a lesson important to a culture, that is passed down through many generations

foreshadowing – hints inside a piece of writing about what will happen later in the story

fragment – an incomplete sentence that begins with a capital letter and ends with a punctuation mark

freewriting – a way for a writer to pick a topic and write as much as possible about it within a set time limit

friendly letter – a kind of letter used to share thoughts, feeling, and news

future tense – a form of a verb that names an action that will happen later

gender – the masculine, feminine, or neuter form of a noun or pronoun

generalization – a statement meant to describe a whole group
Example: Everyone loves a parade.

glossary – a list of important terms and their meanings that is usually found in the back of a book

graphic – a picture, photograph, map, diagram, or other image

graphic organizer – a visual device, such as a diagram or chart, that helps a writer plan a piece of writing

greeting – the part of a letter that begins with the word *Dear* followed by a person's name; also called the *salutation*

heading – a title within the body of a text that tells the reader something important about a section of the text (Literature & Comprehension)

heading – the first part of a letter that has the writer's address and the date (Writing Skills: Composition)

helping verb – a word that works with the main verb to show action; for example, *has*, *have*, *will*, *do*, *did*, *can*

hero – a character who must struggle to overcome problems in a story and whose actions and traits are admired by others

historical fiction – a story set in a historical time period that includes facts about real people, places, and events, but also contains fictional elements that add dramatic interest to the story

homophone – a word that sounds the same as another word but has a different spelling and meaning

hook – a surprising idea or group of words used to grab the reader's attention, usually at the beginning of a work

how-to paper – a paragraph or essay that explains how to do or make something

hyperbole – exaggeration
Example: Steve was so hungry he could've eaten 50 steak dinners.

idiom – a group of words that does not actually mean what it says; for example, *raining cats and dogs*, *a month of Sundays*

illustration – a drawing

illustrator – the person who draws the pictures that go with a story

imagery – language that helps readers imagine how something looks, sounds, smells, feels, or tastes

imperative sentence – a group of words that gives a command or makes a request

independent clause – a group of words that has a subject and a verb and can stand alone as a sentence

independent part – about a sentence, a group of words that has a subject and a verb and can stand on its own as a sentence

index – an alphabetical list at the end of a book or magazine that tells the pages where a subject or name can be found

infer – to use clues to make a guess

inference – a guess that readers make using the clues that authors give them in a piece of writing

informative essay – a kind of writing that informs or explains

inside address – the part of a business or formal letter that comes after the heading and before the greeting, made up of the name and address of the person to whom the letter is written

intensive pronoun – a pronoun used for emphasis, but not necessary to the meaning of the sentence
Example: I *myself* don't agree with that statement.

interjection – a word (or words) that expresses strong feeling

Internet – a global communications system of linked computer networks

interrogative sentence – a group of words that asks a question

introduction – the first paragraph of an essay, identifying the topic and stating the main idea

introductory element – a word, phrase, or clause that begins a sentence

introductory sentence – the first sentence in a piece of writing

inverted order – of a sentence, order in which the verb comes before the subject

invitation – a kind of personal letter or a form in which the writer invites someone to attend a party or other special occasion

irregular verb – a verb that does not add *–d* or *–ed* to the present form to make the past and the past participle

journal – a notebook where a writer regularly records experiences and ideas

journal entry – a response to a specific prompt or an instance of recording one's thoughts and experiences

keyboarding – using a word processing program to produce a piece of writing

legend – a story that is passed down for many years to teach the values of a culture; a legend may or may not contain some true events or people

limiting adjective – an adjective that is a number or an amount; for example, *seven, two, few, several*

line – a row of words in a poem

literal meaning – following the usual, or exact, meaning of words

literature – made-up stories, true stories, poems, and plays

logical order – a way to organize that groups details in a way that makes sense

main character – an important person, animal, or other being who is central to the plot

main clause – another name for an independent clause

main idea – the most important point the author makes; it may be stated or unstated (Literature & Comprehension)

main idea – the most important point of the paragraph (Writing Skills: Composition)

map key – a guide to what the symbols on a map mean

media – all the ways by which something can be shown, shared, or expressed

metaphor – a figure of speech that compares two unlike things, without using the word *like* or *as*
Example: The cat's eyes were emeralds shining in the night.

modifier – a word or phrase that describes another word

monologue – lines spoken in a play to show that a character is thinking or talking to himself

mood – the emotions or feelings conveyed in a literary work

moral – the lesson of a story, particularly a fable

myth – a story that explains how something came to be and that usually contains magical figures as characters

mythology – all the myths of one group of people

narrative – a kind of writing that tells a story

narrator – the teller of a story

nominative case – the form of a noun or a pronoun used as a subject or a predicate nominative

nonfiction – writings about true things

nonliteral meaning – a figure of speech; a word or phrase that exaggerates or changes the usual meaning of the word or words in the phrase

noun – a word that names a person, place, thing, or idea

novel – a fictional story of length

number – the form of a word that shows if it is singular or plural

object – a noun or pronoun that follows a preposition or an action verb

objective case – the form of a noun or pronoun used as a direct object, indirect object, or object of a preposition

object of a preposition – a noun or a pronoun that follows a preposition and completes its meaning

object pronoun – a pronoun in the objective case; for example, *me, him, her, us, them*

onomatopoeia – the use of words that show sounds; for example, *moo, woof, quack, squash*

opinion – something that a person thinks or believes, but which cannot be proven to be true

order of importance – a way to organize that presents details from least to most important, or from most to least important

order words – words that connect ideas or a series of steps, or create a sequence, such as *first, next, later, finally*

organization – of a piece of writing, the way the ideas are arranged

outline – an organized list of topics in an essay

pace – the speed, and the change of speeds, of a speaker's delivery

paired passages – a set of passages that are related in some way

paragraph – a group of sentences about one topic

paragraph outline – a list of paragraph topics in an essay

paraphrase – to restate information in one's own words

part of speech – the category that words belong to according to how they are used in a sentence, such as *noun, verb,* and *adjective*

past participle – the principal part of the verb used to form the perfect tenses

past tense – the form of the verb that tells what has already happened

pattern of organization – the order by which details are arranged

period fiction – a fictional story set in a historical time period that depicts how people lived and acted during the time

personal narrative – an essay about a personal experience of the writer

personal pronoun – a word that takes the place of one of more nouns; the personal pronouns are *I, me, you, he, him, she, her, it, we, us, they,* and *them*

personification – giving human qualities to something that is not human
Example: The thunder shouted from the clouds.

perspective – the way someone sees the world

persuasive essay – an essay in which the writer tries to convince readers to agree with a stand on an issue

phrase – a word group that acts as one part of speech; for example, an adjective phrase or an adverb phrase

plagiarism – use of another person's words without giving that person credit as a source

plot – what happens in a story; the sequence of events

plural noun – a word that names more than one person, place, thing, or idea

poem – a piece of poetry

poet – one who writes poetry

poetry – writing that uses language, sound, and rhythm to make readers feel, experience, or imagine something

point of view – the perspective a story is told from

positive form – the form of an adjective or adverb without any special ending

possessive case – the form of a noun or a pronoun that shows ownership

possessive noun – the form of a noun that shows ownership

possessive pronoun – the form of a pronoun that shows ownership

predicate – the verb or verb phrase in a sentence

prediction – a guess about what might happen that is based on information in a story and what you already know

prefix – a word part with its own meaning that can be added to the beginning of a base word or root to make a new word with a different meaning

preposition – a word that begins a phrase that ends with a noun or pronoun
Examples: In the phrases "over the bridge" and "to me," the words *over* and *to* are prepositions.

prepositional phrase – a group of words that begins with a preposition and usually ends with the noun or a pronoun that is the object of the preposition

presentation – an oral report, usually with visuals

present tense – the verb form that tells what is happening now

prewriting – the stage or step of writing in which a writer chooses a topic, gathers ideas, and plans what to write

principal part – one of four basic verb forms—present, present participle, past, past participle

problem – an issue a character must solve in a story

process – a series of steps that explains how to do something

process paper – a paragraph or essay that explains how to do something

pronoun – a word that takes the place of one or more nouns

pronoun–antecedent agreement – the way a pronoun and its antecedent match in number and gender

proofreading – the stage or step of the writing process in which the writer checks for errors in grammar, punctuation, capitalization, and spelling

proper noun – the name of a particular person, place, thing, or idea; proper nouns begin with a capital letter

publishing – the stage or step of the writing process in which the writer makes a clean copy of the piece and shares it

purpose – the reason for writing

question – a kind of sentence that asks something

quotation – a report of exact words spoken or written, usually placed within quotation marks

quotation marks – punctuation that encloses a quotation, or the exact words of a speaker or writer

realistic fiction – a made-up story that has no magical elements

reason – a statement that explains why something is or why it should be

reference – a work that contains useful information for a writer such as an encyclopedia, a dictionary, or a website

reflexive pronoun – a word that refers back to another noun or pronoun in the sentence and is necessary to the meaning of the sentence
Example: The politicians voted *themselves* a pay raise.

regular verb – a verb that adds *–d* or *–ed* to the present form to make the past and the past participle

research – to find information through study rather than through personal experience

research report – a type of essay based mainly on the author's research

return address – the name and address of the sender, written in the upper left corner of an envelope

revising – the stage or step of the writing process in which the writer rereads and edits the draft, correcting errors and making changes in content or organization that improve the piece

rhyme – the use of words that end with the same sounds; for example, *cat* and *hat* rhyme

rhyme scheme – the pattern of rhymes made by the last sounds in the lines of a poem, shown by a different letter of the alphabet to represent each rhyme

rubric – the criteria used to evaluate a piece of writing

run-on – two or more sentences that have been joined without a conjunction or proper punctuation

salutation (of a business letter) – the greeting of a business letter, which usually says, "Dear (name of recipient)"; it is followed by a colon

salutation (of a friendly letter) – the greeting of a letter, which usually says, "Dear (name of recipient),"

search engine – software that searches for websites, usually by keywords

second-person point of view – the telling of a story, or addressing a piece of writing, directly to the audience, using the second-person pronoun *you*

sensory detail – descriptive detail that appeals to any of the five senses—sight, hearing, touch, smell, or taste

sensory language – language that appeals to the five senses

sentence – a group of words that tells a complete thought

sentence combining – joining two sentences that have similar parts into one sentence

sentence expanding – adding details, such as descriptive words and phrases, to sentences

sequence – the order in which things happen

setting – when and where a story takes place

shades of meaning – small differences in meaning between similar words or phrases

showing language – words used to create pictures in the reader's mind, rather than words that merely tell what happened
Example: The sun blazed on the street, and my bare feet sizzled like a frying egg each time I took a step.
[as opposed to] The sun was hot, and my bare feet burned each time I took a step.

sidebar – a short text within a larger text that tells something related but not necessary to the main story

signature (of a business letter) – the part of a business letter following the closing, consisting of the writer's signature above the writer's typed name

signature (of a friendly letter) – the end of a letter where the writer writes his or her name

simile – a comparison between two things using the word *like* or *as*
Example: I didn't hear him come in because he was as quiet as a mouse.

simple predicate – the verb of a sentence without any of its modifiers, objects, or complements

simple sentence – a sentence that is one independent part, a group of words with one subject and one verb that express a complete thought

simple subject – the subject noun or pronoun without any of its modifiers

singular noun – a word that names one person, place, thing, or idea

solution – how a character solves a problem in a story

source – a provider of information; a book, a historical document, online materials, and an interviewee are all sources

spatial order – a way to organize that arranges details by their location

speaker – the narrator of a poem

speaker tag – the part of a dialogue that identifies who is speaking

stanza – a group of lines in a poem

statement – a kind of sentence that tells something

story map – a kind of a graphic organizer that helps a writer plan a story

structure – the way a piece of writing is organized

style – the words the writer chooses and the way the writer arranges the words into sentences

subject – a word or words that tell whom or what the sentence is about

subject pronoun – a pronoun used as a subject or predicate nominative

subject–verb agreement – the way a subject and verb match when both are singular or both are plural

subordinate clause – a group of words that has a subject and a verb but cannot stand alone as a sentence; also called a *dependent clause*

subordinating conjunction – a word that is used to introduce a dependent clause

suffix – a word part added to the end of a base word or root that changes the meaning or part of speech of a word

summarize – to tell in order the most important ideas or events of a text (Literature & Comprehension)

summarize – to restate briefly the main points of a text (Writing Skills: Composition)

summary – a short retelling that includes only the most important ideas or events of a text

superlative form – the form of an adjective or adverb that compares more than two things

supporting details – the sentences that give information about the main idea or topic sentence

supporting paragraphs (body) – a series of paragraphs that give information to support the thesis of an essay

suspense – uncertainty about what will happen

symbol – an object that stands for or represents something else; for example, a heart is a symbol of love

symbolism – the use of symbols in writing

synonym – a word that means the same, or almost the same, as another word

table of contents – a list at the start of a book that gives the titles of the book's stories, poems, articles, chapters, or nonfiction pieces and the pages where they can be found

tense – the time that verbs show, such as present, future, or past

text feature – part of a text that helps a reader locate information and determine what is most important; some examples are the title, table of contents, headings, pictures, and glossary

thank-you letter – a kind of friendly letter in which the writer thanks someone for something

theme – the author's message or big idea

thesaurus – a reference work that gives synonyms and antonyms for words

thesis – the most important point, or main idea, of an essay

thesis statement – the sentence that states the main idea of an essay

third-person point of view – the telling of a story by someone outside of the action, using the third-person pronouns *he, she,* and *they*

time line – a line showing dates and events in the order that they happened

time order – the arrangement of ideas according to when they happened

tone – the author's feelings toward the subject and characters of a text (Literature & Comprehension)

tone – a speaker's attitude as shown by his or her voice (Writing Skills: Composition)

tone – the writer's attitude toward the topic or subject (Writing Skills: Composition)

topic – the subject of a text (Literature & Comprehension)

topic – the subject of a piece of writing (Writing Skills: Composition)

topic sentence – the sentence that expresses the main idea of the paragraph

trait – a quality of a person or character

transition – a word or phrase that connects ideas

unity – when all sentences in a paragraph or all paragraphs in an essay support the main idea

URL – the Internet address of a website; stands for *uniform resource locator*

verb – a word that shows action or a state of being

verb phrase – a main verb and one or more helping verbs

villain – a bad or evil character who often works against the hero of a story

visual – a graphic, picture, or photograph

visualization – a picture of something in one's mind

voice – the way a piece of writing sounds

volume – how loud or soft a speaker's voice is

website – a place on the Internet devoted to a specific organization, group, or individual

Works Cited page – a list of sources cited in the text of a research report

writer's craft – the techniques a writer uses and the decisions a writer makes to develop an essay

writing prompt – a sentence or sentences that ask for a particular kind of writing